1970

This book may be kept

Books by Thomas Caldecot Chubb

THE LIFE OF GIOVANNI BOCCACCIO

ARETINO: SCOURGE OF PRINCES

DANTE AND HIS WORLD

DANTE
And His World

The Giotto Dante (located in the Bargello at Florence), although almost certainly executed after Dante's death, is the only portrait definitely done by someone who knew Dante during his life.

DANTE

And His World

By

THOMAS CALDECOT CHUBB

Little, Brown and Company • Boston • Toronto

Published simultaneously in Canada
by Little, Brown & Company (Canada) Limited

PRINTED IN THE UNITED STATES OF AMERICA

To my brother-in-law, J. RUSSELL PARSONS,
with admiration and affection and in appreciation
of a friendship which began in 1921

È gentilezza dovunque è virtute
Siccome è 'l cielo dovunque la stella.

Tu lascerai ogni cosa diletta
Più caramente, e questo è quello strale
Che l'arco de l'esilio pria saetta.
Tu proverai sì come sa di sale
Lo pane altrui, e come è duro calle
Lo scendere e'l salir per l'altrui scale.

Thou wilt leave everything that thou hast held
Most dear to thee, and that will be the bolt
The bow of exile arrows at thee first.
Thou wilt find out how much doth taste of salt
Another's bread, and how hard a road
Is going up and down another's stairs.

Paradiso XVII, 55–60

Contents

Contents

List of Illustrations

Introduction

IN undertaking to write a full-length biography of that great Florentine and amazing human being who, at the apogee of his powers, "walked in heaven and hell and purgatory as if they were the paved streets of his Florence" and set down what he saw there in concise Tuscan speech, I take some risk of being numbered among those who rush in where angels fear to tread.

For not about any single book, even the Bible, have so many words been written as about those hundred cantos in *terza rima* which the author, without circumlocution, called *Commedia*, but to which title later generations have added the adjective "divine."

Not even about Abraham Lincoln or William Shakespeare or Napoleon Bonaparte has there been so much comment and explanation as there has been about the author of this *Comedy*, the Dante di Alighiero degli Alighieri whom today we call Dante Alighieri, or (since a good wine needs no painted inn sign) simply Dante.

It has been stated that even to keep up with the current flooding of the more than six-hundred-year spate of exegesis, analysis, adulation, commentary, and criticism would be a full-time job, leaving no time to study what has been written in the past.

I go even further. It is my personal contention that if all the writings about the man and his books were laid end to end, they would reach from the entrance to hell (surely somewhere near the Solfatara north of Naples, which still fumes and sends up acrid smoke) to and up the mountain of purgatory, and then on to the tenth heaven, or empyrean. There are students who are prepared, though even here they do not all come to the same conclusion, to tell you just how many miles (or kilometers) that was.

Nor have these *chiosatori* fallen into any one category.

There have been poets like Geoffrey Chaucer (whose wife of Bath speaks of "the wysë poetë of Florence that hightë Dant"), Ugo Foscolo,

Giosuè Carducci, Gabriele D'Annunzio, Byron, Shelley, James Russell Lowell, Henry Wadsworth Longfellow, and T. S. Eliot.

There have been scholars like Isodoro del Lungo and Michele Barbi as well as our own Charles Eliot Norton and C. H. Grandgent.

There have been historians like rugged and cantankerous Thomas Carlyle, who placed Dante among his "heroes" — among the men who shaped the world — and storytellers like Giovanni Boccaccio, turned by love of his great predecessor into a phrase-by-phrase analyst.

There have been those who knew Dante personally — possibly the fellow Florentine who wrote what he modestly called the *Ottimo Commento* (Best Commentary); and certainly the poet's sons, Jacopo and Pietro.

There have even been the anecdotists and the street-corner tellers of tall tales. Dante attracted one and all.

Yet as I am confronted by this array of talent, I cannot help remembering a story related about the American artist Frederic Remington. Back in the 1880s, he told his Eastern friends that he was going West to paint Indians.

"But everybody has painted Indians," they objected.

"*I* have never painted Indians!" said Frederic Remington.

I also recall an observation by the late Professor Barbi, who said that Dante is so universal and so full of matter that he must be restudied constantly. There is no age, he indicated — and by implication, no serious student — that cannot add something new.

This I will attempt to do.

I have the greatest respect for the array of patient and enlightened men who, with love and intelligence and sometimes with an ingenuity which matches that of Sherlock Holmes, have attacked every aspect of the Dante problem. I have no quarrel with those who call Dante a theologian. Certainly he was deeply concerned with theology. I do not disagree with those who call him a philosopher. If he was not a philosopher — one who *loves* acquiring *wisdom* — there is no meaning to the word.

Obviously, of course, I am in complete accord with those who cast Dante in the role in which most of us think of him.

Considering only one facet of the Florentine's character, Ugo Foscolo observed that "the more Dante is looked on as a historian" — or a theologian or a philosopher, he might have added — "the more he eludes you, and arises as a poet."

It hardly needed saying.

But behind the poet, behind even the great poet — and behind the historian and the philosopher and the theologian and the polemicist (he was that too) was the man himself.

It is primarily about the man himself that I intend to write.

Here I take my text from Carlyle.

Speaking — with inaccuracies and exaggeration, of course, but with a sort of fundamental, basic truth — he says this of the son of Alighiero:

"An unimportant, wandering, sorrow-stricken man, not much note was taken of him while he lived; and most of that has vanished in the long space that intervenes."

Then he goes on to drive his point home.

"But we will not complain of Dante's miseries: had all gone right with him as he wished it, he might have been Prior, Podestà, or whatever they call it, of Florence, well accepted among his neighbors — and the world had wanted one of the most notable words ever spoken or sung."

Dour Thomas delivered these sentiments during the course of a lecture, and as usual he played to the gallery. After all, he had to be dramatic to hold his audience. We must evaluate them accordingly.

Dante was not unimportant — not even in the sense that Carlyle meant.

Nor has most of what was known about him vanished. Some has, of course, but enough is left to go on.

But he did wander, and he was sorrow-stricken, and the testy Scotsman was entirely correct when he implied that but for this, we might never have had the *Commedia*, with its not merely "notable" but soul-shaking words. For the *Commedia* is not a book which could have flowed gravely from the pen of a man who had done nothing but marry happily and sit by a Florentine fireside.

The wanderings and the sorrows were necessary — not merely for the writing of the great poem, but for most of Dante's other achievements, which were considerable. The wanderings, and some other frustrations! They will, therefore, be a principle concern of this book.

« 2 »

A collateral, but equally important, concern will be to place Dante in his world and in his time.

"No man" — this quotation has now been repeated so often that it is almost stale — "is an island, entire of itself," and by the same token no man can be accurately studied as an isolated being. It is useful as well as interesting to know what was happening throughout the whole world at various points in his life.

This likewise I intend to set down. For the moment, I will omit both what was taking place in Dante's own city and in that fair land which he proudly, if prematurely, called Italy. It will be more appropriate to narrate this during the course of the story. But here — beginning at the extreme northwestern corner of Europe, and proceeding in a counter-clockwise direction — is as good a place as any to consider the rest of the globe.

In Norway, and indeed in all Scandinavian lands, the great outward surge of adventure had spent itself. This surge had given us Leif the Lucky, who penetrated the dangerous fogs of the Newfoundland Banks to reach the coast of North America. It had sent Harald Haardraade (who died at Stamford Bridge in England just twenty days before the battle of Hastings) to stand guard in Constantinople, and to do battle for the Empress Zoë in Sicily, North Africa, and Syria. It had produced Rollo (of Normandy), William the Conqueror (of England), Roger Moneybag (of Sicily), and, of course, Tancred, who established his own kingdom in Asia Minor.

But now these stirring days were more distant — in the number of years elapsed — than the American Revolution is from today. The sailors of the whale's bath, the founders of Russia, the mercenaries of the Byzantine Empire, the Viking raiders of half western Europe ("Defend us, O Lord, from the fury of the Northmen!" chanted monks from Ireland to southern Italy) now devoted themselves to hunting, fishing, and agriculture; to taming the wold and its wild animals; to cutting down their pine forests; and to developing (under the compulsion of an unsuccessful war) trading relations with the Hansa ports of Baltic and of North Sea Germany.

(They were also reading the sagas of the great Iceland poet Snorri Sturleson. Snorri died about twenty years before Dante was born.)

Indeed, despite the fact that Dante mentioned Haakon V (very sarcastically as "*quel di Norvegia*") in *Paradiso* XIX, perhaps the person most remembered in Scandinavia during his lifetime is the so-called Maid of Norway, whose story most people know. Lovely flaxen-haired little Margaret, daughter of Eric II (Eric the Priest-Hater), was born in the year in which Dante, having attained his majority, took over the management of his late father's affairs. She died tragically in the bleak Orkney islands in the same year that Beatrice died. At the time she was seven years old.

Scotland, on the other hand, was enjoying one of its brief periods of glory. It was conquered by Edward I in 1294, when Dante was twenty-nine, but it refused to stay conquered. The "Scots wha hae wi' Wallace bled, Scots wham Bruce has often led" were contemporaries of the great poet. It was in 1297 (when Dante was thirty-two) that Sir William Wallace, an unknown knight, appeared in the North to lead the Highlanders, wearing the already traditional kilts, in a wild, and for a time successful, uprising.

Wallace was defeated at Falkirk in 1298. He then took to the heather, and it was not until seven years later that he was betrayed and taken to London where he was hanged, drawn, and quartered after the savage custom of the times.

But his mantle was assumed by Robert the Bruce, and in 1314 (when Dante was not quite fifty) Robert crushed and destroyed the English army on the green and fertile plain traversed by the meandering Bannockburn (Bannock Brook), which you can still see from the walls of Stirling Castle.

Incidentally, it was King Robert's daughter Marjory who married Walter Fitzalan, known as "the Steward." The name became Stewart or Stuart. Contemporary with Dante, then, was the founding of this royal line.

England, during Dante's lifetime, stirred and was filled with memorable accomplishments too.

Three kings sat on the English throne between Dante's birth in 1265 and his death in 1321: Henry III (1216–1272); Edward I (1272–1307); and Edward II (1307–1327). Although they were father, son, and grandson, they were in no way similar in character.

Henry III, son of that villain of England's history, Magna Carta John, was known as "the artist king," and he clearly deserved the title, for more than anyone else he was responsible for Westminster Abbey, which was built almost entirely at his command.

His part of it was completed in 1270, and the date is important to remember. The now gray, massive, and venerable edifice was brand-new and white and shining when Dante was a five-year-old boy.

Edward II did not even have art to justify his unsavory reputation and his weak and ineffectual rule. That he was handsome in a blond effeminate way no one denies, but today he is most frequently remembered as an easily swayed sodomite, who was dominated by his French favorite Piers Gaveston until the latter's murder, and then by his English favorite Hugh le Despenser, and who was motivated by hatred of his wife and queen. With his favoritism and his folly, he brought about the anarchy which was the true cause of the Wars of the Roses. Not until Henry Tudor would England again be a great power.

Yet, at that, Edward did at least leave one modest footprint on the sands of time. Born at Caernarvon Castle in 1284 (when Dante was nineteen), he had the distinction, if it be one, of being the first heir to the English throne who was known as the Prince of Wales. This is one more matter which still concerns us today which had its origin in Dante's lifetime.

But with Edward I, who ruled during thirty-five of Dante's fifty-six years here on earth, it was another matter. The "better issue" (*migliore uscità*), to use Dante's phrase, "of the king of simple life" (i.e., Arrigo — Henry — of England) was neither a vague dreamer and artistic like his father nor dissolute and a pervert like his son. He was sometimes known as Longshanks and sometimes as the English Justinian. Either title became him.

It was Edward, for example, who marched triumphantly through a divided Scotland to carry off the Stone of Scone and bring it to his father's abbey, where it has remained, except for a brief interlude a few years ago, ever since. It was Edward who defeated William Wallace. It was Edward, too, who conquered and tamed Wales, surrounding the supposedly impregnable Snowdon fastnesses by land and sea, and starving the elusive Llewelyn ab Gruffydd into submission. It was he who built the mighty castles of Conway, Caernarvon, and Harlech, using them to make the Welsh English, although not even today have they been completely persuaded to use the English language.

But it was also Edward who caused English law to be codified. (It was in Edward's reign that the first Inns of Court were set up.) He saw to it that an edict was passed requiring all men having an income of twenty pounds to assume the duties of knighthood (1278); another that no one might grant land to the clergy without permission of his overlord (1279); and a third one that feudal entail be perpetuated (1285). It was Edward also who, in 1295, convened the so-called Model Parliament, from which, many feel, modern representative government is derived. "What touches all," he said, "must be approved by all." In 1303, he promulgated the merchant's charter, whereby merchants were granted full immunity and full safe-conduct in return for an agreed-on new schedule of customs dues.

During the lifetime of Dante, then, Edward made England strong; he gave it law; he made its government at least modestly the concern of its people; and he perhaps led it to take its first step toward commercial greatness. This is a great deal.

Edward did one other thing which must be considered, for although it would be deemed brutal by present-day standards, it had an important indirect effect upon Dante. In 1290, he expelled the Jews from his kingdom. This left the moneylending business wide open to Christian usurers, and the Italians, mainly from Florence or Siena, flocked in. Wealth flowed back to Italy, much of it to the city in which Dante now lived as a young man. The struggle for control of this wealth was at the back of a political conflict in whose quicksands he would find himself engulfed.

« 3 »

Of the other countries in western Europe, somewhat less need be said, and for various reasons.

The Iberian peninsula, with its harsh climate and its gleaming, dramatic saw-toothed mountains (*sierra* means saw), was a backwater.

To be sure, during most of Dante's life, Portugal, that quadrilateral enclave against whose long beaches pound incessantly the tall, gray Atlantic rollers which in those days must have seemed to come from nowhere, was ruled by its best-loved medieval monarch. Diniz (Denis or Dionysius) the Farmer was a poet of some ability who, besides laboring to improve agriculture and trade and by establishing the Portuguese navy setting the stage for Prince Henry the Navigator, did much to raise the cultural level of the court and the nation. Among other things, he brought education in Europe to its farthest western point by founding the University of Lisbon in 1290.

To be sure, Christian Spain — it was then divided into Navarre, which crouched against the western Pyrenees, León, Castile, and Aragon — had anticipated the future by pushing the Moors back into a greatly reduced kingdom of Granada. To be sure, Spaniards — or at any rate Spanish monarchs — were giving Dante's peninsula a forewarning of what would happen two centuries later. Pedro III, Jaime II, and Fadrique II (Peter, James, and Frederick) were not greatly admired by Dante, but they did establish Spanish rule as close to Italy as Sicily. To be sure, Catalan *almogávares*, having become the world's most ruthless and most notable professional soldiers, ranged and fought from the Balearics and from Tunis to the Sea of Marmara. To be sure, great cathedrals (Barcelona in 1298, Gerona in 1312) were arising; great palaces like the Alhambra were being constructed; and although there was no one comparable to the earlier and Moorish Averroës, some kind of learning did flourish under James the Conqueror and Alfonso the Learned. But the fact is that Spain was far from the *trecento* mainstream, and when Dante or any of his Florentines thought of the land "whence Zephyr comes," they thought mainly of the pilgrimage to the shrine of St. James at Compostela. Certainly they did not think of Spain as a great nation. It would not become a great nation or even a nation until Ferdinand married Isabella just in time for Columbus.

France, however, *was* a great nation, and here is something interesting to note. It is generally believed that the great powers of Europe were born in the late fifteenth or early sixteenth centuries under Louis XI (King Spider) of France, Henry VIII of England, the Ferdinand and Isabella we have just referred to, Suleiman the Magnificent, and, more distant and a little later, Ivan the Terrible of Muscovy. But the truth is that at least England and France had a try at greatness long before that, and it was only because of civil conflict in England and, in France, a long series of mediocre if not downright weak monarchs that the job had to be done all over again.

France was made great by Philip the Fair (Philip IV, who ruled from 1285 to 1314). This tall, vigorous grandson of St. Louis, with his large frame, blond ringlets, eyes as blue as steel, and simple way of eating and drinking, was one of the outstanding monarchs in French history, and his ruthless and successful *coup de main* against the Knights Templars (an act whose brutal efficiency neither Hitler nor Stalin ever surpassed, for its prelude was the arrest in a single night of all fifteen thousand members of a battle-trained corps) achieved a shift of power which quite obviously diverted the channel of the river of history. Nevertheless, I shall say no more of him or of France here. They are too intimately connected with important phases of the Dante story and — like Italy — should be discussed as that story unfolds.

I omit Germany (the Holy Roman Empire), which was in a period of decline and weakness, for the same reason. But it is fitting to mention, even if only in passing, a small corner hidden in the Alps in which, almost unnoticed, another important step toward the future was being taken.

It was on August 1, 1291 — immediately following the death of Rudolf of Hapsburg (Habichtsburg, "Hawks Castle") and when Dante was twenty-six — that the men of Uri, Schwyz, and Unterwalden united to form a loose federation which became known as the League of the Three Forest Cantons. This was the beginning of Switzerland.

It was on October 7, 1307, that Werner von Stauffacher, Walter Fürst, and Arnold von Melchthal, each with ten followers, met on the high meadow of Rütli, which overlooks Lake Lucerne, and there signed a document which has earned the place a name with Runnymede and Independence Hall. William Tell — if there was a William Tell, which now is generally doubted — would have been among their number.

It was in November 1315 that the Swiss, swinging their deadly "morning stars," poured down the mountainside to defeat the Austrians and thus demonstrated that what men had won men could and — if it were precious — *would* defend.

Incidentally, if Dante was the contemporary of William Tell, he was also the contemporary of another famous outlaw. As we leave western Europe, it might be interesting to observe that it has now been fairly well established that Robin Hood lived in the reign of Edward I, not Richard Coeur de Lion. Among other evidence for this is the fact that it was in Edward's reign that the longbow, borrowed from the defeated Welsh, became the English national weapon.

« 4 »

Eastern Europe — and indeed the East as a whole — seems to have figured less largely in Dante's mind and possibly in the minds of his fellow Florentines. But the trade records (Pegalotti and a whole array of account books), the *Commedia*, and even some of Dante's other writings show that neither he nor they were entirely unaware of it.

Certainly Dante spoke plainly enough of *"quel di Buemme"* (he of Bohemia) and with even greater scorn than he spoke of *"quel di Norvegia."* "He neither true worth knew nor wanted to," he wrote of this last of the Premyslids in *Paradiso* XIX. In *Purgatorio* VII he said that this king's father, Ottokar, "was much more virtuous even in swaddling clothes than Wenceslaus his son, a bearded man, who stuffed himself with leisure and with lust." He had a word for Ostericchi (Austria), and he knew about the thick armor of ice "which more like glass than water seemed" that in winter covered the Danube and the Don. He lashed out at the king of Rascia (Serbia) for counterfeiting Venetian money (being a good Florentine, tampering with coin of the realm seemed a particularly grievous sin to him), and he was amused but pleased at the peasants from "Croazia" who came to Rome to goggle at the Veronica. He was conscious of at least three Byzantine emperors – Constantine, whom he reproved for taking the Roman eagle eastward; Justinian, whom he praised for his bridle (i.e., his laws); and Anastasius (but he turns him into Pope Anastasius II), whom he incorrectly supposes to have been misled into heresy.

But his eyes went even farther toward the rising sun. He had something to say about Jerusalem and the crusades, which were no longer directed thither. He was aware of the great subcontinent whose borders marked the farthest advance of Alexander of Macedon. He had something to say about the Indus. He even knew about the mouths (plural) of the Ganges. In his *Quaestio de Aqua et Terra*, he set them down as the eastern limit of the habitable world.

It might be well, therefore, to dwell, even if briefly, on the lands to the east.

As far as Europe was concerned, and to some degree as far as Asia, the most important event at this time – and indeed it was world-shaking – was the terrible incursion of the Mongol nomads led by a grandson of Genghis Khan. This took place nearly three decades before the birth of Dante, but its effects were exceedingly apparent all through and even beyond his life.

"In the year of Christ 1238," says an ancient chronicle, "the Tatars, who had come out of the East" – another chronicle says, "who had come down from the mountains of Gog and Magog" – "and conquered Turkey and the land of the Cumans, passed into Europe and there divided into two groups. Of these, one tribe went into the realm of Poland and the other tribe went into Hungary, and in the said realms they fought many and savage battles. And after this plague of Tatars had gone by, there was so great and so cruel a famine in the land that mothers ate their own children, and the large part of a mountain which was made of a substance called chalk they used up and devoured instead of flour."

This, incidentally, was neither the first nor the last in the long series of incursions by yellow-skinned and slant-eyed raiders from the East which began when Attila's ancestors invaded the dying Roman Empire in 372 and ended when the Turks were driven back from the walls of Vienna in 1686.

(The Turks shaped themselves into the people that we know in modern times during Dante's lifetime, for it was in 1290 — when Dante was twenty-five — that Osman I became ruler of Turkic tribesmen living near the shores of Lake Van, so founding the Ottoman dynasty, which reigned until 1920.)

But it was clearly the most devastating.

At the time of Dante's birth, eastern Europe from Poland to the Ukraine and then back to Hungary was a black and smoking waste on which the plowman, "that gray-haired enemy of the wold," hardly bothered to turn up the soil. Why sow for others to reap?

Yet even amidst the confusion, steps toward a better world were taken, and Dante knew of many of them. This is shown in some of the things he wrote.

It was during his lifetime — specifically it was between 1301 and 1308 — that the ancient Magyar (Turco-Tatar, and hence Asiatic) dynasty of Hungary came to an end and was replaced by French rulers.

It was during his lifetime, in 1310, that Wenceslaus III of Bohemia (our Czechoslovakia) was replaced by John of Luxemburg, son of Dante's Henry VII.

It was during his lifetime that German merchants — and artisans — began a peaceful penetration of Poland.

It was not long before his birth that Alexander Nevski defeated the Livonian knights on the ice of Lake Peipus and thus removed enough pressure from the west for the grand princes to begin building modern Russia.

It was during his lifetime that the first important Balkan state began to take shape. In 1281, Dragutin seized the Serbian throne and, although his reign was short, his nephew and his grandnephew were able to create a mighty Serbian empire whose art — just to name one of its achievements — was similar to in some ways and almost as great as that of Dante's friend Giotto.

Farther to the east, it was during Dante's youth that the great Kublai Khan ruled Cathay, the most civilized country in the world till then. He became emperor of China in 1271 and died in 1294.

It was to Kublai's capital, Khanbalik (Coleridge's Xanadu, modern Peiping), that Marco Polo directed his steps when he made the long overland journey which ultimately took him through most of China and much of southeast Asia. He left Acre in 1271, a boy of seventeen, and returned to Venice in 1295. It was in 1298 that he dictated his book with its unbelievable traveler's yarns (most of which have turned out to be true) to a fellow prisoner of war, Rusticiano of Pisa, as they languished in a Genoese dungeon.

There is, of course, no evidence that Dante read it, and, to be honest, the probability is that he did not. Yet he did visit Venice once, if not two or three times, and there Mark of the Millions (Marco Millioni) was already a legend. His achievements were Rialto conversation. The brilliant "*drappi Tartari e Turchi*" of which Dante spoke in his *Commedia* may have been a reflection of Marco Polo. They probably were Chinese silk.

Dante was contemporary with another reaching out into the distance — the disappearance into the unknown and mysterious Atlantic of a Genoese and two Venetian seafarers. More will be said of this during the course of the book.

« 5 »

So much for the captains and the kings! But as we thus wander through the world the poet lived in, there are still a few more things which should be mentioned.

Dante's great poem with its harsh realism and even occasional sardonic humor yet soaring idealism has sometimes been compared to a Gothic cathedral with its leering gargoyles and heaven-reaching arches and spires. It is, therefore, significant that many of the finest Gothic cathedrals already stood in Dante's time. Notre Dame, commenced in 1163, dates chiefly from the early thirteenth century. Rheims was well begun. Chartres did not look very different from the way it does today. Substantial parts of Canterbury were completed. Amiens was built largely between 1220 and 1288.

(On a scale more comparable to the exquisite miniatures which were now beginning to decorate manuscript after manuscript, the Sainte-Chapelle, with the blues and crimsons of its stained-glass windows, was completed seventeen years before Dante was born.)

There were cathedrals in the world of the spirit too.

St. Dominic had died in 1221 and St. Francis in 1226. But St. Bonaventura was alive during at least part of Dante's life, and so was St. Thomas Aquinas. Dante may have seen one or both of them, but it is rather unlikely, and if he did it is not probable that he talked to them, because he was only nine when both died.

He was also a contemporary of Duns Scotus (1265–1308), that learned philosopher from the land of kilt and heather whose name by ironic transposition has given us the word "dunce"; of Jean de Joinville (1224–1317), whose history of St. Louis of France is perhaps the finest of all medieval biographies; of Jean de Meung (1250–1305), author of the latter part of the *Roman de la Rose* (an Italian adaptation in two hundred sonnets, *Il Fiore*, was once credited to Dante); and of the great German Albertus Magnus, who was Thomas Aquinas's teacher.

Finally, he was a contemporary of Roger Bacon. "Friar Bacon" — as Robert Greene called him in one of the more tumultuous Elizabethan plays — was a Franciscan, and he was in such good standing in his order that he was asked to write one of his earlier treatises by none other than Pope Clement IV himself. But his scientific and experimental approach was too advanced and too experimental for his day, and this "*doctor mirabilis*" (remarkable doctor), as he was called, was twice imprisoned by his own order. One of these imprisonments lasted from 1277 to 1292.

Like Leonardo da Vinci, Bacon was in advance of his times. He foresaw the possibility of circumnavigating the globe, propelling boats by mechanical means, flying, and improving sight by proper adjustment of lenses; and he may — but equally well may not — have invented the telescope and the microscope and have discovered cells with nuclei.

But his popular fame rests on the legend that he invented gunpowder — and almost blew himself up so doing. It is entertaining to think of him inventing it just as Dante was preparing to descend into hell.

« 6 »

It is against this backdrop — and against the backdrop of his own Florence and of an Italy which he made his own — that I would like to tell the story of Dante. So doing, I shall be undertaking a task which for a long time has been in my mind.

Amusingly enough my first encounter with Dante was in a book of satirical drawings which I saw when I was ten or twelve years old. There he sat — or there, rather, sat two Dantes, each lean-faced and somber. In front of one was a round straw-covered bottle; in front of the other a bottle tall and lean. Under the drawing, as nearly as I recollect, was this jingle:

> I sometimes wonder whether Dante
> Drank Benedictine or Chianti.
> But I will have it as you say,
> For I can draw him either way.

It was almost a brief analytical essay. The Benedictine of heavenly theology! The Chianti of his Tuscan common sense!

The name of Dante stayed with me, and thereafter I encountered it frequently indeed — as who does not that studies either the literature or the history of the Western world. But it was not until 1924 (when I was two years out of college) that it became really important to me.

Then I lived for a while at Candeli, just a few miles east of *"la gran villa Sovra il bel fiume d'Arno"* in which Dante said that he was born, and not far from the plain of Ripoli, whence, leaving Beatrice for a while, the youthful poet marched with the Florentine army to Campaldino.

The month was May, and Tuscan May, like Oklahoma June, has a way of busting out all over. The leaves on the split, gray olive trees shimmered like silver. Poppies nodded — but did not seem somnolent — between the rows of bending wheat. Wisteria poured over an ancient stone-gray pool in a spilling of fragrant lavender florins. Lizards flashed metallically as they darted across the sunlight. Later on the nightingales sang their hearts out, and the fireflies which Dante would include in his poem made the dusky perfumed hillsides into an animated Milky Way.

Under these circumstances it was natural to turn to the son of Alighiero and, after some brief delight with Maurice Hewlett's *Earthwork Out of Tuscany* and then in Italian *I Fioretti del Glorioso Messer San Francesco e de Suoi Frati* (the *Flowers of St. Francis*), I began stumbling through the *Divine Comedy* in the original. It was learning Italian the hard way, but soon I could at least say *"Taci, maladetto lupo!"* to our landlord's German sheep dog when he came barking up to me.

I then began reading some of the things written about Dante, commencing with Edmund G. Gardner's useful little primer. My copy of it, bought on the Via Tornabuoni, still stands on my shelves. Despite all I have read since, I still find it as helpful as any book there is, with the possible exception of the Honorable William W. Vernon's line-by-line analysis.

Ever since that time I have wanted to write about Dante's life, and once — when I had just completed a life of Boccaccio — I was specifically asked to do so. But I must have sensed — for at that time I had not read it — T. S. Eliot's wise judgment: "The majority of poems one outgrows and outlives, as one outgrows and outlives the majority of human passions. But Dante's is one of those one can only just hope to grow up to at the end of life."

Even now, I confess, I feel some trepidation.

"For who in our time," asked Boccaccio — I quoted this when I wrote about Giovanni more than three decades ago — "can approach the minds of the ancients and expose the secrets of those long gone from this mortal life or rediscover the sentiments they had? Surely that would be more divine than mortal."

If this came to my mind when setting down the biography of a relatively simple man like the urbane and gay-hearted author of the *De-*

cameron, how much more must it do so when I turn to his great predecessor!

At that time I invoked all the Latin and Italian muses who had guided the pen of the man from Certaldo. I do so again, and I invoke Virgil too.

But I also need some Christian orisons.

"Ara vos prec!" (Now I beseech you pray!) says Arnaut Daniel in *Purgatorio* XXVI.

I too beseech your prayers.

DANTE
And His World

I

The Roots of the Tree

LIKE virtually every other person who has left his footprints upon the sands of time, Dante Alighieri was at least in part the product of his age. And since the vital spirit which made possible the "Age of Dante," as it later came to be known, was derived from the economic revival of western Europe with its concomitant development of busy, independent-minded towns and communes, it is appropriate that he should have been born in one of the more actively commercial and perhaps the most independent-minded town of the era.

It is equally appropriate that he should have come from a commercial and a busily trading family.

For that the Alighieri surely were — at any rate, during the years immediately preceding and immediately following Dante's birth. This is indisputably established by the documents. At least thirty-two are available, and of these only three do not deal directly or indirectly with business or property.

Grandfather Bellincione, for example, is mentioned in these documents eight times. In one, he is witness to a loan. (In matters like this, there seems to have been mutual accommodation, one businessman witnessing another's agreement just as now one businessman serves to another's board of directors.) *"Presentibus Bellincione Alaghieri, Ciuto Mezanelli, Braccio Belcari et Gualfredo q. Rodolfini,"* reads the notarial Latin. The sum was not great — twelve pounds (*"libbre"* or *lire*), eighteen *soldi* (*"solidi"*) Pisan money. But we all know what little drops of water and little grains of sand add up to, and so did they in late-medieval Florence.

Once he is witness to a sale of land.

On another occasion he is noted as being present at a meeting of the "ancients, councillors, standard-bearers, rectors, and *capitudini*" who on November 10, 1251, ratified a treaty made by Florence, Lucca, and Genoa against Pisa. This is taken to indicate that he was a Guelph (the merchant as opposed to the aristocratic party in those days), a leader in one of the guilds, and in the good graces of the Primo Popolo, which between 1250 and 1260 gave Florence what was perhaps the first attempt at something even remotely resembling municipal democracy since the days of the ancient Athenians.

Five times he takes part in a complicated real estate transaction in association with his son Alighiero — we will call him Alighiero II to distinguish him from an earlier Alighiero I, of whom more later — and his other sons Brunetto, Drudolo, Bello, Gherardo, and Donato. Alighiero II was Dante's father.

Cousin Gualfreduccio di Bello Alighieri — son of Bellincione's brother and hence brother to the turbulent Geri del Bello whom Dante met in hell, and well he deserved to be there — is mentioned once. There he is stated to have taken an oath of compliance before the consuls (i.e., the governing officials) of the guild of the Calimala merchants. This oath was taken on December 7, 1237, and was effective for ten years. Gualfreduccio thus became a member of the guild dealing in imported cloth, which in the Florentine guild hierarchy ranked second only to the Guild of Judges and Notaries.

Incidentally, Gualfreduccio's father Bello was a member of the latter guild. He was thus entitled to strut through the streets of Florence in a long red cloak lined with miniver. To be sure, his pay may have been low. In some instances a judge received only a florin a month, which may have led to the venality and corruption which caused the writer of novellas Franco Sacchetti only a century later to exclaim that he would rather have his son a gambler than an officer of the court. But at least he had prestige and dignity. It would seem that the Bello branch of the family had acquired just a shade more status than the Bellincione branch.

Uncle Brunetto appears sixteen times — five times in connection with the family land sale already mentioned. Three times he witnessed a loan of money. Once he witnessed the release of a claim against one Dagomari and his son Grazia — thirty-two pounds, five *soldi* Pisan money. (At this time the famous florin had not been coined yet.) Almost immediately thereafter he lent the same pair sixteen pounds, twelvepence (*denari*). The next day (why this change of heart, or maybe the price accounts for it?) he sold this and other claims against Dagomari and Grazia to a certain Aldobrandino di Pugliese for forty-seven pounds. The claims amounted to only thirty-seven pounds, twelve *soldi*, and eightpence. Once (I assume the Belluzzo of the document to be in error for Brunetto) he witnessed a promise to repay one Albertino di Dino the value of a horse. Once — and this is his only large transaction — he was one of the guarantors of a loan of a hundred one pounds, thirteen *soldi,* and fourpence. This was on December 22, 1249. On August 30 of the next year, he was relieved of any responsibility for its repayment.

Brunetto is also — on February 11, 1260, when he may well have been in his forties — noted as being elected one of the foot soldiers of the *carroccio* which was led against the Ghibellines in a Siena war.

For the benefit of those who are not sufficiently familiar with the military procedures of the tradesmen-turned-soldiers to understand what this "big cart" was and what it was used for let me cite a Dante contemporary, the chronicler Giovanni Villani.

"And note that the *carroccio,* which was led by the commonwealth and people of Florence, was a chariot on four wheels, all painted red, and two tall red masts stood up thereupon, whereon was fastened the standard of the arms of commune. It was dimidiated red and white. It may still be seen today [i.e., in Villani's time] in San Giovanni.

"This *carroccio* was drawn by a great pair of oxen covered with red cloth. He who drove them was a freeman of the commonwealth.

"It was led by the *popolani*" — not the proletariat but the plain citizens, the merchant-burghers — "in time of war, and to guard it were chosen the best and strongest and most virtuous among the foot soldiers of the *popolani,* and round it gathered all the force of the people."

This alone indicates considerable Guelph status.

Another document, dated May 17 of the same year, does a little more. It reads as follows:

"Given at the headquarters of the army. The below named have been directed to make and widen the streets in the camp with the help of one from the household of the *podestà.*"

The *podestà* was the chief executive of the municipal government.

"*Burnettus de Alagheriis porte Sancti Petri*" was among the six — one from each section of the city — who were listed.

Did Brunetto then personally take part in the disastrous battle of Montaperti, "whose rout and whose great slaughter the Arbia did color all blood red" (*Inferno* X)?

It was in this battle — the Florentine losses were twenty-five hundred dead with fifteen hundred taken prisoner — fought along the banks of an insignificant stream that still flows sluggishly between reedy thickets that, according to Villani, "was overthrown and destroyed the First People of Florence, which had continued in so many victories for ten years."

And if so, what was his role?

Michele Barbi throws cool if not icy-cold water on the old story of a

Dante uncle who, like a Tuscan Roderik Dhu, stood back to the wall — or rather back to the *carroccio* — while the fighting raged around him and thus, as he told about it later, became a hero to young Dante and possibly even inspired him to the fierce patriotism which was one of his most notable characteristics.

For Dr. Barbi points out that the May 20 order of the *podestà* and *capitudini* directs that of the one hundred fifty-two Florentines named to this guard only twenty-three were actually to serve, receiving "*pro salario et mercede, soldos decem pro unoquoque illorum*" (for salary and wages, ten *soldi* apiece). He indicates that there is no proof that Brunetto was one of the twenty-three. He also reminds us that there is definite proof that Brunetto was alive at least until 1306. He contends that none of those who had defended the *carroccio* — which was taken and dragged in triumph through the streets of Siena — could possibly have survived.

But the fact remains that Brunetto was part of the Florentine host; that he was enrolled among those selected to defend the banner of the city; that he either defended it or would have done so if he had been required to; that he was very clearly not among the cavalry, who, when the battle was going badly, tarnished their reputation by fleeing.

Plainly then he was regarded as a man whose valor could be depended on.

But that is not surprising.

During the course of this book, many faults and many feelings will be ascribed to various of the Alighieri, including Dante. Lack of courage will not be one of them.

« 2 »

Of the other Alighieri — uncles Drudolo, Bello, Gherardo, Donato, and father Alighiero II — the documents have something to say too.

Drudolo is recorded as one of four witnesses to a loan; Bello as the witness to a guarantee that a horse purchased by the already mentioned Dagomari del fu Grazia would be paid for within two months; and Gherardo — who was a *campsor*, or a member of the Bankers Guild — and Donato as engaged in similar activities.

Alighiero II seems to have been even more active.

On March 22, 1246, for example, he is set down as having loaned Leonardo de' Franceschini nine pounds, eighteen *soldi*. Two days later, one Arrivero "acknowledges" having received from him thirteen pounds, four *soldi*. Two days after that, he lends Ricco, son of the late Mercadante, one hundred ten *soldi*. In 1247, he witnesses a loan of twenty-nine pounds, seven *soldi*, and six *denari*. (In this transaction we can recognize the £, s., and d. of the English monetary system. It came from Italy.) In

1257, he lifted up his eyes unto the hills. On October 20 of that year he loaned twenty pounds, eight *soldi* (approximately one thousand 1920 gold *lire*) to the widow Benincisa of Montemurlo.

Montemurlo, only three years before a stronghold of the Counts Guidi, was in the foothills of the Apennines about four miles west of Prato. Even today it is a little hamlet with only some three thousand inhabitants, but in those days it scarcely numbered as many hundred. It clustered about the foot of Montemurlo Castle, which still looks down on it.

For drawing up the document which covered this loan, the notary received two *soldi*, but no mention is made of interest, which in those days was considered low when it was twenty percent. It is possible that Dante's father was dealing generously with a poor widow, but more probably the omission was to avoid charges of usury, which was practiced generally but severely frowned on by the Church. Even in the Age of Dante it was advisable to read the small print. The Florentine merchant — like the merchant of Venice — very rarely gave up willingly his pound, or even his ounce of flesh.

These were personal matters, but Alighiero II was also deeply involved in Alighieri — as opposed to Alighiero — business. Indeed, there is good reason to believe that Bellincione — who may have been born as far back as 1175 and if so was growing old — regarded him as his fit successor in the management of the family's affairs. He was quite possibly the eldest Bellincione son. Renato Piattoli sets his birth at *circa* 1210, but even if it was later, his place at the head of almost every family list is further evidence.

But furthermore Bellincione thought highly of son Alighiero's ability. It is hardly surprising. Bello (but he was a brother, not a son) as a member of the Guild of Judges and Notaries; Gualfreduccio (but he was a nephew) as a member of the Foreign Cloth Guild — the cloth was mainly woolen cloth, bought abroad and refined in Florence; and Gherardo as a *campsor* of the Bankers Guild had, as we have already noted, a certain status. But the other Alighieri were often, if not always, in trouble.

This high esteem of Bellincione for Alighiero is perhaps nowhere better brought out than in a complicated exchange of property which took place in Prato toward the end of March 1246.

Prato — so that we may understand the matter better — was the scene of many Alighieri operations. (Even Montemurlo was in the environs of Prato.) This little city was, and still is, a miniature Florence situated about twelve miles to the northwest on the right bank of the sometimes torrential small Bisenzio River. To the north, it is shadowed by the tall (about three thousand feet), forested Monti della Calvana. Besides city walls, its monuments include the massive, rectangular Palazzo Pretorio (this stood in Dante's youth, but not in 1246) with its unusually dignified outside stairway; the Duomo, which was built in the tenth century and given most of its present form (but not its white and green marble facade) in 1211; and an imperial castle (known as the Fortress) complete with Ghibelline (i.e., indented) machicolations, which was built by Frederick II between 1237 and 1248.

But in the mid-thirteenth century it was the center of a minor wool industry and an important market town as well. To the south of it and to the east and to the west is a small concentration of fertile farmland. For running northwestward from Florence for approximately twenty-four miles is a flat, rich valley averaging four miles in width. It is sheltered in every direction by mountains. It is fertilized by floods at reasonable intervals. Even today, it is golden with wheat and corn, green with trailing vines, and every color one can imagine with commercially grown flowers. It was not very different in the time of Dante's father. It was a good land to invest or speculate in. It was a good land to buy or sell.

Evidently the Alighieri did both. They acquired land for their own use, but they also speculated. If they bought, they also sold.

One of these transactions took place on March 21, 1246 — just one day before Alighiero II loaned money on his own account to Leonardo de' Franceschini, and three and five days respectively before he made similar advances to Arrivero di Randieri and to Ricco di Mercadante, all three of these operations also in Prato.

"*Millesimo ducentesimo quadragesimo quinto, duodecima kal. aprilis, ind. IIII*ᵃ" — in 1245 (but remember the year did not change on January 1 in those days), twelve days before the calends of April, in the fourth indiction, "Bellincione Alighieri of Florence, and Alighiero, and Brunetto, and Drudolo, and Bello, and Gherardo, and Donato, sons of the said Bellincione," the latter with the consent of their father, this father and the said brothers asserting that the said Bello and the said Gherardo were eighteen years old and more and that the said Donato was fifteen years old and more, "did sell, hand over to, give, yield, and deliver for his own property and forever to Messer Tosingo, son of the late Pugliese," the following:

(1) an income of five *moggia* (a *moggia* is said to have been eight bushels) and seven *staiori* (bushels) less one quarter *staioro* of high-quality pure wheat "according to the Pisan standard";

(2) six pieces of land at Tavola (on the southern side of the valley), "which land they assert to be eleven *staiori* or more" (a *staioro* being the amount of land which required for its planting a bushel of seed);

(3) their rights and interests in five pieces of land located in Tavola,

Campia di Ronco, Limite (down the Arno near Empoli), Gualfredingo, and "near the wood lots of the parish of San Giusto."

In return for all this — in return, that is, for a guaranteed income from a plot of land of a size which required forty-six and three fourths bushels of wheat (thirty-one modern bushels) to seed it adequately (provision 1); outright possession of six plots of land at Tavola (provision 2); and whatever rights, presumably through long-term leases, the Alighieri may have had to five other pieces of land (provision 3) — Messer Tosingo agreed to pay them the sum of one hundred forty *libbre*.

For those days, this was quite a sum.

But "the same day, in the same place, and before the same witnesses" the authorization was changed. He now was to pay it not to the Alighieri family but to one designated member. "Bellincione," said this second document, "together with Brunetto, Drudolo, Gherardo, Donato, and Bello, sons of the said Bellincione, gave full power and permission to the said Tosingo di Pugliese to give and pay with their approval and consent to Alighiero, son of the said Bellincione, the money which the said father and sons made with him in regard to an agreed-upon amount of land."

Presumably to give and pay it to Alighiero as agent for the other Alighieri. This Tosingo did — one hundred *libbre* that same day and forty *libbre* on April 27.

Thus at the probable age of thirty-six — certainly he was not any older — Alighiero II became the effective manager of an important Alighieri enterprise.

At least, that is how I interpret the matter.

Renato Piattoli, who uncovered the document, seems to agree with me.

"This whole complicated affair," he says (he is speaking of this Prato transaction only), "was a matter of family arrangement in a family which was deeply involved in business."

The kind of business, he continues, which any Florentine capitalist might carry on.

"All the Alighieri were engaged in operations of this sort. They were engaged in them in a more or less aboveboard manner, more or less honestly. Their only excuse was that business was business."

« 3 »

Business seems to have been very good business as far as Alighiero II was concerned, for at his death he left Dante and Dante's brother Francesco a more than modest property.

It is worth enumerating. Most of it was in or near Florence.

There was a farm with houses, tenant shacks, a barnyard, a vineyard, cultivated ground, olive and other trees, "all forming a single estate and located in the *popolo* of San Marco di Mugnone, and bounded on the first, second, and third sides by the street and on the fourth side by the heirs of Berto the cuirassmaker."

There was a second farm with farmhouse, barnyard, cultivated ground and trees "located in the *popolo* of San Miniato di Pagnola in the Florentine *contrada* [countryside legally under the jurisdiction of the city] in the place called Le Radere, which on the first side is bounded by the road, on the second side by the moat, on the third by the lands of the bishop of Fiesole, and on the fourth by the heirs of Litto de' Corbizi; together with certain other pieces of land located in the said *contrada* and surrounding the said farms and land."

(This last holding can still be easily identified. It is now occupied by the Villa Bondi. It is hidden behind high walls and somber cypresses on a secondary road that leads from Florence to San Domenico on the way to Fiesole.)

There were two pieces of property in the *popolo* of Sant' Ambrogio. One seems to have consisted of land only, but in the other, which was bounded on the first and second sides by the street, on the third side "by the heirs of Corso the baker," and on the fourth side "by the heirs of Miglioruccio," there were rentable small houses.

Finally, there was the Alighieri city home. This is the place in which the Alighieri lived when Dante was born.

This city home was described as "a certain house in the *popolo* of San Martino del Vescovo, on the first side bounded by the street, on the second by the heirs of Simone di Neri de' Donati, by Donna Bellina, widow of the late Chierico di Messer Martello de' Donati, and by Tizio di Giammoro, and on the third by Ciocco or by others, and on the fourth by the Mandoli."

But in spite of this explicit description, its exact location is still a matter of dispute. The most that can be said with certainty is that it was in the complex of medieval-looking houses on or near the present Via Dante Alighieri. Some of these still stand.

In addition, there may have been property at Badia di Ripoli in the flat, sunny plain south of the Arno, and there are hints of property or interests at Prato, Pistoia, Lucca, Siena, Pisa, and Arezzo, although some of these may have been acquired later by Alighiero's sons.

Two farms, then, on the gay, exuberant hillsides which almost encircle Florence and which in those days were already gemmed to a distance of three miles by the gleaming villas which Boccaccio would so charmingly describe in his *Decameron!* Both were north of the city.

Two profitable bits of urban real estate — for at least some hold that it was increased income from rising city rents which provided the cash accumulations which brought about the birth of capitalism!

And their very adequate residence!

"Before his expulsion from Florence," wrote Leonardo Bruni, who was one of the poet's earliest biographers, "Dante, although not of extraordinary wealth, was not poor either; but he had a modest patrimony. It was sufficient to live on in comfort."

It would seem to have been a little more than that. Certainly Dante did not possess wealth comparable to that of the Bardi and the Peruzzi, who "were acquainted with all the holes and corners of the known world" and who not only had their Florentine business but could rake in cash or credit from agents and correspondents in Pisa, Genoa, Venice, Cagliari, Barletta, Rome, Avignon, Paris, London, and Bruges, to say nothing of all over the Mediterranean and the Levant. But he had generously independent means.

« *4* »

But the Alighieri, at least in their own opinion, were something more than successful, if small, capitalists. They did not claim to belong to the castled nobility, dwellers in and defenders of many an eyrie which "like an eagle's nest clung to the crest of purple Apennine" and which overlooked and often threatened Florence. It would not have been prudent to do so.

But they did believe that they belonged to one of the city's old families. And this was an aristocracy too — if of another sort.

Here is how Giovanni Boccaccio tells about this in his *Life of Dante:*

"Florence, as well as most other noble Italian cities, took her beginning from the Romans. In the process of time, she grew larger, became full of people, and began to appear not merely a city but a power. But not many centuries afterward, Attila, the cruel king of the Vandals" — actually it was Totila — "killed or dispersed all or the greater part of its citizens" and reduced the city itself "to ashes and ruins."

Thus it remained "for more than three hundred years." But after that, it was rebuilt by Charlemagne, "the most clement king of the French, raised to the imperial throne," and he, in order to achieve this purpose, collected "the few remnants which could be found of the descendants of the ancient exiles" and brought them back to their ancestral home.

"Among these new inhabitants — perhaps one who superintended the rebuilding, or was assigned the houses and streets, or gave this new people the necessary laws — there came from Rome, as the story runs, a noble youth of the family of the Frangipani, called by all Eliseo. He, by chance, after he had accomplished the principal purpose for which he was to come, became a permanent resident of the city, drawn either by love for the place which he had so recently helped to reorganize; or by the pleasant site, to which he foresaw that heaven in future must be favorable; or by some other sign. After him he left a large and worthy family of sons and descendants, who, abandoning the ancient surname of their ancestors, took that of him who had founded the family and became the Elisei.

"As time went on, and as son succeeded father, there was born and lived in the family a brave knight, remarkable for his deeds and wisdom, whose name was Cacciaguida. To him was given as a bride a damsel of the Aldighieri family of Ferrara, esteemed for her beauty and character as well as for her noble blood, with whom he lived for many years and by whom he had many children."

The damsel's name was Aldighiera.

To a son, this Aldighiera gave the name of Aldighiero. Later the *d* was dropped and it became Alighiero.

"The worth of this man brought it about that all who descended from him forsook the name of Elisei and called themselves Alighieri — a practice which has lasted to our time."

All this should be read and thoroughly digested, for although large parts of it — particularly those dealing with a supposed Roman descent — are now rejected by almost all serious scholars, it was clearly the official Alighieri story.

They — and Dante — firmly believed that they were sons of Rome and not base quarry workers from Fiesole or low-born farmers from "Campi or Certaldo or Figline." (Oddly enough, Boccaccio came from Certaldo.)

They — and Dante — firmly believed in their knightly ancestor Cacciaguida.

They — and Dante — believed in Aldighiera.

Nowhere is this more apparent than in the fifteenth canto of the *Paradiso*. There, as Dante moves upward toward revelation, he encounters an intense gem of light that first addresses him in sonorous Latin, skillfully reduced by the poet to *terza rima*, and then, in the succeeding two cantos, gives a vivid concentrated history, biography, and autobiography which narrates (and in my opinion establishes) more about what Dante was — or what he felt in his heart he was — than do any or all of the notarized documents that have been or that may in the future be found.

O leaf of mine, who brought me so great joy
Even as I waited for you, I was your root . . .

                              He from whom you took
Your cognomen and whom the mount [of *purgatory*]
      has circled
On its first ledge a hundred years or more
My son was, and was your great-grandfather . . .

To such a tranquil, yea, to such a fair
Citizen way of living, to so worthy
A people, in so very sweet an inn,
Mary, prayed by my mother, delivered me,
And in that ancient Baptistery of yours,
I, in one day, became Christian and Cacciaguida . . .

Moronto was my brother, and Eliseo.
My lady came to me from the Po Valley.
It was from her that you your surname got.
Then followed I the Emperor Conrad,
Who girded me with belt, thus knighting me —
So had I won his favor with my good deeds.
I went with him against the wickedness
Of that foul creed whose followers usurp,
Through the pope's failure, lands that we should rule.
There was I by that race of evil men
Liberated and set free from this false world,
The which has so debased so many souls.
And thus I came through martyrdom to peace . . .

      From that day in which "*Ave*" was said
Unto that birth by which my mother, now sainted,
Did lighten herself of the burden which was me
Unto the Lion five hundred and fifty times
And thirty more had come the planet Mars
To warm itself again under his paws . . .

My ancestors and I were born in that place
Where the first boundary of the last ward is reached
By him who is rider in your annual race.
Suffice it of my forebears to say this.
Of who they were and from whence they came hither
It is more modest to be silent than to speak . . .

Six separate statements in all, and if one turns to them in Dante's Italian rather than contenting himself with my or any other translation he will note that they are compact and beautiful poetry.

But he should note also that they expressed — very tersely and very explicitly — what Dante considered to be the truth.

Just what did this truth amount to?

Some of it has already been stated, but I will risk repeating it.

First, the voice which came to him from the flame was that of his first recognized and provable ancestor—he was the root of the tree from which Dante leafed. There was an earlier Adamo, but he is only a name.

Second, this ancestor had a son from whom Dante took his cognomen (i.e., surname) and this son shared the family's and Dante's sin of pride. This was Great-grandfather Alighiero I, of whom more will be said very shortly.

Third, he (the ancestor) was born in Florence, and was christened Cacciaguida in Dante's beloved — if as yet unmarbled and undecorated — "*bel San Giovanni*"; he had two brothers, Moronto and Eliseo (this may have been the basis for the Elisei story, for Eliseo had descendants still living during Dante's lifetime, some of whom were exiled for Ghibelline activities during Dante's youth); and his wife did indeed come from the Po Valley.

Ferrara is in the Po Valley, and Ferrara is full of Aldighieri. The Boccaccio statement would thus seem to be substantiated — although Parma, Verona, Bologna, and a few other places also claim the honor of being the home of Dante's maternal family. In this connection, incidentally, there are some who contend that these Aldighieri were of Teutonic origin, the name being the same one which produced our modern Alger. The poet Carducci supports this theory. It is contested by the critic Zingarelli. It is not very important. Almost all northern Italians have some German blood.

The passages cited also establish that Cacciaguida joined the bannered army of the Emperor Conrad III which was transported down the Danube to Byzantium and then marched across Cappadocia toward the Holy Land. This was the famous Second Crusade, which was enlivened by the presence of the glamorous Eleanor of Aquitaine.

They establish that he was knighted by Conrad — presumably for valor on the battlefield. They establish that he was slain by the infidels. The date is 1147. They give us a basis for establishing the date of Cacciaguida's birth. From the date on which the "*Ave*" was said — i.e., the date of our Lord's conception — to his birthday Mars had completed its orbit 580 times. To do this takes approximately 1091 years.

Finally — in his own way, roundabout but one which every Florentine would understand — Cacciaguida tells Dante that he (Cacciaguida) and his forebears were born and lived not far from the Mercato Vecchio (now the Piazza della Republica) in the *sesto* (ward or quarter) of the Porta San Piero. The annual horse race — for a handsome strip of red and white cloth — ended in that quarter. The Mercato Vecchio was its first boundary.

He also gave a broad hint that he too believed in a lofty ancestry. Modesty — to paraphrase what Dante had him say — prevented him from telling who these distinguished ancestors were.

But more probably Dante simply did not know.

« 5 »

Cacciaguida's son Alighiero I was the one to whom Aldighiera gave her name. Only a few things are known of him, and there is no evidence that he followed his father's soldierly and knightly career, although he certainly did resemble him in some other ways. Indeed it is probable, if not certain, that it was this Alighiero who established his family as burghers, and it is even more probable that it was he and his brother Preitenitto who moved the Alighieri into the seething little *popolo* of San Martino, where from then on they lived.

In this *popolo*, he and Preitenitto very shortly began to demonstrate the litigious nature which was so characteristic of the Alighieri. In fact, their first appearance is in a lawsuit which apparently they lost.

This is what the document says:

"In the year 1189, on the fifth day after the ides of December, in the presence of Berco, son of Mincello; Luterio and Giugno, sons of Zampo; Astoldo, son of Chiarissimo; and Passavanto, son of Bencivenno, Preitenitto and Alighiero, sons of the late Cacciaguida, under penalty of twenty *soldi* and under injunction of the consuls and whatsoever *podestà* may be in power do promise and make agreement with Tolomeo, parish priest of the church of San Martino, and with his successors that within eight days they will cut down and destroy the fig tree which has been planted close to the walls of San Martino, or any other fig tree that they may subsequently plant. If they do not do this, the said priest of San Martino or anyone else designated to act for the church may cut down and destroy the said fig tree without any interference from the said Preitenitto and Alighiero or their heirs. If they do contradict or interfere they shall pay over the above-named penalty."

A word of explanation is perhaps needed. In the days we are talking about, a fig tree was sometimes planted to give shade from the dazzling Florentine sun, but it was used even more often to establish a property line. It looks as if the two brothers were reaching out a little. It looks as if they were quietly trying to take over a little church land. In this they were balked by the alert priest.

But Alighiero I made another contribution to Alighieri history, and to those of us who are concerned mainly with his great-grandson Dante Alighieri it was a much more important one. He allied the family with the famous Bellincione Berti, who was the same kind of symbol of old-time simplicity and citizen virtue to the Florentines that Cincinnatus had been to the Romans and George Washington is to us. He allied it with the good Gualdrada, who had become another Florentine legend.

This Gualdrada — if you can believe Boccaccio and others — was Bellincione's daughter. She was noted for her beauty.

As the story tells it, the Emperor Otto IV paid a state visit to Florence, and to please the Florentines he agreed to attend their great annual festival. This took place — or rather culminated — in the square where the Duomo now stands but which was then occupied by the ancient church of Santa Reparata.

"Now it befell that, as is the custom of the day, there came the wife of this Messer Berti to the church, and she brought with her this daughter who was still a maiden. This daughter placed herself at one side with the other young women, but so great was her charm and her fair speech that almost all of those standing there turned to look at her.

"Among them was the emperor, who, after having greatly praised her beauty and manners, asked Messer Berti, who stood beside him, who she was.

"To this Messer Berti replied: 'She is the daughter of one to whom it would be pleasing to tell her to kiss you if you so desire.'

"The girl heard these words, so close was she to him who said them. And, very much disturbed by the opinion of her which her father seemed to have, namely that whenever he wished it she would allow herself to be kissed less than chastely, she rose to her feet and, showing something of shame on her visage, said: 'My father, do not be so generous in promising away my modesty. For I assure you that if I am not forced to permit it no one will ever kiss me except he to whom you give me in marriage.'

"For the which speech the emperor commended her, swearing that for his part too he agreed that none should have to do with her except honestly and with a pure heart. Wherefore he called into his presence a young man called Guido Bevisangue, who was later called Count Guido Vecchio, and assured him that he wished him to marry her. As dowry he gave him great holdings in the Casentino and among the Alps. And all the Counts Guidi are descended from the said marriage."

Alighiero I almost certainly married this good Gualdrada's sister.

"From these Ravignani" (Ravignani was Bellincione Berti's family name; he was Bellincione di Berto de' Ravignani), wrote Dante's son Pietro, "were descended — that is to say from the said Messer Bellincione of the said house — the Counts Guidi (according to what I wrote about *Inferno* canto XVI) through the Lady Gualdrada, his daughter. His three other daughters were married as follows: one into the house of the Donati; another into the house of the Adimari; and another into the house of this writer, that is into the house of Alighieri. And in all of these houses because of the said Bellincione there are many named Bellincione."

Grandfather Bellincione, for example! Cousin Cione! Possibly even the various Bellos and Belluzzos!

« 6 »

What is the import of all this?

It has already been noted that most scholars — whether rightly or not — have rejected the theory of Roman ancestry as at best unproven, and the good Gualdrada story is at least as vulnerable. The dates are wrong. When Otto IV visited Florence, Gualdrada was a middle-aged and comfortably married woman. Guido Bevisangue (Guido Drinkblood — there is a romantic story about how he got this name) was Gualdrada's father-in-law, not her husband. Furthermore the Counts Guidi held their titles and their lands long before Otto of Guelph claimed the imperial throne, or even before he was born.

But just as Dante believed that he was descended from the Romans, he believed too that the good Gualdrada was his great-grandaunt. It is also a fact that what a man believes — particularly what a man like Dante believes — is often just as significant as what is really true.

Most analysts of Dante's character and development have deemed that not merely his greatness but the very shape and form of his greatness was forged by three events. The first was his love for, and the death of, Bice or Beatrice. The next was his long and unjust exile. The last was the collapse of his noble (if visionary and impossible) dream of an ideal empire which would do man's business on earth while a reformed and no longer worldly papacy took care of heaven's business.

These may have hammered out the sword, but the amazing metal out of which the sword was hammered was an alloy made of the modern (and by modern I mean late thirteenth- and early fourteenth-century) Florentine and the haughty aristocrat who could lift up his nose arrogantly and thank God he was not like other men — and therefore *be* unlike them.

The last quality surely came from Alighiero I. This plain citizen who had felt sure enough of himself to marry the sister of the good Gualdrada and the daughter of the almost legendary Bellincione Berti — Villani, who was not related to Berti by marriage or otherwise, calls him "the greatest and most honored knight in Florence" — gave him his pride. And it was pride — it was the feeling, referred to above, that he was not quite as others were — which gave Alighiero I's great-grandson the endurance to go on with a task which was beyond any labor of Hercules in spite of all rebuffs and every frustration that could be devised by fate and man.

Dante was not always happy about this pride, for to him pride was the sin for which he was most likely to have to atone when it came his turn to visit purgatory in reality.

(As we have seen above Alighiero I was still doing penance for it after more than one hundred years when Dante made his imaginary visit to the first cornice.)

He fleered at it with his most effective sarcasm. *Paradiso* XIII:

> O our poor, petty nobility of blood,
> That thou dost make men glory down below
> Where faltereth our keen desire for good
> I never more will find astonishing,
> Since here where will from virtue does not swerve—
> I mean in heaven—I do glory in thee!

But we who read Dante today can be grateful for it. For if he had not had this pride we would probably not have the great poem which still shakes the souls of those who read it almost six hundred and fifty years after its last lines were written down.

II

Florence Within Her Ancient Circuit of Walls

TO this nobility of blood — whether it was poor and petty or whether it represented worth and valor handed down from ancient Rome — Dante's mother contributed too. To the innate Alighieri sense of genealogical superiority — evidenced by the fact that whether or not they were descended from the Roman Frangipani they did use the Frangipani coat of arms with its evenly divided red and blue — came a similar sense of innate aristocracy from the woman who, if we can accept Virgil's words to the poet in the eighth canto of the *Inferno*, should "blessed be" because "she bare thee."

Or so, at any rate, we believe. To those who insist on documentary evidence, the only incontrovertible statement which can be made is that the woman who bore the great poet was named Bella, and that she brought Alighiero II a dowry which was still intact when it figured in a legal settlement made between Dante's sons and his brother in 1332. Bella, for the record, is an *accorciativo* — a nickname or familiar name — for Gabriella. The name of the poet's mother was Gabriella.

But it is generally, or at least widely, accepted that she was the daughter of Durante di Scolaio degli Abbati, Dante thus taking his name, as had now become a well-established Alighieri practice, from the maternal side (Alighiero I from his mother Aldighiera, Bellincione from his grandfather Bellincione Berti).

The Abbati were on an even higher social level than the Alighieri.

"Of the Ghibellines of the said *sesto*" (i.e., Cacciaguida's and Dante's Porta San Piero), reported Villani, "were the Caponsacchi, the Lisei [Dante's Elisei], the Abbati, the Tebaldini, the Giuochi and the Galigai."

But the Abbati were more than Ghibellines. They were magnates and even noblemen.

They were Ghibellines too, the most notable member of the family having been the famous — or infamous — Bocca degli Abbati. It was Bocca who, in the midst of the battle of Montaperti, pretending to side with the Florentines, came up to the Florentine standard-bearer Messer Jacopo degli Pazzi and, riding beside him, struck the said Messer Jacopo with his sword, cutting off the hand which supported the banner.

"And immediately Bocca was set upon and killed," continues the story.

Dante later put Bocca into hell, but that does not preclude his being one of the poet's relatives. For when the son of Alighiero spoke in the name of eternal justice, neither blood — nor even love or friendship — stood in his way.

But Dante was something more than the scion of a good family whom, in the Giotto fresco on the walls of the chapel of the *podestà* in the Bargello, one can see dreaming of a past which perhaps had never been and of a future equally remote from probability.

He was also a Florentine, sharing the Florentine faults and virtues, hating the city because he loved it, eloquent as its street-corner mountebanks, realistic although high-spoken, analytical although often moved by prejudice, even shrewd.

Many of these qualities came from his father — from the Alighiero II who, as we have already seen, although his lineage was not unlofty, was willing to move about in the marketplace and there drive a hard bargain for a small plot of land or a handful of *libbre, soldi,* and *denari*. But many came from Florence itself — from that city which, according to a Dante contemporary, "is in the province of Tuscany, built under the sign of Mars; richly favored with an imperial river of sweet water which divides it almost in half; its air temperate; protected from hurtful winds; its citizens very courteous; its women handsome and well attired."

A Florence which had come into being almost on the day on which Dante was born. A merchant-burgher Florence, "valiant, but proud and quarrelsome" — and also adventurous. A Florence which stood at the very threshold of three hundred incomparable years which would equate it with Periclean Athens and with the England of Queen Elizabeth as matchless both in the spirit and in the world.

To be sure, Dante lived in an earlier Florence too — but only in imagination.

"And note," said Giovanni Villani describing that earlier time, "that in those days and for a long time before and after the citizens of Florence lived soberly and on coarse food, and in respect to their manners were sometimes uncivilized and rude. Both they and their wives were clad in rough garments, and many wore skins without lining and caps on their heads, and all wore leather boots. The Florentine ladies were content with one close-fitting garment of scarlet serge. The women of the people were clad in green fabric. One hundred pounds was considered the common dowry for wives, and two or three hundred pounds was held to be excessive. Most of the maidens were twenty years old or more before they were wedded. After such habits and plain customs then lived the Florentines, but they were true and worthy to one another and to their commonwealth, and with their simple life and their lack of affluence they did greater and more virtuous things than are done in our times with more luxury and with greater riches."

Dante described this early Florence too. Again (*Paradiso* XV and XVI) he put the words into the mouth of his ancestor, Cacciaguida:

> Florence within her ancient circuit of walls,
> From whence she still hears daily terce and none,
> Lived peaceably and soberly and decent . . .
>
> She wore no bracelets then and no tiara,
> Nor ruffled petticoats, nor had she girdle
> More dazzling to see than she who wore it.
> Not yet, by just being born, did daughter bring
> Fear to her father. Her dowry and the age
> She married at were both appropriate . . .
>
> Houses were not so large that they seemed empty,
> Nor yet had Sardanapalus come
> To teach what could be done in sweet chambers . . .
>
> I saw Bellincion Berti clad in leather
> With clasp of bone. I saw his lady too,
> Come from her mirror with unpainted face.
> I saw a Nerli and a Vecchio
> Content go about clad in rough sheepskin,
> As were their wives with spindle and with thread . . .
>
> O happy days! Then everybody knew
> Where he would buried be, nor was poor wife
> Left in an empty bed for journey to France . . .
>
> And so one mused fondly beside the cradle
> And soothed her little baby with the prattle
> That mothers and fathers take delight to use.
> Another, drawing the thread from her distaff,

> Told to her eager children ancient tales
> Of the Trojans, of Fiesole, and of Rome . . .
>
> In those days would have been as great a marvel
> A lewd Cianghella or Lapo Salterelli
> As would be Cincinnatus or Cornelia today . . .

It would be a reasonable estimate to say that this Florence did not have more than five or six thousand inhabitants. It covered approximately sixty-six acres of ground. And almost up to its brown walls came the thick forests of medieval Italy. They were dense and impenetrable, but through them ran primitive roads — in many cases little more than cart tracks — down which was brought produce from clearings worked by peasants in various stages of dependency.

"We must begin," writes a modern historian, "by thinking of it as a village whose usually deserted streets were brought to a certain amount of animation upon the customary market days."

He perhaps "overexaggerates." Six thousand inhabitants are too many for a village. It would be better to call it a small town. But certainly it was very far from being a metropolis or even an important city.

« 2 »

The Florence of Dante's childhood was neither a village nor a small town any longer.

In 1172 — for expansion had begun even then — a second circle of walls was constructed, and this enclosed an area at least three times as large as did the first circle. More than two hundred acres is a fair guess. But by the time Dante was nineteen, not even these new walls enclosed enough land for the swelling population. Nor, for that matter, was their military usefulness enhanced by the fact that a sprawling collection of hospitals, monasteries, and even the houses and palaces of citizens who had influence now crowded their top. In 1284, therefore, work was started on a third circle, although even that part of it which faced Prato was not completed until 1299.

This third circle — it was forty feet high, square and solid, with Guelph (i.e., plain and unindented) battlements, and with a perimeter of five miles — multiplied by more than seven times the area of the city. This was now fifteen hundred acres.

For those who know the modern city, the boundaries of this wall ran from the present day Porta al Prato (near the Cascine Gardens) east-northeastward past the Fortezza da Basso to the Porta San Gallo. Thence with a slight elbow they turned southeastward to the Porta alla Croce.

Then southwest to and across the Arno (with a gap for the river, of course), westward along the present Via di Belvedere and the southern edge of the Boboli Gardens to the Porta Romana. Finally north (again with a few elbows) to the Porta San Frediano. Thence to the river again.

Cacciaguida's five or six thousand inhabitants had grown to forty-five thousand. This made a reasonably big city — at least by the standards of the time.

Dante's Florentines, too, were different from Cacciaguida's.

Pope Boniface VIII, who, as we shall see, had every reason to know them, defined them succinctly.

On February 22, 1300, this pontiff was borne in solemn procession through the streets of Rome to St. John Lateran. There, clad in rich pontificals, he proclaimed a papal Jubilee in honor of the thirteen hundredth anniversary of the birth of our Lord.

"Until its last day, and retroactive to the preceding Christmas, in reverence for the nativity of Christ shall be granted supreme and full indulgence after this manner: that to whatsoever Roman who, during the course of this said year, shall visit continuously for thirty days the churches of the blessed apostles St. Peter and St. Paul, and to all other people who are not Romans who should do likewise for fifteen days, there should be granted full and entire remission of all their sins, both their guilt and the punishment thereof, they having made or to make confession of the same.

"And I further order that on every feast day of the year be shown publicly the handkerchief of our Lord" — this was the Veronica, the kerchief or veil upon which Christ wiped His face as He went to the cross and on which His visage was said to be clearly seen — "and, besides feast days, upon every Friday of every week for its greater devotion."

This Jubilee was an almost unbelievable success.

The winter was unusually severe — possibly even as severe as that of 1168, when the Arno froze solid and the people held foot races and horse races on its glassy surface, or conducted wrestling matches, or sat at tables on the ice and played chess or draughts or backgammon. Blizzards howled through the Apennine and Alpine passes, nor did "the great snows that prevent any from leaving their houses" desist in some parts of Italy until the month of April.

But when the spring came, it was like a melting freshet.

"A vast army," wrote a man from Parma, "was seen to pass daily in and out along the Claudian Way.

"Barons from France and other lands made it up. They were sometimes attended by a cavalcade of forty or fifty horsemen. And well nigh all the houses on this same Claudian Way were turned into inns and sold food and drink to the foreigners. And every day they were thronged with people."

"Frequently," said a second observer, "did I see men and women trod underfoot, and I myself more than once barely escaped the same fate."

This chronicler dwelt upon another aspect of the Jubilee.

"Day and night," he reported, "two clerics stood at the altar of St. Paul" — presumably San Paolo fuori le Mura on the Via Ostiensis, which next to St. Peter's was and still is the largest church in Rome — "with rakes in their hands raking in *pecuniam infinitam*."

This was corroborated by Ptolemy of Lucca, who had once been St. Thomas Aquinas's personal confessor. He estimated the daily oblation to have been "*1000 libbras provinciales*" — one thousand Provençal pounds!

But besides "the barons from France and every other land" — which must have included everywhere from the Golden Horn to distant Norway — there came another group of men who were especially noted by the aging but observant pope.

These were the foreign ambassadors, who were presented to him one by one as he reclined in his great ornate bed and to each of whom he held out his finely shaped hand with its dark, glittering ring.

Let us hear their names read out by the appropriate official of the papal household.

"The ambassador of the king of England — Messer Ugolino de' Cerchi.

"The ambassador of the king of France — Messer Musciatto Franzesi."

Boccaccio's unsavory "Monsieur Mouche" of the first story of the *Decameron!*

"The ambassador of the king of Germany — Messer Vermigli Alfani.

"The ambassador of the king of Bohemia — Messer Ranieri Lazeri.

"The ambassador of the emperor of Byzantium — Messer Simone Rossi."

One source has it "the ruler of Russia," but this is obviously a mistake.

"The ambassador of Lord Alberto della Scala, lord of Verona — Messer Bernardo Ernari.

"The ambassador of the khan of Tartary — Messer Guiscardo Bastari.

"The ambassador of the king of Naples — Messer Manno degli Adimari.

"The ambassador of the king of Sicily — Messer Guido Tabanca.

"The ambassador of the republic of Pisa — Messer Lapo degli Uberti.

"The ambassador of the lord of Camerino — Messer Cino di Diotisalvi.

"The ambassador of the grand master of the Knights of St. John — Messer Bencivenni Folchi."

Twelve of them in all, and every single one a Florentine!

Nor were they the only ones from Florence in Jubilee Rome.

Geri Spini was there. He, as the pope's moneyman, was already beginning to spin the web of intrigue that would be so disastrous to Dante and to his city.

Villani was there. The young banker on whose chronicle I have already drawn and will draw over and over again was twenty years old in 1300, and he states plainly that the inspiration which led him to begin his great history came from what he saw in Rome.

Giotto was there. His portrait of Pope Boniface is all the proof we need. It was clearly done from life.

I contend, finally, that Dante was in the Eternal City. Describing the myriad spirits of the damned in one of the pouches of Malebolge (*Inferno* XVIII), he wrote this:

> As did the Romans, because of the great crowds
> In Jubilee year, this method adopt
> So that the people might cross over the bridge:
> Namely that on one side the throngs faced the castle
> And went toward St. Peter's, but they came back
> Toward the Capitol on the other side.

This is a very clear description of a method of traffic control not unlike the use today of one-way traffic. The bridge leading to the Castel Sant' Angelo and thence to the great church as divided by a barrier which some say was composed of liveried men. The long file of those proceeding toward Vatican Hill kept on one side of this barrier. Those returning kept on the other side. Dante saw it.

The pope, then, must have seen Florentines everywhere.

He gave a gesture of exasperation.

"Who are these Florentines?" he asked petulantly. "Who are they?"

One of his cardinals tried to soothe his irritation.

"I do not know," he replied. "Yet, your holiness, the city of Florence is a good city."

"Nonsense!" flung back Boniface. "Nonsense! Nonsense! Florence is not a good city, but the greatest of cities. She feeds, clothes, and governs us all. Indeed, sometimes she seems to rule the whole world. I tell you she and her people — I tell you Florence and the Florentines — are truly the fifth element of the universe!"

They were indeed!

« 3 »

It was these Florentines — quintessential but also flesh and blood — who built the local habitation in which Dante, like his Branca d'Oria (but not like Branca in any other respect), "ate and drank and slept and put on clothes." It is this quintessential — but also brick and mortar — Florence made by these Florentines which we must now examine.

Viewed from a distance, it was almost the same city which we see today, a riant, if sometimes hazy, panorama of red-tiled roofs and a red-tiled cupola, with here and there a brown or a marble-encrusted bell-tower, and, if you stand in the right place, the pencil smudges of six bridges crossing the thin pewter-colored river. In the time of Dante, it seemed very similar. Then as now the city rose "proud, dark, and threatening against a somber background of hills covered with cypresses, with oaks, with fir trees, swaying in the *tramontana* breeze," I have some reservations about the red-tiled roofs and the red-tiled cupola, but bridges already crossed the pewter-colored river and they were often mist-enwrapped from the heat haze of the Florentine summer, or the winter fog. The most notable difference would have been the hedgehog array of towers lifting into the air above the strongholds of the *consorterie*, or tower societies. For obvious security reasons, these had been reduced to a maximum height of fifty feet when the merchant class in 1250 began its first try at power, but they still bristled like the raised spears of an army. Only in San Gimignano can you see them today.

Within the city, however, it was another matter, for although even in the time of Dante Florence was a crowded city, it was not quite the warren of closely packed houses and dusky tunnel-like streets it would later become. The very names Via Vigna Nuova (New Vine Street) and Via Vigna Vecchia (Old Vine Street) remind us that there were farms and vineyards not merely within the third, but even within the second, circle of walls. The more than occasional watering troughs for animals also added a rural note.

Gardens were numerous inside the city too. The nightingale sang where today there is scarcely space — and, since the automobile has replaced the horse, scarcely the food either — for a sparrow. There were the perfume and the exuberance of Tuscan flowers.

Many of these gardens were in the very heart of the city. One Ghano — the rest of his name is not known — had lush grass and burgeoning roses around his house, which was not very far from the Alighieri home, and there, before they had their own palace, the priors sometimes used to meet. Somewhat to the east, on land owned by that Ser Durante de' Chiaramontesi whom Dante would denounce for fraud, was a grove of thirty-five hundred orange and lemon trees. There was another orange grove at the corner of the Via Ghibellina and the ancient Via de' Fosse, now the Via Giuseppe Verdi. The Alfani laid out — in 1284 — a garden in the parish of San Michele Visdomini. That was also well within the city. The Frescobaldi had a famous garden in the Oltrarno — Across the Arno — quarter. Most of the convents had verdant lawns with pergolas surrounded by cypresses and fig trees. In the Florence of the last years of the thirteenth century, it was easy to have a green thought in a green shade.

Only a handful of the now familiar Florentine buildings had been built when Dante was born, and not very many more were built while he still lived in Florence. The Baptistery — his *bel San Giovanni*, to which "with other fleece, yea, and with other voice" he never ceased hoping he would return — dated back to Lombard days if not earlier and, although the breathtaking Ghiberti bronze doors were still more than a century in the future, most of the surfacing with white and green marble from Prato had been completed, as well as many of the grave and somber mosaics. The Badia had been founded in 978 by the Marquis Hugo's mother Willa. She had been won over to religion and a virtuous life by Florence's first fiery politician-reformer St. Romuald. If in any way she resembled the Willa so robustiously described by Bishop Liutprand of Cremona, she certainly needed it. Sant' Annunziata — but the list of small churches could be expanded considerably — was begun in 1250 and Ognissanti not long after 1251. San Miniato al Monte looked down on "the well-guided city" as it had for a long time — it was built in 1018 — and it already had its present facade. I have already spoken about the bridges. There had been a bridge on the site of the Ponte Vecchio in Roman times, and Dante's Ponte Vecchio was built before 996. It was destroyed by flood in 1333, but the present Ponte Vecchio, built in 1345, cannot be very dissimilar. The Ponte Rubaconte (now alle Grazie) was built in 1237. The Ponte Santa Trinità was built in 1252. There was also a bridge on the site of the Ponte alla Carraia. The first stone of the Bargello — in those days the palace of the *podestà*, or military city-manager — was laid in 1254.

But Santa Maria Novella, so rich in associations with both Dante and Boccaccio, was not begun until 1279, when the poet was fourteen years old. Orsanmichele — and not in its present form at that — was not begun until 1285, nor Santa Croce until 1295. The slow work on the Palazzo della Signoria, now called the Palazzo Vecchio, did not start until 1298. It was built out of stones from the Uberti palaces which had been torn down after the final Ghibelline overthrow in 1266, and its very shape and location were determined by a tough and characteristic idosyncrasy of the Florentine character. The Guelph citizenry refused to have a single foot of their municipal palace stand upon Uberti land. A still-existing bias on its northern side resulted.

Dante never saw, either, Giotto's beautiful campanile, and quite obviously he did not see either the Pitti Palace or the Uffizi. Obviously too — although he certainly witnessed and may even have played a part in the first steps of the conversion of the old Romanesque Santa Reparata into Arnolfo di Cambio's dramatic Santa Maria del Fiore (the Duomo), he knew nothing of the heavy, rusticated stone palaces of the days of the Medici (like the Strozzi Palace on the Via Tornabuoni and the Medici-Riccardi Palace on the Via Cavour) which today give the city such a feeling of authority and power.

But in spite of the gardens and the grass, and in spite of the fact that so many of the edifices we know today had not yet been erected, we must not think of the *gran villa* as in any way empty or rural. It is true that forty-five thousand people do not need forty-five thousand houses — especially not in medieval Italy! But certainly they need more than a handful, and more than a handful there were.

Here some statistics are useful. In 1260, the Ghibellines caused to be torn down one hundred ten palaces and six hundred smaller buildings; yet there was still a city. Despite this — and conflagrations and other whole-sale destructions — Florence remained on the map.

In connection with the conflagrations, it should be noted that while brick and stone buildings were by no means unknown in the time of Dante, a substantial number of houses were still made of wood.

"Keep handy," warned Pace da Certaldo, "at least twelve large canvas sacks in which to put your belongings if a fire breaks out in your neighborhood, and also a thick piece of rope long enough to reach to the ground so that you can escape from the window."

He said nothing about buckets of water. Evidently when a fire broke out there was nothing to do but save your own hide.

« 4 »

But if there were wooden and crudely built houses in this Florence, there was also magnificence. The *nuova gente* — the merchant-burgher capitalist class — was both buying and building. Its members had the means to do this.

This is not the place — nor for that matter the book — in which to go into the whole complicated story of the guilds and their origins. But its outlines must be noted. In 934, the Florentines could record the activities of Amalpertus, deacon and doctor; in 1038, of Giovanni, "who is called a turner"; in 1076, of Barone, a shieldmaker; in 1091, of Benzolus, a potter; in 1113, of another Giovanni, maker of wooden shoes; in 1193, of Rein-aldus, a loom-maker; and even as late as 1211, of one Albizzo of Ferrara, a ragseller on the Lungarno.

These obviously were independent craftsmen, artisans, and/or huck-sters, and such independent workers of every kind there continued to be — at any rate for a while. But early indeed they began to organize themselves into *arti*, or corporate entities. These were the famous Florentine guilds.

By the time of Dante, these guilds were both firmly established and all powerful. When he was a youth, every male over sixteen — except, presumably, those who were excluded because of noble birth or for other reasons — was obliged to join either a guild or a trade association. Those who did not were known as *scioperati*. Literally, this meant "men without employment," but to the Florentines it connoted "shiftless vagabonds." Twenty-one in number, the guilds brought Florence to a peak of prosperity which was without equal during the Middle Ages except at Byzantium.

The members of the Bankers Guild became the moneylenders to Europe. These *mercatores Tuscie* — but they were also known as "Lombard dogs"! — were noted at the famous Champagne fairs by 1100, while by 1200 Florentine banking houses were established in England. At the time he was placed under papal interdict, Magna Carta John was doing business with sixty-nine of them! Again in England, they financed Edward I. In France, they lent money to Charles of Anjou, to Philip the Fair, and possibly to St. Louis.

The agents and the buyers of the Wool Guild — the famous Arte di Lana — were everywhere too. Closely associated with the Umiliati — the Humble Fathers of St. Michael of Alexandria, who came to Florence in 1238 bringing with them improved working conditions and more efficient techniques — the members of this guild were at least slightly oriented toward religious houses and did much of their buying from monasteries in such strange places as Boccheselle in Chenti (Boxley in Kent), Stalleo in Guarvicche (Stoneleigh in Warwick), Guizzopo (Worksop near Nottingham), Guesame (Eversham), Miense (Amiens), Bosella (Brussels), Inghiemino in Arnaldo (Enghien in Hainaut), Merusolle (Melrose), Gonellasso (Galloway), and Chilosola (Kelso). But the shrewd Florentines who were sent out from the guild's handsome headquarters near Orsanmichele were too aware of the varying excellencies of the different fleeces to be restricted to this one kind of source. From Portuguese Algarve — Tuscanized into Garbo — came the best wool, but Spanish wool, from merino sheep brought into the peninsula by the Romans and crossed with native stock, was also excellent. Both of these were sold as *lana di Garbo*, and they brought the highest prices. But even in England, the Wool Guild's agents sometimes bought directly from sheep-raisers in Codignaldo (the Cotswolds) and Scrisestri (Chichester). According to Villani, in 1308 the Wool Guild employed thirty thousand persons, operated two hundred workshops in Florence and the immediate *contrada*, and manufactured each year between seventy and eighty thousand pieces of cloth having a total value of two hundred thousand gold florins.

But it was not merely the Wool Guild and the Bankers Guild which raked in by the sackful coins both clipped and honestly minted.

The ancient and honorable Arte di Calimala (Foreign Cloth Guild) purchased cloth from abroad, then processed it and dyed it with the famous Florentine dyes, which were so fast that "the Venetians must confess that they learned this art from us" and so vivid that the consuls of the guild after 1279 were given the exclusive right to make the cloth used in the red robes of the cardinals. It was a very profitable business.

The innkeepers entertained travelers from every part of the accessible world.

The armormakers and swordsmiths, the harnessmakers, and the always turbulent butchers (with their coat of arms showing a goat rampant) and bakers had trouble keeping up with the demand amid a people that both fought and feasted.

It is not possible to estimate the private wealth of Florence at this time. But less than thirty years after Dante's death, the public funds were estimated to be twenty million gold florins. They were not very much less during his lifetime.

Some part of this wealth was put to public use. It went into the construction of the churches, the municipal buildings, the bridges, and the monasteries which have already been noted and which inspired Dino Compagni to his exultant words. But there was much private building too, for the moneymen of the Western world saw no reason to hide their light under a bushel. Wealth creates wealth, and one way to show that you had the wealth to do this was to live in size and spendor. The wool merchants with their worldwide interests, the managers and proprietors of famous — sometimes even those of obscure — countinghouses where all that glittered actually *was* gold, even some of the humbler guildsmen began to move into residences so magnificent that not even the popes and the monarchs with whom the Florentines now began to deal as equals could despise them.

The "*palazzo*" of the Tosinghi, for example. This did not compare either in fragile grace or marble filigree with contemporary palaces in Venice, but it was far from being the modest home of a private citizen. Its facade was one hundred sixty feet tall and decorated with handsome columns. It had a tower almost two hundred fifty feet high. It was the tallest building in Florence.

The "*palagio*" of the self-made Cerchi was another. This faced, and was near, the Badia and so was in Dante's own part of the city. It had been the Ravignani home, but became the property of the Counts Guidi when Guido Vecchio married the good Gualdrada. It literally squatted over the Porta San Piero and, since the Cerchi were thought of — to use a modern phrase — as social climbers who had bought their way into respectability, it was often pointed at as an example of what the world was coming to. Dante may have been among the pointers.

There was the house of the Baldovinetti in the *popolo* of Santo Stefano. Since a *trecento* drawing still extant shows us its appearance, we can at least know what the exterior of a Florentine mansion was like. On the street-facing, or front, side of the ground floor was a large gate which led to shops and offices — the shops and offices of the Baldovinetti — and beside this was another door, perhaps half the size of the first one, leading to a stairway and to the living quarters. The building was three stories high and each story had three windows on each side. These were closed with wooden shutters. The roof was slanting and seems to have been covered with slate.

Another imposing edifice was the Palazzo de' Mozzi across the Arno and near the Ponte Rubaconte. This is still standing. The Mozzi were important people, and their home sheltered such persons as Pope Gregory X, Cardinal Giacomo Savelli (later Pope Honorius IV), and the pacificator Cardinal Latino during their various visits to Florence.

A fourth edifice which Dante saw was the Palazzo de' Frescobaldi. We can see it too, for it has recently been restored. It was a favorite of French royalty, many of whom — for better or worse — stayed there.

Finally, there was the great Palazzo Spini, which also still stands — and, also thanks to restorations, with something of its old appearance — at the corner of the Lungarno Acciaiuoli and the Via Tornabuoni. It was built by banker Geri Spini in 1289. Dante, then, could see it slowly taking shape, and later on would have cause to regret this. For in those days — but not now — it had arches which connected with buildings across the street, and hence it could be, and was, used to control the Arno crossing. It has a gay immortality in that the banker Cisti (*Decameron* IV, 2), hoping for favors there, sent Geri "a small pitcher of new Bolognese ware, full of his good white wine." But more important — and to Dante, disastrous — it was the headquarters of the Donati and other Dante enemies during the Black-White struggle for power, of which we will hear in due course.

« *5* »

In spite of the greenery and the gardens which have already been noted, these palaces — and others too numerous to note — did not always stand apart from their neighbors on open ground.

They, and the mean hovels and the modest citizen houses too, were more often on narrow streets which, if by 1290 they were already paved — at that time even the streets of Paris were still deep and slimy mire — twisted and bent without any logic (other perhaps than to go around the land belonging to some influential property owner) and were kept dark and gloomy, but also cool, by numerous overhanging stories and buttresses. Sometimes a vault or covered gallery crossed from one side to the other — there was one of the latter at the Arte di Lana building — and connected two houses belonging to the same family or the same company. These added to the cool and to the darkness. Often there was a wooden balcony. There were numerous tabernacles and shrines, usually with an image of the Virgin Mary, and these often drew crowds that emphasized the narrowness. There were numerous loggias and porticos. Wherever the *vicoli* (small squares that often amounted to little more than an enlargement of the street) were large enough, there was a stone well. There was at least one well in each of the fifty-seven *popoli*. Women and maidservants used to gather there to gossip.

Some of these passages between buildings give the flavor of old Florence by their name alone.

There was the Via di Calimala (Foreign Cloth Merchant Street), which ran from the Mercato Vecchio to the Mercato Nuovo. This was short — not much more than one hundred fifty yards long — but even so it held a substantial part of the wealth of Florence. It was dominated by the Cavalcanti Palace and was filled with talk about the latest prices in Paris, St. Denis, Troyes, Bourges, Marseilles, Toulon, Avignon, Montpellier, Carcassonne, and Toulouse.

There was also talk on it of the latest and most brilliant colors. *Scarlatto d'oricello*, for example, which was specially prescribed for all robes of state and for ceremonial hangings and tapestries. The secret of its manufacture was carefully guarded, but it was known to be made of a small admixture of madder with the *oricello* (white moss) dye which was discovered in the Levant by one Nardo Alamanno, who thereafter took the cognomen of Rucellai (famous indeed in later Florentine annals) for himself and his family.

The Via di Calimala was sedate and orderly, neither indecent, blasphemous, injurious, nor provocative language — the punishment was imprisonment — being permitted within its purlieus. But lest the restraint on Florentine tongues be too great, near at hand was Il Baccano, or Rowdy Row, called this because of the noisy shouting of its apprentices as they tried to attract customers to their employers' shops.

Another prosperous street was the Via Por Santa Maria, which ran southward from the Mercato Nuovo to the Ponte Vecchio. It was the home of the small but exceedingly wealthy Silk Guild. It was also noted as a favorite resort for practical jokesters. Even a century earlier the jurist Buoncompagno had observed that the medieval Florentines were "great buffoons." One of their ideas of high humor was to place butts of dirty water under the shadow of the Torre degli Amidei or the Torre di Leone. A chain would be stretched across the street. When some pompous and overstuffed merchant passed he would trip, and if he fell into one of the buckets he would immediately be the target for a volley of ordure or even stones from the small boys who always lurked in the neighborhood.

Today's Via Calzaioli (Street of the Shoemakers) is another medieval street. In Dante's day it was divided into three parts — the Corso degli Amidei, presumably the headquarters of that aristocratic family; the Via de' Pittori (Street of the Painters); and the Via de' Cacciaivoli (Street of the Cheese Vendors), the last filled with the sharp, appetizing aromas which came from the cheeses of every size, shape, and color that hung upon the walls of its shops.

There was also a Vicolo del Guanto, where practiced their trade the dressers of kidskin and calfskin and the makers of military-looking gauntlets and delicate gloves for ladies. For fairly obvious reasons, it was regarded as a trysting place for lovers.

There was a Via del Fuoco (Furnace or Fire Street), where the ironmongers worked. The fiery glow and smell of sulfur around their forges may have given Dante a foretaste of the lower regions.

There was a Via dei' Pelliccieri, where the skinners and the tanners held forth.

There was — and still is — a Via Vacchereccia, or Cow Pasture Street. Oddly enough, it had little to do with cattle but was the working place of goldsmiths and niellists.

« 6 »

This, then, in Dante's time, was the city which he called Fiorenza but which now, far less poetically, is known as Firenze or Florence.

To the north — and even beyond its newest walls — it sloped upward to the Apennine foothills. Here it was less crowded, and the buildings were of a different sort. On the long and even then relatively broad street which led to the city from the San Gallo Gate — it is still called the Via di San Gallo — there were, for instance, relatively few private dwellings. Instead, there was a succession of monasteries and convents.

But to the south — and hence across the Arno — it was another matter. To be sure, certain of the fine edifices described above were located there, as those owned by the Mozzi and the Frescobaldi. In addition the Velluti (called this because they had made their fortune from the manufacture of velvet), some of the Bardi, the Nerli, the Rossi, and the Manelli with their quick daggers came from this quarter. But basically the Oltrarno was a concentration of slums. One section was even called the Borgo Pidiglioso — in modern English, Louseville.

The river itself was both good and bad. Even as early as 1283 there was a tidy *lungarno* which extended from the present-day Ponte alle Grazie to the Ponte alla Carraia. This is a little more than a thousand yards. It was a place where young people walked — Dante among them.

But in other respects the stream was less attractive. Slightly to the west was a large island called Sardegna (Sardinia) because of its shape. Originally there was a fuller's mill on it, but in 1277 this was replaced with mills for grinding wheat. There was a city-established fishery on one bridge. On another, the goatskin tanners had their workshops. (Only the Ponte Vecchio with its goldsmiths and pursemakers was clean and pleasant.) In between was the poorhouse of Altrafonte. All along there were mills of every sort — a great menace in time of flood, since like "the mill on the Po" described by Riccardo Bacchelli in the modern novel of that name they floated and were apt to break loose in time of flood and wreck everything in their path. There were numerous water gates, each with its congeries of ferries and fishing boats. There was, of course, every kind of hovel and shack.

Obviously none of these contributed to the river's purity and crystal clarity. For their waste was often highly colored and always it stank.

But not merely along the Arno, north of it and south of it as well, Florence certainly offended fastidious nostrils.

"Street hygiene," said one of its modern historians, "left something to be desired."

Every kind of refuse was cast into the public way. Only the best houses had privies. Citizens not fortunate enough to have one made use of the ruins and abandoned buildings between the first and second circles of the walls. In 1297, the stench in front of the church of San Lorenzo was so great that it almost prevented the congregation and their priests from attending Mass.

To the scent of the sewer was added a barnyard odor that was characteristic of the medieval city. For not only could chickens, geese, and cows be seen almost on every hand, but pigs roved and rooted as their appetite and fancy moved them.

"Whoever is acquainted with Florence," wrote Sacchetti, "knows that on the first Sunday of each month it is the custom for men and women to go to San Gallo in company, and that they go there rather to make merry than to seek a pardon. Upon one of these days, Giotto set out to go there with some friends, and as he paused for a while in the Via del Cocomero [Watermelon Street, now the Via Ricasoli] to tell some tale or other there passed by some of these pigs of St. Anthony, and one of them, upon a sudden wild rampage, went between his legs in such a manner that he fell down upon the ground.

"Helped by his companions, he got up and shook off the dirt, nor did he curse at the pigs nor say a word to them. Instead, turning with a half smile to those who were with him, he said this:

" 'Well, well! Can you blame them? I've gained thousands of *lire* with their bristles, and I've never so much as given them a pail of swill!' "

The Tantony pigs! Those porkers belonging by charity to the Holy Church. They will be referred to later by Dante in one of the most scathing passages of his great poem.

They were almost as sacred as the cows of India, and fully as free-roving.

That is until the feast of St. Thomas!

"San Tommè chi piglia il porco per lo pè!" Day of St. Tommy, when you grab the pig by his feet and put him in your tummy!

On that day it was reasonable not only to butcher a hog, but even to steal him from your neighbor if you could, or smuggle him past the ever-watchful city customs.

« 7 »

In this city which I have described lived the Florentines. They lived in the handsome edifices, in the citizen houses, in the *casolari* (tenements) and slums. And out of them they poured upon every occasion. They poured into the Florentine street.

For even as in ancient Byzantium, where brocaded noblemen jostled garlic-reeking artisans along the crowded Mesé, the street was everything. The street and the *mercato*, the piazza and the *vicolo*.

Space was at a premium, rents high, and business houses, monasteries, and even private dwellings let their activities overflow outward — just as they do even today in many a town in Italy.

Many an artisan, for example, sat under the painted sign which hung over the front of his shop as he stitched a leather sole to a shoe or worked on a silver cup. The chapter of San Lorenzo leased the loggia of its hospital to barbers, bakers, and retailers. Grain merchants sat beside their piled-up sacks of grain in front of exquisitely beautiful Orsanmichele. Many of the lesser money changers or pawnbrokers did their business nearby, or on the Via Tavolini, or even in the Oltrarno quarter. Those who belonged to a guild were allowed to have a chair, a table, a table-cover of green baize, and, of course, a sack of gold and a wooden or metal bowl filled with small coins. But there were unauthorized money dealers as well, more or less shady in their operations, and these too were in the streets.

In the meantime, transportation had to be taken care of. There were no carriages, and litters had not yet come into use. Noblemen and soldiers rode, some of them arrogantly like the young man of the Adimari family who pushed his way through an alley with his legs spread out so that the plain people he passed would have to polish the tips of his boots. "Appropriating the property of the commune!" Dante testified. Maybe he was one of those whose robes were rubbed by the young man's boots.

The plain people walked.

Merchandise and materials were transported on the backs of sturdy little donkeys. If you can believe the story — and why not? — some of the donkey drivers would, a little later on, mingle verses from "the book of Dante" with the "*Arri! Arri!*" with which they drove their *asinelli* along. A similar story is told of a blacksmith singing from "Il Dante" as he beat out red-hot iron on his anvil. Dante did not appreciate either honor. He is said to have exchanged figs — the most vulgar and insulting gesture known to Florentines — with the donkey driver. He scattered the blacksmith's tools and implements all over the alley. "You have ruined my business!" — the blacksmith was clipping short, and otherwise garbling, Dante's verses — "Take no offense if I should ruin yours!"

Through the midst of this melee moved hawkers of every kind of feminine commodity and secondhand dealers who urged all and sundry either to purchase the wares they were offering or to sell them things for which they had no more need.

The ladies who thronged around them did not come from their mirrors without rouge as had the wife of Bellincione Berti.

"Who is the greatest master of painting in the world?" asked an artist of his colleagues one day. "Cimabue? Or Giotto? Or Buffalmaco? Or Stefano?"

"The women of Florence," replied the sculptor Alberto Arnoldi. "They rub here, they chalk there, they make a pale and yellow face into the likeness of a rose. They try even to improve the handiwork of God."

In authorized places, vegetable dealers, both male and female, offered farm produce from their handcarts.

The crowd thickened when the public crier proclaimed lost goods or when he announced a death, for which he was paid by the deceased's family. The people gathered, too, when the herald of the commune read out a law or a sentence, or proclaimed a bankruptcy or the appointment of a guardian or curator.

Blind beggars abounded. With their dogs, canes, and wooden platters, they could be seen everywhere but particularly near those churches where a reputed miracle drew many people. They did very well.

"I have been blind twelve years," said one, "and I have amassed a thousand pounds."

"I was born blind," said another, "and am now forty-seven years old. If I had kept all I gained, I would be the richest man in the world or in the Maremma!"

Cutpurses and pickpockets were apparently numerous too. Their favorite hunting ground was in the markets. They usually operated in pairs, one having a sharp pair of scissors and the other attracting the victim's attention. Very often they ended up having their pictures painted on some conspicuous wall just as nowadays the photographs of men wanted can be seen in post offices. It was one way of having your portrait done by Giotto.

But it was not merely business, whether legitimate or otherwise, that intruded on the Florentine scene. The Florentines loved entertainment. Indeed, as a careful historian notes, this love was carried to such a point that it became a public interest. There were, for example, magnificent pageants supported by the city itself when Clemence, daughter of the Emperor Rudolf, passed through the city on her way to Naples to marry the son of the heir to the throne of that city; when Charles II, also of Naples, arrived with his wife, three sons, and a daughter-in-law for a short state visit; and also when Cardinal Latino came at Pope Gregory X's order to attempt a pacification between the Guelphs and the Ghibellines. All these were held during Dante's youth.

Civic in its size too and almost civic in its intent was the great festival given in 1283 by the Rossi and their neighbors of the *popolo* of Santa Felicità in the Oltrarno quarter "in honor of the merchants and the artisans and especially the Guelphs." A company of a thousand white-clad youths and maidens was assembled under a Lord "whose name was love."

"This said company devoted itself to naught but games and diversions together with dances both by knights and ladies and the people. Other honorable folk moved about the city with trumpets and other instruments and they joyfully and gaily took part in banquets and feasts. This court lasted for almost two months and it was the most noble and renowned that was ever held in Tuscany or Florence. To which court there came from other cities and lands many gentle troubadours and many jesters, and all were received and provided for with due honor.

No less dazzling were the city's great religious celebrations. Of these, the most important was the festival of St. John the Baptist, the city's patron saint.

Three days before the festival, a herald, to the sound of trumpets, proclaimed that all who were fifteen years old or more must carry their candles to the Baptistery and to San Pier Maggiore. At the same time the decoration of the piazzas in front of the two churches was begun — the one in front of the Baptistery at the expense of the city, the one in front of San Pier Maggiore at the expense of the Wool Guild. Over each of them a "heaven," or canopy, was stretched. Forty feet above the ground and held by ropes attached to iron rings which were affixed to the walls of the buildings, the canopy was originally of simple azure cloth but later it was richly decorated. In the middle were the lily of the commune and the red cross of the people. Around the edges were the standards of the corporations and magistracies.

In midmorning on June 23, the long procession began. It was headed by the clergy wearing their brocaded dalmatics and the other rich vestments with which they did not think it inappropriate to honor the ascetic who had lived in the desert on locusts and wild honey. They carried all the relics which the city possessed. They were followed by the lay confraternities, each preceded by a band of musicians.

The cortege started from the Duomo, still covered with the scaffolding of its constructors; made a circle of the streets, some of which had been transformed into ballrooms and on all of which the shops displayed their finest wares; and then returned to its starting point. At vespers came the offering of candles by the guilds and companies. Before each one was borne a waving gonfalon. Later selected members put on feats of acrobatic skill, while others on stilts and fantastically garbed to represent spirits or giants moved rowdily about through the crowds.

Each parish of the *contado* also sent a representative. These village "first citizens" assembled at San Felice Oltrarno. Thence, with lit torches and following blaring trumpets and whining bagpipes (which, by the way, originally came from Italy, not Scotland), they crossed the Ponte Vecchio on their way to the center of the town. These too were accompanied by jesters and buffoons, to the great delight of the crowd.

Ahead came the priors themselves — and it is interesting to note that Dante's priorate embraced this late June celebration — six in number and accompanied by their official staff. Among them were the Guelph captains, before whom a noble youth upon a prancing steed carried a silken banner with on it the Guelph eagle gripping a serpent. Then followed the knights, the more important citizens, and the foreign ambassadors. After these came emissaries of the cities and of the castles and towns which had submitted to Florence. Here civic pride roared from hoarse and sometimes vinous throats as candle after candle, often carved into the shape of the submitting castle, was humbly offered as a tribute to the city's power.

On the next day, there was a solemn divine service, yet even in this the man who conducted it usually made a bid for popular favor.

"Do not preach upon usury," cried a poor woolworker at a Florentine service, "for none of us has money to lend. All of us are poor as a hare."

"*Beati sunt pauperes!*" the preacher replied. "Blessed are the poor!"

Later in the day was held the long-awaited horse race. It started in front of the church of Ognissanti; went down the Via Vigna Nuova; crossed the Mercato Vecchio; then down the Via del Corso and the Borgo degli Albizzi; and ended at San Pier Maggiore. There trumpets, beautiful ladies on the red and white cart on which the prizes were displayed, the judges on a wooden platform, and the priors and magistrates from tapestry-decorated windows greeted the winner. Not more than twelve horses were allowed to enter. Some were ridden by their owners.

« 8 »

There were, of course, private amusements too.

The apprentices, for example, having munched their onions and their bread and cheese with perhaps some hard sausage and Trebbiano wine, often indulged in impromptu *calcio*, or football, among the tethered beasts and the stalls of this or that market. Doubtless they caused as much confusion as once did a trained crow who in the Mercato Vecchio starting pecking two mules "laden with cloth which had just come from the presser." This set the mules to rearing and plunging, and by the time they were brought under control they had wrecked the stalls of the butchers, kicked over the baskets of Lisa the fruitseller, and trampled "all the vegetables of Monna Menta." Ultimately the *podestà* had to intervene between the heads of the Wool Guild and the Butchers Guild, who were by now hurling objurgations at each other.

Edgecumbe Staley speaks of a game of "*palla e maglio*" — ball and bat — which he says was the ancestor of cricket. Since he was an Englishman, I will not contradict him.

Jousting was also popular — in the form of both hand to hand conflict and tilting at the ring. A favorite jousting ground was Peretola, four miles northwest of Florence. There, despite the fact that the Church frowned on tournaments and would not bury a man killed in one in consecrated ground, the young men of the city used to hie, mounted on blooded stallions equipped with bright and flying horsecloths, tooled saddles, and jangling bells.

But it was not merely the young and agile who tried their hand at this sport. Sacchetti — once more, Franco Sacchetti — tells the sad story of one Agnolo di Ser Gherardo who despite his gray hairs decided that he could run a course with the best of them. He hired a horse from a livery stable in the Borgo Ognissanti and out he jogged. But when he got to Peretola some of the young bloods put a thistle under the tail of his steed and he came back through the Porta al Prato like a Florentine John Gilpin. He got no sympathy at home. As she pried him out of his armor, his wife gave him a tongue-lashing for his seventy-year-old folly.

Fistfighting was popular, and it was much practiced until a 1294 *consulta* (ordinance) forbade it on the grounds that it led to feuds and vendettas. But feuds were also a Florentine "pastime." They were bloody and remorseless, and they lasted from generation to generation. "A feud," ran a Florentine saying, "less than a hundred years old has not cut its eyeteeth."

Another popular diversion was a game called *il Veglio della Montagna* (the Old Man of the Mountain). This was a masquerade in which the Old Man and his oriental assassins moved about the city, supposedly playing tricks but often committing crimes. It was declared illegal, but the law was little enforced.

On the more gentle side, Tuscany — and Florence — became a center of music and the dance. The very names *canzone* — song (*chanson*), now lyric poem — and *ballata* — ballad, from *ballare*, to dance — indicate the close connection with singing and the dance, for much of the poetry of the day, including Dante's, was either sung or danced to. Dancing was an integral — and often intricate — part of every celebration, including, or perhaps especially, weddings. Singing was identified more with the Church. Indeed many of the confraternities — such as those marching in the great St. John's Day procession — were essentially confraternities of laud singers. But singing had its social aspects too.

It was customary, for example, to sing under the window of one's ladylove accompanied by lute, guitar, or violin. Such performances were called *mattinate*, or morning songs. They met with no disapproval when they were conducted at that time of the day, or even in the afternoon, but when this lover's caterwauling became nocturnal it evoked enough complaints to call forth a statute providing a fine and the confiscation of the offending instruments.

But along with the animated Florentine life; along with this love-singing whether by night or by day; along with the business activity; along with a fierce and savage politics which will be discussed in due course; along with a flowering of art which almost simultaneously set Nicola and Giovanni Pisano to chipping marble and Buffalmaco and Andrea Tafi and Giotto to painting frescoes, there was one other field of activity which must be noted.

Suddenly in the city of the red lily there was a proliferation of the ability to write poetry — or at least verse — which is perhaps without parallel in any other place or time.

Here a small amount of historic background is necessary. Although there are some dissenters and although some of their arguments are appealing, it is generally agreed that rhymed poetry came to Sicily from Provence during the enlightened reign of the last Hohenstaufen emperor, Frederick II. It had flourished in Provence but had vanished thence, partly because it had become ingrown and deliberately obscure (like much of the most critically acclaimed poetry of today) and partly as a consequence of the brutal Albigensian Crusade (1208–1226) which destroyed not only a so-called heretical sect but one of the most enlightened civilizations of medieval Europe. From Sicily, it moved to central Italy. To Bologna, for example — where King Enzo, Frederick's poetry-writing son, was imprisoned for seventeen years. To Arezzo. From central Italy, it came to Florence.

Be that as it may, it was well established in Florence by the time of Dante's birth. A Vatican manuscript, for instance, preserves 999 sonnets and *canzoni* of this time, and of these 453 are by Florentines. Two hundred and five, it should be noted, are anonymous, and some of these may be by Florentines too.

These 453 poems — and many others — were written, too, by men, and in one instance a woman, of almost every imaginable occupation and of virtually every class.

Pacino de Ser Filippo Angiolari and Gianni di Forese Alfani served terms as gonfaloniers of justice. Lapo Salterelli was a judge. Dino Compagni was a prior and held other offices. Torrigiano de' Rusticelli was the most distinguished physician in Florence. Because of his long-winded medical treatises, he was known as "the supercommentator." Migliore degli Abbati, Chiarino Ghibetri, Sennuccio del Bene, Lambertuccio Frescobaldi and his son Dino were either merchants or important bankers. Orlanduccio Orafo, on the other hand, was a goldsmith, while his adversary in a famous poetic contest was a capain of the crossbowmen. Guido Cavalcanti — Dante's "first," if somewhat older, "friend" — was an aristocrat and to some degree a dilettante. Pace da Certaldo — he is the one who in a prosaic moment told the Florentines how to protect themselves when fire broke out — was a notary. Gianni Alfani — another Gianni Alfani — belonged to the Silk Guild. The Compiuta Donzella (accomplished damsel) was a young lady of good family and good breeding.

The subjects were as various as the men — and the women — who wrote them, for in those days — or in those days in Florence, at any rate – a poem was not simply a literary exercise. You wrote a poem when today you would write a letter to an editor. You wrote a poem when today you would write a book review. You wrote a poem in place of an epistle offering condolences or congratulations. You wrote a poem telling how to be a businessman or a knight.

But basically they could be fitted into one of five categories.

Love.

War – including Florentine victories and Florentine defeats.

Politics.

The decay of the old Florentine morality.

And satire.

In the last, the Florentines showed great gifts for invective, but equally great gifts for sarcasm.

> When God created Master Messerin,
> The whole world cried: "Behold a miracle!
> He's bird and beast and he is man as well.
> Something of each to making him went in."
> His neck is like a duck's, long, tough, and thin.
> Like a giraffe's his long and slanting back.
> But all too human is, they say, alack
> His simpering face, in color cramoisie.
> In singing, he's melodious as a crow.
> In intellect, a poor dumb animal.
> But lo, he wears the clothing of a man.
> When the Lord made him, the results were small.
> In fact, I think He shaped him but to show
> That what the Lord God wants to do he can.

Finally – like this poem by Rustico di Filippo, who, oddly enough, was a Ghibelline aristocrat – they were all written in the vivid, earthy, resilient Florentine tongue which was now not only being spoken by the banker at his bench and the hawker at his street corner but had even begun to replace crabbed medieval Latin in legal documents. They were all filled with the pungent, pithy, popular phrases of the Florentine tavern and the Florentine *mercato*. It was much the same with Shakespeare in his London. It is always so when the arts become lively and great.

The man about whom this book is written was one of these Florentines. He too wrote about love – if it is necessary to use paper to state this. He too wrote about war and politics and the decay of the old Florentine morality. On occasion, he too wrote satire, and once he even indulged in the rough and tumble of a *tenzone*, which is literary polemics.

He too used the Florentine *volgare* – in fact, he established it, perhaps against his intention, as the foundation upon which the Italian language would be built.

But although he wrote it better than anyone ever has or ever will, neither in the fact of using it — nor even always in the way he used it — was he a precursor. And sometimes he was even a follower.

In this matter, then — as in so many others — once again was he the product of his times.

III

The Poet as a Young Man

JUST as we cannot know certainly — and yet are reasonably sure — who Dante's mother was, so we can be reasonably sure of — and yet cannot know certainly — the year of his birth, the day and the month in which he was born, and, except for those who push critical skepticism to its last limits, the place where he first saw the light of day.

I use the phrase "those who push critical skepticism to its last limits" advisedly, for of his birthplace at least there can be no well-founded doubt.

To be sure, the faithfully kept baptismal registry in which, presumably, his name was entered has disappeared. We do not have, therefore, the same kind of evidence which we have in the case of Shakespeare, whom we know to have been baptized *in* Stratford on Avon *on* April 26, 1564.

But there is other evidence, and it seems conclusive.

Dante himself states (*Inferno* XXIII) that he was born and grew up "in the big city by the Arno." Other than Florence, there were only two cities upon the famous river to which the adjective could have been applied. But clearly neither Arezzo nor Pisa is meant.

"Those hills" — that is to say, the hills of the Fiesolans — wrote Fillippo Villani, nephew of the more famous Giovanni Villani, in his *De Origine Civitatis Florentiae,* "beneath which thou" — that is to say, Dante — "wert born."

In *Paradiso* XXV, Dante speaks of Florence as "the fair sheepfold where I slept as lamb."

In *Purgatorio* XXIV, he describes it as "the place where I was set to live."

In *Inferno* X, the famous warrior Farinata degli Uberti recognizes him as a Florentine by his way of speaking.

> "Your very accent makes it more than plain
> That you are native of that noble city
> To which perhaps I brought too much annoy."

Even deeper in hell (*Inferno* XXXIII), Count Ugolino of Pisa, gnawing the skull of the Archbishop Ruggieri, also identifies him by the way he pronounces certain words:

> "A Florentine
> You truly seem to me whenas you speak."

Loquela is the word used by Farinata for accent, and the Florentine *loquela* was as distinctive then as it is today. Just one example: the Florentine almost always changes *c* to *h*. Instead of *questa casa* (this house), he says *huesta hasa*. For *io sono a Prato* (I have gone to Prato), he says *io sono andatho a Pratho*. Other examples will suggest themselves.

Guido Guerra (*Inferno* XVI) and others know that he has come from their city from the garb he wears.

> "Halt now, who by thy clothing seemst to be
> One who has come from our so wicked city."

The long gown, or *gonella*, which is so familiar to us in almost every picture of Dante! The pointed *cappuccio*, or hood, which had turned what had once been a Roman toga into something very different!

Further supporting testimony is as follows. Dante calls himself a Florentine in his book on the Italian language *De Vulgari Eloquentia*. He inscribes himself "*Florentinus exul immeritus*" (a Florentine and an undeserved exile) in a letter to his fellow poet Cino da Pistoia. He writes himself down as "*humilis Italus Dantes Alagherii Florentinus*" (a humble Italian, Dante Alighieri, the Florentine) in his epistle to the princes and the people of Italy. He denominates himself "*Dantes Alagherii Florentinus*" in another epistle, his scathing communication to the Florentines. He uses similar expressions in his letters to Henry VII and to the college of cardinals. In his letter to Can Grande della Scala, lord of Verona, he makes himself known as a Florentine "by birth, but not by conduct."

It might be argued — and indeed it has been — that some of these phrases would apply just as much if he were a Florentine citizen but not born in Florence. This could be said of *some* of the passages cited, but not *all* of them.

Moreover, the only even slightly plausible point which can be made against a Florentine birth comes from the fact that the Alighieri were a Guelph family. The Guelphs were exiled after the battle of Montaperti (1260) and supposedly did not begin to return until 1267, or two years after Dante was born. Indeed, "Zerio di Belli Aleghieri" — this is taken to be uncle Geri di Bello — was specifically noted as being in Bologna, a Guelph rendezvous, in 1266. Must not Alighiero II have been in exile too?

But it is also true that the Alighieri, although Guelphs, were not important Guelphs, and it is almost certain that Alighiero II's wife was a member of an extremely notable Ghibelline family.

One of three things, then, could have happened.

Because of his relative obscurity, Alighiero II was not exiled with the other Guelphs.

Because he was connected with the Abbati, he was not exiled with them.

Because of his relative obscurity or because of his connection, he *was* exiled but not in exile's strictest form. He was sent merely to *confino* in a nearby subject town. This was like house arrest or being put on bounds. Gabriella lived there with him, but came back to the city to have her baby.

« 2 »

There is little, if any, more reason to feel any uncertainty as to the year in which Dante's birth took place.

"The glory of the Italian race," wrote Giovanni Boccaccio, "was born in our city when the imperial throne was vacant through the death of Frederick in the year of the saving incarnation of the king of the universe MCCLXV [1265] while Pope Urban IV sat in the chair of St. Peter."

In citing the author of the *Decameron*, it should be pointed out that Boccaccio was eight years old when Dante died; that he knew not only Dante's daughter and possibly his sons but also his sisters and his cousins and his aunt; that he lived in Dante's city; and finally that he was the founder of a Dante cult which has never ceased to flourish and as such was an assiduous collector of what today we would call Danteana. I bring up this matter because there are some who feel that the gay-writing man from Certaldo could not very well be a responsible authority. I consider him highly responsible and will turn to him again and again.

But it is not merely upon Boccaccio that we may rely.

"In the year 1321," wrote Giovanni Villani, "in the month of July, Dante Alighieri of Florence died in the city of Ravenna. He died in exile at the age of about fifty-six years."

Subtract 56 from 1321 and the result is 1265.

He was born in 1265, said Leonardo Bruni, who, although he did not compose his *Life of Dante* until the beginning of the fifteenth century, clearly had access to contemporary sources, *"a little after the return to Florence of the Guelphs who had been exiled after Montaperti!"*

The italics and the exclamation point are mine. Bruni not only gives further support to a 1265 birth, but seems to indicate an earlier return of the Florentine exiles than is generally accepted. This adds a fourth possibility to the three I have given above — the possibility that Dante's father was indeed an exile, but that he had returned before Dante was born.

But Dante himself supports 1265 as the year of his birth. For example, he does so in the opening lines of the *Commedia*.

> *Nel mezzo del cammin di nostra vita*
> *Mi ritrovai per una selva oscura.*

> Midway upon the pathway of my life
> I found myself within a darkling wood.

But what was this midway point of life?

This question was asked both by Dante's son Pietro and by Benvenuto da Imola, another early and well-informed commentator. Through similar reasoning, they came to virtually the same answer. I give that of Pietro di Dante because it is more concise.

"The psalmist says: 'The days of our years are three score and ten, and if we live longer it will be in labor and sorrow.' And therefore the midway point is thirty-five."

Dante, then, was thirty-five years old when he commenced his imaginary journey through hell, purgatory, and heaven, and he has made it plain to us that his encounter with Virgil which begins it took place on Good Friday 1300.

Take 35 from 1300 and once again you have 1265.

Indeed, it is only when we try to determine an actual birthday that we run into difficulties, and even in this matter we can come closer than might be expected.

For Dante himself has established his birth as having taken place within a thirty-day period, writing this about it in *Paradiso* XXII:

> As, reader, I do hope to see again
> This heavenly triumph—and for this I weep
> My sins full often and do beat my breast—
> I swear you would not swifter snatch your hand
> From flame you thrust it into than I saw

> The sign that follows Taurus and was within it.
> O glorious stars! O light filled to the brim
> With power! You from whom—I do acknowledge—
> Comes all my genius, such as it may be!
> *In you arose, in you did likewise set,*
> *He who is father of all mortal life*
> *When first I breathed and knew the Tuscan air.*

The sign that follows Taurus is Gemini. At the present time the sun is in Gemini between May 22 and June 21. But in 1265 — partly because of the precession of the equinoxes and partly because of the change from the Julian to the Gregorian calendar — the sun moved into this sign somewhat earlier, probably between May 14 and June 14. Dante, therefore, who certainly should know when he was born, set his natal day as having fallen in late May or early June.

Giovanni Boccaccio tried to pinpoint it even closer. He sought to eliminate June from consideration.

Between October 25 and sometime in December 1373, the aging and ailing novelist gave a series of lectures upon his great predecessor in the ancient church of Santo Stefano alla Badia not much more than a stone's throw from Dante's home. The notes on which he based these lectures have been written down, and are now known as *Il Commento alla Divina Commedia* (Commentary on the *Divine Comedy*). In them, he deals with Dante's birthday in this way:

"A worthy man named ser Pietro di Messer Giardino of Ravenna, one of Dante's most intimate friends and disciples, related to me that he was told by Dante himself as he lay upon his deathbed in the sickness which finally took him away that he had passed his fifty-sixth birthday by as much time as had elapsed from the latter part of May until this present time."

The English scholar Dr. Edward Moore has argued from this that Dante's bitrhday was May 30, 1265 — "or at most two or three days earlier" — but it is not necessary to be so precise.

We can accept Dante's somewhat wider bracket and find it sufficient to say that as May ended or June began in the year of our Lord 1265, there was born in the city of Florence to Alighiero II degli Alighieri and to Gabriella degli Abbati this Dante di Alighiero degli Alighieri whom we find it difficult not to remember even after six hundred years.

The day and the month were propitious. Gemini, as the author of the *Ottimo Commento* has pointed out, "is in the house of Mercury, and Mercury signifies, according to the astrologers, literature, learning, and science, and to this direction it inclines those who are born when it is in the ascendant or particularly when the sun is in it."

They were also appropriate.

Observed Folgore da San Gimignano, who was perhaps twenty when Dante reached the prime of his life:

> For June I give a little hill whose crown
> Is broidered with a gracious stand of trees.
> There thirty villas make a handsome frieze.
> Twelve castles stand above a little town.
> Near all of these a thousand streams flow down,
> Fed by a little stream as clear as glass.
> They move through meadows with bright flowers strewn
> And cool a meadow's smooth and short-cropped grass.

Late May was not notably different.

"Violets," noted Folgore, "and roses dazzle the eyes."

Poppies too. Myrtle. Campanulas.

The lark — and Dante was later to notice this himself and set it down in one of his most exquisitely lyrical passages — rose into the air, burst into song, and then paused to rejoice in its own song's sweetness.

The sky was bluer than the deepest deep blue of the Mediterranean, and down it slowly drifted unimaginably fleecy white clouds.

What a time for a poet to be born!

« 3 »

He was baptized on Easter Saturday the year following.

Here we have to do with ancient Florentine custom. Today baptism is a relatively private affair. Only the parents, the godparents, and such relatives and friends as the family chooses to invite are present. But in the time of Dante it was a public, almost a municipal, ceremony.

Furthermore, in the time of Dante, all baptisms took place upon the same day. The only matter in question was the year in which the baptism took place. If the baby were born before March 25 — the day of the Annunciation, on which officially the Florentine new year began — he was baptized almost immediately. If he were born after March 25, he was not baptized until a year later.

Dante was born after March 25, and therefore was baptised in 1266. Sometime after "the third Sunday in Lent" his godparents-to-be dropped a black bean into the official urn — if it had been a girl, a white bean would have been dropped — and then presented his name to the church authorities, by whom a careful scrutiny was made.

Thereafter he became part of a mass ceremony, the size of which was more than startling.

"Church records," says Robert Davidsöhn, "show that between fifty-five hundred and six thousand children were baptized every year."

The careful German historian of Florence adds that the males exceeded the females by as much as seven percent.

It is not hard to reconstruct what took place.

First, there were numerous celebrations and ceremonies which, again according to Davidsöhn, "because they took place in the spring must have made a good contribution to infant mortality." These were private. They must have involved much drinking of the sharp and heady Tuscan wine and much eating of the already famous Florentine food.

Unquestionably the Alighieri stood host to such a gathering. After all, Dante was the first scion of a family which did not place a modest value on itself.

There the baby was shown to all present, who admired him effusively as they were supposed to do.

Then he was taken through the seething mob.

The actual rite would be performed in the ancient Baptistery, which has already been described and which then faced the relatively modest Romanesque church of Santa Reparata (the cathedral of those days) as it now faces the black-and-white-striped Duomo. The space available was, therefore, little if any larger than the present-day Piazza San Giovanni. But into it were crowded not merely six thousand squalling and swaddling-clothed infants, but twelve thousand or more godparents, twelve thousand parents, and a goodly number of wet nurses, to say nothing of the hucksters, the sellers of food and of souvenirs, and the merely curious. The odor of sweat and garlic must have been suffocating, and the noise must have been deafening. But the Florentine, whether participant or spectator, took it in his stride.

Finally the building was reached, and there Dante was presented to a priest.

Then came the brief ceremony. It had to be brief, for, even if we assume that the baptizing continued without interruption for twelve hours, the eight priests who were present would have to have each baptized more than sixty infants in every hour.

"In the name of the Father, the Son, and the Holy Ghost — Durante."

Or maybe simply Dante.

But it accomplished its purpose.

Let us turn to Dante to see what this purpose was.

> Here where I was — or so it struck my ears —
> It was not weeping, it was only sighs
> That set the eternal air to shuddering.

> This came from sorrow without pain or torture
> Known by a crowd — it was a very great one —
> Of children and of women and of men.
> My good master to me: "Why askst thou not
> What spirits be the ones thou seest here?
> Now I would have thee know ere thou goest farther:
> These did not sin, but though they merits had,
> 'T was not enough, for they were not baptized."

This is in *Inferno* IV. In *Paradiso* XIX, he reaches the same conclusion by another road.

> Thou saidst this: "One is born upon the banks
> Of Indus River. There they do not speak
> Of Christ, nor do they read of Him nor write.
> Yet every wish and deed of his is good.
> He does not sin in either word or act
> As far as human reason can perceive.
> Yet he was not baptized, hence had not faith.
> What is the justice that condemns him then?
> Was it his fault that he does not believe?"

The meaning is plain in English, and it was equally plain or more so in Dante's crisp Italian. *If you are not baptized, you cannot be saved.* You cannot come to heaven. It did not make any difference whether your parents or guardians had been neglectful; or whether you had died before the day came around; or whether you lived in distant India; or whether you had been born too soon like the great honorable pagans of whom Virgil was only the most beloved by Dante. Nor did justice have anything to do with it. Or, to put it another way, inscrutable are the ways of God, and man — including Dante, as he will make plain on more than one occasion — cannot always comprehend them. But he must accept them. He must understand that God is Goodness, and that anything that Goodness does is good.

But to Dante and to almost every well-ordered and well-organized medieval mind, baptism was something a great deal more than a protective device. It was also the first step toward Christian citizenship.

Citizenship was very important to Dante; and in fact when this intense offspring of a restless but persistent money changer and the aristocratic damsel who had become Alighiero II's wife wanted to describe heaven he could think of no better phrase than "that great Rome where Christ was Roman." Heaven, a city. Christ, its citizen.

Now, in the arms of a godfather or a godmother, and long before he personally controlled his own actions, he had taken that step.

Later he would take other steps, and later we will hear about them.

But these were his own doing, and therefore he would first long since have had to cease to be an infant in swaddling clothes. First he would have had to grow up.

Of this growing up — of this gradual changing from an infant to a boy to an adolescent and finally to a young man — we have much material for theorizing and for speculation but fewer hard facts.

Certainly the early biographers do not give us many.

Boccaccio, for example, seems to have been far more concerned with a dream Dante's mother is reputed to have had than with the details we would wish so greatly to know.

"It seemed to this gentle lady," he wrote, "that she was under a lofty laurel tree in a green meadow hard by a clear spring, and here she felt herself give birth to a son. He in a brief time, feeding only on the berries which grew upon the laurel tree and drinking of the waters of the clear spring, seemed to her to become a shepherd and to strive with all his heart to lay hold of the leaves of the laurel tree whose fruit had fed him. And in striving for this he seemed to fall and, rising, to have become no more a man but a peacock.

"This dream is now clear to all, although it was not then understood by her or by others."

But in other areas, the author of the *Decameron* was exceedingly sketchy.

He did point out that even during Dante's infancy there appeared "many signs of the future glory of his genius," but he did not tell us what they were, except to say that from the beginning of boyhood, after "he had learned the first elements of letters, he gave himself up to the study of the liberal arts. In these, he became marvelously expert. He became thoroughly familiar with Virgil, Ovid, Horace, and other famous poets. He was not only fond of knowing them, but he strove to imitate them in lofty song. He made a proper division of his time, and strove to learn history by himself and philosophy under various masters. His acute mind explored the most profound depths of divine theology."

Elsewhere Boccaccio pointed out that Dante was "marvelously logical"; "that he seems to have been an astrologer" — one must remember, however, that in the Middle Ages the line between astrology and astronomy was not cleanly drawn — "and one cannot be that without arithmetic and geometry"; and that "they also say that he heard lectures on moral philosophy and that he learned it incredibly well." But this may refer to a later period of Dante's life.

Leonardo Bruni added very little to what "this delightful and charming Boccaccio" had to say.

He too pointed out that in his boyhood Dante was put under teachers of letters and "at once gave evidence of greatest genius." He noted that Dante lost his father "during his youth," but that "under the encouragement of his relatives and of Brunetto Latini he gave himself up not only to literature" but to other liberal studies. But for all this he did not shut himself up at ease from the world, but, living and moving about among the other young men of his age, he approved himself gracious and skillful and valiant in every youthful exercise.

Besides this, Bruni indicated that Dante was to play an important part in "the business of the commonwealth."

There was nothing in this second biographer's book about dreams or laurel trees or peacocks.

On the contrary he made it plain that he was annoyed at his predecessor for passing over "the weighty and substantial parts of Dante's life" while he recorded trivialities.

"It came, therefore, into my heart to write another life of Dante, not in disparagement of Boccaccio, but as a supplement."

This he did.

It is packed with truth, and there is documentary evidence for one of its important statements. Alighiero II's name is among those signed to an agreement dated February 7, 1277. He is referred to as "the late Alighiero" in a release made by his son not later than March 25, 1284. The poet's father could not have died until after the first date and must have died before the second one. Actually there is a strong presumption that he died between February and August 1277. At that time, Dante was twelve years old.

It is known also that Dante's mother Gabriella (Bella) died even earlier — probably when the poet-to-be was five or six — and that his father then remarried. The poet's stepmother was Lapa di Chiarissimo Cialuffi. It is known that Dante had a half-brother, Francesco, and a half-sister, Tana or Gaetana. He also had a full sister. Her name has not been preserved.

As long as they both lived, Francesco was his older brother's loyal friend and close associate, as was also — although less intimately — Tana, who married one Lapo Riccomanni, a small-time money changer and land speculator like Dante's father. This seems to have been Lapo's second marriage.

The sister whose name is not known to us was married to Leone Poggi, a *banditore*, or public crier, employed by the city of Florence. They had a son, Andrea.

Andrea "marvelously resembled Dante in his features" — this comes from Boccaccio — "and also in his carriage, being somewhat hunch-backed, as Dante was." He was unlettered — "*huomo idioto*" is the Boccaccio phrase, but it does not mean idiot — "but had great common sense, and his speech and his life were well ordered and praiseworthy."

Gradually a picture comes into focus. We are shown a serious young man, but one who was able and eager to take part in the more high-hearted activities of his less intellectual contemporaries. We see one who already showed signs of the genius which was to lift him so high, but who lived in no ivory tower, nor ever would.

To a degree, we are even permitted to know his personal appearance. He was of modest height — not more than five feet five or six inches tall — and after he had come to maturity he walked with a slight but noticeable stoop. (But he was not *gobbo* — he was not a hunchback like nephew Andrea Poggi.) He always wore good clothes of a fashion appropriate to his station and his years, but they were never ostentatious. His face was long, his nose aquiline, his eyes large. His jaws were large too, and his lower lip protruded over the upper. They were almost Hapsburg jaws.

"His complexion was dark, his hair and beard thick, black, and curling."

(He himself refers to his beard in the *Commedia*, and yet oddly enough not a single Dante portrait shows him other than clean-shaven.)

Incidentally, the dark hair and black beard later became the subject of many a Dante anecdote.

"Do you see the man who gives us his shadow as he walks in front of us?" said in Verona one old woman to her companion as the poet passed her by. "He is the one who goes to hell and back again, and brings us back tidings of our friends who are below."

"I can well believe it," replied the other. "Can you not see how his beard is crisped and his complexion is browned by the smoke he found there?"

But the idea that Dante, or someone well known to him, visited the infernal regions almost at will was part of the stock-in-trade of almost every storyteller.

"What do they do in hell?" asked Signore Bernardo Visconti, lord of "Melano," in one of Franco Sacchetti's tales.

"They cut to pieces, they quarter, they rend and hang neither more nor less than your lordship does here."

"What is your proof of this?"

"I held discourse not long since with one who had been there, and it was from this man that Dante the Florentine learned that which he wrote about matters pertaining to it. He is dead, alas, but if you do not believe me send one to see."

Details can be added — and the picture sharpened — if we turn to his writings — all of them — and are willing to accept it that facts often lie hidden in the supposed fiction.

This I am willing to do.

It becomes apparent, for example, that Dante was the son of a self-contained and at least relatively harmonious household. It becomes apparent that he respected his father, whether or not he loved him, and that even more he respected the institution of fatherhood. It becomes apparent that he loved his mother or his stepmother as the case may have been.

About neither father, mother, nor stepmother did he, to be sure, speak by name and specifically, for it is only in Cacciaguida passages that he is other than reticent about his family. But his generalities are extremely revealing.

Let us take up the father first.

Purgatorio I:

> I saw before me only one old man,
> But he more worthy seemed of reverence
> Than any father was from any son.

Paradiso XXXI:

> Forth from his eyes and on his cheeks there shone
> Beatifying joy and pious mien
> Such as befitting is to loving father.

In *Convivio* IV, 24, " 'Hearken, my son, to the admonition of thy father,' " he quotes Solomon as saying.

"Wherefore," continues Dante, "just as, so soon as he is born, the child clings to his mother's breast, in like manner, so soon as the first gleam of thought appears in him, he should turn to the correction of his father. His father should teach him, and let the father see to it that he give no example himself contrary to the words of his teaching. For we see that every son by nature looks more to the prints of the paternal feet than to those of others."

A few paragraphs later:

"The Apostle says: 'Children, obey your father in all things, for this is the will of God.' And if the father is no longer living this obedience must be transferred to him who in his last will is bequeathed as a father; and if the father dies intestate obedience is transferred to him to whom the law commits the son's government."

It has been argued that these words are less than warm, and likewise that Dante more than hints at fatherly misconduct — that he reproves his father as much as he evinces love or respect for him. It has also been argued that they go forward to Dante's own sons rather than backward to his father — that he was lecturing himself rather than his sire.

Here again we can only hazard an opinion, which I do: backward not forward. I think he was speaking *of* his father, not *to* his sons.

Dante's love for a mother (or a stepmother) and his understanding of a mother's love for her child are also expressed over and over.

Paradiso XXX:

> There is no babe who turns his head more swiftly
> Toward his mother's breast when he awakens
> Very much later than he usually does.

Paradiso XXIII:

> Like as a baby who toward his mother
> Reaches its arms when it has had its milk
> Because its soul so overflows with love.

Paradiso XXII:

> Like to a mother when she comforteth
> Quickly her very pale and breathless son
> With her calm voice which always reassures him.

Inferno XXIII:

> My leader with quick movement snatched at me,
> Just as a mother, wakened by the roar,
> Sees the flames race toward her, blazing red,
> And takes her child and flees, nor does she halt —
> Having more care for him than for herself —
> More than to snatch and put on a scant shift.

Does this last, incidentally, reflect some actual childhood incident? Were the Alighieri involved in one of the many fires which, as we have already seen, in those days so often and so disastrously swept Florence? Did Dante with his own eyes see Lapa di Chiarissimo Cialuffi snatch up little Francesco or little Tana in her arms and escape half clad into the

Florentine night? Or was this just one of the many episodes in the crowded life around him when he was a boy?

I speak of Lapa, for I am convinced that it was the stepmother rather than the mother, that it was Lapa rather than Bella, about whom Dante wrote.

To be sure, there is some evidence pointing in another direction.

Paradiso XVI:

> The most degenerate people in the world,
> If they'd not been as stepmother to Caesar
> But rather as mother to a dear-loved son,
> There is one now, a Florentine merchant and trader,
> Who'd have been hounded back to Simifonti,
> There where his grandsire used to beg for bread.

And there are other passages (*Paradiso* XVII, for example) which tell the same story.

But these seem to me obviously, and indeed almost provably, literary.

Even granting that Dante was precocious, a mother who had died when he was still a toddler could hardly have been more than shadowy to him.

It was Lapa whom he saw nursing a brother and a sister.

(The other sister — the one who married Leone Poggi — being, as we have already noted, Bella's daughter, was but little younger than Dante.)

It was Lapa whom he saw caring for them in their childish illnesses and comforting them in their childish frights.

It was Lapa, too, to whom Dante saw them run in fear or childish grief (*Purgatorio* XXX), and it was before her that he saw them with their heads bowed and their feet shuffling.

Purgatorio XXXI:

> Like children who all tongue-tied and abashed,
> Their eyes cast on the ground, stand shamefacedly,
> Listening and conscious-stricken and repentant.

Incidentally, it is even possible that Dante derived some of his later strength from the fact that he had a stepmother instead of a mother. If Lapa had been his mother, he could have rushed to her arms as did Francesco and Tana. Instead, he had to stand by himself.

But he stood by himself in warm and friendly surroundings. Lapa gave him her affection, and even if we put the coolest possible interpretation upon the poet's relationship with his father, there was nothing in it to embitter him. Any bitterness which might subsequently leave its imprint upon his character was not small and personal but came from the slings and arrows of a fortune that was, almost more than one can imagine, outrageous. Any bitterness which he might later feel was on a larger scale.

« 5 »

When he was six years old, or at most seven, Dante took another step forward in his development. He began to go to school.

He did so in a city in which education was rapidly increasing in importance — just as with us today.

"We find," wrote Giovanni Villani, "that there are between eight and ten thousand boys and girls [in Florence] who are learning to read and write. Between one thousand and twelve hundred boys" — boys only, be it noted, for after they had learned their letters (usually under a governess or aged tutor) girls studied only dancing, singing, and domestic science — "are learning the abacus and algorism in six schools. Those who in four big schools are learning *grammatica* and *loica* number between five and six hundred."

At this point a few observations should be made. Villani's figures are for 1339, at which time the population of Florence was one hundred thousand. When Dante was a schoolboy, the population was perhaps fifty thousand. A suitable adjustment must be made.

We should also say something about the subjects taught. The abacus was an instrument used for computing in medieval Europe, and still used in the Orient. Algorism was the relatively new Arabic art of computing with nine figures and a zero. It had been but recently introduced — by Florentines who traded in Babylon (Cairo) and Alexandria — but it was increasingly used in commercial transactions even in Dante's youth. *Grammatica* was the study of Latin. *Loica* was logic.

We think that Dante studied all of these subjects. Obviously he had learned how to read (as had virtually every boy and girl in Florence), and his knowledge of mathematics, which was not able, makes it equally certain that he had been taught arithmetic and algebra — at the house of an *abbachista* and between the ages of eleven and fourteen, like every other Florentine youth who had any thoughts whatsoever of engaging in anything mercantile, as who among any but the working class did not.

But although he was not destined for either the Church or the law and had not thoughts of becoming either a doctor or a notary, we believe that he studied Latin and logic too. He speaks of himself as a bad Latinist but not as someone who did not know the language at all. It was only to philosophy and to theology that he did not apply himself until later in his life.

We think, too, that we know the textbooks he used. Or, at any rate, some of them.

"Our forebears," wrote Giovanni Domenici in the next century, "were illuminated in the way that they educated youth. Our moderns are blind. The first things they taught were the psalms and after that the doctrines of our religion. Then they moved on to the morality of Cato; *Aesop's Fables;* the worthy teachings of Boethius; the virtuous lore of Prospero as he drew it from St. Augustine; the philosophy of *Eva Columba* or the *Tres Leo Naturas;* together with the versified scriptures of the *Aethiopum Terras.*

"And other books, none of which led to evil!" he added.

The world was going to the dogs, Domenici implied. The younger generation was being exposed to every kind of bad influence.

What, more specifically, were these writings?

The psalms are obvious, and so too are "the doctrines of our religion." Aesop is hardly less so.

"*Isopo,*" wrote one of Dante's early commentators, "is a little book which boys read. In it are certain stories which teach good conduct."

It was also known as *Isopotto* or *Yzepet.*

In all probability, Dante's *Aesop* was either a prose version translated from the Greek of Phaedrus — or so said the translator — by one Romulus or a rhymed version by Walter the Englishman.

But the "morality of Cato" had nothing to do with either Cato the Elder or Cato the Younger. It was a series of one hundred forty-four distichs on moral subjects composed in the fifth century by another Cato, Dionysius Cato. The "worthy teachings of Beothius" was clearly not the famous book of philosophy about which we will hear more in due course. It was more probably a simplified verse translation of Boethius.

The "virtuous lore of Prospero" was Prosper of Aquitaine's dull rendering of St. Augustine into verses which a child was supposed to memorize.

The *Eva Columba* was the Old and New Testaments reduced to epigrams. It took its title from the first quatrain.

> Eve was a white dove, then became a black one,
> Made this by the deceiving fraud of the poisonous snake.
> Adam the innocent he stained too with his filthy spots.
> Then the dragon victor gave a fig leaf to their innocence.

The *Tres Leo Naturas* was a bestiary. It described the habits of such real or imaginary animals as the lion, the unicorn, and the panther, but it linked them all to Christ.

The *Aethiopum Terras* was a dialogue between Truth and Falsehood. It matched the true stories of the Bible with the lying fables of the pagans. Moses was opposed to Deucalion, Sampson to Hercules, Joseph to Hippolytus. Theological explanations — in a language which was supposed to be understandable to the young reader — were added. They were somewhat more repetitious than eloquent. In those days there was no objection to laboring a point.

We also know Dante's teacher — the man who, for the not inconsiderable sum of something between sixty and one hundred florins *per annum,* put the elements of knowledge into the head of as illustrious a pupil as any instructor was ever destined to have. At any rate, we know his name.

There was in the parish of San Martino — where the Alighieri had their home — one *Romanus doctor puerorum* (Romano, boys' schoolteacher), and this Ser Romano seems to have been a close friend of the Alighieri. He vouchsafed for them in a lawsuit and evidently was associated with them in other matters.

With Romanus as a neighbor, it does not seem likely that they would go farther abroad.

Finally we know something about the school — also called a *bottega,* or shop. It was in a nearby street, and if Romanus was like other teachers it probably was in a rented building with a garden.

Let us try to visualize it. On sunny days classes may have been held outdoors, but for the most part — and always in winter — the students were crowded into a small room which smelled of mold and damp stone. A wicker cage with a blackbird perched in it hung in the corner. Children have to be amused as well as instructed, and since a blackbird can be taught to talk perhaps it imitated their halting recitations.

There would have been some bare benches for the pupils; a desk for the master; some goose quills and a knife to keep them sharp; some murky ink; some strips of parchment.

And, of course, the birch rod always handy.

Not very long after, Antonio Pucci, the people's poet — the same one who was to call Dante "the lordly astrologer" — wrote a sonnet upon education.

"When a little child is naughty," he said, "he should be punished with a switch. When he is seven or more, with a belt or a strap. When he is fifteen or more, he should be cudgeled until he asks for pardon. When he is twenty or more, he should be sent to prison. When he is over thirty, he should be permanently expelled."

With his eye on the birch rod — for he was as lively as he was keen of mind — with his ear tuned for the blackbird's song, and with a mind ready to absorb every kind of fact laid before him, Dante trudged to just such a school for at least four or five years and then went on to other schools.

Under his arm probably in codex form were the treatises we have referred to above. Parchment being bulkier than paper, they were a heavy load for a lad to carry, although in modern printed form they would have made a book of not more than one hundred pages.

But carry them he did, and after he had carried them he learned from them and remembered them.

When, for example, at least thirty years later, he set down in his *Convivio* the story of the cock and the pearl, he said that it came from "*Esopo poeta*" and that Aesop had related it in "his first fable." When in *Inferno* XXIII he told about the frog and the mouse, he said that his mind had turned back to "Isopo."

The lion and the leopard, mentioned by him toward the beginning of his *Commedia*, do not roam the Italian hills, although the wolf does. Presumably he first heard of the lion and the leopard in the *Tres Leo Naturas*, although not much later there was a captive lion in Florence which broke loose and caused great consternation.

It seems almost equally probable that his knowledge of the Bible, his severe impartial morality — he judged even himself — his choice of Boethius rather than some other philosopher, and the pairing of Christian with pagan which he was to do so successfully in the *Purgatorio*, all can be traced to these schooldays and these treatises.

It is even possible that the Virgil of the *Commedia* himself — Dante's "courteous master," his "lofty doctor," his "sweet pedagogue," that "comfort" of his who guided him from the wild wood wherein he was lost to the very portals of heaven — was at least partly based upon the man who conducted a school for young Florentines within close walking distance of the Casa Alighieri. For in the pages of the *Commedia*, Virgil with his white beard, his spontaneous eagerness to instruct, and his calm, firm discipline is much more like a medieval — or even a modern — pedagogue than he is like the poet laureate of Augustus's Rome.

« 6 »

But Dante Alighieri was shaped and educated, and his character was formed, by many more things than the small Latin and less Greek which he learned either from Romanus the schoolteacher or from the Romulus who translated fables. He was also shaped and educated by the doings of his energetic family. He was taught by the people whom he met or saw or heard about in Florence. An impress was put upon his wax by life in the city and by life in the country round about. He would spend a considerable part of his time in the country for reasons which we shall shortly learn.

For Dante did not ever live aloof and to himself, but was rather much more like the poet in Robert Browning's "How It Strikes a Contemporary."

> If any beat a horse, you felt he saw;
> If any cursed a woman, he took note,
> Yet stared at nobody — you stared at him
> And found, less to your pleasure than surprise,
> He seemed to know you, and expect as much.

Modestly dressed — what Boccaccio said about his clothes has already been reported — but gifted "with a retentive memory and a penetrating intellect," he noted and observed all that happened around him and stored it in his mind.

The family first — for the family of all things was the closest to him.

Much has already been said about the Alighieri in the years before Dante's birth, and what we see of them during his boyhood and early manhood shows that they had changed very little.

To get down to specifics, there are still surviving seventeen documents pertaining to the poet or his immediate family dating between 1268, when Dante was three, and 1289, when he was twenty-four. With two exceptions—but these two exceptions are notable — they deal with matters civic or political, or with matters of business or finance.

Let us examine a few of them and see what they tell us.

In 1268, one Chiarissimo del fu (son of the late) Ardimanno acknowledges that he has received in custody from Brunetto di Bellincione, *superintendent of the Pagliazza prison of the commune*, Uberto di Falconieri dell' Impruneta, and promises that he will either return him to prison or pay any fines imposed.

Brunetto was Uncle Brunetto.

In 1269, Geri, son of the late Bello Alighieri — Cousin Geri, that is — is awarded twenty-five *libbre* because his house had been "somewhat damaged" when the Ghibellines came to power.

In 1270, Gherardo di Bellincione — Uncle Gherardo — acts as a guarantor in some court proceedings.

In the same year, Belluzzo (presumably Bello) and Donato Alighieri — both uncles — sell rights which they had in some property at Prato. Donato makes Belluzzo his attorney for this transaction.

In 1275, Brunetto compels the city of Prato to pay one Ser Torello forty-eight *soldi* "because he went to Florence in the matter of Brunetto

Alighieri and spent four days there." (Evidently the expense account is not a modern invention.)

In 1276, both Geri and Bellino act as witnesses — one of a loan, the other in a lawsuit.

In 1280, Brunetto is recorded as a member of the general council and also of the Council of Ninety.

In 1283, Cione is recorded as being absent from a meeting of the Council of the Captain.

In 1288, Brunetto receives sixty-four gold florins from the guarantor of a loan he had made.

In 1289, Bellino witnesses a deed.

The next two documents deal with matters far more complicated.

It will be recalled that in 1189, Alighiero I and his brother Preitenitto had been haled before the consuls and directed to cut down a fig tree which they had planted upon land claimed by the church of San Martino and the monks of the Badia who by then owned it.

The fig tree had long since become firewood, but the Alighieri conviction that the plot upon which it had grown was really theirs was strong as ever, and when sometime before 1276 they learned that the rector and the monks were planning to build upon it, they resorted to direct action. Under the probable leadership of Brunetto — and apparently with the approval or at least consent of their neighbors — they dumped a pile of "large and small stones" upon the disputed piazza. They would do a little building themselves.

Needless to say, the church authorities did not waste any time in striking back. Waving an array of deeds and titles, they marched up to Judge Maffeo, "assessor" of the *podestà*, Currado da Palazzo. (Dante's "good Currado," none other — we will meet him again later in this book.) In their spiritual garments, they demanded far from spiritual rights.

These were given them forthwith and fully, whereat — and to say this is also needless — the Alighieri and their neighbors entered an appeal. They were not more than partially successful, for this, dated September 11, 1277, was the final verdict:

"The masters and the measurers of the commune shall diligently and legally assign the land according to the Florentine custom, and they shall give it to the syndics of the church and monastery with permission for them to build thereon."

But at least there were three protective provisions:

(1) "that these syndics agree to tear down and destroy the walls in question if it shall ever be proved that they have built without right"; and

(2) "that they may not build in the street near the property of the Abbati where there is a well five *braccie* [about nine feet] distant, which land was sold by the monastery to make said well"; and

(3) "that they may not build closer than three and three quarters *braccie* to the pavement where the west gate of San Martino is."

The second document — or perhaps set of documents — deals with physical violence. It — or they — bears dates between November 2 and November 14, 1280.

"Before you, the lord *podestà* of Prato, I, Spigolato, called Balzano [Piebald], son of the late Iunta, denounce the following persons:

"Paragino, son of the late Feretti, and Donna Diletta, his wife; the priest Ubertino, rector of the church at Narnali, and Donna Borisa, wife of the late Iunta and now mistress of the said priest; Ghita, daughter of the said Borisa; Giana, daughter of the said priest and of the said Donna Borisa; Piero de Capezana, son-in-law of the said priest and husband of the said Giana; *and Geri and Cione, brothers, and sons of Bello Alighieri.*

"I declare that all of these, in the public street, with arms and men, by force and in an evil manner, with malice aforethought, took from me, Spigolato, one Pagano da Camaino, who was under ban of the commune of Prato and was a prisoner in the hands of the commune. They wounded him in the hand and in the arm so that blood flowed, and they seized and wounded the said Balzano. They hurled him onto the ground and threw him into a ditch. This was on the public street going toward Pistoia near the Porta Gualdimari. Furthermore they dragged the said Balzano as far as Narnali and farther."

Master Piebald must have had a rough time of it. Narnali is a good two miles from Prato, and the road is dusty and would be hot even at the time of year when all this happened, for it runs — between olive trees — straight as an arrow through a reasonably narrow valley which is protected on almost every side by a rampart of blue hills. The rowdies were nine in number, and though four of them were women, an Italian woman — particularly if she is a priest's mistress or a priest's bastard child — when she rages can be first cousin to a maenad. Piattoli says that they had been visiting the tombs of their ancestors. To me it seems obvious that they had been drinking. It is not known why they wanted to rescue Pagano, who was a Lombard woolworker.

This was on November 2. Between November 3 and November 8, one after another of the accused persons appeared before the Prato magistrates and swore that he had not done what he was accused of doing. They were released under surety.

Bello and Cione did not appear, however, and were sentenced *in absentia.*

"They not coming before me, I, Dominus Bonifazio, judge, instruct and order the public crier to proclaim their banishment with a fine of one hundred gold *libbre* each for seizing the said Pagano and a fine of two hundred gold *libbre* each for wounding Balzano."

This ban would not be lifted unless the two troublemakers came before the judge "between today and tomorrow." They did not. In all likelihood, cooled off and hence able to appreciate that discretion was the better part of valor, they had concluded that under the circumstances Florence was a healthier place for them to be in. Insofar as it was possible — you cannot fine an absentee, but you can confiscate his property — the sentence was unquestionably carried out.

All this — and the lawsuit and the various other Alighieri complications — must have been the subject of many an evening conversation in the house facing the church of San Martino. Surely Dante must have listened attentively, for he was twelve, and then fifteen, years old.

It is not hard to imagine the surroundings. Although not comfortable by modern standards, the Florentine house during the Age of Dante was no longer the dark and smoke-filled hovel of but a little earlier, for the Florentines, according to Villani, "readily had adopted every kind of improvement."

The walls — sometimes even the beams — were decorated by painters, although often with nothing more than the arms of the family, the *popolo*, or the city. Glass windows had come into use, but most windows were still covered by shutters or by oiled or waxed cloth. The beds were covered by canopies and closed in with curtains. These curtains were often of rose and yellow, green, or heavenly blue silk. Carpets were considered indispensable. Mirrors had long been in use. They had frames of wood. Cupboards and chests were plentiful, but there were very few tables. There appear to have been writing desks. For the rich — and probably even for the merely well-off like the Alighieri — there were wax torches and wax candles. If there were no fireplaces, there were at least numerous small braziers. These were in every room.

Nor, in these homes, did the Florentines lack service, for one did not have to be a magnate to have those who did menial work for him. *Serve* (housemaids), *ancelle* (lady's maids), *cameriere* (waitresses), and *nutrici* (nurses) were found in almost every Florentine family. Some Florentines even had Saracen or Maltese slaves.

The Alighieri were not likely to have been an exception. Certainly they would at least have had a housemaid, and the tastier or more varied food which had replaced the simple would at least have been placed upon the board by a countrywoman trained for the purpose.

As they ate it, they talked over their various affairs.

That infamous lawsuit brought on by the grasping hands of greedy priests!

How could they have lost it? And how could the appeal have turned out almost as badly as the original case? Was not the man who then headed the Florentine government good and honorable? Was he not a Guelph, one of their own faction? But there are some things — and people — you cannot circumvent.

"*Di questo ingrasso il porco Sant' Antonio*," a boy who listened to all this would write years later (*Paradiso* XXIX), "*ed altri assai che sono ancor più porci.*" On this grows fat the pig of St. Anthony, and others who are even greater pigs.

Dante, as we will have ample opportunity to discover, was a great Catholic Christian — short of the saints, possibly the greatest one who ever lived. But he always differentiated between the faith and those who said they were its captains and its soldiers! He did not think he was attacking religion when he attacked the Church.

He also heard his father and his uncles discuss the status of this loan or that hypothecation.

"It is well and wise to know, Bellino, that this Messer Guido del fu Ugolino will never and can never repay all or any part of the loan you made him. You must turn to Rinaldo di Malaspini, who guaranteed it."

He heard them discuss the doings of the Council of Ninety or the Council of the Captain. Could men, who as businessmen must know, depend on the promises of Lucca or Genoa?

Finally, he heard them discuss how to handle Geri and Cione so they would neither get into trouble themselves nor embroil the family. Evidently the two had emerged from the fracas with reputations untarnished, for at least one of them subsequently held office and both mingled in municipal affairs.

Yet they must have troubled the Alighieri.

"Doubtless they will not come to a good end!" must have been the family verdict.

Nor did one of them.

As, in the *Commedia* (*Inferno* XXIX), Dante walks through that part of hell where the sowers of discord are punished, he addresses his guide, Virgil, thus:

> "Within that hollow
> On which I held so fixedly mine eyes,
> Methought I heard one of my own blood weeping
> The sin for which he now doth pay so dear."

Virgil replies:

> "Do not break
> Thy thought upon him ever from now on.
> Attend to other matters. Let him stay there.
> I saw him at the little bridge's foot.
> At thee he pointed. He threatened with his finger.
> I heard someone call him Geri del Bello."

Evidently Dante's cousin of the Prato fracas had involved himself in one broil too many. In consequence, one of the Sacchetti family came upon him and thrust a knife between his ribs!

« 7 »

But the youthful Dante did not spend all of his time in the Casa Alighieri, listening to tales of the legal deviousness of the monks of the Badia or to boastful accounts of the violence and pride of his relatives.

He walked about the city too.

He looked at the bakehouses, to which it was the custom of the Florentines to send "a pipkin containing a chine of meat or sausages made of I know not what" to have these cooked for them. There he saw the scullions, sweating and half naked, using their long iron hooks to plunge gobbets of meat into the seething cauldron. Later, when he came to write about hell, these would provide him with a vivid simile.

He strolled past the Mercato Vecchio.

He loitered for a while to hear the street-corner preachers with their false relics. He watched the artisans at their trades.

He was also exposed to some of the *dramatis personae* whom he would set down in his great poem, writing about them as vividly as Boccaccio or any other novelist.

There are, Davidsöhn points out, seventy-nine people specially mentioned in the *Inferno,* and of these thirty-two are Florentines and eleven are from other parts of Tuscany. In the *Purgatorio,* there are four Florentines and eleven Tuscans. But evidently — in Dante's mind, at any rate — virtue in his native city was in short supply, for only two Florentines can be found in the *Paradiso.*

Dante did not, of course, encounter all of these people in person. Some of them he was merely told about.

The great Ghibelline captain Farinata degli Uberti, for example, had died in 1264, the year before Dante was born. He was the one whom the poet encountered (*Inferno* X) half buried in a fiery tomb which reminded him of those "at Arles where the Rhone stagnates."

But men talked about him, for although he had crushed Guelph Florence he was a hero even to the Guelph Florentines.

"This Farinata," wrote one of them, "was tall of stature, manly of visage, strong of limb, gravely continent, soldierly eloquent, polite of speech, very wise in council, bold, quick to act, and ever strong in feats of arms."

He had ensured the Ghibellines their victory at Montaperti, for when their leaders went to King Manfred for help and he gave them only one hundred horsemen instead of the fifteen hundred they had expected, he prevented his fellows from returning angrily to Siena.

"Do not refuse any aid from Manfred, however small!" he cried passionately. "Let him send only his standard with them and we will set it in such a place that he must aid us further!"

So it turned out.

But when the Florentines had been crushed, and the Ghibelline leaders, meeting at Empoli, decided either to destroy the city or to reduce it to an open village, Farinata intervened.

"While I have life in my body, I will defend it with my sword in hand!" he cried to his colleagues.

There, just as he would later in the *Commedia*, he stood haughtily.

They were obliged to accede.

But there were some whom Dante probably knew and probably had talked to, or at least whom he saw with his own eyes as he and they shared the city in which he grew up.

There was Filippo Argenti, to name one.

"He was a big burly man," wrote Boccaccio, "and the most despiteful, choleric and humorsome one ever to have lived.

"This Filippo Argenti of the Cavicciuli," wrote Coppo di Borghese Domenichi, "was a very rich knight who sometimes had the steed he rode shod with silver, and from this he got his name. He was dark complected, vigorous, and of marvelous strength, but above all he was easy to anger, even for the slightest cause."

It was this anger which Boccaccio celebrated in the *Decameron*, and it was also this anger — although the fact that the Cavicciuli were notably hostile to Dante may have contributed — which won him a place in the *Commedia* (*Inferno* VIII).

> When we were plowing through the stagnant pond,
> Before me up rose one besmeared with mud
> Who said: "Who art thou—come before thine hour?"
> And I to him: "I come, but do not stay!
> But who art thou who hast become so foul?"

He answered: "Thou dost see—one who laments!"
And I to him: "Weeping and in deep grief
Ever remain, O thou most evil spirit,
For I do know thee, filthy though thou art!"
Thereat he clutched the gunwale with both hands
Until the wary master snatched him loose,
Saying: "Get down there with the other dogs!"
Then did he put his arms about my neck
And kissed my face and said: "Indignant soul,
Blessed be she who bare thee in her womb!
This was an arrogant person while he lived,
Nor did he one good deed to deck his name.
Therefore, his shade here rages furiously.
How many up there now are held as kings
Who here like pigs shall wallow in the mire,
Nor leave behind them aught but an ill fame!"
And I: "My master, would I could but see
Him being plunged and soused into the stew
Before it comes to pass we leave this lake!"
And he to me: "Before the other shore
Is plainly seen, thou shalt be satisfied,
For it is fitting that thy wish be granted."
Shortly thereafter, I saw such a rending
Of him to pieces by that muddy crew
That I still praise and thank the Lord for it.
All of them cried: "Have at you, Filippo Argenti!"
Whereat the evil-tempered Florentine
Savagely tore himself with his own teeth.

There was Ciacco (*Inferno* VI), who appeared in the same *Decameron* story. Ciacco is a nickname. It means Hoggy or Hog.

"This man," said Boccaccio, "was not exactly a court hanger-on, but he was wholly given over to the vice of gluttony, and he always associated with the gently born and very rich, especially those who ate and drank well and delicately. If he was invited to dine with them, he always went."

There was Agnèl Brunelleschi (*Inferno* XXV). Of a well-established family and wealthy enough to make thievery unnecessary, "this Agnello even as a little boy stole the purses of his father and mother. Later he broke open the strongboxes of banks and committed other burglaries."

There was Cianghella (*Paradiso* XV, but there to be contrasted with virtuous Cornelia), "an arrogant and impatient woman who went about the house with a cap on her head and a rod in her hand."

Sometimes she flogged her housemaid, and sometimes she flogged her cook, and once when she went to Mass and the other women did not give place to her she "laid violent hands on them, snatching at the hair and headdress of some and scratching the skin of others."

She lived at Imola for a while, but then returned to Florence.

"What more? She had many lovers and lived very lewdly."

There was "Cianfa" Donati (*Inferno* XXV). Like Agnèl Brunelleschi, he was a thief, but that did not keep him from being elected to the Council of the Captain.

There was Sassol Mascheroni (*Inferno* XXXII).

"Sassol Mascheroni," wrote the Anonymous Florentine, "was of the Toschi clan of Florence, and having an old uncle, a rich man who had only one son, he thought 'If I kill this lad, I will remain the heir of my uncle.'"

With an accomplice, he arranged to have this done and then left Florence so that he would not be suspected.

"Later he returned to the city and took over the inheritance of the old man, who was now dead. But in the end the deed was known. He was arrested and, having confessed, put into a cask lined with projecting nails and rolled through the streets. Then his head was cut off."

There was Andrea de' Mozzi (*Inferno* XV), who became bishop of Florence.

"This simple, fatuous man often preached publicly to the people of Florence, saying many ridiculous things. 'The providence of God,' he said, 'is like a mouse hidden in the beams of a house. He sees whatever is done therein, but nobody sees him.' 'The grace of God,' he said, 'is like the dung of goats. It falleth down from above, yet it is dispersed everywhere.' 'Great is the power of God,' he preached. He held out in his hand a turnip seed. 'Ye see how small and tiny it is.' Then he took forth from his cloak a huge turnip. 'Behold how marvelous is God who from so small a seed makes this.'"

Somewhat later Bishop Andrea was transferred to Vicenza. Supposedly this was because of his unseemly way of living, but possibly it was because the less sophisticated Vicenzans could better tolerate his style of preaching. But he was placed in hell for another reason. Like several other distinguished persons, he was supposed to have been guilty of sodomy.

Another whom Dante may have seen — although this is a little less certain — was Jacopo Rusticucci (also *Inferno* XV). Jacopo was also in the hell of the sodomites.

"Jacopo was a Florentine knight," said Benvenuto da Imola, "a *popolano*, but exceedingly polite and high principled. He might have lived happily enough if he had not had a wicked wife. But he was married to an evil-tempered woman with whom no one could live. Therefore, he gave himself over to shameful things."

Also (mentioned in *Inferno* XXX), there was Gianni Schicchi. It is surprising that Boccaccio never put him into one of his stories.

"This Gianni Schicchi," wrote the Anonymous Florentine, but others wrote about him too, "was of the Cavalcanti family in Florence." Here is one of the things they tell about him.

"When Messer Buoso Donati" — Buoso was a rich and prominent Guelph — "lay dying, he wished to make his will and leave much to many people, but his son Simone argued with him urging him not to do this. Simone kept up this talk until one day Buoso died.

"Then, fearing that Buoso might already have made a will as indeed the neighbors said he had, he kept secret his father's death and, not knowing what else to do, he went to Gianni Schicchi and asked him what he should do.

"Gianni was one who knew how to imitate any man there was both in his voice and in his actions. He especially knew how to imitate Messer Buoso, for he knew him very well.

"Gianni said to Simone: 'Get a notary and tell him that Buoso wishes to set down his last testament. I will get into his bed — we will hide Buoso behind it — and I will cover myself up well, and I will put on a nightcap, and I will make you the kind of will you wish. To be sure, I will expect some kind of reward.'

"Simone agreed to this. Gianni got into the bed and, when everything was in order, he began to counterfeit the voice of Messer Buoso so that it seemed to be Messer Buoso himself.

" 'Item, I leave twenty *soldi* to the Opera di Santa Reparata [the governing board of the old cathedral] and five *libbre* to the Frati Minori [the Franciscans] and five *libbre* and five *soldi* to the Predicatori [the Dominicans].' "

Lest the false Buoso appear unduly stingy it should be pointed out that in those days a *libbre* was not the modern *lira* but a pound.

"He continued in the same strain, leaving this and that to God but little else, and this pleased Simone greatly.

"Then he came to more important matters.

" 'And I leave,' he continued, 'five hundred florins to Gianni Schicchi.'

"Said Simone to the supposed Messer Buoso: 'You need not put that in the will. I will give them to him as you leave them.'

" 'Simone, let me do this in my own way. I will make such provision for you that you will be satisfied.'

"Simone kept silent. He was afraid that Gianni would expose the fraud.

"Gianni went on. 'And I leave to Messer Gianni Schicchi my brood mare.' It should be known that Messer Buoso had the finest brood mare in all of Tuscany.

" 'O Messer Buoso,' cried Simone, 'he cares very little for this brood mare. He likes her little.'

" 'I know what Gianni Schicchi wishes better than you do!'

"Simone began to burn up with rage, but out of fear he contained himself.

"Gianni Schicchi continued: 'And I leave to Gianni Schicchi the one hundred *libbre* that I am owed by such and such a neighbor. But the residue of my estate I leave to Simone as my sole heir. With this provision, however. That he be obliged to execute all my bequests within fifteen days. If not, my whole estate is to go to the monks of Santa Croce.' "

Finally during these early days Dante encountered — but not in any chance meeting in the street — still another person whom he would later put in hell, and this man, next to himself, was perhaps the most distinguished Florentine of the time. Certainly he was the most learned.

This was Brunetto Latini, whom we have already noted as being one of those who urged the poet to pursue his studies.

Dante (*Inferno* XV) says as much himself, and says it in one of his most moving passages:

"If had been granted in full measure my prayer,"
I answered him, "you surely would not yet
Be banished from the ranks of living men.
For in my mind is fixed and fills my heart
The good, the dear, and the paternal image
Of you who in the world hour after hour
Taught me how man wins immortality."

Earlier in the same canto, he had identified him. Using the respectful *voi* (you) instead of the familiar *tu* (thou), he had cried out in anguish: "O Ser Brunetto, are you indeed here?"

"A worldly man," Villani calls Brunetto, "but we have made mention of him because he was a master in making the Florentines cultured, and in making them speak well, and in knowing how to rule and guide our republic according to the precepts of politics."

Born, we think, in 1210, he was "by profession a philosopher and by business a notary."

He was exiled in 1260, went to France, and, "when he was almost old," learned French and "to please the *grandi* and noblemen of the land wrote a very beautiful book, *Le Trésor*." *Le Trésor* was an encyclopedia of universal knowledge.

After the battle of Benevento (1266), when Manfred was slain and the Ghibelline cause lost, he returned to Florence, where he became one of its most prominent citizens. He became secretary to the Florentine government (*scriba consiliorum communis Florentiae*), president (*console*) of the notarial guild, one of the guarantors of the peace between the Guelphs and the Ghibellines imposed by Cardinal Latino, and one of the two syndics sent to negotiate an offensive and defensive alliance (directed against Pisa) with Genoa and Lucca. In 1287, he was prior. In 1289, he was public orator. He died in 1294 at the age of eighty-four and was buried in Santa Maria Maggiore.

Yet despite his distinguished career, despite Dante's affection for the man, and despite the fact that he was buried in consecrated ground, Dante placed him not merely among the damned but among those in the infernal regions who were guilty of unnatural practices.

This is hard to understand. To be sure, sodomy — at least in popular belief — was so prevalent in medieval Florence that the German verb for it was *florenzen*. But it was something which Brunetto especially condemned.

"There is a crime," he wrote in *Le Trésor*, "which is more heinous than adultery, and that is to lie with a male."

In *Il Tesoretto*, which is a rhymed Italian version of *Le Trésor*, he said this:

> Worthy of scorn
> Is adultery,
> But a greater sin,
> It seemeth to me,
> Committeth the one
> Guilty of sodomy.

It was once generally thought that Brunetto was Dante's schoolteacher. This is now recognized to be improbable. Brunetto was fifty-five when Dante was born, and by the time Dante came to schoolboy age he was far too deeply involved in Florentine affairs to conduct a school or even to tutor an individual lad.

Yet, even at that, he may well have had an intimate connection with Dante. After Alighiero II's death, Brunetto may have become the guardian whom Dante says every father should name in his last will. If so, the small trader who is so often regarded with such scorn must have had better judgment and more enlightenment than is usually ascribed to him.

« 8 »

But it is not to be thought that Dante knew only the wicked or the ones he called wicked. Living as he did in that part of the city which was known as the Sesto di Scandolo — Quarrel Ward is the usual translation but Disorder Ward might be better — it was logical that he should come into contact with a few more sinners than saints. But in Florence — and even in Dante's part of Florence — there were good people too. Dante knew many of them. A few were his close friends.

One of the latter was Casella — or, as some say, Scarsella — the musician. Dante placed him in purgatory (*Purgatorio* II), where at the poet's request this "*Casella mio*" sings one of the poet's own *canzoni*.

> "O love that in my mind doth discourse so,"
> So very sweetly did he then begin
> That in my heart its sweetness soundeth still.

Scarsella was a composer as well as a singer. In the Vatican library, there can still be seen the manuscript of a poem by one Lemmo da Pistoia, and on it is inscribed "*Casella mi diede il sono*." Casella set me to music!

Casella was also a gay, high-hearted fellow, as is demonstrated by the fact that on June 13, 1282 — well within the time limits of this chapter — he was haled before the authorities of nearby Siena and fined "for having been found wandering about the streets at night."

Wandering and singing, no doubt, his heart warmed to the cockles by generous imbibings of that warm, rich, and ruby-red *vino da pasto* which still is made from grapes growing on the "calcareous-clayey" soil of hillsides round about Colle, Gambassi, San Casciano, Certaldo, and Poggibonsi!

Such conduct — we have already noted — was not pleasing to sober citizens nor to their wives.

But it was stimulating to a musician.

Casella doubtless paid his fine and went on singing.

Another Dante friend who made his way to purgatory was the man known as Belacqua, or, in English, Master Drinkwater. This appellation may have been ironic. His real name seems to have been Duccio di Bonavia.

"This Belacqua was a citizen of Florence who manufactured the heads of lutes and guitars and who was the most indolent man in the world. It was said of him that he used to come to his shop in the morning and never rose from his chair except to eat and sleep."

Dante, it is said, used to rebuke him for this laziness, and one day Belacqua thus answered him:

"Have you not read Aristotle, my learned friend?"

"I have indeed."

"Then you should know that Aristotle has said that by sitting still and keeping quiet a man becomes wise."

"By the Holy Virgin!" cried the poet. "By the Holy Virgin! You must be the wisest person in the whole world!"

Dante must surely have known, too, a third person whom he remembered later and did not send to nether regions. This was Piccarda of the illustrious Donati family. She is one of those two Florentines whom he saw fit to enthrone in paradise.

If he did not know her, certainly he knew her story.

It was a scandal which shook even the not easily shocked city. Florentine tongues had done wagging enough when the beautiful daughter of a rich and powerful clan had suddenly shorn her golden hair to become a nun of Santa Clara. They would have much more to wag about only a little while later. In 1282 (when Dante was seventeen), or perhaps in 1288, Piccarda's brother Corso (of whom we will hear a great deal more in due time) suddenly put aside all his business in Bologna, where he was *podestà*, and came galloping back over the lofty Futa Pass and then down to his native city.

Why this posthaste clatter of hoofs across the Apennines?

"Rossellino della Tosa of the Tosinghi family is eager to make an alliance with the Donati. He wishes to marry a Donati daughter."

The Tosinghi were prominent and powerful, but they were also notably depraved. Indeed, the "banquet of the accursed Tosinghi women" was a legend in the story of Florentine women. But what difference did that make to the ambitious Corso?

Torches flared in the night, and armed ruffians beat at the convent door. The nuns screamed — possibly not all in fear — and the abbess, statue-like and dignified, tried to interpose. It was unavailing. Corso never started what he did not mean to finish. Screaming herself and struggling as a Donati could struggle, Piccarda was dragged out into the night. Shortly thereafter — by a complaisant priest and with armed men still standing around — she was married to Rossellino.

"Whereat," says a contemporary, "she almost immediately fell ill, and finished her days, and became thus the bride of Christ to whom of her own free will she had pledged herself. And they say that the said illness and her mortal death were bestowed upon her by Him who is the giver of all grace. Thus He answered her prayers."

Dante later tells her story — in *Paradiso* III, where he meets those who have indeed broken their vows but not through any fault of their own.

> "In thy world I a virgin sister was,
> And if thy memory look back aright
> My greater present beauty will not confuse thee,
> But thou wilt recognize I am Piccarda."

Then she continued with her story.

> "Her perfect life and her high merits enheaven
> A lady higher up," she said, "under whose rule
> There are on earth those who put on the veil
> So that until death comes they wake and sleep
> With that Spouse who doth every vow accept
> Which love doth make conform unto His will.
> As a young girl, I fled the world to gain her,
> And thereupon I did put on her garb
> And pledged me to the pathway of her order.
> But then men more accustomed to evil than good
> Seized me and haled me forth from my sweet cloister,
> And what my life became God alone knows."

« *9* »

All the persons we have so far discussed were Florentines, but there were others who were not natives of his city whom the young Dante must have either seen or heard of as he moved about the streets. Here are a few of them.

One of Dante's great stories — indeed it is one of the great love stories of all time — is the story of Paolo and Francesca which he tells in *Inferno* V, and with at least one of its protagonists he must have had personal contact.

In 1282, the Florentines created a new office — the *defensor artium*, or defender of the guilds. From March in the year of its creation until February 1283, this office was held by Paolo Malatesta da Rimini. One of the Victorian writers on Dante paints a sentimental picture of Dante once holding Francesca in his arms — and later placing her in hell. This is, of course, chronologically impossible. But it is inconceivable that he did not see that handsome golden-haired young man whom he would one day equate with Paris and with Tristan. He may even have talked to Paolo — and this was the Paolo of the story — and by him first have heard mentioned the star-crossed young lady whose nephew, oddly enough, was to be his last patron and protector.

It is equally inconceivable that he did not see Charles of Anjou — "*colui dal maschio naso*" (he of the male nose) and "*nasuto*" (big nose) he would call him in *Purgatorio* VII — for although he was only seven when Charles came to Florence in state, the occasion was a memorable one. It was one of those great pacifications between Guelph and Ghibelline which were so often attempted, and the whole population of Florence was assembled on the sands in front of the Rubaconte Bridge, "great scaffolds of wood having been erected in that place" for Charles and the other lords to stand upon.

"This Charles," wrote Villani, "was wise, prudent in council, and valiant in arms, harsh and much feared by all the kings of the earth, great-hearted and of high purpose, steadfast, firm in every adversity, faithful to every promise, speaking little and acting much, scarcely smiling, chaste as a monk, catholic, harsh in judgment, and of a fierce countenance, tall and stalwart in person, olive-colored, large-nosed. In kingly majesty, he exceeded any other lord."

With Charles came the "Emperor Baldwin of Constantinople" — the deposed Byzantine emperor — and Pope Gregory X.

Baldwin has nothing to do with the Dante story, but although Dante never specifically mentions Gregory by name it seems likely that one of the pope's acts, the incident occurring when Dante was ten years old, made its contribution to his concept of what the papacy, to his sorrow, had become.

The Guelph-Ghibelline pacification having come to naught, Gregory left the city in a fury and placed it under papal interdict. But on December 18, 1275, as he returned from the Council of Lyons, he found it necessary to pass through Florentine territory. He did this without fanfare, but because of his own ban he could not enter the city and so arranged to be led secretly around it but near the old walls.

"But the Arno was so swollen by rain that he could not cross the ford but must needs cross by the Rubaconte Bridge. So that, not being able to do otherwise, he entered into Florence, and while he was passing over the bridge and through the Borgo San Niccolo he took off the interdict and passed on, blessing the folk. But so soon as he was without, he renewed the interdict and excommunicated the city afresh!"

It is less likely that Dante had any personal memory of either Catalano de' Malavolti or Loderingo de' Carbonesi. He was too young.

These were the two hypocritical rogues with whom he deals so sarcastically in *Inferno* XXIII.

> "Jovial Friars we were, and Bolognese.
> I Catalano and the other Loderingo
> Are named, and we did jointly rule your land —
> By custom and of old ruled only by one —
> To keep the peace, and what our rule was like
> You still can see in ruins round the Gardingo."

Dante still could!

To clarify the story, "to keep the general peace between the Ghibellines and the Guelphs of Florence, the city sent for two lay brothers from

Bologna, one of each party. It gave to them mutual government and rule, each one to be the *podestà* of his particular party. The Guelph was Fra Catalano and the Ghibelline Fra Loderingo."

This was in 1266.

Their rule lasted for a year and then came to the end that government by two irreconcilable factions always does. The stronger faction — in this case, the Guelph faction — won out.

"For false dealing" — there must always be an excuse — "Fra Loderingo was driven from the city."

But if Dante had no personal contacts with the two "crowing cocks," as the Frati Gaudenti were also called, he heard plenty of talk about them. For they were intrinsic to Florentine political debate.

He heard more than talk about one other person whom he surely saw as he grew up in Florence. This was Adam of Brescia, about whom (*Inferno* XXX) he would write one of his most poignant passages.

> "Look you, and give heed
> Unto the bitter fate of Master Adamo.
> While yet I lived, I had all I desired.
> Woe's me, now one drop only of water I crave.
> The little streams that from the verdant hills
> Of Casentino flow down into the Arno,
> Making their way in brooklets cool and fresh,
> Are ever in my mind — and not in vain —
> Since just to see them parches me far more
> Than does the scurf that robs my face of flesh.
> That rigid justice which now scourges me
> Uses the very place wherein I sinned
> To make my sighs burst forth from me in flood.
> There is Romena! There I falsified
> The coin that had on it the Baptist's seal,
> For which I left my mortal body burned.
> But could I see here, damned and tortured,
> Guido or Alexander or their brother,
> I would not give that sight for Branda's spring.
> One of them's here already, if the raging
> Shades who inhabit this place do tell the truth.
> What good is that to me whose limbs are bound?
> If I were even now only so nimble
> That I could crawl an inch a hundred years,
> I should already have set out on the path
> To seek for him among the scurvy folk,
> Although it is eleven miles around,
> Here where the valley is but a half mile wide.

> Because of them I'm with this sorry tribe.
> 'T was they persuaded me to counterfeit
> Florins by adding three carats of base metal."

"This was Master Adamo of Brescia," wrote the Anonymous Florentine. "He was a very skilled coinmaker. He was brought into the Casentino" — a hill country between Florence and the crest of the Apennines — "at a time when the counts of that place were on very bad terms with the Florentines. At that time, the lords of Romena and of the lands around it were three brothers — the Counts Aghinolfo, Guido, and Alessandro. They persuaded him to coin florins like the coins of Florence. They were of the right weight but not of the right material, for they were of twenty-one carats when they should have been twenty-four, so that they had in them three carats of copper or some other base metal. Many of these florins were spent, and in the end Master Adamo came to Florence and spent some himself. He was arrested and burned."

This burning took place in 1281. Apparently it took place at Consuma, or more properly the pass of Consuma, where, amid pines and chestnuts, the winding road from Florence to Poppi and Bibbiena crosses the lofty mountain chain of the Pratovecchio. There — to impress the Guidi counts — the execution (according to Landino, who wrote only one hundred fifty years after the event) was carried out "on the old road where a heap of stones is still to be seen today, and the peasants, who live about there now, affirm that their grandparents had it from their old people before them that it was so."

It is thought that Dante witnessed this burning. In *Purgatorio* XXVII, he shrinks to go through the purifying fire because his vivid imagination conjured up the picture of "human bodies I had once seen burned." It is thought that this is a reference to Master Adamo. But if he did not see the fiery end of the Englishman — Adamo was born in England — who came to Brescia and then Tuscany, there were other burnings he could have witnessed. For the records with their frequent listings of "twenty *soldi* for faggots" and "ten *soldi* for oil" show that this form of punishment was common in Florence. But Dante had also seen murderers buried alive head down — this too is noted in the *Commedia* — and if his eyes were open he had seen a man forced to swallow molten metal and two others slowly boiled alive. As he painted his picture of the tortures of the lower regions, he had only to look around.

« *10* »

Whether or not, however, Dante, on foot or on muleback, did go to Consuma, whether he merely heard about Master Adamo or indeed joined the not inconsiderable throng that followed the Arno to Pontassieve and then turned to the left and climbed slowly upward in order to see the counterfeiter pay his scorching penalty for tampering with the sacrosanct Florentine coinage, it is quite clear that the poet, when a young man, did not spend all his time within the city walls. It is clear that he came also to know the Tuscan countryside.

This came at least in part as the inevitable consequence of new responsibilities which I will now explain.

It has already been noted that Alighiero II died between 1277 and 1283.

Now, according to Florentine custom and law, a boy put on breeches and was considered a young man at the age of fourteen, but if his father was living — unless the said father gave special consent — he did not attain formal majority until he was twenty-five. Even then there was almost always a ceremony before a judge or notary.

"Be thou henceforward a man and master of thine own actions. From now on thou canst act as the head of thy family, and as a Roman [*sic*] citizen!"

But if a boy's father was dead, he attained his majority at eighteen. There is still extant a document which shows that Dante did just that.

This document records that sometime between March 24, 1283, and March 25, 1284, "Dante, son of the late Alighiero of the *popolo* of San Martino del Vescovo, sold to Tedaldo, son of the late Orlando Rustichelli, all claims, either real or personal, which he may have against Donato, son of the late Gherardo del Papa, or against certain properties of his in the *popolo* of Santa Maria at Ottignano and in the *popolo* of Sant' Ambrogio. Against these properties, the father of the said Dante was owed twenty-one *libbre* by the said Donato and by his brother and his sons."

But if he disposed of property — which, incidentally, he could only do if he had attained legal manhood — he also retained property, and some of the property which he retained was real estate in the form of operating farms.

Dante, it should be clear, had ample time to devote himself to this property, and particularly to Le Radere on the road to Fiesole with its thickets of yellow-flowering broom and squat scrub oak. But it was more than a question of having leisure. Absentee ownership had as many dangers then as it has today, and, poet though he already was, Dante was shrewd enough to see them.

With his younger brother — later this younger brother was to become the businessman of the family — tagging at his heels, he must very often have gone from white farmhouse to white farmhouse sticking his nose into every possible corner. He must have talked to his tenants, inspected the outhouses and barns, and overseen the livestock and the crops, thus making as sure as he could that the people living there understood that he was vitally interested in everything they did and did not do. He had to be, for his land was the major source of his income.

He must also have walked the fields and tramped the woodlands. Certainly he was not clad, as he did this, the way we see him in his pictures. Tight hose, a homespun or fleece-lined jerkin or coat, a Florentine cap, and rough or country shoes is far more likely.

This exposure to the countryside is reflected in every single book he wrote, but it is particularly reflected in the *Commedia*. To Dante the philosopher and Dante the theologian — and also to Dante the observer of the city which he loved but chastised — must be added Dante the bucolic poet.

For in some ways his bucolic passages matched those of Virgil and Theocritus.

Here are just a few of the things which he described in them.

Frogs (*Inferno* IX, *Inferno* XXII, *Inferno* XXXII):

> And just as frogs before their enemy,
> The adder, swiftly dive into the pond
> Till every one lies huddled on the bottom.
>
> And as within the water of a ditch,
> The bullfrogs squat with only their nose showing,
> Their feet and even their body being hid . . .
> And one still stays there and the other leaps.
>
> And as, that he may croak, the frog keeps
> Nose out of water in that season when
> The peasant woman dreams of gleaning her crop.

An angry bull (*Inferno* XII):

> Just as a bull is when he breaks his halter
> The moment he is felled by mortal blow,
> And knows not where to go but lunges blindly.

Oxen (*Inferno* XVII, *Purgatorio* XII):

> He twisted then his mouth and thrust forth his tongue
> As doth an ox when he would lick his nose.

Shoulder to shoulder, as oxen who are yoked,
I walked along beside that burdened soul.

Goats upon a hillside (*Purgatorio* XXVII):

Like goats, now drowsy as they ruminate,
Who had lept here and there and who had skipped
Upon the craggy slope ere they had eaten.

Sheep (*Purgatorio* III):

As sheep are when they come into the fold
By ones and twos and threes, and they all stand
Timid with eyes and muzzles to the ground,
And what the first one does the others do,
Huddling around it if it comes to a stop,
Silly and quiet, yet they know not why.

(These sheep must truly have impressed him, for he speaks of them —
and in the same manner — in the *Convivio*.)

But Dante also (*Inferno* XVII) described dogs scratching at their fleas.
These must have been the noisy, savage, white dogs of the *contadini*
which you can see — and hear — in Tuscany even today. He described a
huge hog running and biting when he is let loose from his sty (*Inferno*
XXX); he described the ant pausing to touch its feelers to another
ant — I myself have seen them do this — as it marched, single of purpose, up
or down the white wall of a Florentine villa (*Purgatorio* XXVI); he
described the industry and the instinct of the bee (*Paradiso* XXXI).

He had something to say, too, about the noisy gabble of starlings
(*Inferno* V), the flight and the feeding of doves (*Inferno* V and *Purgatorio* II), the long line of cranes across the sky (also *Inferno* V), and the
ways of storks on the housetops (*Purgatorio* XXV), and swallows (*Purgatorio* IX) as they piped about the eaves.

(The last, of course, he could have observed in the city. They piped
then, as they still do, around palaces and towers.)

He portrayed — and very vividly — a peasant patching his hedgerow
fence with a pitchforked bundle of thorns (*Purgatorio* IV).

Dante was likewise incredibly observant of the beauties of the earth
around him and the heavens above this earth — of flowers and frost, of
autumn and of spring, of clouds and of mist, and of the fireflies which
even today dazzle the Tuscan night.

Flowers and frost (*Inferno* II):

> As little flowers, by the chill of night
> Bent down and closed, when the sun shines on them
> Open their petals and stand up on their stems.

Autumn (*Inferno* III):

> As in the autumntide the leaves fall
> One after another until the branch sees
> All of its treasure spread upon the ground.

Spring — as uncertain in Tuscany as it is elsewhere (*Inferno* XXIV):

> In those days of the young and budding year
> When the sun's rays are tempered in Aquarius
> And the long nights have moved toward the south,
> When nothing but hoarfrost copies on the ground
> The image and replica of her white sister
> And what she draws there lasts but a short while,
> The countryman whose fodder is running short
> Gets up and smites his thigh, returns inside,
> And grumbles like one who knows not what to do.
> But then goes forth again all filled with joy
> Because the world has changed its face again
> In time so short, and he takes up his crook
> And forth unto their pasture drives his lamblings.

Mist and clouds (*Purgatorio* XVII):

> Think now, my reader, if ever amid Alps
> You found yourself in mist through which you saw,
> Not otherwise than mole does through his skin,
> How when the thick and very drenching vapors
> Began to dissipate themselves, the sun's
> Sphere did thereupon shine through them ever so wanly.

Fireflies (*Inferno* XXVI):

> As many as the rustic, his repose
> Taking upon a hillside when the one
> Who keeps the world warm the least hides his face,
> And in that hour when fly yields to gnat,
> Fireflies sees, there in the valley below him
> In which he tends his vines and plows his field.

But it was not merely in moving about his farms where the *contadini*, stripped to the waist and the color of walnut or mahogany, went about their business, nor in walking over hill and dale while overhead the skylark sang and then paused to hear the melody of its own singing (*Paradiso* XX), that Dante was exposed to life under the blue sky.

He also took part in livelier and more jocund countryside activities.

One of the more spirited of his earlier writings is the famous so-called "hunting sonnet."

> Now brachets bark, and huntsmen cry hulloa,
> And hares start up before the hue and cry,
> And greyhounds swift to slip their leashes try
> As over the fair hillsides they would go.

To be sure, he indicated that he himself did not wholeheartedly take part in this particular day's merry doings, for the sonnet continued as follows:

> Ah this, ah this, should bring delight I know
> To a light heart and one that's fancy free.
> Hence I, by love's thoughts weighed down heavily,
> Am mocked by one who would not have it so.
> He gives me this advice. I hear him say:
> "It should be joyous to one gently born
> To take delight in all this woodland sport,
> Leaving the ladies beautiful and gay!"
> But I, who fear that Love will hear report
> Of this, shamefaced and sadly turn away.

But that was just a passing mood.

In his sonnet sequence, *The Months of the Year*, Folgore da San Gimignano tells us that the young men of Siena hunted "stag, agile roebuck, and wild boar"; that they angled for eels, trout, lamprey, salmon, dentex, sturgeon, and "every other finny thing that's known"; that they went hawking with "goshawk, hobby, peregrine"; and also that they jousted upon gaily caparisoned steeds and threw snowballs at the damsels standing in the square.

The young men of Florence did the same, and Dante was a young man of Florence.

In the *Commedia,* he speaks of a boar breaking through the underbrush (*Inferno* XIII), of very many phases of falconry (*Inferno* XVII, *Inferno* XXII, *Purgatorio* XIII, *Paradiso* XIX), and of a man watching the frondage for the small birds he would net (*Purgatorio* XXIII). In more than one place he gives clear indication that he knows how a bow is drawn and its arrow released. In *Purgatorio* XXIV, he has something to say about a jouster riding full tilt at his target.

All of these observations are precise and sharp. They could only have been made by a man who knew what he was talking about. Dante did know what he was talking about. There is no question that he wrote out of personal experience.

« *11* »

There are two other matters relating to Dante and to his experiences between his birth in 1265 and 1290, when he became twenty-five, which should here and now be discussed. The first is his probable visit to Bologna. The second is his marriage to Gemma Donati and its likely or even possible date. Both have been the subject of much discussion and some controversy.

Let us take up the stay at Bologna first.

Although even this has been challenged, it is as certain as anything can be that Dante sojourned more than once in the famous university town, and it is almost equally certain that his first stay there was early in his life.

"The first elements of his education he got in Florence," wrote Boccaccio, "and from there, as to a place richer in such food, he went to Bologna."

Read in the context of the whole Boccaccio *Life*, this seems to me the clear meaning:

Upon completing his elementary education — *almost immediately after* completing his elementary education — he went to Bologna.

But among Dante's own writings can be found even more convincing proof of an early visit there, for among his youthful sonnets there is a notable one, *Non mi poriano già mai fare amenda* (They need not ever make amends to me), that specifically refers to the Garisenda which is Bologna's own "leaning tower," while another phenomenon which can be noted when you observe it is later (*Inferno* XXXI) described so precisely as to make it impossible that the writer had not seen it with his own eyes.

This is the passage:

> As Garisenda appears to one who looks
> Upon its leaning side when a cloud passes
> Drifting in the opposite direction to its slant,
> So did Anteus seem to me who stood
> And saw him bend.

Even today this is something that impresses those who observe it. If you look at this tall tower's lofty top as fleecy white clouds float down the Italian sky, the tower appears to be falling.

But a copy of this sonnet, set down in the neat and charming callig-raphy for which he was famous, has been found in the register of Enrichetto delle Querce for 1287. Enrichetto was a Bolognese notary who later became proconsul of the Bolognese notarial guild and after that Bolognese ambassador to the papal court at Avignon. It was the custom of Bolognese notaries thus to transcribe poems which caught their fancy.

The poem, then, was written no later than 1287, and so Dante must have paid his first visit to Bologna during or before that year.

At one time it was thought that he had come to Bologna even earlier.

A legal document dated 1286 refers to "a Florentine by the name of Dante." This now appears to have been one Dante degli Abbati, and so unless Dante for reasons unknown used his mother's maiden name it could not have been him.

Another document shows that in 1285 "a certain Aldighieri" offered a ruffian named Giovanni twenty *soldi* to have another scholar whipped. This is the kind of thing that a nephew of Geri del Bello might well have done, but Aldighieri was a relatively common name on the Bolognese side of the Apennines and there is no evidence whatsoever that this Aldighieri was Dante Alighieri.

Nevertheless — whether in 1287, 1286, 1285, or even earlier — to Bologna he went, and in so doing he exposed himself to a life that was as notable for its rowdiness as it was for its learning. Its learning was very great.

Even in the Florence of his time, scholars were a turbulent lot. They claimed the right to stone to death and drag through the streets their political rivals, or more likely the political rivals of those who had won their favor. Street battles with the harassed and pushed-around guards of the signory were a frequent, if not a daily, occurrence.

But in Bologna there was an added cause for riots and disturbances. Its ten thousand students came from every part of Italy, and indeed — largely because of the high reputation of its law school — from many if not most parts of Europe. Those who had managed to get through the passes of the Alps and the Apennines, who had survived the deep snows, the impossible roads, and the bandits which infested the roads, found them-selves grouped together into so-called "nations" which spent as much time fighting each other as they did in acquiring knowledge.

But the nations sometimes banded together to extort concessions from the townspeople (one such concession: even when Bologna was at war with a student's native city he could remain at his books) or to boycott professors who charged too much or taught too little.

When they were not doing this, or were not — for they did study sometimes; they had to — listening to lectures which by modern standards were incredibly long-winded and pedantic, they plunged into a wild life of gluttony, drunkenness, rioting (often without cause, just for the sake of rioting), theft, and singing bawdy goliardic songs.

The goliards — so that we may know of them — were lawless wandering scholars of the Middle Ages. They pretended to worship a mythical Pope Golias, and their satire and their blasphemy were incredible.

Since they attacked the Church, the Church declared them its enemies. "No clerk shall be a jongleur, a goliard, or a buffoon," said a 1289 decree.

But it could not enforce this pronouncement.

The goliards were equally renowned for their high-hearted living.

"Wine, women, and song" is a goliardic expression.

And some of this song was stirring poetry, as can be seen in the fragments which remain.

Unquestionably Dante encountered these goliards — or rather their spiritual descendants, for the true goliards were of an earlier century. His own sharp sense of satire almost shows this, as does his sense (not always commented on) for grotesque comedy. But there is no reason to suppose that he was one of them.

More likely — in fact, almost certainly — he was a sedate and serious student, eagerly absorbing what was offered to him, for all that he later showed that he knew makes it clear that he missed no opportunity for learning. He learned at Florence and he learned at Bologna. As we will discover later, he did not ever stop learning.

How did this sedate and serious student live in the brown city by the summer-dry Reno which was famous even then for its fine food?

Who were his teachers?

Who were his literary friends?

To each of these questions, we can give at least a fragmentary answer.

Clustered about the city's two tall leaning towers — the 154-foot Garisenda, which has already been discussed, and the nearby 318-foot and far more famous graceful Asinelli — was a group of *hospitia*, or inns, which were probably no less noted for sour (or watered) wine and for shabby and soiled linen than those Sacchetti would describe a century later. But at least they were run by Florentines, and some of these Florentines came from famous Florentine families.

Feo di Gianni *Soldanieri*.

Brandaglia di Ruggero *Nerli*.

Bindo di Jacopo *Brunelleschi*.

Giacomo de' Benci, an agent of the banking house of *Peruzzi*.

(It should be noted that these inns were often also the shops and branch offices of notable Florentine firms.)

Sangallo dei *Portinari*, whose last name will be of considerable importance to us later on.

Professor Livi, who has studied Dante's life in Bologna more than any other man, has concluded that as a scholar in the city Dante stayed at one of these inns. He even indicates a possible specific host: Baldo di Jacopo da Passignano. Baldo was a merchant, but he was also a poet and an author. His most famous work was the *Liber Spei* (Book of Hope). It seems reasonable that a merchant-author might have sheltered Dante. But it is still only a guess.

Dante's instructor — or at least the most renowned of his instructors — was almost certainly a Florentine too.

In describing the hell of the sodomites in which he found Brunetto Latini (*Inferno* XV), Dante had Virgil go on to tell him this:

> "To sum up, know that all of these were clerks
> And men of letters, great and much renowned,
> But sullied while they lived with the same sin.
> There Priscian walks amid that wretched crowd,
> And Francesco d'Accorso. If thou hast
> A craving for such scurf, him that thou seest . . ."

The list continues.

The poet, it is apparent, did not have much esteem for the moral conduct of the pedagogic profession.

For this he was much criticized during his life, nor did this criticism subside with his death.

"I myself," said Benvenuto da Imola writing nearly one hundred years later, "was angry indeed when I first read these words. But then in 1375 I went to Bologna!"

Sodomite or not, Francesco the son of Accursius, or d'Accorso — for he is the one who concerns us — was one of the most distinguished law teachers of his day and age. He had one of the most distinguished legal minds.

His father Accursius of Bagnolo (a little town southwest of Florence) had been a distinguished legalist too, and when he died (in 1260), Francesco (born in 1225) succeeded him. He became a professor of civil law.

But in 1273, Edward I passed through Bologna on his return from the Holy Land and persuaded him to come to England. He lectured at Oxford, where he was given in return free lodgings at the king's manor, also known as Beaumont Palace. The angry Bolognese proscribed him as a Ghibelline and confiscated his property.

But when he returned to Bologna 1281, the property — and his pupils — were restored to him. This was in part because of a witty tale he told the magistrates.

"Once upon a time," he said, "a father, because of his poverty, left his native land and journeyed to a far country. He had been there many years when one day he encountered men from his own city. Moved by pangs of love, he asked them for news of the sons that he had left behind.

" 'They have done well, and they are now rich,' he was told.

"At this, he decided to return, and when he came to his home he found that it was indeed true, and so he asked them to return his property to him since he was their father and their lord.

"This they refused to do.

" 'We are the ones who gained this wealth. It had nought to do with you.'

"To the law courts he then went seeking justice, and the law courts gave it him.

" 'The father is master of everything his sons have gained or own.'

"Honorable lords, my scholars are my sons, and they and what they have gained belonged to me."

This is not the only witty tale told by or about Francesco. His tongue was sharp and penetrating.

Nor was moral turpitude his only vice. He also practiced usury — and that even against his own pupils.

But he did teach as no one else could teach, and he continued until his death in 1293. Scholars came from everywhere to listen to his lectures. In all probability, Dante was one of them.

Dante at Bologna had literary acquaintances too, but the name of only one of them has survived — the *"poeta Veneziano* [Venetian poet], Giovanni Quirini, with whom he had literary correspondence."

Quirini outlived Dante and wrote a splendid tribute to him after his death. But they also were friends when young blood coursed and youthful pulses beat splendidly.

Quirini wrote this to Dante in their earlier days:

> Not kind and human but like dragon fierce
> And cruel doth show herself, haughty and venomous,
> Thy lady fair, savage and orgulous.
> Just thinking of her my heart doth wound and pierce.

He was not, incidentally, speaking of Beatrice!

But Dante, in this city, did more than listen to learned lectures and exchange writings with poetic friends. As he had in Florence, he walked about the streets and came to know their everyday life.

He learned the Bolognese language and in his *De Vulgari Eloquentia* had something to say about it, as we will see later.

He knew the Bolognese slang. For yes they said *sipa* instead of *si*, and they called the ravine on the outskirts of the city into which they threw executed criminals the *salse*, or saucepots.

He was aware of the city's gutter way of living and heaped scorn upon it. There are more Bolognese panders in hell, he said (*Inferno* XVIII), than people now living in Bologna.

One of these he must have known.

It was still told of Venetico Caccianimico how he had sold his sister to the blond-haired and bestial Azzo d'Este.

"This marquis, having heard of Ghisolabella's beauty, and having, because of his friendship for Messer Venetico, seen her several times, left Ferrara incognito and knocked at Messer Venetico's door."

Messer Venetico pretended to be astounded to see him there, and observed that he must be upon important business.

"The marquis, because he knew the soul of Messer Venetico, took him into his confidence and said that he loved Messer Venetico's sister more than anyone else and that he knew she was in the house. Wherefore, and after many prayers, Messer Venetico consented and yielded to the will of the marquis and departed from the place and left her behind. After some dispute, the marquis had his will of her."

When Dante was in Bologna, Venetico was an old man, but the people still talked of the scandal. He did not need the money which Azzo reputedly gave him, for he was wealthy in his own right. Why did he betray his sister?

Dante did not ask the reason, but inexorably, as he always did, he sentenced him (*Inferno* XVIII) to eternal punishment. With the pawn-broker Vinaccio Bencivenni of the Ubbriachi family (a Florentine but apparently established in Bologna), whom he identified by the goose argent upon a field gules embroidered on his purse, and Pier da Medicina, one of the *cattani*, or military captains, of the Bolognese territory, who was almost as inveterate a troublemaker as Geri del Bello, he was one of only three associated with the city whom Dante placed in hell.

« 12 »

Of Dante's marriage to Gemma Donati not even this much can be said.

It is known that on February 9, 1277, a marriage contract was drawn up between Dante and Gemma, Gemma being the daughter of Manetto

Donati, a neighbor and a prominent citizen. The dowry was two hundred florins, which was not small.

It has been argued that the marriage took place almost immediately. Child marriages — particularly when they were family alliances — were not infrequent. Guido Cavalcanti — Dante's "first friend" and himself a great poet — was married to the daughter of Farinata degli Uberti when he was only nine. Dante's father, it is argued, was ill at the time and realized that he was probably dying. He wished to put his son's affairs in order.

Other authorities place the marriage a great deal later.

The plain fact is that we do not know.

Nor, in a sense, is it important. For, except for bearing the poet three — or possibly four — children and bringing them up successfully under extremely difficult circumstances, Gemma played very little part in Dante's life.

IV

A Short History of the Fount of Joy and Valor

I T was during this period, it was as Dante grew to manhood and maturity, that "the fair and gay city of Florence, the fount of valor and joy, the flower of cities, Fiorenza" — this description comes from Chiaro Davanzati, a Dante contemporary — attained its maturity too.

How this came about is something which we must know. The physical aspect of Florence has already been described; and so have its workmen and its artisans, its gay blades and its sedate older citizens, the rich men, poor men, beggarmen, and even thieves who gave the city an intentness and an animation which have not more than once or twice been equaled during the long story of mankind. But equally important is the city itself — how it became what it was as a city and a state and as a city-state, and what it was that it became.

Let us begin with legend. There has grown up a type of student who dismisses this kind of protohistory as ignorance embroidered by fantasy, and indeed one of the most competent modern writers upon Florence, speaking of an early chronicle, *Il Libro Fiesolano*, remarks, "It is hard to believe that this sort of uncontrolled invention was ever considered to be entertaining." But he also says that in spite of this, "Whoever is curious about Dante's historical background cannot overlook these ancient compilations."

He cannot overlook them, he forgot to add, because however much they have been discredited by the more scientific modern approach, the stories which they related were implicitly believed by virtually everybody in Florence in the days when Dante grew up. By the butcher in his stall. By the housewife speaking stridently from her doorstep. But likewise by the grave-faced judge or notary, the latter with his long fur-trimmed robe.

Important to us, they were believed by Dante. They shaped both his feelings and his thought.

What were these stories — or these fables — which Dante and others believed?

Giovanni Villani tells us — and in some detail.

"We find in the Bible histories, and in those of the Assyrians," he writes, "that Nimrod the giant was the first king, or ruler, and assembler of the gatherings of the people," and that "of his pride and strength he thought to rival God," and that further "to the end that God might no longer be able to hurt him by a flood of water, he ordered the building of the marvelous work of the Tower of Babel. Wherefore God, to confound the said pride, suddenly sent confusion upon all mankind, which was at work upon the tower, and where all were speaking one language [to wit, Hebrew] it was changed into seventy-two diverse languages, so that they could not understand one another's speech."

In consequence of this confusion, the world shortly thereafter was divided into three parts, and of these parts "the third was called Europe."

"This Europe was first inhabited by the descendants of Japhet, and the third son of Noah," and of these descendants one of the most notable was a certain Attalus, or Atlas.

"Atlas, with Electra his wife, arrived in Tuscany, which was entirely uninhabited by human beings and, searching by the aid of astronomy through all the confines of Europe for the most healthy and best spot which could be chosen by him, he took up his abode upon the mount of Fiesole. And there he began to build a city."

It was predestined for greatness and fame.

Because it was near the sea and because of the mountains which surrounded it, "better and more salubrious winds" prevailed there than anywhere else in the world. Furthermore, "It was well provided with fresh water led to it by a marvelous conduit." And, it was founded "under the ascendant of such a sign and planet that it gives more sprightliness and strength to its inhabitants than any other part of Europe."

Finally, it had a prudent ruler.

Atlas, Villani concluded in proof of this, "had the city walled with very strong walls, wondrous in their masonry and thickness, and with great and strong towers, and there was a fortress on the top of the mountain, as can be seen by the foundations of the said walls. This city multiplied and increased its inhabitants, so that it ruled over the surrounding country to a great distance. And note that it was the first city built in the third division, and therefore it was named *Fia sole* — Be thou alone."

Rome — this is the second step in the legend — was descended from Fiesole.

Atlas had two sons, Italus and Dardanus, and after consulting an oracle, it was decided that Italus should remain in the town founded by his father and that Dardanus should seek his fortune elsewhere. He went to Asia Minor, and there "upon the shores of the Grecian sea" he too built a city which he called, after his own name, Dardana. But later is name was changed to Troy after his grandson Trojus.

When Troy fell — "owing to the sinful lust of Paris for Helen" — its princes fled in all directions. Among these was Aeneas, who, after many adventures which are well celebrated in the *Aeneid*, came to Latium. There, some fourteen or fifteen generations later, his descendants founded Rome.

"At the time when this Rome was still ruled by the government of the consuls, Catiline, a very noble citizen, a dissolute man but brave and daring in arms and a fine orator, but not wise, formed a conspiracy. He purposed to slay the consuls and part of the senators, and to destroy their offices, and to overrun the city, robbing and setting fire to many parts thereof, and to make himself ruler. He would have done this if he had not been warded off by the sense and foresight of the wise consul Marcus Tullius Cicero."

Catiline fled and with a part of his followers came to Tuscany, where he established himself at Italus's town, Fiesole, which "he caused to rebel against the rule of the Romans, assembling all the exiles from Rome and from many other provinces with lewd folk disposed to war and ill doing."

The Romans sent an army against him. He was defeated and slain, and his followers fled to Pistoia.

"And therefore it is not to be marveled at if the Pistoians have been and still are a fierce and cruel people!"

But the Fiesolans continued to fight — and not without success. They slew Fiorinus (a Roman general) and with him slew his wife and children. It was only when Julius Caesar and his soldiery, with an impressive list of Roman "counts," set his camp before their city that they gave in.

"The city was taken, and despoiled of all its wealth, and was destroyed and laid waste to its foundations." Then Caesar descended to the plains, and where "Fiorinus and his followers had been slain" they began to build their own city.

One consul undertook to pave all the streets. "This was a noble work and gave beauty and charm to the city. To this day fragments of these streets are found." Another Roman leader "caused water to be brought in conduits and aqueducts, bringing it from a distance of seven miles." Gnaeus Pompey — Pompey the Great, of all persons! — "caused the walls of the city to be built of burned brick, and upon these walls he built many round towers." His colleague, a Roman lord, "caused a Capitol to be built after the fashion of Rome. This Capitol stood where today is the piazza called the Mercato Vecchio."

The city was then peopled "by the best of Rome, and most capable, sent by the senate from each division of Rome, chosen by lot from the inhabitants. And they admitted too among their numbers those Fiesolans who desired to abide and dwell there."

When Caesar had fixed the boundaries, he wished to call it Caesarea after his own name, but the senate would not permit this.

"And so by many at first it was called Rome the Lesser. Others called it Floria because Florinus had died there. But afterwards it was, through long use of the vulgar tongue, called Fiorenza, that is, Flowery Sword."

These, then, were the tales of "the Trojans, of Fiesole and of Rome" which, as Cacciaguida has already pointed out, were told to Dante and to other intent, dark-eyed Florentine children as they clustered about a mother or a grandmother while she did her household tasks.

He was told other things too.

He was told how Minias (San Miniato), "the firstborn son of the king of Armenia," had been beheaded by the cruel emperor Decius "where now stands the church of Santa Candida alla Croce al Gorgo." And when the head of the blessed Miniato had been cut off, by a miracle of Christ he set it on again, and on his feet passed over the Arno, and up to the hill where now stands his church. And when San Miniato came to that place, he gave up his soul to Christ."

He was told how Totila, "a barbarian, born of the province of Gothland and Sweden," after destroying much of Italy, promised Florence his aid against Pistoia.

"The foolish Florentines (and for this cause they were afterwards called blind) opened the gates to him, and admitted him and his followers into the city." Once there, he invited the greatest and most powerful men in Florence to come before him, and as they passed one by one through an entry he caused them to be massacred.

"And after that Totila had thus wasted it of inhabitants and goods, he commanded that it should be destroyed and burned, and that there should not remain one stone upon another. And this was done."

Dante was also told how Charles the Great (Charlemagne) caused the city to be rebuilt and that it was at this time that some of his ancestors came to it. But this has already been related.

« 2 »

It is curious — but perhaps, on second thought, it is not entirely curious — to note that neither history nor archaeology completely refutes these ancient stories. Atlas, of course, did not found Fiesole, nor did a fleeing Trojan chieftain found Rome. But civilization was almost certainly introduced to central Italy by a people whose original home was not only in Asia Minor, but in a part of Asia Minor which was right next door to Troy.

The Etruscans, whose intensely concentrated capacity for living has not even today been entirely diluted in their Tuscan descendants, are one of the major historical mysteries in Europe. But it is now generally agreed that they were from Lydia. Lydia lies alongside of Phrygia, and it was in Phrygia that arose those topless towers of Ilium whose burning caused Aeneas and other Trojan princes to take refuge in lands to the west.

The arrival of the Etruscans in Italy was around 1000 B.C. — plus or minus, as the saying goes. Nor did it take them long to establish themselves there. By 900 B.C. they had begun building at least the earlier of the twelve cities of the Etruscan League — Vatlona (Vetulonia), Tarquinia, and Caere (modern Cervetri). Not much later they were trading their wheat, wine, olive oil, and timber for the iron of Spain, the tin of distant Britain, and the gold, silver, jewels, and pottery of Egypt and Syria. By 616 B.C. there was an Etruscan king in Ruma — i.e., Rome.

Faesulae (Fiesole) was not one of the twelve lucumonical or league towns, but it was certainly built by the Etruscans and in all probability it was built by 700 B.C. (It may have been built as early as 900 B.C.) Its hillside situation — common to most early Etruscan towns — was the consequence of insecure times, as were the massive "cyclopean" walls, whose huge blocks and almost invisible interstices were a tribute to both engineering skill and resolute willpower. Fragments of them still remain. They are the walls of Atlas described by Villani.

Florence was this hill town's daughter, born when the times became secure. During their first days in Italy, the Etruscans had to do battle not merely with the various native tribes but even with the marauding and yellow-haired Gauls who poured into the peninsula under various chiefs named Brennus (Brann, or Brian, is Celtic for king) and once even stormed the Capitoline at Rome, which was saved only by the cackling of geese. Then came the long struggle with the Romans. But when the latter had finally triumphed, law and order was established from the Alps to Sicily, and it was then thought prudent by at least some of the Fiesolans to come down from their mountain stronghold and settle in the more convenient valley.

This was in 200 B.C. The new settlement was called Fluentia — from *fluere*, to flow? — but soon it got its present name. There were two Fluentias, or Florences. The Etruscans built their Florence somewhat to the east of the medieval city but well within the limits of modern

Florence. It was leveled to the ground by Sulla in 82 B.C. But in 59 B.C. a new Florence was constructed, and since this was done under the terms of the *lex Julia*, adopted during the consulate of Julius Caesar, it is not hard to see how the legend that he founded the city came into being.

But not even this new Roman Florence was much more than a Roman *castrum*. Roughly square in shape — as Roman *castri*, or camps were — it measured approximately five hundred yards upon each side. It was bounded on the north by the present-day Via Cerretani and Piazza del Duomo, on the east by the Via Proconsolo, on the south by the Borgo Santi Apostoli, and on the west by the Via Tornabuoni.

Nor was it ever more than moderately important. Florus, to be sure, in his condensed history for Roman schoolboys does refer to it as one of the *municipiae Italiae splendidissima*, but he does this for propaganda purposes. Pliny, the naturalist, thought that *Fluentia vel Florentia* deserved inclusion in his list of Roman-Etruscan towns. It also had the forum, the aqueducts, the baths, the theater, and the temples of a Roman *municipium*, and later, as a suburb developed, an amphitheater for shows of gladiators and wild animals. But so too did many another small Roman city — Arretium, Perusia, Spoletium, and perhaps even Sena, or Siena. The principal importance of Roman Florence lay in the effect it had upon the medieval Florentine mind.

After the Caesars had gone, even this Roman Florence almost disappeared. But it was not destroyed by Totila, or by any other of the barbarian chieftains who one after another poured into the peninsula. It was destroyed rather by the conditions which these barbarian invaders created.

Following Rome's fall, there was a brief Byzantine interlude, and then Visigoth, Vandal, Ostrogoth, steppe-born Magyar, and even Saracen and Northman pirates followed each other in rapid succession.

The aqueducts and many of the city walls were torn down. The plowed fields became woodland or wasteland. Such of the hard-working Roman *coloni* (tenants and small farmers) as survived became the slaves the Guidi (the Wieds), the Cadolighi, the Aldobrandeschi, and others. They are the ancestors of the later peasant class.

Anarchy compounded by bandit exactions took the place of order and of rule.

"Men" — this was said of a later period, but it applied even more emphatically to the desperate last half of the first Christian millenium — "could not sow nor reap nor dwell in the farmsteads."

Such agriculture as there was was carried on either within the walls of surviving towns or under armed protection.

"This they must do by reason of the marauders who were multiplied exceedingly, and used to seize men and hale them off that they might ransom themselves for money. They also carried off their oxen and either sold them or ate them. Those who refused to give ransom they would hang up by the feet and draw their teeth, or they would put toads into their mouths, which was more bitter and abominable than death."

Trade also virtually disappeared — and for the same reasons.

But a city — any city — is dependent upon order and commerce.

"What really happened at Florence," said the late Professor Ferdinand Schevill, "was the very opposite of striking drama. The town slowly vegetated to decay."

In this, he added, it "repeated the experience of every town in the peninsula."

Mighty Rome, for example, at one time had less than thirty thousand inhabitants!

"Too indolent and discouraged to remove the debris, the few remaining inhabitants raised such new shops and shelters as they might require upon the steadily accumulating garbage piles until every trace of the Roman buildings had been covered up and the slowly rising medieval city was lifted to a level anywhere from four to ten feet above its Roman predecessor."

« 3 »

It was not until the year 1000 approached — the fateful year which according to the superstition of the day was to bring the end of the world — that this slow but continuing decay began to end and that the trend, after five or six centuries, was upward.

Since the days of Alaric, the invaders from the north had been for the most part bringers of ruin whose one thought had been how much treasure they could seize, how many acres they could take over, and how many edifices they could make roofless or tear down. But now the idea of empire was restored, and empire intrinsically means law and order.

Charlemagne was its first proponent. To many he was but another barbarian chief, but when Pope Leo III paid a political debt by proclaiming him heir to the Caesars and crowning him Roman emperor in the ancient — not the present-day — basilica of St. Peter's on Christmas Day 800, the great German-speaking French monarch began to act like one.

In Italy, particularly, he moved against the old disorder. He replaced the self-aggrandizing administrators set up by the Lombards with new ones called *comites*, or counts, who were responsible to him personally. He appointed *scabini*, or tax-collector assessors, and, realizing that local needs must be considered even by a strong central government, he usually named to this office a local citizen of some prominence. Over these, to be sure, he placed *missi domenici* (agents of the sovereign lord). But these were not oppressors. They were to see to it that the administration, both fiscal and otherwise, was carried out as soundly as possible and carried out for the benefit of all.

Charlemagne also formally reopened the ancient trade routes, and to further their convenient use he set up so-called *civitates* (places where merchants could foregather) in the cities, *mutationes* (relays) in the villages, and *mansiones* (trade hostels) in the countryside.

Once again a light began to shine.

Unfortunately, however, the benefits brought by this Karl der Grosse did not outlast his life, for his son Louis the Pious was weak and ineffectual, and his grandsons even more so. Anarchy returned. But in 936 there was a strong emperor again. Otto I and his successors were also Teutons by birth and education, but they had a clear understanding of what Rome meant, and by frequent visits to Italy and by both military and diplomatic skill they reconstituted the organization which would become the Holy Roman Empire two hundred years later. Almost at the same time the papacy began to struggle out of a muddy slough of sordid finances and rotten immorality. Pope John XI was the bastard son of Pope Sergius III and the notable Roman harlot Marozia. He died in 936. But by 999, Sylvester II could be called "a moderate reformer," while by 1073, Gregory VII — the short, corpulent, glittery-eyed son of Tuscan peasants who was born Ildebrando (Hildebrand) di Bonizio degli Aldebrandeschi — not only had begun to restore papal conduct to a high level but also was attempting to make his Church the paramount power in Europe. In both efforts, he had considerable success.

This rise to temporal power of the West's spiritual chief and the resultant struggle for primacy with another temporal power, the emperor, was the most important Italian political fact of the whole Middle Ages. But it was a struggle for power and not for plunder, and each of the two contestants needed a prosperous Italy — hopefully, it would be on his side. They saw to it that Italy was prosperous. The trade which was revived by Charlemagne and then disappeared again had, in consequence, a second rebirth. From Venice, but more important to this story from Pisa, from Siena, and from Florence, the ships and/or pack trains began to move out again; and when they returned they were laden with other bales of merchandise or with weighty sacks of gold.

« 4 »

It was out of these new prosperous conditions that local self-government arose or, to be more exact, became important — not only in Florence but throughout Italy.

It is not hard to see why.

The first rulers — at any rate, in Florence — came from the Church; and these rulers — at any rate, again, in Florence — were a very worldly crew. They are best typified by Bishop Hildebrand (not to be confused with the Hildebrand who became Pope Gregory), who with his "wife" Alberga and his numerous sons lived, *circa* 1020, in an episcopal palace just west of San Giovanni and conducted himself like a feudal lord.

Their rule did not last, however, nor did that of those who followed them: saintly men like St. Romuald and his followers who (*Paradiso* XXII) "within the cloister firmly set their feet," or the more politically expert Guarinus who dared thunder at the bishop's doughty lady: "You accursed Jezebel! How dare you open your mouth? You ought to be burned at the stake!"

They were not sufficiently attuned to actual and pressing needs.

Even in the darkest of the Dark Ages, there was a basic municipal or locality housekeeping which had to be done. This had always been necessary, but it became increasingly important now that trade had been revived. And since in the confusion there was no one else to undertake the task, the localities and the municipalities did it themselves.

Their methods were highly pragmatic, and it is doubtful that they greatly concerned themselves — as, with many words, historians have been doing ever since — about whether the institutions they set up were derived from Roman law or from German custom. Almost automatically those with common interests simply banded together. In the country or in the small country town, the unit thus formed was the *vicinia* or *vicinanza* (neighborhood). In the city it was the *populus*, or parish.

Parish or neighborhood, each group had, of course, its leader, and this leader was from the beginning the one who impressed his neighbors or his fellow citizens as its most forceful member.

But behind this leader were the people themselves met in assembly, for it was the people who had given him first his informal, and later on his formal, powers. These assembles were called *parlamenti* or *arringhi*. It is interesting to note that *parlamentum* comes from *parlare*, meaning to speak. *Arringhum* has given us our word harangue.

At first these assemblies were spontaneous gatherings, but eventually they had legal status. Usually they were convened on Sunday. After morning Mass, the inhabitants of a *populus* (or a *vicinia* if it was a small neighboring village) would gather into the open space — it was not yet called a piazza, but usually a *campo* or field — and there listen to the local most important citizen eloquently but with homespun common sense expatiate upon their problems and on how to solve them. If the issue were

The Palatine Dante (an illustration in watercolor in the National Library in Florence) shows a Dante slightly older than the Giotto Dante. It was executed in the early fifteenth century.

important enough, the *popolani* from the various parishes would flow in to some central place like the flat, large square in front of Santa Reparata.

Was there a bridge to be built? The *arringhum* shouted that they must build it.

Was the road to be repaired? The assembly approved, and out came the citizens with their shovels and their pickaxes.

Had the walls fallen into ruin? A *viva voce* decided it. They then put to work their stonecutters and their masons.

It was the same when there was a castle which must be destroyed.

"Monte Crucis est cruciatus!" the citizens shouted exultantly as they marched back from tearing down Monte Croce.

This was in 1155.

But Monte Croce was very far from being the only castle upon which the Florentines laid their hands.

In 1107, they destroyed Monte Gualandi, a stronghold of the Counts Alberti which looked down on the highway to Pisa; and in 1138, in the autumn when the ripened grapes were pale green or deep purple on the vine, they marched south and destroyed the castle of Pitigliano. This was near Colle, and well on the way to Siena. But between those dates, Villani alone tells of a half dozen of those turreted strongholds — each one, to borrow a phrase, "like an eagle's nest perched on the crest of purple Apennine! — which this new entity, a strong-headed and independent-minded *municipium*, took and then toppled from its pride of place.

And, of course, both before and after, there were many more!

They toppled them with the new Florentine citizen-army, which in a sense was the *arringhum* in action.

At its head, to be sure, was a small band of knights, who had already (by the middle of the eleventh century, that is) been organized into a *societas militum*.

But behind these *milites* followed the *pedites*. These *pedites*, or foot soldiers, were the ordinary Florentines. They were the artisans and the mechanics and even the day laborers who were called up from their shops and benches — or from working in the ditches and streets — by the tolling of every bell in the city. They did not wear armor and their weapons were whatever they could hastily snatch up. The blacksmith would pick up his mighty hammer, the carpenter his mallet, the laborer his pickaxe or shovel, and the maker of farm implements his sickle or scythe. To be sure, there were pikes, swords, and daggers, but the point is that every man had his own kind of weapon, anything that could strike a foeman down.

Clad in their workday clothes, wearing leather breeches and perhaps even a leather jacket, carrying in front of them a banner of a simple cloth half red, half white — for in those days there was no lily of either color — they followed the pennoned cavalry with the firm steps and resolute purpose of those accustomed to do whatever job was given them. Through the valleys they tramped, and then up steep slopes to those hilltop masses of huge feudal masonry which sheltered the arrogant aristocrats who — they were convinced — menaced their newfound well-being.

They were the numerical strength of the Florentine fighting force, and it was probably they who made it so frequently unshakable. Like the French at the Bastille six centuries later, they tore down these refuges of their enemies with their bare hands.

But it was not merely to assaulting nearby castles that the *arringhum* gave its shouted approval.

Should they help one of their neighbors — particularly when it was in their own self-interest to do so?

In 1117, the Pisans — at that time friendly, although later they would be an enemy — organized a fleet of galleys and other ships to send against Majorca, which at that time was in the hands of Saracen pirates. But just as they were about to set sail, the army of the commonwealth of Lucca marched toward their city.

What should the Pisans do? If they sailed, Pisa would be taken, but to draw back did not seem to their honor.

They bethought them of the city up the Arno.

"Wherefore they took counsel to send ambassadors to the Florentines, and they begged them that they would protect the city."

Understanding full well the importance of curbing these raiders on a commerce from which they too benefited, the Florentines agreed.

"They sent thither armed folk in abundance, horse and foot, and, in respect for their women, they would not enter the city, and made a proclamation that whosoever should enter the city should answer for it with his person."

One Florentine disregarded this edict. He was promptly sentenced to be hanged.

"Thereon they raised a gallow and did their execution."

Before the *arringhum* were also laid matters of state and high policy.

How to deal with the emperor, for example?

With a strong emperor, like Frederick Barbarossa, who would attempt to restore the imperial authority?

With a weak emperor who would make concessions?

How to reap the most advantage from either? How to clip the wings of the *potestas,* or imperial agent, with his hated Teutonic regime, which was so strongly established down the Arno at San Miniato del Tedesco?

Florence could not be strong as long as the Germans held this little city.

All these — and the housekeeping matters cited above — were laid before this assembly of the people. The *arringhum* settled them with a shouted vote.

Yet it must not be assumed from what has been said that this early and to an extent improvised Florentine government was — or at any rate remained — a true democracy in the sense that we now understand the word. The *arringhum* was indeed a gathering of the whole people, but long before Dante's time it did not so much take action as, urged by an oratory made up of eloquence and pithy sayings, it ratified actions taken by another and much smaller body. This smaller body — whether its members were called consuls or *boni homines* or *anziani* — was the true ruler of the city. With very few exceptions, it was made up of noblemen or at least magnates. They were "the big man" and not "the little fellow." To be sure, almost from the beginning this small group was assisted by a council of one hundred and fifty. It is not known how the council — which in default of public buildings met in a lesser church such as San Piero Scheraggio — was elected. But this too was basically an oligarcho-aristocratic institution, acting in the interests of the best and most important (i.e., noblest or richest) families and clans.

« 5 »

Not very far from the beginning of the twelfth century, a new and disturbing element was added to the Florentine scene. This was the savage struggle for ascendancy between the Guelphs and the Ghibellines, the two famous political parties whose birth — or more accurately, whose appearance in Italy — was to set in motion forces whose impact upon Florence would shape its history well into Dante's young manhood and even beyond.

As might be expected, the Florentines had a legend to account for them.

"In the year 1215" (by our calendar 1216) — this is from the so-called pseudo-Brunetto Latini, but other chronicles tell the same story — "Messer Mazzingho Tegrimi had himself dubbed knight at a place called Campi, and invited thither all the best people of the town. When the knights had sat down to meat, a buffoon snatched away the full plate of Messer Uberto dell' Infangati, who was paired at table with Messer Buondelmonte de' Buondelmonti. That angered Messer Uberto, for which anger Messer Oddo Arrighi de' Fifanti roughly reproved him. In reply Messer Uberto told him that he lied in his throat, at which Messer Oddo tossed a plate full in his face. The whole assembly was in an uproar.

When the tables had been taken away, Messer Buondelmonte struck at Messer Oddo with a knife and gravely wounded him."

That was the beginning, but worse was to follow.

"As soon as the company had returned home, Messer Oddo conferred with his friends and relatives. Among them were the Counts of Gangalandi, the Uberti, the Lamberti, and the Amidei. Their advice was that peace should be made and that Messer Buondelmonte should take for wife the daughter of Messer Lambertuccio de' Amidei. The bride-to-be was a niece of Messer Oddo. A marriage contract was made, the peace was arranged, and the wedding was to take place the next day."

But at this point "Monna Gualdrada, wife of Messer Forese Donati," sent secretly for Messer Buondelmonte.

"'Sir knight, you are forever disgraced if you take a wife out of fear of the Uberti and the Fifanti. Leave her and take my daughter!'

"He resolved to do this, and when on the following morning the guests of both parties had assembled, Messer Buondelmonte passed through the gate of Santa Maria and went to pledge troth to the girl of the Donati family. Her of the Amidei, he left waiting at the church door."

Needless to say, this insult "enraged Messer Oddo greatly," and once again he summoned his friends and relatives.

"When they had gathered, he complained in strong terms of the disgrace put upon him by Messer Buondelmonte."

Different kinds of advice were given.

"Some counseled that Messer Buondelmonte be given a cudgeling, others that he be wounded in the face."

At this point, Messer Mosca de' Lamberti spoke up:

"'Whoever beats him or wounds him, let him see to it that his own grave is dug. Here a clean decision is needed. *Cosa fatta capo ha!*'"

A thing done — this is the literal meaning — has a head to it. Halfway measures never settle anything!

"Thereupon they decided that revenge was to be carried out in the very place where the injury had been done, and thus it came to pass that when on Easter morning" — with his bride at his side we know from other sources — "in a doublet of silk and with a wreath upon his head, he came riding over the bridge [the Ponte Vecchio], no sooner had he arrived at the statue of Mars than Messer Schiatta degli Uberti rushed upon him and, striking him with a mace, brought him to earth. At once, Messer Oddo was on top of him and opened his veins."

"Murder Incorporated" in the medieval Florentine manner!

Immediately the city was in an uproar. The body of the slain man, his white garments now stained with red, was placed on the bier, and the bride took her seat there, holding his head on her lap and weeping audibly. As it moved through the streets of Florence, the city rose in arms. Before night fell, conflict raged so violently from tower to tower and from street to street that the *podestà* had to intervene.

Nor did the fury expend itself in a night and a day.

"For," said another chronicler, "this death was the cause and the beginning of the accursed parties of the Guelphs and the Ghibellines in Florence. Long before, to be sure, there were factions among the noble citizens by reason of the strife and questions between the Church and the empire, but now the city was permanently divided."

Those of the Buondelmonte faction became the Guelphs. Those of the Uberti faction became the Ghibellines.

"Whence followed much evil and disaster."

It is clear Dante agreed with this verdict and it is clear also that he accepted the story at face value, as he did almost every Florentine legend. *Inferno* XXVIII:

> He cried out: "Oh remember likewise Mosca,
> Who said, alas, 'A deed done hath a head!'
> This was a seed of evil for Tuscany."

Paradiso XVI:

> "O Buondelmonte, it was ill thou fledst
> Thy wedding at another's soft persuasions.
> Joyful would many be who now know sorrow
> If God had only let the Ema drown thee
> The first time that thou camest to the city."

About the latter passage, a word of explanation is necessary. The Buondelmonti were one of the numerous country-noblemen families that came to Florence when their castles were destroyed by the citizen armies, and to reach it they had to cross the little Ema River. If they had drowned in it, Florence would have known internal peace.

This, of course, oversimplifies a complex matter, for even though the Buondelmonte story was true, the strife which was to bring the city of the lilies so much heartache (and yet help to make it great) did not come merely from a young man's impetuous marriage, nor from Gadfly — which is what Mosca means — de' Lamberti's sharp and overquick tongue, nor from Messers Uberto and Oddo's ready blades.

It arose also from inevitable pressures.

I have purposely not gone into the official structure of the Florentine government as it came to be adopted. It changed too often and is not here pertinent. But control of such legal bodies as from time to time there were had long been contested by naturally antagonistic groups. On the one hand — and even here we simplify — were the noblemen and the aristocrats with their rowdy "tower societies" of armed followers who ruled segments of the city as they had formerly ruled segments of the countryside. On the other hand was the rising merchant class, which seriously objected to this hegemony. Among other things it was bad for business.

Power is where power resides, and each of these two groups, therefore, had no choice whatsoever but to seek the residence of power. Made to order for their purpose were two factions which had come into being in Germany as a result of a fifteen-year civil war (1197–1212) which was fought there for possession of the Italian imperial throne. Candidate of one faction was Otto IV, who was the great-grandson of Duke Welf of Bavaria. His followers called themselves Welfs. By the relatively common change of German *w* into Italian *gu*, this in Italy became Guelphs. Otto's adversaries — first Philip of Swabia and then Philip's half-German, half-Norman nephew, Frederick II — had among their many strongholds the castle of Waiblingen in south Germany. "Waiblingen!" was one of their battle cries. This in Italy became Ghibelline. In the beginning, the Guelphs were the imperial party and the Ghibellines the papal party, for Frederick II as a boy was a ward of the pope and greatly enjoyed papal favor. This did not last and later he was twice excommunicated. The Guelphs then became the papal party and the Ghibellines the party of the emperor. That way they remained.

In Italy — but more particularly in Florence — each of the two factions into which almost every city was divided gravitated to one or the other of these parties and, although there were exceptions for local and even for family reasons, it was in general the Ghibellines who drew the old, largely Germanic country lord with those in the city who adhered to him. The merchant turned to the pope and was apt to be a Guelph. This was natural, for the nobleman — although he sometimes fought him and always tried to restrict his power — found an emperor, especially a distant one, congenial. But the merchant was inclined to take sides with the pope. For one thing the pope needed money, which the merchant could supply — and was glad to for a fantastic rate of interest. For another, the pope was not defending old interests. He therefore — at any rate for the time being — could rely on the new.

Ghibelline and Guelph! The old order and the new! It was out of their conflict that the Florence which was known to Dante came into being. It was because from, say, 1215 to, say, 1282 the old (the Ghibellines) was locked in so deadly a conflict with the new (the Guelphs) that there was born the strong and muscled republic with the implements to control its own destiny and the will to use them.

"Never," cried Betto Brunelleschi to a later emperor, "have the Florentines lowered their horns to any lord, nor will they."

His ability to say it and his will to say it came into being at this time.

« 6 »

In this contest which was fought out so long and so hard it was the old order which drew the first blood.

Frederick II, far more Sicilian and Norman than German, was an able and percipient monarch, and when, in defiance of the pope who was his guardian, he assumed imperial power, he saw clearly that however eager he was to make his realm into an enlightened and modern state, he must be conservative and reactionary in respect to its towns. Particularly in respect to his Italian towns! For neither in Lombardy nor — and this concerns us more — in Tuscany could he afford to have a group of independent entities fighting their own wars, making their own trade agreements, and doing their own business without any regard whatsoever to his needs and to his policies.

During the first years of his reign, he was, to be sure, obliged to proceed with caution. To Florence — as to every other city — he sent representatives to assert and to exercise his traditional rights. But when they were ignored, or even humiliated, he did nothing about it.

Then on November 27, 1237, at Cortenuova near Crema in northern Italy, he defeated and in fact crushed the league of Lombard cities, which lost ten thousand men either slain or taken prisoner.

From then on, Frederick could do what he wanted to.

For the time being, he still proceeded circumspectly. To be sure, he replaced the popular *podestà* Rubaconte da Mandello with Gebhart of Arnstein, a German; but Gebhart very carefully did not make any excessive demands. All he required was that future *podestà*'s be ratified by the emperor before appointment.

Gebhart's successors were less restrained, however, and when in 1246 the emperor's natural son Frederick of Antioch was made vicar-general of Tuscany, word went from mouth to mouth that Ghibellines would take over the city. Already there had been disturbances — as for example in 1245, when a crowd, equipped with arms and ropes, threatened to take unofficial action if a group of heretics, said to be of the imperial party, were not officially condemned. But now brawl followed brawl, and disorder followed disorder, until early in 1248 the riots and disturbances reached such a peak that the emperor, through his representative, intervened. He sided with the Ghibellines. Fully organized — although they had already been driven underground — and now for the first time, headed by *capitani de' Guelfi*, the Guelphs took the only counteraction they could. On Candlemas Day (February 2) they fled to the surrounding hills, where some of them at least had castles and retainers. This was the so-called "first exile" and more than one chronicler would point out that it set a tragic precedent.

Almost at the same time, the victorious Ghibellines set another precedent which if less tragic also had grave future consequences.

Unable to lay their hands upon their Guelph adversaries, "they changed the ruling of the city the way they thought best, and caused thirty-six fortresses of the Guelphs to be destroyed, palaces and great towers."

One of these towers — it arose from "a beautiful building faced with marble columns" — was one hundred thirty cubits (approximately two hundred feet) high!

"The Ghibellines also attempted something yet more impious."

There was on the Piazza San Giovanni another sky-tall edifice known as the Guardamorto because it overlooked the communal cemetery. It was one hundred twenty cubits high.

"And forasmuch as the Guelphs resorted greatly to the church of San Giovanni, and all the good people assembled there on Sunday mornings and there they solemnized their marriages, the Ghibellines purposed to raze this said tower. They caused it to be propped up in such a wise that when fire was applied to the props it should fall upon the church of San Giovanni."

This was done.

"But it pleased God that when the tower came to fall it avoided the church and fell directly upon the piazza.

"Wherefore all the Florentines marveled, and the *popolo* rejoiced greatly."

They had better things about which to rejoice greatly before very long. On December 3, 1250, Frederick died at Fiorentino in Apulia. It had been predicted by astrologers that he was to die in Florence, and so he had avoided that city. But not even an emperor can escape his doom.

Almost immediately, the cry of *"Viva il Popolo!"* rang through the city.

In the streets and around the churches gathered a seething populace that was now ready and eager to accept government by Guelph magnates instead of Ghibelline magnates.

Why not?

The Guelphs at least were Florentines and had their interests irrevocably bound up with Florence. They were not absentee landlords operating against the city's interest. They might tax but they would not saddle with vexatious taxes to support the distant causes of a far-off emperor. What they did would be for the city — and its citizens.

Almost immediately, therefore, word went to the hills, and the exiles, flushed with a recent and conclusive victory over the Ghibellines at Figline, responded immediately. To the sound of bells and trumpets — and possibly even flaunting the red lily upon a white field which they would officially substitute for the white lily upon a red field in 1251 — they marched through the Porta Romana to their beloved city just a little less than three years after their hasty exit.

With them, they brought their consolidated ideas as to the kind of government which they — and, they hoped and believed, the Florentines — were now convinced they required. It was to be a people's government — people, I repeat, to the Florentines meaning the merchant-burghers and not the proletariat. For that reason it was called the Primo Popolo, or First Democracy. But again, it was not a democracy in the way we understand democracy today.

In many ways, however, it lived up to its name. The *podestà* was retained, and he was not shorn of many of his powers. But a new office, captain of the people (*capitano del popolo*), was created and he was given twenty-four companies of militia which he could call up when he needed them. The *popolo* thus not only had legal authority, but the power to assert it. At the same time, the districts as such were given direct participation in the government. A board of twelve *anziani* was set up, and two of these *anziani* were elected from each of the *sesti* (liberally "sixths," but in our sense wards, or voting districts) into which the city was divided. These *anziani* were charged with general supervision of the state and of its finances. In other words, they combined the powers of a chief executive with those of a board of estimate. With this began the first rudiments — but indeed they were little more — of government of the people, for the people, and by the people. For once a man is chosen by his immediate neighbors, he is inevitably subject to their pressures, and by the same token he begins at least tentatively to speak for them, whatever his theoretical position may be.

« 7 »

The Primo Popolo remained in power for exactly ten years, and during this time it "won so many victories and boasted such power and grandeur" that this decade could well be called one of the great periods of Florentine history.

It was during this decade that the Florentine bankers — and the merchants who were so closely associated with them — established themselves as a European institution. They also began to move into control of the city, a control which — with only a few interruptions — would last until the Medici became grand-ducal some three centuries later. To be sure, it is almost certain that artisans and shopkeepers participated in the new government, but they were subject to the influence of these more important citizens.

It was during this decade — actually it was in 1252 — that Florence began to coin and to issue its famous gold florin. This coin was stamped with a lily on one side and with the image of John the Baptist on the other. Its weight and the purity of its metal were studiously determined and thereafter carefully maintained. The result was that it assumed a position among world currencies which before was only held by the *nomisma* (bezant) of Byzantium, and in later days by the British pound sterling and the American dollar. To a very great extent Florentine prosperity was based upon this florin, for its fixed value at a time when tampering with the coinage was the rule rather than the exception conferred a stability which made Florentine business highly desirable.

It was during this period that much important medieval building was completed or begun. But this has been adverted to in an earlier chapter.

Finally, it was during the government of the Primo Popolo that the Florentine republic first became imperialistic. Previously it had fought most of its rivals as a protective measure, but now it tried to dominate them.

Sometimes to do this the Florentines used their purse instead of their sword, and indeed one of their first attempts at expansion was to lease the little silted-up port of Talamone from the Aldobrandeschi family. Oddly enough, the Sienese did the same thing only a few decades later, and then (*Purgatorio* XIII) Dante found it appropriate to laugh at them.

> Thou will see there the empty-headed folk
> Who count on Talamone, but will lose
> More hope than they did seeking hidden springs.
> Those would-be admirals will lose more than that.

But when Florence did it, it was another matter.

But the Florentines also moved into the actual aggressions to which their expansionist policy committed them. Pistoia, Montecalcino, Montepulciano, Poggibonsi (then called Poggibonizi) and San Gimignano were only a few of the smaller Tuscan towns which felt the heavy hand of their now powerful neighbor and were obliged to make one sort of accommodation or another.

Pisa — alarmed by the apparent strength of a league which consisted of Lucca, Genoa, and Florence, and torn by internal dissension — broke down and yielded. The once-proud maritime city — she had once sent one hundred twenty vessels, commanded by her archbishop, to aid the Crusaders in the Holy Land — gave her rival the privilege of importing and exporting through her territory without paying any duty.

Even Siena gave in.

She agreed to come to the aid of Florence in time of war, and not to shelter Florentine exiles in peacetime.

But here the Florentines had overstepped themselves. They had reckoned without either Sienese resilience or the tenaciousness of Siena's Ghibelline allies. The result was the battle of Montaperti, which has been discussed twice in earlier chapters. It took place on September 4, 1260, and nine days later, on September 13, the defeated Guelphs, "without being banished or driven out, went forth with their families, weeping, and betook themselves to Lucca."

On September 16, "the exiles of Florence" — i.e., the Ghibellines — "which had been at the battle, with Count Giordano and his German troops, and with other Ghibelline soldiers of Tuscany, entered the city without hindrance, and immediately they made Guido Novello of the Counts Guidi *podestà*." Except for what they had taken them with them, the merchants were not even left with their moneybags. The new Ghibelline rule had begun.

It did not, however, last even as long as its predecessor.

First of all, the pope entered the picture. His reason for this was obvious. Unless he were to give up the idea of being a temporal ruler, he could not brook so great an augmentation of imperial power. He immediately took two steps. First, although he needed money badly, he made it plain that he would borrow from Guelph bankers only.

Next he sent emissaries to France.

There Charles of Anjou — he of the big nose, whom we have met before — was offered the throne of Sicily together with the realm of Apulia if "he would be the champion of the Holy Church." Needless to say, Charles accepted.

With five hundred knights and a thousand bowmen, he set sail from Marseilles in twenty crowded vessels. He had no difficulty in landing at the mouth of the Tiber.

On February 26, 1266, he and Manfred met near Benevento.

"Tell the sultan of Nocera," he cried — this was in reference to Manfred's supposed atheism and his Saracen troops — "that today I will either put him in hell or he will send me to paradise!"

He was not sent to paradise.

For although the blond, handsome — *biondo era e bello e di gentile aspetto*, says Dante (*Purgatorio* III) — Manfred struck bravely "into the thickest of the fight" crying "Ho, knights for Swabia!" it was not enough. He was completely routed.

"Chi comprà Manfredi?" Who will buy Manfred? cried one of his own base-born camp followers who had found him almost hacked to pieces and slung him across the back of a donkey which he used to transport his wares.

Nine months later — on November 11, 1266 — the Florentines revolted, and although the Ghibellines had ample strength to put them down, Count Guido Novello, who commanded their troops, asked merely for the keys to the city, "caused a cry to be made" to see whether all the German mercenaries were accounted for, and then "took the wide road to the old Ox Gate," went past the Piazza Sante Croce then outside the city walls "where as yet there were no houses," through the Borgo de' Pinti — "there stones were cast at them" — and on to the Cafaggio.

By nightfall, having circled the city, he was in Prato.

The next day, he and his followers returned. In battle array, they came to the Carraia Bridge and demanded that the gate there be opened to them. The Florentines shouted back refusal. "And when they would have made a dash for the gate, they were shot at and wounded." That was in the middle of November, and the Florentines forthwith set about to reorganize the city. But they proceeded cautiously and in January of the ensuing year they even made a peace in which both Ghibellines and Guelphs were restored to their rights. It did not last for long. For shortly thereafter, the Guelphs, "feeling themselves strong," and "emboldened" by the defeat of Manfred, "sent secretly to King Charles and he sent back Count Guy of Montfort with eight hundred French horsemen." Guy arrived in Florence "on Easter Day of the resurrection in the year of our Lord 1267." Even before he got there, the Ghibellines had fled into the night. "And never afterwards did they return to their estate." To the day, it was the fifty-second anniversary of the Buondelmonte murder. Florence was a Guelph city from then on.

« 8 »

It was in this Guelph city that Dante spent those formative years which we have just been considering and which for another few chapters we will still consider. He grew up as Florence became Guelph. And since this Guelph Florence was one of the more important factors which made Dante what Dante later became, it is not inappropriate to examine some of the Guelph happenings which occurred between Dante's birth and his attaining legal manhood, and which he was either told about or saw.

One of them has been discussed already. But it needs elaboration. For it was the first step in an important chain of events.

I refer to the episode of the Frati Gaudenti, the two *podestà*'s who in 1266 jointly shared executive authority. Their appointment — one of them Guelph, the other Ghibelline — was a Ghibelline attempt to forestall the future. Even before Benevento the Ghibellines could see the handwriting upon the wall in large and clear characters. This sharing of authority was an attempt to circumvent what it predicted. It was an attempt to retain part when the whole was plainly just about to be lost.

It was not successful.

For the two *podestà*'s did not govern either jointly or separately. To assist them in their administration, to give them counsel, and "to provide for the spendings of the government," there was set up "a council of thirty-six members. These were merchants and artificers, the greatest and best that there were in the city.

"And the said Thirty-six met every day in the shop and the court of the consuls of the Calimala."

They acted as men would who met in this stronghold of the Foreign Cloth Guild. They acted like merchants and artificers. In other words, although some of them were Ghibellines, they acted like Guelphs.

They made, for example, "many good ordinances for the common weal of the city, among which they decreed that each one of the principal arts [i.e., guilds] should have its own ensign and its own standard." This was "to the intent that if anyone in the city rose in force of arms, they might under these ensigns stand for the defense of the people."

(Some of these ensigns should be noted. That of the judges and notaries had a large golden star upon an azure field. That of the merchants of the Calimala had a golden eagle mounted upon a white globe upon a field of red. That of the moneylenders — the bankers — had a red field sewn with golden florins. That of the Wool Guild had a red field on which was a white sheep. That of the physicians and apothecaries had a red field, "thereupon St. Mary with Christ in her arms." Others were equally colorful.)

They integrated these same arts into the general government — or began to think about doing this.

They gave consideration to a systematic study of law revisions. Under these new laws, Ghibellines would take second place, although they were not supposed to know this.

They gave consideration to what today we could call political patronage.

The government of Florence had at its disposal the captainships of various fortresses as well as other dignities and small and great offices.

How could these be used to help establish power?

But it was not the waving panoply of guild banners that dismayed the Ghibellines, nor was it the cautious hints of future law reform.

It was the more dangerous, inescapable fact that the Guelphs, once organized for war, now were organized for rule and government. The various Guelph entities began to group themselves into a Guelph *massa* — today we would call it a machine — and this *massa* did not attempt to conceal that it aimed at domination.

"For which reason, the Ghibelline magnates began to have their factious fears aroused. They determined, therefore, to put the town in an uproar, and to destroy the office of the said Thirty-six. With their armed troops, they sallied forth from their houses, crying, 'Where are these thieves that we may cut them to pieces?' "

But the Guelphs — and the citizens who supported them, for the class division between the *popolo grasso* (the wealthy burghers) and the *popolo minuto* (the small shopkeepers) was scarcely yet in being — were not intimidated.

The Thirty-six straightway adjourned. The populace gathered in "the wide street of Santa Trinità." A barricade was thrown up, and when Ghibellines tried to break through it, "the people boldly defended it with crossbows and by hurling missiles from the towers and houses."

These were the riotings which caused Guido Novello to flee the city, and note that they took place before the official Guelph return. Then, as we have seen, the Guelphs did return, accompanied by French troops. Very shortly too they made the lord to whom these troops owed allegiance their chief executive. Charles of Anjou became *podestà*, and ultimately his term of office was extended for some thirteen years.

He did not govern personally, however, but through a vicar-general.

Or rather seem to govern.

For the true seat of authority was the Parte Guelfa. Not only did it control the Council of One Hundred, the General Council, the Council of the People, the Council of the Captain of the People, and the other councils in which constitutional authority was supposedly vested, but through its own councils and its own officials it began to intervene directly in the conduct of the Florentine state, bypassing theoretical legal entities and acting because it knew it could.

One of these officials, incidentally, was the so-called "accuser of the Ghibellines."

He was literally that. He was the head of a small secret service which was assisted by a volunteer corps of informers made up of virtually every Guelph in Florence.

It was his duty to divide the Ghibellines into two groups, the *ribelli* and the *confinati*. The *ribelli* were the really dangerous Ghibellines. They were the ones who fled the city. They were sentenced to death *in absentia*, their houses were subject to destruction, and their property of every kind was confiscated. The *confinati* were either placed in something similar to house arrest or sent into limited exile. The limited exiles were compelled to leave the city and assigned to a specific place of residence.

Their lot was very miserable.

"You ask us to leave Bologna!" cried a group of them. "Where shall we go? Facing your displeasure, who will receive us?"

But if they did not obey, they became *ribelli*.

The triumphant Parte Guelfa took another step, and this was even more effective. When Ghibelline property was confiscated, it was sold, converted to money, and the money distributed. One third went to the Florentine treasury, one third to Guelphs whose houses had been damaged or torn down (as, for instance, Dante's cousin Geri), and one third to the party strongboxes. It was thus disseminated beyond any hope of recovery if the Ghibellines should ever return.

Dante was a year old when the Frati Gaudenti were given power. He was eighteen months old when Guido Novello fled the city. He was two years old — or very nearly two years old — when Guy de Montfort and his French horsemen permanently brought back the Guelphs.

He was four years old at the time of the next Guelph triumph.

"In the year of Christ 1269," writes Villani, "and in the month of June, the Sienese, whereof Messer Provenzan Salvani was governor, with Count Guido Novello, with the German and Spanish troops, with the Ghibelline refugees from Florence and from other cities in Tuscany, and with the forces of the Pisans, to the number of fourteen hundred horse and eight thousand foot, marched upon the stronghold of Colle di Valdelsa, which was under the lordship of the Florentines."

The latter, taken by surprise, could only muster eight hundred horsemen (and virtually no foot soldiers), but under the leadership of Messer Aldobrandino of the Pazzi family these few charged recklessly into the Sienese ranks and, where prudence would have failed, a bold act succeeded.

"Count Guido Novello fled" — once again! — and Provenzan was taken prisoner.

"They cut off his head and carried it through the camp on a lance."

Perhaps because it was the first public event which Dante could remember personally and not merely hear talked about, this battle made a lasting impression on him, and he wrote about it twice. Once he wrote about Sapia, said by some to be Provenzan's aunt, who out of envy, although herself of Siena, prayed for Sienese defeat.

Purgatorio XIII:

> My fellow citizens were at Colle
> And ready to do battle with the foe
> When I prayed God for that which God did will.
> Routed they were, and then they knew the bitter
> Footsteps of flight, and when they were pursued
> I felt a joy beyond all joy there is,
> And so I lifted my exultant face
> And cried to God: "Now I no longer fear thee!"
> As does the blackbird for one day of spring.

He had her say this too:

> Sapient I surely was not, although Sapia
> I had been named, who from the hurt of others
> Did get more joy than from good fortune of mine . . .
> I cleanse me here of my so guilty life.

But he had a good word for Provenzan. To be sure he put the great leader into purgatory, because "he was presumptuous in bringing all Siena into his hands."

But he put him into purgatory, not into hell. Oderisi d' Aggobio in *Purgatorio* XI gives the reason:

> "When he was living gloriously," he said,
> "Freely and in the Campo of Siena,
> Laying aside all shame he stationed himself,
> And there, to ransom a good friend of his
> From pains suffered by him in Charles's prison,
> He acted so he trembled in every vein."

This is the story. One of Provenzan's friends had been taken prisoner by King Charles and, unable himself to provide the money needed for his release, Provenzan sat down in the famous Sienese square and, with begging bowl in hand, sought a contribution from every passerby until he had enough. To Dante, who knew what pride was — and humiliation — this was a truly Christian act.

« 9 »

Colle should have been a coup de grace to the Florentine Ghibellines, and indeed it seemed as if it was. They had lost control of the city, and now the one ally who could restore them from without had gone down to defeat too. The Guelphs rode the crest of the wave — and they acted accordingly. It was following Colle that they implemented the harsh laws which have been discussed above; drove out the last Ghibelline; and, emulating what their adversaries had done to them, tore down so many Ghibelline houses that the city looked as if it had been ravaged by an earthquake.

Yet the Ghibellines did not give up the struggle. Failing at home, they looked for help abroad and, of all people, they turned to their old enemies.

"If you would control Italy, you must have order in the cities," they told Charles of Anjou.

"If you would have a crusade and would rescue the Holy Land, there must be peace between Christian and Christian," they told Pope Gregory.

The result was the attempted pacification of 1273, which, as has already been noted, came to naught.

But in 1278, there was another pacification and it was more successful.

"In these times," wrote Giovanni Villani, "the Guelph magnates of Florence — having rest from their wars without and fattening upon the goods of the exiled Ghibellines — began to strive among themselves. Hence there arose in Florence many quarrels and enmities which led to deaths and the shedding of blood."

On one side were the Adimari, and on the other side the Tosinghi, the Donati, and the Pazzi. The other Florentines were divided between the two factions.

"Wherefore the city and the Guelph party were in great peril!"

Now, in other words, not having Ghibelline to contend with, Guelph was fighting Guelph.

"From the which thing," Villani continued, "the commonwealth and the captains of the Guelph party sent their solemn ambassadors to the court of Pope Nicholas" — Nicholas III of the proud Roman Orsini family, who, after three other popes, had succeeded Gregory X — "that he should take counsel and give aid in making peace among the Guelphs of Florence." If not, the Guelph party would be broken up. "And in like guise the Ghibelline refugees sent their own ambassadors to the said pope to entreat him to put into effect the peace treaty which Pope Gregory had commanded between them and the Guelphs of Florence."

What an opportunity for "the son of the she-bear" (*Inferno* XIX) who was so "eager to advance his cubs" — i.e., his Orsini relatives — that he was willing to risk damnation for it!

Guelph must be made to take Ghibelline into partnership. Ghibelline must accept Guelph as an associate. Then the Guelphs would have delivered the city into Pope Nicholas's power, and the Ghibellines would be grateful to him.

"For the foregoing reasons, the said pope ordained a mediator and a legate" — his nephew, Cardinal Latino de' Frangipani, "a man of great authority and learning" and certainly related to Dante's supposed Frangipani family — "who departed from the Romagna and came to Florence on the eighth day of the month of October in the year of Christ 1278."

His orders were explicit. Bring the quarrelers to heel.

Cardinal Latino did so with very little waste of time.

To be sure, there were the customary festive ceremonies. The citizens and the clergy marched out to greet him with the banners waving and with their famous *carroccio*. Later, jousts were held.

The cardinal made a goodwill gesture too.

"On the day of St. Luke the Evangelist in that same year and month, the legate blest the first stone of the new church of Santa Maria Novella, which pertained to the order of the Preaching Friars, whereof he was a brother."

Then he summoned the city's leaders and got down to business. These were the papal terms:

Uberti must make peace with Buondelmonti.

"This was the third peace between them," noted a chronicler acidly.

The Ghibellines and their families must be freed from all sentences of banishment.

Ghibelline property must be restored.

The Ghibellines must be given full freedom of movement and action "save that to some of the chief leaders it was commanded for the more security of the city for a certain time to be under bounds."

Finally, a new form of government was ordained. There is no point in discussing the five councils which were set up as part of it, for at the most they were modifications of councils which already existed. But the executive was another matter, for in it lay the meat of the cardinal's plan for controlling the city. It was a body of fourteen citizens known as the Quattordici, which is the Italian word for fourteen. Three of its members must come from the *sesto* of San Piero Scheraggio (near the present Palazzo della Signoria), three from the Oltrarno *sesto*, and two from each of the other four *sesti*.

But there was another restriction on its membership, and it was more important. Not more than eight of its members could be Guelphs. Six of them must be Ghibellines.

The hated enemies of the ascendant merchant-burghers were not only returned to the city but made part of the government. It was a very bitter pill.

But Cardinal Latino made the Florentines swallow it — and publicly. For no sooner had he exacted adherence — with substantial bonds to see that they kept their word — from the leaders of the city than he summoned the Florentines into one of their old-time *arringhi* and prepared to address it. This was in February 1279.

The gathering was held on the wide, ample piazza in front of which the new church, so recently blessed by the cardinal, was slowly rising. Platforms were erected, together with great wooden scaffoldings. These were covered with brightly colored cloths, while a blaze of banners hung from every building.

A rostrum had also been built, and to it the cardinal mounted to make "a noble speech with citation of great and very fine authorities as behooved the matter."

Then he came to his climax.

In front of the vast assembly "he caused the representatives of the Guelphs and the Ghibellines to kiss one another on the mouth, and there were one hundred fifty on each side."

To the Ghibellines this was all the victory they needed. To the dream-loving Florentines it meant peace and an end to disorder. They greeted it with great joy.

But the government of the Quattordici lasted no longer than any other imposed form of government, and for the same reasons. The force which established it was not maintained. Nicholas died in 1280, and the popes who immediately succeeded him had other interests. It ran counter to the spirit of the city. The Guelphs, not the Ghibellines, were the Florence of the day and of the future. You cannot very often halt the times.

What would happen shortly was foreshadowed clearly by an action taken by the Guelphs in 1281. Over the heads of their minority Ghibelline colleagues, they succeeded in passing a law which required magnates — and magnates only — to put up a bond of two thousand *libbre* to guarantee their good conduct. In the same year another law was passed, giving the *podestà* a militia of one thousand citizens with which to keep the peace.

Then, in 1282, the Guelphs informally set up the government of the priors. In the beginning it was a shadow government, nominated and dominated by the Guelph merchants. At first there were three priors, but later the number was increased to six. Every prior had to be a member of one of the so-called seven greater guilds. In 1283, they made this informal government formal. The Quattordici was abolished. The Guelph merchant-burgher priors took over the city's rule.

« *10* »

How does all of this relate to Dante?

Let us examine the events chronologically as a way of finding out.

Dante was fourteen years old when Cardinal Latino addressed the

Florentines in the piazza of Santa Maria Novella, and since he was an alert boy, interested in everything that went on about him, one would like to think he was part of the jostling crowd.

He was sixteen when the law was passed which required magnates to put up a bond for their good conduct.

He was seventeen when the priorate was instituted.

He was eighteen when the priors formally took office.

Incidentally, they took office almost right under his nose. They were elected for a term of two months — and could not succeed themselves. One was chosen from each of the *sesti* and "during their term of office they remained shut up in the Castagna tower near the Badia so that they need not fear the threats of the powerful, and they were given the perpetual right to bear arms, and they were given other privileges and they had six servants and six bodyguards."

The Castagna tower was just across a small square from the Casa degli Alighieri.

Step by step, then, the government of Florence under which Dante lived, a government which would be as important to him *and* to his writings as any other thing that impinged upon him, took its final shape and form between the year in which he was born and the year in which he attained his majority.

« *11* »

The world occupied his attention too — or at any rate those happenings in the world which had some bearing on the fortunes of Florence.

Here are some of the events which we know or we believe he must have noted as he grew up.

The Sicilian Vespers. These took place on Easter Monday, "which was the thirtieth day of March," in 1282 — the same time that the government of the priors was being set up in Florence.

This uprising was set off by a single incident.

"The inhabitants of Palermo, men and women, going in a body on horse and on foot to the festival of Monreale three miles outside of the city (and so also went the Frenchmen and the captain of King Charles), it came to pass that a Frenchman in his insolence laid hold of a woman of Palermo to do her villainy. She began to cry out, and the people being already sore and moved with indignation against the French, the retainers of the barons of the island began to defend her."

Thereupon a great fracas began with men killed and wounded on both sides. The Sicilians had the worst of this.

"Straightway all the people returned in flight to the city, and the men flew to arms crying, 'Death to the French!' "

Under the hot Sicilian sun everybody who said *oui* instead of *si* was stabbed, clubbed to death, or hacked to pieces. The revolt spread to the rest of the island, and in a short time more than four thousand of Charles of Anjou's followers lost their lives.

It is now known that this apparently spontaneous burst of fury had been carefully plotted — by Gian da Procida, some of whose amorous adventures have been narrated by Boccaccio and others. They were working in the interests of — and paid by — the Palaeologus emperor of Byzantium (Michael VIII), who feared Charles would claim his throne, and by Pedro III of Aragon, who wanted to claim Charles's.

The sea battle of Meloria. Offshore, and about midway between the Arno mouth and Leghorn, there were, and still are, shoals of sand and mud known as the Secche di Meloria.

Above these shoals, on August 4, 1284, by a combination of deception and seamanship, the Genoese navy literally annihilated the proud Pisan fleet. Seven galleys and thirty-four lighter vessels were sunk. No count was made of the slain, but more than nine thousand prisoners were taken to Genoa. They were never ransomed, but rotted out their days in Genoese dungeons.

Meloria was one of the great naval battles of the Middle Ages. It changed history as well as made it. For it took Pisa permanently from the ranks of Mediterranean naval powers. But to the Florentines it meant something even more important. It meant that Pisa, after this devastating loss of manpower, would be a far lesser adversary even on land.

The capture in 1287 of the prince of Salerno, the future Charles II (the Lame) of Naples, that rash young prince who as an older king would be rebuked by Dante for selling his daughter Beatrice in marriage to Azzo, the evil old marquis of Este.

Purgatorio XX:

> That one who once stepped captive from his ship
> I see sell his daughter, while bargaining
> As corsairs do when selling their she-slaves.

The capture was not without its ludicrous side. Charles was entrusted with the command of the Neapolitan fleet, but he was given strict orders not to engage the enemy. However Ruggiero di Lauria of Genoa, who commanded a Spanish squadron, evidently judged the young man's character correctly and decided to taunt him. On the morning of June 2, 1284, setting every brightly colored sail he had, he flauntingly entered the Bay of Naples and challenged Charles to stop him. Charles took up the dare and sailed out, but he allowed his ship to become separated from its fleet and it was surrounded. Only at the pleading of Queen Constance of Aragon (Manfred's daughter) was he spared beheading and sent to Spain a prisoner.

The death of King Charles I of Naples in Foggia. This took place on January 6, 1285.

"Lord God," were his last words, "as I truly believe that Thou art my Savior, so I pray Thee that Thou have mercy on my soul; and as I did conquer Sicily more to serve the Holy Church than for my profit and from covetousness, so do Thou forgive my sins."

Quite a pious justification of grand larceny!

Less noticed, the death in the same year of Philip III of France at Perpignan and the succession of Philip the Fair, which would have such consequences to Italy and also to Dante.

Finally, the pitiful end of Count Ugolino dei Visconti, his sons, and his grandsons. This took place in 1288.

Count Ugolino, a Guelph leader who played both sides of the street even to betraying his own son, was not a particularly admirable character.

The Pisans were quite certain that he was responsible for their defeat at Meloria and therefore were quite happy to deliver him into the hands of the Archbishop Ruggieri, head of one of the rival factions. Then the tragedy began.

For the Pisans replaced Ugolino with the great Ghibelline captain Guido da Montefeltro, who hastened to Pisa.

"And when the said count had come to Pisa in the said month of March, the Pisans" — possibly to impress him with their resolution — "which had put into prison Count Ugolino and his two sons and his two grandsons in a tower on the Piazza degli Anziani, caused the door of the said tower to be locked and the keys thrown into the Arno, and refused to give the said prisoners any food, and in a few days they died there.

"For which cruelty the Pisans were blamed throughout the whole world — not because of the count, who for his treacheries and crimes perchance deserved such a death, but because of his sons and grandsons, who were innocent boys."

Dante joined in this chorus of shocked horror.

Inferno XXXIII:

> Faugh, Pisa, shame and scorn of all the people
> In that fair country in which *si* is said.
> Since all too slow to smite thee are thy neighbors,
> Would that Capraia and Gorgona'd move
> To make a dam across the Arno mouth
> So that all dwelling in thee would be drowned!

But, as will be discovered in due course, Dante may have written these lines when he had other reasons for vituperating Pisa than his revulsion at this horrible deed.

But if Dante witnessed these events — or was told about them — he did not take part in them. All of his political and governmental activities — and they were many and important — took place somewhat later. But even when he was still a youth, he did serve the Florence which would always be his fatherland. He served, however, in a manner more appropriate to his years.

As with almost everything else which entered into him deeply, he alludes to this service in his *Commedia*.

Inferno XXII:

> I have indeed seen horsemen breaking camp
> To launch attack, and seen them make their muster,
> And sometimes I have seen them flee posthaste.
> I have seen scouts ride out across your land,
> O Aretines, and armed bands galloping,
> And clash of tournaments, and joustings run.
> I have heard trumpets blown and bells rung,
> Drums beaten, and seen signals made from castles.
> I have seen foreign and domestic arms.

Inferno XXI:

> Thus once I saw foot soldiers quake with fear
> As they came out of Caprona under treaty
> And saw themselves surrounded by their foe.

In the first of these passages, he refers to the Campaldino campaign, which was fought out on a level field in the Casentino, a wide Apennine valley high in the mountains to the east of Florence. There the Florentine Guelphs routed a Ghibelline army largely under Aretine leadership and later marched to Arezzo, where they wasted militarily important time by contemptuously running horse races under the city walls, and "hurled asses with miters on their heads" to show their scorn of the archbishop of Arezzo, who had been slain.

The Caprona incident took place in a campaign against Pisa.

Dante may also have fought at Poggio a Santa Cecilia, also in the Aretine country, and taken part in an earlier (1283) march against the city at the mouth of the Arno. This is the contention of Isodoro del Lungo, a nineteenth-century scholar, and it is given some support by a supposed statement by Dante cited just below.

The Campaldino campaign first.

"In the memorable and mighty battle that was fought at Campaldino," wrote Leonardo Bruni, "he, being of military age and well seen to, marched with the advance guard. So doing, he was in the utmost peril. For the engagement was between the squadrons of cavalry — that is to say, knights — of whom they on the side of the Aretines overcame the squadron of Florentine knights with such fury that, scattered and routed, they must retreat to the foot.

"This battle Dante describes in a letter of his, and says that he was in the fight, and draws a plan of this battle.

"I say then that Dante was found fighting valiantly for his country, and I could wish that Boccaccio had made mention of this fact rather than of his falling in love and such like trifles. But what can you expect? His discourse is ever of drinking who loves wine."

In this battle, says another lost letter reported by Bruni, he was "not raw in arms," but in spite of that he "knew much dread."

"But at the end I knew the greatest pleasure!" he quotes Dante as saying.

Why not? The taste of victory is always sweet.

Dante's presence at Caprona is equally well substantiated.

"Be it noted," wrote Benvenuto da Imola, who was a friend of Boccaccio and had reliable sources of information, "that the author was personally in the army there. He was twenty-four years old and he saw what happened there. So he could freely make that comparison" — the comparison in the lines from *Inferno* XXI just cited — "since he relied upon his own memories."

But we have circumstantial evidence equally convincing. A *consulta* of 1285, dealing with an excursion against Pisa, orders all shops and stores to be closed and everybody in the city to be prepared to give aid to the army.

"Let there be chosen," it continues, "four men from every district and two men from every parish in the city to make up companies of fifty of the ages between fifteen and seventy."

Dante was twenty at this time. And while the decree obviously referred to the *pedites*, it was not likely that a young cavalryman would be backward. Dante plainly was not.

Of these two campaigns, Campaldino was by far the more important. Here is how it is described by a contemporary.

"In the said year [1289], in the month of May, the horsemen of

Florence being returned from escorting Prince Charles [who became Charles II, the Lame], a host was gathered against the city of Arezzo because of its outrages." The Aretines had greatly offended Florence by tossing their Guelph *podestà* into a cistern, where incontinently he died. "The banners were given out on the thirteenth day of May. They bore them to the Badia at Ripoli."

There, in the dazzling bright sun, they paused to deliberate. From their position at the Badia, they directly threatened Arezzo, and many advocated that they proceed up the Valdarno to attack it. By doing this they would protect the great houses — owned by the Guelph leaders, of course — of the *contado*. But others said that they should march to Pontassieve and then strike eastward, leaving the river and climbing toward Consuma.

"There were many speakers, but finally *a ballot was taken*. The route to the Casentino was chosen." In other words, the route to Pontassieve and then over the Consuma. "And notwithstanding that it was the most dangerous and doubtful way, it turned out for the best."

It turned out for the best because the Aretines were surprised.

"On the day appointed the Florentines set out. They went along bad roads where if the enemy had found them they would have had bad hurt. But God did not permit this."

Finally they arrived at Campaldino. There they halted and formed in battle order.

"The captains of the war placed the picked cavalry in front and those with large shields were drawn up to support them."

It was at this time that the Aretines first noticed them.

"Then the bishop of Arezzo, who was nearsighted, asked: 'What walls are those?' He received the answer: 'They are the enemy's shields!' "

At the same time, the Florentines received instructions from one of their leaders.

"In the old days," cried Messer Barone de' Mangiadori, "the wars in Tuscany were won by attacking well, but now the manner is changed. Victory comes by standing steady. I therefore counsel you to stand firm and leave the attack to them."

This the Florentines, as ordered, did.

"Then the Aretines attacked so vigorously and with such force that the main body of the Florentines fell back for some distance."

This was the retreat in which Dante took part.

The battle continued, however, and was very stubborn.

"New knights were made on both sides. Messer Corso Donati attacked the enemy flank. Messer Vieri de' Cerchi, with one of his sons at his side, acquitted himself right well."

Corso, whose sister was Piccarda. Vieri, Corso's later great adversary.

"Arrows fell like rain. The sky was covered with clouds. The dust was very great."

Finally, in spite of bravery — and cowardice — on both sides, the Aretines were routed.

"They were defeated not owing to want of valor but by the overwhelming number of their enemies. The Florentines captured many flags and took many prisoners. They slew many of them, which brought great loss to all of Tuscany."

The Aretines were also defeated because of a dramatic change in the weather. This too is described by Dante in one of the great passages of the *Commedia*. In the purgatory of the negligent (*Purgatorio* V) he is addressed by one of the Aretine leaders!

> Then said another: "So that thy desire
> To climb to the high mountain may be fulfilled,
> Out of thy charity do thou aid mine.
> I was of Montefeltro. I am Buonconte.
> Giovanna, nor any other, cares for me,
> Wherefore I walk with those of downcast brow."
> And I to him: "What violence or chance
> Took thee so far away from Campaldino
> That even now none knows your burial place?"
> "Oh," answered he, "below the Casentino
> There flows a little stream called Archiano.
> It rises in the Apennines above the Hermitage.
> To that place where it has this name no more
> I stumbled with my gaping gullet slit,
> Fleeing on foot and bloodying the plain.
> There my sight failed me, but I cried out: 'Mary!'
> With my last word. And in that place I fell
> And nothing but my body there remained.
> I tell the truth. Tell thou it to the living.
> God's angel took me, but then one from hell
> Cried: 'Thou from heaven, wherefore dost thou rob me?
> Thou takest away with thee his life eternal
> All for a single little tear he shed,
> But I'll do otherwise with what remains.'
> Thou knowest well how in the air is gathered
> That humid vapor which doth water become
> Once it has soared to where the cold condenses it.
> He joined that evil will which aye seeks evil
> Then to his mind, and moved the mist and wind
> With that fell power which his nature gave him.

> Thereat the valley, as the daylight ended,
> From Pratomagno to the peaks, he covered
> With cloud which made the sky above so dense
> That all the pregnant air was turned to water.
> Then fell the rain, and into every gully
> Poured all of it the earth could not absorb,
> And, as is fitting to a swollen spate,
> It rushed so swiftly to the royal river
> That there was nothing that could hold it back.
> My frozen body somewhere near its mouth
> The raging Archiano found, and tumbled
> Into the Arno, and unloosed from my breast
> That cross my arms had made when pain assailed me.
> It rolled me along its banks and over its bottom.
> Then with its branches and gravel it covered me."

I know from personal experience that no lines Dante ever wrote were more realistically accurate. Not very long ago I visited the Campaldino battlefield and, as I drove back with Pratomagno's magnificent chain upon my left, without warning blue-gray clouds began amassing, and then suddenly it began to pour. Until then the little streambeds had been dry and filled with round gray stones, but now they became raging torrents. In a modern automobile, I proceeded comfortably and was not even delayed, but it was not difficult to imagine how differently must have fared the fugitives from the wrath of the victorious Florentines. Their only hope was that the rain must have blinded the pursuers too.

Campaldino took place in 1289 on the eleventh of June, a time of year when even in this mountain valley the wheat fields were beginning to turn golden and red poppies and other flowers of blue and yellow gleamed between the rows of grain. Two months later Dante was surrounded by a different kind of scenery. He had come down out of the hills. An accomplished and battle-tested cavalryman, he now rode with his pennoned fellow warriors along the southern edge of the massive, roughly oval-shaped mountain "because of which [*Inferno* XXXIII] the men of Pisa Lucca cannot see." Here was no crisp Apennine air. Instead the brutally hot sun of midsummer in Tuscany beat down impartially upon the soldiers tortured in their armor and the brown-skinned *contadini* who, stripped to the waist, could endure it.

Here, fortunately, there was no fighting either — or no serious fighting.

Perched on the top of a sheer cliff that was almost peach-colored (yellow with distinct undertones of pink) and that overlooked the meanderings and the canebrakes of the lower Arno stood a sturdy castle almost the same color as the rocks it crowned. (Today it is a ruin, and the cliff, converted to a quarry, is being chiseled away.) From its tower — at any rate as soon as morning haze had burned away — could be seen the gleaming white marble of a mighty cathedral and the Baptistery with its round dome and the half-finished leaning tower which would bring men to Pisa through the centuries. Beyond, a line of blue slightly darkened by distance, was the sea.

Caprona — for the castle was Caprona — had an importance of its own. There were many such strongholds upon many a hillside, but this dominated the route from Florence to the rivermouth. It must be taken and neutralized.

Scarcely, therefore, had they finished with Arezzo than the Guelph rulers invested Caprona with fifteen hundred horsemen and ten thousand foot soldiers. The besieged garrison looked to Pisa for aid, but no aid came. Before long it was short of food and water, and an emissary was sent to the besiegers.

"We will lay down our arms if you will spare our persons."

This was agreed to.

But as the defenders marched out, the men waiting outside showed less restraint than their leaders did.

"Hang them!" they shouted. "Hang them! Hang them!"

Whether Dante joined in the shouting is not known, but he certainly was among those who stood armed and ready as the beaten men emerged. He noted their white faces and bedraggled appearance, and he noted, too, their relief when they realized that the pact would not be violated.

Then he and others of the Florentine contingent turned their horses' heads toward home. With spurs and bridles jingling, they jogged toward Florence. Across the Arno at Pontedera. This was at the moment in Florentine hands. Under San Miniato of the hated Teuton vicars. It was now Florentine too. Through Empoli — an *emporium* (hence its name), or marketplace, even in the days of the Romans. Through Montelupo, called this — i.e., Wolf Mountain — because its castle was built in 1202 to destroy or at least dominate Pistoia's Capraia (Goat Pasture).

"To destroy goats we need only a wolf!" cried the Florentines.

Through Lastra a Signa with its solidly built walls.

The presumption is that they entered Florence by the San Frediano Gate.

« *13* »

As they did so, Dante, jogging with them, had good reason to be content. If he was no hero, he had least conducted himself in a creditable manner. He was twenty-four years old — indeed, well on his way to the important twenty-fifth birthday, which in the medieval concept was the threshold to mature life. He had long since begun to establish himself as a poet. When he was eighteen, according to his own testimony, he "had already learned the art of saying words in rhyme" and since then had been busily intent on making this ability known "to the foremost verse-makers of his time."

He had also found something moving and important to write about — something befitting a poet whom, according to the fashion of the day, "we are invited to picture not as a cavalier trotting his horse down a leafy path, but as a pale youth walking slowly down a narrow street, or sitting pensive in a city square."

Pale even though he had fought at Campaldino! Pensive even though he had served at Caprona!

Less than ten months later, however, he had something to be pale about as fate struck him a shaking blow.

What this blow was can now appropriately be narrated. It came as the climactic episode in a long and famous (but not always understood) story — a story which had begun when Dante was very young indeed.

V

The New Life

ONCE again we turn to Boccaccio for our information.
In his biography of Dante, he wrote this:

"In that time of the year when the soft and gentle breezes of heaven reclothe the earth in a gay garb and when all is made merry and jocund by a variety of flowers amid the green leaves, it was the custom in our city for men and women to gather together, each in his own district and each among his own special friends.

"Thus it came to pass that, among others, Folco Portinari, a man who at that time was held in high esteem by his fellow citizens, invited his nearest neighbors to take part in a celebration which he gave in his own house upon the first day of May.

"And among those bidden to come was Alighiero" — Alighiero II, the poet's father — "of whom we have already spoken. At his heels trotted Dante, who had not yet completed his ninth year. He followed him as young boys usually follow their fathers, especially when they go to a feast.

"There he mingled with others of his own age — for there were more than a few such, both boys and girls — and when the first courses had been served, he began boylike to play with them such games as his youthful age permitted.

"Now among these many children, there was a daughter of the above-mentioned Folco. She was known as Bice — although Dante always called her by her real name, which was Beatrice; was perhaps eight years; and was as pretty as a girl of her age could be. She had, too, gracious and pleasing manners, and her ways and her words were far more sedate than one would expect from so young a girl. Besides that, her features were delicate and well formed, and over and above her beauty, she was so candid and winsome that many people said she was like a little angel.

"Such as I paint her then, or perhaps even more lovely, she at this feast was seen by the eyes of Dante — not for the first time, I believe, but for the first time with the power to make him fall in love. And thereupon — and although he was still but a little lad — he embraced her sweet image with such affection that from that day forward it never departed from his heart. No, not so long as he lived!"

But we do not have to rely upon Giovanni for an account of this meeting. Dante told about it too. Seventeen years after it took place, to be sure, and in more stilted and more symbolic language, but with a vividness that bespeaks an unforgettable experience and something that had really happened.

"In that part of my memory" — this is the first sentence of the first book he was ever to write — "before which little could be read, there is a rubric which says: *Incipit vita nova!*"

Here beginneth a new life!

Then he continued with a factual account.

"Nine times since my birth had the heaven of light already almost returned to the same point in relation to its own revolution when the glorious lady of my mind first appeared to mine eyes. That lady was called Beatrice by many who did not know what they were calling her!

"She on her part had lived just long enough for the heaven of the stars to have moved one twelfth part of a degree toward the east."

This was a reference to the so-called "precession of the equinoxes" — that apparent slow movement of the fixed stars from the west toward the sunrise which was first noted by the Greek astronomer and mathematician Hipparchus between 160 and 125 B.C. In Dante's day, it was believed it would take thirty-six thousand years for the full cycle to be completed. On that basis, the time taken to move one twelfth of a degree would be eight years and four months.

"So that she appeared to me almost at the beginning of her ninth year, and almost at the end of my ninth year did I behold her.

"She appeared to me wearing a dress of a most noble hue, a subdued and modest crimson. It was cinctured and adorned in a manner which was appropriate to her tender age."

Next the first consequences of her appearing thus:

"At that moment, I declare upon my word that the vital spirit which dwells in the secret chamber of the heart began to tremble so mightily that it was apparent in the least of my pulse beats. As it trembled, it uttered these words: '*Ecce Deus fortior me, qui veniens dominabatur mihi.*' Behold a god who is stronger than I am, and who, coming, masters me."

In medieval belief, the vital spirit controlled the emotions.

"At that moment, the animal spirit which dwells in the lofty chamber to which the spirits of the sense carry their perceptions began to marvel much. Speaking especially to the spirits of sight, it said these words: '*Apparuit iam beatitudo vestra.*' Now doth your happiness appear to you."

The animal spirit was supposedly seated in the brain. It would receive tidings of Beatrice's beauty.

"At that moment, the natural spirit which dwells in that part whence nourishment is distributed began to weep. And weeping, it spoke thus: '*Heu miser! Quia frequenter impeditus ero deinceps.*' Woe's me! Full often shall I faint now!"

The natural spirit, seated in the liver, was that which keeps one alive.

"From thenceforward," concluded Dante, "Love held lordship over my soul which so early had been bound to him. He began to have such mastery over me through the power which my imagining gave to him that I must needs do all he wished me to. He commanded me many times."

It is interesting – and, as we will shortly see, it is important – to compare somewhat carefully these two step-by-step accounts of the same episode.

They agree in certain points, and do not really differ in others.

Boccaccio, for example, carefully points out that the little girl who would grow up to be she of whom Dante would write was known as Bice. It is almost as an afterthought that he adds that here real name was Beatrice. Dante says that she was known as Beatrice. His addition was that most people did not realize the significance of this name. Beatrice means "bearer of blessedness." But he himself called her Bice at least twice. Once was in the *Commedia*.

Boccaccio describes her as the daughter of a specific and identifiable Florentine. Dante has nothing to say about this.

Boccaccio states that Dante met her upon a specific occasion. Dante merely says she appeared to him.

Boccaccio describes her beauty and manners in some detail. Dante is content to call her glorious.

Boccaccio points out that Dante had seen Beatrice—and one assumes that he had seen her many times—before the springtime festival at the house of her father. This does not seem improbable since Folco Portinari and Alighiero degli Alighieri lived in the same part of Florence if they were not actual neighbors. But Dante stresses the word first.

Dante, however, describes the dress Beatrice was wearing, and he does this convincingly and as one who vividly remembered it. Of this, Boccaccio, who usually went in for accurate descriptions, says nothing at all.

But if they differ — and it is only slightly — upon the matters referred to above, they agree — and very fully — upon everything which is really essential.

They agree, for instance, that a boy named Dante Alighieri did actually come to know a girl named Bice — or Beatrice — and they agree that this meeting took place when Dante was not quite nine and when Beatrice was little more than eight.

They agree that it was an apocalyptic meeting.

They agree that almost immediately Dante's pulse began to beat faster and that something happened to him which he was never to forget. Boccaccio describes this with a characteristic, if sometimes flowery, realism and directness. To a degree at least, Dante blurs the melody of a lark song with his attempt to be scientific. (When he wrote his account of the meeting, he had just begun to saturate himself with book learning, and he was full of it.) But they agree upon the basic fact.

« 2 »

It is necessary to note this agreement — the agreement, that is, between the poet's poetic autobiography and the words of his first and most devoted biographer — for there have been some who have doubts as to the identity of Beatrice, while a few even doubt she ever existed. To a degree at least, the latter consider her a figment of the poet's fancy.

Francesco Buti was perhaps the first to do this.

"Some people," he wrote in 1584, "would like to believe that Beatrice was a woman of flesh and blood. This is not so."

But even as recently as 1958, a competent scholar still felt able to have reservations.

"It would be impertinent," wrote Maurice Valency in his *In Praise of Love*, "at this stage to suggest that the *Vita Nuova*" — the book from which we have taken Dante's account — "is a work of the imagination, a sort of novel like *Fiammetta*, were it not for the fact that since Boccaccio wrote his life of Dante in 1364, it is traditional to assign a certain historicity to these events, and to assume that the daughter of that Folco Portinari who died on 31 December 1289, the Bice Portinari who married Simone de' Bardi, was in fact identical with the Bice of the sonnet *Io mi sentii svegliar* and the Beatrice of the *Vita Nuova*. Perhaps she was. But the fact is that the tradition which connects the glorious Beatrice, the 'blessing of Florence,' with the wife of a Florentine merchant is based chiefly on the testimony of 'a trustworthy person' three quarters of a century after the event, and from a scholarly point of view, this is disturbing."

Between Buti and Valency many others have shared this role of doubting Thomas. Among the most notable was Father Mandonnet. To him Beatrice was Beatitude or Theology.

But she was Wisdom to Biscioni; the Emperor to Rossetti; the Ideal Church to Gietmen; Dante's Thought-word, his Sectarian Faith, his Soul and Spirit personified to Perez; and the Ideal Woman to Bartoli and others.

I cannot agree with these gentlemen, but go along with Guido Mazzoni.

"At this time of day," he wrote, "denial of the reality of Beatrice is an expression of a would-be scepticism rather than an actual doubt."

Both logic and evaluated evidence show that Signor Mazzoni is right.

Let us go into the matter of the "realiable" — or the trustworthy — witness first.

When, as he approached sixty, Boccaccio began his lectures on Dante, he supplemented his earlier account of Beatrice with these corroborating words:

"At this point" — he was discussing canto II of the *Inferno* — "it does not seem inappropriate to say something about the one to whom the author refers in various parts of his work, for he did not always speak of her in an allegorical manner. This lady — according to what was told me by someone worthy of trust who knew her well *and was very closely related to her* — was the daughter of a worthy man named Folco Portinari. His family had long been citizens of Florence. And although the author always called her Beatrice which was her true name, she was known as Bice, and he settles this matter once and for all by testifying to it in the *Paradiso* when he says: 'But that great reverence which queens it over me wholly by the mere sound of *B* and *ice*.' She was as praiseworthy in her manners and in her open ways as a lady should and could be. She was adorned with beauty and charm. And she was the wife of a knight of the Bardi family, whose name was Simone."

Mr. Valency — and other skeptics — also make a point of the fact that Boccaccio's first comments were set down in 1364, and another point could certainly be made of the fact that Boccaccio's lectures — from which the second comments are taken — were not delivered until 1373. But Boccaccio did not necessarily receive the information on which they were based either ninety or ninety-nine years after the event. The author of the *Decameron* was an alert boy of eight when Dante died, and he lived — except for a short period in Naples — Dante's city. In Dante's city which had by then begun to understand what it had lost in Dante.

Nor was there any shortage of those who had known Dante and his lady, or known those who had known them. I will name only one of them. Boccaccio's stepmother — and for a while, even if bitterly, he shared his father's house with her — was Margherita de' Mardoli of the same San

Martino parish in which the Alighieri lived, and Margherita's mother was the daughter of one Salto dei Portinari who for a time had been a guardian of Folco's children. She was, then, a relative of Bice. But there were other possible sources of information. After all, Giovanni's father Boccaccino had been an important employee in the great banking house of Bardi, and among his fellow employees there must have been some who could remember Messer Simone and his lovely wife. There was also the talk of the Florentine piazza and the Florentine street. This was often vicious and malicious but it was not ever wholly inaccurate.

Besides that we have the words of almost all of the earlier commentators.

Commenting – in 1324, when Dante had been dead only three years – on that same *Inferno* II which had elicited Boccaccio's observations was a notary, Graziuolo, who may have known Dante in Bologna. He wrote: "This lady was the soul of the excellent Madonna Beatrice who was the daughter of the late Messer ———— " Here there is a lacuna. Evidently Ser Graziuolo, who lived on the wrong side of the Apennines, did not have enough information to complete the sentence.

But it was filled in a subsequent Italian translation: "daughter of the late Folco of the Portinari."

Jacopo della Lana in 1328 spoke of "Beatrice whom while she lived seemed more beautiful than any other to him."

Andrea Lancia in 1334 referred to "that Madonna Beatrice whom he loved with all his heart."

The anonymous author of some thirteen hundred and thirty-seven "explanatory notes" also named her by name and indicated that she was a Florentine.

But perhaps the most conclusive evidence came from Dante's own son Pietro.

He too commented on *Inferno* II.

"And since here," he wrote, "for the first time is mentioned Beatrice of whom much is lengthily said, and especially in the third cantica, the *Paradiso*, it should be set down that a lady whose name was Beatrice, and who was noted for her charm and for her beauty, truly lived in the city of Florence in the time of the author. She was born into the family of certain Florentines whose name was Portinari. And as long as she did live Dante courted her and loved her, and in her praise wrote many rhymes."

Because these words appear in only one manuscript of Pietro's opus, those who die hard insist that they were interpolated later. Investigation seems to prove the contrary. And if they were not interpolated, they must be credited. For who was more likely to know accurately the name of the lady about whom Dante wrote than one of Dante's own sons?

But Dante's own words made Beatrice flesh and blood.

This is how he reacted to their meeting in canto XXXII of the *Purgatorio*.

> So eager and intent were then my eyes
> After a ten years' thirst to sate themselves
> That every other sense of mine went blank.

You do not write thus about Theology — or about Wisdom — or about the Emperor — or about the Ideal Church — or even about the Ideal Woman.

To be sure, the lady of his great poem came to have an allegorical meaning too.

"Of the women who hear themselves called 'angels,'" wrote Étienne Gilson with a twinkle, "very few expect to be treated as symbols."

Whether she expected it or not, however, Beatrice was one of those few.

But behind the symbol was Bice, daughter of Folco. Of this there can be no reasonable doubt.

« *3* »

If there can be no reasonable doubt as to the reality and the identity of Beatrice, there can be little more as to the circumstances under which she and Dante met. They were consistent with the way life was lived in Florence during the second half of the thirteenth century, and especially with the way it was lived by Folco Portinari and by his neighbors, who included Dante's father.

It has already been noted that Folco was a man of some standing in the community. This is an understatement. He was something more than that.

In discussing the origins of Florentine municipal government, we have already noted the importance of the *vicinia* and the *popolo*. But the *vicinia* — which was the rural version of the *popolo* — often grew up around the castle.

"A castle," observed Ferdinand Schevill, "consisted of a tower with barns and stables, enclosing one or more courts, and with a sturdy wall, unscalable except with ladders, enveloping the whole compound. To this fortress-like residence, as soon as an enemy appeared, the cultivators of the surrounding fields flocked for safety, bringing with them all they held dear, their families, their animals, and their chattels. In the frequent sudden emergencies of that lawless epoch, the peasants of whatever degree served as the garrison of the castle, performing the military duties required by the occasion; and in return they were endowed with a number of rights, among them the very important right to appoint a gateman, or *portinarius*, to act as caretaker of their goods."

From one of these *portinarii* — moved to the city — it is reasonably probable that Folco Portinari was descended. He was, therefore, one of those new citizens like Caponsacco (Head-in-Bag) — incidentally Folco's wife was Celia dei Caponsacchi — and Infangato (Muddy Breeches) and even Bellincione who, when the boundary of Florence was still "at Galuzzo and at Trespiano" (these were then villages and are not more than two or three miles distant), "unto the market had already descended" to seek and make their fortune.

Gatekeeper's descendant or descended from a gate militiaman, he succeeded in doing this. This the record shows very plainly.

He matriculated into the Merchants (presumably Bankers) Guild in 1259 — this means that he was probably not born before 1234 and that he may have been born as late as 1243 — and he became one of its consuls in 1288, if not earlier. He was one of the fourteen *buonomini* nominated by Cardinal Latino — see chapter IV — to keep peace between the Guelphs and the Ghibellines. He was a prior from August 15 to October 15, 1282, and he was again a prior from August 15 to October 15, 1285, and from October 15 to December 15, 1287. This makes him a Guelph, for only Guelphs were priors. Incidentally, he was one of the very few citizens to hold this important office three times.

Folco was also noted for his public charities. He was buried in his own chapel in Santa Maria Novella in a marble tomb bearing the Portinari arms of a gate and two lions rampant, over which hung a portrait of the Virgin Mary painted by Cimabue and paid for by Messer Portinari. On it was carved this inscription:

"*Hic iacet Fulcus Portinarii qui fuit fundator et edificator huius ecclesie et ospitalis S. Marie Nove et decessit anno MCCLXXXIX die XXI Decembris. Cuius anima pro Deo misericordia requiescat in pace.*"

"Here lies Folco Portinari who was the founder and builder of this church and hospital of Santa Maria Novella and who died in the year 1289 and on the day of December 21. May his soul rest in peace through God's mercy."

If these words can be taken literally, it was something of a donation, for Santa Maria Novella is one of Florence's biggest and most important churches. But more probably they refer only to a private chapel.

The hospital he did endow, however — in the year 1288 and on the twenty-third of June.

"In the name of God, amen" — it is said that Folco was inspired to draw up this deed by the insistence of one of his servants, a certain Monna

Tessa — "by this public document be it made known that Folco, son of the late Ricovero de' Portinari of the *popolo* of Santa Margherita in Florence, on this of today, presents to the venerable father, Messer Andrea" — Andrea de' Mozzi, whom, as we have seen, Dante would later put in hell — "by the grace of God, bishop of Florence, a certain petition of his, the purport of which is as follows:"

First of all, "outside of the walls of Florence and near to the church of Santo Gilio" — but Sant' Egidio on the street of that name is now completely engulfed by Florence — there shall be given over certain houses to shelter the poor and the needy.

"Second, in one of these houses there shall be built an altar, and this altar shall be consecrated by the bishop, who has given indulgences for a year and forty days to all those who attended the ceremony and has promised forty days indulgence to any who visit it upon the anniversary of this consecration.

"This done, I, the said Folco, out of reverence to God and to the Virgin Mary and for the repose of my soul and the souls of my parents, beg that of the worldy goods which God hath bestowed upon me, I may endow it so that in perpetuity there may always be a priest and his servant there and that they may dwell there and be decently nourished, and that there may always be candles kept burning.

"And these are the goods with which I beg permission to endow this church.

"First of all a piece of land and a vineyard and plowed fields with a large house three stories high and a wine cellar and a bakehouse and with two cottages and a hayloft and an orchard, and this property is in the *popolo* of Santa Maria di Fornello.

"Second a piece of land with plowed fields and a vineyard.

"Third . . ."

He lists nine of these pieces of land in all. Some of them are noted as having a woodlot of oak or chestnut trees.

"Also the undivided half of forested land in the *popolo* of Santa Brigida. Also a silver chalice; three sacerdotal robes and a chasuble; a copper thurible; a missal; two antiphonaries, one for daytime services and one for evensong; a book of martyrs; a psalter and a hymnal; a bed and a chest.

"And to govern this church I pray that there be named a rector who may conduct the services in this church, and that the said Folco and his male children and all his descendants of the male sex have in perpetuity the right to name this rector.

"And I also pray that for the peace of my soul and for that of my parents I may endow the above-named hospital for the poor with three hundred *libbre* and also with the furnishings and the beds which I now enumerate:

"A coffer and a trunk.

"Seventeen beds furnished with straw mattresses, featherbedding, sheets, coverlets, and other bedclothes.

"Also a copper caldron and a copper bucket.

"But I reserve for myself and for my male children and for my male descendants the right in perpetuity to appoint the superintendent of this hospital too, and I pray that this superintendent in times to come may employ neither lay brother nor lay sister without the license and permission of myself or my male sons or my male descendants, and that if a lay brother or lay sister is employed without this permission, their employment is not valid nor shall it be continued.

"With the exception of this, the said Folco or his above-named descendants shall receive no other privilege now or in times to come from this hospital or its superintendent except in such matters as are specifically provided for by law."

It was a deed which with only modest modifications could be drawn by a wealthy philanthropist even today — and not merely in Florence or in Italy. Nor have the ripples produced by this public-spirited act ceased their spreading. Folco's little Santo Gilio, clustered about with farms and farmhouses, some of the latter already occupied by the ill and by the poor, is now embraced by the huge, imposing Arcispedale (Arch-hospital) of Santa Maria Nuova. This covers a large city block, and besides that has reached out to acquire Careggi, once a Medici villa in the nearby hills and now a training school for nurses. The seventeen beds have become the largest hospital in Florence. The effects of Folco's donation have lasted for almost seven hundred years.

But Folco was something more than a civic leader, a successful businessman, and a generous giver. He was also a Florentine, and a Florentine at a time when the city of the lily was beginning to throw off some of the shackles of the somber Middle Ages. To much shaking of heads on the part of the conservative, the coarse gray or brown homespun of earlier and simpler days was giving place to the "sky-blue cloth" noted not many years later by Sacchetti, and to the blue and the crimson which we begin to see in pictures by Giotto and others, and to cloth shot through with threads of actual and metallic gold.

But there were other changes too.

The love of entertainment which, as we have already noted, was so intrinsic to the Florentines as to become a matter of public concern was now beginning to become manifest, and although the famous Rossi celebration (also already noted) which brought people to the Oltrarno section from all over Europe did not take place until 1283, and although the Calendimaggio — the May Day which was brought down from the north — was not officially celebrated until 1290, there was plenty of festivity beside the Arno. Much of it took place in the spring.

But then, why not? Were not the Florentines descendants of the ancient Romans and did not the Romans celebrate the Floralia by visiting the grotto of the nymph Egeria on its middle day — approximately May 1 — and bearing to her branches and flowers? But celebrating the May is almost universal in temperate climes, for something in the heart suddenly lifts when the black and apparently dead trees become vested with the fragile first green. This is resurrection. This is immortality.

Long before the Calendimaggio became a formal festival, small sheds known as "courts" were built in the smaller piazzas to celebrate this joyous occasion, and the walls of many of the houses were draped in brocaded silken cloth. Garlanded couples moved through the city singing to the accompaniment of cither or violin.

Banquets were also given to men and women, and on May 1, 1274, Folco Portinari, an established citizen with an important wife and five sons and five daughters, gave just such a banquet.

It was this which Dante and his father attended.

As they walked the short distance which separated the two houses, the street would have smelled of rain-washed dust and flowers. Vines would have trailed from window ledge and balcony. Overhead the sky would have been blue, and down it would have drifted fleecy clouds.

Inside the Portinari garden there was the sound of music, for it was not merely in the street or under some lady's window that songs were sung as someone played some instrument. Lutes — newly introduced from Germany, if you can believe Cecco Angiolari, a sarcastic contemporary poet — tinkled and plunked. A lute is something like a mandolin. Rotas (an early guitar), sackbuts (a primitive slide trombone), lyres, rebecks, and fiddles: these, or some of these, contributed to the harmony. There may even have been a violin or a *mezzo cannone*. The latter was a short, curved flute.

With the music there was, of course, feasting.

According to legend, macaroni was introduced into Italy by Marco Polo, and if so it could not have been served by Folco. (Yet even here there is conflicting evidence. An earlier legend says that Frederick II made spaghetti popular after he smelled some cooking as he rode past a humble kitchen in Naples. Only a hundred years after Dante, Sacchetti spoke of it with such familiarity that it long must have been part of the Italian diet. Then as today, Italians wrapped it around their forks for convenience in eating. Sacchetti also speaks of ravioli "without a pasta crust," which is a little hard to figure out.) Nor would there have been its almost inevitable present-day concomitant *salsa di pomodoro*, for tomatoes were discovered with America.

But there would have been sausages, "stuffed" — again Sacchetti — "with I know not what." Even from Roman days, the Italians were famous sausagemakers. There would have been a variety of cheeses. Huge earthenware platters laden with a loin of lamb or beef, a chine of pork, or with capons, veal, or mutton, would have been brought in from a nearby cook shop. There would have been *insalata* — salad, the unsalted — and such fruits as were in season at this early time of the year. However, there would not be any out-of-season garden products. From the time of the Romans until the very recent past, such were not served in Italy.

There also would have been ample wine.

"The cult of wine," it was observed only a little later, "is so great that for a long time most Italians have employed every possible means to serve only the best, so that not content with importing it from every part of the land, they have even sent for young shoots so that they could improve their own vines."

The same writer noted that visits to "the tower of grapes" — i.e., drinking deeply — were frequent.

"When they were at their supper, the Florentines made greater use of their glasses than of their platters," was an often-quoted saying.

"There are diverse sorts of grapes," reported an English visitor. "*Uva canaiuola*, good to eat or for wine; *passerina*, a small grape, good only for wine; Trebbiano, the best grape for white wine; *zebibbo*, dried for Lent; *moscatella*, with a taste like musk; *uva grossa*, not to eat nor to drink, but a few of these put in a great vessel of wine giveth it color."

Out of these grapes and others were pressed the Vernaccia, the Leatico, the *vin santo*, the Carmignano, the Pomino, and even the Chianti which were the most in demand even then.

Less than a century later, the average annual wine consumption in Florence was fifty five thousand *cogni*. A *cogno* was ten barrels. This is more than five barrels a person.

After the feasting, the entertainment.

In a private garden — such as that of Folco — much of this must have been the dancing to song which has already been referred to. But it is possible — although not necessarily probable in view of the dignity and reputation of the host — that the men gathered in little groups to indulge in the gambling which was rapidly becoming such a vice among the Florentines.

One of their gambling games was *mosca*. Here each player set a coin in front of him on a table, and the one on whose coin a fly first alighted took the stakes. The devices used to lure a fly were sometimes a little more notable for their ingenuity than for their compliance with a spirit of fair play.

They also played *zara*.

This was a dice game. Three dice were thrown, and if they came up less than seven or more than fourteen, the thrower lost.

Dante had plainly seen *zara* played — and frequently — for he described it vividly in *Purgatorio* VI.

> Now when a game of *zara* doth break up,
> Sorrowfully cursing the loser lingers on,
> Replays each throw, and tries to learn from bad luck.
> The lucky one goes off. A crowd goes with him.
> One goes in front. Another jogs at his back.
> One at his side says: "Please don't forget me!"
> He pushes on, gives something to this and that one.
> And when they've snatched his gift, they melt away.

It should be noted that gambling was illegal in Florence — indeed, when Florentine merchants went abroad they had to swear not to gamble — but for a while it was permitted at Calendimaggio, and one can assume that it was also permitted on May Day at this earlier time.

« 4 »

As their elders diverted themselves in one way or another, or watched or took part in the dancing — or if they were women indulged in another form of feminine amusement for which only the tongue is needed — it is not unreasonable to assume that the young people also collected in groups as described by Boccaccio.

What were some of these diversions?

Fra Salimbene, a jovial and observant Franciscan monk who says that he began his book in "this present year, A.D. 1284," reports a boys' game "where they lay hand upon hand upon their knees, and each, seeking to get the better, withdraws his hand from below and strikes it upon the hand above." It is still played — and many ocean leagues from Florence.

There were other children's games too — a version of hopscotch is only one of them — and many are still played with expressive gestures and musical jabber of voices upon small piazzas and up side alleys from Venice to Naples even today.

But for the most part the boys stood with the boys, and the girls with the girls, and simply looked at each other.

What is more natural than that Dante, as he stood with the other boys of his age, should suddenly have had his attention taken by this serious yet gay little girl who was clad in tasteful but modest dress of a color that could not but arrest the eye? He had, of course, seen her before, but then she had been a baby. Now at eight — at least to Dante, who was a keen, dark-eyed nine — she was a young lady. What is more natural than that she should suddenly have become someone whom he could note and remember? What is more natural than that later on — and after many other things had happened — he should have decided, and have convinced himself, that they all began to happen that day?

But even as we acknowledge this, do we have to accept the rest of the story?

Was heaven indeed about him in his infancy? Did it trail clouds of glory?

At that moment, in that place, upon that occasion, was there, as Boccaccio indicated and as Dante himself seems to have indicated, apocalyptically born the immortal exaltation which was never to cease soaring until almost a half century later it had taken the poet far beyond any earthly infatuation to that Love which is God, the Light Eternal, and that moves the sun and all the other stars?

Or is this something that he imagined later?

That is possible too.

For we can all of us thus tamper with the truth which is deeply hidden in our hearts. Nor do we always realize that we have so tampered with it.

Dante himself hedges a little upon this important matter.

Again in the *Vita Nuova:*

"Love directed me, and more than once, to seek out and behold this beautiful angel. During my childhood, therefore, I often went to where she could be seen, and I discovered that she was of so noble and laudable bearing that certainly these words of Homer could be said of her: 'She seemed not the daughter of a mortal, but of a god.' "

But then common sense made him shade the picture a little.

"But even if the image of her, which stayed with me always, gave Love the strength to rule over me, yet at no time did it permit him to do so without the council of reason. At least in those matters in which this council were useful!

"But since," he concluded, "to dwell on the things suffered and done at so early an age seems like idleness, I will turn away from them. I will pass by the many things which might be drawn from the copy from which they were derived."

What can we deduce from this?

That Dante did indeed fall in love with Beatrice, but that his inate good judgment told him that he aspired for someone far too lofty? After all, the Portinari were among the wealthiest and most distinguished families in Florence, whereas the Alighieri, if of old lineage, had come down in the world.

It has happened before and since. Boys have indeed fallen in love at the age of nine and this love has sometimes lasted for the rest of their lives. Equally, lovers have sometimes — if sadly — shown common sense.

Or were his eyes and his fancy merely drawn lightly toward this very pretty little neighbor's girl so that he paid her much attention but only later found it necessary to crown her with a golden halo?

I would suspect the latter, for this was a very difficult time in Dante Alighieri's life. Not more than three years after Folco's festive May Day, Dante's father died, and thereafter — except insofar as Brunetto Latini shared the responsibility — he was left to the mercies of a pack of uncles, whose qualifications (or, rather, lack of qualifications) to serve *in loco parentis* should already be apparent. His financial situation was of questionable stability, and he was gloomily betrothed to Gemma Donati and may even have been married to her. Clearly it was no time for romantic lady-service like that of the troubadours whose works he would soon be reading so avidly.

But from time immemorial, young men have looked over the back fence and liked — whether she was golden-haired or dark-haired — the girl whom they saw there.

At ten, at eleven, at twelve, at thirteen, at fourteen, at fifteen, at sixteen, and at seventeen, as the occasion offered itself, Dante did indeed do exactly this.

It is obvious that he and Beatrice must have met frequently. The strange thing would have been if they had not.

In my judgment, however, love is too strong a word to apply to any feelings he might have had for her. Let us say more modestly that she was someone whom he found it good to look at and from time to time think about.

That is enough.

« 5 »

But at eighteen it was another matter.

Here is how Dante reported it.

"I come now to those words which are written under more weighty paragraphs.

"After so many days had passed that nine years were precisely completed since the above-written appearance of this most gentle lady, and on the last of those days, it happened that this wonderful lady appeared to me clad in robe of purest white. With her were two other ladies who were older than she was. And as she passed me by, she turned her eyes to where I stood most fearful, and of her ineffable courtesy she gave me a salutation of such virtue that it seemed to me I saw the uttermost bounds of blessedness."

This is the famous meeting by the Ponte Santa Trinità on the Arno which is so celebrated in song and story — and in art. We can date it precisely. It took place on April 30, 1283. "Standing on the corner watching all the girls go by!" Thus, in the words of a present-day song, this meeting was humorously described by one who saw the painting of it which has now been reproduced on Florence's most popular postcard, and Dante may well have been so standing, for, as we will see, he still had an eye for others of the opposite sex even when he most loved Beatrice.

But now — and I think for the first time — his heart really did increase its tempo, and the world suddenly dissolved into a haze.

"The hour when her sweet salutation reached me," he continued, "was assuredly the ninth of that day" — this would have been four in the afternoon; the gorgeous springtime sun was westering toward Signa — "and as that was the first time that her words set forth to come to my ears, such sweetness possessed me that as one drunken I departed from all people and withdrew to the solitude of my room, and began thinking of this most courteous one."

Incidentally, there is a slight inconsistency here. This is the first time Beatrice ever spoke to him, Dante says. Yet he met her when she was eight, and frequently went to places where she could be seen in the ensuing years.

"And as I thought of her, a sweet sleep fell upon me, and sleeping thus I had a marvelous vision."

Here it is.

In the midst of a cloud of flame, there appeared to him a "lord of terrible aspect" who said to him in Latin: "I am thy master." In his arms was a naked woman lightly clad in crimson drapery whom Dante recognized immediately as the lady of his encounter. In his hand he held a flaming object. "Behold thy heart!" he said. Then he awoke the lady and made her eat the heart.

"Thereafter he stayed but a short time before his gladness changed to bitterest weeping, and thus weeping he gathered this lady in his arms and it seemed to me he went toward heaven with her. From that time onward, my natural spirit began to be impeded in its action because my mind was given over wholly to thinking of this most gentle lady. Therefore in a short time I became of so frail and weak a state that the sight of me weighted upon my friends."

It was the normal, and indeed almost conventional, reaction.

"Why so pale and wan, fond lover? Prithee, why so pale?" wrote Sir

John Suckling some three centuries later. He added: "Will, when looking well can't move her, looking ill prevail?"

Beatrice's poet, however, did a little more than mope and pine. Then as now, a young man who had learned how to use his pen could sublimate, and Dante, after he had indulged his feelings for a while, sublimated them into the first poem — although we know that he had written earlier ones — which can definitely be ascribed to him. It should surprise no one that it is not the best he ever wrote.

> To every captive soul and gentle heart
> Into whose hands doth come this present word,
> That they may speak their thoughts, nor stand apart,
> Greetings I give from Love who is their lord.
> Already had sped a third part of the hours
> Wherein each star there is, shines glittering bright,
> When to mine eyes suddenly Love appeared.
> I tremble sore when I recall his sight.
> Jocund he seemed. He held my heart in hand.
> And in his arms he held my lady fair,
> Who, wrapped in a mantle, peacefully there slept.
> Thereat he wakened her, and then the brand
> That was my heart she ate in humble fear.
> Thereafter, he did go his way and wept.

But if this is not one of Dante's great — or even particularly good — poems, it at least shows that already at this early age he had begun to move along the particular poetic path which he was to follow so assiduously and with such success.

In *Purgatorio* XXIV — and in the *Purgatorio* as in the *Inferno* and the *Paradiso* you can find Dante's final, considered thought upon virtually everything that was of importance to him — he carried on a discussion of poetic theory with Bonagiunta of Lucca, a minor poet contemporary with him, and when Bonagiunta called his attention to another, and this time really great, poem which Dante had written, the latter set down his self-analysis as follows:

> And I to him: "I am but one who, when
> Love doth inspire, note and, in the manner
> He speaks to me within, make plain without."

"Look in thy heart and write!" as Sir Philip Sidney put it.

Bonagiunta — but we must remember that it was Dante who put the words into his mouth — acknowledged that the appraisal was accurate.

> "O brother," said he, "now I see the knot
> That bound the Notary and Guittone and me
> This side the sweet new style [*dolce stil novo*]
>   which I do hear.
> Now I see plainly why it is your pen
> Follows so closely behind the dictating lord.
> This does not happen to the rest of us . . ."

In other words, Dante, according to Dante, recorded literally, and sometimes almost photographically, everything he knew and, more important, felt. One can agree with him. He always was to a degree, and he became increasingly, a realist, a fact which for obvious reasons has not always been noted. This is apparent in even the most decorated of his love poems and his most abstruse odes to philosophy. It is doubly apparent in his *Commedia*, in which are described the cities, plains, mountains — and people — of hell, purgatory, and heaven almost as one might describe the cities, plains, and mountains of Italy, which is one reason why the *Commedia* can be read today.

The sonnet to Beatrice — or, more accurately, *about* Beatrice — also began to establish Dante's reputation as a poet.

It has already been stated that as he began to write he sent some of his compositions to the more notable of his contemporaries. This sonnet was one of them. It elicited replies and three of these replies survive. One was from Dante da Maiano, a second from Cino da Pistoia, and the third from Guido Cavalcanti.

In tone, they differed greatly.

Dante de Maiano, for example — that other Dante who perhaps would not even be known were it not for his relationship with Dante Alighieri — lashed out with a savage and a sarcastic attack.

(Later he became a great admirer of the man he now scorned, and eulogized that Dante's "fine and firm and golden way of speech proves true the good things that men say of you.")

> On that you send me and my judgment seek:
> I looked at it and briefly answer thee,
> O great good friend of mine, scarce known to me,
> Thrusting into your nose truth's pungent reek.
> Of this your trade and craft these words I speak:
> "If you are sane, if you of mind are sound,
> Wash well your private parts, for I have found,
> Not from your lips, forsooth, but from your breek
> Comes that which makes you say fantastic things . . ."

The rest is equally coarse and at least as physiological. In effect he told Dante that if he kept on writing like this he should consult a doctor. We would say a psychiatrist.

Cino da Pistoia, however, and Guido Cavalcanti recognized Dante's ability.

"You made Love happy," cried Cino. "Hence he came to give you what your heart demanded."

Guido was even more exuberant. Dante would have every worth and joy and good that man could know.

Indeed, the second of the two poets, who was then a mature twenty-eight, responded so generously that from then on, and by Dante's own testimony, he became the first of Dante's friends.

Recognition by these two men was significant and important. It was also reassuring. For next to Dante — and some feel that this aloof, introspective man (he has been called "a Florentine Hamlet") who "was one of the best logicians in the world and an excellent natural philosopher" was in some aspects of his work Dante's equal — Guido was the foremost poet of the new writing, and Cino followed closely at his heels.

Beyond that, their lives already paralleled — and would continue to parallel — that of Dante to an extraordinary degree.

All three were members of that new and at least partly self-made bourgeois-noble class which did not find business or a profession and making money incompatible with a sense of social superiority or a literary career. Guittoncino de' Sinibaldi — that was Cino's lofty-sounding name — was born into a noble Guelph family of Pistoia. But he held various public offices, taught law, and practiced as a notary. Guido belonged to an ancient clan which had grown rich in commerce and trade. Shops and dwellings owned by the Cavalcanti and either used by themselves or rented out occupied much of central Florence, and besides this they had castles and extensive estates in the Valdelsa and the Valdipesa, both southwest of the city at the edges of the Chianti country. But no Cavalcanti forgot to claim descent from the German nobility and, like Dante, relationship with the good Gualdrada.

All three suffered the anguishes of exile. "I exhort you," wrote a "Florentine undeservedly in exile" (Dante) to the "exile from Pistoia" (Cino) in 1305, "so far as in you lies, to arm yourself against the darts of Nemesis." Inasmuch as Guido's exile is inextricably a part of Dante's own story, I will say nothing of it until later.

Both Cino and Guido gained much of their reputation from poems addressed to a lady or ladies. Cino addressed his poems to a Selvaggia who is the predecessor of Petrarch's Laura both in herself and in the quality of the poetry which Cino wrote to her. Who she was is not known. Guido was more earthy and had had more than one lady. The most important of them was a certain Giovanna whom he sometimes called Primavera, or My Lady Spring. She was a close friend of Dante's Beatrice. Another was a certain Mandetta (probably Mandette) who lived in Toulouse in southern France. Mandette's eyes, Guido said, had driven him to distraction, and from that we can assume that she was a typical daughter of the Midi. To both of them, but particularly to Mandette — "Go to Toulouse, O little song of mine, and softly steal to her, the golden one" — he wrote poems of an extraordinary delicacy and lilt. They are among the more refreshing of the age of Dante.

« 6 »

But if Dante now knew true love, its course lived up to the proverb and did not run smooth. More accurately, it did not run unaccompanied by a curious kind of complication which made the whole story of his attitude toward Beatrice very different from the love stories of many of his contemporaries — who, one after another, were sonnetizing the fair ladies of all Tuscany in perhaps one of the greatest outbursts of love poetry that there has ever been.

Certain aspects of his character brought this about — as did some attendant circumstances that pertained both to him and to the lady of his heart. Although, for example, and not much later, he would write poems to Florentine beauties to whom he gave such names as Violetta, Fioretta, Pietra, and Pargoletta (Little Maid), in this instance it did not comport with his concept of making plain without that which love spoke to him within to hide the identity of the real person who had so deeply moved him behind some symbolic name. This Cino had done with Selvaggia. At the same time, he could not be self-confidently open like Guido Cavalcanti, whose aristocratic assurance permitted him to move from Giovanna-Primavera to Mandette and back again while cheerfully proclaiming both of them. He could not, either, have the brash vulgarity of Cecco Angiolari, another contemporary and another who, like Dante da Maiano, would one day attack him in a sarcastic sonnet. Cecco caterwauled about his unrequited pursuit of his leathermaker's daughter Bettina in almost as many of these fourteen-line poems as Dante, Cino, and Guido wrote between them, and in these poems he was always specific and sometimes insulting.

Instead a deep-rooted reticence — and perhaps some other considerations — made it necessary for the son of Alighiero to conjure up a veil of mystery. For the moment, at least, he could not celebrate Bice — or even Beatrice — for the whole world to wonder at. Or so he thought. For the moment, Dante, who one day would hide nothing, had to be studiously reserved.

Chance gave him the needed opportunity.

"One day it came about that this most gentle lady" — i.e., Beatrice — "sat in a place where words about the Queen of Glory were being chanted, and I was in a seat from which I could behold my beatitude. And midway between her and me there sat in direct line another gentle lady. This lady gazed at me and seemed to marvel much. She marveled that my gaze always seemed to end upon her."

Others apparently marveled too, Florence being a city which paid much attention to who was looking at whom, and so as he walked out into the square he heard people talking about him.

"Look at what a state this lady has brought him to. Behold, he wasteth away!"

Then they gave the lady's name.

"And by their naming her, I learned that they were speaking of the one who sat in the middle of the direct line which began with Beatrice and ended with mine eyes. This comforted me greatly for it assured me that my secret had not that day been made known to others by my look."

It also gave him an idea.

"For straightway I decided to make this lady a screen of the truth, and such a show did I make of this that in a short time my secret was known to most of the people who had been talking about me."

It is a charming story, and one that is entirely convincing. In those days, the church was the center of all parish activity, and if — as is apparent from Dante's account — men and women still sat apart at the services which all attended, it is clear that a curtain no longer separated them. Sermons were long, and eyes had time to wander. What is more likely than that Dante should go to Santa Margherita — which was Beatrice's church; San Martino was his — and that there, on a spring morning when the almond blossoms foamed outside, he should let his eyes fall upon the one who had so recently bewitched him? What is more probable than that another young lady — who by chance sat between Dante and Beatrice — should intercept the look and believe with others that it was intended for her?

The only question to be answered is how seriously Dante came to take her.

Did she remain the lady of the screen? Or did she come to be a good deal more to him?

There is some evidence in favor of the latter.

This is a sonnet which he wrote to Guido Cavalcanti at about this time:

> Guido, I would that thou and Lapo and I
> Were placed by an enchanter's magic wand
> Upon a little bark by breezes bland
> Wafted where'er we would across the sea.
> I would that no foul days incontinently
> Or wind or storm our pleasant course might stay,
> But, having but one mind among the three,
> We might together long to be alway.
> And Monna Vanna and Monna Lagia too
> And she that stands the thirtieth on the roll
> I would the enchanter might magic to our side,
> And that our talk to love should aye be true . . .

Vanna we know. She is the Giovanna-Primavera we have already referred to. Lagia was the ladylove of Lapo Gianni, another poet. But who was the thirtieth on the roll? Almost certainly the lady who had looked at him in church.

Incidentally, Dante himself explains this obscure reference. "I say that at this time when this lady was a screen of Love I took the names of sixty of the fairest ladies in Florence, and I composed an epistle in the form of a *sirventese*."

In it, these ladies were listed and praised. But Dante did not think it worth preserving.

Beatrice's name was in this poem, and Dante paused only to note that it was ninth in place. Nine — as has already been mentioned — was becoming an important number where Beatrice was concerned.

But there is further evidence than the sonnet to Guido with its enchanting portrayal of the three poets and their three ladies drifting idyllically over limpid waters that leads us to the conclusion that his involvement with the lady he had seen in church and said that he pretended to love only to protect Beatrice went far deeper than that.

Much of it comes from Dante himself.

"It became necessary for this lady" — almost immediately after Dante had composed the *sirventese* — "with whom I had so long hidden my desire to depart this city and to go into a far country."

As the wife of a merchant who had been sent to France or elsewhere?

This has been contended but there is no evidence either for or against.

"Wherefore I was much disquieted, *much more than I myself would have believed possible before it happened*."

I supply the italics, but I will shortly try to justify them.

"And thinking that if I did not speak somewhat sorrowfully of her departure people would be very quickly aware of the fact that I concealed something, I decided to utter my great grief in a sonnet.

"I will write it down."

Here it is — or here, at any rate, is its first stanza:

> Oh ye who do upon Love's way pass by,
> Observe now and descry
> If any sorrow deep as mine ye know.
> I only ask that ye attend to me
> And then determine and see
> If I'm not inn and hostelry of woe.

It is not a sonnet — it has twenty-one lines, not fourteen, and the verse structure is different — but its words are so eloquent (not only in the beginning, but right up to the last line wherein the poet tells his readers that "deep in my heart I slay myself and weep") that they could not possibly have been written for a proxy. Not even if Dante swore this, as he tried to do. For the record, they also foreshadow one of the great passages of his later writing. At the moment it was he who was *d'ogni tormento ostello*. In *Purgatorio* VI, it would be "slave Italy" which was "hostelry of woe." But there is no reason why a writer should not borrow phrases from himself.

« 7 »

Not very long after the lady's departure, Dante was "compelled" to leave Florence too and, as luck would have it, "to go toward that place where now dwelt that gentle lady who had been my defense, although the ending of my journey was not as far away as the place where she was."

He was "in the company of many," and because of this and because of certain phrases he used — *in quelle parte*, for example, and *andata* (foray) — which had military connotations, it has been assumed that he was on a military expedition.

But he may equally well have been on his way to Bologna and to his studies. Then, too, he would have had many companions, his rowdy fellow students. Then, too, he would have been "compelled" to go, as have been snail-paced scholars from time immemorial. For Dante does not seem to have been an eager book learner during his earlier years.

Scholar or soldier, he did not go willingly.

He made no bones about it.

"The journey misliked me — so much that hardly could my sighs give vent to the anguish which I felt."

Not even the sight of "a stream, fair, swift and clear" could lift his spirits.

This is taken to be the Arno — although the description hardly fits it today — and as further evidence of a military expedition. There was no stream, nor is there any, between Bologna and Florence to which the adjectives could apply.

Then suddenly he saw something which lifted his heart, a cloud of dust on the horizon. It grew nearer, then settled into recognizable shapes. Horses, prancing as they were with difficulty restrained. Mules, patiently plodding under their burdens of bales and baggage. On foot, men —and women too — wearily marching with staffs in hand and clad in *schiavine*.

A party of pilgrims — with probably some merchants and a few knights and men-at-arms too. Even for one wearing the cross, it was prudent in those days to have an armed escort.

One of them recognized Dante.

Guido Cavalcanti? We know that Guido had indeed been a pilgrim — that he had been one of those who set forth on the long, difficult journey to Santiago (St. James) de Compostela in the metal-rich mountains of the extreme northwestern corner of Spain. These pilgrims were so many that the Milky Way became known as the Road to St. James because of its fancied resemblance to the wavering and bobbing torches.

(For the purposes of his writing, Dante did not consider him to be Guido or anyone else. He was rather "that most sweet lord who held mastery over me by virtue of the most gentle lady." He was Love himself disguised as "a pilgrim lightly clad and wearing coarse apparel." A coarse woolen robe, sandals, and of course carrying a staff. But actually he was a real person and someone who knew Dante well.)

He stepped forward and spoke to the young poet.

"I come from that lady who has long been thy defense," he said, "and I know that her return is not to be. Therefore I have with me that heart which I made thee have for her. Bear it to this other lady who shall be your defense even as this one was."

And he named her to him, Dante indicated, "so that I knew plainly who she was."

He knew her well enough to take the advice given.

"After my return, I set out to seek this lady. And, not to waste words, I say that in a short time I made her so much my defense that many people spoke of it beyond the bonds of courtesy."

To leave riddles, this devotion (or pretended devotion) to the new lady of the screen was so ardent that it convinced everybody.

Florentine gossip (*pettegolezzo*) set to work and this Florentine gossip had and still has at its disposal poisons such as even the Borgia never dreamed of.

"This weighed upon me very heavily," said Dante.

Evidently it weighed heavily on someone else too — Beatrice!

"And for this cause — that is to say, this outrageous rumor which seemed to accuse me of vice — that gentle one who was the destroyer of all vice and the queen of every virtue, as she passed by a certain way denied me her most sweet salutation in which lay all my beatitude."

On Dante, the effect was devastating. I have suggested that the first lady of the screen took at least a part of Dante's heart, and the same thing could be said of the second lady. But now he realized that they at most were passing fancies. Beatrice was the sun. They were the stars or the faint, fickle moon.

And now Beatrice had snubbed him.

(If anyone still entertains a doubt that Beatrice was a real woman, this little incident should remove it once and for all, it is so entirely human. Folco Portinari's daughter, who was the most dazzling of Florentine beauties, knew that Dante had been drawn to her ever since she was the neighbor's little girl, and she knew too that more than once he had been in love with her. But now his eyes — and his sonnets — were for this hussy. So she passed him with her nose in the air and not even a *buon giorno*. This is not something done by Theology or any other highfalutin abstraction!)

His pride was hurt too, and I think I have already pointed out that pride was a notable Alighieri characteristic of which Dante had his share.

First of all, as he had done before, he went to a solitary place — "to bathe my grief in tears" — and then he returned to his chamber. Here he had one of his numerous, and usually convenient, visions. He dreamed of a young man (Love) who told him: "I am the center of a circle, to which all parts of the circumference bear an equal relation." This obscure statement he refused to explain, but later on he said something which was easier to comprehend. Beatrice, he said, who is the enemy of all vexations, believes that Dante has vexed this lady, and that therefore she will not speak to him. (Beatrice must have done some rationalizing herself.) Finally, he told Dante to write a poem to Beatrice. It should be in the third person and should tell her that through her Love had made him his servant.

Dante did so, but still struggled for his freedom and even went so far as to debate with himself whether love were good or evil.

At this point "it came to pass" that Beatrice "came to a place where many gentle ladies were assembled, to which I was conducted by a friend who thought to do me great service by taking me to where so many ladies were displaying their loveliness."

Dante's reputation as a lady's man is again emphasized.

It was a Florentine wedding party. It was a custom in Florence for ten friends of the bride and fourteen of the groom to take part in the wedding feast which was the first entertainment which the bride gave in the home of her new husband.

"So that thinking to please my friend, I agreed to stay in his company in the service of the ladies."

As he did this, all at once he felt a tremor begin at the left side of his breast and quickly spread over all parts of his body.

"Then I covertly laid my body against a painting which surrounded the hall" — i.e., which covered its walls — "and fearing lest anyone be aware of what I suffered, I raised my eyes and gazing upon the ladies saw Beatrice among them. Then were my senses destroyed so that no more than the spirits of sight remained."

Some of the company noticed that he had turned pale and several of the ladies began to mock him.

"Whereupon my friend took me by the hand, and leading me from the sight of those ladies asked me what ailed me."

Dante pulled himself together and pondered an answer.

"Verily," he said at last, "I have now set my feet on the point of life beyond which no one must ever pass if he hopes to come back."

We have a modern phrase for this: "the point of no return."

Dante had come to the point of no return in his love for Beatrice.

Through his changed appearance, all Florence knew this — but they would have anyway — and one day as he approached a group of ladies one of them, "a lady of very sweet speech," called out to him.

"What is the good," she asked laughing, "of loving this lady since you cannot bear to be in her company? Tell us. For certainly a love like this must come to a strange end."

Dante had already noticed that Beatrice was not one of their number, and this made it easier for him to talk, for in her presence he was tongue-tied, which is not surprising.

"I once loved her but for her salutation, but since it now pleases her to deny me this, Love has placed all his beatitude in that which cannot fail me."

At these puzzling words, the ladies all began to speak among themselves and, perhaps because any one of them would have gladly taken Beatrice's place, "even as we behold rain sometimes mingled with snow" Dante heard the prattle of their conversation mingled with sighs.

"What is that?" asked the lady who had first spoken to him.

"In those words which praise my lady," replied Dante.

At that moment, he laid the ground for a decision which would ultimately give Italy and the Italian language their greatest writing.

For "pondering these words" only a little later, "I proposed to take evermore for the matter of my speech that which would be praise of my most gentle lady."

The flesh, even as he talked, had become spirit, and Beatrice by being recognized as unattainable would be attained.

But since, even as he took care of the Alighieri business interests and lived the life of a young Florentine, he was a poet above everything else, this attainment in the first instance was literary.

"I vow," we can imagine him saying, "that from now on I will leave the shadowed alleys of my passing fancies and tread only the sun-drenched highway. From now on every line I write will be of Beatrice."

Nor did he wait long to carry this out.

"It soon happened that passing by a way along which flowed a river whose waters were most clear" — once again the clear river — "so great a desire to speak took possession of me that I began to wonder what style I should use. I decided that it was not fitting to speak of her unless I spoke to her in the second person and not to every lady but only to such as were gentle and not mere women."

He returned to Florence and a few days later he began to write.

> Ye ladies who indeed know greatly of love,
> To ye my lady I would now commend,
> Not that I of her praises could reach the end,
> But that this speaking easement to me prove.

This is the *Donne che avete intelletto d'amore*, which, by the way is the poem Bonagiunta spoke about. It should be read in Italian. It is one of the great love poems in any language.

A little later he wrote a second poem.

> *Amor e cor gentil è una cosa*
> *Siccom' il Saggio in suo dittato pone.*

> Love and the gentle heart are but one thing
> Even as the Wise Man sayeth in his rhyme.

The Wise Man is the poet Guido Guinicelli of Bologna, who died when Dante was eleven years old. In *Purgatorio* XXVI Dante with entirely uncharacteristic modesty calls him "the father of me and of my betters."

There were undoubtedly other poems, but they are not specifically identified.

« 9 »

It was at this time — one would like to think — that Dante rode off to fight at Campaldino and Caprona. We have already told you that he came back with heart singing. No wonder, for in it was an unfinished symphony which was bursting to come forth.

VI

Morte Villana

A S far as can be determined, it wasted no time in doing so.
The chronology of Dante's poems — and indeed the chronology of the whole canon of his writings — is something which can only be established deductively, and so it is entirely possible that both the *Donne che avete* and the *Amor e cor gentil* were written before rather than after the Campaldino and Caprona campaigns. Dante may even have written them while he was in military service. If so he would not have been the first poet — nor the last — to do this. From Aeschylus, who fought at Marathon, to Rupert Brooke and after, the list is long of those who have taken up the pen during the intervals between using the sword.

But wherever — and whenever — these poems were put on paper, the next sonnets in his ever more soaring canticle in praise of Folco Portinari's daughter were certainly written after Dante's return from the war.

Their contents makes this evident and obvious.

Let us assume that he rode back from Caprona late in August 1289 — and certainly he must have ridden back no later than early September. The grapes, rich purple (but dusted with a faint white must), would have hung in heavy clusters, and the doves and other birds which fed upon the grain wasted by the reapers would have been almost too fat and heavy to fly. By the time that they did fly, by the time of the *vendemmia* when these grapes had been gathered and brought to the presses, by the time that you could smell new wine in every house, by the time pompions, chick-peas, a few kinds of beans, and some of the late melons were all that you could see in the stalls of the Mercato Vecchio, he was back again to his normal life.

Part of this normal life was to revere Beatrice.

August became September; September, October; and October hurried golden to its end.

It was All Saints' Day, when it was traditional to eat goose, either roasted plain or stuffed with quince or "with larks and little birds," and so the aroma of the fowl which had once saved Rome was wafted down the narrow streets.

But on All Saints' Day — as on other festivals — it was also traditional for young women to gather in groups to sing and to perform slow dances.

Dante — from a distance, it seems likely — saw one of these groups.

He wrote a sonnet about it — and about someone who was one of its members.

> Of gentle ladies I did see a band
> On the All Saints' Day which has just now passed,
> And one among them who was first not last.
> Why, even Love saw her at his right hand.
> Light from her eyes danced a gay saraband.
> It seemed to me a spirit bright as flame.
> It so consumed me that I gave the name
> Of angel's to her face, serene and bland.
> She gave her greeting unto everyone
> Who worthy was, calmly and benignantly.
> She moved all, heart and soul, to virtue's path.
> I do believe that she from Heaven came down
> That our salvation she might come to be.
> He who is nearest her, most blessing hath.

Beatrice? Although he does not mention her name, who else?

Shortly after, he began for the first time to enhalo her. Until then, she had been a woman. Now she was a little more.

But even that was not enough.

"After I had treated of love in the aforewritten rhyme" — to be sure he is speaking of the *Amor e cor gentil* and not the sonnet translated above, which is not in the *Vita Nuova*, although it should be — "there came upon me the desire to say some words in praise of this most gentle one. In them I wished to show how Love is awakened by her, and not only does she awaken it where it sleeps, but even where before it had no power she miraculously brings it forth."

And so he wrote this:

> My lady carries love within her eyes:
> Hence all who look at her are lovely made.
> He who doth pass her by must turn his head,

And him she speaks to, tremble in such wise
That his abashéd face grows pale and wan,
And he doth sigh for every fault he has.
Anger and pride before her footsteps run.
Ah ladies, help me honor her and praise!
All sweetness, every modest thought there is,
Is born in his heart who her speaking hears.
Blessed is he who first did her behold.
And when she doth but smile, what she appears
Cannot be held in memory or told.
It is too rare and noble a miracle.

The gradual progression of Dante's writing — and therefore presumably his feelings — about Beatrice is clearly illustrated.

For this time he not only spoke from the heart, but he spoke from the heart specifically about his lovely lady.

Hitherto he had not done this. He had written about a dream and Beatrice. He had written about ladies who understood love and Beatrice. He had written about love and a gentle heart and Beatrice. Lately he had written about All Saints' Day and Beatrice.

But this poem was about Beatrice herself.

About Beatrice herself, and only one other.

Dante.

For Dante surely was the one who had to turn his head if he did but pass her by. It was surely Dante who trembled when she spoke to him; whose abashéd face grew pale and wan; who sighed — being that kind of person and one given to introspection — for every fault he had.

Most clearly of all, it was assuredly Dante who hoped that anger and pride — which were notable Dante and Alighieri defects — would run before her footsteps.

Then he might be worthy of her — which was the goal of all his dreams.

« 2 »

This he assiduously strove to bring about, and perhaps he had made progress, when his relationship to her and also the hovering premonitions that every deeply feeling lover must have were tested and brought into focus by something which deeply affected Beatrice and therefore affected him too.

"After the passage of not many days" — i.e., not many days after he had written the sonnet we have just discussed — "even as it pleased the glorious Lord who denied not death to Himself, he who had been the father of the most gentle Beatrice departed from this earth and unto eternal glory."

To speak more plainly, Folco Portinari — the generous benefactor, the successful banker, the civic-minded Florentine, but more important to this story "the good father of a good child, since the lady was of surpassing goodness, and her father (even as by many it was believed, and it was true) was good to the highest degree" — died suddenly of causes which have not been recorded.

The date of his death was December 21, 1289.

He may have been in his middle forties. He was certainly not as old as sixty.

He was not, however, unprepared. On January 12, 1287 — or just a little less than three years before his decease — "while by God's grace he was still sound of mind and body and in order to be ready for any fatal event," he had set down his last will and testament. It was notarized by Tedaldeo del fu Orlando Rusticchelli of Florence and witnessed by six friars of the Penitential Order of Jesus Christ in their own church of Santo Gilio without the Walls, which, as already noted, Folco had helped them build. Evidently Folco wanted the church to oversee the disposition of his worldly goods as well as the disposition of his soul.

It is an interesting and illuminating document.

First of all, as might a modern testator, he humbly commended his soul to God, and then he chose his place of burial. He further directed his heirs "to pay every decent and necessary funeral expense."

To make sure that this was done, he made two specific bequests each of fifty *libbre*. They were for the maintenance in perpetuity of a caretaker and a chaplain.

After that, he turned to charity. In the next paragraph of his will, he left, in his own words, one hundred *libbre* — but when the specific bequests are totaled they amount to three hundred fifty-one *libbre* — to thirty-eight named religious houses, of which eleven were in Florence and none was farther away than Camaldoli (in the Casentino) in one direction and Volterra in the other. The list is an impressive one, both in demonstrating Folco's generosity and in showing the large number of religious institutions in the city and nearby.

Then he remembered those whom, the Lord tells us, we will have with us always.

"Item, to the paupers and beggars of Florence, four small *denari* each, up to a total of eighteen *libbre*."

It was only when he had done this that he turned to his own family, but these too he dealt with adequately and even generously.

To his wife "Monna Celia, daughter of Gherardo Caponsacchi" he left "over and above the dowry which he had received with her, all his woolen, linen, and silken garments" and also "that piece of land which the testator himself had bought, in part from Tegghiaio Diotisalvi and in part from Giovanni Galletti, as is attested by Spigolato Aldobrandini, a notary."

To his natural sister Nuta — evidently the good Folco's own good father had strayed at least once — he bequeathed the right to bed and board in the Portinari house "for as long as she doth live," and he also directed that she be paid the sum of twenty-five *libbre* from his estate.

To his unmarried daughters Vannia, Fia, Margherita, and Castoria he left eighty *libbre* each.

To his grandson Niccolò, son of Bando Falconieri and Folco's daughter Ravignana, he left fifty *libbre*.

These taken care of, he constituted his sons Manetto, Ricovero, Pigello, Gherardo, and Jacopo his residuary legatees — they and their own sons *per stirpes* and not *per capita*, as is still customary — but noted that in the case of Manetto and Ricovero the fifteen hundred *libbre* "which have been inscribed in their names in the books of the company of Messers Uliviero, Bindo, and Giovanni de' Cerchi" should be counted as a part of their share.

To all this — "in order to take away from his sons and heirs and from their consorts any cause for dispute which could possibly arise" — he appended an inventory of the houses and real estate owned by him either outright or jointly with the heirs of (cousin) Doccio Portinari.

This listed "the old house of the Portinari which had recently been repaired by the testator and by Grifo Assalti and by Salto Portinari" in the *popolo* of Santa Reparata; a house in the *popolo* of Santa Maria in Campo; a palace with towers in the *popolo* of Santa Margherita — this was unqestionably the Folco Portinari home, the place where Dante first saw Beatrice; and two dwelling places, one of them imposing enough to have belonged to a prosperous goldsmith.

Quite an array of profitable city property — and that in a time when rents were steadily rising!

But it could go to Folco's male descendants only.

"Item, I direct that no woman and no descendant through a female line shall inherit these homes, cottages, etc., whether by provision of a will or from one who died intestate."

He also set up a protocol for settling disputes between his sons and the businessmen who now held so much of their fortunes. If any question arose as to sums of money allegedly owed to Folco's estate by the Cerchi banking house, or by him to the Cerchi, "the simple statement of Uliviero must and should be credited."

Finally, he appointed guardians for his minor children. His sons Manetto and Ricovero. Grifo Assalti. Salto Portinari. Uliviero and Bindo de' Cerchi.

Two brothers. Two close relatives, for Salto was certainly a cousin and Grifo seems to have been. Two of their father's business associates.

Of the latter, Uliviero should be particularly noted.

He was the famous Vieri de' Cerchi, pompous — "the braying ass of the Porta," one of his enemies would call him — self-assured, and self-satisfied, but nevertheless one of the important Guelph leaders. We have already noted Vieri as one of those who fought at Campaldino, and we will see him again later. At that time he would be "the businessman in politics," and no more successful in that unfamiliar calling than most businessmen. But he was a leading banker in this city of moneymen.

Folco — as far as could be judged correctly — only associated with the best.

« *3* »

But it was not with Folco's associates nor was it with Folco's will that Dante was concerned deeply when Folco died.

It was with the feelings and sorrow of a young lady. It was with the feelings and sorrow of "Bice, who was his daughter and the wife of Simone de' Bardi," to whom Folco, who overlooked nothing and no one and certainly not one who was perhaps dearer to him than anyone else, had also left fifty *libbre* even though — since she was married to Simone of the house of Bardi — she was rich in her own right.

He was also concerned with death itself. Death which impartially and undeterred took the just and the unjust, the good and the wicked. Death whose ways and robberies human understanding could not explain.

Dante had been concerned with death before.

"After the departure of this noble lady" — he is speaking of the first lady of the screen — "it was the pleasure of the Lord of the angels to call unto His glory a young lady very lovely in appearance who was held in high esteem in the city, and I looked upon her body bereft of its soul lying in the midst of many ladies who wept their hearts out. Then I remembered that I had once seen her in the presence of my own fair lady, and I could not refrain from writing two sonnets. I called the first of them 'Weep, Lovers!' and the second *Morte villana*."

"Weep, Lovers!" is relatively pedestrian, but *Morte villana* (Churlish death) — incidentally, the second poem Dante called a sonnet when it was something else, in this case a *ballata* — was a deep-felt cry of anguish.

O churlish Death, of pity enemy,
Thou who of grief the timeless mother be,
Thou ineluctable in thy dire judging,
Since thou dost give me cause for sorrowing,
My grave brow furrowing,
My tongue grows weary in but chiding thee.

And since I'd show of grace your beggary,
I must set down and must tell openly
Your wickedness, guilty of every wrong,
Not because from good folk it lieth hid,
But to make angry at it
All those whom Love would nurture tenderly.

Thou hast from this age courtesy removed,
And virtue too, for which all ladies care.
In her gay youth, and loved,
Thou hast, thou hast destroyed this lovely fair,
Nor will I tell you who this lady might be
Except by naming her good qualities.
He only who merits heaven, and to it flies,
Can hope — and can deserve — her company.

All this about a person whose only power to inspire Dante's pen came from the fact that he had once seen her with Beatrice!

It was a secondhand and vicarious sorrow which called forth these compelling words.

But now *morte villana* had struck again, and this time it had struck someone closer to him — Beatrice's father.

He reacted predictably, and has set down the circumstances of his reaction.

"It was the custom of the city for women with women and men with men to go together to the place of mourning, and therefore many ladies had assembled where Beatrice was."

They knelt before the bier, paying their respects to Folco, and then said the usual perhaps perfunctory but necessary words of condolence.

The men waited outside, Dante among them, and as he waited some of the ladies who had left the place of mourning passed close beside him.

They talked of Beatrice.

"She was weeping piteously," said one of them.

"She is so grief stricken," said another, "that anyone who sees her almost dies of pity herself."

Then they went on their way, and Dante suddenly felt his own eyes flood with tears. He put his hands before his face so that no one would see him. He too started to walk away.

But it occurred to him that if he remained where he was he would hear more of Beatrice, and so he stayed.

"And as I tarried in the same place, other ladies passed by near me, and I heard them discoursing."

One of them said this:

"How can we ever be happy again now that we have seen her sorrow?"

After that still others came by, and one of them saw Dante.

"Look, he is weeping too. He is weeping as much as he would have if he had seen her even as we have."

Said another:

"He is not himself. He is like another person. His sorrow has completely changed him."

Dante listened to them.

"And as I thought about what they said, I decided to put it down. I decided to put into rhyme how it would have been if I had questioned them, and they had replied. I made two sonnets. I called the first of them *Voi che portate* (Ye who do bear) and the second *Se' tu colui* (Art thou the one?)."

Sonnet number one — Dante to the ladies:

> Ye who do bear yourself in humble wise
> And with your downcast eyes deep sorrow show,
> Whence come ye now and whither do ye go,
> Whose pallor makes ye wear compassion's guise?
> Have ye now seen my lady, seen her eyes
> Weeping, her visage drenched with tears of woe? . . .

Sonnet number two — the ladies to Dante:

> Art thou the one who of our lady fair
> Oft spoke, but who now speaks to us alone?
> This doth thy voice and way of speech declare,
> But thy look makest thee seem another one . . .

It cannot be said that either sonnet was more than adequate. Even "Weep, Lovers" with its opening line "Weep now, ye lovers; Love himself doth weep" had more lift to it, and that poem, which I have already called pedestrian, was written — as was *Morte villana* — about someone who meant relatively little to him.

Why? What was the reason? This is something I have tried to puzzle out.

Here we have Dante's first intimate, indeed almost personal, encounter with sorrow — I exclude the death of his mother because he was so young when she died, and that of his father since his father, although respected, was not really close to him — and suddenly we find him almost tongue-tied.

Why, at this impact, did words fail him?

There is no question that he was moved by Folco's death and even more by Beatrice's grief for it, for if we probe the halting words and concepts we can find deep feeling. But he could not bring it to the surface.

Perhaps — this is the only suggestion I can make — it was too close to him. He who would later be able to lay bare the inmost recesses of his soul with almost photographic accuracy was now still too inexperienced to do this. He could only be good — at the age of twenty-five — when he was literary. But you cannot be literary when the scalpel probes your heart.

« 4 »

Not long after Folco's death, Dante fell ill himself.

"It came to pass," he said, "that a grievous infirmity fell upon some part of my body. For many days, I suffered the most bitter pain. In consequence, I became so weak that it behooved me to lie upon my bed motionless. I was like one who cannot stir."

What the illness was he does not say, and obviously it is impossible for us to diagnose it nearly seven centuries later, especially since he does not give many, if any, of its symptoms.

But clearly it brought with it a high fever, and with the fever came delirium. Through the Yuletide — which is almost always dank in Florence — and on into January, he tossed and fretted under his covers in the Casa degli Alighieri. His nights were an uneasy sequence of sleeping, waking, and then sleeping again. In the daytime, dawn moved toward noon and then on to the early darkening of a winter even. Everything was at once blurred and exquisitely clear. Sometimes the very bed curtains seemed like the tapestries of an undeterminable corridor.

And then suddenly he struggled through pain to a cool vision.

"I say that on the ninth day" — but we must always suspect the accuracy of nine when Dante uses it about Beatrice — "a thought came to me which was of my lady."

He thought about her and began to live again.

"I thought about her for a while, and then took up my feeble hold on life."

As he did this, he began to feel sorry for himself, as ill people when they are beginning to recover often do.

"For seeing how little was my power to endure — even in health it was little — I began to weep within myself because of my weakness."

Then suddenly the dagger thrust, and after that the nightmare.

"Do you realize" — this clutched at him as he said in inwardly — "that Beatrice herself will one day die?"

Beatrice herself! It was as if it had actually happened.

"And thereat" — as he tossed on his bed — "such great dismay did take possession of me that I closed my eyes and shook and suffered like a man possessed.

"Then I had the vision. I saw the faces of women with disheveled hair and they cried: 'Thou shalt die too! Thou shalt die too!' After them came other women even more horrible in appearance, who said to me: 'Thou art already dead.'"

At this time his fever-ridden mind began to wander.

"I did not know where I was but the disheveled ladies swept past me, weeping and wondrously sad, and I thought that I saw the sun grow dark and the stars begin to show and I thought too that there were mighty earthquakes."

Then, in his feverish tossing, he imagined that a friend came to him.

"Beatrice will die? Beatrice is dead already!"

At this, Dante imagined that he gazed heavenward and there saw a multitude of angels. "In front of them was an exceedingly white small cloud. They sang hosannas."

Now he doubted no longer.

"True it is our lady lieth dead."

Why, then, should he himself want to live any longer?

"Sweetest Death, come to me and be not churlish!"

(*Non m'esser villana* — here we have *morte villana* again.)

"Now come unto me who do so greatly desire thee. Thou seest that I already wear thy color."

That, at any rate, is how he recorded it later. But more probably, weakened by his illness and once again yielding to self-pity, he buried his head in his pillow.

"I want to die!" he probably sighed. "I want to die. There is nothing to live for."

Nor was what followed thereafter out of pattern.

"As I uttered these words, a young and gentle lady who was joined to me by closest ties of kinship" — it is generally thought that this was Dante's sister Tana — "stood beside my bed, and believing that these words were a lament for the anguish of my sickness" — which, of course, if you think about it, they really were — "began herself to weep with dread."

At this, the other ladies in the room, realizing from Tana's tears that Dante himself was in great anguish, led her away from him, and knowing that he was dreaming, drew toward him and tried to awaken him.

"Sleep no more, and do not be discomforted."

"Beatrice!"

Then of his own accord he opened his eyes and knew that it had all been delirium.

He turned to them, abashed yet grateful.

"He seemed like dead," said one.

"Let us comfort him," said another.

"What," asked a third, "were you afraid of?"

"I will tell you."

Then he related all that he had seen in his dream.

"But I concealed the name of the most gentle one."

He forgot that he had already cried it out.

Later on, when he was "healed of this infirmity," he decided to make a poem about it.

"I proposed to say words about what had happened to me, and therefore composed a *canzone* about it."

> A lady, kindhearted and of tender age,
> And decked with every human excellency . . .

The whole poem is one hundred twenty-eight lines long, and in these one hundred twenty-eight lines it sets down the episode very literally.

This is what Dante intended it to do.

"This *canzone* has two parts," he explained. "In the first I say, speaking to a person I do not name, how I was roused from an empty dream by certain ladies; and in the second I say how I told it to them. The second part begins here: *Mentr'io pensava* [While I was thinking].

"The first part divides in two. In the first I tell what certain ladies, and what one alone, said because of my dream during the time preceding my return to real consciousness. In the second I tell what these ladies said after my delirium had ended. It begins here: *Era la voce mia* [So sorrowful was my voice].

"Then when I say *Mentr'io pensava*, I say how I told this vision to them, and concerning that, I make two parts. In the first I tell about this vision as it happened. In the second, after telling them at what point they awakened me, I thank them and thus end. And this second part begins here: *Voi mi chiamaste* [Ye did recall me]."

These comments illustrate another Dante characteristic. No matter what he did, he knew what he was doing, and, at least as far as his writing is concerned, he was always in control. Here is a poem that arose out of one of his more moving experiences — a poem which truly came from the heart — yet he takes it apart as if he were a professor of the most pedantic nature presenting it in the classroom. Nor was this the only poem which he so analyzed. There are twenty-nine others in the *Vita Nuova* — from which this comes — and three in the later *Convivio*. Of each one, Dante tells either what he meant in it or what he decided later that he meant. But even in the *Commedia*, the hand is firmly on the rein. Without straying to the right or to the left, he takes even this poem down a chosen path.

« 5 »

In the meantime, life — and Dante's part in it — moved on.

It has been suggested — and this is based on accepting Dante's account as reasonably accurate — that he fell ill in late December, and that he had his disturbing fever-dreams just after what we call, though the medieval Florentines did not, the first of the year. But we do not have to pin it down so exactly. It is enough to say that he became sick in winter when, as has already been noted, the houses were cheerless and dank, when there was sometimes snow but more often penetratingly chill rain, and when the sky, which in other seasons was cerulean, became a dismal and discouraging gray.

It seems evident that his recovery took place in early spring. At this time, the tops of the surrounding mountains were still white (often, this white melted in the day, was renewed each night), but the countryside was precociously blooming. Around the already ploughed fields (this he would have to imagine, for he was still in the city), the *biancospino*, or white hawthorn, was getting ready its exuberant foam. Tiny little yellow violets grew in the shady places and there were crocuses of every imaginable hue. The myrtle was in bloom and everywhere there were jonquils and narcissus. It was perhaps too early for the nightingale to have commenced his throaty song, but the Franciscan bird, the skylark, with his hood and his brown robe, was not silent. You could hear the cuckoo and perhaps the turtledove.

Even here on the small paved square which fronted the Torre del Castagno there was renewed life and a feeling of expectancy.

It was a time in which to get well.

Dante did.

Pale from his recent illness, he sat in front of his house in a rectangle of white sunlight.

He watched the people go by.

Thus watching them, he had another of his encounters.

"After this empty dream of mine, it happened that, sitting in a certain place deep in thought, I felt my heart begin to tremble as if I had been in the presence of my lady. Then there came to me a vision of Love, and I thought I saw him coming from that place where she was, and that he said joyously to my heart: 'Remember to bless the day when I took thee captive, for thou hast cause to do so.' And when I heard this, I thought that my heart was so glad that it did not seem to be my own. So changed was it from its former state.

"And shortly after these words in which my heart spoke using the tongue of Love, I saw a gentle lady coming toward me. She was famed for her beauty and at one time had been the much beloved ladylove of my first friend. The name of this lady was Giovanna but because of this same beauty — or so people believe — she was given the name of Primavera, and this is what people called her."

Guido Cavalcanti's Giovanna-Primavera again!

"Then looking beyond her I saw the wondrous Beatrice approach."

They passed very close by, "the one after the other," and speaking to their pale friend, one hopes.

"And as they thus did, I thought Love spoke again in my heart. He said to me: 'The first is named Primavera only because of the way she came today. For I moved the giver of her name to call her Primavera, which is to say "she will come first [*prima verra*]" on that day when Beatrice will reveal herself to the vision of her faithful one. And if you will consider her true name, that also means Primavera, for Giovanna comes from John and John was the forerunner of the True Light and he said: "I am a voice crying in the wilderness to make ready for the coming of the Lord."' Then I thought Love said these further words to me: 'He who thinks deeply would call Beatrice Love, for she truly resembles me.'

"Whereupon," concluded Dante, "I decided to write something in rhyme about this, and sent it to my first friend. For I believed that his heart was still drawn to the beauty of this gentle Primavera."

In spite of his strayings down a garden pathway with Mandette!

He did.

He wrote a sonnet.

> I felt within my heart stir suddenly
> A fond, dear spirit which had slumbered there.
> Then from afar came Love. He did appear
> So joyous I scarce knew who he might be.
> And thus he spoke: "Now honor pay to me!"

Laughing, what time he said this, at each word.
He stayed with me awhile, till gazing toward
The place whence he had come miraculously,
I Monna Vanna and Monna Bice beheld.
Unto the place in which I was, they came,
One marvel the other marvel following.
Then Love did say — by memory this is spelled:
"This Primavera, Love that hath for name.
She is so like to me in everything."

But no sooner had he composed this poem than he began to have certain reservations.

He set them down.

"Here a person worthy of having his difficulties explained might be perplexed. He might wonder what I was about when I spoke of Love as if he were not merely an intelligent but a corporeal being."

For this, said Dante, is false. Love does not exist as a being but as the quality of a being.

Yet Dante speaks of him as a being.

"I speak of him as coming from afar, and inasmuch as coming implies locomotion and — according to the Philosopher — only a body can move, it is apparent that I assume Love to be a body. I also say that he laughed and that he spoke. These things being peculiar to human beings, it also appears that I assume him to be a man."

But how could he justify doing this?

"In order to make such things plain, be it first understood that of old there were no versifiers of Love in the vulgar tongue, but only in the Latin tongue. Nor have many years passed since poets in the common tongue appeared for the first time."

One hundred and fifty years, Dante estimated.

"And the first one that began to compose in the vernacular tongue was moved to do this because he wished to make his words intelligible to a lady who had difficulty in understanding Latin verses."

But "they who compose in rhyme are no other than poets in the vernacular," and since "it is right and seemly" that greater license be vouchsafed to poets than to writers of prose, it is right and seemly for them to make use of it.

It is right and seemly for them to speak to animate beings as if they had sense and reason, or to make them speak to each other or even to address imaginary beings or abstract qualities. This the classic poets had done. Virgil had addressed the winds in the person of Aeolus. Lucan had spoken of Rome as an animate being. Horace had even carried on a conversation with his own poetic ability.

"Tell me, O muse!" Horace had cried.

Modern poets had every right to do the same.

But only when it was useful and necessary.

"And in order that no witless person may take advantage of what I have said, I say that none of these poets spoke without good reason, nor should those who now write rhymes speak this way either, unless in their minds they have an interpretation of what they have said. For it would be a crying shame if anyone should in his lines make use of figures of speech or rhetorical adornment and when he was later asked not be able to explain the real meaning.

"But," concluded Dante acidly, "my first friend and I know of many who rhyme in this stupid manner."

Quite a tirade to be appended as a footnote to a love poem!

But, once again, entirely in character.

But this sonnet plays another role in the Dante story besides serving as a springboard for a lecture on his theory of poetry. It also expresses, or at least hints at, a shift of emphasis in Dante's attitude toward Beatrice.

What are its most significant lines?

> I *Monna* Vanna and *Monna* Bice beheld.
> Unto the place in which I was they came,
> One marvel the other marvel following.
> Then Love did say — by memory this is spelled:
> "This Primavera, Love that hath for name.
> She is so like to me in everything."

It will be observed that *Monna* is italicized.

"Italian scholars say," writes P. H. Wicksteed, "that though maiden ladies may be addressed as 'Madonna,' only married women can be described as 'Monna.' Beatrice was now married."

We, of course, do not need this help to know that. Folco's will makes it plain that she had been married for at least three years.

But this was the first time that Dante addressed her as a married woman, and the only time before *Paradiso* VII that he called her Bice.

He also put her in the company of Monna Vanna, and certainly Vanna was something quite a great deal more than the far-off and idealized lady of a poet's vision. Presumptively, she was not merely the dark lady of Guido Cavalcanti's sonnets but his mistress.

She was flesh and blood. She was accessible. She was a woman.

Did Dante, as he saw Folco's daughter walking with Vanna, put her, even if briefly, even if only in imagination, in the same category?

He was young — but not too young — and we have already had many reasons to know that he was far from unsusceptible.

On that lovely spring morning, did his pulses beat more than just a little faster?

Had the one who made them beat thus come some part of the way toward earth from Heaven?

I personally believe that she had.

It was not, however, a mood which lasted for long.

Although for a short moment Beatrice may have seemed to him another Vanna — or another lady of the screen — he soon returned to his old distant adoration. March became April, April became May, and he returned to his old dedication. He became again the poet celebrating his *princesse lointaine*. He returned to seeking happiness by praising her.

He did this in his old way, but with greater skill.

Commenting on the Vanna-Bice sonnet — and not without a modicum of self-praise — he wrote as follows:

"This gentle lady of whom the preceding words were spoken came to such favor among people that when she passed by, everybody ran to behold her. This brought great joy to me. And when she came near to any man, modesty so possessed his heart that he dared not lift his eyes nor respond to her greeting.

"I say that she showed herself so gracious and so pleasing that everyone who looked at her felt within his heart a sweetness so soft and so seemly that they knew not how to describe it. No one could ever look at her without being constrained to sigh. These and things even more wonderful proceeded from her by her power. For this reason — and because I wanted to sing in her honor again — it became my purpose to write down words which should make understood the wonderful and excellent effects she had."

To do so, he wrote this sonnet:

> So seemly and so modest, I aver,
> My lady is when she to others doth speak
> That every tongue there is grows dumb and weak
> And not a single eye dares look at her.
> When she is praised, she goes upon her way
> And still wears her humility as a gown.
> She is like one from heaven to earth come down,
> Its miracle upon earth to display.
> She is so wondrous she enraptureth
> Who looketh on her, and a sweetness gives
> No one can understand who doth not prove.
> Upon her lips there moves and lives
> A spirit so full of gentleness and love
> That to the soul it says: "Sigh!" under its breath.

« 6 »

But it was not merely upon dazzled young men that Beatrice cast her transfiguring spells and exerted her so admirable powers.

She was beloved by the young women who strolled with her and sang with her too.

This Dante also set down in rhyme.

> He sees salvation plainly, who doth see
> My ladylove midst other ladies fair,
> For those who go with her constrainéd are
> To thank God for her grace most reverently.
> Yea, of such great virtue is her beauty
> That other ladies envy never feel,
> For it with love doth vesture her full well,
> And with good breeding and faith wonderfully.
> Just seeing her humbleth everyone
> And doth not only make her seem lovely and kind
> But honors all the rest who do stand nigh,
> And in her acts such gentleness is shown
> That no one is there who can bring her to mind
> And thereupon not for love's sweetness sigh.

Two lines of this should be repeated.

> *E sua bieltate di tanta virtute*
> *Che nulla invidia all'altre ne procede* . . .

> Yea, of such great virtue is her beauty
> That other ladies envy never feel . . .

Compliment could hardly go higher. For if Beatrice was the reigning beauty of Florence, and if she gathered all the other beauties around her, and if none were jealous of her, then she must indeed have been a paragon.

As Dante believed her to have been!

Brush stroke by brush stroke, the portrait was being incomparably limned.

But something was still needed to complete it.

Dante, who used his head as well as his heart, knew what it was.

"A little while later, I began to think one day of what I had said of my lady in these two sonnets, and it came to my mind that I had not yet told of the effect she had on me, and that, therefore, I had not yet completed my speaking. I decided to write down something which should tell how completely I was in her power and what her virtue wrought upon me."

But he "could not relate this in the brevity of a sonnet" and so he began a *canzone*.

> So long, so very long hath held me Love
> And me accustomed to his mastery
> That as he long ago was cruel to me
> Now he is kind . . .

He continued slowly. This was to be the final word and it had to be worked out carefully.

> Therefore when he bereaveth me so of my power

A pause for thought.

> That do my spirits seem to flee in haste,
> Then does my frail soul feel
> Such sweetness that my face turns white as death.
> Thereat Love takes me so greatly in his power
> That he makes my sighs speak for me.
> They go forth, calling
> Upon my lady to grant her grace to me again.
> This she does every time she sees me
> So modestly it passeth understanding.

One line.
Two lines.
Ten lines.
Then there came a knock at the door.
Someone stood there with incredible tidings.
"I was still at the purpose of my *canzone*" — still slowly and painfully scratching out the lines — "and had finished only this stanza when the Lord of Justice called this gentle lady to dwell in glory under the ensign of that queen, the Virgin Mary, whose name was in very great reverence on the lips of this gentle Beatrice."

Beatrice was dead! The lovely, the lighthearted, the gay, the beautiful one lay, pink and white wax, and would no longer either scorn him or smile at him.

When did this happen?

"I say that according to the Arabian style, her most noble soul departed in the first hour of the ninth day of the month; and according to the

Syrian style, it departed on the ninth month of the year, because the first month there is Tisrin I, which with us is October. And according to our style, she departed in that era — that is to say the years of our Lord — wherein the perfect number was completed nine times in that century in which she was placed, and she was of the Christians of the thirteenth century."

This is a curious way of describing something so intimately important, but it must be remembered that Dante wrote these words sometime later when his feelings had grown less intense.

Convert the Arabian calendar — about which Dante had learned from the writings of Alfraganus, who was born in Samarkand (then called Fergana, hence the Persian astronomer's name) — into the Western calendar and you will find, since their year began in October, that their ninth month was our June.

It was our eighth of June, for, as Alfraganus also tells us, the Arabs began their day at sunset, and therefore the first hour of the ninth day their style was the first hour after sunset on the eighth day our style.

The year was 1290. Ten is the perfect number, and 1290 was that year in the thirteenth century in which the number ten had come up for the ninth time.

On June 8, 1290, and in the early evening, then — almost six months after Folco's death and not much more than six days after Dante's twenty-fifth birthday — Beatrice left this mortal world, and what he had dreamed about in his nightmare became reality.

There is a theory — advanced by Wicksteed and others — that she died with the poet's name upon her lips.

This is pleasingly romantic — it would be heartwarming to give to it complete credence — but it has to be acknowledged that there is no specific substantiating evidence either from Dante or from anyone else.

Yet there is at least circumstantial evidence that he had become important to her.

Speaking of her death, Dante says that he could relate more but would not for three reasons. First, to do so would not comport with the purpose of what he wrote. Second, his pen lacked the ability to describe it as it should be described. And third — and this should be noted and weighed — it would not be fitting to do this, "for so doing, it would behoove me to become a praiser of myself, which thing is both unseemly and blameworthy."

But how could Dante, by talking of Beatrice, praise himself?

Only if she had great faith in his ability, and had spoken of it warmly. "You are good. You are gifted. There is no one more talented than you in Florence. But — and by what you say you feel for me — you could do better."

Even in her last days she may have said something like this, even as she actually lay dying.

But that is something we can only guess at. We can never really know.

VII

A Lady at a Window

I T is not always easy to measure grief, and this is particularly so when the grief is that of a poet. For a poet is not ever immune from being carried away by his own words, and therefore from being led astray by them from the straight and narrow path of literal accuracy.

Yet there is no doubt that Dante was deeply shaken.

He would have been shaken even if he had not loved Beatrice. For here was this young lady of extraordinary beauty and charm, with warm and laughing eyes, with a gay and generous nature, and, with all that, wealthy and well married. One who, as the modern saying goes, had everything. And then almost without warning she lay hushed and still in a silent chamber, no breath coming from her delicately modeled nostrils, her faint smile immobilized forever.

No longer would she come dancing up to him — or to anyone else — at a May Day festival, and thus and very early do her first bewitching. No longer would he — or would anyone else — see her walk along the Arno clad in gleaming white and in the company of two older women, and just because she walked there add something to the ineffable season. No longer would she tilt her chin loftily as she looked at him — or at anyone else — and thus prove that she was as feminine as she was inimitable. No longer would she lift up his heart on an effulgent Florentine morning when she and Vanna strolled past him as he was recovering from his illness.

It has been observed that we never do anything consciously for the last time without a feeling of loss, and even the most obtuse of us must surely recognize that we have done something for the last time when we look upon the pale image of someone whose life has closely impinged upon our own.

Beatrice's life had indeed closely impinged upon that of Dante, and so even if he had not loved her, he would have felt this loss. Even if he had not loved her, he would have been moved.

« 2 »

But Dante did love Beatrice, although he seems to have loved her in a curious and complex fashion which is difficult to understand even when you set it in the framework of the love conventions of Dante's own time. It is almost impossible for those of us who judge it within the framework of the love mores of today.

He did indeed love Beatrice in part as an abstraction.

He did indeed love her as the unattainable and therefore as the ideal and the to-be-sought-for.

But he also loved her as a woman and as Bice Portinari.

(Perhaps only at times, but certainly sometimes.)

She was a saint enshrined in the niche of a cathedral. But she was also Eve and Isolt.

And he knew too what it was like to love someone and to lose someone who was also Isolt and also Eve. Otherwise he could not have written his story of Paolo and Francesca.

Let us look at this story for a moment.

"You must know," wrote the so-called Anonymous Florentine, "that for a long time there was war between Messer Guido of Polenta and Messer Malatesta da Verrucchio, the lord of Rimini, but when both sides had grown weary of fighting, they made peace by mutual agreement, and in order that it might be the better observed, they concluded a family alliance."

Madonna Francesca, the daughter of Messer Guido, was to be wedded to Gianciotto, the son of Messer Malatesta.

But unfortunately Gianciotto "although wise and prudent" was physically deformed — his name means "limping John" — and when Guido was warned that his daughter might not accept him for husband, he arranged to have the groom's handsome brother Paolo take his place as a proxy.

"This is your intended husband," she was told.

She fell in love with him forthwith.

"But when the marriage had taken place and she found herself by the side of Gianciotto and not Paolo, she was ill pleased. She perceived that she had been tricked, and she would not lay aside the love she had given to Paolo. Whereupon he, although at first it was repugnant to him, let himself return her love."

The inevitable, of course, happened. One day they were secluded together and read about Lancelot and Guinevere.

"So reading, they yielded to their desires. And as they continued to do so on various occasions, a retainer of Gianciotto's observed it."

This retainer wrote Gianciotto, who was absent on public business. Gianciotto returned posthaste and one day surprised his brother and his wife.

In his hand, he held a weapon.

Not quite gallantly, Paolo tried to flee.

"And certainly he would have escaped had not a link in the habergeon he was wearing caught on the point of a nail in the trapdoor, and he in this way remained hanging. Gianciotto rushed at him with a halberd, the lady ran between them, and Gianciotto as he brought down this weapon, thinking to strike Paolo, struck his wife and killed her. Then in like manner he killed his brother."

But it is not this relatively commonplace triangle which makes the story of this particular set of star-crossed lovers significant. It is the deep and sensitive feeling which Dante puts into it as he recounted it in *Inferno* V.

There, blown before the wind which symbolizes the lightness of their conduct, he sees most of the famous lovers of history.

"Who are they?" he asks Virgil.

> "The first one of the ones there, of whom news
> Thou wouldest have," he said to me thereat,
> "The empress was of many languages . . .
> She is Semiramis of whom thou readest.
> She succeeded Ninus and she was his wife.
> Hers was the land where now the sultan rules.
> The other is she [*Dido*] who loving slew herself
> And thus betrayed the ashes of Sichaeus.
> Then Cleopatra comes, that lustful lady.
> See Helen who did bring so long and evil
> A time, and see too the great Achilles . . .
> See Paris, see Tristan . . ."

But among the many who were tossed hither and yon by the infernal hurricane, he noted some who were more familiar to him.

Two in particular.

"Poet," he said to Virgil, "I would speak to them."

"Thou shalt," replied Virgil. "When they come nearer, pray to them in the name of love."

Dante did, and they responded.

> As doves who are by their deep longing called
> On wings wide-poised and strong to their sweet nest
> Do flight them through the air as they do wish,
> These flew forth from the band where Dido was
> And came to us through the malignant air.

One of them spoke.

> "O living creature, gracious and benign,
> Who moves to visit us through the perse air,
> Us who did tint the world all bloody red,
> If He who king is of the universe
> Our friend were, we would pray Him for thy peace,
> Since thou hast pity for our perverse woe."

Then she told her story, which was already known to him.

> "Sitteth that city in which I was born
> Upon that seashore where the Po descends
> To find him peace with all his tributaries."

In other words, she was born in Rimini, which was on the Adriatic, and with some stretching of the imagination was not far from the Po mouth.

Later she came to Ravenna.

What befell her there?

> "Love that doth swiftly take captive the gentle heart
> Did make that man a prisoner with the fair body
> That hath been reft from me. The manner still grieves me.
> Love which absolves no person beloved from loving
> Made me so greatly long to do him pleasure
> That, as thou seest, the longing is with me still.
> Love did conduct us to a single death.
> May Caïna await the one who took life from us."

Dante bowed his head. He bowed it in such grief that Virgil asked him what he was brooding about.

> When I began, I thus replied: "Woe's me!
> How many the sweet thoughts, the sweet desires
> That brought those two unto their dolorous end!"

Then he turned to Francesca and asked her how it came about.

> And she to me: "There is no greater woe
> Than to recall thee of a happier time
> In time of misery, as thy teacher knows . . .
> We read together to our delight one day
> Of Lancelot and what love moved him to.
> We were alone and suspected not our hearts,
> Yet many a time the reading urged our eyes
> Together, and it made our faces pale,
> But not till one point did it conquer us.
> When we read that the longed-for smile was kissed
> By such a famous lover, then that person
> From whom I never now shall find me parted
> Did kiss me on the mouth, all trembling.
> Gallehault was the book, and he who wrote it.
> That day we did not further read in it.

This is very different from the lurid story told by a chronicler with a taste for scandal and sensation (the Anonymous Florentine). It is instead love written about by someone who understood what love was and what it incredibly did. It is love written about by someone who had learned what love was — and not from a book and not from a troubadour tradition but from his own deep and innermost feelings.

For that reason it is useful to look over again some of its more penetrating phrases.

La bella persona che mi fu tolta. The fair body that hath been reft from me.

Amor, ch'a nullo amato amar perdona. Love which absolves no person beloved from loving.

Oh lasso! Quanti dolci pensier, quanto disio menò costoro al doloroso passo! Woe's me! How many the sweet thoughts, the sweet desires that brought those two unto their dolorous end!

Nessun maggior dolore che ricordarsi del tempo felice ne la miseria. There is no greater woe than to recall thee of a happier time in time of misery.

Soli eravamo e sanza alcun sospetto. We were alone and suspected not our hearts.

Questi, che mai da me non fia diviso. That person from whom I never now shall find me parted.

Love poetry more remarkable has not ever been set down, for it takes the gamut of deep feeling and from it borrows the notes to create an intricate music wherein longing, the need to love, frustration, sorrow, and, incredibly, triumphant joy are so inextricably blended that not a note could be added or subtracted without flawing perfection.

But these are Dante's songs, needs to love, frustrations, sorrows, and triumphant joys. He must have known them. He must have experienced them.

It must, therefore, be recorded that at least one of the phrases that expressed them was used by Dante when he wrote *in morte di Beatrice* (about Beatrice's death).

> *Partissi della sua bella persona*
> *Piena di grazia l'anima gentile.*
>
> From her fair body did go forth her soul
> That was so lovely and so full of grace.

Bella persona!

About Francesca this was said — and about Beatrice.

The fact should here be noted, so that no one will fall into any misconception — even at the risk of repetition it should be noted — that Messer Simone de' Bardi, the prosperous and well-established banker, the Guelph councillor, the future Black intriguer, had no reason whatsoever to fear that Dante might play Paolo's role; and that he may even have smiled — and been a little flattered since it implied he had good judgment when he selected a wife — at the spate of sonnets, *ballate*, and *canzoni* which the gravely good-looking poet had composed about Bice.

(They were now on the lips of almost every gay young man and young lady of the city.)

But it is also true that a fair body must be worn by someone flesh-and-blood and mortal.

Beatrice.

When she died, Dante felt a flesh-and-blood and mortal grief.

« 3 »

As was to be expected, he expressed it in words.

"*Quomodo sedet sola civitas plena populo,*" he began. "*Facta est quasi vidua domina gentium!*" How doth the city sit solitary that was full of people! How is she become as a widow, she that was great among the nations!

This, uttered by the prophet Jeremiah and taken from the first verse of the first chapter of his Lamentations, is all that has been permitted to survive of a long letter describing the city as "left, as it were, widowed and deprived of all worthiness." It was addressed to "the chief people of the land."

Dante deliberately suppressed the rest of the epistle.

He gave a reason.

"And if anyone should reprove me because I do not here set down the words which follow, I give this for an excuse. My intention was from the beginning not to write other than in the vulgar tongue."

Not to write other than about Beatrice, that is.

"And a like intent," he said, "I know had my friend" — i.e., Guido Cavalcanti — "to whom I am writing this" — i.e., dedicating all that he said about Beatrice — "namely that I should write to him only in the vulgar tongue.

"Therefore," he continued, "inasmuch as the words that follow those cited are all in Latin, it would be beside the purpose to write them."

It is reasonably convincing, but there may have been another reason too.

Because the letter *was* in Latin, and because it was addressed to the magistrates of Florence, it is not only possible but probable that it was official rather than personal, and that it was not merely addressed *to*, but written *for* the city's "people of importance." The Portinari, after all, were a prominent family; Folco had been an outstanding citizen; and Beatrice herself was one of Florence's most loved young ladies. Public condolences were in order, and Dante was the obvious choice to give them expression. As will be seen, it would not be the last time he wrote a letter of this sort, sometimes even signing it with another person's name.

But Dante's grief was personal too, and he expressed it in a personal manner.

Here too Boccaccio helps us. He writes this in his *Trattatelo in Laude di Dante* (Treatise in Praise of Dante):

"As everybody can plainly understand, there is nothing stable in this world, but if there be anything which is especially subject to change, it is our life. A little too much cold, a little too much heat, and before we know it we are brought from being to not being, the weight of which universal law Dante must needs learn from the death of another person before he learned it from his own.

"The beautiful Beatrice had nearly reached the end of her twenty-fourth year when, as it pleased Him who is all powerful, she left the anguish of this world and departed to the glory which her own merits had prepared for her. At her departing, Dante was left to such sorrow, grief, and tears that many of those nearest to him believed that there would be not end to them except his death. The days were like nights and the nights were like days, and no hour of either passed without laments, without sighs, without copious tears. Because of his weeping, because of the pain which his heart felt deep within it, and because he now took no care of himself, he seemed like a man distraught to those who looked at him. He was lean, unshaven, and so completely transformed that not only his friends but everyone who saw him felt pity for him, although, to be sure, while this tearful life of his lasted he let himself be seen by few others than his friends."

The author of the *Decameron*, of course, exaggerated — and likewise he wrote in the manner which had come to be expected of one who had written so many popular romances.

(Not merely the "hundred merry tales" on which his reputation is based, but the *Filocolo*, which retells the old French love story of Fleur and Blanchefleur, and *Amorous Fiammetta*, which is about his own youthful dalliance with the daughter of the king of Naples, and the *Filostrato*, which told Chaucer — and Shakespeare — about Troilus and Cressida.)

But even under the flowery language, there lurked some basic truth. Dante, after the earth-shaking June 9 which had taken Beatrice, was not the Dante he had been before.

It is not surprising, then, that he became gaunt and haggard, and it is not surprising that he neglected his appearance and his former and well-established concern for careful dress.

Nor is it surprising that, at least as far as was possible for a man who had a family and financial cares, he withdrew to solitude and brooding.

Even under ordinary circumstances — again we rely upon Boccaccio — "he was especially fond of being alone and at a distance from people in order that his contemplation might not be interrupted."

But these were not ordinary circumstances.

More than once in his many writings, Dante refers to a *solinga camera* — a solitary chamber — to which he could repair. We can assume that it was in the staid medieval house which was reconstructed in modern times at the corner of the Via Dante Alighieri and the Via Santa Margherita. In it there would have been a table (or a desk), a chair, some kind of lamp, quills, parchment, and the ingredients with which to make some exceedingly black ink.

Thither — and as his soul did harbor earthquake — he betook himself with increasing frequency, and there he let his thoughts take shape.

Finally they did.

"After mine eyes had wept for a long time and were so weary that I could not ease my sorrow, I thought that I would ease it with some dolorous words. I purposed, therefore, to make a *canzone*, wherein, lamenting, I should discourse of her."

"*Gli occhi dolente*," it began.

Those eyes which do bewail the heart's deep woe
Have in their weeping suffered such great pain
That they by weeping have been conqueréd.
And now if I should wish to make grief go —
My grief so great that by it I am slain —
Laments by me must needs be utteréd.
And since I do recall I spoke and said
About my lady when she was alive,
O gentle ladies, to ye willingly,
To no one else should now my speaking be
Save to the gentle hearts which in you thrive.
Then weeping will I speak of her, for she
Hath unto heaven gone upon swift wing
And with me hath left Love all sorrowing.

Unto high heaven hath Beatrice gone,
To that realm where the angels do know peace.
She dwells with them. Ye ladies hath she left . . .

There are five stanzas in all, each fourteen lines long, followed by a short concluding *tornata* of six lines which bids the "song" go forth upon its weeping way and find again the dames and damsels to which its sisters — that is, Dante's earlier poems about Beatrice — had once brought gladness. A total of seventy-six lines or perhaps five hundred words. In the sedate, compact measures of its deep feeling — but again, like anything else by Dante it must be read in Italian to get its full value — in its gravely expressed emotion, in the very calmness of its grief, it is clearly as good as anything which Dante had so far written. Indeed, in many ways it was his first great poem.

It was also one of his more important ones. For it marked the first, but far from tentative, steps toward what would be Dante's final attitude toward Beatrice. It was in this poem, to be sure, that Dante used the phrase *bella persona* which I so greatly stressed, but it was also in this poem that he first placed Folco's daughter in the empyrean.

"Cold" — he anticipated Boccaccio's words and perhaps even supplied them — "did not take her from us, nor did heat, as is the case with other lovely ladies."

He continued:

It rather was her great benignity.
For so the light of her humility
The heavens pierced, and with such power there shone
That it made marvel the Eternal Sire
So much that to Him came the sweet desire

To summon to Him her perfection.
Yea, He did lift her to His eternal choir,
Because He knew that nowhere on this earth
Was there aught worthy of her gentleness and worth.

God, in other words, did not find heaven complete without her. That is why He took her.

Taken literally it was little more than the lover's ultimate word of praise, and as such it was echoed by at least one other poet who wrote Dante to console him.

"*Gia serai in ciel gita!*" To heaven thou art gone! apostrophized Cino da Pistoia. Dante had said: "*Ita n'è Beatrice in l'alto cielo.*"

Beata l'alma che lassa tal pondo e va nel cielo. Blessed the soul by life's affliction wearied who goes to heaven.

Di che vi stringe il cor . . . che avete in cielo la mente e'l intelletto? With whom do you burden your heart . . . who have in heaven your mind and intellect?

Finally — and this as well as the lines beginning *Beata l'alma* and *Di che vi stringe* was addressed to Dante:

This [*Beatrice's death*] should not evil be
Unto your soul, which still may have the hope
To see her in heaven and be held in her arms.

But Dante's poem must not be taken literally. We must soar as he began to soar. Umberto Cosmo, one of the warmest if not the most scientific of those who have written about Dante, thinks of the poet's whole life after Beatrice's death as a return to her. Its culmination he calls *l'ultima ascesa* — the ultimate ascent. It was a long journey and one that was far from unfaltering, but in the end Dante reached his goal. Although he himself (I think) did not realize it, the journey began with this poem.

« *4* »

In those first days of sorrow and loss, other persons than Dante and the poets of his circle mourned Beatrice, and most of them in their mourning turned to Dante.

One of them was Manetto Portinari, Beatrice's oldest brother and the guardian of her younger brothers and sisters.

This is how Dante reports what he did:

"After this *canzone* had been composed" — i.e., the poem which placed Beatrice in heaven — "there came to me one who as friendship is measured was the closest friend I had after the one I called first, and he was so closely united in kinship to this glorious lady that there was none closer to her. And after he had talked to me for a while, he begged me to compose something for a lady who had died, and he tried to deceive with his words so that it would appear to me that he spoke of another lady who had also died recently."

But Dante was not deceived. He knew Manetto too well and he knew also of the young man's deep affection for his sister.

"Wherefore, perceiving that he was speaking solely of this blessed one, I said that I would do what he had prayed me to, and then having pondered I decided to make a sonnet and to give it to my friend in order that it should appear that it had come from him."

Here it is:

> Come ye, and listen to my every sigh,
> O gentle souls. This pity bids ye do.
> Forth from me, most disconsolate, they go.
> If they did not, of grief I sure would die.
> For lo, these eyes of mine as debtors are —

Debtors! Even a banker's phrase was used!

> And more times than I'd ever wish — to me
> For weeping for my lady piteously.
> I thought to ease my heart in weeping for her.

He continued into the sestet, still speaking for Manetto.

> And very often will you hear them call
> Upon this gentle lady who hath stole
> Unto the high realm by her virtues earned
> As they disprize this world, in the deep pall
> Of gloom which doth enwrap the sorrowing soul,
> Since it by its salvation hath been spurned.

As a tour de force, it was perhaps successful, but on its own merits it was something less than that.

Dante knew this, and he said so plainly.

"After I had composed this sonnet and, realizing who he was to whom I would give it as though it had been written by him, it came to me that it was a poor and naked thing to have set down for a person who was so closely related to so glorious a lady. Therefore even before I gave it to him I composed two stanzas of a *canzone*."

The first was "for him truly" and the other was Dante himself.

"Although," said Dante, "to one who does not look closely both seem to be composed for one person."

But they were not.

"For anyone who does examine them closely will see well that two different persons are speaking, for one does not call her his lady and the other does."

Stanza number one:

> *Quantunque volte, lasso, mi rimembra*
> *Ch'io non debbo giammai*
> *Veder la donna, ond' io vo si dolente* . . .

> How many times, alas, shall I remember
> That I must never more
> The lady see for whom I walk in sorrow . . .

The word to remember is *la*. The speaker is concerned with *the* lady. Stanza number two:

> *E' si reccogli negli meie sospiri*
> *Un suono di pietate*
> *Che va chiamando Morte tuttavia.*
> *A lei si volser tutti i miei desiri,*
> *Quando la donna mia*
> *Fu giunta dalla sua crudelitate* . . .

> There gathers, there is gathered, in my sighs
> A sound of agony
> That goes forth calling Death forevermore.
> To him now turneth all of my desires
> Since my lady
> Has by his cruelty been smitten sore . . .

My lady, note; not *the* lady.

This is curious and very revealing. Here is Dante in the early days of his deep, soul-shaking anguish and he finds time to see (figuratively speaking) how many poems he can inscribe on the head of a pin.

One for Manetto.

One for himself.

And yet this is the same person whose profound, absolutely clear, and absolutely sincere thinking and writing will, when he comes to the *Commedia*, make him without equal or even near equal among the poets of the Western world.

But Dante obviously did more than brood and write introspective poetry for himself and for others during the weeks and months and even during the full year which followed Beatrice's death. Specific information is exceedingly scarce and indeed the only document between 1283 and 1295 dealing with him in any way is one that shows him witnessing a power of attorney which one Guiduccio da Ciampolo da Petragono obtained from Maschio del fu Bernardo so that he might plead a law case in a city court. We know, however, that he was a man of many vocations and avocations, that he was now head of the senior branch of the Alighieri family, and that he was now, having celebrated his twenty-fifth birthday, his own master under any Florentine circumstances.

It seems safe, then, to assume that as he sorrowed he also went about his business as he always had — that he kept accounts and perhaps did a little banking, that he managed the Alighieri farms and other holdings, and that he took care of his brothers and his two sisters, being now their legal guardian.

He had to. There was no one else to do it. He must have, since there is no evidence that his affairs fell into more than the usual Alighieri minor disarray.

Yet as he did this, Beatrice never completely departed from his mind and sometimes she poured into it and enveloped it.

Dante tells us of such a time.

"On that day on which the year was completed when this lady was made one of the citizens of the life eternal, I was sitting in a certain place, and there, as my mind went back to her, I painted a picture of an angel upon certain tablets."

Dante, we thus discover, was a painter as well as a poet.

"And as I was putting it upon canvas, I saw beside me certain people to whom honor was due. They were looking at what I was doing and, according to what I was told later, they had already been there for some time before I noticed them.

"But when I did see them, I arose and greeted them:

" 'Someone was with me but now, and therefore I was in thought.'

"At that they departed and I returned to my work, namely to the drawing of angels."

It is an episode which has arrested the attention of many, not the least of them Robert Browning, who also understood love although in a different manner, and who has written about it in his "One Word More."

Certain people to whom honor was due.

The grave citizens of his own *sesto.* Perhaps a prior wearing his gold chain of authority, for the priors still held their meetings in the Torre del Castagno. Or a gray-bearded and long-robed notary dangling his seal of office. Or a pompous and heavy-set judge or canonist with his haughty mouth and self-assured face and wearing his red gown and cape of vair.

Someone was with me but now.

Who but Beatrice?

Dante's very abstraction makes the story convincing.

"In his studies," reported Boccaccio, and certainly this could include painting, "he was most assiduous both in the time which he gave to them and in the fact that no interruption whatsoever could distract him from them. Indeed, people who are worthy of being believed" — Boccaccio's sources were always "worthy of being believed" — "tell this tale about him which shows how he gave himself to whatever had absorbed his interest.

"He was in Siena once and happened to be in an apothecary's shop when there was brought to him a book which had long been promised to him. It was well thought of by worthy men, but he himself had never seen it.

"Unhappily he did not have the opportunity to take it away with him, and so he leaned himself upon a bench in front of the shop and put the book upon this bench and began to examine it eagerly.

"Now it so happened that on account of a great festival which was being held in the city, a company of well-born young men began and carried out a tournament and passages of arms in the very district where he was and right before his eyes.

"And as is always the case in such affairs, and what with the applause and with the sound of music, the bystanders made a great deal of noise, and although other things happened too which would have distracted the attention of anyone else — dancing by beautiful women, for example, and many youthful sports — there was no one who saw him stir from where he was or even lift his eyes from the book.

"It was about the hour of none" — about three in the afternoon — "that he began to stand before the bench, and it was not until after vespers" — the time of sunset — "that he had read it all and went his way.

"After it someone asked how he could keep his eyes from so fine a celebration which had been carried on before his eyes.

"He replied: 'I heard nothing of it.'

"And so to the questioners a second cause for wonder was not improperly added to the first."

Thus he spent his days, dreaming or doing his business. Then he went back to his poetry.

After his long silence — for there is no evidence that he had composed a single poem since he had written the two for Manetto — he wrote a sonnet.

It had two opening quatrains, both of which he decided to preserve.

> There had, yea, there had come into my mind
> The gentle lady who for her great worth
> Had been placed by the Most High far above earth
> In the heaven of humility where Mary we find.

This obviously was written before Dante had taken up his paintbrushes. But the second opening quatrain was written later.

> There had, yea, there had come into my mind
> That lady gentle, mourned by Love indeed,
> And at that very moment which inclined
> Ye to look on the thing which I then did.

Thus, and characteristically, he took notice of changed circumstances. Then he continued.

> Love, who now in my mind perceived her,
> Was wakened straightway in my wasted heart
> And said unto my sighs: "Go thou! Depart!"
> Wherefore each one went forth, a sorrower.
>
> Weeping, they issued forth from out my breast
> And with the voice that often doth endow
> Sad eyes with dolorous tears that have no end.
> But they that issued forth, and with the most
> Anguish, came saying: "Noble spirit, thou
> A year ago to heaven did ascend!"

Even in Italian, it was a lame and halting effort, hardly less perfunctory than the sonnet which he had written for Beatrice's brother.

But now there was a reason. For in spite of Beatrice's sudden resurgence in the white-hot book of his memory, time had gradually been doing its inexorable work, and his life was now entering on a new, if not a durable, phase.

« 6 »

Boccaccio tries to tell us what it was, but for once he lets his imagination and his prejudices lead him from the facts.

"But even," he writes, "as we see that anguishes, when they are long suffered, become easy to bear, and similarly that in time all things grow less and then perish, it happened that in the course of several months Dante was able to remember without tears that Beatrice was dead. With better judgment, as sorrow began to give place to reason, he came to realize that neither weeping, nor sighs, nor indeed anything else could bring him back his lost lady.

"Accordingly, he set himself to endure the loss of her presence with much patience, nor did much time pass before his sighs too began in great measure to pass, never to return again. He, then, who up to that time had obstinately kept his ears shut to all consolation now began to listen to that which was said for his comfort."

By his friends and his relatives, that is, who were, as we have seen, greatly disturbed about his well-being.

"They found a young girl," continues Boccaccio, "who was suitable for his station, and with arguments that appeared to them the most convincing they made known to him their intention. And without going into all the details, after a long discussion and considerable passage of time their arguments were effective and he was married.

"O blind minds!" cries Giovanni in horror. "O darkened intellects! O vain reasoning of many mortals! What sort of man would he be who, because he said that the heat was too scorching, would take himself from the sweet air of Italy to the burning sands of Libya? Who, to warm himself, would move from the island of Cyprus to the eternal shadows of the Rhodope Mountains? What physician would endeavor to drive away a high fever with fire, or a chill which penetrated to the very marrow of the bones with snow or ice?

"His relatives and friends gave Dante a wife in order that his tears for Beatrice might cease. But although his tears no longer flowed, I am not sure that his love for Beatrice passed away. Indeed, I do not believe it."

The author of the *Decameron* and *Il Corbaccio* (*The Old Crow*, a book which savagely attacked a widow who had made a fool of Giovanni) could have spared himself his eloquence — and his misogyny.

Dante's psychological mood is accurately described, but despite apparent agreement by many noted Dantists, it was not Gemma Donati who brought Beatrice's lover consolation.

Nor was she married to him for that purpose.

As a matter of fact, in all probability she was already married to him.

It has already been stated that no one can say when Gemma and Dante, were joined in matrimony, probably in the same little church of San Martino del Vescovo which appears so often in the Dante story.

But we do now have reasonable evidence that they were married before

June 8, 1290, when Beatrice died. For in 1921, there was discovered in the archives of Lucca a notarial document which was dated October 21, 1308, and was witnessed by one "Johannes filius Dantis Alighierii" — one Giovanni, the son of Dante Alighieri. Although, as always, there are some doubters, it is now generally accepted that this Giovanni, the son of Dante Alighieri, was the son of our Dante Alighieri and not of someone else who just happened to have the same name. It is also generally accepted that since he publicly proclaimed himself the son of Dante he was legitimate — in other words, that Gemma was his mother.

But in order to qualify as a witness, it was necessary to be at least eighteen years old.

Giovanni, son of Dante, could not, therefore, have been born later than October 21, 1290.

At the latest, Dante must have been married by February of that year.

But if he did not marry Gemma to forget his grief, he did seek consolation elsewhere and in a manner which would have been far more suitable for description by Boccaccio's lively pen.

He suddenly found himself emotionally involved with another fair Florentine. She was the one whom he was later to canonize as "the daughter of God, the queen of all things, the most beautiful and noble philosophy," and about her he would write the only one of his books (the *Convivio*) — but by no means the only one of his poems — which had for its subject a woman who was not Beatrice.

Curiously enough, since guesses about Dante and about everything that happened to him and about all those he even casually mentioned are not ever in short supply, no one has ever seriously hazarded a guess as to her identity and her name.

Dante tells us about this episode himself.

"Then sometime afterwards" — sometime, that is, after he had written the sonnet both versions of which began "There had, yea, there had come into my mind" — "I found myself in that place in which I recalled times past, and I stood there so very pensive and with thoughts so very sorrowful that they gave to my outward appearance a dreadful dismay."

That place in which I recalled times past.

Those very streets which Beatrice had walked — perhaps even a small piazza in front of the Casa Portinari.

At any rate, a place steeped in memories of Folco's daughter.

"Then" — self-consciously — "I looked up to see if any beheld me."

Someone did.

"I saw there a gentle lady who gazed at me from a window very compassionately."

So compassionately, indeed, that it "seemed as if all the compassion in the world were gathered in her."

When did all this take place?

Dante tells us this too (*Convivio* II, 2).

"I say — indeed I begin by saying — that after the departure of that Beatrice who lives in heaven with the angels and on earth within my soul, the star of Venus had twice revolved in her circle which brings her to view in the evening and in the morning when that gentle lady of whom I make mention in the *Vita Nuova* first appeared to me."

This could hardly be more explicit. Venus, it is well known and was in Dante's day, revolves around the sun in 225 days. It was, therefore, 450 days after the death of Beatrice when he saw looking down at him this lady who was so compassionate.

(There are some who insist that Dante refers to the synodic period of Venus rather than to its revolution about the sun. This is 584 days. The time involved, if this were true, would be 1168 days and this would bring us to a date which is not compatible with other Dante chronology.)

One year, two months, and twenty-four days. Transfer this to the calendar and you come to the first day of September 1291.

It was on this date, when autumn after the long Moloch-like scorching of Tuscan summer made the heart glad again, that Dante lifted up his eyes not unto the hills but to something which, if nearer, still exalted him.

As he did, they flooded.

"Wherefore" — this is how he continued the story — "and since when those who are in anguish see that someone else has compassion for them they feel compassion for themselves, mine eyes began to wish to weep, and not wishing to have her see me in this abject state, I departed from before the eyes of this lady. But I said to myself: 'It must be that love dwells with her.' "

It was not an unpromising start.

Notwithstanding this, he did not fall in love with her at once.

Instead, he let her help him brood about Beatrice.

> Mine eyes the great compassion did divine
> That was most plain upon your countenance
> When you gazed on the feature and presence
> Which oftentimes because of grief were mine.
> Then I perceived that you were thinking on
> The nature of my life of dark and gloom,
> Whereupon fear did in my breast find room,
> Thinking my vileness in mine eyes were shown.

> Therefore I left you, for I was aware
> The flooding tears that gushed forth from my heart
> Were truly stirred by looking upon you.
> I then said to my sadness: "It must be true
> That love is with her, does not stand apart,
> And that is why I weep as I walk here."

But even as he wrote these lines — even in these lines if you read them carefully — there was a hint of other things to come.

« 7 »

The lady, however, did not have to struggle with any such complexities. Her response was far more simple and less fabricated. She did, as we say today, what came naturally. Perhaps not the first time she saw him — although even that is not impossible — but certainly very soon, this fair lady, who must have been one of those he often saw about Beatrice, felt a dangerously warm surge of emotion toward the heartbroken (and famous) young man whose feelings she correctly judged to be vulnerable.

Dante tells us about this too.

"It then befell that whenever she beheld me she became visibly compassionate and of a pallid hue as if of love."

He also tells us of his own reaction.

"Whereupon I remembered me of my most noble lady who often showed herself to me of the same color. And, therefore, and truly being able no longer to weep or to ease my sorrow, I went many times to this sympathetic person who by her look seemed to draw forth tears from my eyes."

Here we have a very simple account of the first steps in the logical development of a human relationship.

Dante mourned Beatrice, but the white-hot intensity of his sorrow had been burned down to dull embers by the healing process of the passage of more than a calendar year. But he still mourned her — or thought he did — and since his poems about her in her life and after her death were on the lips of every Florentine, most of Florence talked about this mourning. A young lady who had heard this talking sat at her window. There beneath it stood Dante. First she felt her heart go out in pity, and then she loved him.

But pitying him or loving him, she wanted to comfort him.

"If only I could make him forget Beatrice!"

Then:

"If only I could take the place of Beatrice!"

Dante, however, did not want to forget Beatrice.

The Naples bust (National Museum, Naples) is attributed by some to Donatello, but more generally to "an unknown sculptor of the fifteenth century." It has been copied over and over, and is perhaps the best known of all Dante portraits.

He wanted to remember her.

Indeed, as we have just heard him say, he was drawn to the lady of the window because she took his thoughts to Folco's daughter.

He was also drawn to her because of her compassion.

She understood him!

Because she understood him, he went — as we have also heard him say — many times to see her.

To have her share his tears for Beatrice.

To have her weep with him.

It was all very platonic — in the beginning.

As has happened both before and since.

But that kind of a relationship does not last for long. Not in the thirteenth century, and not today. And certainly not if the young man is Dante with his intense feelings and the lady is a young woman suffused with sympathy.

It did not.

"I came to such a pass" — this is the next thing which Dante felt constrained to report — "that the sight of this lady began to delight me far too much, so that many times my heart was filled with anger at myself. Indeed, I held myself to be exceedingly base.

"Many times," he continued, "I cursed the inconstancy of mine eyes.

"'Come,' I said to myself, 'you were always able to make anyone weep who beheld your grievous state, and now you would forget it because of this lady who looks down at you.'

"'For I' — Dante's heart is still speaking — "will recall her to you often since not until life has gone from you should ye cease weeping.'"

Then, reported Dante, "sighs most heavy and choking" assailed him.

"And in order that this conflict which I had within me should not remain known only to the one suffered it" — i.e., to Dante himself — "I composed a sonnet."

It reiterated what he had argued above.

The very tears ye wept so bitterly,
O eyes of mine, and for a time so long,
Made to weep too of other folk a throng.
Their hearts felt pity as ye plainly see.
Yet her now I do think ye would forget
If I could be a traitor for my part
And your impulse thereto I did not thwart
By making ye remember her ye wept.
Your fickleness doth set me pondering,
And it affrighteth me until I fear
To see the lady that now looks on ye.

> For ye should ne'er forget till death is here
> Our lady who is now among the dead.
> This said my heart, and then I heard it sigh.

But not even these fourteen lines — eloquent or merely hairsplitting — could stem the inevitable.

Almost at the outset, the lady at the window had begun to delight him too much. Now, as he put it, still thinking of Beatrice, merely seeing her brought him "into so strange a state of mind" that many times he thought of her as one who pleased him overly.

"I thought of her thus: 'This is a gentle lady. She is fair and young and wise, and she hath appeared to me because it was Love's will that she did, and so my life may find peace.' "

Still the platonic, or little more than the platonic.

"But many times I had about her still more loving thoughts, and my heart consented to them and that I should plead them."

But Beatrice? What about Beatrice?

"But when my heart had consented, I thought once again and this time I let my soul convince me. I said to myself: 'Ah, what is this thought that in so base a manner seeks to console me so that it scarcely permits me to think of anything else?' "

Yet why shouldn't it?

He was talented, filled with exuberance and vigor, and at not more than twenty-seven had barely crossed the threshold of *gioventù*, or young manhood, which begins at twenty-five and according to Dante gets its very name from *giovare*, to know joy.

So he presented the other side of the question.

"Then there came to the surface another thought. It said to me: 'Since thou hast suffered such tribulation, why dost thou not withdraw thyself from thy great bitterness?' "

Why not indeed?

Amor, ch'a nullo amato amar perdona.

And he was indeed loved by this lady at the window, whoever she may have been.

"Wherefore since I had wrestled many times within myself, I desired to utter some further words about this struggle, and since they that had pleaded for the lady had won the battle of my thoughts, I decided that it would be fitting to speak to her directly and so I composed this sonnet. It begins: 'A gentle thought [*Gentil pensiero*].' "

> A gentle thought and one that says words too
> Cometh so very often to dwell with me
> And it of love doth speak so dulcetly

That it doth make the heart consent thereto.
The soul rebukes this heart with these words: "Who
Is he who comes now to console our mind,
Whose innate virtue is so potent too
No other thought a place with us can find?"
The heart replies to her: "O brooding soul.
This is of Love new inspiration,
Who his desires doth offer to bestow.
All of his life and power — yea the whole —
Came from the eyes of that compassionate one
Who deeply was perturbed at our great woe."

The second line of the sestet is the important one. *Questi è un nuovo spiritel d'amore.* This is of Love new inspiration!

Even as he wrote this sonnet, Dante still struggled as he strove to remain faithful to his old love.

"A gentle thought," he repeated, "and I say *gentle* in so far as it discoursed of a gentle lady, for otherwise it was most base."

But that should not deceive anybody.

For this was no longer a light and casual flirtation with someone with whom — as Milton says he did with Amaryllis — he could sport in the shade. He was now deep in a new enamorment and, next to the enamorment with Beatrice which took him from hell through purgatory to heaven, few things in his life would affect him more deeply.

This he himself came to understand when, a decade or so later — again in *Convivio* II, 2 — he could look at both Beatrice and the lady of the window with at least relative detachment.

"And as I have said in the little book just cited" — his *Vita Nuova,* of which more will be said shortly — "it was more her kindness than my choice which made me consent to be hers. For she showed herself to be moved by such a flood of sympathy for my widowed life that the spirits which dwelt in mine eyes became indeed enamored of her. And when they had thus become enamored, they so wrought upon my inmost being that I was both content and willing to make their image my own.

"But since" — and now he reviewed the story — "love is not born in a moment, nor in a moment does it wax and reach perfection, but requires the passage of time so that it may be nourished in the mind (and this especially when there be thoughts of another to hinder), there had to be — before this new love reached its perfection — many a battle between the thought which fed it and those other thoughts which ran counter to it and still held the fortress of my mind in the name of the glorious Beatrice.

"For one part of my being urged me to look forward and the other part was in the possession of my memory and made me look behind."

But finally the new conquered the old, and this is something important to remember. The lady of the window conquered Beatrice.

"For those thoughts which looked forward and which kept me from turning my face in any way backward grew stronger every day which the other could not do. This seemed to me a miracle. But it also seemed to me so hard to endure that almost I could not endure it.

"Wherefore almost crying out aloud to excuse myself for a fickleness which seemed to show I lacked every steadfast quality, I directed my voice toward that quarter which preceded the victory which had been won by the new thought" — i.e., the heaven of Venus — "and I began by saying: *Voi che intendendo il terzo ciel movete.*"

> Ye who by thinking the third heaven do move
> Hark to the discourse which is in my heart,
> Nor can be told to others so strange it is.

It was at least as good as anything which had yet come from his pen. Indeed, with the possible exception of those other *canzoni, Donne che avete intelletto d'amore* and *Gli occhi dolenti per pietà del core*, it was better than anything he had composed for Bice Portinari.

When was it written?

It would be useful for us to know this, for it celebrated the culminating summit of his love for his new lady.

« *8* »

Oddly enough — for precise chronological touch-base points in the life of Dante are few and far between — it can be determined with reasonable exactitude.

In *Paradiso* VIII, Dante recounts his meeting with Carlo Martello, eldest son of Charles II of Naples and Anjou, titular king of Hungary, crown prince of Naples, husband of Clemence of Hapsburg, and the father of the beautiful and blond Clemence of Naples, whose later marriage to Louis the Obstinate of France would plunge her into the tragedy and shabbiness of the disintegrating French monarchy.

> And among those who in the front rank were
> So clear *hosanna* sounded that thereafter
> I never did not long to hear it again.
> Then there drew one of them much nearer to us
> And speaking by himself began: "We are ready
> To do thy pleasure that thou have joy of us.

> We do revolve with those celestial princes
> Within one circle, one circling, and one thirst,
> Of whom thou in the world did one time say:
> *Voi che intendendo il terzo ciel movete.*
> And we so full of love are that to please thee
> No less sweet would a little silence be . . .
> Much didst thou love me, and had reason to,
> For had I stayed on earth I would have showed you
> Much more of my affection than its leaves."

But we know when Charles passed through the city of the lilies.

He was at Siena on March 2, 1294, and on March 7 of the same year the Council of One Hundred voted the funds to pay for the canopy under which the handsome young prince was to make his formal entry. This canopy was of white silk embroidered with gold, and although Carlo with his queen and four princes of the blood rode on caracoling horses, it was carried by young Florentines who walked on foot.

With Charles, reported Villani, was "his company of two hundred knights with golden spurs, French and Provençal and from his kingdom. They were all young men, invested by the king with habits of scarlet and gold. Their saddles all bore one device. Their palfreys were adorned with silver and gold, with arms quarterly, bearing golden lilies and surrounded by a bordure of red and silver, which are the arms of Hungary. And they appeared the noblest and richest company a young king ever had with him."

With him was a famous dwarf, who, according to a document dated May 12, 1290, was paid a princely salary, together with musicians, jesters, buffoons, and professional street singers.

The last, "in a good voice" according to the Franciscan Ubertino da Casale, "chanted the deeds of Roland and of Oliver" from that old favorite *I Reali di Francia* (The Charlemagne Cycle) — and they may well have also chanted a new favorite such as the latest poem by Dante or Guido Cavalcanti.

"And in Florence he abode more than twenty days, awaiting his father King Charles and his brothers, and the Florentines did him great honor, and he showed great love for the Florentines, wherefore he was in high favor with them all."

He departed from the city in April 1294. By August he had died of the plague.

Voi che intendendo must, then, have been written before April 1294, and of course after September 1, 1291, when he first saw the lady at the window.

But not much before, for it is obvious that it was fresh and new when Carlo heard it.

Here are some further lines from the poem:

> "Thou art not slain. Why, thou art but dismayed,
> O thou our soul, thou who lamentest so."
> Then said a young and gentle spirit of love;
> "For that fair lady whose power thou dost feel
> Has so transmuted that life that thou hast
> That thou hast fear of it, being faint of heart.
> But marvel how pitying and modest she is,
> How wise and courteous though of high degree,
> And think to call her 'Mistress' evermore.
> For if thou dost not now deceive thyself
> Thou shalt behold such glittering miracles
> That thou shalt straightway say: 'O Love, true lord,
> She is thy handmaid. See to it that she please thee.'"

Dice un spiritel d'amor gentile. (*Spiritel d'amor*, for the second time.) It was again springtime. Charles was in Florence with his bright retinue. Life was overflowing and gay — it was no longer widowed life. And there was someone, young and tenderhearted, to whom he could give his heart. For the moment, Beatrice, herself become as white and still as marble, lay in Santa Maria Novella, or in Sant' Gilio, and was out of his mind.

« 9 »

But not for long.

Charles rode out of the city, and the interlude ended.

Why?

Was this poet of the praise of love — and of the service of love even in its most wordly aspects — at heart a puritan?

And thus in a strange way an unshakable idealist?

"Once, and only once, and for one only."

That was Robert Browning's way of describing it.

Or had he never really forgotten Beatrice?

Or was he surfeited with too much tenderness and pity?

It has happened to others.

Or did the lady, instead, tire of him and jilt him?

He himself lays it to a return of common sense.

"Against this adversary of reason there arose in me one day, and almost at the hour of none, a vivid vision in which I thought that I saw the glorious Beatrice in the very crimson garments in which she first appeared to my eyes, and she seemed to me youthful and of the same age she was when I first saw her. Then I began to think of her. I began to remember everything about her in the order that it happened, and my heart began to repent of the desire with which for certain days it had allowed itself to be possessed, and that against the changeless laws of common sense. And when this evil desire had been cast forth, all my thoughts turned toward the gentle Beatrice. And from that time I began to think of her with all my shamed heart."

He began to sigh too. Sighs, as we have seen, came easily to him.

He also began to weep.

"Through this rekindling of sighs, the tears which had ceased began to flow again and in such a way that mine eyes appeared to me two things whose sole desire was to weep, and through this weeping they came round about of a purple hue such as appears when some torture has been received."

Finally, he began to write again.

About Beatrice.

About the grief that many felt for her.

He wrote a sonnet about his weeping eyes and followed it with a second sonnet about his desolate city.

This second sonnet he has discussed in some detail.

"After this sorrowing of mine, it so happened that at the season when many people go to inspect that blessed image which Jesus Christ has left us to show us his beautiful countenance" — the Veronica, which was then in St. Peter's at Rome — "some pilgrims passed along a street in the middle of the city, and it seemed to me that they went very pensively. I thought about them, and then I said to myself: 'These pilgrims seem to me from a far country, and I believe that they have never heard my lady spoken of and that they know nothing about her. They are instead thinking of their distant friends.' I added: 'I know that if these were from some nearby place they would seem to be troubled as they passed through the dolorous city.' Then I said further: 'If I could keep them for a while, I would make them too weep before they left the city because I would say words which would make whoever heard them weep.'

"Wherefore, when they had passed from my sight, I decided to make a sonnet in which I would reveal what I had said to myself, and I composed this one which begins: 'Ah pilgrims!' "

But even as he wrote it he realized that pilgrim was not an accurate term. And always he had to be accurate.

"I said pilgrims," he explained, "according to the wider sense of the word, for pilgrims may be understood in two ways. In the wide sense, whoever leaves his fatherland is a pilgrim. In the narrow sense, none is called a pilgrim except one who is journeying to or returning from St.

James. There are three ways for properly naming those who journey for the worship of the Most High. They are called palmers who journey overseas, for many times they bring back palm branches. They are called pilgrims who journey to Galicia. And they are called romers who journey to Rome, and it was there those I called pilgrims were going."

The sonnet, then, should have begun: *Deh romeri* rather than *Deh peregrini* as it did.

When it was written down, it went abroad as all his other writings had.

Whereupon two gentle ladies read it and then sent to him.

"We pray you of your goodness to send us our own copy of these words in rhyme."

But Dante thought that "because of their nobleness" they deserved better than that.

He did indeed send them the sonnet about the pilgrims, and he also sent them the earlier sonnet "Come ye, and listen" which he had composed for Manetti Portinari.

And then, specially for them, he composed a special sonnet.

Oltre la spera, it began. Beyond the sphere.

> Beyond the sphere that widest circlest
> There goes a sigh that issues from my heart.
> In it a new faculty, at weeping Love's behest
> Planted, forever seeks the loftiest part.
> When it doth reach the place of its desire,
> It doth perceive a lady honored and praised
> Who shineth and with such effulgent fire
> The pilgrim can but gaze on her amazed.
> It sees her such that when it telleth me
> I cannot understand, so subtle its praise
> Unto the heart that it to speak doth incline.
> I know, though, that it talks of my lady,
> For very often *Beatrice* it says,
> And then I understand, dear ladies mine.

In his praising of the lady he had, then, taken one step further. Once he had placed her with the angels. Now he put her in the loftiest heaven of all.

« *10* »

But if the praise was high, it was the last poem he would write about Beatrice for a very long time. For even as he wrote down these words he had a revelation, and he came to a conclusion.

Beginning perhaps a year after Beatrice died and continuing up to and including the time — probably late in 1294 — when he returned to her after his involvement with the lady of the window, Dante had slowly been gathering his writings about the lady he was to make immortal into a small and compact volume. This is the book which we call the *Vita Nuova*. It was made up of the poems he had written to Beatrice and to or about the other three ladies who appear in the Beatrice story, together with the running commentary from which I have taken frequent excerpts in this and in the preceding chapters, and out of which — with a few assists from the *Convivio* — has been reconstructed much of the story of his love.

Although there was some slight precedent for it in the *vidas* and the *razos* — the lives and the prose commentaries — attached to the poems of certain of the Provençal troubadours, nothing really like it had been done before. For it not only set down Dante's poems — those of them he wished remembered — but it set them down in context. In the context, that is, of his relation to the lady, for they told little or very little of his daily affairs.

Yet while he was still making this book he realized — and almost suddenly — that it would be inadequate.

As was normal for him, he realized this — or said he did — in a vision.

"After this sonnet, there appeared to me a wondrous dream, and in it I beheld things which made me decide to write nothing more of this blessed one until such time as I could treat of her more worthily. And to attain this I now bend every possible effort, and this she knows full well. So that if it be the pleasure of Him by which all things live that my life continue for some few more years, I hope to write of her what hath never been written of any other woman. And when I have done this, may it please Him who is Lord of grace that my soul may be permitted to behold the glory of its lady — that is the blessed Beatrice who gazes in glory on the face of Him *qui est per omnia saecula benedictus.*"

I hope to write of her what hath never been written of any other woman!

Only one other poet gave himself — and accepted — such a challenge. John Milton. He said this:

> Of man's first disobedience and the fruit
> Of that forbidden tree whose mortal taste
> Brought death into the world and all our woe . . .
> Sing heavenly Muse, that on the secret top
> Of Oreb or of Sinai didst inspire
> That shepherd who first taught the chosen seed

In the beginning how the heavens and earth
Rose out of chaos, or if Sion hill
Delight thee more, and Siloa's brook that flowed
Fast by the oracle of God, I thence
Invoke thy aid to my adventurous song
That with no middle flight intends to soar
Above the Aonian Mount, while it pursues
Things unattempted yet in prose or rhyme.

But Milton's proud boast was made when he was a man in his middle fifties and after he had already begun his epic.

Dante was not thirty and had scarcely fledged his wings.

VIII

All Men Do Naturally Desire Knowledge

THERE is some reason to believe that he had begun these efforts already, and that the last paragraph in his little volume about Beatrice was simply an attempt to fit into a pattern and to dramatize a new phase of his life which, as he wrote it, was well under way. But even as we say this, we run into some problems of chronology which are difficult, if not impossible, to solve in a manner which will leave everybody satisfied.

To be sure, Dante has provided us with "coordinates," but they are not always clearly stated, and it is usually left for us to determine where they are and what they mean.

Let us look over carefully a few of the passages in which they may be found.

Convivio II, 13:

"To start from the beginning again, I say that when to me had been lost the first delight of my soul as has been made mention of above I remained pierced with such sadness that no consolation had any effect on me. However, after a certain while, since I could neither console myself nor could anyone else console me, my mind, which was casting about for a way to make itself whole again, determined to fall back upon the method which another unhappy man had used to find solace for his own grief.

"And so I set myself to read that book of Boethius which is not known to many people and in which he tried to console himself when he was a prisoner and had been driven into exile. And hearing further that Tully had also written a book in which as he talked about friendship he had introduced the words of consolation which that excellent man Laelius spoke upon the death of his friend Scipio, I set myself to read that book too.

"In the beginning I found it difficult to understand the meaning of either, but finally I did understand them — at any rate as much as the knowledge of Latin which I had, and such little ability as was mine, permitted me to do. But by this ability I had already begun to perceive many things as in a dream as may be seen in the *Vita Nuova*.

"And just as it often happens that a man goes in search of silver and without even intending to finds gold instead, the same being set in his way by some occult cause but perhaps without God's command, so I who sought to assuage my grief not only found a cure for my tears but the words employed by these authors and their knowledge and their books.

"And as I pondered on them, I came to the conclusion that Philosophy, who was the mistress of these authors and of their knowledge and of their books, must have been a thing supreme. Then I imagined her as being made in the likeness of a gentle lady, and since I could not imagine her as doing anything which was not compassionate, my sense did have such a longing to gaze on her that I could hardly turn my eyes away from her.

"Therefore, impelled by this image which I had made of her, I began to frequent those places where in very truth she was revealed — that is, to the schools of the religious and to the disputations of the philosophers. So that in a short time — perhaps some thirty months — I began to have such a sense of her sweetness that my love for her banished and expelled every other thought."

Convivio III, 1:

"Oh how many nights there were when the eyes of others, closed in sleep, did take their rest, but mine gazed fixedly upon the dear dwelling place of their love!"

Convivio I, 1:

"As sayeth the Philosopher" — i.e., Aristotle — "at the beginning of his First Philosophy" — i.e., his *Metaphysics* — "all men do naturally desire knowledge."

But "of this most noble perfection, many are deprived for diverse causes."

Some of these lie within and some without.

"Inside, there may be two defects or impediments, one of the body and the other of the soul. It is a defect of the body when some of its parts are not made perfectly as with the deaf and with the dumb and the like. It is a defect of the soul when vice has such supremacy over it that it is given over to the pursuing of vicious delights and is so deluded by them that for their sake it holds every other thing cheap.

"Similarly, without two matters may be apprehended. One of them compels a man to other activities, the other leads him to laziness. The first is those family and civic cares which rightly occupy most men so that they do not have the leisure for speculation. The second is the unhappy character of the place in which a person is born and nurtured which is devoid not only of all opportunities for study but of far-away learned men."

The first two of these causes "are not to be blamed, but are to be excused." The two others — although one more than the other — "deserve both to be blamed and to be despised.

"Manifestly, then," he concluded, "only a few may attain to that state which all desire, and almost numberless are those who live all their lives starving for this universal food."

Was he one of those few?

« 2 »

What, exactly, did Dante try to tell us as he set down the above, and how will this help us reconstruct this part of his life?

(1) That as soon as Beatrice died he plunged into devastating grief, but that "after a certain while" he found a way to emerge from it.

(2) That this was to read deeply the thoughts of Boethius and of Cicero (Tully) as expressed in the former's *De Consolatione Philosophiae* and the latter's *De Amicitia*.

(3) That as he read the two men deeply he dredged from them every single thought that was not too profound for his limited familiarity with Latin — but this is his judgment, not ours — and his lack of formal education to permit him to understand.

(4) That one thing led to another, and as he plunged into the writings of the ancient and then the later Roman he was so moved and so influenced by their wisdom and their words that he sought even further knowledge.

In other words, he went back to school again. But not to the humble trivium (grammar — i.e., Latin — rhetoric, and logic) and the only slightly less modest quadrivium (arithmetic, music, geometry, and astronomy). To the schools of the religious — the university-taught monks — and to conversation with every learned man who lived in Florence.

(5) That he made rapid progress — such rapid progress, indeed, that within two years and six months he was ready to hold his head up in any learned company.

(6) That this was not surprising since with his intense and passionate nature he threw himself into his new preoccupation without regard to either time or health.

That the latter suffered have no doubt. It has been noted that Dante studied both by night and day. This being the case, some of the distraught and haggard looks which have been attributed to his feelings about Beatrice may have come from long hours spent with his books in his upper-story room far from the marble *camino,* or fireplace, which at that only erratically heated even the *sala matronale,* or great living room, in which it was situated. Unquestionably, he was well wrapped. He certainly wore the long robe, or *zimarra* — Petrarch, it should be remembered, left Boccaccio fifty florins so that he could buy one of these fur-trimmed garments to wear on dank and chilly evenings in not too distant Certaldo — which was the scholar's substitute for central heating.

But even though he was wrapped in it, he shivered.

Nor did he have enough light to study by, and this had consequences too.

There was in Florence a famous edifice built by one of the Counts Guidi, and it was known as "the house of mirrors" because the sunlight glittered on the transparent panes of its innumerable windows. But in general — and probably in Dante's house — a kind of oiled fabric took the place of glass, which was expensive and difficult to obtain, and through this even the intensive sunlight of Tuscany filtered thinly.

The chance of eyestrain was considerable, and Dante, like many others, became its victim.

He writes about this — also in his *Convivio.*

Convivio III, 9:

"It also may happen" — he is discussing the changed appearance of a heavenly body — "that by reason of weakness or exhaustion the sheath of the pupil becomes much bloodshot, or through infirmity or illness."

Then everything seems red.

"And when the sight is enfeebled, a certain dispersion of the vision takes place, so that things no longer seem knit together but sprawling, much as do the letters when we write upon damp paper. And that is why many, when they have it in mind to read, remove the writings to a distance in order that the image may enter the eye more smoothly and more clearly, and in this way the letters be better defined."

Many people? Or Dante himself? Was Dante, then, clinically far-sighted?

"And so too a star may seem blurred, and of this I had experience in the year in which this ode" — that is, the *Amor che nella mente mi ragiona,* "Love that discourseth to me in my mind" — "was composed. For through greatly overtaxing my sight by zealously reading, I so weakened it that the stars all appeared to me as shining through a kind of white haze. It was only by giving my eyes a long rest in cool and dark places and by cooling my eyeballs with clear water that I regained those powers of vision which I had lost and returned to my former good sight."

(7) That there were but four possible impediments to a life devoted to learning and by implication Dante was not held back by any of them.

Physical or mental defects.

No.

A dissolute way of life.

Not, at any rate, at that time.

Family and civic cares.

Either he disregarded them or they too came later.

An environment which was uncongenial to the pursuit of scholarship.

Hardly!

Florence was not yet Periclean Athens, but as we will see shortly it was not a Sahara of the intellect. In it there was plenty to stimulate the mind.

Dante also tries to tell us when all this took place, but here he is almost as cloudy as his vision.

Did he mourn Beatrice, turn to his "compassionate lady," return to Beatrice, write down (somewhat juvenilely even his most ardent admirers must admit) his love for her in the *Vita Nuova*, suddenly discover that his equipment was inadequate, and having discovered this resort to books and teachers? Or were his studies and his enamorment with the lady at the window carried on at the same time?

The first makes for an orderly story and in a sense it is the one Dante tells himself, but there are certain serious objections to accepting it.

As noted in point five above, he stated that his arduous devotion to philosophy and to teachers of philosophy lasted for thirty months, but if we add thirty months to the date of the ending of his involvement with the compassionate lady we come to October or November 1296, and at that time he was deep in other activities.

He also (point one) observed that he had begun his love affair with learning "a certain while" after the death of Beatrice. The Italian words are *dopo aliquanto tempo*. "A certain while" might well take us to September 1291, the date when his enamorment with the lady at the window began.

Furthermore (point six), his serious eye trouble came to him at a specific time — the time when he composed the *Amor che nella mente mi ragiona*. But this poem is very clearly part of the cycle of poems which he wrote to the lady at the window.

But the compassionate lady cycle — this poem and others — can, as has already been shown, be very definitely dated by its relationship to the arrival and the departure of Carlo Martello. Count back thirty months from this and you come to September 1291, which is the date we have already arrived at.

The second theory, then, is the more tenable. Dante's preoccupation with study did begin early and it ran side by side with his infatuation for the lady of the window. It was in or near September 1291 — and even as he loved Bice's successor — that he began his fierce application to everything man had written and thought. Incidentally, this would make his later identification of the lady with Philosophy less incongruous.

He was not totally unprepared for this change of interest. The *Vita Nuova* itself — the book which according to his own statement led him to this new hunger for learning all he could — is plain evidence of this. For in it there were a series of explicit references which showed that — thanks to Master Romano and Ser Brunetto Latini — he had far more than a passing acquaintance with learning. He quotes or refers to the Greek astronomer Hipparchus (born in Nicaea in Bithynia *circa* 160 B.C. and first cataloguer of many of the stars); Alfraganus; Virgil (the *Aeneid*); Lucan (the *Pharsalia*); Horace (the *Ars Poetica*); Homer (but only as quoted by Horace); and even Ovid (the *Ars Amatoria*), despite the fact that he was denounced by the monks as well as by medieval taste.

It is also clear that he was deeply familiar with the Holy Scriptures.

It likewise seems probable, if not certain, that he had long had beside him the mighty masterwork of Uguccione de' Bagni of Pisa. This was an enormous dictionary — in our sense of the word it was almost an encyclopedia — which was commonly known as the *Magnae Derivationes sive Dictionarium Etymologicum* (The Great Derivations or Etymological Dictionary.) Its popularity is attested by the numerous manuscripts which have survived — some of them interlined or their margins scrawled upon by industrious annotators. There was hardly a man of learning in the Age of Dante who did not have it at his side.

But now Dante set himself to the acquisition of knowledge with the much more substantial enthusiasm of a mature person — of a mature person who no longer sought to learn because almost every child was made to, but because learning satisfied a need that was both urgent and overpowering. You will recall that Dante spoke of seeking silver and finding gold. It was more as if he had discovered that like Moses in the desert he could strike his staff against the bare and heat-split rock and forth from it would gush clear and refreshing water.

At first he did this seeking on his own and by himself, without benefit of instructor or instruction.

At the moment, it was not necessary to have either.

For despite the curious phrase (quoted earlier in the chapter) in which Dante asserts that the philosophical masterpiece of Theodoric's great *magister officiarum* (almost "Secretary of State") was not known to many — possibly he means *understood* by many — *The Consolation of Philosophy* by Anicius Manlius Severinus Boethius (480–524) was perhaps as easy to obtain and, for a keen mind, to understand as anything written between the last days of the western Roman Empire and the great dawning of the twelfth and thirteenth centuries.

Boethius the man was well known too.

His wide reputation for great learning, his rise to almost supreme power, his dramatic fall from favor, the cruelty of his death — "a cord was twisted for a very long time around his forehead so that his eyes started out of his head, and then at last he was slain with a club" — and the general belief that he had died as a Christian martyr, which he had not, made this last of the Romans and forerunner of the medieval schoolmen a popular hero.

The circumstances under which his book came into being contributed to his reputation.

In prison — this is the story — Boethius neither pined nor beat his head in hopeless fury. Instead in his cell at Pavia he set down his faith and his unshakable belief. Recalling his one-time wealth, "his noble father-in-law, his chaste wife," his excellent children, he did, to be sure, cry out — as Francesca da Rimini would later — in a sort of heart-wringing anguish that "in adversity it is the most unhappy kind of misfortune to have been happy." But he also remembered "that there likewise remaineth a beholder of all things, which is God.

"Wherefore flee vices, embrace virtues, possess your mind with worthy hopes, offer up your prayers to the highest Prince. For there hath been imposed upon you a great necessity of attaining probity."

Words like these had made what he had written a handbook for those whom fate had bludgeoned and who wished to stay unbowed.

"Read him," some of his friends surely told Dante.

"Read him," Dante's own heart echoed, remembering what he had learned about him as a schoolboy. He did.

Boethius began thus:

> I, who did write my songs with youthful zeal,
> Must now, alas, intune them mournfully.
> Now to a tattered Muse I must appeal.
> Now tears runnel my cheeks disconsolately . . .
> As old age, sped by evil and unsought,
> Doth come, grief having on her years laid,
> And white hairs, here too soon by sorrow brought,
> And wrinkles on trembling flesh half dead.

A little further:

> O fortunate death, who spares our sweetest years
> But comes in sorrow, called by frequent woes,
> Why are you deaf now to a wretch's tears?
> Why are you loath my weeping eyes to close?

After that:

> When fickle fortune favored me with vain
> Gifts, she did almost do away with me,
> But now that her face clouded is, 't is plain
> My weary life drags on interminably.

Finally:

> Why do you say that I was fortunate?
> He that has fallen fortunate never was.

"While I thought over all this" — Boethius now resorted to prose — "and made up my mind to commit to writing my sorrowful laments, it seemed to me that I saw a woman standing above me. She had a grave countenance and bright, clear eyes, and her perceptions were quicker than those which nature doth ordinarily afford. Her color was fresh and bespoke still lively vigor, yet she was of such an age that in no way could she be thought of as belonging to our century. Her stature was hard to determine. Sometimes she did not exceed the height of common men, and sometimes she seemed to touch the heavens with her head. With cunning workmanship, her garments had been made of the finest threads, and these had been woven by her own hands into a fabric which would last forever. But a certain duskiness caused by negligence and time had darkened their color, even as pictures are usually darkened when they are kept in a smoky room. In the lower part of these garments was placed the Greek letter *pi* and in the upper part the Greek letter *theta*."

Pi for *praktike* and *theta* for *theoretike*!

"In her right hand she had certain books and in her left hand she had a scepter."

Who was this lady?

Boethius tried to answer.

She stood by his bed, he said, and seeing that the muses of poetry still stood there she cried out angrily: "Who hath permitted these tragical harlots to have access to this sick man? They will not only comfort his grief with wholesome remedies but also nourish them with sugared poison."

She then laid her hand upon his brow and with the corner of her garment dried his eyes.

"Thereat the mists of sadness dissolved. I looked into the sky again. I recovered my senses. Then recognized I the face of my physician, for gazing at her steadily I saw before me my nurse Philosophy, in whose house I had dwelt from my youth.

" 'O mistress of all virtues,' I said to her, 'why hast thou come down from the pole of the heavens into this our solitary banishment? Art thou come to bear me company in being falsely accused?'

" 'Should I,' she replied, 'foresake thee, my disciple, and not share the burden which has been imposed upon thee by those who hate my name? Should I not partake of thy anguishes? A thousand times no! For Philosophy has never thought it lawful to turn away from the innocent in their time of trouble."

My *nurse* Philosophy! With Dante, who was obviously led to her by Boethius, she would become my *lady* Philosophy.

Then she continued, Dante listening. In the ensuing pages she took up matter after matter which troubled him now or would trouble him later. What she said was indelibly imprinted on his memory.

Here were some of her messages:

The importance of divine reason, and the fact that everything which had happened to Boethius — or would happen to anyone else — was the result of its influence and not of blind chance.

"Wherefore, fear not; out of this little spark will be kindled thy vital heat."

The fact, too, that there is no one who has not known in some way the slings and arrows of adversity:

"For who hath so entire a fortune that he is not in some part offended with the condition of his estate?"

The impossibility of achieving peace except in one's own heart:

"O mortal men, why do you seek felicity without? It has been placed within you."

The little value one should place upon the things of this world:

"They who have much, need much; but they need little who do not measure their wealth by the superfluity of ambition but by the necessities of nature."

The fact that misfortune tests loyalties:

"Dost thou esteem it a small benefit that this rough and harsh Fortune hath made known to thee the minds of thy faithful friends?"

The benevolence of the Almighty.

"God cannot do evil."

The necessity for being firm and resolute.

"A wise man must be no more tormented by adversity than a brave captain by the sounds of battle."

The matter of life and death:

"It hath the same import as those things I proposed before — the sun rising and the man going."

The basis for an ideal state:

"Those men" — this was borrowed from Plato — "should be happy if either the students of wisdom did govern them, or if those who were appointed to their rule would give themselves to the study of wisdom."

The injustices of political calumny:

"But thou seest to what a pass being innocent has brought me. Instead of the rewards of true virtue, I enjoy the punishments of wickedness wherewith I am falsely accused."

Also:

"Now, being conveyed five hundred miles off, I am condemned for bearing the senate too much goodwill."

The puffed-up vanity of certain mortals:

"For, if among mice thou shouldst see one who claimed jurisdiction and power over the rest, to what laughter would it move thee." "But thou hast learned by astronomical calculations that the whole earth compared to the heavens is no bigger than a pin point."

The important thing about nobility:

"I judge it to be this. That it imposeth a necessity upon those who are noble not to suffer their nobility to degenerate from the virtue of their ancestors."

The relationship between foreknowledge and free will:

"Why deemst thou their solution incorrect who think that free will is not hindered by foreknowledge? The free will of man remaineth unviolated."

I set down these excerpts because it is important to see clearly that Dante not merely read Boethius but to some degree was shaped by him. He was, of course, consoled by him, but he was molded by him even more. This will be increasingly apparent as we are exposed to more and more of Dante's writings. Obviously this Roman of the days after Rome had fallen is present on more than one page of the *Convivio*, but his influence did not end there. Not a single thing that Dante wrote up to and including his greatest masterpiece, not a single one of his thoughts is the same as it would have been if the man who had dared to look up to heaven even when it was farthest away from him had not constantly stood at his side.

« *3* »

There is no less reason why Cicero and his *De Amicitia* should not have fallen into Dante's hands.

Here, however, we must correct a misconception and one which was particularly popular in the late nineteenth century, when it was advanced by such notable scholars as John Addington Symonds and Jakob Burckhardt. This is that following Rome's fall not only was there a period justly called the Dark Ages, but it was so filled with barbarian ignorance that the light of the past was almost completely extinguished, so that when finally there came that astonishing resurgence of the human spirit which in its broader sense has become known as the Renaissance (rebirth) and in its narrower the Revival of Learning, it had only been through a series of accidents that much of what we cherish had survived.

To an extent this misconception is based upon Boccaccio's famous visit to Montecassino as he reported it to Benvenuto da Imola.

"He stated," reported Benvenuto, "that, while he was in Apulia, moved by the renown of the place, he went to the noble monastery and, eager to see the library, which he had heard was magnificent indeed, he humbly begged a monk who stood by that he would be so good as to let him see it. Showing him some steep stairs, the latter said stiffly: 'Mount these. You will find it open.' Boccaccio went up them with a high heart and there found that the place which held so many treasures had neither lock nor door. He saw moss growing around the windows and at the entrance. He saw the books and bookshelves deep in dust, and when, wondering, he began to pick up and turn the pages of this book and that book, he found that there were many ancient and very noted books there but that from many several pages had been torn and that from others the margins had been cut away and that most of them had been defaced. Returning to the cloister he asked the monk why the books had been so shamefully disfigured. The fellow replied that when certain of his fellow monks wished to earn two to five *soldi* he would scrape off one volume and from it make some little psalters which they would sell to boys, or from the margins they would make gospels and breviaries which they sold to women.

"Now, scholar," concluded Benvenuto, "give yourself a headache in this writing of books!"

The misconception was further based on Boccaccio's and Petrarch's efforts to learn Greek, an effort which led them to put up with the filthy habits and the utter villainy of black-bearded Leontius Pilatus — "a Greek from Calabria" and a complete scoundrel — in the hope that he would not only translate the *Iliad* and the *Odyssey* but also teach them Homer's language.

It was also fostered by the intellectual snobbery of the members of Platonic — and other — academies from the days of the Medici onward.

These gentlemen of the late fifteenth and early sixteenth centuries were indeed learned, but they were flushed with self-esteem, and like others of their kind they did not consider anything had been read until they had read it.

And when a pope would pay as much for a Petronius as for a province, there was indeed very often plenty for them to peruse.

But even in these days before — supposedly — the lights were lit again, even when Aristotle and some others could be read only in crude Latin translations, even when Boccaccio's books on the genealogy of the gods, the fortunes of great men and great women, and mountains and fountains had many of the qualities of a cathedral gargoyle, the great writings of the past were not completely forgotten, nor were the classic authors (at any rate the Latin classic authors) completely ignored.

In the very monasteries upon which the author of the *Decameron* heaped such scorn — St. Gall in Switzerland, Montecassino, elsewhere in Italy, too many places to name in France, England, and Germany — many of their compositions not only survived but were studied and treasured.

I name only a few of them.

The more famous, and some of the less famous, poets, such as Claudian (he, too, of the falling Roman Empire), Statius, Valerius Flaccus, Lucan, Ovid, Horace, Juvenal, Persius, and Martial.

The novelist — and arbiter of fashion — Petronius.

The comedy writers Terence and Plautus.

The historians Sallust, Sidonius Apollinaris, Cassiodorus, and Suetonius.

The grammarian Macrobius and the rhetorician Quintilian.

(Many of these in a single monastery in France.)

And, of course, Boethius. And, of course, Cicero.

Of these, none was more admired than Cicero.

More admired or more read.

Nor were this admiration and this reading something new.

St. Augustine studied the Roman orator, and in the early days of Christianity when — as with all revolutionary movements — ideological purity was of great importance, St. Jerome, by his own statement, was rebuked by an angel for being a Ciceronian rather than a Christian.

Somewhat later, and in distant France, Nicholas, the secretary of St. Bernard of Clairvaux, is said to have sighed over the charms he found in this Roman author and in the Latin poets, a charm notably absent from clerkly writings.

The English scholar John of Salisbury (1115–1180), who had studied under Abelard and was present at the murder of Thomas à Becket, "was steeped in Cicero." Abelard was too, although perhaps less notably. But the list could go on and on.

It would have been a little startling, then, if the eloquent orator — and writer — who had been born in Samnite Arpinum (Arpindo today) in the foothills of the Abruzzi Apennines, and who, except for when he studied at Athens or served in Asia Minor as a governor, lived and died in Italy should not have been admired and read in his own country.

In point of fact, he was.

By the same token, editions of his works became plentiful. A twelfth-century catalogue of the great library at Cluny, for example, lists four manuscripts of Cicero's *Letters*, four of the *Orations*, five of the rhetorical works, and seven of Cicero's philosophical writings. But copies of at least his rhetorical and philosophical works were in almost every library worthy of the name. Many of them had some of the *Orations*. They were eagerly sought after during this so-called unenlightened era. Hence the editions were many. The copyist with his quill pen and his durable lamp-black ink was as conscious of "best sellers" as is the publisher of today.

Just as had the book by Boethius, one of these manuscripts came into the hands of Dante.

The *De Amicitia*.

Cicero, he began to read, was told by Quintus Mucius Scaevola, the augur, about the discourse which Laelius had given to his two sons-in-law, Fannius and Scaevola, just a few days after the death of Scipio Africanus.

"The heads of that discussion I committed to memory," said Cicero. This, abbreviated, is how he continued.

"And then, just as I wrote as an old man speaking to an old man when I wrote about old age, so I now wrote a book about friendship speaking as a friend to an intimate friend. In the first book Cato spoke, but now it is Laelius. I wish then that you could turn your attention from me for a while and imagine that it is Laelius who is speaking. Gaius Fannius and Quintus Mucius Scaevola have come to the house of their father-in-law. They begin a conversation. Laelius replies.

" 'You are a philosopher,' Fannius begins, and Scaevola corroborates this. 'You are the kind of person that not merely the common herd but all educated men are wont to call a philosopher. And so people ask me — and they ask Scaevola too — in what manner you bear the death of Africanus, who was not only a man of the greatest excellence but also your very close friend.'

" 'I consider that nothing evil has happened to Scipio,' Laelius responded. 'If any has happened, it has happened to me.' "

Why?

" 'For unless he desired to live forever — which he did not — what has he not attained which it is lawful for a man to wish for?' "

Scipio had every kind of public honor.

Cicero listed them.

And this without any self-seeking on his part.

Besides this, Scipio was devoted to his family, and how dear he was to the state is shown by the profound mourning at his public funeral.

" 'What more could the addition of a few years have brought to him?' "

Moreover, Scipio ascended to heaven.

" 'For from the high degree of his worth it would seem that he went to the gods above rather than to the gods below.' "

And there *are* gods above and gods below, and men can go to them!

" 'I say this for I do not agree with those who lately have begun to contend that the soul dies with the body. I hold rather with the authority of the ancients — and especially of that man who has been adjudged by the oracle of Apollo to be the greatest philosopher of all — that human souls are divine, and that when they have departed from the body the way to return to the skies lies open to them, and that those who are the best and the most righteous will return upon it the most speedily.' "

Yet suppose that the ancients were wrong.

" 'If another contention is true — namely that the death of the soul and of the body go together and that consciousness is forever lost — then if there is no good in death neither is there any evil. For if oblivion is the end, it is just as if we had never been born at all.' "

Thus, as he confronted that which all must confront, the pagan philosopher joined the Christian stoic in saying something to Dante in his hour of perplexity and sorrow that would bring him courage and strength.

The pagan philosopher!

I try to say this with at least some small part of Dante's regret and reverence.

For if — since Virgil was born before Christ and so could not be saved — the poet could not put his master and guide in any place other than hell, it is obvious that he must do the same with every great intellect — Cicero included — who had likewise been born too soon.

Yet it is equally obvious he loved them and revered them.

Inferno IV:

> We then approached a noble castle's foot,
> Seven times circled by a lofty wall
> And well defended by a brooklet fair.
> We crossed this stream almost as if dry-shod.

> Through seven portals did we enter it
> And then came to a meadow of fresh green.
> People were there with serious and calm eyes,
> And they had great authority in their looks.
> They spoke few words and these in a soft voice.

Who were some of them?

> I saw Electra with many people around her,
> Among whom I knew Hector and Aeneas
> And armèd Caesar with gyrfalcon eyes.
> I saw Camilla and Penthesilea
> And on the other side saw King Latinus,
> Lavinia his daughter seated with him.
> I saw that Brutus who did drive off Tarquin,
> Lucretia, Julia, Marcia, and Cornelia,
> And standing all alone great Saladin.

Then he came to the important ones:

> I lifted up mine eyes a little bit
> And saw the master of all those who know
> Seated amid the family of philosophers.
> All of them looked at him. All did him honor.
> Then saw I Socrates and I saw Plato,
> Who of all others stood the nearest to him.
> I saw Democritus, who said all is chance,
> Diogenes, Anaxagoras, and Thales,
> Empedocles, Heraclitus, yea, and Zeno.
> I saw the good collector of all qualities,
> Dioscorides, I mean. I saw Orpheus,
> *Tully*, and Livy, and moral Seneca,
> Euclid geometer, and Ptolemy,
> Hippocrates, and Avicenna, and Galen,
> And Averroes, who *The Great Commentary* wrote.

Tully, of course, was Cicero. He too was in the infernal regions —
although at least he was in that pleasant part of them which was entered
by the seven gates (the trivium and the quadrivium) of learning!

But Cicero — or Tully — did considerably more than join Boethius in
teaching Dante how to show firmness in the face of an ultimate assault.

He also set a value on something without which standing firm would
hardly be a thing to test our souls for.

Let us see what it was.

"This is my first opinion. Friendship cannot exist except among good people, for friendship is nothing more than a complete unity on all points in goodwill and affection, so that I am inclined to think that with the possible exception of philosophy no better gift has been given to man by the immortal gods.

"Love — from which friendship gets its very name [*amor, amicitia*] — is the prime factor in uniting goodwill.

"For there is nothing more lovable than virtue, and nothing that more inclines to love.

"So that we think friendship should be sought not because we expect to gain something from it but because all its advantage lies in love itself. Those who, like cattle, seek any pleasure are widely at variance with us. No wonder. For those who can look up at nothing lofty, nothing glorious, nothing divine have debased all their thoughts.

"What excellent philosophy! For those who take friendship out of life have taken the sun out of the universe.

"We ought to take note of any man who shows himself weighty, constant, and firm in friendship as coming from a very rare and almost divine class of people."

For *friendship*, as Cicero suggested, read *love*. For *Scipio Africanus*, I suggest, read *Beatrice*. For *Laelius* read *Dante*.

Omnia vincit amicitia — but *amor* too.

Love conquers all.

Including death.

Laelius's friendship (love) for Scipio! Dante's love for Bice Portinari!

This love, however, cannot be self-seeking.

It should be sought — to repeat — "not because we expect to gain something from it, but because all its advantage lies in love itself."

It was perhaps as he read this that he began to have his first doubts about the lady in the window.

And so started on a loftier road.

« 4 »

But even as this happened, even as Dante slowly read the two books, even as he furrowed his brow trying, as so many did in these later years of the Middle Ages, to dredge from old-time wisdom modern and personal meanings, he became increasingly in love with knowledge for its own sake. This is not surprising. Drinking begets thirst and he had certainly drunk deeply from both Boethius and Marcus Tullius Cicero. Now all at once he wanted to know not merely that which would shore up his own stability but that which would construct for him a framework for the universe, which would explain to him the inexplicable, which would give him a firm rock on which to stand.

Acquiring this kind of knowledge involved, however, walking along a pathway which was so steep and difficult that it would have been almost impossible to tread it unassisted and alone. Guides were needed. Fortunately they were available. In the city of the lilies, there was more than one person who had some sort of technical instruction and therefore could both talk and teach.

There were also at least two important and well-established schools. The Dominicans had founded a *studium* at Santa Maria Novella not long after 1221. The Franciscans set up their own center of learning at Santa Croce only a little later. Less is known of it, but it was in existence at least by 1277.

Dante apparently attended both of these schools, although not necessarily as a regularly enrolled scholar. He was by then a little old for that.

Notebook in hand, he listened to the lectures. Because he was so obviously influenced by St. Thomas Aquinas and because St. Thomas was a Dominican, it is assumed that he attended the school at Santa Maria Novella the more regularly. But his knowledge of Franciscan doctrine and his obviously warm feeling for the little poor man of God — for whom he clearly felt a much deeper affection than he did for the *santo atleta* (the holy athlete), "courteous to his own and to his enemies cruel," who had come from Callaroga in Spain to preach and even to fight in the terrible Albigensian Crusade — make it almost certain that he attended Santa Croce too. Moreover, he speaks of the "schools" — not of the "school" — "of the religious."

What did he learn at them?

What also did he learn when he listened more informally to "the disputations of the philosophers"?

Who were his teachers?

Who were the philosophers he listened to?

Let us take up the last two questions first.

Robert Davidsöhn, the learned German who one day in the last century came to Florence and was so enraptured by what he saw that he then and there decided to devote the rest of his life to studying its history, has given us a list of "possible Dante lecturers."

In reality, they were "probable Dante lecturers."

Let us see who they were.

Fra Scolaio Squarce d'Oltrarno. He was in the Dominican order from 1277 to 1320. He was reported to have been "very literary, a brilliant stylist, and an excellent singer."

Giovanni di Ruggiero Tornaquinci. He was born in 1270 (or five years later than Dante) and entered the order in 1283. He was a reader and later he became prior (of the monastery, not one of the priors who governed the city). His name shows him to have been well born. The Tornaquinci were one of the old Florentine families. During Dante's lifetime they changed their name to Tornabuoni, which for some reason showed they were on the side of the people.

Simone Salterelli. Salterelli was also an established Florentine name. Simone taught ancient history, liberal arts, and physics, including medicine. He later became Bishop of Parma, and died in 1312.

Fra Uberto Guido — he, however, must be called only "possible" since he did not join the order until 1298. Fra Uberto was born at the castle of Nipozzano, which still from its Apennine slope looks down upon Pontassieve between vines and olive trees. In all probability, he belonged to the Counts Guidi family.

Messer Buonaccorso degli Elisei del Arco di Pietà. He was a relative of Dante's. A Ghibelline exile, he was recalled by the pacification of Cardinal Latino, but he could not resume the teaching of law. He could, however, talk.

Ottavante di Guidalotti de' Rigaletti. He was a law professor.

Messer Boninsegna de' Becchenugi of an important commercial family. He also taught law.

(But all of these men were philosophers too. All dabbled in every form of learning.)

Mino da Colle. His real name was Minotto di Naldo da Colle, but Dante called him Mino Mocato, which may or may not have been a scandalous nickname. (*Moccare* with two *c*'s means to earn a trifling sum, and it also means to blow one's nose.) Mino was a poet — an exceedingly minor one — and like many another exceedingly minor poet he eked out a miserable living by giving a course in the *ars dictaminis*, or art of writing. It was thorough, if pedestrian. He began with punctuation.

Dante refers to him in his *De Vulgari Eloquentia*. With Fra Guittone of Arezzo, Bonagiunta of Lucca, Gallo of Pisa, and even Dante's beloved Brunetto Latini, he speaks a "municipal" rather than a "curial" language — that is, he uses a street-corner rather than a cultivated choice of words.

Taddeo Alderotti was another, to whom Dante may have listened and with whom he may have talked. Taddeo succeeded "Maître Aldobrando of Florence" as that city's first physician. And just as Messer Aldobrando had ingratiated himself with his fellow citizens and with posterity by the extremely modern treatise on medicine which he brought out in France, so his successor's greatest claim to fame was his *Libello per la Conserva-*

zione della Salute (Guidebook on How to Keep Well), which, with an eye to the main chance, was dedicated to a rich and powerful citizen.

Taddeo, like Messer Aldobrando, advocated a hygienic life. He urged setting-up exercises, cleaning the hair with a comb, washing the hands and face with cold water (all these things were in the morning), clearing the throat and nose by coughing and snuffling, cleaning the teeth and gums with pulverized bark. He said that fumigation with dried rose petals or sandlewood cleared the brain. He said that from time to time you should chew fennel, anise, or gullyflower cloves. You should engage in physical labor before meals and you should chew everything thoroughly. After meals you should again wash your face and hands (remembering that dirty hands infect the eyes, but also that you can cure eye ailments by sleeping with a covered head), again clean your teeth, and then take a thousand steps. If you suffer from cataracts, you should follow a special diet, rest in bed, take certain prescribed medicines, and finally if necessary resort to surgery.

But Taddeo was much more than a physician. He was interested in every kind of knowledge, and among other things translated Aristotle's *Ethics*.

Dante said it was a poor translation.

But poor or not, it drew the poet toward the old man whom Villani was to call "the most learned medical man in Christendom."

There is considerable likelihood too that if Dante did not actually hear Pietro di Giovanni di Olivi (reader at Santa Croce from 1287 to 1289) speak, he had at least listened to talks by men whose thinking and feeling had been shaped by him.

Olivi, whose sermons were renowned, was one of the greatest and most eloquent of the leaders of the Spiritual faction in the Franciscan order — i.e., the Franciscans who believed in the strict interpretation of St. Francis's rule as opposed to the Conventuals, who abjured absolutely strict poverty and said that the order could build great churches, live in well-endowed convents, and own property — and, although Dante's understanding of the fact that in God's house there are many mansions was clear enough for him to take either side in the controversy, equally clearly he had been exposed to the Spirituals' point of view.

« 5 »

But if it seems likely that Dante, as he sought knowledge, turned to some or even all of these men; if he may well have heard Fra Scolaio talk or even sing; if he may have been taught a variety of matters by Giovanni Lisei, Messer Ottavante di Guidalotti de' Rigaletti, and Messer Boninsegna de' Becchenugi (and their notebooks show that lawyers and notaries were among Dante's earliest admirers); if he probably did more than heap scorn upon Mino Mocato; if he studied philosophy — and perhaps medicine — with Taddeo Alderotti; and if, even, there is a reasonable possibility that he became saturated with Franciscan feeling by Olivi or his followers (some have contended — incorrectly — that he became a lay brother), there is one person about whom there is absolutely no doubt.

This is Fra Remigio Girolami, one of a handful of extraordinarily eloquent preachers who held forth in the city at this time. Among others were the very much younger Fra Giordano da Rivalto and the world-traveling Fra Ricoldo Pennini, who rode on the Pope's business from Acre to Azerbaijan and then on to Nineveh and other places in the Near East.

When Pennini returned, he preached to huge throngs of gaping Florentines — and he wrote a book too — about the Old Man of the Mountain with his mysterious assassins; about the cedars of Lebanon; about riding camelback to and through Armenia; about giving sermons in Arabic for a year; and about the marvelous lands in the Near East where under the rich earth there were salt mines and petroleum and hidden gems, while on every side you saw lovely gardens in which grew rare, delicious fruits.

"These," he cried, puzzled, "the Lord in His infinite wisdom hath given to the infidel, while Christians are persecuted and slain, or forced to dwell in deserts and caves."

But Fra Remigio was perhaps more eloquent than either of them. He was a native Florentine. He was born in the *popolo* of San Pancrazio, which lay just to the west of Dante's own *popolo* of San Piero Maggiore, in the very heart of the city. Hence, like Dante, he had absorbed the lively, picturesque, expressive Florentine way of speaking with the milk on which he had been suckled as a baby.

This he made use of to bring the sermon from the cloister to the marketplace or the street, and he was enormously successful in doing so. But his sermons were not always or even often in good taste, for as he moralized and expounded he used equivocations, plays on names, forced jokes, and even bawdy byplay.

Indeed, it is almost certain that it was Fra Remigio who inspired Dante's diatribe against a certain kind of preaching which is found in *Paradiso* XXIX:

> Ye down below go not on "the one path"
> When ye philosophize: so much transports ye
> Love of display and always thinking about it.

Yet even this is suffered here on high
With far less indignation than when are scorned
The Holy Scriptures, or they are perverted.
Do ye not know the price in blood it cost
To sow these in the world and how he pleases
Who very humbly doth adhere to them?
All now do strive for show, everyone makes
His own inventions, and these are the subject
Of every preacher. The Gospel is not named.
One says unto us that the moon turned back,
What time Christ suffered, and interposed itself,
So that the light of the sun could not shine down.
He tells a lie. This light did hide itself
Of its own choice, so that to Spaniards and Hindus
As well as Jews the eclipse was manifest.
Florence has not so many Lapi and Bindi [*Toms, Dicks,*
     and Harrys]
As fables such as these that the year long
Are tossed hither and yon from every pulpit,
So that the innocent sheep who know nothing
Come from the pasture fed on empty wind;
Nor does not knowing the harm they did excuse them.
Christ did not say unto his first disciples:
"Go forth and preach idle words unto the world."
He unto them did give the true foundation,
And that alone sounded from their mouths,
So that the ones who would fight for the faith
Used the Evangels for their swords and shields.
But now with jests and with buffooneries
Men go to preach, and if they get a laugh
Their cowls puff up with pride. They ask no more.

Fra Remigio, however, was something more than just a popular preacher. He was also a man of learning — at any rate, as learning went in those days. He had studied in Paris and when he returned to Italy it was to hold a chair as a professor in the *studium* at Santa Maria Novella.

Moreover, his interests were wide, and in his readings and his writings he found a place for medicine, mathematics, politics, canon law, mechanics, and even magic. He wrote about *teatrica* (since he wrote this under the heading of mechanics, presumably it had to do with mechanical devices used in religious plays). He composed a treatise on the Song of Songs, and studies on the essence of things, the tribulations and decay brought about by party strife, and the admissability of compromise in religious negotiations. Many years, if not centuries, before there was the most elementary archaeological knowledge, he even tried to delve into a mystery which still fascinates: the identity and the provenance of the Etruscans.

But it was not these aspects of Fra Remigio which drew Dante to the white-robed friar. It was his knowledge of and his sympathy for that man who is now generally conceded to have been the most influential Catholic scholar of the Middle Ages: St. Thomas Aquinas, otherwise known as "the angelic doctor," who set Catholic doctrine upon a foundation of solid rock by bringing every part of it which was not based upon revelation into at least a working concord with the ancient Greek philosophers, and particularly with Aristotle, in Dante's opinion the greatest of them.

This is not a book about St. Thomas, and therefore I must perforce be brief. But so important was he to Dante — and to every other thinking man of Dante's time — that something must be said about him even at the risk of being inadequate.

As Dante claimed to be, Thomas was of noble birth. His father was a nephew of the Emperor Barbarossa, and his mother was descended from the Norman princes of Sicily.

(A century later one of his not-too-distant relatives would have the doubtful honor of going down in history as the husband of Boccaccio's mistress Fiammetta.)

He was born in 1225 in his father's castle of Roccasecca near Aquino and about forty miles from Naples; got his early schooling at nearby Montecassino; and then at the age of fourteen went to the University of Naples. It was an odd place for him to have gone, for Duns Scotus taught there at the time — he lectured on Averroës — and it was a hotbed of Greek, Arabic, and Hebrew influences. Indeed, so worldly was its atmosphere that his brothers decided to become troubadours, and one of them, attached in this capacity to the court of the free-thinking Frederick II, urged Thomas to join him there. Instead, in 1243, he entered the Dominican order.

Almost immediately, he was sent to Paris to study theology, but his mother arranged to have him kidnaped; took him back to Roccasecca; kept him a close prisoner for a year; and used every means to win him from his vocation, including, it is said, introducing a beautiful young woman into his lonely cell.

They were unsuccessful, and he continued his journey to the city by the Seine. There he met the amazing German scholar Albrecht or Albertus of Cologne, who is more generally known as Albertus Magnus — Albert the Great. Under him he studied from 1245 to 1248.

Albertus not only taught him but believed in him.

Because of his stolid manners and his plodding and careful approach some of Thomas's fellow scholars called this gentle-mannered fellow with his broad face and yellow hair "the dumb ox of Sicily."

Albertus would have none of this.

"Dumb ox, you call him? Dumb ox? Well, he may seem a dumb ox to you. But I tell you the whole world will re-echo to the lessons which they will learn from his lowing!"

Thomas believed in Albertus too, and when the latter was called back to Cologne — protesting that this took him from both religion and philosophy — to organize a *studium* there and later to become the reluctant bishop of Ratisbon, the man from the kingdom of Naples followed him.

He stayed in Cologne for four years, but in 1252 he was in Paris again. There, in 1256, he received the degree of Licentiate in Theology and shortly afterward that of Master of Theology.

(But the faculty of the university refused to admit either him — or St. Bonaventura — to the Society of Masters. Professional jealousy does not seem to have been a modern invention.)

The next three years he spent in bitter controversy. Against William of St. Amour, the official spokesman of the university. Against Siger of Brabant for his alleged support of Averroës and of Averroës's teaching that the soul is not immortal. (Dante, in *Paradiso* X, would defend Siger.) Against many others.

Then he returned to Italy to teach in the pontifical *studium*, which had been moved from Anagni to Orvieto and finally to Viterbo.

But in 1268 he went once more to Paris — it always drew him.

In 1272, he was recalled to his native Naples. Charles of Anjou wanted him to recognize his alma mater.

Two years later, Pope Gregory X summoned him to attend the Council of Lyons.

He set out from Naples on muleback, intending to ride the length of Italy and then over or around the Alps. But even before he reached Rome, he fell ill and took to his bed at the Cistercian monastery of Fossanova near Terracina and not more than a mile from the then malarial Pontine Marshes. On March 7, he died there.

Dante (and others) said that he had been murdered — by Charles himself, who feared that Aquinas would work against him in papal councils.

Murder, however, was not necessary. The Pontine climate and the rigors of medieval travel were sufficient.

He was only forty-nine years old.

But in those forty-nine years he had created and set down perhaps the most voluminous collection of philosophical, religious, and even political writings which had ever been assembled by a single man since the Aristotle whom he — and because of him, Dante — so admired and so sought to use.

(Aristotle, it should be noted, lived to be sixty-two.)

Even a list of his writings is little less than astonishing.

He began with the commentaries on the Bible which won him his licentiate.

Then, in 1254, he wrote a similar work on the *Sentences* of Peter Lombard.

Shortly thereafter he wrote his *Quaestiones Disputatae* and his *Quaestiones Quodlibetales*. (These expressed tentative opinions on certain theological problems with which he would deal more confidently later.)

Next he undertook a series of comments upon Boethius; upon the pseudo-Dionysius (supposedly a convert of St. Paul's, but really a Syrian who lived around 500 A.D.) and upon more than a dozen of the more important works of his beloved Stagirite, Aristotle.

These were merely preludes, however, and as he approached the supposed middle point of our life, he began the two very huge works upon which his reputation rests today. The *Summa Contra Gentiles* — a work upon Christian ideas written for the specific purpose of converting Moslems and Jews — was begun in 1259 and finished in 1265. It was five volumes long. The *Summa Theologiae*, in which unfinished book the author stated that he would treat of "those things which pertained to sacred doctrine and with such brevity as the subject matter allows," filled twenty-one volumes, and in them there were thirty-eight treatises, six hundred thirty-one questions or topics, and ten thousand observations or replies. (St. Thomas's complete published works would take ten thousand pages with double columns.) Yet no one can deny that it was as brief as it could be.

Taken as a whole — and in this case the whole is clearly greater than the sum of the parts; studied and correlated; added up and evaluated, it becomes apparent that this mighty production was a monument to something important and even shaking which was about to happen to the human mind.

For unlike St. Augustine, who — at any rate, if you can believe what he says in his *Confessions* — was drawn to God by the wild turbulence of an emotional yearning, St. Thomas appealed to and lived in a world of reason. It is almost — *but not quite* — true that he believed that anything must be proven to be accepted as valid, and that anything valid *could* be proven so. Even Diety itself.

And it must be proven by that which we observe and see.

"*Nihil est in intellectu quod prius non fuerit in sensu,*" said Aquinas. There is nothing in the mind which was not first in the senses.

Nothing — and that is an all-embracing word.

This being the case, it is in no way surprising that this patient, soft-spoken Italian of Germanic blood, whose aim was "not merely to find out what others had thought, but what the truth of the matter is," and who having found it expressed it in language equally suited "to the studious minds of his fellow monks or to the simple intellects of common folk," should have set afire person after person in western Europe.

It is not surprising that he should have been read and expounded in Florence, where minds were beginning to be extraordinarily sharp and keen.

It was Fra Remigio who expounded him in Florence.

It was appropriate that he should do so. For one thing, both men were Dominicans, and as early as 1286 the general chapter of this organization had imposed upon all Dominicans the duty of defending St. Thomas and his teachings.

But Fra Remigio was also one of St. Thomas' students, and a good friend. Who knows? He may even have sat beside him in the refectory on one of those many occasions when Thomas was so absorbed in his study that his plate was snatched away from him without his even knowing it. He may even have attended the dinner with Louis IX (St. Louis) at which, rapt in his thoughts, Thomas smote the table and cried:

"I have an irrefutable argument against the Manichaeans!"

"Bring him pen, ink, and parchment," commanded St. Louis, in no way offended.

It was equally appropriate that Dante should have turned to the man from Roccasecca.

Many thousands of words have been written on the question of whether or not Dante was a Thomist, but with all due respect to the learned authors, it is only marginally pertinent. Thomism was all about and everywhere, and what Thomas Aquinas wrote upon prime matter and substantial form, upon the soul and the body, upon proofs of the existence of God, and even upon such mundane matters as the family, the sovereign people and its representatives, and the duties of a ruler — to select a few from many — was as much a part of the intellectual equipment of every intelligent man of his time as is some sort of an idea of the Einstein theory today. To that extent, Dante could no more not be a Thomist than he could escape breathing the circumambient air.

Far more important is when and how he came really to know the great philosopher.

Here, once again, an all-conclusive answer cannot be given.

Anybody who compares the twentieth section of the *Vita Nuova* with St. Thomas's *De Anima*, book 11, chapter XVI, will discover that Dante, in dividing the sonnet there commented on into two parts and then explaining them, so closely followed not merely the technique but the very phraseology used by Aquinas as to make it virtually indisputable that this was an imitation.

But equally, anyone who traces the changing influence of St. Thomas as one Dante book succeeded another must concede that the poet's study of the philosopher was continuing.

Nevertheless, it seems highly probable that it was in the years which immediately following Beatrice's death — in the years between 1291 and 1295 — and under the tutelage of Fra Remigio that Dante had his greatest exposure to the man whom he was later to call light, illumination, life, and *benedetta fiamma* (blessed flame). Here his own observations on the effects of his study give corollary evidence. Cicero and Boethius were relatively easy. They could hardly have kept him awake nights. It was Aquinas who set him week after week to burning the midnight oil, who ruined his eyesight and impaired his health even as he molded his soul.

« 6 »

During this period something else suffered too. Or so it would seem.

For it is not more than two years later that two very revealing documents were drawn up. They are dated April 11 and December 23, 1297.

Document one:

"Dante and Francesco Alanghiero [*sic*] Alighieri of the *popolo* of San Martino acknowledge having received the below-named sum from Andrea di Guido de' Ricci — namely 227½ Florentine florins of honest weight — and this is notarized by Ser Dato di Jacopo of Carrara."

For the record, this debt was still unpaid in 1300.

Document two:

"On December 23, 1297, Dante and Francesco, brothers, and sons of the late Alighiero degli Alighieri of the *popolo* of San Piero Maggiore, acknowledge the receipt of 400 gold florins from Jacopo del fu Litto dei Corbizzi, who lent them on behalf of himself and of Pannochia Riccomanni" — she was a woman and could not do business on her own account — "under the security of Messers Durante Scolaio degli Abbati" — Dante's supposed grandfather — "Manetto de' Donati" — Dante's father-in-law — "Neddo del fu Riccomanni degli Adimari, and Spigliato del fu Spigliato da Filicaia."

It would seem that Dante — and the younger brother who always tagged at Dante's financial heels until he became old enough, and a good enough businessman, to manage the affairs of both — had let everyday matters fall into rack and ruin.

It would seem that the Alighieri farms were being neglected.

It would seem that whatever small loan business had been inherited from Alighiero II had disappeared.

It would seem that the brothers Alighieri now had to pay interest instead of receiving it.

(Maybe that is why Dante, in his *Inferno*, was so hard on usurers.)

Why?

A plausible explanation is that Dante was now spending so much time at his books — or daydreaming with his head in the clouds as he tried to find the answer to the unanswerable — that he did not have any time, nor did he have the desire, to pay the necessary attention to those *libbre*, *denari*, and *soldi* without which you cannot live in Florence any more than anywhere else.

Yet it is equally possible that the financial embarrassments which must have set tongues to wagging did not come from time wasted — as many Florentines must have regarded Dante's studiousness — in spinning scholastic cobwebs, but from another phase of Dante's life, from a new and very uncommendable way of living into which he now plunged himself almost as if in reaction to the ardors and endurance — and the discipline — of the last few years.

IX

Thy Life So Vile

 T is a matter first reported to us—and in some detail—by Guido
Cavalcanti, who certainly should have known what he was talking
about.

This "first friend of Dante," it should be particularly emphasized, was
in no way straitlaced – as should be more than plain to anyone who
remembers his relationships with Florentine Primavera-Giovanna and
Provençal Mandette. He did not set himself harshly difficult or impossible
standards.

"Deep in a thicket," he wrote in one of his poems — and he was clearly
not talking about either of the above-named ladies — "I found a shepherd lass, and she was far more lovely than a star."

He continued:

> Her eyes were filled with love. She was rose wax.
> With dainty crook she shepherded her lambs.
> She went barefoot. Her feet were laved with dew,
> And she did sing as if in love with me.
> She was dressed up in every pleasing grace.

What then?

> I greeted her forthwith most lovingly,
> And she thereat did answer with sweet words
> That she alone in the fair thicket was,
> But added: "Know thou that the dove of Cupid
> Has told me I will soon a dear one have."

When she thus told me she was fancy-free
And in the branches I heard small birds sing,
I said unto myself: "The time hath come
For someone to embrace this shepherd lass.
But I will only ask her for a kiss.
Perhaps she will then seek to know my arms."

Ah, she then took my hand, lit up with love,
And said that she had given me her heart.
And then she took me to a leafy grove—
Within it there were flowers of every hue—
And there for me had such sweet entertainment
That I do swear I saw the god of love.

It is quite an idyll, if one dares call it that!

One cannot help thinking, indeed, of Robert Herrick, who lived and wrote a little more than three centuries later.

Rose wax, said Guido Cavalcanti.

"Gather ye rosebuds while ye may," said Herrick, adding that "Old Time is still a-flying!"

The Florentine aristocrat-poet certainly gathered them — and very infrequently from the same rosebush.

Nor did this deep and moody fellow — who curiously enough despite his introspection and unhappy pondering wrote poetry that is like a garden when it is still dewy — see any reason why he should not.

But when Dante strayed from what Guido thought to be the straight and narrow path, it was another matter. Then the older poet — Guido was at least forty at this time, and Dante not quite thirty — became a moralist and let Dante know it.

He wrote him this sonnet:

I come to thee in dream again and again,
And that thy thoughts are base and vile I find,
And so I mourn thy onetime noble mind,
And all the many virtues from thee ta'en.
One time thou heldst much company in despite.
Now 't is from thee that hurries the ignoble crowd.
Thy rhymes did once so praise me I was proud
To treasure every line that thou didst write.
But now I dare not — thy life being so vile —
Take pleasure from a thing that thou dost say,
Nor myself in thy presence even show.
Yet do thou read and reread this sonnet awhile.
Then will the evil spirit that haunts thee so
Be thrust from thy vile soul and go away.

It is quite a tirade, and as such should be examined carefully. We should examine both its phraseology and its overall tone. Hopefully we can learn much.

The phraseology first.

The word *vil* or some form of it is used three times.

E trovate pensar troppo vilmente. And that thy thoughts are low and vile I find. *La vil tua vita.* Thy life being so vile. *Si partirà da l'anima invilita.* Be thrust from thy vile soul and go away.

The word *noioso*, or a form of it, is used twice.

La gente noiosa. The ignoble crowd. *Lo noioso spirito.* Thy vile soul. Then the overall tone, which is scornful.

Once Dante fled from the crowd, now the crowd flees from him.

Guido once treasured every line Dante wrote, now he does not dare to do so.

Guido and Dante were once boon companions. Now Guido does not even wish to be in Dante's presence.

But even as he thrusts these daggers at Dante, he reminds him that it was not always so.

"Thy onetime noble mind!" he cries.

And it may become noble again.

Let Dante merely read and reread Guido Cavalcanti's sonnet. "Then will the evil spirit that haunts thee so be thrust from thy vile soul and go away."

It is clear that Dante had fallen, or was thought to have fallen, into evil ways.

It is clear that Guido Cavalcanti, no angel himself, felt it necessary to take pen in hand and chide him publicly.

It is also clear that this was the true time — although in the *Commedia* it takes place on April 8, 1300 — when Dante strayed from the *diritta via* (the way of righteousness) into the *selva oscura* (the darkling wood) where he found the three allegorical beasts of lewdness or luxury (the leopard), pride (the lion), and avarice (the she-wolf).

At that time, he reached the nadir of his earthly pilgrimage.

He has Beatrice say the following of this nadir in *Inferno* II:

> "My friend — but he is not the friend of fortune —
> Upon the desert hillside is so hindered
> Upon his road that he turns back in fear,
> And I do fear he is so far astray
> That I may well have roused myself too late
> To help him. That is what I hear in heaven,"

But Beatrice had not arisen too late, as will become apparent as we proceed with the story.

« 2 »

What was this nadir of Dante's? What was the slough and mire into which he had sunk?

The German Witte and the Swiss Scartazzini say that it was nothing more than intellectual error with a blameworthy neglect of theology. They are, of course, not the only ones who find it difficult or distasteful to believe that the man who was unquestionably the greatest Christian poet who ever wrote could have descended to the very depths.

To me this shows a complete lack of understanding both of human nature in general and of Dante's. To me Dante never could have reached heaven if he had not gone first into hell.

"Though I lie in the gutter, I can look upon the stars!" cried a modern poet.

Dante appears to have lain in the gutter for a while.

But the last line of every cantica of his *Commedia* has him looking on the stars.

But again, what kind of a gutter? This is important.

Boccaccio offers a suggestion.

"In the midst of such virtue and learning as has been shown above to have been in this marvelous man," he says, speaking of Dante's personal life, and his words have been attacked by six centuries of the poet's admirers, "licentiousness also found a most ample place, and not only in his youthful, but in his mature, years.

"Which vice," he continues — but hardly in character — "although it be natural and common and, as it were, necessary, cannot be commended or even excused."

But Dante himself indicates that he knew more than a little about the kind of living which this would imply.

Purgatorio XXIII:

> Sardinia's Barbagia is by far
> More modest in the conduct of its women
> Than the Barbagia is wherein I left her.
> O my sweet brother, what wouldst have me say?
> That future time already comes in sight,
> Nor will this hour be ancient when it does,
> When from the very pulpit shall be denounced
> Those brazen-faced, immodest Florentine women
> Who go about with bare breast, showing their teats.

> What low barbarian, nay what Saracen,
> Doth need, to make her walk decently covered,
> Either spiritual or other discipline?
> But if these shameless ones did only know
> That which swift heaven is storing up for them
> They would already have mouths open for wailing.
> For if my foresight doth not here deceive me,
> They will taste grief before the cheeks are bearded
> Of those who now listen to lullabies.

In my judgment, Boccaccio told the truth, but not the whole truth.

Dante may have lived licentiously in this period of reaction against his almost health-destroying pursuit of knowledge, and in his reaction to both sorrow and a more orderly pursuit of love.

In that case, licentiousness is not more than marginally too strong a word.

Nor is *vil*.

Certainly dissolute is not.

But licentiousness, *viltà*, and dissoluteness do not tell the whole story, which is better expressed by saying that at this time Dante's life was just generally disorderly. He was doing at thirty what he might better have done a decade earlier and what most men do at that much younger age. At this time, he was living in a generally disreputable manner. With all that this implies!

« *3* »

As might be expected, he did not live disreputably alone. He had a companion — the man, incidentally, upon whose lips he had placed the denunciation of Florentine women which we have just read.

Again let us turn to *Purgatorio* XXIII. Dante is looking at a group of shades who are "so shriveled up to naught but rind by hunger" that "the sockets of their eyes did seem like rings that have no gems."

He continues with his description:

"Whoso," he says, "upon man's visage doth read *omo*, would surely there have recognized the *m*."

This refers to the fact that the capital *M* of Dante's time framed by two *o*'s greatly resembled the nose between two eye sockets. Through hunger, the eyes had sunk so deep they had disappeared.

Then he comes to the point:

> I was still wondering what had so famished them,
> For not yet manifest the reason was
> That they so lean were and so covered with scurf,

When lo, sunk very deeply in their skull
Eyes stared at me. A shade looked fixedly
And then cried loudly out: "What grace is this?"
Never would I have recognized his visage,
But in his voice it was made plain to me
That which his aspect certainly had concealed
And this spark did rekindle in me all
My recognition of the changed countenance.
I knew again the face of my Forese.

The face of my Forese!

It was Forese Donati, son of Simone Donati, brother of Corso and Piccarda Donati, and also cousin of Gemma Donati, Dante's too frequently neglected wife.

"Stay not from speaking to me!" Forese cries.

Dante does what he is asked. He says this:

"That face of thine which I did weep in death
Now makes me weep for it with no less sorrow,
Seeing it so deformed."

Then he sets their friendship in time:

"Forese, from that day
In which you changed world to a better life
Five years not yet have rolled around till now."

Forese, then, had died in 1295 or 1296.

Dante continues, defining this friendship.

"If thou bringest back to mind
What thou to me was, and what I to thee,
Even today the memory will grieve thee."

But now their paths have diverged.

"From such a life I was taken by the man
Who walks in front of me the other day
When round in heaven still appeared *his* sister —"
I pointed to the sun. "He from the deep
Night me hath led, and from the truly dead,
Still wearing mortal flesh, who follow him."

Again, what kind of life did Dante abandon?
What kind of life did he share with Forese?

What did Forese and Dante do together in that vanished time of their mutual youth when each meant so much to the other that even in the place of purgation where all earthly longings are supposedly cleansed away they looked back to it with nostalgia and sorrow?

From what life had Dante been taken by the man who walked in front of him — i.e., by Virgil?

« 4 »

Some of this has already been stated, but much more is made plain by an extraordinary *tenzone*, or poetic contest, which was carried on between the two men — a sequence of six sonnets, three by each, which was discovered in the last century and for a long time was not widely thought to be authentic.

Dante could not have written such ribaldry, said his admirers.

But the weight of evidence indicates that it is authentic, and it should be read carefully and examined thoughtfully.

Sonnet one — Dante to Forese:

> Who hears Forese Bicci's hapless wife
> Coughing her head off would perhaps aver
> She spends her winters in some climate where
> The chill ice crystals cut her with sharp knife.
> Even in August she is frozen stiff.
> In any other month, then, think of her!
> But it would do no good, with hide or fur,
> Countryman-style to quilt her, on my life.
> For her rasped cough, her rheum, her other pains
> Come not to her from humors, inborn, old,
> But come because she sleeps in bed alone.
> Her mother weeps, whose woes are multifold,
> As she "I could have married her" complains
> "For one fig to Count Guido had I known."

Sonnet two — Forese to Dante:

> The other night I too coughed off my head
> Because I had no quilt to cover me,
> But when dawn broke I was moved instantly
> To venture forth to gain more than my bread.
> Now hear you to what place Dame Fortune led.
> A casket full of pearls I thought to see,
> Or red coined florins that shone goldenly.
> Instead I saw your father lying dead,
> Cast in the ditch and tied with Solomon's

Knot or some other sage I do not know.
I crossed myself and faced the breaking day,
Whereat he cried: "O untie me at once
For love of Dante!" I did not know how,
And so I turned aside and went my way.

Sonnet three — Dante to Forese:

You too will have your knot of Solomon,
Bicci Novello, made of partridge breast
Or, worse for you, of mutton chine well done
Whose parchment takes revenge on what you taste.
Indeed, you'll find yourself in San Simon
Locked up if you don't flee the coop in haste.
Just giving up your gluttony alone
Is now too late. You must fork up at last.
Yet I have heard that you have learned a trade
So profitable—if it's true indeed—
That you'll recoup your losses great and small.
Of summonses you need no more be afraid.
You can stay here. And yet I bid you heed
The Stagni's end. For they got hanged. That's all.

Sonnet four — Forese to Dante:

Repay St. Gall before you leer and sneer
At other people's abject poverty.
God knows you've used in full its charity,
You and your friends, the winter of this year.
But if you must needs beg, as it seems clear,
Why always come to us so whiningly?
There's Altrafonte Castle generously
To give you all you need of food and cheer.
Yet I'm convinced you'll have to sweat and swink
With Tana and Francesco still alive,
Since your Belluzzo has no truck with you.
You'll end up in a paupers' ward, I think.
Yes, I see Dante—who'll take all we give—
Guzzling in rags there with the other two.

Sonnet five — Dante to Forese:

Bicci Novel (I don't know whose son he,
Nor will unless his mother should apprise)
Has swilled so much in his foul gluttonies

That he must needs resort to robbery.
And so good folk with purse at belt who see
Him coming near to them if they are wise
"That fellow," warn, "carved up from chin to eyes,
Is the most notable brigand there could be."
His father too in bed quakes and grows cold
For fear the rogue red-handed will be ta'en,
Who's his no more than Christ was Joseph's son.
Of Bicci and his brothers this is told:
It's born in each his ill-got gains to take
And this the other's wife bestow upon.

Sonnet six — Forese to Dante:

That you are Alighieri's son no doubt!
It sticks out clear and plain in the revenge
You took so swift and sure when his exchange
Of eagles very lately was found out.
But though they'd quarter you or cut your throat
Why in such haste, sir, do you peace arrange?
It's time they filled your saddlebags with change,
Two mules who were too burdened to trot.
For this—I understand and I repeat—
You will be clubbed and drubbed, and by the one
You held to be your brother—and your friend.
But if by any chance I should relate
All who would thrash you, long ere I was done
I'd use up all the numbers, nor reach end.

It would be well to examine these sonnets too.

What — it would be well to ask — were these two young men about town trying to say to each other, admittedly in a spirit of rough-and-tumble fun but not without certain savage, sarcastic barbs which show that Dante at least (who as the series progressed seems to have shown less control of his temper than Forese) had strayed more than a little beyond the boundaries of good feeling and good taste?

To be sure, because of the packed economy of the eighty-four lines and their many allusions to episodes and events which for obvious reasons have not been recorded, scholars have disagreed on this for as long as the poems have been known. Nor are they ever likely to come to unanimous and solidly provable conclusions. Yet guesses can and should be hazarded, and if they are made thoughtfully they may not be far wrong.

Sonnet one:

"You, Messer Forese, who are called Bicci after your grandfather or some other worthless rogue, are a night wanderer and a chaser after low women. True, your wife is at least partly to blame. She is a poor miserable creature who coughs her head off as she shakes and shivers with so great a chill that not even the warmest country covers would set her blood to flowing."

(Yet it should be noted that, in *Purgatorio* XXIII, Forese speaks of his wife with touching affection.

"How have you come here so soon?" Dante asks him.

> Thereupon he to me: "Ahead of time
> To drink down the sweet wormwood of my torments
> My Nella brought me with her bursting tears.
> She with her devout prayers and her sighing
> Hath drawn me from the slope where I should have waited,
> And she hath freed me from toiling through other circles.
> For very dear to God and very precious
> My little widow is I loved so much."

It was a human *Commedia* as well as a divine one.)

"But that is not her fault. It is yours. She does not shake and quake because a cold or other fever grips her, but because she has to sleep alone in an unwarmed bed while you go nighthawking. Yet she brought you a good dowry and certainly she could have found a better husband. Have you heard her mother on the subject? 'Why for a fig,' she cries, 'why for just lifting my finger, I could have married her to one of the great Counts Guidi.' "

Sonnet two:

"It's not, Dante, my wife who coughs her head off. It is I. And that is because I generously gave her my own covers. You have me wrong on something else too. I was not abroad in the night pursuing women. I was looking for something better — good hard money. What did I find? Not a strongbox filled with pearls and florins. I found your father. He was tossed into a ditch like other heretics. Fra Solomon of Lucca or some other inquisitor had him bound and tossed there. I crossed myself for he was a damned soul and at that he cried out: 'Save me! For the sake of Dante, save me!' But that was too much even for me to do, and anyway it was cock's-crow. So I turned my back on him and came home."

Sonnet three:

"You are tied up by your own kind of Fra Solomon, Bicci Novello, Bicci the Second, and this knot is not heresy but the partridge breasts you guzzle on, or the well-done roast of mutton you stuff your guts with. But take good care. The skin of that mutton has been turned into parchment and on it the order for your arrest has been written. In that way the slaughtered sheep will get even with you. Yes, if you don't take to your heels and that right swiftly, you'll soon find yourself in San Simon prison. Just giving up your gluttonous ways will not be enough. You must also pay up your old debts. But I hear that you've now learned a trade that will take care of them, and so you fear duns no longer. I say you'd better watch out. The Stagni turned highwaymen too, and they got hanged."

Sonnet four:

"Before you mock other people's poverty, why don't you pay back what you've taken from the poorhouse yourself? I'm talking about St. Gall's. You and your friends have sponged on it all winter. Anyway, if you have to beg, why do you always come to me? There's always that home for illegitimate children, the castle of Altrafonte by the Arno side. It should give you food and drink. But I'm afraid that you may have to work for a change anyway, for you now have your sister Tana and your brother Francesco on your hands, and cousin Belluzzo has announced that he is through with helping you. Or you could end up as a pauper, living at the expense of your *sesto*. That's what probably will happen. Yes, I can see Dante and the other two dressed in rags and living off what charity we give them. I can see that."

Sonnet five:

Bicci Novel — and if you throw illegitimate at me I reply that only your mother knows whose son you are — I repeat that you have swilled so gluttonously that now you have to turn robber to pay for it all, so that anyone with a purse at his belt starts to tremble when he sees you coming. 'That carved up fellow,' he cries, 'is the most notable wallet snatcher in all Florence.' Your father trembles too, but for another reason. Although you are no more his offspring than Christ was Joseph's son, he fears that you will be caught red-handed. But if you are not caught even worse will happen, for you and your brothers bestow your booty — and more beside — upon each other's wives. You are better brothers-in-law than you are husbands."

Sonnet six:

"Well, I know well enough who your father was. It was Alighiero, all right. This very plainly shows in the valiant way you avenged the wrongs that had been done to him. They threatened to hang, draw, and quarter you — or at least to cut your throat — and so you came to an agreement with them. Naturally, you were well paid for this. Where else did you get the two muleloads of money you are boasting of? But if you got paid that didn't help you with your so-called friend and brother. You must have swindled him with the others, for he's ready to give you a dusting. And so are a great many others. There aren't enough numbers to set them down."

It is, of course, obvious that none of this was intended to be taken absolutely literally.

Dante accused Forese of abandoning his wife, or at least of being unfaithful to her. He accused him of gross gluttonies. He accused him — and some of Forese's own lines almost seem to substantiate this — of getting the necessary funds for this at stiletto point. He warned him he risked being hanged. He accused him of being a bastard. He accused him — at least by implication — of being unduly attentive to his sister-in-law.

Forese accused Dante of having a heretic and sharp dealer for a father. He accused him of living off charity. He accused him of being a coward.

But these charges were not made in formal documents laid before the priors — or the Council of One Hundred.

They were made in a series of sonnets written to entertain.

Nevertheless, when you go in for satire based on personality, you must at least heap your scorn on characteristics which your victim is believed to have.

It certainly is not contended that Dante lived on what was given to him by his friends, but at the least his relatively lean purse must have been notable and noted. It is not contended that he quaked in his boots when he saw an adversary — he had taken part in at least two battles, as we remember — but he must surely have had the reputation of being less eager to use sword or dagger than some of his associates; you will remember that cousin Geri del Bello complained that he had not been avenged. Nor is it contended that his father was actually condemned as one of those who with Epicurus — and with Farinata and Cavalcante Cavalcanti — were forever enclosed in the burning tombs of the sixth circle of Inferno, or that he got into difficulties with the law for devious financial transactions. But Alighiero II could not have been thought of as a devoted churchman or as one whose business methods were beyond even a suspicion of reproach.

So too with Forese, who at the very least must have been something of a libertine; who clearly did not fill his purse from his friends' charity but by other more direct methods; and who was certainly — to use a phrase borrowed from the Bible — "a glutton and wine bibber" as well as a friend of publicans and sinners.

It would seem that this gluttony and this wine-bibbing were the most conspicuous of Forese's characteristics, for he was not put into the hell of either the violent or of those who had loved more well than wisely but into the purgatory of those who were paying the price of their inordinate appetites.

But Dante seems to have been — or to have become — extremely conscious of the dietary excesses of some of his contemporaries. *Purgatorio* XXIV. Again it is Forese who is speaking.

> "This" (with his finger he pointed) "is Bonagiunta,
> Bonagiunta of Lucca, and that other face
> Beyond him, far more haggard than the rest,
> Once held the Holy Church in his embrace.
> From Tours he was, and now by fasting purges
> Bolsena's eels and his Vernaccia wine."
> Then many others he named me one by one,
> I did not see one of them darkly scowl.
> I saw hungrily gnash their teeth on nothing
> Ubaldin della Pila and Boniface . . .
> Who shepherded many people with his staff.

It was a short catalogue of those who, as the phrase goes, "did themselves well," and, even as today, among them there were men of many different kinds. Bonagiunta was a poet. We have already heard him talking about poetry. The man from Tours was Simon of Brie — the Brie which still gives us one of the world's finest cheeses. He was first the chancellor of Louis IX of France, then a cardinal, and finally, through the influence of Charles of Anjou, became Pope Martin IV. "He was a good man and exceedingly prudent, but he lived extravagantly." Accordingly to legend, he was excessively fond of eels from the Lago di Bolsena, which he kept in milk and then had stewed in the sweet, tangy white wine from near Genoa which is still called Vernaccia. Supposedly he died — in March 1285 — from overeating this favorite dish.

The others named by Dante were similarly accomplished at the board in the banquet hall, and enjoyed a similar repute.

At this time of his life — but at this time only — did Dante too?

« 5 »

It seems almost certain that it was also at this time that Dante wrote the only other of his less than serious poems which has survived, and it too throws some light on this phase of his life.

This was a forty-four-line *discordo* — literally "discord" — a very hard poem to translate, for almost all its effect of playfulness and irony comes from the fact that it is written in three languages (French, Latin, and Italian), and this effect is naturally lost when the poem is reduced to a single tongue.

I therefore reproduce it both in the original and in an English translation, hoping that at least some part of what Dante intended will thus be conveyed.

Aï, faux ris, pour quoi traï aves
Oculos meos? Et quod tibi feci
Che fatta m'hai cosi spietata fraude?
Iam audivissent verba mea Greci!
E selonch autres dames vous saves
Che' ngannator non è degno di laude.
Tu sai ben come gaude
Miserum eius cor qui prestolatur:
Je li sper anc, e pas de moi non cure.
Ai, Dieus, quante malure
Atque fortuna ruinosa datur
A colui che, aspettando, il tempo perde
Nè gia mai tocco di fioretto il verde.

Ah, thou false smile, why hast thou drawn to thee
Mine eyes? And what to thee have I then done
That thou on me hath wrought such pitiless fraud?
Already to the Greeks my words are known!
Like other women thou knowest certainly
That the deceiver merits neither praise nor laud.
Thou knowest 't is true joy—and not a gaud—
That fills the sad heart that is eased of its load:
I hope for this, for myself have no care.
Ah God, what evils are,
And what dire fortune, bestowed
On him who waits and, waiting, his time loses
And never sees the blossoms of the roses.

Conqueror, cor suave, de te primo,
Che per un matto guardamento d'occhi
Vous non dovris avoir perdu la loi;
Ma e' mi piace che li dardi e li stocchi
Sempre insurgant contra me de limo
Dont je serai mort, pour foi che je croi.
Fort me deplait pour moi,
Ch' i' son punito ed aggio colpa nulla;
Nec dixit ipsa: "malum est de ipso";
Unde querelam sisto.
Ella sa ben che se'l mio cor si scrulla
A penser d'autre, que d'amour lesset
La faux cuers grant paine en porteret.

Conqueror, soft and gentle heart, of thee first!
I say that because eyes madly looked at you
You still from guarding the law should never swerve.

Yet would your slings, yet would your arrows too,
Against me from the slime now do their worst,
Yea, though it slay me, for I faith observe.
Yet it displeases me without reserve
That I who have done no wrong chastisement must take,
Nor does she cry out: "On him be a curse!"
Then I could complaints rehearse,
For she doth know full well that if my heart should break,
Thinking of her who by love doth bind and tie,
Her false heart great pain will endure thereby.

Ben avrà questa donna cor di ghiaccio
E tant d'aspresse que, ma foi, est fors,
Nisi pietatem habuerit servo.
Bien set Amours, se je non ai socors,
Che per lei dolorosa morte faccio
Neque plus vitam, sperando, conservo.
Ve omni meo nervo,
S'elle non fet que pour soun sen verai
Io vengna a ri veder sua faccia allegra.
Ahi Dio, quant'e integra!
Mes je m'en dout, si grant dolor en ai,
Amorem versus me non tantum curat
Quantum spes in me de ipsa durat.

This lady has a heart of ice indeed,
And is so bitter 't is impossible
She ever will show pity to her slave.
And if there be no succor, Love knows well
Cruel death, and for her sake will be my meed,
Nor hope for longer life will I then have.
I'll ache in every nerve
If she does not of her goodness grant to me
That I may see her face with great joy shine.
God, she is fair and fine!
Yet so I grieve her that this cannot be.
She has not love for me, I do aver,
Even half as great as the hope I have in her.

Cianson, poves aler pour tout le monde,
Namque locutus sum in lingua trina,
Ut gravis mea spina
Sia saccia per lo mondo. Ogn'uomo senta:
Forse pietà n'avrà chi mi tormenta.

Song, thou mayst now go forth through the whole world,
For written as thou art in languages three

> How sharp my thorn may see
> All in the world, and then, of all men known,
> Perhaps she who torments me may pity show.

In the mind of anyone who reads this poem, a question almost inevitably arises. Who was the woman to whom Dante wrote this erudite and witty tour de force? What Florentine was herself learned enough and witty enough to appreciate it?

The answer is that it was not written *to* a woman but *about* one. Nor was it written *for* a woman. It was written for the entertainment and diversion of Forese and the other high-spirited young men with whom Dante now consorted.

Who were they — besides Forese and, of course, Guido Cavalcanti?

Clearly Betto Brunelleschi. Later, in Florentine politics, he would become one of Dante's most implacable enemies, but now they were close friends.

"Messer Brunetto," Dante wrote him in an extremely charming sonnet, "this fair little maid I send to you to keep the Eastertide."

The little maid is generally thought to have been a copy of the *Vita Nuova*.

Dino Frescobaldi.

Lapo Gianni.

Casella.

Lazy Belacqua — Master Drinkwater.

(But all of these we have met before.)

And quite probably Giotto, the painter, with his fellow painters Bonamico and Bruno.

Giotto — whose painting of Dante (it is the only provably contemporary portrait of the poet, and was done by one who had seen him) can still be seen in Florence on the wall of the Bargello — was born in 1266 or 1267 (hence he was a year or two younger than Dante), the son of a substantial farmer who lived near the village of Vespignano a few miles northeast of Florence. According to Vasari, his artistic abilities were discovered by Cimabue when the older artist, tramping through the countryside, came upon a young boy who, as he tended his father's herds, was drawing a sheep on the bare face of a rock with homemade charcoal.

Cimabue took him to Florence, where, "aided by his natural gifts" and taught by the man who had discovered him, "he not only, while still a boy, equaled the work of his master, but became such a good imitator of nature that he cast aside the clumsy manner of the Greeks" — the Byzantines — "and revived art with a good and modern way of painting."

He also lived a trecento *vie de Bohème,* during the course of which his wit and high spirits became legendary.

We have already heard of his encounter with a Florentine pig, but that was not the only entertaining episode in which he took part.

Once, for example, a yokel who from the farm had risen to wealth and importance even as had Giotto, came to him and asked him to paint him a coat of arms. Giotto did, but to the symbols of the fellow's new knighthood — a casque, a gorget, a pair of armlets, two iron gloves, two cuirasses, a pair of greaves, and a lance — he added a shovel and a plow!

But the artists of Dante's day and age went in heavily for practical jests.

Bonamico — known as Buffalmaco, or Big Buffalo — was especially prolific in these. He is celebrated both by Boccaccio and by Franco Sacchetti.

Upon one occasion, with the assistance of his friend Bruno, he persuaded a third painter, Calandrino, "a simple-witted man and of strange usances," that a stone called heliotrope could be found in the bed of the Mugnone and that it would render one invisible. It could be recognized by its black color. With Bruno and Buffalmaco urging him on, Calandrino found a sack of these and carried them home. The guard at the city gate, primed by the two jokers, feigned not to see him. But when he reached his house in the Cantoalla Macina his wife berated him for being late for dinner, whereupon he rushed at her in a fury and "cuffed and kicked her in every part as long as he could wag his arms and legs."

On another occasion, Buffalmaco was commissioned by the city of Perugia to paint a picture of Sant' Ercolano, and, while he was painting it, "hidden behind planks and matting as is the custom with painters," the people so harassed him with foolish questions that it entered into his head to depict the saint crowned "not with laurel like the poets nor with a diadem of glory like the blessed but with a garland of mullets." Then he decamped. "They have their decree and I have my mullets!" he cried when they tried to order him to come back.

On a third occasion, being compelled — this was when he was still an apprentice — by his master, one Tafo, to get up before dawn and begin his work, he caught thirty large beetles and ingeniously attached to them tiny wax candles. He then convinced Tafo that they were demons and that the only way to get rid of them was to stop working at night.

« 6 »

But at the very time Dante was consorting with these fellows — or with their counterparts; while he watched them eat, drink, and be merry, although he did not always eat and drink and was not always merry himself; while he roved of nights in rowdy company; while he flung sonnet after sonnet at Forese Bicci; while he entertained his companions by writing his *discordo* (and perhaps other *discordi* which are now lost to us), it seems likely that he was also seriously engaged in trying to gain the affection of one more of the not more than four or five ladies (the two ladies of the screen, the lady at the window, this lady, and a later one) who besides Beatrice take definite shape and form for us as we study his life.

I refer to the one who is known to us only as Pietra, or the Stony-hearted One. She has been variously identified as Pietra di Donato, described as Dante's sister-in-law; as Pietra degli Scrovegni of Padua (if it was she, the affair must have taken place much later, as some believe anyway); as a countrywoman from the Casentino; as a generous hostess whom he wished to compliment extravagantly — while keeping in the good graces of her husband by praising her inaccessible virtue; and even — this seems almost incredible — as Gemma Donati, Dante's wife.

To her — whoever she may have been and whenever his pursuit of her took place — Dante wrote four somewhat lengthy poems, the four poems of the so-called Pietra cycle. They are as poignant and as effective as anything (before the *Commedia*, that is) that he ever penned. Among them perhaps the finest was the *Al poco giorno ed al gran cerchio d'ombra.*

> To day's swift ending and the circle of shadow
> I've come, alas, and to the whitening hills,
> Now that all color's faded from the grass.
> But for all that my longing changes not its green,
> It is so rooted into the hard stone
> That speaks and hears as if it were a woman.
>
> And like the hills this lovely lady is
> Who stands as chill as snow does in the shade,
> For no more moves her than it moves a stone
> The sweet season that now warms the hills
> And brings them swiftly back from white to green
> By covering them with flowers and with grass.
>
> When on her head she wears a garland of grass,
> She banishes from our mind all other ladies,
> For so are mingled waving gold and green
> That love itself must hide now in the shadow—
> Love who hath locked me in the little hills
> Far more securely than in walls of granite stone.

Her beauty has more virtue than precious stone.
The wounds she gives may not be healed with grass,
And therefore I have fled o'er hill and dale
To 'scape the wiles of such a dangerous lady,
Yet from her sunshine nothing can give shade—
Nor hill, nor wall, nor any leaves of green.

Awhile ago I saw her dressed in green
So beauteous that she might have wakened in stone
The love which I feel even for her shadow.
Therefore I sought in a fair meadow of grass
Which lovely was as was any lovely lady
And was girt roundabout with lofty hills.

Yet of a truth rivers will flow uphill
Before this damp and sappy log of wood
Will catch on fire (as ladies are wont to do)
For me who would be willing to sleep on stone
All of my life and to pasture on grass
Only to see her garments cast a shadow.

However dark the hills do cast their shadows
Upon the fairest green, this youthful lady
Will make them vanish like a stone covered with grass.

Thus in English.

But it should be read in Italian.

And read in English or in Italian, certain things should be noted. First, the word *pietra* (stone) occurs in every stanza. Second, the colors green and gold are stressed (perhaps the lady had golden hair and wore a green dress when Dante first saw her.) Third is the repetition of the concept of chilliness; shadow is used over and over again, as are whiteness and snow and cold, and there is one instance of the word *gelata*, which means frozen. But the lady of the *discordo* also had a *cor di ghiaccio* (heart of ice).

Here incidentally, if only briefly, a question is raised. Might she and Pietra have been the same person? Personally I do not think so. I believe Pietra was a real woman and the lady of the *discordo* someone invented to amuse Dante's friends. We will, of course, never know.

But whether they were the same person or not, and whether Dante loved Pietra at this time or somewhat — even a great deal — later, the phase of his life which we have just been discussing did not last for long. He soon moved out of it to begin upon another phase. The new phase was just as important in the shaping of Dante into the man who could write the *Commedia* as was his love for Beatrice. It was as important as his wandering in the *selva oscura*.

This new phase will be our next concern in Dante's life.

But first we must look at Florence between 1289, when Dante came back from Campaldino and Caprona, and 1295, when this new phase begins. We must learn what happened during these years, and next during the years which immediately followed them. We must see what the city was like then. With the help of the Florentine archives; with the help of Giovanni Villani, the wool vendor who became a great historian; with the help of Dino Compagni, the silk merchant turned politician (but not always an especially good one); with the help of other chroniclers and even novelists; and of course with the help of Dante himself, this will now be our task. With their help, we will set the scene.

X

The Sack of Envy

EVEN for Florence, which was not then or ever noted for internal tranquility, even for this city of crooked streets and narrow alleys from which violence, armed with a blade, could issue with impunity to do its evil work, it was a period of unusual turbulence. We will hear of rioting, marketplace brawling, and disorder, nor was this always or even often the end product of personal vendetta although personal vendetta was common enough in that place and in those days.

The seething was, rather, political, as — to borrow a phrase from Dante (*Inferno XXI*) — the "cooks and scullions" of civic controversy plunged their hooks into the simmering stew of Florentine life, thrusting down those who had risen to the top and dredging up those who had sunken, and so on *ad infinitum*.

We have already noted that Dante's own quarter, the Porta San Piero, was known as the Sesto di Scandolo. This name could now be properly extended to include the whole city, which might well be called La Città di Scandolo. The towers had been torn down or truncated, and there were no more tower societies, but group still fought group, family family, and sometimes fraction of a family another fraction, with the old animosity; and all, in the new prosperity, had money aplenty to hire ruffians and bravos to help them out.

Dante well describes the resulting bitterness and chaos.

In *Inferno* VI, those being punished for their gluttony lie upon the ground and are beaten by a drenching rain.

One of these half rises and asks the poet if he can recognize him.

Dante cannot. "Tell me who thou art!" he implores.

> And he to me: "Thy city which so full
> Of envy is that the sack overflows
> Held me in its embrace during lovely life.
> My fellow citizens called me Ciacco,
> And for the damnable sin of gluttony,
> As thou must see, this deluge pelts me.
> But I am not the only wretched soul,
> For all these others pay for the same sin
> With the same penalty."

Ciacco. We have met him before.

But who was he?

Because he was witty and eloquent as well as a bon vivant, it has been suggested that he was Ciacco dell' Anguillara (Ciacco from Anguillara, or Ciacco the Eel Vendor's Son?), a minor poet of whom nothing is known but his name and the one unimportant sonnet which is all of his writings to survive.

This does not seem likely. It is more probable that he was nothing more than a Florentine who had grown legendary for his ventures in good living.

That made him a typical Florentine.

"For," said Benvenuto, "the Florentines, although they are generally moderate in their eating and their drinking, exceed all others in gluttony and drunkenness when they do indulge."

Dante questioned him:

> "Thy sufferings
> So grievous are to me they make me weep,
> But tell me, if thou knowest, what will befall
> The citizens of my divided city.
> Tell me if any are just. Tell me the reason
> Why such great discord hath assaulted it."

Ciacco's answer is explicit.

> And he to me: "After long contention,
> They will come to bloodshed and the homespun party
> Will have the other out with much injury.
> But afterwards—and that within three years—
> They too will fall and the other come to power,
> Thanks to the one who shifts this way and that.
> High will it holds its head for a long time,
> Keeping the other bitterly oppressed,
> However thou knowest grief and shame therefrom.

> The just men there are two, and no one heeds them.
> Pride, envy, and avarice—these, these are
> The three hot sparks that have inflamed their hearts."

Master Hogfat's words — Hogfat is another good English equivalent for Ciacco — should be examined carefully, for they are as accurate historically as they are compact poetically.

The one who shifts this way and that. Pope Boniface, who took a long time, Dante would have us believe, in making up his mind what course of action would best further his interests.

The just men there are two.

Dante and Guido Cavalcanti?

Dante and Dino Compagni?

Dante and some still unguessed-at Florentine leader?

Neither of the first two seems likely and we have no clues as to who the third might be.

Only one thing is certain — Dante was one of them. In due course, we will see why.

Then three inborn Florentine vices or, if you want to be more gentle, defects of character.

Pride — the pride of the old and usually noble families. These anciently established Florentines were greatly distraught at the gains in power and prestige of those who — sometimes not more than a generation earlier — had plodded into the city, reeking of onions or smelling of the barnyard, from "Campi, or Certaldo, or Figline," or from just beyond Galluzzo or Trespiano, and who were now rich and important.

Envy — the envy of everyone for whoever was above him. The serf (only recently — 1289 — freed), the farmhand, and the day laborer for the lesser guildsman. The lesser guildsman for the members of the great guilds. The greater guildsman for the magnates and noblemen — i.e., for the *grandi*.

Avarice — the quest for the almighty florin that obsessed every dweller in the city from the ragpicker and the tinker-tinsmith and the discordant Arno boatman whose harsh wailing as he dredged the river for gravel must have given Dante some of his ideas about the cacophony of the infernal regions to the paunchy and staid banker with his obsequious secretary (who was avaricious too) and his soft and vair-trimmed robes.

"*La gente nova,*" cried Dante, "*e i subiti guadagni orgoglio e dimisura han generata, Fiorenza, in te, sì che tu già n' en piangi!*"

> These self-made people with their sudden gains
> Arrogance and excess in thee have so engendered,
> O Florence, that already thou weepest for it!

"He who today has none," wrote another Florentine, "is rated not better than a beast, and he who has the most is acknowledged the most worthy. Therefore it is wise for a man not only to save what he has but add to it what he can."

Out of the interplay of these characteristics, out of envy reacting against pride, pride against envy, and avarice in turn against pride, all further stirred up by Boniface and opposed only (in Dante's later opinion) by a small handful, came those terrible happenings which had such disastrous consequences to Dante, and which Ciacco predicted and history records.

They were happenings of a new kind and they brought about a new kind of turmoil and disorder. This was not a turmoil born of the more or less clearly defined party conflict between Guelphs and Ghibellines which had been carried on for so long a time. Instead, it was the product of unadulterated, unashamed factionalism based on the naked wish to gain control. Economic and political control. For neither the *parte selvaggia* — the "homespun party" — nor the "other" party were really parties at all. Certainly they were not parties based on any ideological difference. Nor were they based on class. Magnate opposed magnate quite as often as he opposed merchant-burgher, and there were Cavalcanti and Tosinghi and even Donati on both sides of the political fence.

They rarely took their stands for idealistic reasons.

To cite just one example, Baschiera della Tosa, "who deserved to have his share of the honors of the city" — and who, as we will see later, strove mightily to obtain them — sided with one faction. His kinsman Rossellino della Tosa — he was the high-handed young man who had joined with Corso Donati in abducting the latter's sister — sided with the other.

But Baschiera did not split with Rossellino on matters of principle. The latter, as head of the elder branch of the Tosinghi, had taken over distinctions — and property — which he should have shared with Baschiera's younger branch.

"Out of spite," Baschiera sided against his cousin.

"Even the clergy could not avoid siding with one or the other faction," said Dino Compagni.

There is no evidence that they tried.

« 2 »

These struggles for power, this contest for control, did not begin at once.

Again Dino Compagni: "After the citizens had returned to Florence"— after they had returned from Campaldino and Caprona, that is — "the merchant-burgher government" — the Guelph government of wool traders, money changers, and silk importers, to say nothing of lawyers and notaries — "maintained itself in power and prosperity for several years."

Actually from 1289 to 1293.

Back went the bankers to their benches, the green-felt covers of which now gleamed as plentifully as ever with Byzantine *nomismata*, ducats from Venice, French *écus*, English pounds, shillings, and pence, and perhaps here and there coins from Baghdad and Cairo and even Cathay.

The fulling mills by the Arno began to turn night and day again, and the waters of that stream, despite the law, were once more stained with the disagreeable overflow of dying vats.

The goldsmiths renewed their activity.

And if the inhabitants of the squalid Borgo Pidiglioso, which supplied most of the labor, complained that prices were high and pay was low, what could be done about it? How could the increasingly affluent manufacturers of *bigello* (camlet or frieze), *fustagno* (fustian), *arabesco* (canvas-cloth), *schiavina* (Slav cloth), and *villanesco* (peasant serge), or even the importers of expensive English, Flemish, French, and Spanish woolens, make enough profit to afford rich robes and handsome houses if they paid more than the legal minimum — for there was a legal minimum — in wages?

That does not mean, however, that all was peace everywhere. For if there was domestic tranquility, the wars continued.

But the merchant-burghers — or at any rate the merchant-burgher chiefs — did not fight in them as had Vieri de' Cerchi and others on the plain near Poppi.

Instead they left the fighting — and they did not weigh the political consequences of this — to the young sons of ancient families.

"Let us leave the art of war to these bear cubs and these lion cubs whom our fathers chased out of their country strongholds and bound with the chains of citizen living!" they cried. "Let us put fighting into their hands if there is to be fighting! This is their ancestral heritage and it is a useful way to keep them employed! Moreover, if they fight for us, they, the sons of feudalism, will thus be paying homage to the commonwealth! They will thus be acknowledging it as their liege lord and suzerain! True, this will feed their pride, but that makes little difference. It will be enough that this does not prejudice our supremacy, and of that" — when we find the time among our other business — "we will not forget to take care!"

It would be enough, too, if knightly love of adventure did not lead the bear cubs and the lion cubs to commit them to senseless — and expensive — undertakings for which the city, and that meant the merchant-burghers, would have to pay.

"For note," said Giovanni Villani, "that the expenses of the said host" — the Campaldino army which had marched up the Arno and toward Poppi — "were raised by a tax of six and three quarters per-cent" — on what he does not say — "and this raised more than thirty-six thousand golden florins."

But there were adventures that might be as profitable and could be less costly.

An attack on Pisa, for example.

"In the said year of 1290" — Villani tells us this — "the Florentines moved with a host against Pisa. This was done in accord with the Genoese, who came by sea with forty armed galleys, and the men of Lucca were there too in all their strength. The combined host took by force Porto Pisano and Leghorn and laid waste all, and brought down the four towers which stood in the water to protect the port and the light-house of Meloria. They destroyed the latter and made it fall into the sea with all the men who were on it as a guard. And the Genoese brought huge timbers to the port and with these they smashed down the palaces so that the port could no longer be used. Then the Genoese returned to Genoa, and the Lucchese to Lucca, and the Florentines returned by way of the Valdera, where they took and destroyed many castles."

True, they lost the Valdera again — not without some suspicion of treachery on the part of Corso Donati and of other *grandi* — but in due course they won it back.

This was on the night of Olive Sunday in 1291. The Pisan leader was the able Ghibelline Guido da Montefeltro, father of Buonconte, who had died so dramatically at Campaldino.

A move against the Casentino — whose robber barons still molested Florentine pack trains.

"In the same year" — 1290, not 1291 — "they went back to the Aretine, and stayed there twenty-nine days.

"And they laid waste all the lands around Arezzo to a distance of six miles, and there did not remain a vine or a tree or any standing corn. And on their way home the said host went by the Casentino, laying waste to the domains of Count Guido Novello, and they overthrew the castle and palace of Poppi, which was strong and marvelous, and Santangelo, and Giazzulo, and Cechita, and Montaguto in the Valdarno." All in the upper Arno Valley, which was dominated by castles held by the count's pennoned knights. "And by this was carried out the saying of Count Tegrimo the Old, which he said to the said Count Guido after the defeat of the Florentines at Montaperti."

At that time of Ghibelline victory, the craggy and gray head of the house was taken to his cousin's castle, and there he saw an armsroom filled with crossbows, swords, and lances which had been captured from the Florentines. In the dusky hall, they gleamed refulgently.

"What do you think of them?" asked Count Guido.

"They look good to me, or they would look good if I did not know that the Florentines are past masters at lending at usury!"

An excursion into the Mugello — between the Casentino and Florence — where the castle of Ampinana still was a menacing eagle's nest. This took place in 1291.

This castle, too, dominated important trade routes. It beetled, tan in color against the green of oaks and the deep blue-green of cypresses, from one of the numerous gray-faced crags that rose in back of the narrow valley that ran from Borgo San Lorenzo to Dicomano. It lay a falcon's stoop (or less) from the road to Bologna which the Florentines must keep open, and from its serrated walls it was an afternoon's occupation for Count Manfred, the son of Count Guido, who now held the castle, to swoop down on the merchants who plodded by it. It also neutralized Florence's (for the time being) ally, the count of Battifolle, who held the nearby castle of Cattaia.

But "in the said year, the commonwealth sent an army against it, and after a long siege, it surrendered."

This was partly "because of the many missiles which had been hurled into it," but even more "because the said count" — Count Manfred — "was given three thousand gold florins to march off with his ruffians."

The stronghold was torn down to its foundations.

"And from then on the commonwealth treated the people and the villages which had been under its jurisdiction with justice, but submitted them to their own rule and made them give money and services."

This — and the earlier successes at Pisa and at Poppi — the merchant-burghers could celebrate with "gladness and rejoicing" and with the sound of trumpets and bells. Other happenings — both domestic and foreign — brought them less joy.

The great fire in the Oltrarno *sesto*.

"In the year of our Lord 1290 on the twenty-ninth of May, fire broke out in the house of the Pegalotti on the other side of the Arno, and their houses and their towers and the houses of their nearest neighbors burned to the ground. And a Messer Neri Pegalotti with his son was burned to death, and one of the ladies of the family with her three sons and a servant girl, and there was also loss of property."

The Pegalotti were "old and honorable citizens" and among the most important merchants in the city. Their ventures in the Near East were especially notable, and it was only a generation or so later that Francesco Pegalotti in his *Pratica della Mercantura* (it almost might be called *How to Succeed in Business While Really Trying*) would not only relate in some detail the mercantile practices of the day but would describe lands and cities at the edge of Europe with some part of the vividness of Marco Polo.

At the moment, however, "they were almost wiped out," and this was not good news even for their competitors.

(There were other fires too. One in the street called Torcicoda, or Twist Your Tail, consumed more than thirty houses. "But no lives were lost." It was at this time — possibly in propitiation — that "there were erected at San Giovanni for the greater beauty of the church" those columns and the facade of green and white marble which can still be seen today.)

The capture of Acre in the Holy Land.

"In the year of Christ 1291 in the month of April, the sultan of Babylon" — who was not "Tebaldeo," as one chronicler oddly would have it, but Al Ashraf the Conqueror — "having first garrisoned and provisioned Syria, traversed the desert and laid siege to the city of Acre, which was called Ptolemais in the Scriptures and now is known as Acon in Latin, and the sultan had with him so many people, both foot and horse, that his host extended over more than twelve miles."

The city fell, "as was related to us" — i.e., to Villani — "by trustworthy fellow citizens and by merchants who were there at the time."

And who were among the very small handful who managed one way or another to find space aboard the few bright-sailed ships which were able to flee like frightened seabirds to Bari or Brindisi or Venice.

Adult males were slain, "but the young men and the maidens were carried off as slaves, and there were of the slain and prisoners more than sixty thousand, and the loss of goods was infinite.

"Thereafter there remained in the Holy Land no city pertaining to the Christians, and never again was any one of the good cities which were on our [i.e., Italian] shores and borders worth one half of its former profit in merchandise and art. For the port of Acre, by reason of its good situation right on the brow of the sea and well-nigh in the midst of the inhabited world, was a magazine for the world's merchandise both from the East and the West, and all races of men met there to barter, and there were interpreters of every language so that it was like one of the elements of the world."

The harsh action of the king of England.

To break what was virtually an Italian monopoly in the wool trade and in mortgage banking, Edward I in 1290 ordered the sequestration of every bale of wool in England which was owned by an Italian or an Italian firm, and he particularly directed the attention of his officers to the wool sacks piled high on the wharves at St. Botolph's (today Boston, a contraction of Botolph's town), which was then an important seaport on a river flowing into the Wash. St. Botolph's was a major shipping point for commodities destined for Flanders.

At this one place twenty-three hundred bales were seized.

"These had," said a modern historian in an understatement, "quite a considerable value."

The next year, "on the night of the calends of May," an action with similar impact was taken in France. At that time Philip the Fair, acting on the advice of Biccio and Musciatto Franzesi — Monsieur Biche (Master Doe) and wizened little Monsieur Mouche (Master Gadfly) — both Florentines and both "rich and considerable merchants in France" and both obviously not unwilling to bring down their compatriots if personal profit resulted therefrom, "arrested all the Italians in the realm on the pretext of arresting those who practiced usury.

"But he arrested and held for ransom the good merchants too.

"Wherefrom much evil resulted!" said Villani.

To France, "which sank lower and lower."

But also to Florence.

"For note," he concluded, "that between the fall of Acre and these arrests" — and also the confiscations in England and the great fires — "the merchants of the city received great damage and their affairs fell into ruin."

Some of the merchants, that is!

For the basic prosperity of Florence continued to burgeon. It would for another three hundred years.

The merchant-burghers also pondered political matters.

Business and politics can never be completely divorced, much as both businessmen and politicians would like it. And when the business is worldwide business, or at least Europe-wide business, world politics and European politics are of moment.

It was so in Florence.

When, therefore, in 1291 agents of one Florentine company or another, riding a little faster than usual, crossed the Alps and the Apennines with word that an important monarch had departed from this life, the possible consequences were soon a matter of discussion in every warehouse and in every *bottega*.

"*King* Rudolf of Germany has died!" was how the tidings were announced.

Note the word *king*. Rudolf had been elected emperor, but he had never attained imperial honors because he was always too intent upon his affairs in the north to come to Rome.

Opinions on him differ.

According to Villani, he was a man of "energy and valor who from a small count rose to grandeur, and at the same time gained for himself the duchy of Austria and a great part of the duchy of Swabia."

Dante thought somewhat less of him.

Purgatorio VII:

> Rudolf the emperor, who might well
> Have healed the wounds that have slain Italy
> So that 't is long time ere she will revive.

Who *might* have, but who did not!

But Dante's standards for an emperor were high and exacting.

This first Hapsburg was succeeded by a nonentity, Adolf of Nassau. He was slain in battle by Rudolf's son Albrecht, and when the latter, who is generally believed to have been an austere and able man whose keen sense of justice led him to free the slaves and to protect the downtrodden and despised, neglected "the garden of the empire" just as his father had, the poet fleered at him with equal severity.

Purgatorio VI:

> What good is it that great Justinian
> Put bit in mouth if the saddle is empty?
> O German Albert, who abandonest her [*Italy*]
> That hath become unmanageable and wild,
> Thou shouldst now bestride the saddle bow.
> May a just judgment fall upon thy race,
> Therefore, and be so plain and manifest
> That even thine heirs shall live in fear of it.

Why this scorn?

Because Albrecht did not come to Italy and rule.

The merchant-burghers also probably pondered the implications — to them and to Florence and to Italy — of the death of the pontiff.

"In the year of our Lord 1292," wrote Villani, "Pope Nicholas of Ascoli died in the city of Rome. He was a good man and his life was holy and he was a member of the Minorite Friars [the Franciscans]. And after his death the Holy See remained vacant for eighteen months on account of disorders among the cardinals."

From the beginning, it was obvious that there would be a long interregnum, and this posed problems for the merchant-burghers, who liked certainty. To name only one of them, what horse should they bet on? More plainly, to which candidate (or candidates) should they lend money? A defeated cardinal (unless he lost by becoming a pope-maker) was not usually a good risk.

They speculated also as to what the new pope would be like. What would be his attitude toward them and toward Florence? In some ways, it was well they could not see into the future.

Finally — as did everybody else in Florence — they talked about the great and manifest miracles "which, beginning on July 3, 1292, there came to be near the picture of the Virgin Mary on a pillar of the loggia of the garden of St. Michael" — today the Orsanmichele — "where grain is sold."

The sick were healed, the halt were raised to their feet, and, even, madmen regained their senses.

"The Preaching Friars [the Dominicans] and even the Minorites gave no heed to this."

From envy or for some other reason, explained Villani.

But the people did, and from all parts of Tuscany they came in pilgrimage "as they do for every festival of our Lady. And they brought divers images of wax miraculously made until a great part of the loggia around the pillar was filled with them. And so greatly did this increase the wealth of that company" — the Calimala, to which the Orsanmichele belonged — "that many charities and benefits were done, and alms were offered to the poor to the amount of more than six thousand *libbre* a year."

More than six thousand *libbre!*

It was as profitable as their wool trade.

The other guildsmen must have wondered why such golden manna from heaven did not rain on them too.

« 3 »

But even as the merchant-burghers — I use this word wherever *popolo* or *popolo grasso* is meant — thought about or even dealt with such grave or trivial matters, the city seethed around them.

"The nobles and the magnates," wrote Dino Compagni, "began to wax arrogant, and did many wrongs to the *popolani* by beating them and putting other insults upon them."

Villani's account is a little more elaborate.

In the year of Christ 1292, he said, "the city of Florence being now great and powerful in estate, and the citizens thereof having waxed fat and rich and having become arrogant and envious of each other because of too much tranquility, many murders and outrages were committed, and between one citizen and another there were many bloody affrays. Particularly this was true of those powerful nobles both of the town and of the countryside who were known as *grandi*. They assaulted the plain people, who were powerless to resist them. They did violence to their persons and they robbed them of their goods."

Leading them in these new outbursts were none other than "the bear cubs and the lion cubs": the brightly clad cockerels who had fought so gallantly against Arezzo and Pisa and before Poppi and at Ampinana.

Wars ended — at least for the time being — they had no other outlet for their innate violence than pouring into the streets.

To be sure, they tried to justify this.

"We are they who brought about the defeat at Campaldino," they cried, "and now you deprive us of the offices of the city!"

Actually these words are reported as having been uttered during later disturbances.

But they — or words something like them — could have been said then.

But it was not merely the bear cubs and the lion cubs — with their magnate elders who financed them and egged them on — who felt and showed discontent.

All those who did not belong to the ruling oligarchy — which, however, proclaimed itself a *popolo*, or democracy — fumed at their exclusion, and at the harm which they believed this did to them. Beneath the seven greater guilds — the Calimala, the Guild of the Judges and Notaries, the Wool Guild, the Silk Guild, the Bankers Guild, the Skinners and Furriers Guild, and the Physicians and Apothecaries Guild — which in the name of the Guelph party ruled the city, were the five middle guilds (soon but not yet to become greater guilds) and the nine lesser guilds.

The middle guilds included the Butchers Guild, the Ironworkers Guild, the Shoemakers Guild, the Stoneworkers and Woodworkers Guild, and the Secondhand Clothes Dealers Guild. This last guild had an importance which is hard to understand today. Yet the explanation is simple. Goods were durable then and prices high and no one despised used garments. But the secondhand clothes dealers also disposed of booty taken in war and of the rich clothing bequeathed or given to churches and convents.

The lesser guilds included the Winesellers Guild, the Innkeepers Guild, the Tanners Guild, the Oilsellers and Sausagemakers Guild, the Harnessmakers Guild, the Locksmiths Guild, the Armormakers and Swordsmiths Guild, the Carpenters Guild, and the Bakers Guild. Generally speaking, those who had to be subservient (like the innkeepers), or who worked with their hands.

The bakers, their rubicund, sweaty faces streaked with white, were particularly vociferous.

"There are many wealthy citizens," had cried Bernardo Rossi, a baker, addressing the Council of the Captain of the People, "who have money invested in the trades of milling and baking but who take no part in the business themselves. By the high prices they charge for flour they compel us to make inferior bread, and by the high rents they demand for our bakehouses they force us to demand high prices for this bread. This causes hardship among the poorer people — and they blame us."

But all of the middle and lesser guildsmen had grievances, or thought they did, as did the populace, whether crippled beggar or unemployed workman, beneath them.

"Look at these puffed-up peacocks, swollen with their profits," they cried. "They are plain people just as we are. They are *popolani grassi* [fatted ones] just as we are *popolani minuti* [lean and starved ones]. And they make themselves wealthy by taking our little from us. They tax everything that comes into the city. We cannot live any more."

They had done even more than that.

In order to increase their profits upon everything, from the grain which they bought speculatively in Apulia and Calabria to the cloth which the citizens wore upon their backs, the wealthier merchants organized themselves into what they called *catenacci* (heavy chains), really cartels or trusts, and this aroused such animosity that when on June 30, 1290, a general council met to vote on laws which would forbid this practice, it had to be convened secretly. No bells sounded to summon the councillors to San Piero Scheraggio. They were notified by word of mouth. And when the notary called the meeting to order, he merely read them three brief phrases.

Top and bottom, therefore, had good reason to join against the middle. Pride and envy became allies, with avarice their foe.

At first these new colleagues did little but riot and create disturbances, and of this phase of the contest we have no specific account.

(Dino Compagni and even Villani, both cited above, are far too brief to be useful.)

But soon the *grandi*, with their lesser-guild and pleb allies, attempted to attack the very structure of the government.

They had already infiltrated certain of the councils, among them the Council of the Capitudini (Council of the Chief Guildsmen), and when this was convened on November 30, 1292, to select the thirty-six men who would serve as priors during the next six two-month periods, they found spokesmen who would try to modify the priorate itself.

Dino Pecora was one of them and Jacopo da Certaldo was another.

Dino was a member of the Butchers Guild. Probably he was not so much a butcher as a cattle-raiser who sold his stock both on the hoof and as meat. His real name was Aldobrando di Giovanni. Dino was merely a nickname, as was Pecora, which means sheep or mutton. He was a big man, florid of complexion; a brutal man; a noisy man; and an accomplished rabble-rouser. At his orations he usually wore the blood-stained apron of his trade.

Jacopo da Certaldo was a lawyer — and a troublemaker. We will hear of him again.

Dino Pecora spoke first and forcefully.

"Too many are excluded from the priorate," he said, "so let us increase their number. They are now six. Let us have twelve — one apiece for each of the seven greater and the five middle guilds."

Since he was a middle guildsman himself, he could thus become a member of this governing body.

But Jacopo da Certaldo made an even more radical proposal.

"Let there be twelve priors as you suggest — but let there be four from the greater, four from the middle, and four from the lesser guilds."

This was evidently *grandi*-inspired. The lesser guilds would vote the way the *grandi* wanted, which would open, for the latter, a way to power.

But fortunately there were other voices in the council.

Dino Compagni spoke — against the two proposals.

"Let the number of the priors remain six. It is six priors that have brought us to good fortune."

Lapo Salterelli spoke. He too was a lawyer and upon later occasions first would be on Dante's side and then against him.

He, too, opposed changing the priorate.

Others spoke, and then the vote was taken. The motion was to continue with a priorate of six men. Into the urn went the white beans (affirmative) and the black beans (negative). Then a count was made. There were fifty-eight white beans and twenty-eight black beans. The reforms had been voted down.

« 4 »

When you come to analyze it, it was not really close, but it was close enough to "perturb greatly the organized classes that had come into being during the old Florence of the Primo Popolo" — i.e., the greater guildsmen — who suddenly saw a very dangerous threat to their hitherto unchallenged domination.

"Wherefore" — I take up Dino Compagni's statement again — "many worthy citizens among the *popolani* and the merchants set about to strengthen the popular government."

By "popular government" Dino meant the government of guild-controlled priors which was set up in 1282.

They wasted little or no time in doing so.

New priors took office on December 15 — or a scant two weeks after the famous arguments and famous vote — and spurred on by the men (the merchant-burghers) who had elected them, these appointed a committee to draft new ordinances whose sole purpose would be to curb or keep within bounds the pretensions of the *grandi*. These ordinances would be submitted to another council, the Council of One Hundred.

This the committee did, and on January 10, 1293, they were presented, argued about, and then adopted — by a vote of seventy-two to two. These were the so-called Ordinances of Justice which have been called by some the Magna Carta of the Florentine republic.

This is perhaps an exaggeration, but the fact is that they became the cornerstone of almost all Florentine political thinking and legislation for as long as the republic lasted. They had something of the fundamental position of the Constitution of the United States, and at least in theory no legislation could be passed which did not conform to them. *Salve tamen intactis et illibatis manentibus Ordinamenti Justitiae* (the Ordinances of Justice, however, being preserved intact and remaining undiminished): after 1293, this phrase had to be attached to every law.

Nor was their influence limited to Florence.

Not very late in the next century Rome wished to reform its own government and sent for copies.

"And so note," said Giovanni Villani with Florentine pride, "how the centuries do change conditions and states. For anciently the Romans built the city of Florence and gave it laws, but now they send for their laws to Florence."

Yet in spite of their importance, the Ordinances of Justice are not always clearly understood. It is often thought, for example, that they were a whole series of new regulations which appeared with dazzling suddenness almost like a bolt from the blue. Some of them were indeed new, but a good part of them were actually old laws, some of which had been passed as early as 1281. But now they were grouped into a single piece of legislation, many of whose provisions were *canonizzati* (canonized), which meant that at least in theory they could never be repealed.

Old or new, they must be considered, for they were the hammer which on the anvil of events beat into shape the Florence of the immediate future. Dante's Florence. Let us do so — as briefly as we can.

They provided that no one who was not a member of a guild, *and who did not actually practice a trade in that guild,* could be a prior or play any other part in the government.

They provided that no knight could be a prior.

They provided that there should be six priors; that these should serve for a term of two months and not be eligible for reelection for three years; that these should live together in one house (the Palazzo della Signoria — our Palazzo Vecchio was not yet built); that they should eat together there; and that they should neither accept invitations nor give private audiences.

They provided that the priors, as their term of office drew toward its close, should convene the *capitudini* (consuls of the twelve greater and middle guilds — now all considered greater guilds) and the *savi* (wise men or special councillors — the effective meaning is important citizens) to choose their successors.

The Ordinamenti also provided that there should be only one gonfalonier instead of two.

This was the gonfalonier of justice. Like the priors, he was elected for a two-month term, but he could be reelected in two years' time instead of three. (He was elected by the incoming priors, by the captain of the people, by the *capitudini*, and by two *savi* from each of the city's six *sesti*.) He lived with the priors and received the same salary: ten *soldi* a day. Not exactly a magnificent sum, and out of it he had to pay his expenses. But he soon became *de facto*, though not by statute, the seventh and most important member of the priorate, for he was the law-enforcement officer of the city with a guard of a thousand men-at-arms together with one hundred *pavesi* (special troops carrying unusually long shields) and twenty-five crossbowmen to help him enforce the laws. And this made it hard not to treat him with respect.

But perhaps the most important of the Ordinamenti were the statutes directed against the *grandi*, for it was against their disorders and attempts to take over the city that the new laws were principally directed.

Obviously no magnate — or nobleman — could become a prior. The merchant-burghers saw to this.

He could not sit in any of the councils either.

And, although under certain circumstances he was permitted to join one of the guilds, he could never be one of its *capitudini* nor its rector.

He was thus clearly relegated to second class.

Moreover, he himself had to guarantee his own good conduct.

"To cope with their many treacheries" — this was a 1286 law but it was retained in the Ordinamenti — "it is provided and decreed that every male magnate and nobleman between the ages of fifteen and seventy must give security in the amount of two thousand *libbre*."

If he took part in an act of violence from which death did not result, he could be fined up to this full amount. If a death resulted, he must be put to death, his wealth confiscated, and his house or houses torn down. If he had not put up this bond, or if he was contumacious and fled to avoid standing trial, his relatives must pay his fine for him.

In the case of murder, this could be as much as three thousand *libbre*.

Moreover, a man — even he were born a *popolano* — could be declared one of the *grandi*.

At this time, and just as a beginning, three hundred hitherto *popolani* families were thus punitively elevated. Among them were the Uberti (Farinata, the great Ghibelline leader, was this family's most famous member); the Adimari (Filippo Argenti, whom we have already met in hell, was an Adimari, as was the arrogant young sprout who offended Dante by riding through the narrow streets with his spurred boots thrust out so that he could crowd and jostle the plebian scum); the Buondel-monti; the Cavalcanti; the Tornaquinci; the Gherardini; the Bardi; the Cerchi; and the Frescobaldi.

Not every member of all of these families was included, and some of them we will soon see aligned on the side of the merchant-burghers. But it is a catalogue which includes most of the city's then most illustrious families and a clear indication of the new laws' intent.

« 5 »

In the beginning, at any rate, this intent was forcibly and effectively carried out. The Ordinamenti were not simply written on the statute books and then forgotten.

One man — although probably not one man alone — was responsible for this.

"There was," wrote Giovanni Villani, "among the artificers and mer-chants of Florence which desired that life be good an ancient and noble citizen, rich and powerful but one of the *popolani*, whose name was Giano della Bella, of the parish of San Martino" — Dante's parish of San Martino del Vescovo — "who had the counsel and the following of many other wise and powerful men of his class."

Dino Compagni describes him similarly.

He was "a prominent and influential citizen."

He was "a wise, a good, and a worthy man."

He was "of high spirit and of a distinguished family."

But "he resented the outrages committed by the nobles."

A Ghibelline by birth — and therefore he should have been suspect to the merchant-burghers — handsome, outgoing, genuine, and sincere, this dedicated leader, who, however, was "more full of zeal than he was prudent," was one of those high-minded aristocrats who not entirely infrequently have come over to the side of the people. The Romans had such in the two Gracchi; France (although less attractively because of his shabby morals) one in Mirabeau; and the United States in Thomas Jefferson and Franklin Roosevelt.

Giano was not prior when the Ordinamenti were passed, nor did he draft them. They were drafted by Donato di Messer Alberto, Ubertino della Strozza, and Baldo d'Aguglione.

(Baldo is the only one of these we need remember. Dino calls him "a very crafty legalist," and Dante — *Paradiso* XVI — wrinkles his nose before his "yokel stench." He will appear frequently later and as a rule not creditably.)

But if Giano stood on the sidelines at that historic moment, he had already "constructed himself head and leader of the movement" — the reform movement — and when, on February 15, 1293, he took his place in the next priorate, he set out to put the new laws into effect.

At his inspiration, if not at his direct orders, up and down the streets marched the armed guards of the gonfalonier of justice. They had now been increased to two thousand men "with five hundred master woodworkers and stoneworkers and fifty strong and robust pick-wielders each one provided with an excellent pick." Although in normal times the courts opened at ten or eleven in the morning and recessed not merely in summer but on every holiday and festival, to keep these armed guards busy the magistrates now sat day and night.

Giano also insisted on the passage of new laws and these were even more anti-aristocratic.

It was decreed, for example, that if any magnate did not denounce an evildoer he himself could be punished.

(It was also decreed that anyone who denounced falsely could be punished, but this provision was rarely invoked.)

It was decreed that if a *popolano* got into a quarrel with a nobleman the Ordinamenti did not apply but instead common law took over, and that the same pertained in a quarrel between a servant and his master.

It was decreed that if one of the *grandi* wrongfully appropriated the property of a *popolani* he could be fined one thousand *libbre*. But there was no similar provision in the case where a *popolani* wrongfully took over the property of one of the *grandi*.

It was decreed that the *grandi* could not form associations to pay jointly any fines they had incurred. Every man must pay his own fine.

Obviously to be one of the *grandi* was to become every day increasingly subjected to every kind of harassment.

But it was not the laws themselves — many of which were necessary if not just — which caused distress. It was the way they were administered.

Giano was honest and sincere but not all of his followers had his high principles, and the feeling grew that if you were accused you would be sentenced whether you were guilty or not.

Even Dino Compagni, who was a *popolano* himself, had no doubt of this.

"The arrogance of evil men among the merchant-burghers increased greatly," he said, "and they insisted upon 'effectual punishment.' This demand for effectual punishment was carried to such a length that the magistrates feared that if a man who had been accused remained unpunished the magistrate himself would be deemed guilty."

Giano did not help any.

Like most reformers, he was married to his reform and, since his own purpose was altruistic, he found it difficult to believe that self-interest moved any of his supporters.

"Let the city perish rather than the laws not be enforced!" he cried when grievances were laid before him.

In the literal and physical sense of the word, it almost did.

"For," said Dino Compagni, "there were few evil deeds which were not discovered, and many such were punished according to the law.

"The Galigai," he continued (but others say it was the Galli, ancient and probably Ghibelline *grandi*), "furnished the first example of this. A man of that family committed an outrage against two sons of a well-known merchant family. One of the latter was so wounded that he died. They were in France. Wherefore I, Dino Compagni, being gonfalonier of justice, went to their houses and to those of their kinsmen and caused them to be torn down."

This incident, in 1293, led to an evil practice, for although the Galigai were clearly guilty not every condemned magnate was. But if sentence was imposed and the gonfalonier did not carry it out and that thoroughly, he himself was in trouble with the merchant-burghers.

"Thus many of the gonfaloniers perverted justice through fear."

Soon even "the accursed lawyers began to cavil."

They alleged that the Ordinamenti "were a cause of alarm to the magistrates themselves."

Why was this?

They were afraid to convict because if the guilty party were a relative of theirs they might end up having to pay the penalty themselves.

They were afraid not to convict because the laws were now being used "so as to injure the enemies" of the merchant-burghers who now ruled the city and they did not dare offend these holders of such power.

This, the lawyers said, impaired orderly justice. They needed orderly justice for their business — and their fees.

The magnates — and the noblemen — spoke plainly too.

"*Ordinamenti della Giustizia?*" they grumbled. "*Ordinamenti della Tristizia!*"

Not Ordinances of Justice, but Ordinances of Roguery!

"Why look you," cried one of them, "if a horse plodding along the street hits a *popolano* in the face, if in a crowd one man jostles another and without intending any harm accidentally gives him a blow in the face, or if some children of a tender age begin quarreling, an accusation will be made! But ought men to have their houses and their property destroyed for such trifles?"

Very clearly, the answer was no.

« 6 »

Very clearly, too, those who felt that the answer should be no would not waste very much time in doing something about it.

They did not.

Dino Compagni — with his participant's-eye view — tells the story.

Very shortly, he says — probably in 1294, or a year after the ordinances were passed — "certain of the more powerful citizens began to consider various means by which they could subdue the merchant-burghers because of the hatred they bore them."

These powerful citizens, incidentally, were not all noblemen by birth, but "some of them were merely called magnates because of certain accidents."

An *accident* in the Middle Ages meant something which was not inborn or intrinsic — the latter was a *substance* — but which had happened to you.

In this case, the citizens had become magnates because there was a knight in their family, or they had been decreed magnates as a punishment for some real or imaginary offense.

They tried violence first.

"They fetched from Champagne a bold French knight named Messer Gian di Celona [Monsieur Jean of Chalon — probably Chalon in Burgundy rather than the more famous Châlons-sur-Marne] whose strong right arm was more evident than his good faith. This man came into Tuscany, having made an agreement with the Florentine magnates, and he was furnished with powers and charters over any cities he might win."

But these would not take effect until he had performed certain tasks.

He was "to upset the government of Florence" — i.e., the hated merchant-burgher government — by compassing the murder of Giano della Bella.

"Smite the shepherd and the sheep will be scattered!"

This was a proverb of the Florentine *contrada*, and it had pithy, if unprincipled, country common sense. It was now repeated to the Frenchman by the magnate conspirators, one of whom, ironically enough, was Vieri de' Cerchi, who was certainly a "magnate by accident." Vieri would himself be a "shepherd" in due course.

But the murder never came off.

Doubtless, this was not through any fault of Jean's. The little that we know of him indicates a man who would do away with Giano just as cheerfully as he dismembered the roast capon which he ate for dinner.

(Washed down by the good red wine that, according to Fra Salimbene, a jovial Franciscan monk, made the French such famous drinkers.)

But the magnates, although they had no more compunctions, were more cautious. Or perhaps they knew Florence better.

Every time, therefore, that it came to the moment of acting, "they drew back from fear of the *popolani*."

In this instance the *popolani minuti* as well as the *popolani grassi*.

Unlike his predecessors, Giano was the friend of the former and he protected the position of the latter.

So they tried another method.

"Let us destroy him by subtle craftiness!"

How?

"By taking advantage of his credulousness, his sense of justice, and his singleness of purpose."

Little time was wasted in doing this.

On a chilly December day, the tribune of the people was in the church of Ognissanti, then surrounded by green grass and outside of all but the still-unfinished third and last circle of the city walls.

(Today Ognissanti faces a paved square where carriages and their sleepy, tasseled horses stand in the sun; it faces one of the city's best hotels; and its austere tenth-century lines have been hidden by an unhandsome seventeenth-century facade.)

He was busied with a committee at still further amending the laws.

A delegation waited on him. Their faces were made grave by serious business.

"Messer Giano," they said, "while you go about devising new ordinances, consider what is taking place under the old ones. Look, for example, at the wicked deeds of the butchers, who are men full of mischief and evil-disposed. Consider Dino Pecora."

What should he consider?

"He is upheld by the Tosinghi and carries on his business by means both fraudulent and hurtful to the republic. Even in his own guild, proceedings not long ago were taken against him because he fearlessly continued in his malfeasances. He now menaces the magistrates and their officers, and with the support of armed men he goes about committing crimes. But today the butchers stand with him, and they multiply their wrongdoings."

"May I drop dead if I permit this!" cried Giano.

"But there are other people who are making trouble."

"Name them!

"The lawyers! See, they threaten to call the very magistrates to account, and in this way draw unjust favors from them through fear. They keep causes undecided for three or four years, and many cases are not ever decided. And when anyone wishes to discontinue his action or withdraw his defense they will not permit him to do so. To do this, they confuse the issues to be tried and they quibble as to liabilities. They act dishonorably."

It so happened that two of the five who had come to Giano — Baldo d'Aguglione and Lapo Salterelli —— were themselves lawyers, but in his righteous indignation he took no note of this.

"I will make laws against the lawyers themselves! I will check their misconduct!"

Then, continued Dino, when the conspirators had thus stirred up Giano's zeal for justice, they secretly sent to the lawyers and the butchers and the members of the other guilds, saying that Giano was maligning them and that he was proposing laws to be framed against them."

They indicated that action was needed, and plans for action were rapidly formulated.

But fortunately "one day" — one day almost immediately — the plot was discovered.

By our silk merchant-chronicler-politician.

"I, Dino, and some of the committee" — the committee which had been convened to discuss possible amendments to the ordinances — "were about to assemble in the Ognissanti, and Giano was walking in the garden. Then those who were plotting suddenly introduced a deceitful law, the purpose of which all did not understand."

They were not supposed to understand its purpose, of course.

It was that "every city or fortress should be deemed hostile if it sheltered anyone who had been outlawed as an enemy of the people."

"And this they did," said Dino, "because they conspired with certain traitor merchant-burghers to banish Giano and to make the people" — all the people, including the lesser guildsmen and the populace — "hate him.

"But I got knowledge of the conspiracy, my suspicions having been aroused when the plotters drew up a law without consulting their colleagues. I made known to Giano what has being planned against him, and I advised him that if he persisted in his legislation even the mechanics would turn away from him. I advised him to drop his proposals and to speak instead against his adversaries."

This Giano did.

"May the city perish" — this seems to have been his favorite phrase — "rather than such wickedness prosper!"

One by one, and with his old eloquence, he named his enemies — or those whom he believed to have been his enemies.

"Put them to death!" he cried. "They are also the enemies of Florence!"

In this, however, he was not supported by all of his colleagues.

Many of them — and we can assume that Dino belonged to this group — wished first to examine the facts calmly and prudently.

They did not wish innocent persons to be punished, but more than that they did not want those who had conspired merely because they thought the conspiracy was certain to succeed to be pushed into permanent opposition. They would like a chance to win them back again.

"Wherefore we separated in great discord."

This was after a stormy session in which three, rather than two, groups now shouted and stormed at each other. Giano's followers, who urged drastic action. The moderates like Dino and the greater part of his fellow merchant-burghers. The conspirators.

For the same reason, the making — or even the amending — of laws "was not further proceeded with."

But further scheming against Giano was.

Indeed, the need for this seemed to the conspirators more urgent than ever.

For as Florentines — and as practical men — they knew that moderates are not apt to win at any time, and that in times of trouble they almost never do. They knew that Giano would destroy them if they did not destroy Giano.

This they set about to do.

When the others stormed out of Ognissanti, the leaders of the conspiracy remained there. Messer Palmieri di Messer Ugo Altoviti. (He will later stand almost as firmly as Dante in a time of crisis.) Messer Baldo d'Aguglione. (These were both judges.) Noffo di Guido Bonafedi.

Arriguccio di Lapo Arrighi. (But not Lapo Salterelli. He had not yet made up his mind which way the wind was likely to blow.) The notaries Ser Matteo Biliotti and Ser Pino da Segni.

The latter had tried to make a transcript of what had been said, and it was repeated, not without exaggeration.

But exaggeration was hardly needed.

The faction of the *grandi* was in trouble, and the men who had remained at Ognissanti knew it well. As its leaders, they were in even greater trouble.

"So once again they decided they must get rid of Giano. For they greatly feared him, and they feared even more what he might do."

« 7 »

Once again, too, they held a meeting to determine what should be their course of action. This time, however, probably for reasons of security, it was held across the Arno. In the little church of San Jacopo.

Once again there was divided opinion.

"These dogs of *popolani*," cried Berto Frescobaldi, "have stolen every one of our powers and privileges and now we do not even dare enter the palace of the *podestà* to plead our cause!"

He then repeated an old charge and brought it up to date.

"Not only if we stab a *popolano* but if we even beat a servant who deserves it our houses are torn down."

He advocated action.

"I counsel, therefore, *signori*, that we break out of this bondage. Let us take up our arms and sally forth into the street. Let us kill friend and foe alike just so they are *popolani*. Then neither we nor our sons will ever again be subject to them."

But Messer Baldo della Tosa had another opinion.

"*Signori*," he said, "the counsel of the wise knight is good, but it is too dangerous, for if we do not carry out our purpose, all of us will be dead. Instead, let us again try cunning and disunite the populace with mild words. Let us say: 'The Ghibellines are upon us again, and they will take the city.'"

Never mind that many of the *grandi* were themselves Ghibellines. The populace would never think of this.

"Let us say that these Ghibellines will drive us and them from the city, and that for God's sake they should not allow them to rise to power."

Some of the *popolani* would fall into this trap. They would insist that the Ghibellines were indeed the enemy. But others would persist in their hostility to the *grandi*.

"Having thus caused a division among them, let us smite them."

But then, and then only.

This time they would never rise again.

"The knight's counsel was pleasing to all, and they appointed two from each district who should corrupt and divide the *popolani* and should malign Giano."

He only pretends to be a friend to the people. Remember he was born of a Ghibelline family. He himself is a Ghibelline. He has always been a Ghibelline.

But even as they set about to do this events moved faster than their plotting, and the crisis which they sought to bring about came into being of its own accord.

Here again the two men we have relied on so greatly tell the story. Let us hear it from both of them — and as far as possible in their own words.

« 8 »

Dino first:

"While these citizens were thus dissembling," he wrote, "the city was in great turmoil, and it befell that at this time Messer Corso Donati, a most puissant knight, sent some foot soldiers to attack Messer Simone Galastrone, a kinsman of his, and in the struggle a *popolano* was killed and several were wounded. An accusation was made on both sides, and therefore it was necessary to proceed according to the Ordinances of Justice. The trial came before the *podestà*, and one of the doctors of law, hearing the evidence, saw that it went against Messer Corso, but he directed the notary to write down the contrary, so that Messer Corso seemed to be exonerated and Messer Simone the one who should be condemned. The *podestà*, therefore, acquitted Messer Corso and sentenced Messer Simone."

Instantly there was turmoil.

Word spread abroad that the *podestà* had been bribed, and the people surged into the street.

They marched toward his palace.

" 'Death!' " they shouted. " 'Death to the *podestà!* To the fire with him! To the fire with him!'

"And so greatly did the tumult increase that the mob began to pick up faggots and they ran with them to the building."

Then, "in order to please the people," the priors came out, bearing before them the red and white banner of the gonfalonier of justice. They thought thus to quiet the uproar.

"But it increased so much that rioters burned the palace door and stole the *podestà*'s horses and goods."

Egged on by a certain Baldo dell' Ammirato, they went even further. Baldo was a doctor of law "who had many opponents and was in court at the time, engaged in criminal and civil business." At the time, he "had proceedings against himself and he feared to be punished." With the help of every "evil-disposed person who was being sued in court" — and with the help of the mob too — he broke into the cupboards where the records were kept and destroyed them. He tore up "the papers relating to his case" and the cases of such of the other rioters who had actions pending against them. The pieces were scattered to the winds and not one of them was ever found again.

"Many people committed outrages during the rioting. The *podestà* and his household were in great peril. He had brought with him his wife, a Lombard lady highly esteemed and of great beauty. She and her husband, crying that they would rather die than fall into the hands of the mob, fled to the neighboring houses where they were hidden and concealed."

Villani adds a few details.

He dates the disorders. They took place "in the said year of 1294 in the month of January." Actually on January 23 of our 1295.

The people, according to Villani, were well armed, and therefore probably well organized. They assaulted the palace "with arms and with crossbows."

And it was not merely the *podestà* who decided that discretion was the better part of valor.

"Messer Corso" — Corso Donati — "in fear of his life fled from the palace over the rooftops."

This is not without diverting aspects.

Tall and good-looking, his features proud and self-assured, chin thrust forward — all of this somewhat faded by the passage of centuries — he can be seen behind Dante in the painting by Giotto which hangs on the walls of the Bargello (the ancient palace of the *podestà*, where the riots just described took place). Corso was one of the few aristocrats who were idolized by the artisans and laborers.

"Il Barone!" Long live the baron! they shouted as he galloped through the narrow streets followed by a *masnada* of retainers, their pennons fluttering.

But now he gathered his cloak about him and scuttled from chimney pot to chimney pot, wondering if each moment might not be his last.

As we shall see, Corso's disappearance was temporary, but in direct consequence of the riots another prominent Florentine was to disappear permanently.

Giano della Bella.

Here the accounts differ.

"The first to start the uproar, and more from the ill will they bore Messer Corso than from sorrow for offended justice, were Taddeo della Bella and Baldo dal Borgo."

Taddeo was Giano's brother.

Giano was with the priors at the time.

"I will go to save the *podestà!*" he cried.

And thus came into the midst of the disorders.

Villani has another version.

Hearing that Simone had been condemned rather than Corso, "a great number of the people flew to arms, and especially the workmen and the lesser guildsmen, and rushed to the house of Giano della Bella shouting 'To arms! To arms!' and 'Long live the people!' And he, it is said, sent them with his brother to the palace of the priors. But they did not obey him and went to the palace of the *podestà* instead."

But in either case Giano could not control the rioters, and on this matter Dino's story is more precise.

"He mounted his horse, thinking that the people would obey him and retire at his words. But on the contrary they turned their lances against him."

So he turned back.

But not ever again to be an adulated hero.

For the *grandi*, who had always hated Giano, were now joined by "the good people of the city" — by such of the *popolani grassi*, that is, who concluded that if Giano were left in power, or even left with great influence, there would be nothing but an anarchic reign of terror.

"They made a faction together," says Villani, "and determined to elect a stalwart body of priors." By stalwart they meant priors whom the mob could not frighten and who were determined to maintain order. "And, this done, when they were in office these priors conferred with the captain of the people and set forth a proclamation and an inquisition against the said Giano and his followers and confederates."

They charged him with setting the city in disorder, with disturbing the peace of the state, with assaulting the *podestà*, and with violating his own Ordinances of Justice.

At this the common people again poured into the streets. They seethed around his house. They offered to surround him with arms and to defend him or attack the city. His brother even dared to march to the Orto San Michele (Orsanmichele) bearing a standard decorated with the arms of the city.

"But Giano was a wise man, albeit somewhat presumptuous, and when he saw that he had been abandoned by the very men who had been at his side when he made the *popolo* strong, and that their forces with those of the *grandi* were very great indeed, and that the priors were already assembled and armed, he would not hazard a civil war, and, to the end that the city might not be ravaged and also for fear of his person, he withdrew and departed from Florence."

This was on the fifth day of March.

He hoped that the people might call him back, but instead he was condemned. For contumacy! So he never returned.

And many years later, when these turmoils had given place to other turmoils, he died in France.

Not in poverty, however. For he had become the Paris agent of the Pazzi banking house. And such agents were never notably poor.

« *9* »

With Giano driven away, "the smaller tradespeople" — this is Dino Compagni's opinion — "lost all their boldness and energy," and the big people — the *popolani grassi* (some of the *popolani grassi*, at any rate), the *grandi*, and the magnates — set about to consolidate their new position.

As a way of doing this, they proposed drastic revisions of the laws which Giano had made. They proposed radical modification of the Ordinamenti. In particular, they wanted the repeal of that provision which held one kinsman legally responsible for the misdeeds of his relatives and of another provision which said that for guilt of a crime or misdemeanor to be "established by common report" there was needed the testimony of only two witnesses.

"Having their own friends in the priorate" — now we return to Villani — and having made up "the great quarrels among themselves, especially between the Adimari and the Tosinghi, and the Mozzi and the Bardi," they were confident that they could do this.

"And so, on an appointed day, they made a gathering of the folk and petitioned the priors to have the laws amended."

But they had reckoned without the *popolo*. Here the term is comprehensive. Both the merchant-burghers — those who had not temporarily joined with the *grandi* — and the lesser guildsmen and artisans were involved.

"They rose in tumult and they rushed to arms."

The *grandi* rushed to arms too.

They mounted their armored horses and they called in their retainers from the country with such other troops as they could find in the city.

They confronted the *popolani* in three places. One group massed in front of the Baptistery, and there Forese degli Adimari raised a royal standard. (He was probably trying to intimidate the people by making them think that Jean de Chalon, who had left the city when he was not paid, had come back with his five hundred horsemen.) Another group drew up at the Piazza da Ponte, the open space near the Ponte Vecchio. This group was commanded by Vanni Mozzi. A third group, under Geri Spini, gathered in the Mercato Nuovo.

"But the *popolani* all had weapons, and they were many in number, and they had banners and ensigns too. They barricaded the city at sundry points, and they gathered at the palace of the *podestà*, and at the palace of the priors, who at that time abode in the house of the Cerchi at San Brocolo. Wherefore the *grandi* had no power or strength against them, and the people might have overthrown them, but consulting for the best and to avoid civil war, by mediation of certain friars between the better men on either side, both parties disarmed and the city returned to peace and quiet.

"Without any change," Villani adds.

Without any change in the laws, he meant.

But actually there were two changes.

To establish "by public report" that a man had violated the laws, three witnesses were now required instead of two, and it was further decreed that if the offense were capital there could not be more than one offender. In other words, if a murder were done — or even a maiming — there must be a *capitaneus homicidii*, a single guilty person who was held responsible.

This was, of course, greatly pleasing to the aristocrats — to the noblemen and to the magnates — since a whole family could no longer be condemned for the actions of a single reckless member.

The second change went even further. It broadened the very base of Florentine government. Hitherto, as has already been reported, it had been necessary to be one of those who regularly practiced a trade to be eligible to hold office in the commonwealth.

It was now decreed that this no longer need be the case. It was decreed that "*quilibit popularis, dumodo non sit miles, qui scriptus reperietur in libro seu matricola alicuius Artis civitatis Florentie in numero hominum*" of the said guild — that any citizen of Florence, *who was not a knight*, who is found inscribed in the books or on the roll of any guild of the city of Florence — might now serve in the priorate, become gonfalonier, be a member of any of the many Florentine councils, or in fact take any part whatsoever in Florentine government.

Effectively, it meant that, except in the special case of the knight, any aristocrat who wished to come down from his heights to the crowd could, if a guild would accept him, declare himself to be a merchant-burgher.

(A law similar to this has recently been enacted in England. It permits a hereditary peer to make a lifetime renunciation of his title and thus become eligible to serve in the House of Commons.)

This revision was passed by the appropriate councils on July 23, 1295, or just two months after Dante became thirty years old. This happened at a very opportune moment.

XI

Prelude to the Ill-omened Priorate

FOR it was almost precisely at this time that the poet of Beatrice — and of some other ladies — gave up for the time being his writing of sonnets and *canzoni*, his studies of philosophy, and even his young-man-about-town revelries to plunge into the rough-and-tumble of municipal politics.

The revised law made this possible. By his own statement, Dante was an aristocrat, even if only a member of the lesser aristocracy, and although he was a landowner who derived income by leasing some of his property to the cattle-raisers and farmers who were so important to the day-by-day economy of Florence, and although he lent money — and even more frequently borrowed it — he certainly did not practice a trade.

Now he did not have to. He needed only to pay lip service to the commercial interests which controlled the city by enrolling in one of the organizations through which they exerted their influence — by enrolling in one of the guilds.

This he did.

In the Florentine state archives is a collection of volumes which preserve guild records and one of them has this title: *Arti dei Medici e Speziali, Vol. 7, Matricole* (Guild of the Physicians and Apothecaries, Vol. 7, Roster). On pages 46 *verso* and 47, it has this entry:

"The first book, marked *A*, of the enrollments in Florence. It begins in the year 1297."

Then the names are listed. I give those under the letter *D*.

Dino di Bentivegna. Donato di Maffeo. Donato di Spigliato. Duccio di Guido. Dino del Buono. Duccio di Rinieri. Maestro Duccio da Lignano, *medico . . .*

Thirty-three persons in all, one of them Dino del Pechora, which could hardly have been our Dino Pecora of the Butchers Guild. But not until we come to the thirty-second of them is our attention arrested.

"*Dante d'Aldighieri degli Aldighieri, poeta fiorentina.*"

Poeta fiorentina! Florentine poet!

Our Dante, a druggist or doctor!

This certainly is a cause for surprise.

But it so happens that Dante did not have to follow either one of these callings to join this, the eighth in importance among the nine greater guilds.

Nor need he have been a painter. This is the too-ingenious explanation of certain modern students of Dante. Painters, they point out, probably because they were beholden to the apothecaries and their foreign agents for the pigments and dyes out of which they made their colors, belonged to this guild. And Dante had painted a picture.

Rather he was able to join it because, during the poet's lifetime, medicine and philosophy were considered associated disciplines.

And at least locally Dante was considered a philosopher.

"*Vo poetizzando!*" I go poetizing! he once said.

"*Va filosofando!*" He goes philosophizing! said his neighbors.

It was, then, as a philosopher — or at any rate as a dedicated student of philosophy — that he inscribed himself as a member of an association which included not only the doctors and druggists who gave it its name, not only the magicmakers in tempera and fresco, not only the readers of Boethius, Aristotle, and Thomas Aquinas, but (shortly) men of more than thirty other trades, among them the hairdressers and barbers; the goldbeaters; the berettamakers; the stationers; the lanternmakers; the booksellers; the maskmakers; the makers of catgut strings for musical instruments; the bat-and-ballmakers; the perfumesellers; and the sievemakers, all of whom could belong to this guild.

« 2 »

Almost certainly, Dante joined it as soon as he could lawfully do so.

Here is another matter which has sometimes caused debate among Dante students. The *quaderno* — record book — in which Dante's enrollment is noted is clearly stated to have begun with the year 1297 (March 25, 1297, by our style, for that is when the Florentine year began) and the next book with 1301.

An obvious assumption, then, would be that Dante joined the Physicians and Apothecaries Guild after March 24, 1297, and before March 25, 1301.

But this conclusion is flatly contradicted by another document which is also found in the Florentine archives.

This document is dated December 14, 1295.

"In the Council of the Capitudini and of the Savi, the captain laid before the said council for discussion the question of how future priors should be chosen."

Of the nearly one hundred men present, eleven then spoke to the matter.

"Neri Attiglianti proposed that the priors and the *capitudini* each choose" — there is a blank space where the number should be — "from their own *sesto*, and that the vote then be taken in the usual manner.

"Girolamo Salvi proposed that the *capitudini* and the councillors from each *sesto* choose three men from each *sesto*, and that at least three be voted on.

"Dino Pecora proposed that every one of the *capitudini* submit in writing two from every *sesto* and that the councillors from every *sesto* do the same.

"Dante degli Alaghieri" — note the spelling, which differs from one document to another — "proposed that the *capitudini* and councillors of every *sesto* submit in writing" — once again the number is not recorded — "from every *sesto*, and that a vote be taken among all of them."

Other speakers were Ser Bene da Vaglia, Gheri Paganetti, Migliore Guadagni (Greater Gains — what a name for a merchant!) Messer Loteringo da Montespertoli. Messer Oddo Altoviti, Lando Albizzi, and Nello Diotiauti.

By "a sitting and rising vote," the suggestion made by Lando Albizzi carried the day. Because of illegibilities in the manuscript, it is not clear exactly what it was.

But even to have taken part in the debates of this council — let alone to have voted in it — Dante would have to have been a member of a guild.

Not in 1297, then, but in 1295 — and within a few months, if not weeks, after the enactment on June 30 of the revised statute, the poet had complied with the necessary formalities and was enrolled.

He could not wear the velvet hat and the fur-trimmed crimson robes of the *messeri medici* (gentlemen doctors), but with Giotto and Cimabue, both of whom belonged to this guild — and if he had lived two centuries later, with mapmaker Toscanelli and explorer Amerigo Vespucci — he could lean as a fellow guildsman against the counter in a dim and fragrant store regarding the shelves filled with *letti* (pots of ointment), *tazzini* (tasting cups), *fiole* (cruets), to say nothing of perfumes, gloves, sachets and buckles, candied apples, quince and plum jams, dates, manna, myrrh, and spices from Syria and Africa, soap, and endless other "luxuries and foibles" of the day.

He could also become an office seeker and an officeholder.

He had an excellent base from which to do this.

The *botteghe* of the spice-selling apothecaries took the place of the modern barber shop as a center of gossip both personal and political.

The pulse of the city — and of the state — could be felt there.

"Highborn gentlemen and well-to-do *contadini* thronged these marts" — this a modern description of them — "and lent their graces and their foibles to the animated scene."

Who was now allied with whom in the latest struggle to gain control of this guild or that guild?

Whose lute was twangled under whose window?

What member of which banking house was about to defalcate?

All this, as cloves and cinnamon were weighed out — and sold almost for their weight in gold — in a shop from which, by guild regulations emanating from the Palazzo de' Lamberti, flew the red and white guild gonfalon with its device of the Madonna and Child supported by two pots of Annunciation lilies, and which was "kept open daily, except on feast days," and in which only "genuine articles" could be sold.

« *3* »

It is not inappropriate to ponder the possible reasons which led Dante to take this step — the reason why he decided to become a doer instead of a dreamer.

Was he a young idealist stirred to the heart by the reforms proposed and partly carried out by Giano della Bella? Other youthful poets have been stirred by a similar idealism.

Did his land holdings and his other properties make him a businessman against his own deepest inclinations and intentions, and did he go into politics to protect his own interests as other businessmen did before and have done since?

Certainly both Dante and his brother were constantly engaged in monetary transactions.

Nor were they always very particular as to the character of those with whom they dealt.

In 1299, Francesco Alighieri borrowed eighty-three gold florins from Lotto di Cino Cavolini. (Dante was probably associated in this loan. He and his brother always worked in an unwritten partnership.) Lotto was a notorious usurer and he was the son of another usurer whose reputation was even more unsavory — so unsavory, in fact, that in his will he asked his sons to make peace with God for him by restoring his ill-gotten gains, and they did in fact restore part of them.

Yet Dante, who did business with Lotto — or whose brother did — fleered at usurers almost as sagely as he did at simoniacs, sodomites, murderers, and traitors.

Inferno XVII:

> Then did I farther go, and all alone
> Along the seventh circle's farthest edge—
> There where were seated the unhappy people.
> Their grief and anguish flooded from their eyes.
> One side and the other with their hands
> They defended themselves from burning vapor and soil.
> They were in no way different from dogs
> That thrust, in summertime, with paw or muzzle
> When flies and gnats and gadflies bite at them.
> Now when I set my eyes upon the faces
> Of those on whom the grievous flames were falling,
> I could not recognize a single one,
> Yet saw that round each neck there hung a pouch
> Dyed in a certain color with a certain device.
> And when, looking around, I came among them,
> Azure upon a yellow purse I saw
> The visage and the features of a lion.
> Then, going farther on in my inspection,
> I saw another which was all blood-red
> And had on it a goose whiter than butter.
> Then one who had a sow azure and pregnant
> Stamped upon his little and white wallet
> Said this to me: "What dost thou in this ditch?
> Get thyself gone, and since thou livest still
> Know that my fellow townsman, Vitaliano,
> Will shortly take his seat at my left side.
> Among these Florentines I am a Paduan,
> And often do they din into my ears
> Their shouting: 'Let the sovereign knight appear
> Who brings with him the sack with the three goats!' "
> Then did he twist his mouth and he thrust out
> His tongue as an ox does when it licks its nose.

Except for Vitaliano — and the speaker — all of these are identifiable Florentines. The one with the lion azure was a Gianfigliazzi. The Gianfigliazzi lived in the Sesto di Borgo (near the Florentine side of the Ponte Vecchio). They had been Guelphs since the city was first divided into parties in 1215. The one with a goose argent upon a field gules was an Ubbriachi. The Ubbriachi — the name means drunkards — were Ghibellines. The knight with the three goats was Giovanni Buiamonte. He was a distinguished Guelph who with his three sons took part in the disastrous battle of Montaperti (and survived it) and he was gonfalonier of justice in 1293. He alone — but he must have been very old for Montaperti was fought in 1260 — was alive at the theoretical date of the *Commedia*. That is why the other — and less successful — usurers were waiting for him.

Or were none of these the reason, and did Dante plunge into politics as a reaction against his days of riotous living?

This is not impossible either. The subject of this biography had reacted from his involvement with the lady at the window by plunging into his studies of philosophy, and then from the tedium of day and nights in the lecture hall and at his books by turning to a life not very far this side of debauchery.

Did he react from the latter by becoming a civic-minded citizen?

Here dates are not entirely helpful. His "good friend and boon companion" Forese Donati died on July 28, 1296, probably as a result of his abuses to his health, and it was some seven months earlier that Dante first took official part in public affairs. But although — this is implicit, if not clearly stated — Forese did not repent until his deathbed, it does not necessarily follow that Dante roved the streets with him until the very end. He may have — and indeed he probably did — mend his own ways sooner.

However, all this is speculation, and the most we can say for certain is that as he reached thirty Dante the poet became — for a while, at least — Dante the politician, and, in due course, Dante a fairly important politician.

"He was much employed by the commonwealth," wrote Leonardo Bruni.

Boccaccio deals with the same matter.

"It is the nature of temporal things that one is the cause of the other," Giovanni wrote. "His family cares, then" — the necessity to establish himself so that he could support a wife and at least three children — "drew Dante to the affairs of state. In these, the vain honors which are joined to public offices so entangled him that, without noting whence he had started or whither he was going, he gave himself up wholeheartedly and without restraint to the government of the city. In this, fortune was so far favorable to him that no embassy was listened to or answered, no law was passed or repealed, no peace was made, no war begun, and in short no discussion of any weight was undertaken unless he first gave his opinion in regard to it."

No discussion of any weight — and very few discussions of ordinary routine matters! Virtually no discussion of Florentine municipal house-keeping, the ordinary, day-by-day, often humdrum operations which every governmental entity, whether medieval or modern, must faithfully carry out!

That this was so is clearly born out by the second surviving document which deals with Dante's civic activities.

Under the date of *"die V mensis junii"* — the fifth day of the month of June — "in the year 1296," it notes, "the captain of the people" — a certain Fiorino de' Pontecarali of Brescia — "the priors and the gonfalonier being also present, laid before the Council of One Hundred" the following items:

(1) That it might please the said council that of the one hundred *libbre* which might be expended by them during the current month, ten small florins might be paid to one Francesco Lombardo.

(2) That they consider a petition about the matter of the hospital which now faces the Piazza San Giovanni as well as all other matters contained in the said petition.

(3) That they would consider a motion not to receive those exiled by the commonwealth of Pistoia into the city and the *contrada* of Florence.

(4) That those Pistoians who have owned land and property in the Florentine *contrada* for five years be not subjected to the taxes and compulsory loans that were imposed upon other residents.

(5) That they would consider a motion to give the priors and the gonfalonier here present authority to proceed against any person or persons and especially magnates who injure or try to injure any *popolano*.

(6) That they ratify certain appeals and restitutions which were signed and agreed upon before the judge of appeals.

(7) That they act upon a petition laid before them by Ricovero of Milan and Betto Corsi.

(8) That they act upon the petition of the tax collectors and their notary that they be extended a loan of three *libbre* a month for each of them.

(9) That they consider a petition dealing with the prisons made by certain magnates.

"Dante Alagheri spoke in favor of all of these propositions."

They were all carried — by votes of 75 to 0; 72 to 3; 75 to 0; 71 to 4; 68 to 7; 71 to 4; 75 to 0; 74 to 1; and 74 to 1.

Thus for the second time within six months Dante is recorded as having sat in a Florentine council and taken part in a debate upon proposed Florentine official actions.

This time his eloquence was successful.

But note that the issues dealt with were almost all local and almost all routine.

Item one, for example, dealt with paying a sum of money — presumably his salary — to a person otherwise unknown for unnamed service rendered.

Item two dealt with the problems of a hospital — in those days a hospital was for the indigent only — near the Baptistery. Perhaps it was to be enlarged. More likely — since it stood facing Santa Reparata near which work had begun on the new *duomo*, Santa Maria del Fiore — it was to be removed or replaced.

Item six dealt with the approval of certain legal actions and item seven with a petition from two citizens in regard to some unknown business.

Item eight dealt with the understandable wish of those who collected the city's revenues — they did this on the contracted tax-farmer basis so that they were compensated by retaining a percentage of their actual collections — to have an advance which would tide them over until the payments began to come in.

Item nine concerned itself with a complaint against prison conditions. Appropriately this was made by *grandi*. So many of these, unable to pay the confiscatory and often deliberately ruinous fines which had been imposed upon them, had suffered incarceration that one of the most notorious dungeons in Florence was known as the *palliazza dei magnati*, or hiding place for magnates.

(But in that time all Florentine dungeons were notorious! The "black hole of La Berenda" near the ancient Roman theater. The "black hole of the vineyards." The prison of San Michele Palchetto south of the Duomo and near Dante's little San Martino. Their grim walls dripped water. They were dank and chilly. And except for those who could smuggle in enough money to pay outrageous prices, the only fare — since they were operated by private interests to make money — was vinegar which was passed off as wine and bread moldy enough to seem revolting even to the rats.)

Indeed, only items three and four — dealing with Pistoia and her citizens — and item five — which asked for the imposition of still further sanctions on the still troublesome *grandi* — either went abroad or had wider implications.

Pistoia, a small city some twenty miles west of Florence was even more savagely divided than the latter. Here public standards had fallen into such low estate that a thief and blasphemer like the nobleman's bastard "mule" Vanni Fucci could become one of the leaders of the city.

Dante has something to say about Vanni. Calling him "a man of blood and rage," he puts him into hell, and there he is as definite in his evil as Farinata degli Uberti was in his proud patriotism.
Inferno XXIV and XXV:

> "I rained from Tuscany
> Not long ago into this savage hole.
> A beast's life pleased me, not a human being's,
> Beast that I am, and I am Vanni Fucci."

Then Vanni tells what brought him there:

> "I am thrust down so far because I was
> The thief who robbed the riches of the sacristy
> And falsely laid the blame upon another."

This was the famous robbery of the church of San Zeno. Vanni was a leader in this crime.

But not even this villainy — nor the fact that he writhed in hell — tamed Vanni's arrogance.

He taunted Dante and his party with future disasters. "And I do this to make you writhe in woe." Then he turned his scorn on Deity.

> He lifted up his hands with both the figs,
> Crying: "Take that God! 'T is at Thee I make them!"

This was the lewdest and the most insulting gesture known to the Middle Ages.

« 4 »

It would turn out to be extraordinarily unfortunate to have been involved even peripherally in Pistoian affairs.

It was also risky — and would have future consequences — to have become aligned with measures directed against the magnates even though they merely sharpened up and strengthened measures which had been adopted long before.

But these were only three items out of nine. The rest were everyday and innocuous.

That was, however, in 1296.

Beginning in 1300, Dante would be constantly — and consistently — in matters far more grave.

Grave and, as we will find out, perilous.

The Riccardiana Dante (Riccardiana Library, Florence), an illustration of a manuscript collection of Dante's poems, is clearly modeled after the Naples bust, and has itself been the model for subsequent painters, including Raphael.

In these — for the time being at least — he would still speak for the Florentine consensus. He would still vote with the majority. But it was a majority that became less and less effective — though not necessarily smaller — every day.

To find out what these matters were we must for the moment move away from the clustered houses which stood upon the banks of the clear-blue stream (in those days it was not yellow-muddy except in times of flood) which "was born [*Purgatorio* XIV] a little stream of Falterona" in the Tuscan Apennines.

We must journey to Naples — *nea polis*, the new city, it was named in 328 B.C., when it was long since old in wickedness and intrigue — on the half circle of its blue bay.

We must make our way to Paris by the gray Seine, where Dante's new "Pilate," Philip the Fair, was shaping out the first strong French monarchy since Charlemagne — and the last one until King Spider (Louis XI) in the fifteenth century.

"This Philip was one of the handsomest men in the world, and one of the tallest."

Elsewhere he says that the "Iron King" was *"bellisima della persona sopra gli altri del mondo avarissimo come un cane"* (good-looking in his person beyond any other man, but greedy as a dog).

Villani said also:

"He was a wise man and worthy, but by reason of pleasure-seeking, particularly in the chase, he was frequently swayed by ill counsel, to which he readily paid heed."

By the ill counsel of inordinately able but inordinately ambitious men.

Musciatto Franzesi, a few of whose machinations have already been adverted to. (But we will hear more of this manipulator, whose affairs were often "sore embroiled as those of merchants most times are" but who was usually successful.)

Guillaume de Nogaret, "a sagacious and crafty cleric" who was later to become keeper of the seals and secretary of the kingdom.

Enguerrand de Marigny. Geoffroi de Paris called Enguerrand "the best speaker in the land." But his ostentation offended many, for his house at Paris had a golden gable and his luxury outdid that of the king's brothers.

Pierre Flote.

We must also turn to Rome. Looked at realistically, this one time *caput mundi* was (except for the Vatican and the Lateran and numerous small Byzantine churches) a broken-down town where goats clambered over the classic ruins and cattle (watched over by sun-blackened herdsmen) browsed in the Forum. Its population — once more than a million — was less than thirty thousand, and those of its inhabitants who were not dark as Africans were yellow with malaria. Its government, too, was anarchy canonized. Its noblest names were worn by chieftains of *banditti*.

But it was still an immortal cynosure.

"Certainly," wrote Dante in his *Convivio*, "I have the firm belief that the stones of her walls and the very soil on which she is seated are worthy beyond all that men have proclaimed."

And now, for reasons which will shortly become apparent, it was stirring again.

To Naples, then; to Paris; and to Rome.

For the powers that sat by the Bay of Naples, on the Seine bank, and on the seven hills that rise above the Tiber — that is to say Charles the Lame, the foolish and sometimes even addlepated son of Charles of Anjou; Philip the Fair; and the great man who would soon put on the papal tiara — were about to engage in a struggle for hegemony which would involve all of Italy and most of Europe.

It would involve the bankers of Florence and their moneybags.

It would also involve — and deeply — the poet turned philosopher, turned man of government, whose name was Dante Alighieri.

« 5 »

The contest began in 1292.

In that year, as has already been noted, Pope Nicholas IV died, and there followed, as has also been noted, an eighteen-month interregnum.

This — it has been noted too — was "because of 'disagreements' among the cardinals."

But that is oversimplification.

It was not merely that the men charged with making the choice were hardheaded — "each cardinal desiring to make a pope of his own chosing" — but that they were rigidly divided into two parties, both playing for high stakes.

One party "wished a pope that would please King Charles of Naples, and its head was Matteo Rossi of the Orsini."

The head of the second party was Cardinal Jacopo Colonna. It is not stated whom he supported, but it can be assumed that he began by being against anyone whom Orsini favored, for in Rome Orsini and Colonna were mortal enemies. They were the *banditti* chieftains referred to above. It can also be assumed that Cardinal Colonna was looking for political and financial advancement and that he would not fail to listen to a word from France.

The conclave was convened in January 1293 — not in Rome, where the Vatican was still a small, unimportant palace, and where not even the castle of the Holy Angel (the Castel Sant' Angelo) was strong enough to protect the assembled princes of the Church from the hired bravos who served both factions, but in Orvieto, the safely (more than one hundred miles) distant city, which sat securely in an ancient crater. One thousand feet above sea level, this town was protected by sheer, tall cliffs of yellow-brown volcanic tufa, and accessible only by a single road, the gradient of which was twenty-seven percent.

To Orvieto, then, of the wheat-colored Est-est-est wine, hastened the motley throng that was always drawn to such an assemblage. The official emissaries of King Charles or King Philip, and also the official emissaries of many a big or little commune, carrying their messages in a *buta* — a cylinder or box — made of osiers and closed with the royal or communal seal. The spies and the secret agents of the same. The barefoot monk who brought — and sought — tidings in the interest of the king of Naples. The learned clerk with quill pen who did the same for Philip. The buffoon who, between japes, whispered this thing or that on behalf of one or another banking house — and who also reported back rumor or fact on which fortunes could be made.

And besides these the usual camp followers — for an army was gathered at Orvieto even though it was churchly rather than military, and fought with votes instead of crossbows or lances.

The ladies of nearby Bulicame, of which we will say more later, came to the conclave city, adding to its liveliness if not to its virtues, and so too farriers to shoe the mules and horses and to act as horse doctors; wine-sellers with their *botticelli* (kegs) and straw-wrapped *fiaschi;* hawkers of holy objects or of old clothes; tinsmiths; ironmongers; and even fortune-tellers and mountebanks. A gathering for such an important purpose soon became a county fair.

But neither the bribery and threats open or hidden nor the excitement nor the push and pull of contending interests came up with an answer. Days became weeks; weeks, months; and still no pontiff.

The exact date is not known, but baffled and perhaps feeling increased pressure, the cardinals decided to transfer their sessions to another city.

They went to Perugia, where they ensconced themselves behind the massive Etruscan walls. There their long delaying tactics ended — under pressure!

"And being in Perugia and straightly constrained by the Perugians to elect a pope" — at a later conclave the people of Lyons would literally remove the roof from the building in which it met so that inclement weather would hasten an election — "the cardinals, as it pleased God, agreed not to name one of their own number, and they chose a holy man who was called Fra Pietro and was from Morrone in the Abruzzi."

« 6 »

It is hard to imagine a choice more inappropriate, and indeed not until 1522 when Dutch Adriaan Florenz became Adrian VI — he was the last pontiff to retain his own name — was a man less qualified to hold the office elected.

He took the title of Celestine V.

His parents were peasants.

He was eighty years old.

He had been a hermit — this is Villani — "and of austere life and penitence, and in order to abandon the world, after he had founded many holy monasteries of his order, he departed into the mountains above Sulmona."

Staff in hand, sandals on his feet, and clad in the coarse fustian of the anchorite.

This was at the Celestine monastery of Morrone which gave him both his ordinary and his papal name.

"He was a simple man.

"He knew no letters.

"He did not occupy himself willingly with the pomps of the world."

But the papacy was now a world office which had dependent on it — or which it hoped to make dependent — archbishops and abbots from Iceland to Asia Minor, while in Europe the scene was being set for it to pick up the reins which had been abandoned by absentee and uncrowned emperors.

"Two suns," cried Dante, "there were that made good this world."

The empire.

And the papacy.

But now, if things were done right, there could be one sun.

This being the case, the Church did not need an eremite but a Caesar.

The princes of the Church — and those of both factions — realized this almost as soon as they came out of the locked doors.

"The cardinals" — because of his unworldliness and his reluctance to involve himself in their schemes and intrigues — "soon held him in small esteem, and it seemed to them that they had made an ill choice for the well-being and estate of the Church."

And for their own well-being and prosperity which they equated with the same.

But Celestine was aware of his limitations too.

"The said holy father perceiving this" — how could he not since he was harassed night and day? — "and not feeling himself sufficient for the government of the Church, and being one too who loved the service of

God and the welfare of his soul more than worldly glory, sought every way to renounce the papacy."

How to abdicate from his responsibilities.

How to make the great refusal.

Dante called it this and branded it as cowardice. But Dante, as we will see, was hurt by it or thought he was.

Inferno III — in which is described the bleak limbo in which dwell those who refuse to make a choice for either good or evil:

> And I, my head with horror all enwrapped,
> Said: "Master, tell me what is this I hear?
> What people these who conquered seem with pain?"
> And he to me: "This miserable state
> Enduréd is by the sad souls of those
> Who lived their lives *sans* infamy, *sans* praise.
> Here they are mingled with the caitiff crew
> Of angels who not either rebels were
> Nor were they true to God, but were for themselves . . .
> These wretched beings have no hope of death,
> And their blind life is so abject and low
> That there is no one here they do not envy."
> Then I who looked upon them saw a banner
> Which waving in the air did move so swift
> It seemed to me it never could stand still;
> And after it there came so long a train
> Of people that I scarcely could believe,
> Could not believe, death had undone so many.
> Amid them, after I had known and noted many,
> I saw and recognized the shade of him
> Who made through cowardice the great refusal.

How, honorably and in accordance with the service of God, to put aside both the grandeur and the woes that went with wearing the triple crown and to resume his old monastic life.

« 7 »

The man who would show him the way stood in the wings.

"Now among the other cardinals," wrote Giovanni Villani, "was one Messer Benedetto Guatani of Alagna [Benedetto Gaetani of Anagni], very learned in books and in the affairs of the world much practiced and sagacious, and he had a great desire to attain to the papal dignity. He now laid plans to attain it, counting on the aid of King Charles [Charles II of Naples] and of certain of the cardinals who had already pledged their votes to him.

"This Guatani heard that Pope Celestine wished to lay down the papacy. He went to him, therefore, and told him that he could make a new decretal in which it would be declared that for the good of his soul a pope might give up his high office. He cited the example of St. Clement. It was St. Peter's wish that when he died Clement would be pope after him, but the latter for the good of his soul would not have it so, and in his place first St. Linus and then St. Cletus were chosen."

It is reported that Cardinal Gaetani also used other methods of persuasion, but since we are told this only by two writers of fiction, Boccaccio and the author of *Il Pecorone*, it does not quite have the status of fact.

"The truth is" — this is the *Il Pecorone* version — "or this many people say, that the said cardinal sent a man secretly to the pope's bedside, and through a speaking tube this man called out Celestine's name loudly three times.

"The pope finally answered: 'Who art thou?'

"The one with the speaking tube replied: 'I am the angel of God, and I am sent to thee because thou art His devoted servant. He bids me tell thee as coming from Him that thou shouldst hold thy soul worth more than the pomps and vanities of the world.' "

And so — we go back to Villani — "even as the said cardinal had counseled, he made the said decretal. And this done, on the day of St. Lucy in the following December, and in a consistory of all the cardinals and in their presence, he took off the crown and papal mantle, and renounced the papacy, and he departed from the court and returned to his hermit life and to his penance."

In the same year — and indeed only eleven days later — Cardinal Gaetani, "having by his wit and sagacity so wrought that Pope Celestine renounced his high office, followed up what he had begun and went secretly to King Charles with only a few companions. 'King,' he said to him, 'thy Celestine had the will and the means to serve thee, but he had not the knowledge. But if thou wilt work among thy friends among the cardinals so that they will elect me pope I know I shall have the will, and I shall be able.' "

Charles was convinced.

"He promised and agreed that his twelve cardinals" — the twelve cardinals made by Celestine whose votes he controlled — "should give him their support. Both Messer Matteo Rossi and Cardinal Jacopo were at this election, and they, perceiving what was about to happen, gave him their votes too. But the first to do so was Cardinal Matteo Rossi."

Note that Matteo was an Orsini cardinal. This will be important.

"And in this wise was Cardinal Gaetani elected pope."

He was elected in the city of Naples on the vigil of the Nativity of Christ. In other words, on Christmas Eve, December 24.

"But as soon as he was chosen, he departed with his court and went to Rome."

He would go to Naples to be sure of votes, but would not stay there.

"And in Rome" — but in the midst of an out-of-season thunderstorm and to the accompaniment of a bloody street brawl — "he caused himself to be crowned with great solemnity and great honor."

This was in the middle of January.

Thus, amid stage sounds and in a stage setting which seemed strangely appropriate to the *terribiltà* of the man who now mounted the throne of St. Peter, began a papacy which during the nine years it endured would shake all of Europe to its farthest reaches. That it would also shake Florence to its foundations almost goes without saying.

« 8 »

Boniface VIII — for that was the name Cardinal Benedetto Gaetani assumed — was one of the great men of a day and age which produced many such. He may have been one of the great popes of all time. With the possible exception of Innocent II, he was certainly the only great pope between Gregory VII — Gregory the Great (1073–1085) — and the High Renaissance line which began in 1447 with Nicholas V of Sarzana and extended through Pius II Piccolomini, Alexander VI Borgia, Julius II della Rovere (Michelangelo's stormy patron and bully) and Leo X de' Medici.

He was recognized as such by the men of his times.

"He was of extraordinary shrewdness and of very lofty ambitions," said Boccaccio.

"He was a man of large schemes, a lordly man," said Villani. "He sought much for honor and well knew how to advance the Church."

Elsewhere Villani speaks of his "great courage"; of his "great knowledge and memory"; of his "great heart"; of his liberality "to folk which pleased him and which were worthy"; and also of his "experience" and his "caution."

His physical appearance was imposing. When his body was exumed in a later century, it was established that the stories of his great height were in no way exaggerated. He was nearly six feet tall, which is something for an Italian and more for a man of the Middle Ages. (Incidentally his height was made to seem greater by the unusually tall miter he always wore.) It was found also that only two of his teeth were missing. Yet he was more than eighty when he died.

His hands were strong but sensitive, and if we can judge from the statue by Arnolfo di Cambio — and from other statues done during his life — he was not only handsome but placid-looking. This is more than a little surprising in view of certain well-known aspects of his character.

His mind was clear and logical, and his use of words eloquent and convincing. Two of his bulls — the *Clericis laicos,* which forbade Christian monarchs to levy taxes, however disguised, upon the clergy without papal permission, and his *Unam sanctam,* "the most absolute proclamation of theocratic doctrine ever formulated in the Middle Ages," which stressed the unity of Christendom under the pope's headship — rallied men to the side of the Church wherever they were read, and almost overcame the resistance of kings.

He was, too, undeviating of purpose. Once he had set upon an objective nothing could turn him aside until he had either attained it or been defeated.

But Boniface's strength, which was great, and his good qualities, which were many, were counterbalanced by correspondingly bad faults, some of which were singularly inappropriate for a high pontiff.

To begin with, there is almost incontrovertible evidence that he was a skeptic if not actually an atheist. As a young man and even as a young priest, he is reputed to have dabbled in alchemy and magic, and even as he moved upward toward the papacy he continued to surprise gatherings of his fellow clergy with some of his statements.

"The stories of Christianity," he said, "were invented by men" — *inventae sunt ab hominibus* — "as were the fables of the Jews and of the Moslems."

On another occasion:

"The Madonna when she gave birth was no more a virgin than my own mother was."

"It is fatuous," he also said, "to believe that there can be one God in three persons."

Even after he had become pope, Boniface insisted that the dead could not be resurrected — "not any more than my horse can who died two days ago" — and that there would never be a last day and a Last Judgment "because everything created was eternal."

(This last was Averroism pure and simple, and the Church condemned in no uncertain terms the teaching of the Moorish philosopher ibn-Rushd, whom the West called Averroës.)

"Stupid!" he cried to his chaplain who prayed for Christ's mercy on the soul of a knight who had just died. "Stupid! Stupid! What can Christ do? He was a man even as we are. He was not God,"

But he added:

"But Christ was a wise man, although a great hypocrite."

The pontiff was also as merciless as he was single of purpose.

After Celestine V had abdicated the papacy, the old man rode modestly on muleback toward his native mountains. He would stay there awhile and then go on to Slavonia.

But Boniface saw to it that he never reached this refuge.

"It is said," reported Villani, "and it is true, that Messer Gaetani when he became pope caused Celestine to be taken prisoner in the mountains of Sant' Angiolo in Apulia and secretly held him prisoner in the fortress of Fummone in Campania. *There he did not live long.*"

There must not be a possible antipope — not even this bewildered hermit!

Boniface's willfulness was likewise legendary.

"It is not possible to argue with this man," said a cardinal. "It is not safe to argue with him."

Another cardinal is responsible for an anecdote that illustrates the same quality.

"The holy father preached at a dinner one day, to which all the cardinals and bishops and abbots and monks in Anagni were summoned. He began with the words: 'Who am I?' and this he repeated three times because no one answered him the first time.

"Finally a cardinal spoke.

" 'You hold the place of God and St. Peter on earth and what you bind on earth is bound in heaven.' The others echoed these words.

" 'Do you truly believe this?' the holy father then said, and with one voice they said yes.

"Then the holy father told those who were there that they were deposed from office and ordered them to give him their capes and their rings. They all did so.

"Thereupon he continued his preaching, and when he had finished his sermon he said to them: 'You have been obedient to the Church and are worthy of the honors you once held. I give them back to you.' He ordered his servants to hand them back the capes and rings and his notaries to draw up new charters."

But even that did not end the strange episode.

"When he had done this, he went out of the place and told them to wait a little. He went into a chamber and had himself dressed in hose of scarlet presset. He put on gilded shoes and golden spurs and all of his habits were of scarlet. And then he took a sword and issued forth again. 'Do you believe that I am emperor too?' he asked them. They all said 'yes' again.

" 'That I am,' he said, 'and I have thus garbed myself because I am above all Christianity. I bear the cross because I am pope. And the sword in my hand is the sword which the Lord gave to St. Peter to signify that with one edge he should rule over things heavenly and with the other he should rule the earth. And for that reason I have taken this sword."

The onetime Cardinal Gaetani was, besides this, a formidable nepotist. Indeed not until the High Renaissance would a man upon the papal throne so assiduously — and so successfully — advance the fortunes of his many relatives.

As he displayed these characteristics and reached out for greater and greater power, the great fought Boniface when they dared and made deals with him when they did not. The moral deplored him.

Interrupting for a moment his hymn-writing, Jacopone da Todi, the monk-poet, set down this about him in rhymes that were almost doggerel:

> *O Papa Bonifacio*
> *molto ai jocato al mondo*
> *penso che jocundo*
> *Non ten porai partire*

> O Pope Boniface,
> Thou hast cheated the world to its face,
> And when thou leavest this place
> 'T will not be joyfully.

Jacopo also referred to the "astuteness" by which Boniface "thought he would govern the world"; his "wicked tongue" that "spoke nothing but villanies and blasphemy"; and his "redoubled thirst to drink down gold yet not be satisfied."

Dante in his own and more effective way joined Jacopo. In the whole *Commedia*, there is no one whom he attacks more savagely than the Gaetani pope.

Inferno XIX (the simoniac Pope Nicholas III is speaking):

> "Art thou so soon come here
> Into this fiery place, Pope Boniface?
> By some years, then, the writing lied to me.
> So soon then art thou sated by the hunger
> For which thou didst not fear to seize by guile
> Our fair lady the Church and outrage her?"

Inferno XXVII (Guido da Montefeltro):

> "The prince-in-chief of the new Pharisees—
> Having waged war hard by the Lateran,

And not with Saracens and not with Jews,
For every foe of his a Christian was,
Nor one of them had helped to conquer Acre,
Nor one done business in the sultan's land—
Neither his holy office nor his vows
Gave heed to . . ."

Paradiso XII (St. Bonaventura):

"He who sits there, and is degenerate."

Paradiso XXVII (St. Peter):

"He who upon the earth usurped my place,
My place, my place, which is now vacant
In the high presence of the Son of God,
Has made my tomb and cemetery a sewer
Of blood and stench, wherefore the Perverse One
Who fell from heaven to hell is greatly pleased."

St. Peter is made to add:

"The Bride of Christ on my blood was not nurtured,
Nor on the blood of Linus or of Cletus,
To be made use of to acquire gold,
And it was rather to win heavenly joy
That Sixtus, Pius, Calixtus, and Urban
Did shed their blood in agony and tears.
It was not our intention that one part
Of Christian folk at the right hand should sit
Of our successors and one part on the other,
Nor that the keys which were entrusted to me
Should be the emblem of the battle flag
Of those who did wage war on men baptized,
Nor that I should become the sign and symbol
Of false and sold-for-money privileges!"

Boniface may also have been the "*capo reo*" — guilty head — of *Purgatorio* VII; the "*puttana sciolta*" — bedraggled harlot — of *Purgatorio* XXXII; and the "*fuia*" — thieving whore — of *Purgatorio* XXXIII.

Nor at any time did the poet show any recognition of the fact that the pontiff had at least his own kind of stature. Only once — this will be told about later — did he show toward him even a glimmer of compassion. But — as will also be told about later — the author of the *Commedia* had his own special and personal reasons for this animosity. His strictures were not entirely unbiased.

« 9 »

Dante had political reasons too.

Boniface firmly believed — as we have seen — that he was *super reges et regna* (above all kings and kingdoms).

"We would dare to say," he declared arrogantly, "that if all the princes of the world were leagued against us, we would not hold them worth a straw."

In this he was supported by the worldly group of ambitious men who had gathered about him, chief among these being Cardinal Matteo d'Acquasparta, who as vicar-general of the Franciscan order was presumed to speak with authority.

"The pope," Matteo said, "is sovereign king of the temporal and the spiritual. He stands above all, no matter who they be, for he holds his place from God. Therefore he can move against anyone who opposes him as he could move against the infidel."

But it would hardly have been possible for him to be sovereign king — or more than a local lord — without intervening in the affairs of Dante's city. For not only was Florence in some ways the financial center of the world, whose bankers and banking operations he must control if he was to operate effectively as a pope who wished also to be an emperor; it also lay directly athwart the road that led to his designs in north Italy and specifically in Emilia and the Romagna.

Intervene, therefore, he did — very early in his pontificate, although at first very tentatively indeed. He did no more than thrust his finger into the water and after that withdraw it. He was, as the saying goes, merely "testing the temperature of the bath."

How he did should be set down.

It has already been noted that during the struggles which centered around the attempts to remove Giano della Bella from power a French knight, Jean de Chalon, had ridden into Florence with five hundred followers at the behest of the anti–della Bella faction. At least in theory Jean represented the empire, for he was related by blood to Rudolf of Hapsburg, and he had been appointed imperial vicar-general for Tuscany by the latter's somewhat hapless successor, Adolf of Nassau. Adolf gave Jean the specific mission of "taking up the reins of imperial power which no man" — remember what Dante said about Rudolf and about Albrecht — "had taken in his hands for more than fifty years."

But even as Jean's bridle jingled merrily to the tune of imperial benison — and in his purse clinked imperial pay — "he came also by the desire of the newly elected pope."

This matter Monsieur de Chalon had arranged himself. Without consulting either Adolf or Florence, he had jogged to Rome and there listened to Boniface expatiate upon the man who then ruled Florence.

"This Giano," cried the pontiff, "is a rock of scandal and a stirrer-up of discord. He is possessed by an evil spirit."

The pope continued that Giano had conjured up a whirlwind of confusion and seen to it that all concord had been destroyed.

"He has shattered the unity of the Florentines and subverted all their peace."

Then Boniface came to the point.

"Monsieur Jean, I would persuade you to ride straightway to Florence and there form an alliance with all the families and all the party chiefs who oppose this mountain of iniquity. In return I will recognize the imperial pretensions."

Jean listened.

"Your vicarate will have papal confirmation."

That was all he wanted.

"I will do the bidding of my holy father."

Then he left the papal chambers to ride north.

It may be asked why Boniface would have made such a commitment which it is clear he had no intention of carrying out, for the papacy was taking, not giving up. We cannot say certainly, but a possible explanation is offered by one of Florence's more distinguished historians.

"Pope Gaetani certainly could not have believed that these [imperial] attempts would succeed, and so he would have thought it useful and opportune to favor at least in appearance during the early days of his pontificate a direct attempt to restore peace in this region which had been turned upside down by strife. It could not but react favorably upon his authority and the designs which from the beginning he had upon Tuscany if a foreigner, who had with him all the power and prestige of the empire, ended by showing that he was unable to compose their [the Florentines] tangled-up affairs, and to cut the Gordian knot with his sword. Such an enterprise and its probable failure would make the pope an arbitrator and would increase his political power."

To put it more succinctly, if it was demonstrated beyond cavil by Jean de Chalon's lack of success, and Boniface expected this, that the emperor was impotent, it would become apparent that he, Pope Boniface, was the only person to whom the Florentines would turn.

Or, at any rate, those of the Florentines whose ambitions outweighed their fear of falling into the hands of a foreign master.

Thus, even in this relatively obscure and unimportant action, the tall pontiff was taking a long look toward the future. To him politics was a game of chess — *una partita di scacchi* — in which the rewards of a carefully thought out gambit did not come until several moves later.

« 10 »

His next move, however, dealt with the present only. It was concerned, too, with matters which pertained exclusively to Rome.

Before engaging in a career of expansion, it is well for a ruler with expansionist designs to make certain that he is secure at home, and in the case of Boniface this involved him in a no-quarters-given struggle with the second of the two great families that dominated the once-imperial city. The Orsini were on his side. That meant that the Colonna opposed him.

"The Colonna must then be disposed of!"

This he set out to do. Without delay he set into motion plans to fight the men of the column with every means at his disposal — with robbers and *banditti* who were glad thus to legitimize their plundering; with such regular soldiery as the age afforded; and also with treachery.

The latter, incidentally, involved another famous contemporary immortalized by Dante — the great soldier of fortune and "wise and skillful leader" (Villani) Guido da Montefeltro. Just as his son Buonconte da Montefeltro had been snatched from the talons of a demon by an angel because in his last moment he repented, so Guido, in another place described by Dante as *nobilissimo nostro Latino*, was snatched from St. Francis by a devil for his last-minute falling from grace.

Inferno XXVII (Guido is speaking):

> "I was first man of arms, then corded friar,
> Thinking thus girded I could make amends
> For all my sins, and this I would have done
> But for the high priest — and may ill beset him! —
> Who thrust me back into my earlier sin,
> But just as Constantine sent for Sylvester
> In Soracte to cure his leprosy,
> So this man sought me out as his physician
> To heal and weal him of his haughty fever.
> He asked my counsel, but I did not answer
> Because his words a drunkard's seemed to me.
> And then he asked again: 'Let thy heart not doubt.
> I will absolve thee. Then thou mayest teach me
> How to bring Palestrina to the ground.
> Heaven I can unlock and I can lock,

As well thou knowest, for I have two keys.
My predecessor did not hold them dear.'
Then did his weighty arguments convince me
That keeping silence were the worser part
And so I said: 'Father, because thou washest
Me from the sin which I must now fall into,
Know that great promises and small fulfillment
Will bring thee triumph in thine holy seat.'
When I had left this life, St. Francis came
For me, but then one of the black cherubim
Said to him: 'Take him not. Do not do me wrong.
He must come down amidst my wretched souls
Because he did give fraudulent advice.
Since then I have been always at his hair.
He who repents not cannot be absolved,
Nor do repentence and further scheming jibe.
That is a contradiction not allowed.'
O woeful me! Ah how I shook and shuddered
The while he seized me, saying: 'In good sooth,
Thou didst not know that I was a logician!'
And then to Minos bore me."

In an access of devotion — this is the story — Guido, now in his seventies, had taken the habit and vows of St. Francis; divorced his wife; given up his wealth; obtained remission of his sins; and was living in a convent in Ancona. He was summoned from his cell by the pope and promised plenary absolution for any vows he might break if he would show Boniface how to take the Colonna's mountain stronghold.

The old soldier pondered the impregnable walls and then told the pope to use deceit.

"Promise them pardon for their faults — and then when they have surrendered destroy them."

The war with the great Roman family began almost as soon as Boniface took office. The *Ottimo Commento* says that at that time "one of the pope's nephews made love to the wife of Sciarra Colonna," who not being a man to put up with a thing like this struck back. He and his kinsmen — including his wild young cousin Stefano, who in his eighties four decades later would conduct Petrarch through the Roman ruins and talk to him about the fallen grandeur of the city.

In this version, the Colonna struck first. Villani agrees. According to Villani, Stefano Colonna, noting that "the court of Alagna" — the papal court which now sat in Anagni — "moved beasts of burden laden with treasure across the country, held them up and took them and brought them to his own castles." It is said that in one convoy alone he found one million gold florins, to say nothing of other booty. Even for an age of notable brigandry (Ghin di Tacco, Rinier da Corneto, Rinier Pazzo), Stefano's — and Sciarra's — ruffians were accomplished highwaymen.

But it is more likely that hostilities had been carefully planned by the pope, and that at the most these were merely the overt acts which gave him an excuse for beginning them.

"Being greatly aggravated," writes Villani, "by the lords of the Colonna family, who, confident of their great strength, had opposed him in many matters, and even more aggrieved because Messer Jacopo and Messer Piero Colonna had sought to prevent his election, he thought of little else except how to bring them to nought."

Boniface waited for an opportune moment.

Then he took the kind of action which would hurt the Colonna most.

"In the year of our Lord 1297, and on the thirteenth day of May, he deprived the said Messer Jacopo and the said Messer Pietro of their cardinalates and of the many other benefits which they had received from the Church. He likewise deprived all those of the house of Colonna, whether cleric or lay, of every ecclesiastic and secular privilege, and he excommunicated them so they could never have another preferment. Then he had their palaces and houses in Rome destroyed."

In modern terminology, "he threw the book at them."

Obviously the Colonna reacted. But how?

Their first thought was to meet force with force, pouring their factionaries into the streets and defying Boniface in the very seat of his power.

But this, they found, could not be done. Boniface and his allies, the Orsini, were too strong.

Abjectly surrender?

This they would not.

March into the countryside and rally their dependents?

This they did.

They gathered together "a great following" — in Rome and from their feudal domains — and with it moved to Palestrina, to Nepi, and to their other strongholds in the Sabine and Tiburtine Hills.

There, looking down upon fields where grain ripened and the long-horned snow-white cattle browsed upon the Tiber valley's grass, they met excommunication with deposition.

They sent messages to anyone who would read them.

"The pope is not pope — he was unlawfully chosen. Celestine's abdication was extorted — it is not valid."

Then they called on the cardinals to convene a general council.

Boniface's answer was to declare a holy war.

Because of Colonna defiance and because of their attack on what he was pleased to call the Holy Church, "the pope gave indulgence from sin and from penalty to all those who took the cross against the Colonna," and, having assembled a potent force by these means, "he moved an army against the city of Nepi and he beseiged it so long that the city sur- rendered upon terms, but many people died there or fell ill because of the corruption of the air."

Florence took part in this crusade — or hired troops to do so for her.

"The commonwealth sent into the pope's service six hundred cross- bowmen and shield bearers," said Villani. "They had on their shoulders the device of a crusade and before them went the insignia of Florence."

The red lily beside the crimson cross, and this upon a bandit ex- pedition!

Why — for it seems incongruous?

Because Florence was Guelph, and the Guelphs traditionally — and almost always — supported the pope?

Possibly, but I think not.

Or because the divisions which I am sure Boniface foresaw — or else he would not have dipped, with Jean de Chalon, his finger into Florentine affairs — had already begun to fraction the supposedly monolithic Guelph party? And because one of these divisions — the one which embraced the city's hotheads and malcontents plus a certain number of bankers who would do business with (and lend money to) anyone who favored them against their competitors — knew that it could only attain control with outside assistance? And because its leaders wanted this outside assistance on their side?

This seems more likely.

When, therefore, Florentine troops were sent to help the pontiff crush his enemies, it was almost certainly done (whatever arguments may have noisily been put forth in many councils) at the instigation of the would- be obligarchs who were thus paying the first installment on an anticipated debt.

It was the *quid* they offered for an expected *quo*.

« *11* »

The *quo* was forthcoming in due time.

But not immediately. Not, indeed, until the division of the Guelph party had become formal and recognized. Not until the clash of person- alities, which perhaps even more than economics or class feeling was the cause of these divisions, had come to the surface. And even then it took the consequences of a city-shaking scandal to set the stage.

In 1296 (when Giano della Bella had come and gone); in 1297 (the year the Florentines helped Boniface raze Palestrina); and even in 1298, the city by the Arno remained relatively undisturbed, and the Florentines turned most of their attention to time-honored matters.

As they had been doing for at least two centuries, for example, they strengthened themselves in the neighboring *contrada*.

"In the said year [1296]" — this is Giovanni Villani — "the commonwealth and the people of Florence being in a very happy state and wishing to oppose the noble and the powerful of the countryside, and especially the Pazzi and the Ubaldini, who were Ghibellines, gave orders that there should be made two notable towns and castles on the upper Arno. One of these should be between Figline and Montevarchi, and this they called Castel San Giovanni. The other should be at the Arno crossing near the domain of the Ubaldini, and this they named Castelfranco. Also they freed the inhabitants of these towns and castles from all duties and taxes for ten years, wherefore many who had been faithful to the Pazzi and the Ubertini and the Ricasoli and two other counts changed their allegiance and came to dwell in these castles, for which reason in short time they increased and multiplied greatly and became good and large towns."

As they had been doing for even longer, they fought fires, built bridges, and made new roads.

The fires. In 1296, "on the twelfth day of September, a fire began in a house belonging to the Lamberti." This was in the San Prancrazio *sesto* (near and around the present-day Via Tornabuoni). It rapidly became a conflagration. "It burned the houses of the Pilli and the Pilati and the Minerbetti. It did very great damage."

The bridges. In 1297, and "in the month of May," there "was driven the first pile of the bridge at the castle of Altrafonte."

In January 1297, the Sei (Six) — special commissioners charged with road building — requested the priors and their council "that for the honor and beauty of the city and to enhance its business" they be empowered to construct a street running from the Orto San Michele (Orsanmichele) to the palace of the commonwealth and the people (Palazzo Vecchio). This is the present-day Via de' Calzaioli.

But even as the Florentines did this — and went on, too, with the construction of the Palazzo Vecchio, to which the road led, and of the Duomo, and of Santa Croce — and even as they watched with mixed emotions the successful marches and countermarches of Maghinardo da Susinana — Dante's "young lion of the white den" (*Inferno* XXVII), Villani's "great and skillful captain," who was sometimes Ghibelline and sometimes (because Florence had protected him when a young orphan) Guelph — they were engaged in other activities.

They were engaged in the doubling and redoubling of the florin, which was a major preoccupation of the dominant groups in the city. But not always, or often, by methods which were above reproach.

Graft and corruption, to put it plainly, were widely practiced and apparently by some of the most notable citizens and officials, as those — to use a phrase in vogue today — "who knew their way around" used every kind of illegal method to mulct their fellow Florentines and fatten at the public trough.

Dino Compagni tells a story which well illustrates this.

"To safeguard themselves" — and to protect their illicit gains — "the most wicked of the citizens managed to secure the appointment of a poor nobleman of Padua as *podestà.*"

His name was Messer Monfiorito, and they did this so as to have one "who would impose judgments like a tyrant and turn right into wrong and wrong into right as they wished him to.

"He understood their wishes and he carried them out. He acquitted and condemned without regard to law, and he became so presumptuous that he and his household openly sold justice and did not refuse any bribe that was offered to them, whether it was great or small.

"Soon he made himself the most hated man in the city" — for, after all, if you sell justice to one man, you deny it to others — "so that the citizens could endure it no longer, whereupon they seized him and two of his attendants and tortured them with the ropes.

"One of them, Piero Manzuolo, confessed."

Among other things, he confessed that "he had received" — and presumably with Messer Monfiorito's acquiescence and approval "a false disposition in favor of Messer Niccola Acciaiuoli" — a wealthy banker whose son or grandson would be unmercifully castigated by Boccaccio in one of his letters for not giving the storyteller patronage he counted on — "and that therefore he had not condemned him.

"A note was made of this.

"Messer Niccola heard of it. He hastened to his advocate, Messer Baldo d'Aguglione, who found means to gain access to the notary's records, and tore out the pages, and erased from them that part which went against Messer Niccola."

Dante alludes to this action in the *Commedia*. Describing in *Purgatorio* XII the steep stairs that lead from the first to the second ledge of purgatory, he compares them to another stairway, that in Florence which conducted worshipers to San Miniato. This is what he says:

As on the right hand, to ascend the mount
Where the church standeth above Rubaconte
Which lords it over the well-guided city,
The bold and steep escarpment which leads up
Is bitten into by the stairway which made
In those days when the records and staves were safe . . .

The word staves refers to another fraud which was perpetrated during the term of office of the same *podestà*.

"It was the custom in Florence," says the Anonymous Florentine, "to measure salt and other commodities in a measure which was made of staves of wood like a little keg, and at this time a member of the Chiaramontesi family was commissioner of salt." When the salt was given to Messer Chiaramontesi he received it in a full measure, but when he sold it to the people he took away one of the staves and thus made the measure smaller.

"And from this he made considerable profit!"

But the word records clearly refers to Acciaiuoli and to Baldo d'Aguglione.

In this case the guilty were punished.

"For when the notary began to fear that the records he had lent might have been tampered with, he discovered the erasure and accused the two men. Messer Niccola was seized and sentenced to pay three thousand *libbre*. Messer Baldo escaped, but was sentenced to pay two thousand *libbre* and placed under bounds for a year. Messer Monfiorito was put into prison. Many times did the Paduans send to demand him, but the Florentines refused to give him for love or favor. But afterwards he escaped, for the wife of one of the Arrigucci, whose husband was in the same prison, caused noiseless files and other tools to be made with which they cut open the bars and fled."

But this did not end Florence's difficulties when they did this, for one thing leads to another, and malfeasance in high places is like the legendary hydra. If one head is cut off another grows in its place unless you sear it with a red-hot cauter. Furthermore, corruption at the seat of power makes it necessary for you to seize the seat of power unless you are content to be unsuccessful. And there were plenty in Florence — both honest men and dishonest ones, and members of both factions — who would not accept this for their fate.

« *13* »

Our silk merchant tells this part of the story too.

"The city, governed with injustice, now fell into a new danger, because the citizens began to be divided through rivalry for office, one maligning the other.

"Now it happened that certain members of the Cerchi family, men of low rank but successful merchants and very rich ones, who dressed well and kept many servants and horses and put on a brave show, had bought the palace of the counts." The counts were the Counts Guidi and the palace was the ancient Ravignani dwelling from which Count Guido Bevisangue had married the good Gualdrada. It was close to the houses of the Pazzi and the Donati, who were of more ancient lineage but not so rich. "This greatly angered the Donati, who began to feel a great hatred toward them."

But the Cerchi had grievances too.

Messer Corso Donati — Il Barone and "a very ambitious knight" — had recently lost his wife and was now bethrothed to the daughter of Messer Accerito of Gaville. She was an heiress, and because they expected to share in the inheritance her kinsmen would not consent to the marriage.

"But the maiden's mother, seeing that Corso was a very handsome man, concluded the match without any regard to the wishes of the others."

In particular, without any regard to the Cerchi, who were among the offended kinsmen and who forthwith took legal steps to prevent Corso from getting any of the money and lands.

"However, he took her inheritance by force, from which arose much mischief and danger."

Mischief and danger which were almost immediately aggravated by an unfortunate incident.

Even as the lawyers argued, "certain young men of the Cerchi family were detained in the palace of the *podestà* on a matter of suretyship" — they were responsible for fines incurred by members of their family for an affray with the Pazzi and were held while arranging to pay them — "and while they were there a black pudding was set before them. Those who ate it had a dangerous sickness and some of them died, on which account there was a great stir in the city, for they were much beloved."

You can imagine that the Cerchi cried bloody murder.

They did more than this.

"Messer Corso was freely accused of the crime, but the charges were never investigated."

The reason given is that no proof could be obtained.

"Thereupon the rancor grew from day to day."

It was almost as it had been in the days of the tower societies.

Egged on by their elders, the brightly feathered fighting cocks of the Cerchi and the Donati factions began to move through the crooked streets in little groups. They were looking for trouble and they almost always found it.

"One day a number of citizens were assembled in the Piazza dei Frescobaldi for the funeral of a lady. It was the custom at such gatherings for ordinary citizens to be seated on rush mats and for the knights and the doctors to be seated on benches higher up. The Donati and the Cerchi were opposite each other, and one of them, either to straighten out his gown or for some other purpose, stood up."

It is not said whether he was of the Donati or of the Cerchi. It is not important.

"Those of the opposite faction rose and drew their swords. They feared some treachery. The first faction did likewise, and they came to blows."

Indeed, if it had not been for those present who belonged to neither faction there would have been bloodshed. These separated the brawlers and let the funeral proceed.

"Nevertheless, the strife could not be so far quelled that the crowd did not surge to the houses of the Cerchi, and from there they would have gone to attack the Donati."

But a cool head among the Cerchi would not allow it.

A more serious incident took place almost immediately.

"A young man of gentle birth, son of Messer Cavalcante Cavalcanti" — this, it need hardly be said, was Dante's first friend, the poet Guido Cavalcanti — "courteous and bold, but disdainful, solitary, and intent on study, was an enemy of Messer Corso Donati and had several times determined to attack him."

He had good reason for this.

"For Messer Corso feared him greatly because he knew him to be high-spirited, and once when Guido was on a pilgrimage to Santiago de Compostela he sought to have him murdered, but he did not succeed."

"Wherefore," continues Dino, "hearing of this on his return to Florence, Guido stirred up many young men against Corso and they promised to help him."

Then one day as Guido was riding with some of them, and had a javelin in his hand, he encountered Corso and, believing that his little band would follow him, he spurred his horse against Il Barone. As he galloped past him, he hurled his missile. It whistled viciously but missed the mark.

Then he saw that he was alone. His young followers — they were mostly Cerchi — kept at a safe distance.

Corso's followers — among them were Corso's son Simone and "a strong and bold young man, Cecchino de' Bardi" — were less cautious.

"They pursued Guido, but, not overtaking him, they hurled stones at him, and some were thrown at him from windows. One of them hit him in the hand.

"For this reason hatred began to increase, and Messer Corso began to slander Messer Viero. 'Has the ass of the Porta brayed today?' he cried. Guido also he called Cavicchia."

Cavicchia means peg. A square peg in a round hole, perhaps.

Corso also hired one Scampolino, a professional jester, to move from house to house inventing stories about the Cerchi and their allies.

Cavalcanti was an especial target.

"This moon gazer," it was said of him, "is such a large fool that one day when he was playing chess a boy crept up behind him and nailed his cloak to the bench on which he sat. When the game was ended, there he was! He had to send for shears to cut himself free!"

Scampolino was also paid — and well — to move here and there (a jester was always welcome) and pick up any disparaging remark that a Cerchi could be alleged to have made against anyone in Florence. These he was to repeat and exaggerate. The purpose was to build up a reservoir of Cerchi enemies by poisoning men's minds.

The Cerchi answered by turning to politics — ineptly, as we will see later, but full of hope.

The Guelph party, they felt, was for the moment at least controlled by their adversaries, and so they withdrew from its meetings.

"And they began" — instead — "to make advances to the *popolani*" — here very clearly the richer self-made merchant-burghers — "and to the city government. Since they were men of good and genial dispositions who had learned to be very obliging so that they could obtain what they wanted, they were soon on excellent terms with them. They were also on good terms with the magistrates."

But many other citizens were drawn to them too.

The Ghibellines, for example.

"The Ghibellines loved the Cerchi because they had never been wronged by them."

The smaller traders and the smaller merchants "because the conspiracy against Giano della Bella had much displeased them" and they incorrectly believed that the Cerchi had not taken part in it.

Even such self-seeking "persons of importance" as Lapo Salterelli and Donato Ristori, whose only concern was to feather their own nests.

Thus the Cerchi from a family became a faction, and when they became a faction the Donati had to do the same. The Guelphs, in other words, became divided, as a single party always will when it has no outside rival. It was no longer Guelph against Ghibelline, but Cerchieschi against Donateschi. But shortly, as temporary rivalry became permanent division, these family names were abandoned. The Cerchieschi became the Whites, or Bianchi. The Donateschi became the Blacks, or Neri.

These faction names are important to remember, for very soon virtually every Florentine was aligned with one or the other. Dante was no exception. He was a White.

« *13* »

While all this was going on in the city by the Arno, Pope Boniface, the man who would shortly take advantage of it, sat like a spider in his web — sometimes in the Lateran Palace in Rome, but more often in the palace of the Gaetani in Anagni whence his race had sprung.

He had much to think about there. The Colonna had been crushed (although not so thoroughly as to prevent them from later helping to mount and carry out a terrible revenge), and that in a war in which the pontiff had not merely been the commanding general but had endured the hardships of a common soldier. Upon one occasion, for example, his fighting men had outmarched their pack trains and there were no tents with tasseled or silken coverlets. The papal officers grumbled. But not the pope. He simply wrapped his mantle around himself and stretched out upon the bare ground.

France sent her most important officers to treat with him. She sent *her* officers to the pope, not he his officers and legates to France.

Albrecht of Austria had already yielded some of his powers in north Italy to him. He would yield more later. And as we have seen his man, Jean de Chalon, had become the pope's man.

Even England, though obdurate and unbending, was concerned about him.

He could call himself a new Innocent II or a new Gregory — Gregory I or Gregory VII, either one.

As he looked down on the road which led (as all roads are said to do) to Rome, and also past the destroyed strongholds of his enemies, he had every right to be proud and satisfied. He had every right to be content.

He was not, however, and almost as if he were an Alexander looking for new worlds to conquer, his mind went back to Tuscany.

Was not Tuscany a stumbling block in his pursuit of temporal *dominium?*

Did not this important province still elude him?

And what was Tuscany but Florence?

Was not this, then, the time to deal with Florence?

He asked himself this question. And answered it. It was, in his opinion.

That is, if he could find a pretext or an occasion. For then even as now the aggressor had to find high-minded excuses to sugarcoat his command to "stand and deliver."

Even in those days, brigand tactics of simply seizing and making off with were not for heads of state.

The Cerchieschi — the Whites — soon gave him one.

As they made friends, they made enemies.

This was understandable. It was understandable that these men with bloated moneybags should be looked down on — and also envied — by those who had tried to fill their own and had failed to do so. Who were they anyway? "They have come in a short time to great estate and, having reached it, they are not only luxurious and offensive but uncultured and ungracious." It was understandable that the men of older families — and their wives —should turn up their noses at these men of broad girth and coarse red faces who, the former said, still had hands callused from the plow and stank of the barnyard and the stable. It was understandable that the sweaty populace, the artisans and mechanics and the men of even humbler calling, looking for amusement, could be persuaded to hurl offal or even cobblestones at these not so long ago plebians with their now haughty airs.

What is less understandable is why the Cerchi, who are said to have been shrewd — and indeed must have been — should have responded so ineptly. Why they should have taken steps which made them feared as well as hated.

Instead of trying to placate — and win over — some of those who obstructed them, they turned to Florence's most inveterate enemies.

When the Donateschi launched their barrage of slander and vituperation — Corso's jibes about the ass of the Porta, Scampolino's libels and buffoonery — "the Cerchi kept silent, but used their friendship with the Aretines and Pisans as a threat."

The Aretines whom — with Corso as a leader and with Dante in the cavalry — they had defeated at Campaldino!

Their ancient enemies, the men of Pisa!

And the Ghibellines too!

They hinted to the Ghibellines that they might restore their rights and property.

This gave the Donateschi — the Blacks — the opening they needed.

"Your city is being betrayed. The Cerchi have made a league with the Ghibellines of Tuscany."

They saw to it that these words were circulated on every bench, in every booth, at every street corner.

They saw to it too that the tidings went to Rome.

The lord of Malefami — this is another name for Corso Donati, and it is spelled so variously that one cannot be sure whether it means the lord of Does-Ill-to-Me or the lord of Ill Repute — knew well that his ambitions needed an ally.

His and the Blacks' ambitions.

He turned to his friends, the Spini, who were also Blacks.

"The Spini," says Dino Compagni, "were in the pope's service as bankers, and their agent in Rome was Simone Gherardi, a man very experienced in doing their business. With him was the son of a silversmith, a Florentine named Nero Cambi. He was an astute man of subtle wit, but wicked and disagreeable."

Under orders from Florence, Gherardi and Cambi sought an audience with the pope.

"Vieri and his Whites are plotting with whoever would gainsay you. For their own purposes, they will restore imperialist rule and remove Tuscany from your control and influence."

And to support their position they repeated every tale, true or untrue, that was being told in Florence.

Boniface was impressed.

"Send for this Messer Uliviero," he commanded.

Uliviero was Vieri de' Cerchi.

But to Oliver he did not plan to offer an olive branch.

In obedience to the pope's wishes, the head of the Cerchi family — and of the Florentine Whites — rode dutifully south.

But not submissively. He was not that kind of man.

The pope confronted him.

"I command you to make peace with Corso and with the Donati. I direct you to end your quarrels with him. To me you can refer your differences."

"I am at war with no one," said the banker. "Therefore I can make peace with no one."

This is how Cardinal Rossi described Boniface:

"It is impossible to argue with the man. If you do, you are but sharpening a sword against yourself."

Vieri did argue. We have just heard him. And so doing he sharpened a sword both against himself and against his followers.

Should he have done so?

Of him Villani said that in some matters he was wise but in this matter he was "obstinate and capricious."

He could, Villani seems to think, have promised and done nothing.

Instead stubbornly he repeated his answer. Then he returned to Florence.

"Wherefore the pope was moved to anger against both him and his party."

It was an indignation which would have almost cataclysmic effects.

« *14* »

It was an indignation, too, which led to almost immediate action.

An excuse for this was not hard to find.

"It came to pass," wrote Villani, "that a little while after that" — after Vieri had ridden obstinately north — "that certain men of both the one faction and the other were riding, as was their habit, through the city. They were armed and on their guard. And with the party of the young Cerchi were Baldinaccio degli Adimari and Baschiera della Tosa and Naldo degli Gherardini, and Giovanni Giacotti Malispini with more than thirty mounted followers, and with the young Donati were certain of the Pazzi and the Spini as well as others of their company. Now on the evening of the first of May (the *calendimaggio*, that time of festivity and also hot blood) in the year 1300, while they were watching a dance of young ladies on the Piazza San Trinità, one party began to jibe at the other and to jostle each other with their horses. This led to great conflict and confusion in which many were wounded, and as luck would have it Ricoverino, son of Messer Ricovero de' Cerchi, had his nose cut off."

Dino Compagni adds only a few details, but they are significant.

He too stressed the youth of the troublemakers.

"Since this is the more easily deceived than old age, the Devil, that multiplier of evil, began his work with a company of young men who were working together."

But he makes it plain that they were young men of the Donati faction.

"One evening on the first of May as they were at supper together" — probably, like Milton's sons of Eli, "flushed with insolence and wine" — "they reached such a pitch of arrogance that they determined to attack the company of the Cerchi and to use their weapons and their hands."

They knew where to find them.

"On that evening which is the birthday of spring, the women are much given to holding frequent balls in their neighborhood."

And the young men to watching them.

The young men of the Donati faction then, with malice aforethought, rode to the piazza where the young men of the Cerchi faction were looking on as a group of young ladies danced in stately fashion to the sound of lute and dulcimer — and possibly, even, to a *ballata* composed by Dante.

There they deliberately launched an unprovoked armed attack upon their adversaries. It was not a question of steed crowding against steed and tempers rising.

Then, having seriously wounded Ricovero, they panicked. Fearing, and probably expecting, retaliation from the now aroused Cerchi, they fled into the nearby palace-fortress of the Spini family, one of whose members, Piero Spini, is said to have struck the disfiguring blow.

The next morning their emissaries were galloping south. They crossed the Milvian Bridge and came to the Lateran. There Simone Gherardi and Nero Cambi led them into the papal presence, where, on bended knee, they implored his assistance.

"The Whites will now control the city. The Whites are your enemy."

It was all Boniface needed.

At his side, among his many advisers, stood Matteo d'Acquasparta, cardinal of Porto and vicar-general of the Franciscan order.

Boniface turned to him.

"I designate you to be papal legate and pacificator in Lombardy and Tuscany and other parts of Italy."

He called on a secretary to prepare the necessary documents.

"But I intend you to go to Florence."

Go Cardinal Matteo did. On muleback and with a goodly staff of lawyers, notaries, and secretaries, whose baggage and documents made up a sizable pack train. Along the Via Cassia. Past the almost circular Lago di Bracciano. Through Sutri, Viterbo, Bolsena, and Acquapendente. Under Radicofani (where Ghino di Tacco held forth but obviously did not dare attack so important a mission), standing dramatically three thousand feet above sea level. Through Siena. Past Staggia, Musciatto Franzesi's handsome castle, from which one day an attack, and not by Whites, would be staged against Pope Boniface. Finally, into Florence by its Porta Romana.

His instructions were to appear neutral but to favor the Blacks.

"But he accomplished nothing, for he did not receive from the opposing parties the authority he desired."

He did not receive it from the Blacks because the Donati faction did not wish reform but rule and hence did not like the uncertainties implied by his suggestion that all "those of one faction or the other which were worthy to be priors, their names were to be put into a bag together in each of the *sesti*, and would be drawn thence every two months as chance would have it."

Nor were the Cerchieschi more compliant.

"They of the White party which were at the head of the government through fear of losing their power and of being deceived by the pope and by his legate took the worser counsel."

Why should they share what they already had?

They too "would not yield obedience."

"For the which thing," concluded Villani, "the said legate was offended and returned to court" — to the papal court at Rome — "and left the city of Florence excommunicate and under interdict."

As other legates and even popes (Gregory X, for example) had done before him, Cardinal Matteo gathered his robes about him and, after shaking Florentine dust from his feet, decreed that no church bells should be rung, Masses celebrated, marriages performed, or dead buried in consecrated ground until the cross-grained citizens (both friend and foe) had decided to comply with the wishes of their spiritual — and, as it seemed to Boniface, temporal — sovereign.

Nor, when shortly afterwards Cardinal Matteo returned to Florence — actually this was a little later than the time limits of this chapter but it should be told here for continuity — were the citizens any more amenable.

"His aim was now apparent to all," wrote Dino Compagni. "The peace he sought was to humble the party of the Cerchi and exalt that of the Donati."

In other words, all pretenses were laid aside and he moved openly toward his goal.

"This caused very great displeasure, and accordingly" — when, after a day of unproductive negotiations, the cardinal was ensconced in the episcopal palace — "a man of little sense pushed his way near to it, and with his crossbow shot a bolt at one of the windows."

It stuck in the wooden window frame and hung there quivering.

The cardinal was greatly shaken.

Under the armed guard of his following, "he departed thence in fear and took refuge in the house of Messer Tommaso" — Messer Tommaso de' Mozzi — "across the Arno. Wherefore the priors, in order to atone for the affront put upon him, presented him with two thousand new florins. I myself" — Dino, that is — "brought them to him in a silver cup. 'My lord,' I said, 'do not disdain them because they are so few. It is not possible to give more without the sanction of the councils.' He answered that they were pleasing to him, and he looked at them long. But he did not take them."

Because he had already been bought and paid for by the Blacks?

Or because he knew that Boniface had already determined to declare war on the Whites and Matteo did not want to embarrass his probable ruthlessness with a peace offering counted out to him in advance?

Any answer would be a guess.

« *15* »

It is more than unfortunate — but less than surprising, since, as the reader must know by now, the life of Dante must be put together from a fragment of evidence here and another fragment there — that we know little or nothing about the poet and his activities at the time when the above events took place. For it was then that the battle lines were being formed in the contest which would lead to the second of his three great crises — the first was occasioned by the death of Beatrice — and it would be enlightening to know what part, if any, he played in happenings which would so vitally affect him.

But for reasons which elude us, there is a lacuna in the documented record. In particular, the small yellowing notebooks which contain the minutes of the various council meetings held at the time have disappeared, and we have, in part because of this, written testimony of only a single political activity of "that noble man Dantes de Allegheriis" between June 5, 1296, and June 15, 1300. That was his so-called "embassy" to the little neighboring town and republic of San Gimignano and — if one historian can be believed — to the even smaller towns and republics of Poggibonsi, Colle, and Volterra, which took place on May 7 of the latter year.

Here is the official account:

"The general council of the commune and people of San Gimignano, having been convened and assembled, as is the custom, by the sound of bells and by the voice of the crier, and at the order of the noble and powerful knight Messer Mino de' Tolomei of Siena, *podestà* of the said commune, and with Messer Egidio dei Celli of Narni, judge of appeals and syndic of the said commune present, willing, and consenting, the following was propounded and requested:

"That since, by the noble Dante Alighieri, ambassador of the commune of Florence, it had been said and repeated that there is to be convened a parliament and deliberation in a determined place and in the accustomed manner of all the communes of the Tuscan League for the appointment of a new captain, we should accede to this. It was fitting that the syndics and ambassadors of the various communes should convene at the time and for this purpose."

Following this, Messer Primeriano, judge — *Dominus Primerianus iudex* — who was one of the councillors, got up onto his feet and mounted the rostrum. He addressed his fellow citizens.

"Saying that he spoke for the commonwealth of San Gimignano as well as for himself, he said" — among other things — "that the expense of such an embassy would be too great for so small a place. To be sure he did urge that, as long as the commonwealth was on friendly terms with Florence, ambassadors be named and sent to whatever place at whatever time was agreed upon. But he did not wish them to be given unlimited powers. Indeed they should be specifically instructed not to sign any agreement or agreements unless it was agreed in same that no taxes or other charges should be laid upon San Gimignano.

"He was cheered, and his proposal was voted on.

"Into the red jar which held the ayes, seventy-three balls were put, and three balls into the yellow jar for the nays."

It was a scene not hard to visualize, especially since the building and the council chamber can still be visited. San Gimignano, standing on a hill overlooking white roads and dusty olive trees, is not more than twenty-five miles southwest of Florence, and within its walls rise even today fifteen of the seventy-two unadorned brown towers which graced it during the last year of the thirteenth century. One of these — it is more than one hundred sixty feet high — soars airily from the Palazzo del Popolo, a handsome building with arched windows and with Guelph machicolations on its battlements. It is built around a small courtyard, in which, as always in Tuscany in spring and summer, midnight-black shadows contrast with dazzling sunlight. In it — on the second story — is a somber chamber finished in darkish wood which not long ago I found in pacing it off to be about sixty-six feet long by thirty feet wide.

In this chamber, facing the first citizens of Florence's little but important neighborhood, stood Florence's foremost poet, now a civil servant and negotiator. He was neither young nor old — or, perhaps better, he was both. In a few weeks he would be thirty-five years old. *Nel mezzo del cammin di nostra vita.* That was his description of his age. He was intense and not yet disillusioned. His face was serious but not yet creased. And he was a good speaker.

He said and he repeated.

Slowly and carefully, making certain that these men, who must have had the suspicions that small-town men always have of the big city, knew that they needed Florence even though they might fear her, and that Florence needed San Gimignano just as much.

But did he make his point? Was his mission a successful one?

Robert Davidsöhn says no.

"Notwithstanding his eloquence, Dante did not succeed in overcoming the hesitations of the Sangimignanese, who, only two months after he had urged them to renew their adherence to the league, voted to defer action until a representative of Boniface had personally communicated to them the express wishes of the pope."

Zingarelli, however, thinks otherwise.

"The measure laid before the council conformed to Dante's wishes, and when a secret vote was taken only three opposed it."

I stand with Zingarelli. His judgment comports better with the half-a-loaf-is-better-than-no-bread cautious negotiating characteristics of the White leaders who asked Dante to see what he could do.

It is also supported by an almost immediately subsequent happening.

The mission to San Gimignano took place on May 7, 1300, and on June 15, or not quite six weeks later, the Florentine guildsmen honored Dante with the highest office at their disposal.

But let Leonardo Bruni tell us about it.

"Dante, then, having taken a wife and living after the ordinances of the state a decent and studious life, was much employed in the commonwealth, and finally when he had reached the due age he was made one of the priors, not by lot as is the present use but by election as was the custom in those times."

In other words, by the free choice of his fellow citizens.

It was an honor not often attained by one who had gained his fame through poetry and philosophy, and it showed that his political abilities were esteemed by his fellow citizens.

But if an honor, it also led to almost incredible disaster.

"This priorate was in 1300" — from June 15 to August 15, 1300 — "and from it sprang the adverse fortunes of his life."

In a lost letter, Dante is reported to have said the same, only more bitterly.

"All my woes," he wrote, "had their cause and origin in my ill-omened election to the priorate — of which priorate, though I was not worthy of it by prudence, yet by good faith and age I was."

On this Robert Davidsöhn comments with acerbity:

"Politics are for cold and lucid minds and not for the dreaming spirit of poets."

But it was not as simple as that.

It was not Dante's "dreaming spirit" — if it was so dreaming — that got him into political trouble. It was rather that "trying to unite the divided body of the republic" and bringing to bear on this "all his genius, his art, and his learning," he found himself, like all men in the middle, taking blows from both sides.

Then he chose sides — but chose the wrong one. He chose it because, in the city which Ciacco has already so accurately described, it seemed to him the more reasonable one, the more honorable one, the more just one.

But it was not the more practical one — perhaps because it was (within limits, however) reasonable, honorable, and just. And so it lost. And when it lost Dante lost with it. And thus was at the mercy (at least his fortunes were, if not his body) of men who had none of these qualities. Of unscrupulous men. Of vindictive men. Of men who would never forgive an enemy — particularly an enemy whose eloquence and whose reputation made him — in their opinion — very dangerous.

XII

The Lance of Judas

T HE first link in the chain of events which would lead to this consummation so devoutly not to be wished was forged very soon indeed. For, as is so often the case in matters political, the difficulties which
brought Dante and his colleagues such grief were inherited from an
earlier regime. The last link was hammered into shape two years later,
when, for the first time since Carlo Nasuto — Charles of the Big Nose —
a foreign prince intervened successfully in Italy.

"*Fils de roi,*" said his countrymen of this Charles of Valois, who now
tried to follow in his great-uncle's footsteps, *frère de roi, oncle de trois
rois, père de roi, et jamais roi.*"

This referred to his successive, but not successful, attempts to become
king of Aragon, king of Sicily, emperor of Constantinople, and Roman
emperor, which — since he was frequently crowned but never won a
realm — led him to be known both as the Chapel King and Charles
Lackland.

Dante described him less ironically and more bitterly. In *Purgatorio*
XX, the poet tells of his encounter with Hugh Capet, legendary founder
of the then-reigning French line. To him Hugh descants upon "the force
and fraud and rapine" of "the Louises and Philips" who had sprung from
him. Then he says about the latest one:

> That day I see, nor is it long from now,
> Which doth another Charles lead forth from France
> To make him and his people better known.
> Unarmed he comes, or only with the lance
> With which did Judas joust, and this he couches

> In such wise that the paunch of Florence he bursts.
> Thereby not land he gains, but sin and shame,
> And these on him will weigh the heavier
> Because so light accounts he his offense.

Not everybody agreed with this, of course.

More than one admirer, while conceding that Charles — whose descendants, incidentally, were to reign in France until 1589 — "was greatly inferior to his brother [Philip the Fair] in intelligence," nevertheless noted that he "resembled him in physical appearance" and in many other ways. Like his brother he was "tall and handsome with gleaming golden hair and penetrating blue eyes," and, if his gifts for acting decisively and hence ruling effectively were less than outstanding, he was an enlightened patron of the arts to whom we owe both the church of St. Ouen at Rouen with its incredible rose window and the circulation of Marco Polo's *Il Milione*. More important to the age, he was a fine horseman and a dedicated devotee of St. Hubert, patron saint of hunters.

But to Dante and to the Florentine merchants for whom, oddly enough, Dante spoke — at any rate, to Dante and to those of the Florentine merchants who were patiently constructing a state which, if not democratic in our sense of the word, at least tried to govern in the interests of those who produced — he was neither a golden prince, nor a plumed knight-errant, nor a gallant huntsman. He was rather "an ostentatious and needy adventurer" who was far less a *"chevalier sans peur et sans reproche"* than he was a gold-hungry mercenary who was prepared to sell their city, or any other city, to Pope Boniface, or any other bidder, for something considerably more than thirty pieces of silver. And who did exactly that — who sold Florence and pocketed the change.

This sale, it need hardly be pointed out, shook the city to its very foundations.

But its effects upon Dante would be even more devastating.

If only for this last reason, we must find out how it came about.

« 2 »

After the unusually severe winter which has already been noted, there was, in 1300, a more than ordinarily glorious spring. Sapia's blackbird could warble its optimism without fear of offending God. The swallow, whose "lay" when heard at dawn seemed so sad to Dante, could sing again, as could Dante's beloved skylark and as in dark ilex groves could the husky-throated nightingale. For some months now (*Paradiso* XXI), "by natural instinct," on many a castellated tower "the rooks together at the break of day" had shuffled about "to warm their frigid feathers." They did not need to do this any longer. Even at sunrise it was mild and balmy. The cranes, returning from the "sands" (*Purgatorio* XXVI) of Egypt, "made in the air a long line of themselves" as they flew toward the Rhiphaean Mountains (the Carpathians?) or the marshes at the mouth of the Po, the Magra, the Arno, and the Tiber. The long-legged storks were on the rooftops again, the male bird ready to do his grotesque courtship dance. Soon stork fledglings would (*Purgatorio* XXV) "lift up their wings in their desire to fly, then fear to venture forth from the nest and let them fall again."

The eye was gladdened too. The almond tree was in blossom, making many a cypress-guarded hillside a white incandescence. So were the pear tree later to become famous in a Boccaccio story, the peach tree, and the cherry tree. The leaves of the olive tree were a forever-shifting shimmer of silver.

Nor did the snow fall any more. Its delicate flakes, the drifts into which it was blown, and its later melting seem to have fascinated Dante, possibly because he lived in a place where you often saw it on the surrounding mountaintops but infrequently in the streets.

Purgatorio XXX:

> Even as the snow amid the living beams
> Upon Italia's rooftree freezes hard,
> Blown as it is and packed by Slavonian winds,
> Then turns to slush and damply drips away
> When comes a breeze from unshadowed side,
> So that it seems like fire melting a candle.

In short, it was a *dolce stagione* that filled men's hearts with canticles.

(It was also "a sweet season" which was of paramount importance to Dante, and that not merely for political reasons. It was on the Good Friday, Holy Saturday, and Easter Sunday — April 7, 8, and 9 — of that same year, 1300, that Dante supposedly made his poem's pilgrimage, and one is certain that Isodoro del Lungo is not the only person who wondered where the poet actually was during the three days of his imaginary damnation, redemption, and salvation. Was he at Rome to take part in the Jubilee? For it is almost incontrovertible that he did go to Rome during the Jubilee year, and if so he must have gone either just before or just after his mission to San Gimignano. But this is something nobody is ever likely to be able to say.)

But if hearts of some were high as they looked up toward a sky puffed with springtime white clouds, there were others whose thoughts were as deeply disturbed and turbulent as ever.

In particular, the tall pontiff who moved backward and forward between the Lateran and his little city in the hills was frustrated and angry because he was still not able to persuade the Florentines to submit unreservedly to his will.

Indeed, they had not merely not been persuaded, but three times, as we have seen, they had rebuked him emphatically. Vieri de' Cerchi — rebuke number one — had kept his head high even when in the actual terrifying papal presence. Cardinal Matteo d'Acquasparta — rebuke number two — had returned to Rome empty-handed after a futile mission. Dante — rebuke number three — had been defiantly sent to San Gimignano — and to Colle and to Volterra — on a mission which had for its ostensible purpose nothing more than reorganizing and strengthening the Guelph (and, therefore, theoretically pro-pope) Tuscan League, but actually aimed at making certain that this league remained subservient to the Florentine power structure — the anti-pope Florentine power structure — a mission not entirely without success.

And now for some time — at least since late December or the middle of February — Boniface had been hearing even more alarming tidings. The Cerchieschi not only held power, but intended to keep it. And by whatever means were necessary.

Including bribery, overt or covert.

Including open threats and subtle intimidations.

But also including promises and blandishments, which perhaps were the most corrupt of all.

Robert Davidsöhn gives us the necessary background, and also justifies the actions taken. He says that "if it had not been for such illegal doings, the Cerchi could not have succeeded in holding power nor Florence in maintaining its independence in the face of Gaetani greed and the insolence of the Guelph magnates" — i.e., the Blacks.

"The Ordinances of Justice," he continues, "established that just before they left office, the old priors, together with the *capitudini* of the guilds, and, if it pleased them to call these in, certain of the councilmen, acting as a committee, first debated the method of choosing the members of the new priorate, and then proceeded to name them."

In other words, the old priorate — with such assistance as it might wish to invoke — chose the new priors.

But how could you make sure they chose the right ones?

It was easy if you were willing to be practical.

The old priors, the *capitudini*, and every other citizen taking part in this function, once they had discharged their duty, stepped back immediately into the business life of the community, where each one needed the goodwill and often the financial support of those whose goodwill counted.

The goodwill, at this present point of Florentine history, of the White bankers.

The White bankers — the Cerchieschi — made it plain bluntly or deviously that the one way to obtain this goodwill was to show that you thought right by voting right.

If you did not, your bank or your *bottega* or the place where you practiced law was far less frequented by customers or clients, if indeed you had any at all; and when you needed a loan because the argosy that carried your fortunes abroad had foundered, or a wool shipment had not come in from Algarve or England, you would find that the money you had hoped to borrow had already put out elsewhere, or that you could not produce acceptable security.

But if you did vote right, your affairs prospered. For services rendered, you got tangible benefits. Benefits paid in gold florins or in credit for the same. Large benefits, if need be, and if your vote was critical. And not necessarily under the table.

That was the system and the Cerchieschi used it.

Among the six priors who would step down from office on February 15, 1300, were at least three — Donato di Alberto Ristori, Lapo Ammanati de' Minutoli, and Lapo Biondo di Benci — who had a public record of hostility to the Blacks and friendliness to the Whites. Their votes could be counted on. But these were only half of the priorate itself, and very clearly a minority in the larger group which must make the actual decision. A majority must be secured.

Donato's brother, Corso di Alberto Ristori, and Inamo di Lapo Ruffoli, himself a candidate for prior, were enlisted to secure it.

The details of their operations are not known, but clearly they moved backward and forward between the Porta San Piero — headquarters of the Cerchi and those allied to the Cerchi — and those members of the group which did the choosing who were uncommitted.

This was given to certain of them in *cotanti* (in other words, in hard and gleaming cash). *That* was promised or pledged to others. In some cases there were merely hints of future benefits.

But the efforts were successful, and not merely was a priorate which would suit the leaders of the White party elected, but a foundation was laid for securing future similarly suitable priorates.

« *3* »

Not, however, without a Black outcry.

Although, if you can believe Davidsöhn and ordinary common sense, there had been corruption in the naming of priors as long as there had been priors, this time either the action was unusually flagrant or its opponents were unusually vociferous.

"Fraud!" they shouted to the rooftops. "Fraud! Swindle! Dishonest and illegal procedure!"

"Fraud!" the pope echoed. "These cheating merchants!"

For word had been brought to him of the Florentine elections, and he had correctly and angrily evaluated their significance.

If undealt with, it would be a body blow to his pretentions.

But it would not be undealt with, for quickly collecting himself he plotted his own counterattack.

"Let them play their own games," he said. "Their own games with their friends, the *Ghibellines*."

He chose this word carefully, knowing it would antagonize many in Florence.

"I can play my own games. And will. And have to."

For if the Cerchieschi — if the Whites — struggled for survival, he struggled for survival too — survival of his ambitions.

Then he began to play them.

Through Florence spread the story — Boniface arranged to have it spread — that he had written letters — no such letters were ever seen, however — in which he openly expressed his intention of taking away the city's liberties. Or, if he had not written letters, he had said this to the French and German ambassadors as they stood by his bedside in a private audience.

Then suddenly the exact opposite. This time there really were letters. Two of them. Each to a high official who enjoyed papal favor. In both, the pope stated categorically that the rumors circulated about him were false. Far from taking Florence's freedom from her, he wished to give the city greater freedom than ever.

What did this mean? Change of plans? Or an attempt to keep the Whites confused?

The Whites — the Florentine Whites — were themselves in doubt, nor did they deem it prudent to debate the matter in full council. Too many were entitled to attend, and some of them would later talk.

What should be done then?

Only one thing seemed sensible and likely to produce results. Go to the fountainhead of information — go to Pope Boniface himself — and try to find out.

Sometime during the month of March — the exact date is not given or known —six of the most distinguished knights of the city rode toward the Tiber. With them went Lapo Salterelli, added to the party because legal talent was felt to be needed, but in the upshot the mission's most important member. They were members of a formal embassy to the pontiff, and they had been commissioned as such by the priors in a secret meeting. Their official instructions have not been preserved but it is not hard to guess what they were.

Present yourselves to His Holiness, and assure him as eloquently as possible of the firm and unshakable friendship of Guelph Florence. Ask him to give equally firm assurances that he is friendly to Florence too.

But they had secret instructions — these do survive — which were far more important. Or rather certain of the ambassadors had secret instructions, for even here all were not equally trusted by the signory. Get to the heart of the matter. Study and diagnose the state of Roman intrigue. Find out who wants Boniface to seize Tuscany and who wants to leave us free to go our own way. Weigh these men — weigh and evaluate both our friends and our enemies. Try to discover whom Boniface is most likely to listen to. Try to discover what in the end he is likely to do.

« 4 »

In this, they were eminently successful. Boniface, astute as he was, allowed himself to be convinced of White goodwill, and by way of showing how such goodwill would be rewarded, on March 29 he summoned into his presence one of the knight ambassadors, Guelfo de' Cavalcanti, and announced that he had conferred upon his nephew, Tegghiaio di Conte Cavalcanti, an important ecclesiastical benefice.

"We do this by reason of our love for your uncle, Guelfo de' Cavalcanti," read the conferring document.

Nepotism, he appeared to be saying, can work for you as well as against you, for on three counts Tegghiaio was ineligible for the preferment he had received. He was under the prescribed age. He had not taken clerical orders. Only a month earlier his betrothal had been announced.

But if Boniface for the moment overflowed — or appeared to overflow — with affability and warm feelings, not everybody at Rome or at Anagni shared this mood. As Guelfo's nephew basked in papal benefactions, Lapo and the others with him continued their exploring here and there and came up with the fact that there was in the papal court a compact but important group which schemed covertly, when it did not scheme openly, against the best interests of White Florence and White Tuscany.

Prominent among its members were certain of the Colonna family to whom gold — and the desire to be on the winning side — was thicker than blood, and who had sided with Boniface against their less pliable uncles and cousins. Prominent was Jacopo Gaetani, a banker in Pisa and a castellan in Umbria. Jacopo was a distant relative of the pope, but he claimed to be his nephew. Prominent were Francesco da Montenero, at this time a papal chamberlain but later to be provost of Santa Reparata;

the archpriest Antonio degli Orsi, one day to be named bishop of Florence; and Andrea del Cione, who in due course would be made archdeacon of Limoges in faraway Flanders.

Prominent also were Nero Cambi, once prior and now a Spini agent; Simone Gherardi, also a Spini employee; Arnolfo, or Noffo, Quintavalli, who had been a merchant in Genoa but who had returned to Florence to enter Guelph politics; and the lawyer (and notary) Ser Cambio da Sesto.

These names Lapo and his colleagues carefully noted. They noted also that they — and particularly the last four — not merely were close to Boniface but also "enjoyed the confidence of the Guelph magnates." The Guelph magnates of the Black faction, that is. Those Guelph magnates "who would willingly sacrifice the liberties of Florence" if in so doing they would advance their own fortunes.

They noted them, and determined on a course of action.

"We must proceed with extreme caution and on a basis which is legally sound. Also we must not directly involve the pope even though we strongly suspect that the men involved would act only with his approval if not at his orders. And we must direct our attack only against those who are so clearly Florentine that we have an equally clear right to condemn them. We must not, for example, accuse the Colonna, who are Roman, nor that Pisan fraud Jacopo Gaetani. It would also be unwise to prefer charges against clerics — against Francesco da Montenero, Antonio degli Orsi, or Andrea del Cione. This would be to affront Boniface too flagrantly. But we can and should accuse Nero Cambi, Simone Gherardi, Noffo Quintavalli, and Ser Cambio da Sesto of plotting and planning to subvert the Ordinances of Justice and to overthrow the lawful government. We can and should charge them with treason."

But to accuse them of anything, it was necessary to be in Florence, and it would be desirable to be represented on the new priorate. This took office on April 15.

The seven men with their retinue took respectful leave of the pontiff not long after April 1, and once they had disappeared into the distance at least Lapo Salterelli set his horse to a gallop. For he must speak soon and speak fast.

This he did, and with such persuasiveness that when the new priors were chosen he was one of them.

Now he came out into the open.

At one of the first meetings of the priors, he arose and faced his colleagues, and, choosing his words carefully, one by one made plain the alleged schemings and the alleged intrigues of the four Florentines.

This was on April 18, and on the same day a vote was taken. Nero

Cambi was acquitted (lack of proof or friends in high places?), but Simone Gherardi, Noffo Quintavalli, and Ser Cambio were found guilty.

Then the sentence. A fine of two thousand golden *libbre* was imposed on each, and if he did not pay it his tongue would be cut off!

That is, if he fell into Florentine hands. But if he did not his houses could be razed and all his property seized.

Banditori — they were like brightly colored instead of black and white magpies — went to every piazza and important street corner. Bells were tolled and trumpets sounded shrilly. The judgment of the priors was read and proclaimed in sonorous Latin. It was now only necessary to carry it out.

But even as the crowds jostled and shoved — and either muttered in complaint or shouted approval — certain men stepped from their midst, paused at an office for instructions, and then, while the priors with the gonfalonier and his guards were otherwise occupied, slipped cautiously through the Porta Romana and were on their way.

They were on their way to Pope Boniface, sent by the Spini and other Blacks.

"Your enemies now rule in Florence," they said when they were in his presence. "They have thrown aside their masks and act openly. Simone Gherardini has been sentenced — for being your friend — as, too, have Noffo Quintavalli and Ser Cambio. Others will soon be arrested or exiled."

"My friends sentenced?"

"All but Nero Cambi."

Boniface flushed angry red and the veins on his forehead stood out as his hands trembled.

"The woolsellers want war?" he shouted. "Well, let them have war!"

But then he reconsidered. First he would try peaceful methods.

"Let my own emissary go to Florence, and there let him appear before the priors. As they face him, let him conjure them and adjure them under pain of my most extremest displeasure to end all these persecutions and prosecutions. These are my servants they have laid their sentence on."

Promptly he sent a message to the bishop of Florence.

"See to it that these orders are carried out."

After that he caused to be drafted and then sent on its way a formal summons to Lapo Salterelli and to Lippo Rimucci Becchi and to the notary Bondone Gherardi (both of whom had stood at Salterelli's side when he preferred the charges) to proceed posthaste to the Apostolic See and there to explain personally their rash sacrilegious deed.

Lapo's answer was to persuade the priors to convene the Council of One Hundred.

He addressed it vehemently.

"Florentine justice must and always will be independent. Not even the pope can command it."

He followed this statement "with many bitter invectives against Boniface," and in this and in the action, or rather nonaction, which he advocated he was supported by many speakers and apparently by a majority of the council members.

But not even now did the pope go any farther than words. This time, however, the words were considerably stronger.

North to Florence went two more communications. One was a second plainspoken letter to the bishop of Florence, and the other a scorching epistle to Fra Grimaldo of Prato, high inquisitor for Tuscany, who had the authority and presumably the power to bring the recalcitrants to heel.

Let these two men put papal orders into immediate effect. Let them see to it now that not merely the priors themselves, not merely Lapo Salterelli and his accomplices, but every member of the council and every Florentine magistrate gets him to Rome as fast as horse will carry him and penitently humbles himself at his feet. Then Boniface made an exception. Those who had not spoken too bitterly against him, or too eloquently in favor of Lapo, could be represented by attorney. But Lapo, Lippo, and the hapless Bondone Gherardi together with six named councillors must make the trip in person and personally accept papal punishment or censure. Those who disobeyed must be arrested and their property confiscated. And not merely their Florentine property and their property in papal domains. Every ruler in Christendom would be authorized — nay, commanded — to seize anything of theirs that he could lay his hands on. Every Christian banker would be directed to annul their credit.

As he dictated all this, the pope seethed and simmered in his outraged and (as he thought) righteous anger.

"*Hic Lapus lapis est offensionis!*" he thundered, punning badly. "This Lapo is a *lapis* [rock] of offenses!"

Did not this heretic know, he continued, that every human being was subject to the authority of the Church? Else who would correct the sinner and punish the sin? This was particularly true of Florence, the return of whose exiles a pope had brought about when he appointed Charles of Anjou his vicar-general of Tuscany. Had not God made the *successori Petri* — the successors of Peter — lord of every land and every people? Who dared to flout the spokesman of God?

As he thundered this, he also threatened Lapo and his associates with excommunication.

Words only? This is indeed so.

But behind them was an implicit threat of force and arms.

« 5 »

It was at this critical moment in Florentine history that Dante — we might almost say *alas* — stepped onto the center of the stage, assuming for the first time (and, it would turn out, the only time) a position in the Florentine government which had directive powers. Hitherto he had been only a speaker — evidently a convincing and an eloquent speaker — but with no executive authority, with no power to do anything but urge and say. But now his time to speak was ended. He must begin acting. This, and very forcefully, he did.

On June 14, 1300, the priorate of which Lapo Salterelli was the most influential member concluded its term of office, and on June 15, 1300, a new priorate was elected.

The new priors:

Ricco Falconetti, also known as Ricco Spadaio, or Ricco Swordmaker, who would prove to be as tested as was the steel from which he shaped his falchions.

Nello degli Arrighetti and Bindo di Donato Bilenchi, both staunch Whites too.

Noffo Guidi and Neri di Messer Jacopo del Giudice, waverers who would later join the Blacks but now (as later) were at the disposal of those in power.

And Dante Alighieri!

Gonfalonier of justice was Fazio di Guido da Micciole, who, as *collega di Carruccio di Verro* (glassworks commissioner) with ample taxing powers, had used them to harass the feudal noblemen and hence was in the good graces of the merchant-burghers. (But later he would hold office under the Donateschi.)

Their notary was Aldobrandino d'Uguccione, who did considerable business with Dante and his brother, which may have been the reason why he received this lucrative appointment.

That night the eight spent in a convent in prayer and meditation — presumably in the even then historic Badia which was so dear to Dante. The next morning, clad in their official robes — to pay for his, and to help meet the expenses of his family while his farms and other interests were neglected, the poet had borrowed ninety florins from Francesco Alighieri — they marched in solemn procession to the only half-finished Palazzo della Signoria, where they would spend their term of office. There they were formally installed.

Then they began their business, and their first business was some unfinished business left by the old priorate.

It was the custom — and indeed it was now almost traditional — for the priors to act in conformity with the popular will, and to determine what this was it had become their practice to hold frequent audiences in which they entertained petitions from "true men and good" who "wished to see the peaceful state of Florence maintained," or "who loved justice and the well-being of the commonwealth" so well that they therefore "laid before the priors propositions the adoption of which they insistently urged."

Just such a group now stood before the signory.

In their hands they had a document which read as follows:

"On the fifteenth day of June, being present as witnesses Ser Bondone de' Cambi of the *sesto* of San Piero Scheraggio and Ser Biondo and Ser Cione, all notaries.

"Be it plainly known to all those who inspect these presents that in my presence and in the presence of the above-named witnesses I, Sostegno Busatti, gave and consigned to Ricco, swordmaker, to Dante Aligheri, to Nero del Giudice, to Noffo Guidi, to Nello Arrighetti, to Bindo Bilenchi, and to Fazio da Micciole, gonfalonier of justice, the sentence which on April 18 was passed and was put into effect against Noffo Quintavalli, Simone Gherardi, and Ser Cambio da Sesto by Messer Gherardo da Gambara of Brescia, who then held the office of *podestà*.

"This sentence the said priors do accept and reaffirm.

"And they do publish and proclaim the said sentence."

"Sign it!" they urged with all the emphasis they could command. "We urge you to sign it. It is in the best interest of Florence you do so."

In this — although we have no clear proof that he was one of the petitioning group — the hand of Lapo Salterelli is plainly visible. By insisting on procedure against the three popesmen, he had incurred papal enmity. Let others share in it. It would thus be divided and, he hoped, diluted.

It is not known what discussion then ensued — or what part, certainly great, in the discussion Dante played. But sign it the new priors did.

(The notary, incidentally, was not the priors' own notary but one Lapo di Gianni Ricevuto. This Lapo should be noted. He is Lapo Gianni, the poet. He is the Lapo of the so-called boating sonnet earlier set down; the Lapo with whom — and Guido Cavalcanti — Dante wished to drift idly over enchanted waters while they sang songs about Monna Vanna, Monna Lagia, and another lady who was clearly not Beatrice. Dante was, therefore, not the only Florentine poet to engage in high state matters.)

And as soon as they had signed it, word that they had went speeding south as did word of every other papal setback.

The Black magnates saw to this.

"The anti-papal policy of these White Guelphs who are really Ghibellines is now Florence's official policy, since a new signory has confirmed the action of the old signory. You have friends but they are powerless. They will remain powerless unless you aid them. And you have enemies and these have power."

Names were named to him.

Some are already familiar. Lawyer Salterelli. Gherardino Diodati. Five or six others.

But there were new names also, and these the pontiff noted.

Ricco Falconetti. Fazio da Micciole. And Dante.

"A swordmaker, smelling of the forge!" the pope cried. "A corrupt tax collector! And this poet!"

The last in particular was undoubtedly a sower of scandal and a dangerous disseminator of discord!

(Today we would say an agitator and a radical. But actually Dante was a conservative. It was Pope Boniface who was the radical.)

He dwelt on the name. Dante. Dante Alighieri.

And not in a way that would do Dante any good.

Thus, says Davidsöhn, "by the first formal act of their priorate" — and by the angry interpretation which Pope Boniface put on this act — "was placed upon Dante and his colleagues a so-called stigma which affected the whole future of the poet."

« 6 »

The whole future of the poet would also be affected by another action taken by the priors long before the repercussions of the first action had even begun to die down.

The new priors (Dante among them) had hardly been in office a full week when — on June 23, 1300 — on the feast day of St. John, as was the custom, a colorful and solemn procession moved through the canopied streets of Florence to the cheering and the plaudits of the usual crowd. Such a procession has been described already, but it would not be amiss to repeat that in it marched the pomp and circumstance of Florentine life — the high clergy in their gold-embroidered vestments; the priors and the gonfalonier of justice with their attendants; the greater and the lesser guildsmen, even the chief citizens of the surrounding towns.

Spirits were usually high, for the marchers were accompanied by slapstick and by extravagant buffoonery. Heads, to be sure, were sometimes broken. How not in such a rowdy crowd? But they were broken boisterously and not with malice, for the humor was good if rough.

But this time the high spirits turned ugly.

"As the guilds," said Dino Compagni, "were proceeding in an orderly manner to offer their gifts, their consuls, who were walking in front, were assaulted and beaten by certain of the *grandi*."

These were the young bear cubs and lion cubs again — the same ones who had sliced off Ricoverino de' Cerchi's nose and who, led by Corso Donati and his *mesnie*, had sent Guido Cavalcanti flying through the streets.

"You have robbed us of our due rights!" they shouted.

(It was at this time that they made their complaint that although they had won the battle of Campaldino for Florence they now were deprived of their rights as citizens.)

It was a deliberate attempt to create disorder in the hope that it would lead to revolution, a revolution which would put the city in new hands.

It did not succeed, however.

Although contemporary accounts do not state this explicitly, it is apparent that the priors acted promptly and with decision

A quick word went to the gonfalonier of justice, who responded instantly.

A handful of peace disturbers, although most were accomplished fighting men, could do little but scatter like frightened birds when confronted by the gonfalonier's *sbirri*, who, crossbow or pike in hand, moved rapidly into place.

Then the priors faced up to more basic facts.

The men were rioters, but they rioted — and with some hope of success — because of a fundamentally bad situation.

We must attempt to deal with it, they concluded. They did.

"The priors," writes Dino Compagni, "being indignant, sought the counsel of several citizens" — in other words, convened a meeting to which certain Guelph leaders were invited — "and I, Dino, was one of them."

These debated the matter and then came up with a decision in which the hand of Dante is very apparent.

"They placed some of each party under bounds. Of the party of the Donati, Messer Corso Donati and his brother Sinibaldo, Messer Rosso and Messer Rossellino della Tosa, Messer Giachinotto and Messer Pazzino de' Pazzi, Messer Geri Spini, Messer Porco Manieri, and their kinsmen were ordered to Castel della Pieve. And of the party of the Cerchi, Messer Gentile and Messer Torrigiano and Carbone de' Cerchi, Guido Cavalcanti, Baschiera della Tosa, Baldinaccio degli Adimari, Naldo degli Gherardini, and some of their kinsmen, to Serrezana."

Serrezana is the modern Sarzana.

Guido Cavalcanti gives us the clue. Remember he was the poet's "first friend." None other than Dante would have dealt out justice so impartially.

The priors, however, did make one distinction between the Whites and the Blacks.

The White leaders were merely exiled. The Blacks were exiled and fined too.

"Messer Corso Donati, who was the leader in the matter" — this is Villani speaking — "was condemned in goods and in person, as were the other [Black] leaders."

To the amount of twenty thousand *libbre*.

Villani says that they paid these fines.

Dino Compagni, however, paints a picture of White compliance and of Black recalcitrance.

"The Cerchi," he says, "obeyed and went to their place of residence, but those of the Black party refused to go, showing that there was a conspiracy among them."

For a moment the fate of the city seemed to hang in the balance.

For if the Donati, continues Dino, "had taken up arms, they would have that day conquered the city, since the Lucchese at the instigation of the cardinal" — Cardinal Acquasparta — "were coming to their aid."

But for some reason these men who believed in action hesitated, and the opportunity was lost.

For, "hearing that the men of Lucca approached," the priors now had time to write "to bid them not to dare to enter their territory, and to write the villagers commanding them to seize the passes."

The passes through the surrounding mountains through which the Lucchese would advance upon the city.

"It was my business to write this letter," says Dino proudly. He had reason to be proud. He was given this assignment when Dante was one of the priors.

"And both of these matters were so diligently conducted by Messer Bartolo, the son of Messer Jacopo de' Bardi, that in both cases the Florentine orders were carried out."

Two crises in less than eight weeks. And both of them brought to a forceful conclusion.

The Dante priorate had made a very creditable record.

But while it made this record, it first incurred and then reinforced a dangerous enmity — the enmity whose potential for evil was noted in the last chapter.

« 7 »

Only one other matter has been recorded which pertains to Dante during the time of his priorate, and this was personal rather than political. Yet it too could have been used by Dante's adversaries for political purposes, and there is at least a hint that it was.

Dante himself tells the story, albeit somewhat cryptically.

Inferno XIX (he is describing the punishment reserved for simoniacs):

> I saw that on its sides and at the bottom
> The ash-gray pit was filled with many a hole.
> All of one size they were, and all were round,
> Nor did they seem less wide to me, nor wider,
> Than those which in my beautiful San Giovanni
> Fashioned had been to hold the baptizers,
> And one of which not many years ago
> I smashed to save one drowning in it.
> That's the true story. Let this clear all minds.

His commentators, however, are more specific. From the author of the *Ottimo Commento* to Lana and Benvenuto da Imola, virtually every early writer on Dante deals with the matter. I give the account of Benvenuto da Imola because it is complete and adequate, yet reasonably compact.

"You should know that in Florence in the church of their patron saint John the Baptist there are around the baptismal fonts several wells, round in shape and large enough to hold a man."

These "wells," incidentally, have long since been removed from the Florentine Baptistery, but ones just like them can still be seen in the Baptistery at Pisa.

"In these the priests with their dishes of holy water were accustomed to stand so that they could carry out their office more easily and freely in the short time at their disposal. You see it was necessary for them to baptize a great multitude simultaneously and upon a single occasion, since all of Florence was so populous and there was but a single Baptistery.

"And the author here refers back to and talks about an extremely strange thing which happened only a little while ago in the place. Some children, as they often did, were playing in this Baptistery, and one of them jumped with more force than any of the others and went so deep into the well and wedged his limbs so firmly therein that neither skill nor ingenuity could pull him forth. The other boys began to shout: 'Help! We cannot rescue him!' at which a great crowd quickly gathered, but, to

make a long story short, they neither knew how nor were able to set free
the imperiled lad.

"At this point, up came Dante, who was then one of the priors in office.
He saw the boy.

" 'What are you doing, addlepates?' he cried. 'Bring me an axe!'

"And when an axe was straightway brought him, Dante with his own
hands smashed the stone to pieces. It was of marble which shatters easily.
And thus the boy, who by then was only half alive, was saved from
death."

Taken as set down, that was all there was to it — except possibly for
the ironic fact that the boy rescued seems to have been one Antonio di
Baldinaccio de' Cavicciuli and the Cavicciuli would end up as some of the
poet's more vindictive persecutors.

Dante appeared; was flabbergasted by the dithering of the bystanders;
showed initiative; and acted.

But later — as his own lines indicate — this acting would be used
against him.

"This was not a feat of saving life," it would be maliciously spread
abroad, "but an act of sacrilege on the part of one who was a known
enemy of God's Church and of the man who ruled it. For who but a
disrespecter of the Lord and his vicegerent upon earth could have so
desecrated this holy temple? Was there a boy at all? Or if there was a boy,
could he not have been rescued in another manner?"

Thus one more step was taken toward the somber fate which destiny
was preparing for him — a fate which he and we and Leonardo Bruni
have indicated would be filled with nothing but incalculable harm.

« 8 »

Nor did the next step which led to this come much later, although, as a
matter of fact, it was not the Dante priorate but its immediate successor
which initiated the first of the series of actions which would help hurry
on the disastrous end.

It will be recalled that the White leaders had been exiled to "Serrezana," at the foot of the white-marble Alpi Apuane on the border
between Tuscany and Liguria, and it should be noted that although the
guidebooks say that today it is "a *lively* town of 8334 inhabitants situated
on the eastern slope of the fertile plain of the Magra" and therefore an
"important agricultural center," guidebooks have a way of exaggerating. I
found it somnolent and a little melancholy rather than lively when I went
through it in 1961.

In 1300 it was hardly even that. To be sure, it had become an important
center of Church activity in the early Middle Ages, and because many of

the mule trails (they followed the ruins of the Roman roads) used by St. Peter's–bound romeros interlaced there, it had a modest commerce. Its castle, too, is mentioned in a diploma issued by the Emperor Otto in 963, and from 1204 on the bishops of Luni made it their episcopal seat.

But to the Whites who pined for Florence and who took no consolation from the turquoise-blue Tyrrhenian Sea only two or three miles away, neither the castle, the commerce, the procession of pilgrims, nor the bishop himself made any difference. To them, it stank of decay and rottenness.

Why should they have been sent to these Magra swamps — the Magra was scarcely a bowshot away, and in those days, at any rate, its delta was a quagmire fully as malarial as the notorious Pontine Marshes southwest of Rome? Their hated adversaries had been exiled to castles in the Apennines.

Guido Cavalcanti — at least in part — expresses their feelings. In a poem which he may well have sent to Dante, hoping for sympathy, he said this:

> Since I do not hope ever to return,
> Little ballad, unto my Tuscany,
> Go thou then, lightly and swift,
> Unto my lady.
> From her grace thou'lt make shift
> Honor to earn.
>
> Bring thou her news of sighs.
> Tell her my grief and fear.
> But let none of thee beware
> Of thee who's foe to gentleness,
> Or to my misfortune great
> Thou wilt not be received,
> Thou wilt not be believed,
> Which will bring agony
> And when I die a spate
> Of sorrow, and many a tear.
>
> Thou knowst, little ballad, knowst that death
> Pricks me so hard that life abandons me,
> And knowst my heart beats oh! strangely
> And hard as every vital spirit contends for breath.
> So much is my body worn away
> I cannot suffer more pain.
> Do me this charity.
> Take thou my soul, I pray,
> When from me it bursts amain.

Little ballad, to thine amity,
Woe's me, my soul I commend.
Take it in pity away with thee
To my fair dear whom thee I'd send.
Woe's me, little ballad, do smile and say
When thou before her stand:
Here comes thy servitor.
He now stands thee before,
Come to thee at his command,
Love's livery who one time wore.

Go thou, bewildered one and weak,
Who weeping from this grieving heart do come,
And with my soul and with this song speak, speak
Of my worn, weary mind to her.
Thou'lt find a lady so delicate
And of a soul so sweet
That thou'lt delight to follow her forever,
My soul, and to adore her
For her worth ever.

"Since I do not hope ever to return."
"That life abandons me."
"So much is my body worn away."

It should be noted, as we savor these phrases, that the "rich and very talented young man" who had guided Dante down the road to his *dolce stil novo* was a gay and youthful cavalier no longer. Guido was at least forty-five as he penned these lines, and he may have been fifty, which was old by medieval standards. He was worn out by his intense living and his intense thinking. And in the fetid and damp-smelling air of his enforced home, his hands shook with the tertian or quartan fever which had turned a face yellow which was already deeply lined and creased. Not only was he dying, but he knew it.

But if his fellow exiles did not share his gloomy forebodings and if they probably sent no songs to lovely ladies, they did share his homesickness for their beloved city.

And now, it seemed, they had a way of getting back there, for there were those in Florence — those in high places in Florence — who would not want to see Guido come to his end in this desolate hole.

Letters began to go back and forth — stressing and perhaps exaggerating the miasma, stressing but not exaggerating Guido's state of health — and presently they had the sought-after result.

It could have been difficult for the Dante priorate to reverse its own judgment, but its term of office expired on August 15, and the new priorate which took up the reigns of government on the same day was just as strongly White and its hands were not tied.

Therefore, it took action.

Messengers were immediately sent to Sarzana, by whom — "because of the unhealthiness of the place" (Giovanni Villani) — the exiles were told they could return.

Back they came forthwith. Those who have been already named and others. A younger Vieri de' Cerchi, son of the Ricoverino de' Cerchi whose nose had been cut off, and perhaps grandson of the elder Vieri de' Cerchi who does not seem to have been exiled, possibly because he still limped from wounds received at Campaldino. Messer Biligiardo della Tosa. Carbone Gherardini. Messer Guido "Scimmia" Cavalcanti.

This Guido Cavalcanti — Guido "Monkey" Cavalcanti — is said to have been given his nickname to distinguish him from his famous kinsman. But he was the son of the Gianni (Schicchi) Cavalcanti whose ability to ape men's voices and their manners has already been noted. Perhaps he inherited the name from his father.

Guido Cavalcanti, the poet, came too — but in a litter. It is not stated whether his fever permitted him to realize that unexpectedly he had followed his song.

Having returned, "they and the others of the party," according to Dino Compagni, "remained quiet." In other words, shaken by their exile — and by the fear that they might be exiled again and this time fined too — they pursued their various businesses and refrained from politics. At least for the time being.

One of them "remained quiet" for ever.

"Guido Cavalcanti shortly died. And he was a great loss, seeing that he was a philosopher and a man accomplished in many things save only that he was sensitive and passionate."

The exact date is not given but it must have been very late in August, for he was buried on August 29 in the cemetery of Santa Reparata, there where as a young man (*Decameron* VI, 9) he had leaped over the tombstones, hurling back a witty retort at Betto Brunelleschi and his merry companions.

Santa Reparata having become Santa Maria del Fiore, it is not known where he sleeps today.

« 9 »

It was not so with the Blacks. The last thing the Blacks had any intention of doing was to remain quiet — unless it was the quiet of being poised to spring. But this was implicit in their character.

A contemporary — a man who witnessed and even took part in most of the events of the seventeen months of crisis which Salterelli's action began, has thus contrasted the two parties:

"The captain of the Whites" — their captain when they held every rein of power — "did not make himself master of the city as he should have done. His soldiers were not paid, he not having any money and lacking the initiative to lay hands on some. He did not secure any of the towers and buildings. He placed no one under bounds. Menacing words he spoke in plenty, and he paraded around the city enough, but he followed up none of this with deeds. Those who did not know the Whites held them to be rich, powerful, and wise, but anyone who knew anything said: 'They are occupied in trade and are cowardly' — perhaps overcautious would be a better word — 'by nature. Their adversaries, on the contrary, are masters of war, and are both bold and ruthless.' "

A not too well thought out decision by the Dante priorate gave these adversaries a chance to display at least the last two of these qualities. Specifically, it gave the opportunity to the man who for the moment — and for quite a while longer — would be the most effective of the Black leaders. Il Barone, Corso Donati, had long been in evidence but now he stepped forward into the front rank, his purpose being to take charge of the fortunes of Florence before they took charge of him.

For reasons which are difficult to understand, when the White leaders were sent to Sarzana, he and his Black colleagues were banished to a mountain stronghold in the wild region of blue fir trees which had become known as the Massa Trabaria.

Castel della Pieve was indeed an inexplicable choice. It was not merely in papal territory (and therefore out of Florentine control) but enjoyed every strategic advantage. Its lofty height — it lay between some of the tallest peaks of Italy on the one hand and the mountains around Urbino on the other — and its nearness to the latter, which was in the hands of papal sympathizers, made it a secure refuge. But it was not inaccessible. Through the breathtaking Bocca Trabaria (Trabaria Pass — altitude 3400 feet) one looked down — and could easily descend — into the beautiful and fertile "seashell" of the Val Tiberina. From the Val Tiberina roads led to Arezzo, from which Florence could be reached, or via Città di Castello, Umbertide, Perugia, Assisi, Foligno, Spoleto, and Terni to Rome or Anagni.

As long as the White exiles kept their distance, Corso and those with him were content to look, and look only — but from this eyrie vantage point which Dante and his colleagues had seen fit to give them. But when word came that the Cerchieschi had been recalled to Florence, it was another matter. To Corso, especially, it was. For how could he be sure that they would "remain quiet"? In the same circumstances, he would not have. How could he leave his enemies walking the streets from which he was excluded without trying to do something about it?

He could not, and he did not.

"Messer Corso Donati," writes Dino Compagni, "having been placed under bounds at Massa Trabaria, broke them and betook himself to Rome, being disobedient; for which cause he was condemned in person and property."

Presumably he was *again* condemned, for he had been exiled and fined already.

(Villani says that he betook himself to *Castrum plebis* — then Castello, but now Città, della Pieve — in Umbria, and not Rome. There was a papal court there. But probably he was confused by the similar names.)

At Rome — or at *Castrum plebis* — and with the support of Geri Spini who had now joined him, he laid his case before Pope Boniface.

"Florence is in a more evil and uncertain state than ever. The White exiles who oppose you have been brought back to the city, but we, the Blacks, who are your friends, are still kept out. The headstrong captains of the [White] Guelph party" — this seems to contradict Dino Compagni's story of weakness and vacillation (see above), but one still feels that Dino is correct — "do with impunity whatsoever they wish, and they spend money as they need to."

"What should I do about this?" the pope asked.

"Send," cried Corso, "send for Monsieur Charles of Valois, who is brother to the king of France. Call on him to come to the aid of his cousin Charles II of Naples in his Sicilian war, giving him to understand, and giving his brother to understand too, that if he does this you will cause him to be elected emperor of the Romans and will confirm his election, and that pending this you will make him imperial lieutenant for the Church by virtue of those rights which the Church has when the imperial throne is vacant. That will conceal your true purpose. Then make him pacificator of Tuscany — pretending that he will order and control both Whites and Blacks, but understanding that, under Black dominance, he is to bring Florence to submit to you. You will then have the city and the province!"

Have Tuscany! No other words were needed.

He would do what Corso asked.

But first he must prepare the ground — and very carefully.

(Recently Florence had outwitted him. Now he must outwit Florence.)

Given the date of the Whites' recall, it may be assumed that Corso left Massa Trabaria not earlier than September 1300 and probably not later than October. On November 11, Boniface took his first step.

On that day he summoned to the Lateran the ambassadors of Florence,

Bologna, Lucca, Siena, and the small towns of the Tuscan League. A description of the meeting survives. The pope sat upon a high throne which had been placed before his rose-coverletted bed. He wore a scarlet mantle. In his hand he held a small handkerchief with which from time to time he wiped his mouth. Around him stood those cardinals and other clerics who made up the papal curia, and with them were members of their staffs. On one side of him stood a Knight Hospitaler and on the other a Knight Templar. To the clerics he spoke in Latin but to the ambassadors in the *volgare* — in the Italian of Bologna, Lucca, Florence, and Siena.

"I need you and you need me," he told them. "I want your friendship and goodwill. You should want mine."

Then he turned to the Florentine.

"Particularly I need your city's aid and goodwill. I need it in my war against the Aldobrandeschi. These are lawless feudal lords. Except that they are of ancient lineage, they are little different from Ghino di Tacco and Rinier da Corneto."

These two famous highwaymen have already been mentioned. Little is known of Rinier, but Ghino di Tacco, who lived above Radicofani in an eagle's-nest castle whose ruins can still be seen, was an Italian Robin Hood who robbed rich merchants to give to poor students (*Decameron* X, 2), and when a fat prelate fell into his hands would entertain him lavishly as he relieved him of his purse.

"Your good merchants have always stood against feudal lords and long ago you tamed your own Guidi and your own Alberti. Help me now against mine — and persuade the other cities of the league to do likewise."

But even as he spoke, a delegation, headed by Rinaldo of Piacenza, was on its way to Paris to begin *pourparlers* which he hoped would lead to intervention. Their public instructions — like the letters to the bishop of Amiens — were carefully drawn up so as to throw dust in Florentine eyes, and were all sweetness and innocent of any intentions against the city's government or its liberties.

But their private orders were another matter, and these soon came into the open.

For before the end of November, Boniface had deemed it wise to tell the French clergy what they would be expected to do. From the Lateran he addressed to them a papal declaration in which he stated that he proposed not only to send an expedition against Sicily but to bring Florence and Tuscany to heel. He then directed them to give up a year's tithes for this cause. This involved a total sum of 100,000 silver marks.

Having done this, however, he reassured them.

This was not raw conquest, he said, but merely a prelude to a crusade to the Holy Land. But before he could take even the first step which was to rewin Acre, he must be secure at home.

"Sicily must be taken from the hands of Frederick" — Fadrique II of Aragon, "*quel* [*Paradiso* XIX] *che guarda l'isola del foco*" (he who doth lord it over the isle of fire) and who (*Purgatorio* VII) held the lands but not the virtues of his grandfather. "It must be taken from the hands of Frederick and given to one who will do our will."

There must, in other words, be a new king of Trinacria.

"Moreover, Tuscany is now beaten by the waves of disorder. The cities, the localities, the inhabitants who are subjects of their true mother, the Church — all these are in rebellion. They are poisoned by the vice of their ingratitude to her."

Florence must be beaten into submission.

"I have summoned, therefore, the son and the brother of French kings. For when Sicily has been brought to order, and when the rebels in Italy have been put down, we can truly make war against the infidel, and the universal Church of the West can have a sabbath."

To be sure, it was one thing to say all this and another to do it. Just in the matter of money alone, it was no mean business to collect 100,000 silver coins from men — I refer to the French clergy — who "were so greedy and avaricious" that just to sell the favors at their disposal they "employed more brokers than the drapery trade and all the other trades in Paris put together." And besides that, the pope wanted 100,000 *livres tournois* from King Philip himself — who may have thought that he should have been paid rather than pay — and another 40,000 (in return for privileges he could not deliver until the job was done) from the Pistoian bankers Ammanati, who had a branch beside the Seine.

Nor was Charles of Valois easy to negotiate with. Hot and cold. Backward and forward. Dance and footplay. Twist of wrist. Just like a fencing master.

It was not until February of the next year — it was not until February 2, 1301 — that even a preliminary agreement was reached and that he could begin even first preparations.

« *10* »

Yet begin them he finally did, and the strange thing is that even after he had Florence remained unperturbed and undisturbed.

What was the reason?

Had these sharp-witted people been cozened by wits that were even sharper? They who would not have bought an ell of woolen cloth or a pannier full of roots with which to make colors and dyes without pinching and pulling, did they now buy papal merchandise like a pig in a poke?

At least one modern historian thinks so.

"They began to nourish," says Davidsöhn, referring to their reaction to the report of their ambassador after he had attended the bedside convocation, "the most extravagant of hopes."

It is not impossible. You have only to read the *Decameron* to discover that these master gullers were themselves quite often gullible.

Or were they simply too preoccupied with their day-by-day business? This seems somewhat more likely — and in character. It may well be.

But whatever the reason, when tidings came from France, they were either not listened to or disregarded. Not only were no new preparations made to cope with the threatened new danger, but even old precautions were discarded. To give one example, at this time — to reciprocate supposed papal goodwill — most of the Black exiles were recalled. Not Corso Donati. Fatuousness did not go quite that far, and he was still recognized as much too dangerous. But a majority of the more important Donateschi. God was in his heaven — speaking with the for-the-time-being honeyed voice of Pope Gaetani. All was right with the world.

Yet there were some Florentines who did not share the mood of complacency, and one of them was Dante, the supposedly impractical visionary. This is shown not merely by the fact of his participation but by the nature of his participation in an immediately following sequence of events.

Let us take them in order. They are all documented.

April 14, 1301.

"On the fourteenth day of April, in the Council of the Capitudini of the Twelve Greater Guilds and of the Savi, being present too the priors and the gonfalonier, the captain proposed that the method of choosing future priors should be debated.

"Ser Bindo di Ser Guicciardo, a notary, proposed that the *capitudini* and the *savi* of each *sesto* simultaneously should nominate five men from each *sesto* and that then a vote should be taken in conformity with established use.

"Guido Ubaldini proposed that the *capitudini* of each guild should nominate two men from each *sesto*.

"Dante Alighieri spoke in favor of the first proposition.

"A rising and sitting vote was taken and the first proposition was almost unanimously adopted."

Also April 14, 1301.

"On the same day of April 14 with the same persons present.

"In the Council of the Capitudini of the Twelve Greater Guilds and of the Savi, the captain proposed that six good men and true in the six boroughs [*borghi* — the distinction between this and *sesto* is not entirely clear] should be named and that these should proceed to a scrutiny for the choosing of a new gonfalonier.

"Dante Alighieri proposed that the *capitudini* and *savi* from each *sesto* each nominate one man from their own *sesto*.

"A rising and sitting vote being taken, the proposition of the said *savio* (i.e., Dante) was adopted."

April 28, 1301.

"In God's name, amen. The six commissioners in charge of straightening and improving the roads but without hurt to the rights of the commonwealth, having received and heard the petition of interested parties" — to the effect that the Via San Procolo (today the Via Pandolfini), which began almost at the house of Dante and ran through the Borgo Piagentino to the little river, Africo, be widened and straightened — "do appoint Dante Alighieri, with Guglielmo della Piagentina as his secretary, to be superintendent of this work and the official in charge of it."

The purported justification for this roadwork was also given.

It was "very useful and necessary to the men and people of the city of Florence" (1) "so that a plentiful food supply could always be had" — from the farms of the surrounding *contado*; and (2) "so that the common folk of the countryside could proceed in safety and and without clamor and outrage on the part of the magnates and the powerful when they came to the lords priors and the gonfalonier to seek justice."

June 19, 1301.

"On the eighteenth day of the month of June, before the Council of One Hundred, the General and Special Councils, and the Council of the Capitudini of the Twelve Greater Guilds, with the priors and the gonfalonier present, the captain proposed the below-written matters: first, that they should continue to maintain one hundred men in the service of the pope in the manner authorized by Cardinal Matteo [Matteo d'Acquasparta]; and second, that they should receive a mission sent to the priors and the gonfalonier by the town of Colle.

"Ser Ruggiero Ughi degli Albizzi, notary, urged that the aforesaid service of the pope be continued in the manner requested and that the mission from Colle to the priors and the gonfalonier be received.

"Dante Alighieri urged that in the matter of serving the pope nothing be done. In the other matter, he urged following the proposal of the first speaker.

"Messer Guidotto de' Canigiani, judge, urged following the proposals of the first speaker.

"Messer Albizzo Corbinelli urged that the question of serving the pope be laid upon the table.

"Present as witnesses were Messer Gentile de' Gualteroni, judge and assessor of the lord captain, and Albizzo Reddi, crier for the said captain and for the people of Florence, and many others.

"A rising and sitting vote was then taken" — but on the second proposition only, the move to table the first proposition evidently having been successful — "and the proposition of the first speaker in regard to the matter of Colle was unanimously carried. On the said day the said mission was officially received."

On the said day, too, the first proposition came to another vote, but by the Council of One Hundred only.

(Incidentally, the fact that Dante spoke shows that he was a member of this council, and did not attend the earlier meetings either as one of the *capitudini* or one of the *savi*.)

"On the same day and before the same witnesses, the priors and the gonfalonier being present, the lord captain proposed: first that they should continue to serve the pope with one hundred men for as long as it seemed fitting to the priors and to the gonfalonier there present, and that in the said service should remain Messer Neri de' Giandonati, captain of these soldiers, and likewise Ser Torello de' Bronchi representing the notary of the said captain, and that they should serve as they always had, except that the said service should not last longer than the fifteenth of September and that money for this service should be paid only to that person or those persons to whom the priors saw fit to pay it.

"And second, that they should pay three thousand *libbre* to the gonfalonier in the command of those troops so that he could pay his company of foot soldiers.

"Messer Guidotto de' Canigiani spoke in favor of the above proposals.

"Dante Alighieri urged that in the matter of serving the pope nothing be done. He spoke in favor of the second proposition.

"Having made a division by means of ballot boxes and ballots, those in favor of the first preposition were forty-eight; those opposed were thirty-two.

"In regard to the second proposition, those in favor were eighty; those opposed one."

Five separate stands in only a few days more than eight weeks — and all with a single objective! To move Florence toward a position from which she could defend herself.

(1) By setting up the machinery to secure a priorate which would be

steadfast in the face of storm winds. It was particularly important to Dante and his friends that Palmieri Altoviti be named. He *was* named.

(2) By strengthening the city's military posture. This was the true reason for improving the Borgo Piagentino road. If it was straightened and widened, troops from the *contado* — and from the little friendly neighboring towns — could be marched into the city rapidly if the signory faced a sudden emergency.

(3) By opposing anything that could advance the papal cause — even so small a something as sending a token force for a limited length of time to aid Boniface in a cause that under other circumstances Florence could have approved. You do not, he presumably reasoned, do anything that might bring even the slightest chance of victory to an almost certain enemy.

"*Nihil fiat!*" he cried steadfastly. "*Nihil fiat!*"

This was dangerous to say, but it was even more dangerous not to say it.

The first time he was listened to, for it was clearly he — with the support of Albizzo Corbinelli — who forced a postponement and a revised motion with the concurrent necessity of going to another body for endorsement.

But the second time it was another matter. Then those who favored caution were in control, and when a vote was taken they won it. Dante and those who shared his views were in the minority. For such consolation as this may have offered, the margin was slim.

« 11 »

But it was not for their consolation that events would prove them to be right. Yet such was indeed to be the case. For the Blacks, now knowing that there was no other recourse than force, at last — in their own minds, at any rate — were committed to seizing power, and the pope was coming closer and closer to the point where he would openly aid them.

But first there was another meeting — late in June but almost certainly before Dante had spoken so strongly and (even though he lost in the end) convincingly before the convened council. Indeed it may have been the reason for his speaking.

"Being ill content," writes Dino Compagni, "with their recall [the recall of the White leaders]" — and also greatly disturbed by the rumor that four hundred Bolognese soldiers in the pay of the Whites were marching across the Apennines, and because the priors had authorized their followers to arm in self-defense, and besides that "having determined to drive out the Cerchi" — "the leaders of the other party" — i.e., the Blacks — "assembled with their own followers in Santa Trinità."

Once more Santa Trinità! Perhaps because it was so near that Black fortress, the Palazzo Spini, this church of the Holy Trinity drew malcontents like a magnet!

"For this," continued Dino, "they adduced many false reasons."

That they sought the peace of the city.

That they wished to benefit the *whole* Guelph cause (not merely *Black* Guelphs but the Black Guelphs *and* the White Guelphs) and to save it — a thrust at the Cerchi — from the Ghibellines.

That in the interest of the whole Guelph cause, they wished to compound differences with the pope.

But although the above peaceful sentiments were expressed, and although every caution was used — as indeed it had to be, since to keep up appearances, White leaders were invited and some of them attended — the true purpose could not be hidden.

Was a coup d'etat possible?

Could right-thinking people — in Black opinion, right-thinking people were the Blacks and those of the Whites who would go along with them — take over?

"After long discussion, Messer Buondelmonti, a wise and discreet knight" — of the Black party — "said that the risk was too great, that too much evil might come of it, and that *for the present* [my italics] they had better proceed no further.

"So they separated without doing anything."

But not without first hearing a lecture from the Florentine Polonius.

"I, Dino Compagni, was present at the meeting and, desiring peace and unity, said this to them before they departed:

" 'Sirs, why do you wish to throw into confusion and destroy so goodly a city? Against whom do ye wish to fight? Against your own brothers? What kind of a victory would that be?' "

A Black leader answered that they did not meet to fight their brothers but to quell discord and to promote harmony.

"On hearing this, I conferred with Lapo di Guazzo, a good and loyal *popolano*" — but of the Black faction — "and together we went to the priors, taking with us certain of the Donateschi who had been at the meeting. There we acted as mediators, and so appeased the said priors that Messer Palmieri Altoviti, who was one of them, contented himself with sharply reproving them, but did not threaten them."

This was all the Blacks wanted.

"They answered humbly that nothing further would come of their meeting together, and they begged only that certain soldiers who had come at their request should be allowed to depart without being molested.

"And it was so ordered by the priors."

Then, their hands freed, they went back to their plotting.

Beatrice's widower, Simone de' Bardi, went secretly to the count of Battifolle — Simone, Count Battifolle, of the Casentino Counts Guidi — and to his son. With Black money to make his words convincing, he urged them to muster and arm their vassals, and also to accumulate large quantities of bread so that the soldiers (the provenance is not named) "might have whereof to live."

When this was done, the Blacks would strike.

But fortunately the schemes were discovered.

Certain Whites would not go along with Dino's compromise and "they continually kept urging" the signory to punish the instigators of the Santa Trinità meeting.

"They have contravened the Ordinances of Justice," they cried, "and their purpose was to conspire against the government!"

To quiet them, an investigation was ordered, and as it proceeded compromising letters were found. From the count to the Bardi banker. From the Bardi banker to the count.

Not even Dino could urge coexistence any longer. It was destroy or be destroyed, and for once the Whites were frightened into firmness.

"The count and his son and Messer Simone were condemned to a heavy penalty."

(Here there is some irony. Dante was possibly among those who sentenced Beatrice's husband.)

Nor were the other Blacks exempted from punishment.

To be specific, the two counts and Messer Simone were declared outlaws. Any hand could be lawfully raised against them. Those of the Donati faction who had been recalled to the city were sent back to their places of exile, as were others who had attended the meeting, both magnates and *popolani*. The property of the Donati was again laid waste. The sentences passed and repassed against Corso Donati were for the third time renewed.

« 12 »

But even as the Black party seemed finally and definitively crushed, there came tidings which changed the whole complexion of things. They were at least in part unexpected.

After dillying and dallying until neither friend nor foe could be sure of what he would do, Charles of Valois was in Italy.

He reached Turin on July 11; Milan on July 18; Parma on July 25; and Modena a few days later. Everywhere he was treated with a great, if sometimes cautious, respect. The marquis of Este, for example — to Dante he was that cruel *figliastro* (stepson) who had smothered his father with a pillow and who had bought, says Dante also, the king of Naples's daughter from her father as he might a slave girl from a pirate — galloped to him with a sackful of florins, while others offered other kinds of tribute.

Then on to Bologna — hastened, it is said, by the marquis's money, which was given him not "out of love and loyalty" but actually so that he would lead his men thither instead of to Ferrara, where the d'Estes ruled.

There he was greeted by both Black and White embassies.

Said the Blacks:

"Sir, for God's sake help us. We — yea, we only — are the Guelphs of Florence, vassals of the house of France! For God's sake have a care for thyself, for our city is ruled by Ghibellines!"

They also urged Charles to march southward by way of Pistoia. Pistoia was in White hands. This would cause further embroilment.

The Whites, less dramatically, humbly offered him their reverence as their liege lord and offered to serve him in any way he desired.

For the moment, however, he did not heed either.

Certainly he did not go by way of Pistoia, but neither did he enter Florence (with White instead of Black blessings), and it is not probable that he even saw its rooftops and its towers from a high hill.

Instead he made a wide circle, moving southward through the Val di Nievole, near Montecatini, and pausing only at Borgo a Buggiano to receive from the Lucchese a gift of gold and of the rich silken brocades for which Lucca was famous even then. On August 8, he was in San Miniato del Tedesco on the lower Arno, and on August 9 in San Gimignano. From there he proceeded to Siena, where he stayed twelve days.

But not even Siena — although it presented him with five hundred florins and although its *podestà* and its captain stood as godfathers to a newly born son — was his ultimate destination.

Other than himself — and so that he could serve himself — there was only one person he intended to serve and he went to him.

"In the said 1301 and in the month of September," said Villani, "there came to the city of Alagna [Anagni] in the Campagna, where was Pope Boniface, Charles, count of Valois, brother of the king of France, with many counts and barons and with five hundred French knights. This Monsieur Charles was received with honor by the pope and his cardinals, who forthwith made him count of the Romagna."

This was on September 2, and the next day, a Sunday — after the Valois prince had been feted and joyfully received (especially by Charles of Naples, his first wife's father, who gave him four falcons from the royal mews) — he was also proclaimed captain-general in all the territories of the Church, pacificator of Tuscany, marquis of Ancona, and duke of Spoleto.

By papal letter, this was immediately announced to the counts, noblemen, *podestà*'s, captains, and other rulers in the lands and cities affected.

Then, on September 5, Boniface convened a full consistory, and to it, in a speech which was half sermon and half political oratory, he gave his reasons.

"Charles is a Judas Maccabaeus," he began, and he added:

"He is like unto a lion with his thirty-one good qualities, of which I will tell you."

("This lion," muttered the Aragonese ambassador, "has eight vicious qualities, and these make him like unto the Devil.")

"He was a lion," the pope continued, "in the defense of France, and he is a lion cub as he hastens to the defense of the Church. For that reason we wish to honor him above all the other princes of the world. And when we summoned him it was our purpose to summon him in the matter of Sicily only. This was the reason we summoned him, and that he proceed to Sicily is still our intent. But since it is winter, at which time little progress can be made there, we also wish him to carry out that other matter about which we have written him: namely that he reestablish the kingdom of God in Tuscany and restore peace and good estate to our children there."

And note that he did not make him vicar.

"I did not make him vicar because if I did it might seem to substantiate those false Florentines who say that I wish to usurp rule over them and to seize their property."

This was, of course, a lie, the pope said, and the Florentines knew it.

"But why should they not lie? They are usurers who live at the expense of the Church and of the sharp trading which they practice all over the world."

That much for the city by the Arno, and in justification of any action he might decide to take.

Then the pope returned to Charles.

Charles had already been taken care of by the offices bestowed on him. But that was only the beginning.

"Many other things we plan to do for him, and we propose to make him even greater than his brother who is king of France. This I swear by God omnipotent. For we hold him to be *our* brother and *our* son, and he will soon see how much good will we bear him. Here and now, and as a beginning, we order a cash subsidy to be paid to him. Let that be put into writing."

It is recorded that almost at the moment he said this the heavens blazed in warning.

"In the said year of 1301," writes Villani, "and in the month of September, there appeared in the sky a comet with rays of smoke behind. It appeared in the evening toward sunset, and the learned astrologers saw in it grave prophecies of future dangers and damage to the province of Italy and to the city of Florence. They foresaw many revolutions."

But a comet was hardly needed. Ordinary common sense, nothing more than a keen ear and an alert mind, was enough to make it plain as a pikestaff — plain as one of the pikestaffs of the gonfalonier's civic guard — that what bullfighters call "the moment of truth" was now imminent.

For Judas — Iscariot, not Maccabaeus — now stood face to face with the high priest, and this boded no good to the White rulers of the merchant-burgher city.

What would these White rulers do about it?

How would the merchant-burghers deal with the obviously present danger?

What would be the outcome?

That will now be seen.

XIII

If I Go, Who Stays?

FOR even in the bemused city it did not take a very vivid imagination to see at hand the blue and crimson and the gold and lilies of broidered caparison, the tossing of plumed helmets, and the fluttering of silken pennons, nor to hear the jangle of bit and bridle, the whinnying of blooded destrier, and the oath-filled, colorful, expressive language of Paris — and of Tours and Champagne — which François Villon would use so effectively a century and a half later. Boniface was now an armed prophet. It did not take a very vivid imagination to understand against what place and against whom he would direct his arms.

Soon imagination was not needed. From Isola Farnese, a dozen or so miles to the north of Rome on the Via Cassia, Charles of Valois, on September 20 and 21, addressed a series of letters to San Gimignano, to Volterra, to Orvieto, and, it is believed, to Colle, to Arezzo, to Siena, to Lucca, to Prato, and to other Tuscan cities and towns. In these letters he haughtily directed the rectors or priors to send representatives to him at Castel della Pieve. There, on October 4, he would give them his directions and commands in the matter of reconciling the quarreling factions and putting down those who resisted the Church.

Monsieur Mouche — Musciatto Franzesi again — carried on from there. He too wrote a series of letters to the same cities and in these he emphasized a point which Charles obviously could not make openly and officially.

"When you send these emissaries, make sure that you choose men that are devoted — and that are noted for their devotion — to the Apostolic See."

Make sure, in other words, that they are popesmen — that they will do whatsoever he may happen to bid. No temporizers! No one uncommitted!

The message was understood. Only Perugia stood fast, sending Florence a hundred chosen horsemen under one Messer Venciolo di Guiconello. The other cities of the league fell into line. Especially the smaller cities. As ordered, they sent ambassadors to Charles.

It was understood in Florence too.

"There is a proverb," wrote Francesco Guicciardini in a later time of crisis, "that the wise are timid. That is because they know all the dangers and greatly fear them."

The Florentines considered themselves to be wise.

In the Palazzo della Signoria, therefore; in the Palazzo di Parte Guelfa with its grave merlature, lively trefoil windows, and covered stairway; in the Palazzo dell' Arte di Lana; amid the grain sacks of Orsanmichele; in the Old Market and the other markets; wherever a banker had his bench or benches and an artisan his shop, there were hasty and heart-searching revaluations.

How to save the threatened city? More important in many cases, how to save oneself?

« 2 »

But even in this wise, and therefore timid, city, there were a few who were both wise and fearless. Again one of these was Dante, now not merely "one of the lesser, but almost the chief" leader of those who fiercely and steadfastly opposed papal maneuvers because they knew that these would lead to papal domination, and that domination — by the pope or anyone else — would topple the enlightened (and prosperity-bringing) merchant democracy that had been building slowly and carefully for the last one hundred years.

With his words and in his actions, he stood firmly over and over again against the sleepwalking, the lethargy, and the optimism of his fellow Whites — against those who deluded themselves into believing that the best course, in this fateful September and October, was to do little or nothing, and hope for the best.

It is regrettable, therefore — once again it is regrettable — that there is no detailed and day-by-day account of his doings and his urgings at this time. It is regrettable that a man like Dino Compagni did not analyze him as he did Dino Pecora and Corso Donati. It is regrettable that he did not describe Dante's actions with the same careful minuteness that he portrayed those of his own futile self.

But fortunately we at least do have the minutes of three meetings in which Dante took part, and if we examine these thoughtfully and with imagination we may be able to reconstruct at least a partial convincing story.

Once again let us do so.

September 13.

"The thirteenth of September. In the Council of One Hundred, the General and Special Councils of the Captain, the General Council of the Commonwealth and of the Capitudini of the Twenty-one Guilds and of the Savi, convened in the palace of the *podestà*, and in the presence of the *podestà* and the captain, the priors and the gonfalonier, the lord *podestà* proposed that measures be taken to preserve the Ordinances of Justice and the laws of the people.

"Dante urged [here there are three lines of blank space].

"Messer Guidotto Corbizzi urged that whatever powers were needed be left in the hands of the *podestà*, the captain, the priors, and the gonfalonier with such counsel as they might wish to have."

September 20.

"The twentieth day of September. In the Council of One Hundred, the General and Special Councils of the Captain and of the Twenty-one Guilds, the lord captain proposed, the priors and the gonfalonier being present, that it being deemed fitting by the said council that permission be given to the ambassadors of the commonwealth and people of Bologna that on the behalf of the said people and commonwealth they, or someone else they designate, can and are authorized to ship, carry, or have carried through the city and the territory of Florence to the city of Bologna wheat and oats which the said people have had shipped, or are having shipped, by sea to the city of Pisa, subject however to such regulations and rules as may be deemed necessary by the priors, the gonfalonier, and the wheatmasters after they have heard the said ambassadors.

"Present as witnesses were Messer Gentile de' Gualteroni, judge and assessor of the said lord captain, and Lapo Lotteringhi, crier of the said lord captain and of the people of Florence, as well as others.

"Messer Lapo Salterelli, judge, urged that the said permission be granted to the people and commonwealth of Bologna.

"Dante Alighieri urged the same.

"A sitting and standing vote having been taken, it pleased almost all to follow the advice of the said *savi*."

September 28.

"The twenty-eighth day of September. In the Council of One Hundred, the priors and the gonfalonier being present, the lord captain proposed as follows:

"(1) That twenty-five *libbre* of the one hundred *libbre* appropriated for the expenses of the priors and the gonfalonier during the month of September be now paid out.

"(2) Likewise, that sixty-three *libbre* be appropriated to purchase a missal for the chapel of the priors, and that the said money be paid to Bene, priest, rector of the church of San Ruffolo.

"(3) Likewise, that the officials appointed by the priors and gonfalonier are hereby confirmed, and that authority be given to the present priors and gonfalonier to appoint whatsoever officials they see fit and at whatever salary seems good to them.

"(4) Likewise, that the present lord *podestà* be given jurisdiction from the middle of this month of September until the middle of December over all false accusations, false denunciations, and false charges; and that the said lord *podestà* also be given jurisdiction up to the said middle of December over all woundings and assaults, and likewise to the said middle of December over any other crimes committed with any kind of arms if they result in the shedding of blood.

"(5) Likewise, that the accounting to be made by the captain, the priors, and the gonfalonier for the acts in August past or in September be deferred until October.

"(6) Likewise, that Neri degli Gherardini be pardoned.

"(7) Likewise, that one hundred *libbre* be paid to Ser Rustichello di Bernardo, to whom were farmed the wine duties, this because of the payments he made ahead of time and because certain wines paid for by the Pisans were taken back; and that of this sum, as approved by the priors and the gonfalonier, sixteen *libbre* be paid without any conditions.

"(8) Likewise, that the one hundred constables employed by the lords priors and by the gonfalonier should be paid their salary for the six months beginning at the calends of October, and at the customary rate, and that thereafter payment be made every three months.

"Messer Albizzo Corbinelli spoke in favor of the above propositions.

"Dante Alighieri did the same.

"A vote being taken on the first propositions, there were seventy-nine ayes and one nay.

"On the second proposition, all eighty voted aye.

"On the third proposition, there were seventy-eight ayes and two nays.

"On the fourth proposition, there were seventy-nine ayes and one nay.

"On the fifth proposition, all eighty voted aye.

"On the sixth proposition, there were seventy-three ayes and seven nays.

"On the seventh proposition, there were seventy-one ayes and nine nays.

"On the eighth proposition, there were seventy-eight ayes and two nays.

"Present as witnesses were Gentile de' Gualteroni, judge and assessor of the said lord captain and the people, and also others."

These documents, it should be noted, are the last ones (at any rate, the last ones which survive) to record officially Dante's participation in Florentine government. What do they mean?

(1) The September 13 meeting, which was convened to discuss ways of preserving the Ordinances of Justice and the laws of the city – in other words to discuss ways of preserving the merchant-burgher state – was attended not merely by members of the Council of One Hundred and by the greater guildsmen. To the judges and notaries, the wool importers, the weavers and sellers of domestic woolens, the bankers and money changers, the silk merchants, the physicians and apothecaries, the skinners and furriers; and also to the onetime middle guildsmen – the butchers, the blacksmiths, the shoemakers, the master woodworkers and stoneworkers, the retail-cloth dealers and linen merchants; were added the wine merchants, the innkeepers, the tanners, the oil vendors and general provisioners, the saddlers, the locksmiths, the armorers and sword-makers, the carpenters, and the bakers. In other words, an attempt seems to have been made to make participation city-wide.

(2) Although the position taken by Dante at this September 13 meeting is not set down, there is ample space for it. It may have been the notary's intention to set it down later. It should also be noted that at this meeting no vote was recorded. An oversight? Or was there a reason for this too?

(3) The meeting at which Bologna was given permission to transship grain through Florentine territory was planned before Charles of Valois had reached Isola Farnese, and called to order before even the first of his letters – or tidings of the same – could have reached Florence. It therefore looked forward rather than backward.

(4) Although the first two items on the agenda of the September 28 meeting dealt with purely routine matters, at least four of the others (three, four, five, and eight) had a direct connection with newly threatening dangers, while item six may have had an indirect connection.

Perhaps, since this is a biography of Dante, two other things should also be pointed out. In all three of the meetings, he was one of two men recorded as speaking. He and Guidotto Corbizzi in the first meeting. He and Lapo Salterelli in the second meeting. He and Albizzo Corbinelli in the third meeting. In each case where the result is noted, Dante's views prevailed.

What conclusions can we come to from all this — both as they affected the city and as they affected Dante Alighieri?

To me the answer seems easy and hardly arguable. In part, it has been given already.

In the first place, from the moment that Charles stood before the pope at Anagni — and probably from the moment he crossed the Alps into Italy — there was an influential, if small, group in Florence who saw plainly that the presence of the French prince had converted a theoretical menace into a clear and present danger, and who also saw plainly that steps must be taken immediately to deal with it.

In the second place, for the moment at least they were able to persuade the city to take these steps. In the September 13 meeting (of *all* the guildsmen, be it remembered), they were able to offer — and probably to carry — a motion to give the priors full power to deal with internal disorders. In the September 20 meeting, they offered and carried a resolution which was designed to win the friendship of a strong potential ally. In the September 28 meeting, they were able to go even further. Item three (carried 78 to 2) gave the priors and the gonfalonier power to surround themselves with trusted assistants. Item four (carried 79 to 1) bestowed on the *podestà* almost dictorial powers. Item five (carried unanimously) provided that the captain, the priors, and the gonfalonier could postpone until a later month an accounting of their acts. This left them free to focus their attention on present problems. Item eight (carried 78 to 2) saw to it that the priors and the gonfalonier (on whom they counted) should have — most important in these times of agitation — a well-paid, and therefore loyal, guard.

In the third place, Dante was the most vocal — and probably the most effective — of these men. (He was the only one who spoke at *all three* meetings.) He was the most obdurate. He was the most resolute. He was the most inexorably opposed of all in Florence to what today we call appeasement. He was the one who saw the most clearly that if his city was to weather the buffetings that now threatened it, it must, to paraphrase what he would say later in his *Commedia*, stand firmly against the blasts of the tempest and not bend and waver like a reed.

This third conclusion is, of course, only an opinion and a guess — as are also, but to a very much lesser degree, my first two — but it is an opinion which is supported by every recorded position which Dante ever took, and by what at least one thoughtful Dante scholar believes must have been the essence of the position which he took at the September 13 meeting, a position which is not recorded, this being the time when a blank space was left in the minutes.

Nicola Zingarelli goes back to Leonardo Bruni to find a basis for his belief. At an earlier time, he quotes Leonardo as reporting, when the city faced riots and disorders, Dante boldly confronted the city fathers and bluntly demanded that they arm all citizens. He would meet civil disorder with civic resistance. In this later crisis, thinks Zingarelli, Dante did exactly the same. He urged meeting force with force. But since in this case meeting force with force involved military action, the exact proposals had to be "top secret." They were not recorded because this would have given aid and comfort to the enemy. There is only one flaw in the argument. In those days few minutes were that specific. Doubtless, as was his habit, Dante spoke strongly, but possibly the lacuna was merely because of a lazy or an inattentive scribe.

Reverting back to the September 28 meeting, Dante spoke on one other matter which may have had political implications (since the father of the man it involved was a strong White), but in which the position he took was based more probably on a sense of justice than on the desire to do a favor for an opponent of the pope.

In 1298, when Cante Gabrielli (of whom we will heard more later) was *podestà* for the first time, Neri di Diodati Gherardini had been condemned to death for a murder which he allegedly committed in connection with an armed robbery. He fled the city. But now (in 1301) not only was his innocence established, but the brothers of the slain man officially declared and swore to this. All of Florence demanded his pardon and the restoration of his civic rights, and Dante (when he spoke for item six) was one of those who led in the successful effort to bring this about. But the original condemnation was the work of the Donateschi who hated Neri, and so in their account books one more black mark was put against the Dante name. Dante may well also have made an enemy of Cante Gabrielli — for no magistrate likes to have his decisions reversed — and Cante would one day be in a position to do him harm.

« 3 »

But it would not, very clearly, be enough to restrain internal disorders or to place Florence in a posture of defense. Given the nature and the quality of citizen armies (in those days and in other days), given the near certainty that there would be mass defection from the White cause if and when it should appear to be the losing one, it was apparent not merely to the wise but even to the foolish that if Charles should continue to want the city he could have it — especially since his swashbuckling Gallic champions were now supported by the Lucchese, who joined him saying "that they came to do honor to the prince" but actually scenting booty; by the Perugians "with two hundred horsemen" (they had already sent one hundred to Florence, but there was no harm in playing both sides of the street); by Cante of Gubbio (Cante Gabrielli — see above) "with many Sienese"; and by such doughty captains as Malatestino da Verrucchio, the "young mastiff" of *Inferno* XXVII, and Maghinardo da Susinana, whose divided loyalties have already been noted.

No, Charles himself must be stopped. He must be persuaded or directed to call a halt to his advance. But how?

By bearding the pope in his den was the final consensus. By confronting Boniface and convincing him that even for his own purposes discretion was the better part of valor. And, the Florentines soon convinced themselves, it really was. For what, basically, did the pontiff want from their city? Her moneybags, it seemed highly probable, and what the contents of these moneybags would buy! Unlimited use of Florentine cash and credit! But what would happen to these moneybags if Florence were plunged into disorder and destruction? The pope's friends would, of course, survive, but these could not alone supply his needs — not even with unimpaired resources, and their resources would be impaired too. The Spini could not, rich and powerful as they were. Nor could the Bardi, whose tentacles extended from England to Asia Minor. The White Mozzi would be needed as well. And the Frescobaldi. And the Cerchi.

But how could they make Boniface understand this fact, which to them was so patent?

The answer was obvious.

Send an embassy to him. Choose its members carefully. Let them be strong men, but let them also be experienced and skillful. Let them present the White point of view to his holiness and then let them convince him that this point of view could prudently — for reasons of business and money — be the papal point of view, for if the pope granted them only enough freedom so that their affairs — and therefore his affairs — could prosper, in all other matters they would be devoted and loyal.

It was so voted. The exact date is not known, but certainly it was late in September or early in October. Then the ambassadors were selected.

Il Corazza of Signa. (Il Corazza — Master Breastplate — it should be noted, was a nickname. His real name was Guido Ubaldini degli Aldobrandeschi.)

Maso di Ruggierino Minerbetti.

And Dante Alighieri.

In many ways, if not in every way, all three were somewhat surprising choices.

I will give the reason.

Il Corazza, to take the first of them, held the office of gonfalonier of justice from April 15 to June 15, 1300, and it was precisely at this time that three papal favorites were condemned and sentenced. A man of country descent, he was also very closely identified with the *parte selvaggia* (which grew into the Whites) of Vieri degli Cerchi. But he had an advantage which offset all this. He was not a faction man. He was a Guelph — not a White Guelph or a Black Guelph — through and through. Indeed, he was "so deeply imbued with Guelph principles that all other Guelphs seemed lukewarm to him."

This was important.

"The Whites are not Guelphs. They are Ghibellines," cried the Blacks to Pope Boniface and his advisers over and over.

Il Corazza's presence on the embassy would make this statement seem ridiculous.

Minerbetti seemed an inappropriate choice too, but on quite different grounds. Far from being a devoted White, he was not even a member of the *popolo*. "A false [i.e., a pretended] populan," Dino Compagni calls him. Moreover, he was, or had been, a papal servant. When, for instance, a few years earlier than this, Fra Grimaldo of Prato had instigated proceedings in Florence against the kind of Patarine heresy which was associated in Boniface's mind, as in all papal minds, with hostility to papal politics, Minerbetti was the pope's coadjutor. Among the Whites, he was widely regarded as "untrustworthy."

But he, too, had an offsetting virtue. Just as Il Corazza would demonstrate that resistance to the pope was not necessarily Ghibelline, Minerbetti would show that it did not even have to be White. His presence would show that even a papal friend might wish the pope to keep his distance. He would give the embassy an "all shades of opinion" character which would add to its effectiveness. That alone made the risk worth taking — that and the Florentine taste for being devious.

But the naming of Dante to the mission was by far the most extraordinary of all. Indeed, it was so extraordinary that it has led a small but respectable group of scholars to doubt not merely Dante's presence in the group but the very fact of the embassy itself.

This is the gist of their argument.

Dante was more than ordinarily *persona non grata* to the pope, having steadfastly and continuously opposed all papal moves. He had voted to sustain the sentences against the three popesmen. (This could have been more serious than sentencing them in the first place.) He had once, and possibly twice, helped to prevent the election of a compliant priorate. He had (twice on the same day) voted against continuing military assistance to the pope. He had been put in charge of road building, which would — supposedly — make papal aggression more difficult. He had voted for more than one measure directed at putting down subversive activities by papal supporters. And he had voted to pardon an enemy of papal friends.

But by time-honored diplomatic custom, a *persona non grata* is not appointed an ambassador.

They also argue that since a Dante embassy was not mentioned by Villani nor recorded in the Florentine archives, there could not have been one.

I cannot go along with them, however. There is too much evidence to the contrary.

Here is some of it.

Discussing a line in *Purgatorio* XXXII — "because her [the Church's] lustful and her roving eye she turned on me" — the author of the *Ottimo Commento* said: "And of this the author had experience in the time of Pope Boniface VIII when he went there as an ambassador from his commonwealth."

An anonymous commentator on Dante's poem *Tre donne intorno al cor* spoke of him as "ambassador to the high pontiff in Rome in an attempt to restore civil concord."

Boccaccio said that he went to Rome.

Leonard Bruni said he went to Rome.

And Dino Compagni specifically described him as that "Dante Alighieri who was ambassador" to the pope.

Indeed, even the topical, but usually accurate, rhymester Antonio Pucci has a word about the alleged embassy in his *rifacimento* (verse rewriting) of the Villani chronicle.

> He went to Rome, and there the pope, 't is said,
> Would keep him in his service.

In due course, we will see just what construction we should put on these lines, and why, to continue with Pucci's verses, it was "idle chatter" to say that he wanted to accept. For the moment, however, the important thing is that Antonio — like the others — put Dante at the papal court.

But if Dante was named one of the ambassadors — and almost certainly he was — there may well have been some controversy about his choice, and this throws a new light upon a famous Boccaccio anecdote.

"The party that was out of power," wrote Giovanni, "through Pope Boniface VIII had summoned to direct the affairs of our city a brother or a relative of Philip, then king of France, whose name was Charles." At this, all of the chiefs of the party to which he, Dante, belonged met in council to deal with the matter, and in this meeting, among other things, they decided that an embassy should be sent to the pope, who was then in Rome, to persuade the said pope to oppose the coming of the said Charles, or to make him come only in agreement with the party which was then ruling. And when they came to decide who should head this mission, it was agreed by all that it should be Dante himself. Dante pondered about this for a while. Then he said: "If I go, who stays? If I stay, who goes?" just as if he alone of them all were of any worth, and as if through him alone the others were of any account.

"He set great store upon himself," said Boccaccio, almost as if his own innate modesty, which contrasted so strongly both with Dante's haughty pride and with Petrarch's vanity and self-esteem, were offended.

I have another theory, however.

As the pros and cons of sending him were debated, Dante listened attentively; and as he did, it began to dawn on him that he was the only one who was resolute enough, and steadfast enough, and uncowed enough to face the determined pontiff. At this point, he *insisted* on going, using the so-often-quoted words.

From the point of view of the embassy, he was right in insisting. If it were to have even the slightest chance of success, he must be part of it.

But what he neglected to remember was that while he was absent from Florence that city would not have the benefit of his firm and clear-seeing leadership. He could not be two persons in two places. We will have to proceed a little further before we can decide whether the choice he made was the correct one—whether he was the right person in the right place.

« 4 »

He would not, however, be either the right person in the right place or the wrong person in the wrong one without certain difficulties and delays which would have important consequences. For even as they decided to send an embassy to Rome, the Florentine signory came to the conclusion that they would not be able to sway Pope Boniface without allies and assistance, and to get this they turned to the city to which only a little earlier they had done—at the urging of Dante and others—an important favor.

They wasted little or no time in doing so. Hardly had the ink dried which recorded the vote to grant permission to transship *granum et bladum* through Florentine territory when the Bolognese *ambaxtiatores* (agents or commissioners rather than ambassadors) set about complying with the necessary formalities. Then at Porto Pisano near the Arno mouth the precious cargo was loaded onto huge and creaking wains. Convoys of these, drawn by white or silver-gray oxen who tugged and strained to move the heavy loads, followed the winding river until they came to the gates of Florence. At Florence they turned sharply to the left and, to the creaking of leathern bullwhips and the strident shouting of the drivers, began the laborious climb forward to the Futa Pass, from which they would jolt downward to an eager reception at Bologna.

They were followed — or perhaps even preceded — by Florentine emissaries. These, as soon as they arrived, were to wait on the Bolognese, and their instructions what to do then were explicit.

"Bluntly ask the Bolognese to stand at the side of Florence in the matter of Pope Boniface and Charles of Valois. Point out that it is to their advantage to do so, for if the pope, through Charles, should subdue Florence, their own city would be the next he would covet, nor would the fact that it is Guelph turn him aside. Florence is a Guelph city too. Point out that they are able to do so. They still bask in the light of papal favor. Florence does not. Or at any rate the White Florentines do not, for they have shown him not merely once but more than once that they resent and will oppose papal intrusions. Also, if only parenthetically, remind them of the grain which is now being unloaded in the markets. Remind them that this grain came through Florentine territory with the permission of the Florentine White government. Any other way would take longer and be far more costly. Remind them that the Florentine White government could either grant or withhold permission if it were again requested. Then ask them to send an embassy to Rome when we send one. Let this embassy plead for us. The pope will listen to them."

Evidently these words — or the newly swollen Bolognese warehouses — were convincing.

In the seventeenth century, the Bolognese scholar Pasquale Alidosi discovered the following document in the Bolognese archives:

"Alberto Ughetti, *doctor*, Pace Pasi [Pace de' Paci], *doctor*, Ubaldino Malavolti, *doctor*, Iacapo Ignano, *doctor*, and Pietro Mangoni, *notary*, were sent as ambassadors to the pope and to Charles, son of the king of France, at the request of the commonwealth of Florence."

Doctor, it should be noted, signified *doctor of laws*. The city of the Middle Ages' most highly reputed schools of jurisprudence sent four lawyers and a notary. Florence sent two tradesmen (one self-made, the other of an old family) and a poet!

Signor Alidosi headed his abtract as follows:

"1301. Embassy to the pope to deal with matters useful and necessary to the commonwealth. In the first days October *circa* October 1."

The commonwealth of Bologna! Nothing is said of the Florentines!

Yet the first paragraph is not necessarily contradicted by the second one. Obviously Bologna was urged by Florence, and obviously, too, it was influenced by this urging. But since the city on the Reno was governed democratically — and had to convince public opinion and the

powers that appropriate before it acted — the record had to show that
what it did was in its own interest. The point is that it did act, and
promptly. It was one of the few instances in the whole White-Black
story — on either side, it can also be stated — where there was neither
long debate nor undue delay.

« 5 »

It is one thing, however, for duly constituted authority to set up a
diplomatic mission and another for this mission to function properly and
effectively, nor was the Bolognese embassy to Pope Boniface an exception. Despite the Alidosi document, it seems more than probable that the
Florentine mission did not reach Bologna much before October 10, and
that it was not until October 11 that the Bolognese council met and
complied with its request. Given the fact that at least a few days were
needed to make necessary preparations, it could not have been until
October 14 or 15 that the five men with their retainers set out. And that
was only the beginning. To be sure, the bits and bridles of their mounts
slapped and jingled as they moved southward, reversing the route taken
by the grain convoys. To be sure, the brown towers of "Bononia" faded
into the distance. But a number of very pressing problems would have to
be solved before they would be figuratively, as well as literally, on the
road.

Of these, the one that was both the most difficult and the most pressing
derived from the personal interest of one of the ambassadors.

Ubaldino Malavolti, *doctor* and other things as well, had a long record
of public service and is reliably said to have been "a very able sort of
legalist who had served his country well as a negotiator and especially as
an ambassador." Despite Dino Compagni's calling him "pernicious" and
"a man of cavils," this is probably an accurate description. But if he was
able and devoted, he was not so devoted as to put every thought of his
own affairs out of his mind.

Nor did he, in particular, put out of his mind the castle of Tirli near
Firenzuola and not more than four or five miles from the road which he
traversed with his colleagues. Tirli had once belonged to the Malavolti,
but they had lost it to Florence during one of the latter's drives against a
stronghold which threatened their trade routes. As recently as 1298 they
had unsuccessfully tried to win it back "with a mighty array of horsemen
and with brigandry and murders and burnings."

But now diplomatic pressure — strong diplomatic pressure — might
succeed where arms had failed.

It was worth trying.

He and his fellow ambassadors entered Florence through the Porta

Rossa and wound their way through narrow streets to the Piazza and the Palazzo della Signoria.

There the priors awaited them.

But before the latter could do much more than formally welcome them, Malavolti requested a private meeting.

At this, he stated his position, which briefly was as follows:

I and my fellows had been directed to journey to Rome and there in company with Florentine ambassadors to press Florentine interests before Pope Boniface. It was our intention to do so. But we could not and we would not do this if unsettled issues were left behind. And there was such an issue — an important issue. The castle of Tirli and the land about it had long belonged to the Malavolti, but it had been seized by Florence. Unlawfully, and against the interests of peaceful relations between Florence and Bologna. Let it be restored to them. That was justice and it was also necessary. Then the mission could proceed upon its business. But until —

The conclusion did not have to be spoken.

It is not difficult to see that the Florentines could hardly take this in good part, for it asked them to abandon one of the most basic tenets of their foreign and defense policies. But they had no choice. Malavolti, supported by his colleagues, held the whip hand. No restoration of the castle, no embassy. It was as simple as that.

They finally yielded, therefore, but not without acrimonious discussion which almost certainly took several days. The exact date is not known, but it was certainly very late in October when the three Florentines and the five Bolognese left Florence on the last stage of their journey.

But they left too late. Thanks to Malavolti, they did not set out until the pope and his Black allies had crossed the Rubicon. Boniface, who had gone from Anagni to the Lateran, returned to Anagni on October 17. (In his own palace he could more easily remain inaccessible for as long as it fitted his plans.) Almost at the same moment, *"Il Valos"* — the Valois prince — ordered the trumpets to be sounded which bade his followers mount horse and move in cavalcade toward the place the pope had given him.

He was a prince, and he had made his decision. It is not easy to persuade a prince, even a vacillating prince, to change his mind.

« 6 »

Ironically enough the two parties — Charles of Valois with his knightly band and the ambassadors with their more modest entourage — almost certainly met upon the way.

But where?

At Orvieto?

But the ambassadors would hardly have visited this papal city unless the pope himself held court there.

At Ghino di Tacco's Radicofani?

The Valois would not have had to fear Ghino. The ambassadors might have.

At Buonconvento, near the bloody Arbia?

At San Gimignano with its golden wallflowers? ("*I fiori di Santa Fina,*" these were called, after the little city's not-long-dead girl saint.)

At Monteriggioni with its twelve severe undecorated towers?

Dante himself certainly passed in sight of Monteriggioni more than once. He describes it in *Inferno* XXXI.

> For just as on the circle of its walls
> Monteriggioni with towers crowns itself,
> So on the bank which did surround the pit,
> Towered, though showing only half their stature,
> The horrible giants.

At Staggia — at Musciatto Franzesi's Staggia near Colle?

Or, finally, at Siena of the *Galli Senones* (Gauls from the Seine), whose Gallic turbulence seems to have been passed on to their descendants, but who thought of themselves as Roman and used the wolf for a symbol of their city?

I personally believe it was this last place.

There are two reasons for my thinking this. First, it is almost impossible to journey from Florence to Rome or from Rome to Florence without passing through Siena. Second, there is no evidence that Charles stayed for any length of time at any place but Siena until he was actually on his final move toward the Arno. Then he may, but briefly, have paused at Staggia.

It was at Siena, incidentally — but probably after Dante and the others had continued on their journey and probably because they *had* continued and the Valois prince wished to counteract any impression that they might make — that the first skirmishes of the incipient campaign were fought. For reasons which should be entirely obvious, once more, they were still fought with words.

Our authority is Dino Compagni, who also tells us that it was the Black Guelphs rather than the pope who induced Charles to move and that they did this by arranging for "a deposite of seventy thousand florins to be made for his pay and that of his knights."

Dino continues:

"They also brought him to Siena. And when he was in Siena, he sent as his ambassadors Messer Guglielmo [Monsieur Guillaume de la Perche], a Frenchman, his chancellor, who was a dishonorable and bad man although in appearance he was a good man; and a Provençal knight who was the opposite. These brought letters from their lord."

And what did these letters say?

Even as badly translated by "an advocate from Volterra, a deceitful and incompetent man, who acted as their interpreter and who talked in a very confused fashion," they said this:

First, "that the blood royal of France had come into Tuscany solely to bring peace to the party of the Holy Church [the Guelph party, but not necessarily the White Guelphs], and out of the great love which it bore to the city and the said party."

Second, "that the pope had sent him as a lord who might be trusted since the blood of the house of France had never betrayed either friend or foe."

(Except, of course, when it was to their advantage to do so.)

Third and last, "that it should please the Florentines that he should come to Florence to fulfill his office."

Words like these had been spoken and written many times before. They had been spoken by the pope himself and most recently they had been spoken by Cardinal Matteo d'Acquasparta. But never had they been spoken from so strong and proximate a position by one who had so clearly the means to enforce them. Viewed in that light, they were not a proposal but an ultimatum.

« 7 »

This, however, the Florentines did not seem to understand — or, at any rate, the new priorate did not. In view of the deepening crisis, these men had been elected a week ahead of time (October 7), but they did not take office until the legal October 15. On that date they moved from the church of Santa Croce, where they had assembled informally, to the Palazzo della Signoria, where they "frittered away the early days of opportunity," for, said one of them, "we negotiated when we should have sharpened our weapons."

The reason:

"They were good men and above suspicion. And since they were conciliatory and free, and were willing to have the offices divided" — that is to share them between Blacks and Whites — "the smaller traders placed great hope in them as did the White party."

Cried the latter:

"There will be peace."

Peace in our time!

"It is not for us to wear ourselves out" — and compromise "business as usual" — "in preparations. There is no need to disturb ourselves any longer."

"But their adversaries," says Dino Compagni ruefully with the wisdom that comes after the event, "knew that they were weak and peace-loving and thought that they could deceive them."

Dino was one of the priors. He knew whereof he spoke.

Deceive them the Blacks certainly did. And by the most transparent of ruses.

Hats respectfully in hand, they came by prearrangement "fours and sixes at a time as it might occur to them" to the priors in their official palace, and there proffered them honeyed words.

"Sirs," they said, "you are good and upright men, and our city stands in great need of such. You see also that discord reigns among the citizens. It is your duty to end this and to pacify the city. Otherwise it will perish. You only have the power which is needed to do this. So that you can do it we offer you our goods and our persons with honorable and loyal mind."

Dino replied for his colleagues.

"Dear and faithful citizens, we willingly receive your offers, and we will avail ourselves of them and of your counsel."

He and the priors did.

(Later, he would hint that they were obliged to take this course by public feeling, and that he and the other priors "doubted of such offers, believing that they" — i.e., the Blacks — "were covering up their wickedness with false speaking." But that seems to have been an afterthought.)

They sent to the captains of the Guelph party, Messer Manetto Scali and Messer Neri de' Giandonati.

"Honorable captains," they instructed them, "forsake and abandon everything else, and concern yourself solely with making peace with the party of the Church. We place all of the powers of our office at your disposal and we will assist you in any way you ask."

They ordered the city gates to be left open.

They *durst* not close the gates, they would say later. But that was another afterthought.

They banned all provocative actions. Not only were their swords not sharpened, they were not even permitted to be displayed.

They continued their futile audiences with those who planned to overthrow them.

"They could not imagine that anything could ensue but concord, and that for several reasons."

One was that both factions were Guelph, and too long a quarrel — thought the Whites who had played with the idea themselves — might lead to Ghibelline restoration. The other was that "the mutual injuries done by the two parties had not yet reached such a point" that harmony could not be restored by a little generosity — on the part of the Whites — in the matter of political patronage and political plums.

It was before this priorate in the above-narrated frame of mind that Monsieur Guillaume de la Perche appeared with his two colleagues. They bore the letters which have earlier been referred to. These they presented to the signory, and then "with great reverence" they begged permission to present them also to the "great council" of the *podestà*.

When they did, pandemonium — it was carefully planned pandemonium, for the Blacks knew what they were doing — ensued. It was occasioned by what seemed to be almost a mass movement to come to the aid of the apparent victor.

"Many members arose to their feet aflame to speak and magnify Monsieur Charles, and hastened to the tribune, each trying to be first."

Fearing a stampede, the priors would not permit this.

"Yet so many were the speakers that the ambassadors saw that the party which desired Monsieur Charles was greater and bolder than that which did not desire him, and they wrote their lord saying that they had perceived that the party of the Donati had risen very high, while that of the Cerchi had fallen very low."

The priors saw it too.

Yet still hoping against hope, they told Charles's ambassadors that they would reply to the prince with an embassy of their own, but that before they did so they would have to consult another Florentine council, for in a matter of such grave importance they could do nothing without citizen approval.

They then summoned the General Council of the whole Guelph party, and to it also invited the consuls of all of the seventy-two trades which made up the twenty-one guilds. Each one was enjoined to reply in writing whether or not it would be pleasing to the man he represented that Monsieur Charles of Valois should be permitted to come to Florence as a peacemaker.

"All replied by voice and in writing that he should be allowed to come and should be received as a prince of noble blood."

All except the bakers!

"He should be neither received nor honored," their consul said, "for he is coming to destroy the city."

But the bakers, in many ways proletarians before the word was invented, were always recalcitrant.

This settled the matter.

It was no longer a question of keeping Charles from the city, but of how to admit him with the least harm to Florence.

Accordingly ambassadors were named, and Donato di Alberto Ristori — "O thou Dino Alberti who made the life of thy fellow citizens a grief and burden to them!" wrote Dino Compagni later — was commissioned with the assistance of several other lawyers to draft their instructions.

In substance, these directed the ambassadors to tell Monsieur Charles that he might freely come to the city, provided only that he give them letters sealed with his seal in which he stated that he would neither assume any jurisdiction over the Florentines, nor usurp any of the city's rights — whether because the throne of the empire was presently vacant or for any other reason — nor attempt to change the city's laws.

They were also directed to ask Monsieur de la Perche to beg his master not to come to the city on All Saints' Day. For "the common people celebrated the new vintage that day with feasting, and many outbreaks might occur, which by means of the wickedness of bad citizens might disturb the city."

These letters were all important to the priors. It was to obtain them that the mission was sent.

The ambassadors were instructed, therefore, that if they did not obtain them "they should cease to put any trust in Monsieur Charles and should bar his passage at Poggibonsi, the approaches of which they had ordered to be strengthened. And Messer Bernardino de' Rossi, who was vicar there, was ordered to refuse him provisions."

But what was a letter — what were a dozen letters — to the French prince?

He caused one to be written and sent to the priors.

"I, Dino, saw this letter, and ordered it to be copied, and kept it until the prince's coming, and when he came, I asked him if it was written at his command.

" *'Oui, certainement!'* he answered."

Dino — such was his nature — believed him.

Then Charles moved a step nearer — to Staggia. There he was met by Black leaders with seventeen thousand more florins and a plea to abandon his excessive caution and proceed with haste.

"Sire," they told him, "the enemy are vanquished, and they only ask thee to delay for some evil purpose. They are making a conspiracy."

"But they were making no conspiracy," says Dino.

Far from it, they — and Dino in particular — were making one last effort in behalf of harmony.

"Imagining that 'this prince will come and will find all the citizens divided, from which great mischief will ensue,' I thought that by reason of the office which I held and of the goodwill I perceived among my colleagues I might bring together many prominent citizens in the church of San Giovanni, which I did.

"The whole official class" — i.e., the officers of the commonwealth, of the Guelph party, and of the guilds — "were present, and when it appeared to me fitting, I addressed them as follows:

" 'Dear and worthy citizens, who in common have all received holy baptism in this font, reason compels and urges you to love one another as brothers, all the more so since you possess the noblest city in the whole world. But some ill will has come about between you because of rivalry for the offices of state, even though you know that I have promised you under oath to let both parties share them. And now this prince is coming to whom it is our duty to do honor. Put away bad feeling then, and make peace amongst yourself so that he will find you one body. Cast aside all offenses and the wicked desires that up to now have been nourished in your hearts. Let them be pardoned and dismissed from your minds. Do this for the love and the well-being of your city, and in this hallowed place swear good and perfect peace.' "

The approval was almost unanimous.

With these words, Dino continued, "all agreed" and, "touching the Book with their hands," all swore not only to do this but "to maintain the rights and jurisdictions of the city."

Some swore sincerely, but there were others — "wicked citizens" and, of course, Blacks — who "ostentatiously shed great tears" and made "a great show of fervor," but who forswore themselves as soon as the occasion offered and were "chiefest in the destruction of the city."

"For decency sake, I will not tell their names," says Dino. But he did name one — "Rosso della Strozza, a man fierce in aspect and deeds," who not long afterwards "paid the penalty" for his false swearing.

He did not have to name the others. Their names would soon be public property.

For on November 1 — on, that is, the very day on which he had been implored not to enter the city — Charles of Valois, with a following which had now grown to two thousand, rode through the Porta Romana and was in Florence.

He did not cross the Arno, however.

The prince alighted instead at the house of Frescobaldi, which stood just south of the Ponte Santa Trinità and not far from the present Via Maggio.

"He had been entreated to alight where the noble King Charles [Charles of Anjou] and all the other great lords had alighted because there was plenty of room there and it was secure."

In other words, at the convent of Santa Maria Novella.

"But those who were escorting him" — his captains and his other advisers — "would not allow this. They had already made arrangements to occupy a strong position in the Oltrarno section."

They knew that if they could not hold the rest of the city, here at least they could regroup their forces. They were not interested in street fighting — and as a matter of fact were interested in even the Blacks only as far as they could use them. Their purpose was to take and keep.

« 9 »

It was almost at this exact moment — and certainly not more than a few days earlier — that the seven pleaders for the Florentine cause looked down from Monte Maria (in those days it was called Montemalo, or Evil Mountain) upon the golden, undulent Campagna through which, in sinuous curves, moved the Tiber with its tributaries, the Aniene and the Allia, and beyond it the graying Aurelian walls, the battlemented watch-towers, the Byzantine and Romanesque churches, the ruined aqueducts, the fortress-palaces of *caput mundi*.

They may have paused there for a moment, for Rome is always breathtaking. But then their palfreys and jennets, their riders' feet bracing occasionally against the steepness of the slope, began the slow way downward.

They came to the river, crossing it not at the famous Ponte Milvius, which was then in ruins, but at another bridge a little farther south.

But when they reached the Lateran, they were told what we have been told already.

The pope had retired to Anagni.

This created a new problem. Even as the crow flies, Anagni was another fifty or sixty miles farther, but you could not go as the crow flies, for the road twisted as it climbed through hills and mountains. And would Boniface receive them when they got there?

But they had been instructed to confront him, and confront him they would — at any rate, if it were in any way possible!

They proceeded, therefore, to the papal stronghold; stood before the plain, undecorated, unimpressive papal "palace"; requested an audience; and were told that they would be given one.

But not together — the Bolognese and the Florentines must come separately.

The Bolognese Boniface received first, and easily persuaded them that they would help rather than hurt their city if they made common cause with the Florentines.

Then he sent for the latter.

"He received them alone in his chamber," Compagni says.

And when they stood before him, he harangued them in the time-honored manner of would-be and actual dictators.

"Why are the men of Florence so obstinate in opposing me? Why do you place such a bad interpretation upon my intentions? That you do is shown by the fact that you choose such a time to send a solemn embassy to me. That you come before me at this very time when I am sending to you as pacificator one of the greatest princes in all Christendom. Fall on your knees before me! Submit to me! I tell you that in all truth I have nothing in my heart but to promote your peace!"

He let these words sink in. Then before any of them could begin a reply, he said some other words.

"Let two of you return to your city, and they will have my benediction if they persuade Florence to carry out my wishes."

This was said pleasantly, but it can be seen upon examination that it was not a suggestion but an edict.

The Florentines had no choice but to comply.

Two of them, in fact, did return — Maso di Ruggierino Minerbetti, our false populan, and Guido Ubaldini degli Aldobrandeschi.

One remained — Dante Alighieri.

This is the known fact, but what was the reason?

Did Dante *insist* on staying, believing that he was the one person who could win over the pope, and that if he stayed with him he might do this?

Given his notable self-confidence, this is not impossible.

Or did Boniface *make* Dante stay? Did he hold him against his will?

A writer on the period said that the two greatest men and strongest personalities of the late thirteenth and the early fourteenth centuries were the Gaetani pope and the Florentine poet. Did Boniface recognize this fact? Did he keep Dante because he feared him? Did he compel Dante to remain at Anagni — or at Rome — because he knew that, thanks to his machinations, Florence was rapidly falling into chaos, but that Dante could still steel it and stiffen it if he could sit and speak in its councils in this time that tried Florentine souls? Did he retain Dante to immobilize the only force which could still obstruct him?

Since we cannot enter into a man's mind unless he has left us the key with which to unlock its door — and since Boniface did not leave us such keys — we can only surmise. But my surmising leads me to the conclusion that Dante did not stay because he *wanted* to stay but because he *had to* — that he stayed because he was made to stay by a pope who understood tactics as well as strategy, and was prepared to use either or both.

XIV

Even as Hippolytus Was Driven from Athens

TACTICS and strategy accomplished their purpose. For whether Dante's absence from Florence with the concomitant weakening of Florentine will was the principal or merely a contributory cause, it was at this time that Florentine resolution fell apart, and that the succession of timeservers who wanted to make known their burning devotion to the pontiff and his Valois mercenary became a stream in spate.

As the Florentine emissaries proceeded toward Rome, "the priors composing the signory" — making one more futile effort to cope with the situation — "in order not to be held in suspicion by either party, chose forty citizens from both parties," and with these they "took counsel concerning the safety of the city."

In other words, they convened a Special Council.

It might have been better for Florence if they had not, for when the council met, "those having a wicked purpose" — the Black ringleaders — did not speak, knowing that thus they would leave the rostrum to the defeatist, the terrified, and the confused.

The latter hastened to occupy it, Bandino Falconieri being the first.

Waving his arm toward the river across which the French were established, he said: "Sirs, now I am easy in my mind. Before I could not sleep soundly."

Since he was not merely a White but a White leader, Dino Compagni called him a coward, but in his own opinion he was being practical.

He was also long-winded and this probably did as much damage as his words.

"He occupied the tribune half the day, and we were at the ebb of the year."

In other words, as the afternoons shortened and darkness forced early adjournments, he monopolized the attention of the assembly and curtailed the time available for others.

Lapo Salterelli spoke next — Lapo Salterelli who "greatly feared the pope," and who had good reason to fear him.

But he now saw the handwriting on the wall, "and in order to curry favor with his adversaries" — so that he could get back into papal good graces — he began to attack the priors and their gonfalonier.

"Ye are bringing the city to ruin," he cried. "Cause a new signory to be chosen from men of both parties. Recall to the city those who have been set under bounds!"

(He had already recalled one of them — privately. Lapo hoped that Pazzino de' Pazzi, now hidden in his home, would help him when the Blacks returned to power.)

Alberto del Giudice, a rich and spiteful veteran of the plots against Giano della Bella, said the same thing and almost in the same words. Even though the present priorate had scarcely begun to hold office, they should elect their successors forthwith, and then having brought back the exiles, should step down.

"Sirs!" cried Loteringo of Montespertoli, whose rural birth should have made him loyal to the homespun party; "Sirs! Do ye wish my advice? Elect a new signory. Bring back to the city those ye have placed under your ban. Then when ye have done these two things ye may take down the city gates from their hinges."

For, he explained, if you chose a new signory and recall those who have been sent away — and who only stir up trouble because they wish to return — the tranquility of the city would be so assured that it would not need to defend itself against either foreign or domestic enemies.

Panic is contagious, and panic now not only walked in the streets but sat in the seats of the mighty.

Let us do something! Let us do *anything!*

It seems almost certain that if it had not been for Dino Compagni, who was — unexpectedly — firm, there might have been capitulation then and there.

But Dino — and he seems to have dominated the signory — had an inspiration.

"I went to Messer Andrea da Cerreto, a learned lawyer from an old Ghibelline family but now become a Black Guelph" — note how carefully he chose his adviser, selecting not a White but a Black, and one of an old, honored family — "and asked him if a new signory could be chosen without violating the Ordinances of Justice."

Andrea replied that they could not.

That was all that Dino needed.

"For I who had once been accused of such a transgression" — in 1295 when he was gonfalonier of justice — "was determined to observe them. Therefore, I was determined not to allow a new signory to be elected."

He did not allow one to be elected.

Thus — even if in a roundabout way — an immediate crisis was successfully dealt with.

But a second and more serious one was right at its heels.

« 2 »

For it was precisely at this moment that the two ambassadors who had been released by Pope Boniface returned from Rome. Minerbetti, the false populan with his treasonable schemes already ripe. Il Corazza, the naïve Guelph who believed that, since the pope was just as Guelph as he was, all in the long run would be well.

These laid the pope's message — the pope's ultimatum, rather — before the priors, and the priors were consternated. For it was, when you read it through carefully, clearly a demand for unconditional surrender. Put yourselves in my hands. Obey my orders. Trust in my goodwill. And above all do not take any steps which will leave you the least shadow of power.

Become, to use a modern phrase, a papal satellite.

But what could they do about it?

For with Charles and his lances just across the river, the city was defenseless anyway. Or very nearly so.

Once again it was "I, Dino" who supplied the answer.

Yield or appear to yield, and then use this appearance of yielding to separate the pope from the Blacks.

"We can do this if we proceed carefully, for the pope is not irrevocably committed to the Blacks."

To prove his point, he cited a story.

Irked, it ran, that the Blacks still seemed to be waiting for others to strike instead of striking themselves, Boniface growled complaints against them. "They are women! They are mumbling and bumbling old women! And I will not destroy men for the sake of old women!"

But they must act behind closed doors if they were to be successful.

"But we cannot," he was told, "for by constitution and by custom any communication from a foreign potentate must be laid openly before the councils of the commonwealth. Before *all* the councils!"

Bypass the constitution and custom then!

"I take full responsibility for this," Dino wrote later. "I persuaded the priors to withhold the report and I made the ambassadors swear oaths of secrecy."

This done, he "assembled six learned lawyers and caused it [the report] to be laid before them."

Then, still not summoning the councils, but with his colleagues' consent, he "brought forward, supported, and put to a vote a resolution to the effect that the pope should be obeyed, and that a letter should be at once written to him stating that we were submissive to his will."

The letter would also request that the pope dispatch to Florence forthwith Cardinal Gentile da Montefiore "to put us straight."

For word had come to them — presumably from Dante — that Boniface, who alternated between threats and blandishments, was now threatening and insisted on a Florentine *peccavimus*.

If that was all that was needed — and for the moment the Whites thought so — *peccavimus* (we have sinned) they would gladly cry.

If it had not been for Minerbetti, Dino's plan might well have succeeded.

But the false populan went to his Black friends, and "revealed the pope's answer which the Blacks could not otherwise have heard."

Thereupon they also "took council together," for they now believed that the Whites could still make peace with the pontiff.

"If they do this, we are undone," they told each other.

They determined, however, to wait until they saw what course of action the priors would actually take.

But to be ready for whatsoever eventuality.

"If they answer *no*, we are dead men!"

Meaning that if the Whites decided to defy the pope, their first step would be to fall upon the Blacks and destroy them.

"But if they say *yes*, we still have a chance."

For in the interval between White capitulation and the pope's implementation of the same — which, among other things, would involve ordering Charles of Valois to effect a genuine pacification — they could still draw their swords and get what might be refused them later.

"And this they did," wrote Dino. "Immediately on hearing that the priors were submitting to the pope, they armed themselves and began to attack the city with fire and sword."

Leading them was Noffo Guidi, "an iniquitous and pitiless lowerclassman" who had nevertheless an unimpeachable reputation. "For he acted," says Dino, "in the worst possible manner against the city, yet it was his habit to blame in public those very things he did in private, and the doers of them too. He was, therefore, held to be a person of good character at the very moment he was being paid for evil deeds."

At his heels followed a band of the city's dregs, men who for the most part did not care whether Black or White triumphed, but who did care that there was pillaging or plunder. These roved the streets destructively, as smoke coiled into the autumn sky.

It was at this moment — and because of this — that the priors once again vacillated. They reverted to a course of action they had rejected before.

"We were now" — as the disorders raged — "being urged by all the more important citizens to elect a new signory."

And although they still knew that to do so was illegal, this time they agreed.

"More out of compassion for the city than for any other reason!"

As might be expected, the implementation was entrusted to Dino Compagni.

"I attended" — more probably he not only attended but convened — "a meeting in the chapel of St. Bernard where I represented the whole signory, and there I had with me many of the most powerful of the merchant-burgher class because no election could be made without them. These included Cione Magalotti, Segna Angiolari, and Noffo Guidi" — Noffo Guidi! — "of the Black party, and Messer Lapo Falconieri, Cecco Canigiani, and Corazza degli Ubaldini [Il Corazza] of the White party. These I spoke to in the friendliest and most conciliatory manner possible on the whole matter of saving the city. 'I am going to choose a new signory and make it a mixed one' " — i.e., one having on it members of both parties — " 'since rivalry for office causes so much discord.'

"We all agreed and chose six well-known citizens, three from the Blacks and three from the Whites. We chose for the seventh" — i.e., for the gonfalonier of justice — "which could not be divided, a man of so little importance that no one could object to him."

Harmony seemed about to reign.

But harmony was the last thing the Blacks — or their spokesman, Noffo Guidi — wanted, and so even as the names were being written down so that they could be laid upon the altar, as required by custom, he upset the applecart.

"I will now say something," he said, "that will make you think that I am both stern and uncompromising. To accomplish peace you will have to make the Black party in this new signory stronger than the White party."

There is an old saying that there is no anger like the anger of a patient man, and Dino certainly had been patient.

But now his patience was exhausted.

For to do what Noffo had asked him to do would have been to destroy the White party, and since the Whites had put their fortunes into his hands, this would have, in his own words, "put him in the place of Judas."

He flared back at Noffo and his "arrogance."

"Before I committed such a treason," he shouted, "I would give my children to the dogs to eat!"

Noffo's retort to this is not recorded.

"And thus we departed from the assembly," concludes Dino.

This was the last effort made by Dino or by anyone else to effect through compromise a peaceful settlement.

From now on, the struggle would be in the streets.

« 3 »

In the streets — with the cards stacked against the merchant-burgher Whites! For they would soon have more to contend with than Black *oltraggiamenti*, more even than the fact that these Black *oltraggiamenti* and the move toward power of which they were a part would, now that the Blacks had finally determined to start doing something, have the much more than tacit support of the pope.

Charles of Valois was himself getting ready to move. To establish himself in the Oltrarno was a good beginning, and this he had done. Apparently, too, in an aura of gaiety and good feeling, for, according to one chronicler, he was met by "a procession in which were many jousters, bearing silken standards and riding chargers draped in silk," and according to another, he "was much honored by the citizens with horse races and with tilting."

But it was only a beginning. The next step was to cross the Arno, and without too much risk establish himself in central Florence. Until he did this he would not have command of the situation and could not count his mission a success.

But how? That was the question. For the Florentines, even the by now demoralized Whites, were accomplished street fighters. And a knight in armor, especially a mounted knight in armor, needed space in which to maneuver.

Try craft, was the obvious answer, and according to Italians the right one for a Frenchman.

Mask your intentions and use courtesy to cover up what you are devising.

He did.

"Monsieur Charles often caused us to be invited to dine with him," reported Dino.

In the Frescobaldi palace, with its thick walls and its massive iron-bound gates. But the fly would not come into the spider's parlor.

"We answered him [which was true] that our oaths and the law would not permit this, but the real reason for our refusal was that we thought that he might detain us against our will."

Then Charles tried another tactic.

If the priors would not come to him, he would come to the priors — not in their part of the city, however, but in neutral territory.

"He sent to us" — it is still Dino from whom we get our story — "saying that he wished to hold a conference for the welfare of the citizens at Santa Maria Novella outside the city, and might it please the signory to be present."

Might it *please* the signory! Not I command the signory!

"And since" — under these circumstances — "to refuse would be to have shown too much suspicion," the priors "decided" at least partially to disregard the law, and "that three of us should go there, but that the others should remain in the palace."

It was a wise precaution.

For Charles, they learned later, pretending to have suspicions of his own, "had caused his men to be armed and put them on guard at every city gate both within and without."

The alleged reason: "Certain false councillors of his had told him that he would not be able to get back into the city" — not even into his part of the city — "for the gates would be shut against him."

But the real reason was somewhat different.

Actually it had been Charles's plan "if the whole signory had gone to him, to kill us outside the gate, and make himself the master of the city. But it did not fall out this way because only three of us went to him, and to them he said nothing, being a man who did not want to talk but kill."

Charles did not want to talk, that is. His councillors did.

"The barons of the French prince and the evil-scheming Musciatto Franzesi had been continuously besetting the priors with their demands that the custody of the city should be placed in his hands, and especially the custody of the *sesto* of Oltrarno. If that is done, they said, all evil doers will be severely punished. But behind these fair words their real purpose was to acquire authority over the city."

Now, at Santa Maria Novella, they pressed these demands again, and unexpectedly they were half acceded to.

(This seems to me clearly Dino Compagni's doing. He was almost certainly one of the three priors who attended the meeting and, as we have already noted, despite moments of firmness, he was always agreeable to, if not eager for, compromise. It was only later — indeed too late — that he would realize that *umiltà* — literally humility but here sweet reasonableness — "is of very little avail against the wicked."

"The keys of the whole city were denied to Monsieur Charles, but the gates of the Oltrarno were placed in his charge and the Florentines removed from them and the French put there."

Only, to be sure, after a solemn oath had been sworn by Guillaume de la Perche in the name of his sovereign and master.

"I pledge ye," he said, placing his hands within Dino's hands, "that only at the pleasure of the signory will he take upon himself and hold and keep this custody."

"Never," cried Dino, "did I believe that so great a prince and one of the royal house of France would break his faith."

Break it he did, however, and that forthwith.

For "but a small part of the night that followed had passed when, by the gate which we had committed to his custody, Il Valos admitted Gherarduccio Buondelmonti, who had been banished."

Gherarduccio was accompanied "by many other banished citizens."

This was a clear signal to the Blacks.

Far from "punishing them for their evil doing," Charles welcomed them.

Words could not have been plainer.

"This is what I have done for you with such power as has been put into my hands. Get me greater powers and I will do more for you."

At first cautiously, but soon with increasing boldness, this is what the Blacks began to do.

« 4 »

They had begun to do this, as a matter of fact, even before the meeting at Santa Maria Novella.

As a direct consequence of Noffo Guidi's intemperate stand, the priors had persuaded the councils to pass new and severe laws against any who might cause tumult and affrays and, to give these emphasis, they had ordered a block with the headsman's axe beside it to be placed in the Piazza della Signoria. They voted to increase the authority of the captain of the people, and he was ordered to use it. They also strengthened the captain's and their own guards. Among the latter a conspiracy had been discovered. Twenty of them had been paid one thousand *libbre* to murder Dino and his colleagues. They were driven from the palace and were replaced with others whom it was hoped would be more reliable.

But while the Whites did this, the Blacks did not sit idle.

"The prince is in the city," they said. "The pope is with us. In their own minds, our enemies cannot decide between war and peace. Their mercenaries" — this was their harsh term for the White civic guards — "are not paid."

In consequence — and for other reasons — there were mass defections. Even Dino could not help observing this.

"The messengers, our servants, and the sergeants are now betraying us," he cried in anguish.

Noting this — and having ample funds, both the pope's money and their own — the Blacks "set into order everything needful for war." They told their allies to begin marching. They prepared billets near the prince's headquarters for the increasing numbers from Orvieto, Perugia, San Miniato, Volterra, and San Gimignano who were flocking in to join the winners.

Nor did they neglect the city itself. The ancient tower societies, disbanded when the towers were truncated or torn down, had been replaced by *compagni delle vicinanze* (neighborhood societies), and among their membership coin was scattered freely. They would be tremendously important allies if street fighting actually began. The Blacks also laid plans for seizing the Santa Trinità Bridge and for placing engines on the Frescobaldi and Spini palaces. Obviously they sent word to the Black exiles.

Against this — as is so often the case when lawful government attempts to deal with insurrection — the priorate was hampered by its legalistic compunctions. When you defend the law, you do not like to break the law.

"The White Guelphs did not dare to muster men in their palaces because the priors had threatened to punish them and any others who threatened the peace, whether they were friends or enemies."

Dino, who issued these orders, later tried to justify them.

They were for the record, and were not meant seriously.

"These friends should not have believed that their friends" — the priors, that is — "would have put them to death for making preparations to save the city, even though such orders were given."

Then he adds this afterthought:

"However, it was not so much from fear of the law as from avarice that they were neglectful."

Then, as always, preparedness cost too much for certain merchant-minded mentalities.

But that was not all.

At this time "Messer Manetto Scali, in whom the Whites had great confidence since he was strong in friends and in adherents, began to fortify his palace and to place on it catapults for casting stones."

This could not but disturb the Spini, since it lay just across the street from their strategically located stronghold.

One of the Spini, therefore, called cautiously upon his potent neighbor.

"In God's name," he said, "why do we act toward each other thus? We are, when you come right down to it, kinsmen and friends, and we are all Guelphs. Nor do we have any other purpose than to lift from our necks the chains which those shopkeepers would lay upon us. This done, we will prosper as never before. In God's name, help us then! Let us stand together as we should!"

"And in the same manner," said Dino, "the Buondelmonti behaved toward the Gherardini, and the Bardi to the Mozzi, and Rosso della Tosa to Baschiera, and thus did many others behave. Wherefore the White followers lost heart, and the Ghibellines" — who had counted on the Whites to restore to them at least a part of what they deemed to be their rights — "believed that they were being deceived and betrayed by those whom they had trusted. All were filled with consternation."

Divide to conquer!

It had worked beyond their fondest expectations.

"The Blacks, therefore, knowing that their enemies were fear-struck and had lost their energy, made up their minds to seize the city, and on Saturday, November 4, they saddled and armored their horses and began to carry out their plan."

In broad daylight, they galloped through the streets, seeking to provoke incidents.

They succeeded.

One example:

"The Medici, powerful *popolani*" — incidentally, this is the first time, so far as I know, that this famous family is mentioned in a historical document — "in broad daylight, but after vespers, assaulted and wounded a worthy merchant-burgher, Orlanduccio Orlandi, and left him for dead."

There were other assaults.

Yet even at that late hour, the priors, with a modicum of resolution, could have saved the situation, for the *popolo* — the plain people and others not so plain — still stood with them, and in great numbers, "on horseback and on foot," came to the Palazzo della Signoria.

There, one of their number, Catellina Raffacani, acted as their spokesman.

"Sirs, ye have been betrayed. Night is coming on and there is no time for further delay. Send for the militia of the *contado*, and at dawn fight against your enemies."

In the meantime, arrest the peace breakers!

Arrest the peace breakers?

But that would be doing something!

"The *podestà* did not send his officers to the offender's house, nor did the gonfalonier of justice stir to punish the outrage."

Instead, they took refuge in a technicality. Orlanduccio had been wounded, not slain. When a wounding and not a slaying was the crime, it was necessary to wait ten days.

« 5 »

It was at almost precisely this moment that Charles of Valois appeared at Santa Maria Novella and was given qualified jurisdiction over the city, and it was at almost precisely this moment that the White cause was definitely lost.

For the Blacks and the Valois prince who was helping them to do their dirty work hesitated no longer, but let blow follow blow in staccato succession like the onslaught of a pugilist against a foe who has begun to waver.

They guaranteed access to the city by seizing the San Brancazio Gate (actually it was the Porta di San Paolo — San Brancazio was merely its popular name) and driving off a group of stonemasons who were fortifying it with the prior's belated consent. They sent messengers to the houses of their partisans ordering the occupants to be armed and ready by daybreak. (One of these messengers, disguised as a spice vendor, was captured and confessed. But the priors still did nothing.) They also succeeded in disarming the "worthless militia." Or more accurately, they persuaded them to tear down their White banners and slip quietly off. They even convinced a group of Luccan noblemen who hated the Blacks because they had been beaten and robbed by Black magnates that it would be wiser — because safer — to return home. Thus the signory lost another — and perhaps its last — ally. They had greatly counted on these men from Lucca.

That much on November 5. Then on November 6, still not quite yet ready for their final blow, the Blacks called on, and were given an assist by, the French.

"The day following, the barons of Monsieur Charles and Messer Cante of Gubbio" came before the harassed priors and "occupied their time and energy with long speeches" and plausible explanations.

"We swear to ye," they cried, "that our prince holds himself to have been betrayed" — by the Black outrages — "and that he is ordering his knights to be armed, and he trusts that it might be your lordships' pleasure that ample vengeance be taken. For ye may hold it for certain that the prince intends to have these misdeeds punished in such manner as ye would have them punished. Here we stand before ye. Ye may have our heads cut off if there is a word of this not true."

But how, the priors wanted to know, could these words be believed in, when the Blacks still treasonably held the San Brancazio Gate and when it was known to everybody that Corso Donati planned to enter the city?

"Corso? Messer Corso? Ye fear him? But I have heard Monsieur Charles swear with his own lips that he will have Messer Corso Donati hanged!"

Yet even as these words were being said, Il Barone — and surely with the connivance of Monsieur Charles — who had been biding his time at San Stefano a Ugnano down the Arno — galloped up to the city walls. With him were twelve followers. Finding the gate immediately in front of him shut and barred, he circled the city until he came to San Piero Maggiore. There, at the postern of the Pinti, he forced an entry.

"He came into the city like a bold and fearless knight," dispersed a band of fully armed and mounted Whites, and to a crowd of all at once loyal supporters that gathered and grew he issued orders just as if he and not Prince Charles were master.

"Go to the prisons and set free the prisoners."

The Black plotters, of course, the political prisoners — but also every cutthroat, snatchpurse, brigand, highwayman, and other ruffian who had fallen afoul of Florentine law!

And tell them who has freed them and what he wants them to do for him.

But they would have done it anyway.

No sooner had chisel clanked on heavy chains and the evil horde poured from dark cells into the dazzling sunlight than there began a reign of terror that has hardly been equaled.

Dino Compagni:

"Houses began to be burned. Robberies were committed. Maidens were married by force. There were many slayings."

Giovanni Villani:

"The tyrants and the evildoers grew more and more bold. They not only looted the shops and the warehouses but they plundered private homes. They did this for five days. And when they were through in the city they continued their burning and their brigandry in the country, whereby many beautiful and rich possessions were destroyed."

While this went on, Charles did not lift a finger, seemingly so indifferent to the excesses that were being committed that when the smoke from a blazing edifice stung his eyes he was willing to believe that the building was merely a hovel.

Even some of his own household were appalled, notable among them Maître Roger, his sworn clerk or theological adviser.

"Under thee a noble city is perishing!" cried Roger.

"Perishing?" replied Charles. "That I know nothing of, sir clerk."

And when finally he was forced by events to do something — almost to do anything — he acted with his by now almost habitual duplicity.

To the priors he sent two of their old friends — but friends who by now had definitely gone over to him — Lapo Salterelli and the White captain Schiatta Cancellieri.

"Sirs," these told the priors, "surely ye see that Charles is once again filled with anger, and desires that the vengeance taken be ample and that the commonwealth remain supreme. Therefore we think that the most powerful men of both parties should be chosen and sent to him as hostages. Then he will be in a position to impose punishment."

But when the hostages came to him Charles dismissed the Blacks, telling them to return to their homes, but the Whites he kept prisoners. "Without straw and without mattresses, like murderers!"

"O good King Louis [Saint Louis]," cried Dino, "thou who so fearedst God, where is the faith of the royal house of France fallen? O wicked counsellors, who have made a prince of such high dignity not merely a hireling but an assassin!"

But fallen French faith had indeed, and the White government knew that as a consequence it must now fall too.

On November 8, the day after this betrayal, "the priors commanded that the great bell which was over their palace be sounded." This was a summons to citizen action, but the citizens did not respond. "From the houses of the Cerchi not a man came forth," and of the other White leaders "only Messer Goccia and Messer Bindo Adimari with their brothers and their sons" put in an appearance. "And as no one else came, they returned home and the piazza remained deserted."

At that point, the priors bowed to the inevitable. Once again saying that they acted "out of compassion for the city," the priors resigned. A new priorate took office forthwith. But this time there was not even talk of a two-party government. The new priors were all "*popolani* of the worst sort and powerful in their party." Powerful in the Black party, that is.

Six days later these new priors appointed Cante Gabrielli *podestà*. The revolution was now signed and sealed.

Yet even that did not restore law and order. The terror did not cease but merely was carried on now with governmental sanction. And with extortion added to robbery, and with Charles of Valois now among the extortionists.

The old priors, for example, were arrested on his direct order and charged with high crimes and misdemeanors against the Florentine state and having acted "contrary to the honor of the king of France and his own." Specifically, they were charged with having opposed Charles's coming, having sought to usurp his office of pacificator, and having ordered to be fortified towns that guarded the approaches. It was then hinted to them that they could buy acquittal. Their refusal to do this was met with astonishment. 'Surely," said Baldo Ridolfi, one of the new priors, "ye would rather give Charles your money than be sent into Apulia as prisoners!"

But not merely the old priors fell victim to Valois rapacity. Anyone who was either White or not an active Black or merely had accessible money was fair game. Not even acts of friendship brought exemption.

"There was in Florence," writes Dino, "a rich and very worthy *popolano* called by name Rinuccio di Senno Rinucci who had paid much honor to Monsieur Charles at a beautiful estate of his when Monsieur Charles had gone a-fowling with his barons. This man he caused to be seized and imposed on him a ransom of four thousand florins. At the prayers of his friends, however, he released him for eight hundred florins.

"And in similar ways he did amass much money."

Borrowed it, was his own description, but hardly from willing lenders. It is stated that he collected at least twenty-four thousand *libbre*. And all in the space of five days.

In all probability, the Black Florentines collected many times more, notable among the forceful transmuters of *thine* into *mine* being the Donati, the Rossi, the Tornaquinci, and the Bostichi. They "wrought grievous mischief," it is said. "Many did they violently oppress and plunder."

Of all these, the Bostichi perhaps acted the most flagrantly.

"They punished men with the rope in their own houses, which were situated near the Mercato Nuovo in the very heart of the city, and they put them to torture at midday."

Where their screams of agony and for mercy could be heard — and were meant to be heard — by the buyers of fruits and vegetables!

"There are many law courts in Florence!" soon was said throughout the city.

"Where?"

"At the houses of the Bostichi near the market."

All these things happened in November and December 1301, but when the new year dawned the Black domination of Florence entered a new phase. The days of street rioting ended — possibly because the street rioters had run out of booty. But the calvary of the White did not. Now, however, their persecution became legal — it expressed itself in acts vested with every possible judicial correctness, acts decreed by lawfully qualified bodies or persons. And since one of these acts deeply concerned Dante — was in fact one of the three shaking things which shaped his life — it is important for us at least to try to know just where he was and what he was doing as events raced toward their climax and also at the moment that he felt the impact.

« 6 »

Taking the period as a whole, the truth is we cannot exactly say. That is, we cannot say with documented and absolute confidence that he was in such and such a place at such and such a moment, did so and so, and then on another precisely defined date proceeded to this or that other place where he did something different. But the broad outlines we do know. We know that he reached Rome and Anagni before November 1, that he was detained by the pope when the other ambassadors were sent back, that he was finally dismissed (but not until the new priorate was in office and his friends in disgrace), and that he then went to Siena. He was definitely in Siena by the latter part of January. He may have been there considerably sooner.

I myself opt for the earliest date possible.

Siena was much in his poetry and in his mind. So were the Sienese. He wrote much about it and them, his passages about Sapia, Provenzan Salvani, Albero (who was duped by the alchemist Griffolino), and the "admirals" who wanted to make the hill town a seaport having already been cited.

He also wrote about La Pia.

Purgatorio V:

> "I pray thee when thou hast returned to the world
> And thou art rested from thy wearying journey,"
> Said a third spirit following the second,
> "Do thou remember me who La Pia am.
> Siena made me, the Maremma unmade,
> As he well knows who once having wed me
> Did later cast me off with this his gem."

La Pia (The Compassionate One) was a lovely and loved Sienese widow who, after the death of her first husband, married one Nello de' Pannocchieschi, a rough baron who held the Castello della Pietra in the wild Maremma, and who, so said scandal, had her thrown from one of its windows when he wanted to marry another widow.

This story Dante must have heard in Siena.

It must also have been in Siena that Dante learned about the doings of one of those *brigate spenderoccie* — spendthrift brigades — whose doings a little later (but in Dante's lifetime, and before his *Commedia* was completed) Folgore da San Gimignano would celebrate in one of the loveliest and surely the most colorful of the sonnet sequences of the early Renaissance.

Inferno XXIX — Dante is speaking:

> "Was there ever
> A people as empty-headed as the Sienese?
> Certainly not even the French are by a long shot!"

Capocchio, another alchemist, answers him:

> "But include out Stricca,
> Who knew always [*this is sarcastic*] how to live on his income.
> Don't include Niccolò, whose extravagant taste
> First learned how to cook with the clove
> And sowed in that garden [*Siena*] where extravagant tastes flourish.
> Don't include, either, that merry-hearted group
> In whose company Ciacco d'Ascian squandered
> The income from his vineyards and his trees
> And against whom Abbagliato [*Scatterbrain*] matched his wits."

It was perhaps also at this time, and in this place, that his path for the first time crossed that of Cecco Angiolari. Cecco — "a pretty fellow, and well mannered, who could not brook to live in Siena on the allowance made him by his father," says Boccaccio, who describes one of his misadventures in *Decameron* IX, 4 — was one of the rogue poets of all time.

Cecco was a thief, a cutthroat (in 1291 he was hailed into court for stabbing one Dino di Bernardino), a deserter (he was twice fined for leaving his post with the militia), a riotous liver (he was once fined for being in the streets after the third sounding of the curfew), a blasphemer, and apparently (see his sonnets to Corzo di Corzan) a sodomite.

(Yet despite the last, at least half of his poetry was addressed to a certain low beauty, Becchina, "the tanner's daughter," whom he beseiged with tears and imprecations and who finally — but once only — granted him her favors.)

One hundred and fifty of his sonnets survive. They are vitriolic (for the most part) but incredibly vivid. Three of them were addressed to

Dante. I will give one of these if only because it seems to indicate that he and Dante had once been engaged in the same kind of poetic bludgeoning that Dante and Forese Donati had.

> Dante, if I'm a nonsense-talking lout,
> I don't surpass you. This I do declare.
> If I eat stranger's food, you taste their fare.
> If I munch fat, grease fills your starved mouth out.
> If I cut cloth, why then you card the wool.
> If I speak folly, foolishness you spout.
> If I play lord, you are Sir Worshipful.
> If you're a Lombard lean, I'm Roman stout.
> Therefore, praise God, it would be to deplore
> If either of us should the other blame.
> To do this would show little sense I ween.
> That's all. But if you wish to argue more,
> Beware, for I can put you quite to shame.
> I am a gadfly, you a clumsy cow.

To be sure, the context shows that the lines were not written at this time — to me 1306 is as good a date as any. But the same kind of internal evidence makes it very certain that the two poets knew each other personally.

And where better could Dante have met Cecco than in Siena, and when better than at this time?

« 7 »

But whether it was immediately following the fall of the White priorate (as I think, basing my belief on the feeling that Dante could not have learned as much about Siena as he apparently did in a brief bird-of-passage stay) or not until eight or ten weeks later that Dante came to the city of Provenzan, Sapia, and Pia, one thing is certain. He was in Siena when a document was placed in his hands that caused more than his veins to tremble.

It was dated January 27, 1302, and given its urgency it is hard to see how it could have reached the poet more than two or three days later. Because of its overriding importance, I will give it almost in full:

"In the name of the Lord, amen.

"These are the condemnations, or the sentences resulting from condemnations, made, published, and promulgated by the noble and puissant knight Messer Cante Gabrielli of Gubbio, honorable *podestà* of the city of Florence, against the below-written men and persons for the below-written misdemeanors, following an examination by the wise and discreet

Messer Paolo of Gubbio, designated judge by the same lord *podestà* in all matters pertaining to barratries, unlawful extortions, and illicit receipt of funds, who acted with the advice of other judges of the said lord *podestà*. They are written down by me, Bonoro of Pregio, notary of the said lord *podestà* and holding the same office for the magistrates and commonwealth of Florence.

"(1) Against Gherardino, son of the late Diodato, of the parish of San Martino del Vescovo, formerly one of the priors.

"Denounced and accused by Bartolo di Banco of the parish of San Lorenzo for having committed deceit, fraud, and barratry during his tenure of office by arranging to have Guccio, son of the late Messer Cerretano de' Visdomini, offered to God and to the blessed John the Baptist [i.e., pardoned] not for love of God and of the blessed John but because of money and on account of money, receiving from Guccio or from his relatives seventy-two gold florins, etc., and cited to appear, the said Gherardino did not appear, wherefore he was proclaimed banished by the public crier and to have fallen into contumacy, etc."

Gherardino, it will be recalled, was the father of that Neri degli Gherardini who had been pardoned by a council in which Dante spoke forcefully in his favor.

"(2) Against Messer Palmieri Altoviti of the Sesto di Borgo, against Lippo Becchi of the Sesto d'Oltrarno, against Orlanduccio Orlandi of the Sesto di Porta del Duomo — and against *Dante Alighieri* of the Sesto di San Piero Maggiore."

For emphasis, I have slightly rearranged the order of the listing.

"Proceedings were instituted against these men as a result of an investigation made by our office and our court into the following charges which had come to our ears and to the attention of our court through common report:

"First, that the above-named, while they or certain of them held or did not hold the office of prior, or after they had laid down the said office of prior but during the time under consideration in our inquest, committed barratries, made illicit gains, or wickedly extorted either money or property either for themselves or for others. And that they or some of them received money or property, or written or tacit promises of money or property, so that they would elect [designated persons] as the new priors, although not under that name or word. And that they or some of them received certain considerations unlawfully, illicitly, or unjustly on behalf of those who were to be elected or appointed to office in the city or the territory of Florence or in the district or elsewhere so that these would agree to make or not to make [certain] edicts or ordinances, or in return for warrants of authority sent to this or that official of the commonwealth of Florence or given into his hands. And that they or some of them arranged these matters, or did them or had them done, and that to accomplish this they gave, promised, or paid, or had given or had paid or had entered to their credit on the books of some merchant both money and goods either during the time they held office or after they had laid it down.

"Second, that they received from the treasurer of the commonwealth or from the housekeeping or the palace funds of the priors and the gonfalonier more and other properties and moneys than the decrees of the commonwealth prescribed. And that they had committed or had caused to be committed fraud or barratry both in money and in the property of the commonwealth of Florence, and that they had given or spent these against the high pontiff and against Monsieur Charles, and [that they had done this] to resist his coming and against the peace and well-being of the city and of the Guelph party. And that they or certain of them had received money or property from a designated personality or group or entity at the time of and because of fears of agitation in the dependent towns which they had caused or had threatened to have caused by the priors, the commonwealth, and the people.

"Third, that they had committed or had caused to be committed or done frauds, false dealings, false plottings, malicious acts, barratries, and illicit extortions, and that they had schemed or that certain of them had schemed to have the city of Pistoia fall into divisions and sects and abandon the unity it once had. And that they had plotted to have the ancients and the gonfalonier of the said city of Pistoia chosen from one party only. And that they had planned, brought about, or ordained that those who called themselves Blacks should be driven from the said city, and that they also caused the said city to withdraw from its alliance with the commonwealth of Florence and from submission to the Holy Roman Church and to Monsieur Charles, the pacificator of Tuscany."

But not one of the indicted men had responded to the proceedings.

"The said Messer Palmieri and the said Dante, Orlanduccio, and Lippo were, therefore, legally cited and summoned by a public officer of the commonwealth of Florence to present themselves and to appear before ourselves and our court within a certain time which has now expired, and that they and each one of them should make themselves available to us either to clear themselves of the above charges or to excuse themselves of guilt. But they did not come, choosing rather to make themselves liable to be placed under the ban of the commonwealth of Florence by Duccio di Francesco, the public crier of the said commonwealth, and to a fine of five thousand small florins, under which liability they lie by their consent through contumacy in full accordance with what has been provided in the acts of our courts in regard to the above-named offense.

"Wherefore" — and this was the conclusion — "we, Cante Gabrielli of Gubbio, in writing do condemn and sentence the said Messer Palmieri and the said Dante, Orlanduccio, and Lippo, each one of them as follows: (1) to a fine of five thousand small florins apiece to be given and paid to the treasurer of the commonwealth and people of Florence for the account of the said commonwealth; (2) to restore all money illicitly extorted to any who can give legitimate proof of said extortion; (3) that if they do not pay the fine within three days from the day of this sentence, all the property of those who do not pay shall be expropriated, laid waste, or destroyed, and what remains shall belong to the commonwealth; (4) but that even if they do pay the said fine, they or anyone of them who does pay it shall nevertheless remain in bounds outside of the province of Tuscany for two years; (5) and so that [the misdeeds of] Messer Palmieri, Dante, Orlanduccio, and Lippo shall be perpetually remembered, their names shall be inscribed in the statute books, and as falsifiers and barrators they shall forever be ineligible to hold or have any office or benefice in or from the commonwealth of Florence, either in the city, the countryside, the district, or anywhere else, and this whether they pay the fine or do not pay it."

Sanctimoniously it was interpolated that these heavy penalties were imposed on Dante and the three sentenced with him "so that of the seed they sowed they shall reap a harvest fitting to the sowing, and so that they shall be rewarded according to what they deserve with guerdons that befit their merits," and it was reiterated that "by their contumacy" they were "held confessed," and that they were tried under "the laws and statutes of the commonwealth and people of Florence, of the Ordinances of Justice and their revisions," and under "the valid authority" of the *podestà*.

Then came the notarial attestation.

"The above sentences and condemnations were made, pronounced, and promulgated by the said lord *podestà* to the General Council of the commonwealth of Florence sitting as a tribunal, and they were read by me, Bonoro, the above-named notary, to the said council on the orders of the said *podestà*. Present as witnesses were Ser Agnolo, member of the household of the *podestà*, Ser Pace di Tommaso of Gubbio, notary of the said *podestà*, Duccio di Francesco and Albizzo, public criers, and the many others who sat in the said council."

The last phrase deserves particular attention. "The many others who sat in the said council." Cante and his employers were taking no chances. They wanted to make it plain as plain could be that these sentences — and every other sentence they imposed — had a broad base of popular approval, that in no sense were they the end product of star-chamber proceedings. They also wanted it to be part of the record that they had complied with every legal formality — that the defendants had been given a fair trial.

But the whole document deserves careful attention and for many reasons. Dante certainly studied it phrase by phrase by phrase after it was handed to him, perhaps in one of his beloved bookstalls near the Campo — in all probability he studied it in shocked speechlessness. We should do no less.

Its ingenuity was little less than staggering. This was even more evident than the legal correctness.

"The above-named, while they or certain of them held or did not hold the office of prior, or after they had laid down the said office."

"Either for themselves or for others."

"That they or that some of them."

"Would agree to make or not to make."

"Arranged these matters, or did them or had them done."

"Gave, promised, or paid, or had given or had paid."

"Had committed or had caused to be committed."

The specific crimes with which they were charged were equally comprehensively presented. "They or some of them" had "received money or property, or written or tacit promises of money or property" to tamper with the election of a new priorate. "They or some of them" had "received certain considerations unlawfully, illicitly, or unjustly" for agreeing to bribe these new priors to act illegally. They had illegally appropriated, either "from the treasurer of the commonwealth" or from the official funds allocated to the priors, "more and other properties and moneys than the decrees of the commonwealth prescribed," and "they had given or spent these" against Pope Boniface and Charles of Valois. They "or certain of them" had schemed "to have the city of Pistoia fall into divisions and sects" and to have it break away from its alliance with Florence and from its submission to the Holy Church."

It was like an intricately woven spiderweb, in which Dante and his fellows were the trapped flies. It was like the *Arabian Nights* story in which Sinbad wrestles with the Old Man of the Sea. As soon as Sinbad lays hands on him in one shape, he assumes another.

Nor, when the inevitable sentences were pronounced, could they in any possible way be complied with.

Let us consider only three of them, applying them to Dante.

(1) He was to pay into the treasury of Florence a fine of five thousand small florins.

(2) He was to restore all the moneys he had illicitly extorted. (Allegedly extorted, it should be added.)

(3) He must pay this fine or restore this property within three days.

To comply with the first two sentences was clearly financially impossible. It was probably meant to be. Dante was no pauper but he was not rich either. His outstanding debts may have amounted to seven hundred florins and they were certainly at least the two hundred fifteen florins which had to be discharged by his sons when his estate was finally settled in 1332. He had a wife to support and three children.

Possibly he could have hypothecated his city home, his city real estate, and his farms in the countryside. Possibly, but possibly only. For his brother seems to have had a half interest in these properties, and anyway they may have been hypothecated already.

But even if he had been able to pay this fine and make the restoration, he could not have done it in time. The Blacks had seen to that too. Even if a messenger, at the very moment the sentence had been passed, had galloped posthaste to Siena and then galloped back again, the three days of grace would have run out.

Came, then, January 30 or January 31 and the jackals were turned loose, and once again, as in the days of Farinata degli Uberti, large areas in central Florence were piled high with man-made rubble. Dante suffered with the rest. Urged on, it is said, by Boccaccio degli Adimari, who reputedly had once guaranteed a loan to the poet and whose vindictiveness may have been augmented by the fact that this loan had never been repaid, the pickaxe wielders and the demolition experts of the new government marched with menacing tread to San Martino del Vescovo and tore down Dante's house stone by stone.

(This, incidentally, disposes of a legend popular in the last century — namely that a certain dark thirteenth-century building hidden in a narrow Florentine alley was the home of Dante. There is no home of Dante. The present-day so-called house of Dante does indeed in all probability occupy the site where Dante's home once stood. But it was built in modern times.)

While this was going on, looters as well as officially sanctioned appropriators seized everything portable on which they could lay hands, while clerks representing the signory thumbed through the account books of everyone known to have been friendly to the poet in hopes of finding something confiscable. Only his wife Gemma, and, for the moment, his three or four children, were exempt. Neither she nor they were exiled at this time, although this had been the fate of the wives and children of most of the others sentenced. Nor was her property — her own property, that is; the property that came to her as a dowry — either destroyed or taken over. But then Gemma de' Donati was Corso Donati's cousin. If this was a consolation to Dante on the day the sky fell down on him, it was the only consolation he had.

« 8 »

The sky fell for a second time only six weeks later. Specifically, on March 10 of the same year.

On that date Dante was again sentenced — this time even more savagely and vindictively than before — as is borne out by a second "condemnation or sentence" which in the fourteenth century was copied from an earlier document and is preserved in the Florentine archives.

It, too, is worth considering in full.

Like the first sentence, it piously began, "In the name of the Lord, amen," and went on to state that "it had been made, published, and promulgated" by Messer Cante Gabrielli of Gubbio and had been "written down by me, Bonoro di Pregio, notary of the said lord *podestà*."

Then it listed those accused.

Messer Andrea de' Gherardini. (Messer Andrea was the son of Messer Gherardino de' Diodati. To the Blacks, as to other revolutionaries, you were "guilty" if you had a "guilty" father.)

Messer Lapo Salterelli, judge. (His chickens thus coming home to roost, and his attempt to join the winners evidently unsuccessful.)

Messer Palmieri Altoviti. (Involved with Dante in the previous condemnation.)

Messer Donato di Alberto of the Sesto di Porta del Duomo. (Who had drawn up the ineffectual letter to Charles of Valois and who with his brother Corso had been among those allegedly trying to tamper with the priorate.)

Lapo Ammanati of the Sesto d'Oltrarno. (A former White prior and also allegedly one of those who had been willing to use foul means as well as fair to continue White control.)

Lapo Biondi of the Sesto di San Piero Maggiore. (The same.)

Gherardino Diodati. (A second who had already been sentenced.)

Corso di Alberto Ristori. (Brother of Donato, mentioned above.)

Inamo de' Ruffoli. (Another allegedly plotting former White prior.)

Lippo Becchi. (The same.)

Dante Alighieri.

Orlanduccio Orlandi. (Again one of those already condemned with Dante. Perhaps hardly recovered from the wounds inflicted on him by a Black street gang.)

Simone Guidalotti of the Sesto d'Oltrarno. (A fifth former White prior.)

Ser Guccio Medici of the Sesto di Porta del Duomo. (A Medici who went against his clan. Why? And was it from him or from the street-fighting Medici that the first family of Renaissance Florence was descended?)

Guido Bruni degli Falconieri of the Sesto di San Piero Maggiore.

"Against these men," the document continued, "proceedings have been taken as the result of an investigation made about certain matters which had come to our ears and to those of our court" — once again, "through common report."

"And when they or certain of them were convicted of wicked and illicit extortions under the name and fact of barratry, and when these condemnations were announced to them, they or certain of them did not clear themselves of the charges within the prescribed time."

To be specific, "all and each of them were lawfully cited and summoned by an official of the commonwealth who admonished them that it was their duty as commanded by us within a certain time which has now expired."

This official, Chiaro Chiarissimo, "the public crier of the commonwealth of Florence," also warned them that "if they failed to present themselves they would once more fall under the ban, and if they fell under the ban they would renew their contumacy as is provided by the acts and actions of our court."

But they did not appear, and "by not appearing they or certain of them do confess to contumacy as defined by the laws, the statutes, and the ordinances of the commonwealth, and by the Ordinances of Justice and by the decree of our judges and by every law and custom of which we can avail ourselves.

"Wherefore" — the pen dug into the parchment — "if any of the above-named ever or at any time falls into the power of the commonwealth, such a one shall be burned by fire until he die."

Igne comburetur sic quod morietur!

Not merely a fine any longer.

Not merely loss of property.

Not banishment from "the province of Tuscany" for two years — or for some other stated period of time.

Not loss of civic rights for life — or for as long as the Black party remained in power.

Instead, actual and terrifying danger.

For the words written down by notary Bonoro were not used idly or as a mere figure of speech. If Dante or any other of the fourteen who were sentenced with him should fall into Florentine hands, he would be led in chains to a Florentine square and there resinous logs would be heaped around. Nor would the resultant death be the relatively pleasant one of being choked to death by coiling smoke and lack of oxygen. Like the Albigensian martyrs of the previous century, like the worldly Knights Templars ten years later, he literally would be consumed limb by limb while he was still alive.

(Perhaps imagining the flames clinging to and devouring his body rather than the fact that he almost certainly witnessed the burning of Master Adamo and others is why he displayed such a fear and horror of passing through the wall of flame in *Purgatorio* XXVI.)

This forced upon the fifteen men — and many others — new courses of action, for there was now deadly peril in even being near the beloved city unless in strong company.

Although he did not realize it, it also marked for Dante the beginning of the second and a very important phase in his life.

« 9 »

What this was, it is appropriate to let him tell you himself. When he was able to, he did this several times but usually either cryptically or indirectly. But at least twice his words were clear and explicit autobiography. We will consider one of these autobiographical passages now.

Paradiso XVII — and here Dante's ancestor Cacciaguida is speaking:

> "Contingency, although beyond the volume
> Of the material world it doth extend,
> Is clearly painted in the eternal vision;
> Yet therefrom doth not come necessity
> More than does from the eyes which mirror it
> A ship by current drifted down the stream.
> From this, and just as cometh to the ears
> Harmony from an organ, cometh to me
> The sight of what there is in store for thee."

This is by way of explanation. It is by way of telling the medieval reader — and us — how it is possible for God, or for anyone who can see with God's eyes, to foretell things which are still to be established by free choice.

Then the actual prophecy:

> "Even as Hippolytus was driven from Athens
> By his perfidious and cruel-hearted stepmother,
> So thou thyself must needs depart from Florence.
> That is determined, that is already sought for,
> That will be brought about by him who schemes it

> There where — and every day — Christ is bought and sold.
> The blame upon the wronged ones will be put
> In common report, as always, but the revenge
> Will be a witness to the truth that inflicts it.
> Thou wilt leave everything that thou most dear
> To thee hast held, and that will be the bolt
> The bow of exile arrows at thee first.
> Thou wilt discover how much doth taste of salt
> Another's bread, and what a bitter road
> Is going up and down another's stairs.
> And what will weigh the most upon thy shoulders
> Will be the evil and the senseless band
> With which thou shalt fall down into this slough.
> They, all ungrateful, utterly mad and pitiless,
> Shall show themselves to thee. Yet not long after
> They and not thou shall have red faces for this.
> Of this their rash ventures and their brutish folly
> Will give full proof, so that it will seem good to thee
> That thou shalt make a party of thyself alone."

Cacciaguida continues with further details of the days which were to come, but since these are not immediately pertinent we need not consider them until a more appropriate moment.

Finally he reached his conclusion:

> "Son, this is my gloss
> Upon what has been told thee."

By Farinata degli Uberti, by Ciacco, by Brunetto Latini and others in earlier passages of his poem!

> "These are the snares
> That beyond a few revolving years lie hid.
> Yet I would not thou envy thy fellow citizens,
> For thy life shall last far enough into the future
> To see the punishment of their perfidies."

This can be very plainly and very simply stated. I will do so.

From that late October day when the poet set out hopefully for Rome to lay the case of Florence before a pope who already schemed its ruin and his until now more than six and a half centuries later, the mortal body of Dante Alighieri while he lived, his hallowed remains after he had died, never again, never again even briefly, returned or were brought back to that fair sheepfold wherein he was born and grew to manhood. Instead he knew in his lifetime, as I said in an earlier attempt to comprehend and set down his character, "hate and exile, rebuff, self-question, loneliness, hurt pride." He became "a wanderer on the face of the earth." He became "a beggar at the feet of kings." And even after death his city was not able to reclaim him.

Nor did Florence or any notable Florentine seem to care either greatly or a little for a good six decades.

Then Boccaccio (*circa* 1360 in his *Life of Dante*) came to his defense very eloquently, abusing his own and Dante's Florence as he did so.

"O ungrateful city, what madness, what lack of vision possessed thee when with unearned cruelty thou put to flight thy most beloved citizen, thy most distinguished benefactor, indeed thy one and only great poet, and then kept him in exile? If perhaps thou wouldst excuse thyself by the widespread hatreds of that evilly counseled time, why, when the ragings had spent themselves and tranquility was restored, didst thou not repent and recall him? Doth it seem to thee that thou hast so many claims to glory that thou couldst deliberately hunt away from thee this man, the like of whom no neighbor city can boast? Dead is thy Dante Alighieri in that exile to which, envious of his worth, thou unjustly condemned him. He sleeps under another sky than thine, nor mayest thou ever think to see him again except on that day when thou shalt see all thy citizens and their sins weighed and punished by a just judge."

He followed this with an equally eloquent plea "to recover him dead whom thou didst refuse, nay expell, when alive."

This was the first of many attempts to have Dante's body brought to Florence for a final resting place. None of them, of course, succeeded.

« *10* »

But it is not this last, with its indication of a changed point of view, on which we should dwell, nor is it on Boccaccio's effulgent praises. It is rather on a single phrase which brings up a matter which has often, if not always, been brought up by those who study Dante.

That exile to which thou unjustly condemned him.

But was Dante unjustly condemned? At any rate, according to the lights and practices of his time?

The almost unanimous answer has been a ringing *yes*, this *yes* being perhaps most compactly expressed by Robert Davidsöhn in his discussion of the White tampering with the priorate in which many of the poet's associates played an important part. Davidsöhn agrees that such tampering took place, and even that it was necessary. Then he says this:

"Certainly Dante, given his noble nature, does not need to be defended by us here."

He adds:

"The poet would not have lowered himself to the point of participating personally in this sordid business."

And to a point we must agree.

But only to a point.

For as Davidsöhn also says in connection with the same alleged White irregularities, "anyone who takes part in factions and feuds may well, at a given moment, find himself carried along by the whirlwind and plunged into the mud even though his own intentions are the purest and most elevated."

This I hold to have been the case with Dante. It seems certain that he did not personally profit in a monetary sense in any of the intricate dealings which went on. If he had, his financial situation would have reflected it.

But to say that he played no part in the schemes and counterschemes for which he and the others were brought to trial is to cast aspersions on his intelligence. At that time he was a politician and a successful one. As a politician and a successful one, it seems logical that he would join with others in using Florentine money for White purposes in a manner that did not strictly comply with the law. In his *Commedia*, he half acknowledges this.

Inferno XXIII — as he escapes from the demons of the Malebolge (the part of hell where barrators are punished):

> I thought this thought: "Because of us these have
> Been fooled with so much hurt and mockery
> That I believe they must be filled with ire,
> And if this anger's added to ill-will
> They will come at our heels more savagely
> Than a hound snapping at a leveret."
> And I already felt my hair standing up
> In fear as I did look behind myself intently
> To cry out loudly: "Master, if thou hidest not
> Thyself and me swiftly, I'll quake in terror
> At the Malebranche who're in chase already.
> I already hear them baying at our heels.

This is one of the two or three times when Dante appears to fear punishment for himself. Might this not have been because technically — although by no means whatsoever morally — he was a fit target for the claws and talons and the pitchy lake of these tormentors? And because he knew it?

XV

The University of the White Party

B UT whether Dante was guilty as charged or indeed unjustly condemned — "noble and innocent" — as most believe, he paid the full
and devastating penalty of guilt, and he kept on paying for it for the rest
of his life. Nor could he derive much more than literary consolation from
the fact that retribution would strike down one after another of his
persecutors and accusers, and that he would live long enough to see this
happen which he did.

Corso Donati's end came first.

Purgatorio XXIV — Forese Donati is replying to Dante, who has just
told him that the place (Florence) where he has been "put to live from
day to day doth strip herself of good, and doth seem destined to a
tragic fall":

> " 'T is true," he said, "and him for this to blame
> Meseems I see dragged at the tail of a beast
> Toward that vale where sins are not absolved.
> The beast at every step doth swifter go,
> Galloping faster until it smiteth him
> And leaves his body evilly undone."

Actually, Corso — for it was Corso about whom Forese spoke — was
not dragged at the tail of a horse through the streets of the city he once
tried to dominate; yet his end was almost equally ignominious.

Not more than half a dozen years after their coup d'etat, the Black
leaders began to quarrel among themselves, the more conservative Blacks
— Geri Spini, Betto Brunellischi, and Pazzino de' Pazzi — with Rosso

della Tosa, who aspired to become a despot like the Visconti in Milan but thought the time not yet ripe, joining to oppose the more turbulent magnate Blacks who were led by Corso and followed by the city rabble.

The former "had the offices and the government of the city and the people" and the powers that went with having these.

They proceeded to use them.

Calling Corso a Ghibelline who sought to become tyrant over the city, and charging him with putting Florence in an uproar to attain this end, they "first cited him to appear, and then proclamation was made against him. In less than an hour, without giving any longer time for his trial, he was condemned as a rebel and a traitor to his commonwealth. And straightway the priors set forth with the standard of justice, and with the *podestà*, and with the captain and the executioner and their retainers, and with the standard-bearers of the companies, and with the people in arms, and with troops on horse, and went to the house where dwelt Messer Corso at San Piero Maggiore to carry out the sentence."

But although Il Barone, surrounded by "much folks, his friends and kinsmen in arms and with crossbows," seemed ready to meet them, and although he had barricaded the Via di San Piero Maggiore, Twist-Your-Tail Street, the Via San Procolo, and the approaches to the Stinche prisons, when he saw them draw near he lost heart.

Crying that he sought aid, he leaped upon a steed and, although "infirm with gout," galloped out of an eastern gate. He got to Rovezzano but no farther, for there "he was overtaken and captured by certain Catalans" who haled him roughly back to Florence.

Or almost to Florence. For at San Salvi just outside its walls he made a final bid for freedom, promising his captors — who were mercenaries — "much money" if only they would let him escape.

"But they held to their purpose of taking him to the city as was commanded them by their lords."

Then at last he truly panicked.

"In fear of coming into the hands of his enemies, and of being brought to justice by the people, he let himself fall from his horse."

It was the last thing he was to do in this world.

"The said Catalans, seeing him on the ground, one of them gave him a thrust in the throat with his lance which was a mortal blow. He left him there for dead."

Rosso della Tosa died in an accident.

"This man," says Dino Compagni, "having long been awaited by God, seeing that he was more than seventy-five years old, was walking one day when a dog ran between his feet, throwing him to the ground. He broke his knee and a fistula formed on it. While the doctors were torturing him, he died in a convulsion."

Betto Brunelleschi was murdered — by Donateschi.

He had been a prime mover — or so it was believed — in Corso's downfall and death, and for that reason it is in no way surprising that "one day, as he was playing chess, two young men of the Donati family with some others who were their friends came to him in his house and wounded him in the head repeatedly."

He, like Corso, was left for dead.

Yet for some days "his condition was such that some thought he would recover, but after a while, frenzied and without repenting or making his peace with God and with the world, he died miserably."

Says Dino:

"Many rejoiced at his death, for he was a very bad citizen."

Pazzino de' Pazzi was murdered too — appropriately enough by one of the Cavalcanti who learned that he had gone to the dry bed of the Arno with a falcon and only one servant, and thereupon followed him and thrust him through the back with a lance.

"He fell into the water, and they" — young Cavalcanti had friends — "cut his veins and fled toward the Val di Sieve."

Gherardo Bordoni met his end at the small hamlet of La Croce a Gorgo (Crossroads by the Eddy) on the right bank of the Arno east of the city. He had fled thither after an unsuccessful street fight with the anti-Donati Blacks, and was pursued by two of the Spini and by Boccaccio Adimari with his sons and kinsmen.

"They attacked him. He fell on his face. They dismounted and slew him. And one of Boccaccio's kinsmen cut off his hand and carried it home."

For which "some blamed him," says Dino.

Corso's son Simone was fatally wounded while trying to do away with one of the Cerchi.

But even those who played both ends against the middle did not escape.

Lapo Salterelli, for example.

"He died in exile in great misery." Supposedly in France, where other exiles prospered.

All this, however — or most of it — was in the future, the events recorded above mainly taking place in 1307, 1308, and 1309. The present was another matter. Dino Compagni describes this present. "*A parte bianca e ghibellina accorsono molti orribili disavventure.*" To the White and Ghibelline party there befell many horrible misadventures. To them and to Dante with them. For at that time he was one of them, and for the immediate future their cause was his cause.

2

None of these misadventures, however, took place at once, and for that reason none of them took place in the hill city which once (in Montaperti days) had sheltered the enemies of Dante's forebears and in which he heard his own terrible tidings. For as Dino Compagni tells us, "The Ghibellines and the Whites who had taken refuge in Siena did not stay there long. They remembered the old saying: 'The she-wolf plays the harlot!' "

The she-wolf was Siena. She was not thought to be trustworthy.

"Sometimes she gives passage and sometimes she refuses."

Gives passage, that is, to White bands and allows freedom of movement to White and Ghibelline leaders. But the next day halts the same bands and seizes the leaders.

This was a chance the Whites did not dare take.

3

They first went only a little way. To Gargonza, "a fortified castle which was in the possession of the Ubaldini, a Ghibelline family which had been expelled from Florence."

I will let Christopher Hare describe the journey, which is through a country even today savage and remote and deeply scarred with clay pits. His is, to be sure, a work of imagination, if not fiction. But imagination is needed in a work of history. We scamp truth if we are afraid to use it.

"Through the mist of the ages we can picture to ourselves that coming of the banished men. We can see the weather-beaten company slowly ascend the rugged hill path in straggling order — probably late in the evening after a weary, depressing ride. They may have lost their way more than once, for the roads are like rough lanes, dark and over-shadowed with trees, and they find some shepherd lad as their guide to the lonely castle. Perched like a robber hold, the place is prepared for an attack at any moment, and none can approach without a challenge. There is a parley at the gate, the portcullis is raised, the horses clatter across the lowered drawbridge, and lighted on the way by men-at-arms with flaming torches, the motley group passed into the courtyard.

"Tired and hungry, Dante and his companions are glad to dismount and enter into the great hall where they can warm their stiffened limbs before the blazing wood fire on the broad hearth."

This last sentence may surprise, for Dante and his companions came to Gargonza in May. But, as Hare points out, even in the spring it can be icy cold in the Tuscan hills.

"By and by the rude plenty of the evening meal will be spread on the high table, raised on a dais for the lord and his more honored guests, while the commoner sort will feed with the retainers on lower tables spread longways against the walls. We may be sure that as men's tongues are loosened by the good fare and the Tuscan wine, there will be loud, eager talk in abuse of the Neri [the Blacks] and their doings, mingled with noisy jeers and threats of vengeance. They will be too absorbed in this to heed the clanking of metal goblets and dishes, the crunching of bones by dogs under the table, or 'the sharp cry of some ill-bred falcon, for many lords do keep these on a perch behind them.'

"After a long day spent on the road and a heavy supper, there is not much inducement to sit up late; the more important visitors are crowded into the guest chamber while the rest are glad to rest in the hall itself on mattresses of straw placed on the litter of rushes and herbs which is spread over the stone floor."

Sleep is unbroken except as interrupted "by the tossing and coughing of a sick man and an occasional brawl between varlets who had not been able to fight out their quarrel in the daytime."

Otherwise silence.

At the first break of dawn, however, everybody would be up and about his business.

"The grooms would hasten to the stables, the scullions to the kitchen — all men to their various duties; doors are clanging, dogs barking, horns are blown, and the whole fortress rings with cheerful tumult."

The exiles had begun another day.

« 4 »

But not even the early-morning high spirits and the rude evening hospitality kept Dante and his fellows very long at the hilltop castle which stood, and still stands, rectangular and severe amid a bodyguard of cypress trees and the cluster of red rooftops of its attendant town.

There were several reasons for this. For one thing, the Ubaldini were not deemed entirely reliable. As Ghibellines, it was in their very blood and being to be against the pope, and therefore against his allies. But it was thought that they could be persuaded to change sides for money, and in fact rumor had it that approaches had already been made to them. This was not necessarily true, but proscribed men are understandably apprehensive. For another thing, there was a much more secure refuge not more than a dozen miles distant with much more room for their swelling numbers. This had so long a record of hostility to Florence that they felt sure — although this turned out to be wrong — they could forever count on it.

In his life of the poet, Leonardo Bruni has something to say about this.

"Having learned of his ruin," he writes, "and having no other course, Dante decided to join the other exiles."

These included the White leaders new to this fate and the Ghibellines who had grown gray since they had last seen Florence. The latter had hitherto found shelter in Arezzo, Pisa, Pistoia, and Bologna, and in the still-defiant castles of the Apennines.

"They met at Gargonza. There many things were discussed, and it was finally agreed to make their headquarters at Arezzo. Thither, therefore, they hied *en masse*, and when they had reached it, they named Count Alessandro da Romena their captain. They also gave him twelve councillors, one of whom was Dante."

(Here an interesting question obtrudes itself. Who was this Count Alessandro? He is generally supposed to have been the Count Alessandro whom — with his brothers Guido and Aghinolfo — Dante had placed in hell for persuading Master Adamo to become a false coiner. Yet in a letter written to the Guelph leader's nephews at the time of his death in 1304, he refers to their uncle (*patruus voster*) as "illustrious" and as my "noble lord." He says that "his memory will have dominion over me for as long as my life lasts." He speaks of "his loftiness of soul which beyond the stars is now richly recompensed with fitting rewards." He proclaims that "this quality caused him to stand out as it were in bronze above other Italians." But could this have been the same Alessandro? Historians still speculate.)

In Arezzo, the Whites and the Ghibellines, encouraged — but it now seems unduly — by the fact that "Uguccione della Faggiuola, a man of old Ghibelline stock who had there risen to be *podestà*," did one thing more. They formally set up a *massa* (political machine or perhaps even government) in exile. This they named the *Università della parte dei Bianchi della città e del contado di Firenze* — University (central committee) of the White party of the city and the countryside of Florence. (Note that Ghibelline was left out. This was for appearance.) Its purpose was to take the first necessary steps toward an eventual return to the place that had expelled the Whites. First it sought funds, and found them — largely from the Cerchi, who had by now been sentenced too and had fled the city, but apparently had transferred much of their money before this happened. Then it looked for ways to use the funds. These the *Università* — and Dante, who had been named to the *Università* — found too.

« 5 »

The still-surviving abstract of a contract drafted by one Ser Giovanni Buto, a notary from the nearby mountain hamlet of Ampinana, shows what one of the uses was.

"June 8, 1302.

"In the choir of the church in San Godenzo at the foot of the Alps," and in the presence of the necessary witnesses, "it has been agreed as follows by Messers Torrigiano, Carbone, and Vieri de' Cerchi, Messer Guglielmo de' Ricasoli, Messers Neri, Bettino Grosso, Bettino de' Acceriti, and Nuccio de' Acceriti of the Ubertini family, Messer Andrea de' Gherardini, Branca and Chele de' Scolai, *Dante Alighieri*, Mino da Radda, Bettino de' Pazzi, and Lapo, Ghino, Taddeo, and Azzolino de' Uberti:

"That they and that each one of them acting on behalf of them do, after due deliberation, promise and pledge Lapo Bertaldi of Florence, acting for the noble lord Uguccione of Feliccione and for his sons and for all others of the house of Ubaldini and for anyone of them, to recompense, satisfy, and make good out of their own holdings and property all damage, loss of use, and expenses, whether in temporal goods or in ecclesiastical preferment, which they may incur as a result of actions or war made or to be made against the castle of Monte Accenico or against any other stronghold belonging to them or to anyone faithful to them or under their control.

"And they give a bond for this in the amount of two thousand silver marks.

"And as a pledge that they will carry this out they do give a lien to the said Lapo upon all their present and future property.

"And this is guaranteed, etc."

The exiled White merchant-burghers — to explain — had decided to strike back, and as has so often been the case — and still is — with exiles, to strike back with guerrilla or partisan warfare. They would take castles — or try to take them — if need be, but more often they would ravage the countryside, burning farmhouses, trampling the now-ripening grain, cutting olive trees, and rooting up vineyards. To do this — and here goes consistency — they enlisted the assistance of Uguccione of Feliccione, who was one of the very kind of feudal robber baron whom their forefathers, as they tried to establish a citizen government, had spent two centuries trying to destroy or contain.

Nor is an examination of those who guaranteed Uguccione any less revealing.

Torrigiano, Carbone, and Vieri de' Cerchi were sons of Vieri the elder, who was the most important White leader.

Andrea de' Gherardini was a White. He had been sent by the Whites to rule Pistoia in their name during the last days before their government was overthrown.

The Scolaii were Whites, as was almost certainly Messer Guglielmo de' Ricasoli.

For all his Black kinsmen, Bettino de' Pazzi was a White too.

But the four Ubertini — who seem to have played the anomalous role of being both protectors and protected — and the four Uberti were Ghibellines of the most inveterate kind. Indeed one of the latter was a nephew of the greatest of all Ghibellines, Farinata degli Uberti.

Town merchant — onetime town merchant — and the most maurauding type of Ghibelline lord thus stood together. Politics does indeed make strange bedfellows.

And where did Dante, who was one of the signers, stand in this alliance of White and Ghibelline which at long last had come into the open? What did he think of it? As a member of the White party, did he adhere to it?

Boccaccio thought he knew the answer:

"In his days of adversity, the worthy man bore himself with the greatest of fortitude and indeed in only one thing was he intolerant or vindictive — that was in matters pertaining to political parties, and especially after he had gone into exile."

Then he explains:

"A long while ago, the just anger of God permitted almost all Tuscany and Lombardy to be divided into two parties. One was called the Guelph party and the other the Ghibelline. And these two names were so powerful and had such reverence in the hearts of many that to defend the one which one had chosen for one's own against the other, it was not thought too great an evil to lose one's earthly goods, or even one's life if need be."

Dante's ancestors were Guelphs, Boccaccio continues, and as such they were twice exiled from the city, and it was as a Guelph that he held office in the city of Florence.

"But from this city he was exiled, as I have already shown, not by Ghibellines but by Guelphs, and seeing that he could not return, he so changed his sentiments that there was no one more fiercely a Ghibelline and so hostile to the Guelphs as he. And that of which I am the most ashamed is that it is widely known that if any woman even, if even any small child, speaking to him of party matters should condemn the Ghibellines, it brought him to such a pitch of anger that he would even hurl stones at this person if he or she were not made to keep silent. And this animosity continued until his death."

Thus Boccaccio.

But there are some — Isodoro del Lungo is the most notable of these — who will not have it that Dante was ever a Ghibelline. This opinion is at least in part a product of their nineteenth-century liberalism. For to them to be a Ghibelline was to favor the hated Tedeschi (Germans and Austrians), and that in their opinion was something no Italian patriot — and Dante was an Italian patriot — could possibly do.

The truth probably lies in the middle. There is no question that Dante became and died a Ghibelline, but that was later on. On June 8, 1302, he was still a Guelph, and it was as a Guelph that he was asked to sign. As an influential and respected Guelph. Certainly he was worth little as a financial guarantor, for such of his property as Gemma had not been able to retain — or as had not been quietly transferred to his brother Francesco, who in a long life seems almost always to have avoided political involvement — was either confiscated or destroyed. He was a pauper.

But his good name and his general, if not universal, reputation for civic disinterest were something quite different. The Cerchi were money-makers, if not moneygrubbers, and their motive was to get back to making money again. Most of their followers were moved by self-interest, even if it was enlightened. But Dante still served his concept of an ideal city as he would later serve his concept of an ideal state. He buffed some of the tarnish from a shabbying cause.

« 6 »

But it was not merely at San Godenzo, its rosy-pink, brick-facaded Byzantine church clinging, as it still does, to the face of a steep mountainside that looks down on the Sieve valley through which runs a road to Pontassieve and then Florence — it was not merely at this red-tiled fief of the Counts Guidi that Dante did more than yeoman service for the unhappy Whites.

Always a partisan, and always unshakably firm on behalf of any cause which he had espoused or any purpose to which he had dedicated himself, he served the White-Ghibelline alliance (whether or not it was distasteful to him) in many other places and in many other ways. As a counsellor — although his advice was not always taken. As a spokesman — we have already seen one of his letters and will shortly see another. But perhaps most importantly as an ambassador, using the negotiating skills which he had demonstrated successfully at San Gimignano but not at the court of Boniface to win friends and influence people in the struggle with the Blacks.

His first mission in the last capacity took him into the Romagna — specifically to the Forum Livii of the Romans which had come to be known as Forlì. It is widely assumed that this mission took place in the spring of 1304, for it was at that time that Uguccione della Faggiuola had finally — if, as we will see later, temporarily — changed sides, and in Arezzo "had inflicted so many injuries on the White exiles" that a great many of them "went to Forlì, where was Scarpetta degli Ordelaffi, a nobleman, who was vicar of the church" but not unwilling to abet its enemies. But to me it seems more likely that he journeyed to Forlì almost immediately following San Godenzo. It would be in character for him — and desirable for the Whites — to strike when the iron was hot.

In either case, he crossed that rugged part of the backbone or ridgepole of Italy which today is known as the Muraglione, or Big Wall. What doing this was like — what it was like to climb this and the many other mountains he climbed during his life — can be pieced out from many passages in his *Commedia*.

Purgatorio IV:

> Go can one to San Leo, descend to Noli,
> Or mount unto the summit of Bismantova
> With feet alone, but here one must needs fly.

Purgatorio X:

> We climbed up through a cleft between the rocks
> Which seemed that it did bend this way and that
> Like to a wave which draws back and then surges.

This was, of course, an optical illusion. Other mountain climbers have had the same experience.

Purgatorio XIX:

> [Upward we went]
> Between two walls of hard and granite stone.

Purgatorio XIX again:

> Like as a falcon which first gazes at its feet
> And then turns at the call and circles in
> Through the desire for food which moves it thus,
> So I became and so, where was gashed
> The cliff to make a place for the mounting road,
> Did I proceed.

Purgatorio XX:

> We moved along . . .
> The space which was left clear along the cliff
> As one goes by a wall along the battlements.

Purgatorio XXV:

> So one behind the other we moved through the gap.

Inferno XII:

> Necessity impelled me, not delight.

Sometimes he would be obliged to ask for directions from a shepherd who, almost walnut in color and wrapped in a dull-blue homespun cloak, would appear through the damp and chilly mist followed by his bleating sheep.

Purgatorio XI:

> Show us on which side is the shortest road
> That leads us upward. Be there more than one,
> Do thou inform us which the less steep is,
> For he who comes with me, bearing the burden
> Of Adam's flesh with which he vestured is,
> Strive though indeed he do, is slow at climbing.

An answer — not inconsistent, for the pale disk of the sun usually soon burned away the fog — is found in *Purgatorio* I:

> The sun will show to you, which rises now,
> How to climb up the mount the easiest way.

At the day's end, there would be a halt for the night.

Purgatorio XXVII:

> "The sun departs," a voice did then continue. "Evening comes.
> Therefore stay not, but hasten ye your steps
> Before the western sky doth grow all dark."
> The way straight upward went between the rocks
> In such direction that I was cut off
> From the sun's rays which lower sank and lower,
> And few steps forward had my sages and I
> Taken when, from the shadows vanishing, we knew
> That it had set behind my sages and me.
> And then before the vast, immense expanse
> Of the horizon had become one color
> And night had taken all under its rule,
> Each of us on a stone ledge made our bed.

Then he saw the stars — those glittering, intense points of scintillance around which he was to build every climactic moment of his great epic.
Again *Purgatorio* XXVII:

> Little indeed without could we see there,
> But by that little we could see the stars
> Both bigger and more bright than was their wont.

He would have awaked early, and we may assume that he awoke — and that he had laid himself down — at the summit. Such a summit he describes in *Inferno* XXIV ("The breath within my lungs was now so spent by the long climb that I could go not farther but must needs sit me down.") and *Purgatorio* IV ("There did we both make ourselves to sit down facing the east whence we had climbed, for to look backward often doth cheer men.").
Still *Purgatorio* XXVII:

> And with the splendors of the bright predawn . .
> The shadows fled from me on every side,
> And my sleep with them. So did I arise.

But, like the stars, the coming of a new day with its slow suffusion of light always fascinated Dante.
Purgatorio I:

> That sweetest hue of oriental sapphire
> That swelled and gathered with serene aspect
> From the clear zenith unto the first circle
> Did in mine eyes again renew delight.

Purgatorio I again:

> The dawn now overcame the morning breeze
> Which fled before it so that far away
> I could descry the trembling of the sea.

(These last lines were inspired by another view from another mountaintop, but it is appropriate to cite them here.)
Purgatorio II:

> And lo, as at the coming of the dawn
> Through the thick vapors Mars glows ruddily
> Low in the west over the ocean floor,
> So there appeared to me — and may I see it again —
> A light that moved swiftly . . .

EFFIGIE DI DANTE ALIGHIERI DALLA MASCHERA FORMATA SUL DI LUI CADAVERE IN RAVENNA L'ANNO 1321.

IL MARCHESE CARLO TORRIGIANI
CON TESTAMENTO OLOGRAFO DONAVA ALLA CITTÀ DI FIRENZE
QUESTO RITRATTO IN RILIEVO
CHE VUOLSI FATTO VERAMENTE SU LA FORMA TOLTA DAL CADAVERE
E IL MARCHESE LUIGI LO CONSEGNAVA SOLLECITO
A QUESTE REALI GALLERIE NELL' ANNO MDCCCLXV

The Dante death mask (Bargello, Florence) is now thought to be not a death mask but rather an extremely convincing portrait executed at an unknown date, but probably later than the Naples bust.

In the same canto, he spoke also of "the white and rosy cheeks of fair Aurora" which were "turning orange" and said that "on every side now arrowed forth the day / The sun, who with his arrows keen had chased Capricorn from the midheavens." God's world was still fresh enough — as it should be still — for a great soul not to be ashamed of being stirred by simple yet miraculous things.

From the summit near which Dante presumably halted and spent the night, the road descended eastward, but somewhat less steeply than it had ascended from the Tuscan west, and just less than two miles from the Muraglione Pass the poet came to another place which he would describe vividly.

Inferno XVI — and Dante is actually talking of one of the sharper and more difficult descents which he made as he went downward through the infernal regions:

> I followed him, and not far had we gone
> When a sound of water was so near to us
> That we could scarcely hear each other speak.
> For as that river which is first to take,
> South of Mount Veso, a course toward the east
> Upon the left slopes of the Apennines
> (Called Acquacheta there above, before
> It floods below into its lower bed
> And at Forlì of that name is deprived)
> Reverberates above San Benedetto
> Dell' Alpe, where it falls down in one bound
> Where well indeed there might have been a thousand,
> We heard the dark water sound . . .

San Benedetto *in* Alpe — its present name — is, say the guidebooks, "a little village, shut in by mountains, which was founded by the nearby monastery, in which were buried the martyrs Primo and Feliciano, and where Dante stopped to pray." So far so good — and so clear. Dante paused and rested there. But what about the final words of his description? *Dove dovria per mille esser ricetto.* Where well indeed there might have been a thousand.

The most common interpretation is that this was an attack upon the decline of Christian piety — the kind of piety which led men to abandon the pleasures of the world, pleasures which city monks would certainly share, to immure themselves in this lonely place. At San Benedetto there was only a handful of monks where there should have been a throng.

But Boccaccio — and others — understood the words otherwise. In his *Commento alla Divina Commedia,* he said this:

"I was formerly and for a long time in doubt as to what the author meant to say. Then by chance I once found myself in the said monastery in the company of its abbot and he told me that there once was talk among those counts [the Counts Guidi] who were lords to these Alps that it might be well, as in a place that would be very convenient for those who came to dwell there, to build a castle there and to fill it with those who dwelt in the many little hamlets which were vassal to them. But then the one of them who had most ardently pressed the idea came to die, and so the discussions came to nothing. And that is what the author meant. He meant that 'more than a thousand' — that is, many people — might have dwelt there."

But there is still another interpretation which I like better than either of these. This is that the words refer to the cascade itself and not either to Counts Guidi vassals or to monks.

The river, a relative trickle today, then, according to Boccaccio, leaped noisily, "especially when during a rainy season it was swollen with water," in one mighty plunge over a single precipice near the monastery. But in the same space there might have been a thousand little waterfalls, a white welter of Apennine foam!

After San Benedetto, the road continued downward between mountains that were still tall but grew less rugged with every passing mile. Past Portico, overlooked by a beetling castle which is now in ruins, and over a stone bridge which may have been ancient even then. On to tiny Dovadola (Due Vadora — Two Fords) — one of the fiefs of Count Guido Salvatico. Dante may have stopped there, for Boccaccio says that this Count Guido was one of the poet's first hosts. But it is more likely that the count — who was so ardent a Black that one wonders why he received Dante at all — entertained him at Pratovecchio in the Casentino. Finally to Castrocaro, which Dante would flay in one of his more withering passages — a passage which it is not appropriate, however, to quote at the present time.

Now he was in the Romagna, and since the Romagna was the part of Italy that would enter more deeply into his soul and into his thoughts than any other except his own Florence it would be well to set down two of his reactions to it. They seem to contradict each other. But do they?

Inferno XXVII:

> O spirit who art hidden there below,
> Romagna thine is not nor ever was
> Without war in the cruel hearts of her tyrants.

De Vulgari Eloquentia I, 14:

"Let us now cross the leaf-clad shoulders of the Apennines and hunt inquiringly, as is our custom, through the left side of Italy, beginning from the east. Entering the Romagna, then, we observe that we have found in Italy two different types of dialects with certain opposite characteristics in which they respectively agree. One of these, on account of the softness of its words and its pronunciation, seems so feminine that it causes a man when he is speaking to be thought a woman. The other is so bristling and shaggy in its accents that, owing to its rough harshness, it not only distorts a woman's speech, but makes one doubt whether she is not a man."

"*Deusci!*" said the Romagnoli — including the men of Forlì — for yes, and they used *oclo meo* (eye of mine) and *corada mea* (my heart) as terms of affection. Man speaking to man, not man to woman. Yet nowhere were there more savage fighters. A Romagnole cut throats as other men sliced salami.

It was to these fierce-hearted men, who had, however, gentle and effeminate voices, that Dante crossed the mountains to address himself. Forlì is little more than six miles beyond Castrocaro and the road at this point is through a pleasant if narrow valley filled with fruit trees, so this part of the journey could not have taken much time. Moreover, as Dante approached journey's end, his footsteps would have been hastened by eagerness to accomplish the specific purpose with which he had been charged.

"Secure this strategically located city as a base for White-Ghibelline operations," he had been instructed — and perhaps he had helped draw up the instructions himself. "If possible, persuade too the lord of the green claws to continue his support of us."

The "lord of the green claws" (*Inferno* XXVII) was Scarpetta degli Ordelaffi, whose arms were a lion vert upon a field or. He was tyrant of Forlì.

"Let him march to our assistance. If it is his plan to build up an independent domain in these onetime imperial lands which are now claimed by the pope, he will serve himself if he serves us."

To convince him of this would not, however, be easy. Once burned is twice shy, and Scarpetta had already toasted his fingers trying to aid the merchant-burghers and their allies.

Either before or not too long after the agreement of San Godenzo was signed, he had been named captain of an army of seven hundred horsemen and four thousand foot soldiers; had mustered these at the Monte Accenico of the document; and had marched them against Pulicciano above Borgo San Lorenzo. This was a Black stronghold in the Mugello. It was not very well defended, and the men holding it were taken by surprise. The war should have been ended then and there.

But Scarpetta's followers were not Scarpettas, and although the Blacks who marched against this White array — "with caution" — were few in number, the mere sight of bare steel seems to have terrified them, and they panicked.

"The Whites thought themselves as good as captured," writes Dino Compagni, "and therefore retired in disorder, and those who were not fleet-footed enough to escape were made prisoner. For the vassals of the neighboring counts immediately took possession of the passes, where they captured and slew many of them."

Scarpetta had now had all he needed. Angry and even disillusioned, he got back to his own city, where his thoughts about the quaking tradesmen were hardly complimentary.

And now Dante was sent to make him revise these thoughts, and there is some reason to believe he succeeded.

At any rate, he made the effort.

The story is told that to gain Scarpetta's goodwill — and perhaps to replenish his own by now very slender resources — he served as the Forlivese chieftain's secretary. But this has been convincingly denied by the historian Flavio Biondo (1388–1463), himself a native of Forlì and in point of time reasonably close to the event. Dante was not Scarpetta's secretary. The latter's secretary was one Pelligrino Calvi. But Dante apparently did compose some of the letters Pelligrino wrote, and by doing this — by giving the Ordelaffi lord, even though at second hand, the benefit of his reasoning powers and his eloquence — he put the latter in a frame of mind to listen to him. Later events will show that this had results.

« 7 »

At about this time, Dante went to Verona too — almost certainly from Forlì and probably at the urging of Scarpetta degli Ordelaffi.

Here we have another matter that demands examination.

We have already looked at certain of those lines in *Paradiso* XVII in which Cacciaguida eloquently discourses about his famous descendant's imminent misfortunes. In these, after discussing in general terms the bleak days of Dante's exile, he becomes specific.

> "Thy first refuge, thy first hostelry
> Will be the courtesy of the great Lombard
> Who on the stairway bears the sacred bird,
> And he will hold thee in such high regard
> That of the doing and asking between you too
> Will be first that which among others is last.
> With him thou wilt see one so influenced
> By — on his natal day — so strong a star

That every deed he does will be renowned.
Of him the people have not yet taken note,
So young he is, since only for nine years
The wheels of heaven have around him turned.
But long before the Gascon has deceived high Harry
Sparks of his worth and valor will be seen
Whom neither treasure nor effort will deter.
His munificence shall be known to everyone
So plainly that not even his enemies
Will have the power to keep silent of him."

But this first refuge — as a refuge — was not sought by Dante at this time. For at this time — possibly in 1302, but more probably a year later — he was not yet seeking refuge.

Instead, he crossed Emilia and then Lombardy to come to the city by the Adige as an ambassador, not as a seeker for asylum. He sought the help of the Scaligeri as he had earlier sought that of Ordelaffi.

Initially, he seems to have been successful here too. By June 10, 1303, it was reasonably plain that Verona was inclined to join an alliance which to the Whites of Florence would bind Faenza, Forlì, Ravenna, Pistoia, and Pisa. Among the leaders (other than Bartolommeo and probably Scarpetta) would be Bernardino da Polenta, brother of Francesca da Rimini, and Federigo da Montefeltro, grandson of Guido da Montefeltro, son of Buonconte, and ancestor of the great Renaissance dukes of Urbino. That this led White hopes far too high and that Verona not very much later withdrew are another matter. Dante had done what he was supposed to. The failure must be laid to others.

« 8 »

There are only three other matters pertaining to these first years of Dante's exile which should be noted.

(1) There is a possibility that Dante's wife Gemma and perhaps one or more of his sons were now compelled to share his exile. They had been exempted from earlier sentences, but new and more stringently enforced decrees insisted that there should be no exception to the edict that wives and any sons who were over fourteen years old should join their banished husbands and fathers. However we have no specific evidence that either she or they joined Dante.

(2) It is almost certain that even while finding time to go to San Godenzo, to Forlì, and finally to Verona, the poet wandered widely through an area that (except for San Godenzo) was much nearer Florence. This was the Casentino, then held by the Counts Guidi, and whether Guelph or Ghibelline, there was not one of them who would not

proudly receive him. Pratomagno, Porciano, Romena (today a ruin), and Poppi (now handsomely restored) — these are only a few of the Counts Guidi castles that were honored by his presence. But he also walked many miles through the countryside itself, noting the *lucertole* (agile little lizards) that flashed like metal as they darted from sun to shadow, noting the little brooks and streams, noting the dark cypresses, noting the field flowers and the wallflowers.

Two stories have survived which deal with Dante during these days, and although one of them may be apocryphal they are both worth setting down.

One of these he tells himself.

Convivio IV, 11:

"Indeed, I myself have seen the place on the side of a mountain in Tuscany called Falterona where the lowest-born peasant in the whole countryside discovered, while he was digging, more than a bushel of *santalenas* of the purest silver. They had been waiting for him for more than a thousand years."

Falterona, almost fifty-four hundred feet high, is one of the taller peaks in the Tuscan Apennines. On its slope is the source of the Arno. During his wanderings, Dante supposedly climbed Falterona, and as he did so he was shown, the talk of all around, the spot where a poor countryman, grubbing to make a bare living, had uncovered this priceless Byzantine treasure.

The second story is lighter.

Dante, it relates, was staying at a Count Guidi castle when word came to him that an emissary of the Florentine republic was on his way thither — supposedly, at any rate so Dante thought, to ask that he be handed over to him.

The poet did what prudence dictated. He left at once. But on the road he met the representative of his native city.

The man accosted him.

"Where do you come from?"

"Porciano," replied Dante.

"Can you tell me if Dante the Florentine is still there?"

"He was there when I was," said the poet and walked on.

(3) It is highly probable that while Dante was at Arezzo — and for all his moving here and there, he spent much time at Arezzo at this period — he became a close friend of a man whose son was to occupy a place in Italian literature second only to his own.

Among those driven from Florence with Dante was one "Ser Petracco di Ser Parenzo of Ancisa [Incisa], notary for the Reformation," and this

Ser Petracco betook himself to the same hill city which sheltered the poet, where he bought himself a modest villa on a small flowery byway known as the Via, or the Vico, del Orto. There, on July 20, 1304, his wife, Eletta de' Canigiani, bore him a son who was promptly named Francesco. After the custom of the day, Francesco di Petracco. But when the boy came to manhood — and dedicated himself to the Muses — he changed his name to Francesco Petrarca as more melodious. Francesco Petrarca — our Francis Petrarch!

Dante and Petrarch's father may even have shared the same home, for there is a local legend — or was until recently — that not only were he and Ser Petracco fellow exiles but they lived in the same cottage on this little "Garden Street" or "Garden Alley"! This does not seem likely. But a letter from Petrarch to Boccaccio indicates that the two men had many common interests, and spent much time together.

In this letter, he describes their likenesses and their differences.

They both loved study, Petrarch says. But once he was exiled, Petracco put books aside and devoted all his energies to lifting his family out of the poverty into which he brought them. Dante, on the other hand, single-mindedly pursued his purposes — first political and then poetical. And for this reason Petrarch admired him, he told Boccaccio, who had accused him of being jealous of his great predecessor.

« 9 »

But neither Dante's considerable and apparently continuous efforts nor those of his colleagues bore any notable fruit. As perhaps is not surprising, the White cause was in too deep a disarray.

This was a time of disasters and of the *disavventure* we have already referred to. These soon crushed even the least sanguine hopes of the exiles, and gave their endeavors to be restored to their city one way or another the aura of a lost cause.

The *disavventure* began almost at once.

It was earlier set down that Scarpetta degli Ordelaffi had, like the legendary King of France, marched perhaps not ten thousand men but at least forty-seven hundred right up the hill — of Pulicciano — and then, as a result of White pusilanimity, had marched them down again. It was said too that those involved in the rout who did not flee swiftly enough were either captured or slain.

One of the latter was Messer Donato Alberti, who had been the drafter of the letter which the Whites had fatuously sent to Charles of Valois under the illusion that fair words would divert him from looking out for his own interests and purse.

"He was so slow-footed," said Dino Compagni, "that he was seized, as was also a valiant youth named Nerlo, the son of Messer Goccia Adimari, and two young men of the Scolaii family."

To prevent capture, he had put on the garb of a peasant, and in this costume and ignominiously seated on an ass, he was brought before the *podestà*, now Fulcieri da Calboli.

Fulcieri looked at him in astonishment.

"Are you indeed Donato?" he asked.

"I am indeed!" replied the prisoner, who lacked judgment but not courage.

"Then Fulcieri had him put to torture with the rope, and left him hanging there. Furthermore he caused windows and doors of the palace" — the Palazzo della Signoria — "to be opened, and had many citizens summoned under one pretext or another so that they could see the insult and derision he was putting upon Donato."

After that, but apparently not without difficulty, he obtained permission to behead Donato.

"And so he treated all the prisoners."

Adds Dino Compagni:

"And this was not a just decision, but contrary to the common laws. Citizens who, after they have been exiled, seek to return should not be put to death. It was also contrary to the usages of war, for they ought to have kept them prisoners."

But Fulcieri's cruel and arbitrary acts were not limited to men taken in or after combat. He struck out at his supposed enemies wherever and whenever he had power to.

Says Giovanni Villani in his chronicle:

"Wherefore" — because, that is, he had learned of the agreement made between the Whites and the Ghibellines — "the said Fulcieri without warning caused a number of Florentines Whites and Ghibellines to be seized. These included Messer Betto Gherardini, Masino de' Cavalcanti, Donato and Tegghaio of the Finiguerra di Sammartino, Tignoso de' Macci, and, at the petition of Musciatto Franzesi, certain of the Abbati, as well as a sexton of the confraternity of the Calze."

They even included one "Nuccio Coderini de' Galigai *which was but half-witted*"*!* Vindictiveness could hardly go further.

"These were charged with plotting treachery and, whether guilty or not, were made to confess."

And, of course, sentenced and executed.

One of them did not need the headsman's attention.

"The said Tignoso de' Macci" — the gross fellow sweating and groaning in agony — "died under the cord through weight of flesh."

Small wonder that Dante had corrosive words for this *podestà* in the *Commedia.*

Purgatorio XIV — the poet is talking to Fulcieri's illustrious grandfather, Rinier da Calboli:

> "I see thy grandson, and he has become
> The hunter of those wolves upon the banks
> Of the fierce river. He puts them all in terror.
> He sells their bodies while they are still alive
> And then he slaughters them like old cattle.
> Many he robs of life, himself of honor.
> He comes forth bloody from the unhappy forest
> And leaves in such state that for a thousand
> Years it will never be reforested again."

But it was not merely at the hands of Florence that the Whites and the Ghibellines suffered indignity and shame. Divided in their leadership, at loggerheads because of their conflicting interests, they suffered these from everyone who opposed them and in many cases they brought them on themselves.

Not that "the war of the Mugello" — as the events of 1302 through 1304 came to be called — was an unbroken sequence of catastrophes. In its fighting, which was both savage and merciless, the Whites had occasional successes. But none of these had important consequences, and they were always followed by shattering defeats.

Here, but necessarily abridged, is the story.

"The Whites" — I will begin with a White flood tide — "marched from Monte Accenico" — whither they had retreated after Puliciano — "until they had come to La Lastra." This was only two miles from Florence, and was the scene of a later battle. "They burned" — crops and dwellings — "as they went."

The Aretines, who were now White allies, marched to join them.

"They reconquered Castiglione Aretino and Monte a San Savino. They laid waste Laterina. This last place the Blacks could not succor because they were in front of Pistoia."

Laying seige to that city with an army of men from Lucca!

But the Blacks were not the kind to be diverted thus easily from their main objective.

Pistoia would be an attractive prize — among other things, its capture would take a great deal of pressure off the Black Florentine flank — but it was far more important that the Whites and their feudal-lord allies did not establish a strong base of operations which would dominate the roads both to Bologna and Arezzo.

This they immediately set out to prevent.

They left the Lucchese to maintain the beleaguerment, and led by the Marquis Moroello Malaspina — Dante's "hot flame from the Val di Magra" (*Inferno* XXIV) — they set out against the marauding Whites.

Their purpose was to engage the latter.

Again *Inferno* XXIV:

> A battle shall be fought on Picene fields,
> Where fire shall burst so suddenly from the haze
> That blasted by it shall be every White.

Yet, even at that, in the beginning the issue trembled in the balance.

The Whites now "numbered twelve hundred horsemen and very many foot soldiers," and for a change "they displayed great energy in seeking battle."

Unfortunately, however, "they were deceived by certain traitors who took money from their enemies" and then set to work using it to instill a spirit of defeatism.

"You are as good as beaten," they whispered wherever they thought they would be listened to. "Your allies are deserting you. Look at the Pisans. They are not disposed to put good money after bad. They will not stake their fortunes on a battle which they doubt very much can be won."

One of these betrayals is recorded in some detail by Villani.

"In the year of our Lord 1303 in the month of May, the Florentines took suddenly the castle of Montale near Pistoia with four thousand men therein, and they did this because it was yielded to them through the treason of certain of its inhabitants who received three thousand gold florins. This castle was very strong both because of its site and because of its walls and towers, and after they had taken it the Florentines had it torn down and razed to its foundations, and the bell of the place, which was very fine, they brought to Florence and they put it in the palace of the *podestà* to be rung when embassies arrived. They called it La Montanina. And when Montale had been razed, the Florentines from one direction and the Lucchese from the other wasted the land round about, and they were fifteen hundred horsemen and six thousand footsoldiers, and they returned home without any battle."

This particular sale and purchase was arranged by Pazzino de' Pazzi, who at least had the excuse that he was openly a Black. But his cousin, Carlino de' Pazzi, who was or pretended to be a White, also, and at almost the same time, delivered a White-held stronghold into Black hands for Black money.

Again Villani:

"At the time of the said siege of Pistoia" — referred to above — "the castle of Piano di Travigni in the Valdarno rebelled against Florence in favor of Carlino de' Pazzi of the Valdarno, and with the said Carlino were some of the best of the exiled Whites and Ghibellines of Florence, both magnates and *popolani*, and they made great war in the Valdarno" — the guerrilla war which we have just talked about — "in consequence of which" — led by Moroello — "the Blacks went in the month of June to the Valdarno," where, among other things, "they laid siege to the said castle of Piano, and they stayed there for twenty-nine days."

Despite their brilliant commander, without any apparent success!

But "then, and because of the treason of Carlino de' Pazzi, who was given money for this, they retook the castle, whereby many of the best exiles of Florence were taken and slain."

Among these "best exiles" were two close relatives of Carlino, one of them an uncle! For this, Dante would put him in the Antenora of Mordred and Ganelon.

Inferno XXXII:

> "And so thou do not make me further talk
> Know then that I was Camicion de' Pazzi.
> I await Carlino, who'll make my guilt seem less."

For this too, and because of the reign of terror and legal murder which now held sway in Florence, White nerves began to snap and the White cause moved from disaster to disaster.

"In that year," a chronicler was now able to report, "the Florentines" — i.e., the Blacks — "had great victories in every expedition and foray they made. They successfully persecuted the Whites and the Ghibellines."

In the said year (1303), and in the year before it, and in the year afterward!

Moreover disintegration began to follow military defeat. The Whites began to quarrel among themselves — over policy and purposes, but even more about methods. They also began to quarrel with the Ghibellines. Originally White and Ghibelline had worked together, but each had "always doubted that the other was wholeheartedly" devoted to the cause. Gradually, however, "the fact that White Guelph prisoners had been put to death equally with the Ghibellines caused the Whites and Ghibellines to have perfect trust in one another." The acid of failure began to corrode all this. There was harsh thinking, if not harsh words.

It is stated by some that it was at this time, and as a sharer in the above mood, that Dante finally abandoned the men with whom he had been so long associated to go his own way and thus to set up what we have heard described by Cacciaguida — but surely not seriously, surely ironically — as "a party of one man." In proof of this is adduced the fact that there was an important Guelph meeting on May 30, 1303. At this, the White university signed a firm agreement with the Ubaldini, with Forlì, Faenza, Imola, Bagnacavallo, and Cesena — the alliance was widening — with the Polenta of Ravenna and Cervia, and with the *condottiere* (if this Renaissance word can be used so early) Salinguerra de' Salinguerri "for the honor and glory of the pope"— this was to keep up Guelph pretences — "and for the peace and security of Bologna, and of the provinces of Tuscany, Romagna, and Lombardy."

But Dante did not sign the document.

It is contended that he did not sign it because he was no longer a member of the White governing body, having "resigned from it," to use a modern expression, because he was disgusted with its policies and their lack of results.

But the reasons given for his being disgusted are not always the same.

He was disgusted, say some, because the Whites had any dealings with the Ghibellines at all. He was disgusted, say others, because their dealings with the latter were only halfhearted. After all the Ghibellines were the only available leaders with any military experience or gifts.

It is not necessary to believe, however, that his absence from the Guelph meeting can only be explained in this way. Why can it not be explained by the fact that he was too busily engaged in White Florentine business — as he had been at Forlì and Verona, but now somewhere else?

But if he did part company with the Whites at this time, the separation was temporary. For an event was about to take place which would change the whole picture. It would lift Whites and Ghibellines from their slough of despond. It would turn their bleak winter — or they would think so — into glorious summer. It would give them a whole new set of circumstances to deal with. And Dante intended to see that they dealt with them. As far as he could, he did.

« 10 »

It was an event which shook not merely Italy but all of Europe. It should have, for it was not merely Italian but European both in its consequences and in its cause.

Like the sixteenth century when the French king, Francis I, alternately did battle with and intrigued against Charles V (the Holy Roman Emperor who also ruled Austria, Burgundy, the Low Countries, Spain, and most of the Americas) and Henry VIII of England; when Charles either did battle with or intrigued against Francis and Henry; and when Henry, with his red-gold beard and porcine eyes, tried to disengage himself from both so that he would have time for his divorces and his marriages, the late thirteenth and early fourteenth centuries were an age of power politics when Titan battled Titan as each sought hegemony.

Two of the Titans were Philip the Fair and Pope Boniface. They began as friends, and indeed it was with Philip's connivance — or at least with the connivance of Musciatto Franzesi, who spoke for Philip — that Boniface overthrew the Colonna and took the first steps toward acquiring suzerainty over Florence, a suzerainty which was a *sine qua non* if he were to establish a papal state in central Italy.

But soon, and not surprisingly, the two were at swords' points. The reason for this is obvious. Boniface was not content with being the temporal lord of an Italian state which at best could only be the approximate equal of Naples, Venice, and Milan. He was not even content with the pope's theoretical spiritual overlordship of Western Christendom. He wanted it understood that this spiritual authority included temporal authority — and that kings and even the emperor were subject to it.

This, however, clashed directly with the ambitions and the intentions of Philip. The French monarch realized that in Europe France was — *de facto*, at least — the first among equals, but even that was not enough. He wanted to be first with no equals. He wanted at least a recognized temporal overlordship. For the moment, at any rate, he could leave the pope his spiritual overlordship — provided that he did not exercise its powers in France.

But how could he obtain this?

His advisers very adroitly suggested an answer.

"By taking over the vacant imperial throne!"

Philip as emperor? The pope would never sanction this.

"Not in your own name, sire. In the name of your brother, Charles of Valois. Charles will wear the crown, but you will be Charles's master."

"Enguerrand de Marigny, Guillaume de Nogaret, modestly born pantler from Normandy, hard-shrewd now-ennobled former law clerk from the Haute Garonne — Enguerrand, Guillaume, ye have done well for me!" cried Philip.

Then:

"Send emissaries to Pope Boniface."

They were sent, and stood before the pontiff.

"Your holiness has asked help against the Colonna. You will have this help. But on conditions."

What conditions?

"If you wish French support, you must support my brother Valois for emperor."

To promise is easy.

Boniface then and there pledged to King Philip and to Monsieur Charles of Valois that he would make the latter emperor.

"The which promise he did not fulfill," says Villani.

And probably never intended to, for it is not likely that the sage old pontiff could ever have been persuaded to confer power so great upon a potential rival.

"Nay rather in the same year" — the year in which he had promised Philip that he would support Charles — "he had confirmed as king of the Romans Albrecht of Austria, the son of King Rudolf."

Word of this sped to France, where the French king understandably flew into a fury.

"I have been greatly deceived and betrayed by the pope!" he cried. "He shall hear from me and remember!"

Then, from words, he proceeded to action.

First, "In his wrath he entertained and did honor to Stefano della Colonna, the pope's enemy, who had come to France on hearing of the discord which had arisen."

And who hoped that the Colonna and not Boniface would receive France's aid.

Then, deliberately and publicly, he flouted papal-claimed authority.

The bishop of Pamiers, near Carcassonne, was an Italian and had been appointed by the pope. One day armed bailiffs stood at the door of his palace. They cited him to come forth. When he did, they arrested him.

"Come with us in the king's name. You are charged with being a Patarine."

The penalty for this form of heresy was death.

After that, Philip laid royal hands on every vacant French episcopate. He seized and spent their revenues, and sent word to Boniface that the French clergy need concern him no longer. From now on he, Philip, would confer all investitures.

"Wherefore," says Villani, "Pope Boniface, who was proud and disdainful, added indignation to ill-will and became wholly an enemy to the king of France."

The battle royal was on.

It was fought out tenaciously by both sides.

The pope "caused all the great prelates of France to be invited to his court." There he would give them orders as to how to act against the French monarch.

Philip would not permit them to go.

Then Boniface sent the archdeacon of Narbonne to bid Philip "in the name of the pope to acknowledge humbly and with penitence the pope's temporal as well as his spiritual authority."

The king caused the archdeacon to be admitted to his presence, but would not allow him to speak, and when, thus silenced, he presented the papal letter, looked on with approval when another brother, the count of Artois, regaled the French barons by throwing it into the fire.

After this Philip issued orders:

"Guard the frontiers and let no papal messenger or message cross them."

Boniface had only one thing left that he could do.

He excommunicated Philip and the French kingdom.

No bells could toll in any church in France. The Mass could not be celebrated. Marriage could not be performed. The dead could not be buried with Church blessing.

But the bells did toll — and nowhere more clangorously than on the shipshaped Île de la Cité and elsewhere in Paris — as the king of France, "to justify himself and to make his appeal, summoned," at the palace of the Louvre, "a great council of clerics and prelates and all of his barons" as well as the more important laymen of the city to hear him clear himself, and then make countercharges against Boniface, accusing him "of heresy and simony and murder and other base crimes, by reason whereof he ought to be deposed from the papacy."

If it had not been for the abbot of Cîteaux, sentence might have been passed. But this powerful head of the Cistercian order, whose assent was essential, not only "would not consent to the appeal" but "departed and returned to Burgundy."

Then and then only, Philip resorted to direct action.

"With great caution and by the counsel of Stefano Colonna and of other Italians and of men of his own kingdom, he sent a wise and crafty officer, Monsieur Guillaume of Nogaret, into Tuscany, together with Messer Musciatto Franzesi. They were furnished with much ready money, and with drafts on the house of Peruzzi, who did not, however, know what the money was for."

They halted at Musciatto's castle of Staggia, where they bided for enough time to corrupt many of the cardinals and most of the pope's barons.

After that, they set out again.

"In the month of September" — actually it was on September 7 — "in the year 1303, with his mounted followers to the number of three hundred and with many of his friends on foot," and also "with the lords of Ceccano and Supino, and with other [supposedly pro-papal] barons," their new leader, Sciarra Colonna, marched southward through the golden Campagna until he came to Anagni.

Unresisted, he and they entered the city and proceeded, also unresisted, to the Gaetani palace.

"Death to the pope!" they shouted as they stood in front of it. "Long live King Philip!"

As they thundered, a tall, ancient, rugged man confronted them.

It was Pope Boniface himself. Hearing the uproar and seeing himself abandoned by all of his clerics and by most of his servants, he faced his enemies alone.

He did so in the awesomeness of papal dignity. He was seated in his pontifical chair, robed in the mantle of St. Peter, with the crown of Constantine upon his head, and with the keys and the cross in his hands.

"Since like Jesus Christ," he had told the few who did not desert him, "I am taken through treachery and must die by the same, let me at least die like a pope."

For a moment there was a sudden silence. The myrmidons of France and Italy almost forgot what they had been paid for.

Then they remembered again, as Guillaume de Nogaret stepped forward. His narrow eyes flashed. He had been fidgeting with his clothes and from time to time biting his nails, but now he stopped.

"Atheist and dog!" he cried. "At the command of King Philip we are come to take you in chains to Lyons. There a council will try you and condemn you."

The pope flushed, and the statue thus became a living man — someone who could be insulted and injured. Sciarra and his ruffians did just this. They pressed forward to lay violent hands upon the pontiff and upon those who still stood with him. They plucked Boniface's hair and beard and tore his clothing. They abused him with filth and filthy words.

When they had buffeted him enough, they led him off, their captive, and, ironically, as they thus hurried him away, the papal "banner of the keys" floated over his head to demonstrate that his captors were fighting "in defense of the Church" and against an antipope.

They held him prisoner for three days.

Then, surprisingly, he was liberated, and by the same "ungrateful" fellow townsmen who had allowed him to be taken without opposition.

"The people of Anagni, beholding their error and issuing from their blind ingratitude, rose in arms. 'Long live the pope and his household!' they shouted. 'Death to the traitors!' Then running through the city, they drove out Sciarra della Colonna and his followers, with loss to them of prisoners and slain."

But if citizens of Anagni had rescued Boniface, they did not save his life.

Trembling in the impotence of his rage, shattered and shaken by the affront helplessly endured, "he departed straightway with all his court" — the pope on muleback, with pikemen and crossbowmen marching beside him — "and came to Rome to hold a council, purposing to take the heaviest vengeance upon whosoever had offended him."

The council was not held.

For instead, "as it pleased God, the grief which had hardened in the heart of the pope by reason of the injury which he had received produced in him after he had come to Rome a strange malady, so that he gnawed himself as if he were mad, and in this state he passed from his life on the twelfth day of October in the year of Christ 1304."

He was buried in St. Peter's "near the entrance to the doors in a rich chapel which was built in his lifetime." This chapel shared the fate of all of old St. Peter's. It no longer exists. Boniface now lies in the crypt of the new St. Peter's, guarded by his sleeping image from the chisel of Arnolfo di Cambio.

Anagni and the deed done there were soon known throughout Italy and indeed beyond, and even those who bitterly hated Boniface were filled with horror at the outrage to the papacy.

Dante was among them.

He was probably in the Casentino when the tidings came to him, but wherever he was, he brooded on the sorry business and stored this brooding in his mind, whence it would emerge later — as did so many of his broodings — in great lines of poetry.

Purgatorio XX:

> I see the fleur-de-lis come to Anagni
> And in His vicar Christ a captive made.
> I see Him mocked and scorned a second time.
> I see renewed the vinegar and gall.
> I see Him slain between two living thieves.
> I see the new Pilate who is so cruel
> This does not satisfy him, who lawlessly
> Into the Temple carries his greedy sails.

But even as Dante deplored the figurative crown of thorns which had been pressed upon the brow of the aged pontiff in the Ciociaria Hills, he could not help being aware of the hopes it brought. There would now be a new pope, and this new pope could hardly be another Boniface, with his implacable enmity to all those who sought an independent Florentine state and his dedication to crushing anyone who opposed him. This could not but be good news to the Whites. For even if they were not restored to their old place and power, there was now at least a chance that they — and even the Ghibellines — would be treated with something that resembled equity and justice.

« 11 »

A new pope there was indeed — and that after an almost incredibly short interval of ten days.

"After the death of Pope Boniface," wrote Giovanni Villani, "the college of cardinals convened to elect his successor, and as it pleased God they came to an agreement and on October 22 they called upon Pope Benedict XI. He was of Treviso and was born in great poverty. He had almost no relatives. When he was a young priest he was taken to Venice to tutor the children of the Ca Querini. Then he was a preaching friar. He was a wise man and one of holy life, and for his goodness and his worthy conduct Pope Boniface had made him a cardinal."

But it was not the humble birth and the poverty — reports of which must have been exaggerated anyway, since the pope's father was a successful notary — of this Niccolò Boccasini from the Venetian plain, nor was it the fact that he had few relatives and hence few reasons for nepotism which caused "the world" — and most of all the Florentine exiles — "to be cheered with a new light." It was rather that he was not merely "wise and holy" but "steadfast, worthy, and discreet" (Dino Compagni), and that with a notable singleness of purpose he abandoned Boniface's policies and "began many good things," showing in particular "great desire to bring peace among the Christians."

Peace among the Christians!

But what could this mean more than peace between the warring Black and White factions? For warfare between them was not hidden in the mists but was right at the papal doorstep. As it kept half of Italy in a turmoil, it deeply involved the papacy itself.

"Let us end it, therefore," Niccolò, now Benedict, was reported as saying. "Let us end it forthwith, and not by one faction crushing the other but in a Christian spirit of accommodation. Let us end it by each side giving in a little. Let us end it by compromise and through moderation."

Thus, rumor had it, ran the thinking of the new pope.

The rumor was very shortly confirmed by fact.

During "the first fast after his election" — that is, during the Advent ember days of 1303 — Benedict created two new cardinals. One was an Englishman, William Marlsefield, who had actually died four months earlier although news of this had not yet reached Rome. The other was "the bishop of Spoleto, who had been born in the castle at Prato," and this Niccolò da Prato, as he came to be known, himself being "of humble origin" but also "of Ghibelline stock," seemed to Benedict the very man he needed to carry out his intentions.   Accordingly — on January 31, 1304 — he was solemnly named papal legate to Florence and directed to proceed thither as soon as possible in order "to set the Florentines at peace with one another, and likewise with their exiles and all the province of Tuscany."

This he did. As a winter was over and gone, he arrived (on March 10) at the Porta Romana, where he was met by "the people of Florence, carrying olive branches." Why not? Except for the revolutionaries who ruled the city, most Florentines "felt themselves to be divided and in an evil state." They had "the disposition and desire to live rightly." They "loved peace and concord."

The cardinal of Prato — now also the bishop of Ostia and Velletri — took steps to offer them both. To a throng in the Piazza di San Giovanni he delivered "a public sermon and a discourse," telling them the pope's wishes. Then he arranged a series of conferences with the more important citizens. From these, he asked for "full and free authority to set the people at peace one with the other within the city, and with their exiles without." In other words, between Black and Black (between the factions of Corso Donati and of Rosso della Tosa), between Black and White, and even between Guelph and Ghibelline.

With some limitations, this was given him. Thereupon he reactivated the councils and appointed moderate men as priors and as gonfalonier. He also called upon those ruling the city to end exilings and confiscations, and upon all men by letter and by proclamation to submit to his jurisdiction all disputes.

To these pleas, the Whites responded in the affirmative.

Dante had now rejoined them — if he had ever left them — and he was called on to supply the words for their answer. He did so in an impassioned letter which chronologically is the earliest surviving Dante epistle. If, by modern standards, it is verbose, it is also eloquent. Speaking for the party, Dante also speaks for himself, and he does so with many an illuminated and illuminating phrase.

"To the most reverend father in Christ and our beloved lord, the Lord Niccolò, by divine compassion the bishop of Ostia and Velletri, legate of the Apostolic See, and likewise ordained by the Holy Church to be pacificator in Tuscany, the Romagna, the March of Treviso, and the regions adjacent thereto, his most devoted sons, Alessandro the captain, as well as the council and the whole White party of Florence, do commend themselves in all devotion and zeal.

"In submission to his holy admonishments and in reply to his Apostolic Holiness, we, after prayerful consideration, do here reply to the import of the sacred words which you have sent to us and, if we should be held guilty of either negligence or sloth as a result of our delay in so doing, may your holy comprehension lead you to this side of condemning us, knowing, as you surely do, the number and the nature of the consultations that were necessary for the orderly conduct of the affairs of our brotherhood and to maintain good faith with our allies. But if, after you have examined the facts here submitted you, we are still blamed for lack of due promptness, we pray that the superabundance of your goodwill may incline you to indulgence.

"Know, then, that as not ungrateful sons we have examined the letter of your gracious paternity and, since it led us to the threshold of everything which we desire, it filled our minds with a joy so great that no one could measure this with either word or thought. For even in our dreams we have longed only for the weal of our native land, and this, in the guise of fatherly admonitions, is more than once promised to us in your letter. For what else did we engage in civil war? What else did our White banners seek? For what else were our swords and spears dyed red? Only so that those who had madly and lewdly hacked to pieces civic justice should bow under the yoke of righteous law and should be compelled to keep their country's peace! Yea, verily, the lawful arrow of our intentions, leaping from the bowstring we drew taut, sought solely the tranquillity and freedom of the Florentines — sought this and will seek it forever! And if your vigilance moves toward the attaining of an end so dear to us, and if, as your holy endeavors desire, you compel our adversaries to return to the plowed lands of good citizenship, who would dare try to render adequate thanks to you? Father, it is not in our power to do so, nor in the power of any Florentine in this world. But if there is a God in heaven who looks upon such actions as worthy of recompense, may He fittingly requite you who have clothed yourself with compassion for so great a city and are hastening to compose the turmoil of her citizens!

"Whereas, therefore, we are urgently admonished and required by Fra L——, a holy monk and a pleader for good citizenship — and this also was the tenor of your letter — to desist from all assaults and acts of war, and to commit ourselves wholly into your hands, we, as sons most devoted to you and as lovers of justice and peace, do, laying down our swords, submit to your adjudications of our own free will and without reservations, as shall be made known to you by the aforesaid Fra L——, and as shall be declared abroad in due form by public instruments.

"With filial voice, then, we most affectionately implore that your most clement holiness may lave with the balm of tranquility and peace this Florence which has been fever-tossed so long, and that as a loving father you may keep us under your protection — us who have ever been the defenders of our people, us and all those we command. For, as we have never failed in our love for our country, so we look never to stray beyond the limits of your instructions, but in duty and devotion always to obey your commands whatever they may be."

No such spirit of accommodation, however, was manifested by the Blacks. Indeed, why should it be? After all, they now sat in the seats of the mighty, and if concessions were made it was they who would have to give up. The Whites would receive.

The cardinal was able, to be sure, to chalk up certain small but, it would turn out, transitory gains, for there was a peace party among the Blacks themselves, and Niccolò took every possible advantage of this.

The "wealthy merchants," for example, and there were wealthy merchants among the Blacks, "began to be afraid." They were afraid that continuing disturbances would hurt business. The ordinary citizens, and among the Blacks were many ordinary citizens, "seeing themselves in evil estate because of riots and strife," were more than eager for a moratorium in the realm of civil conflict. Even the rich and potent bishop of Florence — himself of the Black della Tosa family, although not always in agreement with it — "favored peace because it would bring with it justice and prosperity."

With this support and believing that a longing for tranquillity was widespread and deep, Niccolò convened the people of Florence for a second time — on this occasion in the Piazza di Santa Maria Novella — "and there in the presence of the signory many reconciliations were brought about, and the parties kissed one another upon the mouth as a sign of this, and contracts of amity were drawn up, and furthermore penalties were imposed" — by a *viva voce* shout — "on any who should violate the agreements."

Thereupon once again olive branches were waved wildly. Huge bonfires were lit. There was a clangor of bells from campanile and tower. The companies of the people marched cheering through the streets.

"With the banners which they had received from him at Santa Croce, they held high festival in the name of the cardinal. And so much did the peace appear to please everyone that, although a great rain came on that day, no one went away, nor did they seem to feel it!"

But even as the Florentines, their clothes drenched and dripping, their plumed hats bedraggled, rejoiced and celebrated, even as Dante, on one of the surrounding hills, felt his heart beat faster as at last he dared to hope that "the cruelty that bars me" from his beloved city might at last be rendered impotent, the Black leaders — or at any rate the more effective of the Black leaders — had other ideas.

"Messer Rosso della Tosa," says Dino Compagni, "was very scornful of the whole business because it seemed to him that the peace had gone too far beyond what he wished."

Here an explanation is needed. What Rosso wanted was enough peace for the Black factions to compose their differences, but not enough for the Whites to mend their fortunes.

"And therefore he made haste to carry out his design."

And this time with the aid of the whole party, for now frightened, the Blacks reunited, and even the Donati followers were willing to let him "do as he pleased, for they were now friendly to him."

What was this design?

Something at once simple and devious.

It was to "delay the peace" until such time as conciliation again "was a thing impossible." But to delay it while seeming to forward it. The cardinal must always think they were on his side.

« 12 »

It is not here pertinent or necessary to give a detailed account of the many things the Black chieftain did or arranged to bring this about. Yet a broad outline is both illuminating and important.

Villani describes Niccolò da Prato as "very learned in matters pertaining to Holy Scripture; innately intelligent; subtle, sagacious, and cautious; and very experienced."

But learning in matters pertaining to Holy Scripture does not necessarily qualify one for dealing with high-handed and strong-willed politicians, nor was experience gained only in the relatively sedate councils of the Church — even the Church of Pope Boniface — in any way a match for the do-now-and-do-not-necessarily-explain-later direct actionism of the Black and strong-arm beneficiaries of the November coup d'etat.

Niccolò also, says Villani, in everything he did tried "to show good and impartial intentions."

But, equally, goodness and impartiality were not what was needed. What was needed was iron purpose and clear eyes.

The Blacks took advantage of these qualities of Niccolò.

Crying piously that, like him, they wanted tranquillity with fairness to all, they systematically created desperate situations. They deliberately engineered foreign involvement and domestic confusion, and, finally, they made use of lies and subterfuge. Let us consider these one by one.

Foreign involvement.

"Those who were in opposition to the pope's will, wishing no longer to endure the burden of the cardinal, induced him to leave Florence with false words.

" 'My lord,' they said to him, 'before you proceed any further in carrying out the peace, make certain that Pistoia will obey, for if *we* make peace, and Pistoia falls into our enemies' hands, we will have been duped.' "

Obligingly the cardinal fell into the trap.

"On the eighth day of May he left Florence, going by way of Campi, where he was lodged in a beautiful country house. The next morning he went to Prato. He had been born there, but had never been there since. There he was received with great honor and much dignity. The streets were arched over and there were music and dancing. On the same day he continued to Pistoia, where he talked with the chief men and the rulers of the city."

But while he was talking in Pistoia, Geri Spini, who had accompanied him, was talking too, and in Prato other Blacks were also talking.

"The most holy father comes with words of peace and reason, but he plans, actually, to take over the city."

The upshot was a debate. Pistoia did grant the cardinal some of the authority he sought, but it was very carefully limited and it was provided that he could not make it over to anyone else (the White Florentines or the pope). But his native Prato actually rose against him. The gates were barred to him, and his friends and kinsmen were driven from the city.

Domestic confusion.

With the White representatives summoned by the cardinal in the pope's name — Petrarch's father, Ser Petracco di Ser Parenzo, was among the first — beginning to appear; with four men selected by the pope — they were respectively from Milan, Lodi, Brescia, and Bergamo, they were not Florentines — "to carry out the universal pacification" beginning to do their work; and with White hopes so on the rise that some White exiles even cautiously returned to the city, it seemed necessary once again to throw Florence into a turmoil, and this the Blacks proceeded to do.

"The della Tosa and the Medici came armed into the Old Market, shooting with their crossbows and then going toward the Corso degli Adimari and down the Calimala. They attacked and tore down a barricade. Messer Rossellino della Tosa then came with his troop to the houses of the Sassetti. He purposed to set fire to them. The Cavalcanti and others came to their assistance, and in this clash of men Nerone Cavalcanti encountered Messer Rossillino. He lowered his lance against him and struck him in the breast, so throwing him from his horse."

(Since the Whites had resisted, even Dino admitting that those who guarded the barricade "had more mind for vengeance than for peace," the Blacks seemed to have an excuse.)

Rioting was followed by arson.

The Black leaders "prepared artificial fire," and then "came to an understanding" with one Neri Abbati, a prior from San Piero Scheraggio — "a wicked and unprincipled man," says Dino reduntantly — to apply it in the center of the city.

"And so, on the tenth of June, he set fire to his kinsmen's houses in the Orto San Michele."

As expected, it became a conflagration, and to make matters worse, another fire was set nearby.

"From the Old Market flaming material was shot into the Calimala, and it spread so greatly that it added to the first fire, and consumed many houses, palaces, and shops."

Nor did heaven help the Florentines.

"In the Orto San Michele there was a large loggia with an oratory of our Lady in which there were many votive images of wax, and when, through the heat of the air, many of these caught fire, all the houses which were near the place were burned, besides the warehouses of the Calimala, and all the shops which were around the Old Market as far as the New Market, and the houses of the Cavalcanti, and the houses in the Vacchereccia and the Porta Santa Maria as far as the Ponte Vecchio. It is said that more than nineteen hundred dwellings were burned."

Then came looting.

"Thieves openly plunged into the blazing buildings to carry away what they could, and whoever saw his property being carried off dared not demand it back, for the city was in utter confusion."

Finally, *the lies and subterfuge.*

Despite his discomfiture at Prato, Cardinal Niccolò did not lose sight of his objective, and continued to press for its attainment. He bent every effort to hasten the negotiations, and promised that when these had come up with a suggested course of action, he would immediately put it into execution. In particular, and to make sure that whatever was agreed upon had a broad base of acceptance, he asked the Whites to supplement the four men they had already sent with fourteen specially chosen representatives who would have full power to act in their name. Then he asked the Blacks to do the same.

Both parties agreed to comply with the request, although the Whites, it must be noted, agreed with reservations. Understandable reservations in the light of past Black conduct. They would come to Florence but they would not venture into the heart of the city, staying rather "in the Oltrarno in the houses of the Mozzi, where they put up barricades and stationed guards so that they might not be attacked."

The Blacks, on the contrary, came before the cardinal, all sweetness and reason.

Who could imagine, they seemed to ask him, such deceit and treachery?

In proof of its impossibility, they made several placatory gestures.

Rosso della Tosa made a show of greatly honoring his kinsman Baschiera, and in turn was greatly honored by him.

Men and women were permitted, if not encouraged, to kiss the coat of arms of the Uberti, certain of whom were among the White ambassadors.

Other White ambassadors were allowed to be ostentatiously protected by friendly magnates.

The populace was allowed to show its enthusiam and approval.

Because of this, and because "the Whites and the Ghibellines" — hoping that if they regained a little, they would be in a position later to regain a lot — "were determined to let themselves be guided by the Blacks and to consent to their demands so that they might have no excuse to draw back from the peace," "the people were filled with great hope."

So for the moment were the exiles.

But even as the Blacks pretended — and succeeded in convincing the cardinal — that they sought accommodation, they were secretly doing all they could to make accommodation impossible.

First, they went to certain magnates — possibly White-inclined, but in all probability of neither party — who had been urged by the cardinal to give the Whites shelter, and to them they delivered a blunt warning.

"Those Whites do not come to you for shelter, but to gather friends in strength, after which they will not leave the city. They will then be conquerors — your masters as well as ours!"

Next they went to Cardinal Niccolò himself.

"Your life is in danger!" they told him.

They offered proof.

Near the Mozzi palaces lived a family called Quartesi who hated the Mozzi, and one of the Quartesi, either of his own accord or quite as likely persuaded by the Blacks who needed an *agent provocateur*, as he was strolling through the city one day, saw Niccolò with his Mozzi hosts and let fly at him with a crossbow bolt.

"You would be well advised to leave the city."

For the second time, Niccolò took the bait.

On the ninth of June, shaking with both rage and fear, he rode from Florence.

He would go to the pope and give him an account of the false doings of those very men — the Whites and Ghibellines — whom, out of Christian charity and what he deemed to be the demands of justice, he had sought to rescue from the pit.

But as he jogged westward up the Arno valley at a churchman's pace, his mind cleared.

It was not, he saw suddenly, the Whites who had dealt falsely, but their adversaries.

It is said that there is no anger like the anger of a patient man, and Cardinal Niccolò, who had patiently tried to do his duty, was now angry.

He would still stand before the holy father, but it was not against the Whites that he would press charges. It was against "the chiefs among the rulers" of the now-Black city. Against Messer Corso Donati, against Messer Rosso della Tosa, Messer Pazzino de' Pazzi, Messer Geri Spini, and Messer Betto Brunelleschi.

This he shortly did, and he must have done so convincingly, for the above-named men, despite the crisis in Florence, were soon at his heels.

They too rode to the papal court, thinking that once there they would "by plausible words, by money, and through the influence of friends be able to wipe out" the bad effects "of the insults put upon the cardinal legate."

But neither they nor the cardinal legate had time to accomplish their purpose.

Nature intervened.

"On the twenty-second of July 1304, Pope Benedict XI died in Perugia of poison placed in some fresh figs which had been sent to him," wrote Dino Compagni.

Villani tells substantially the same story but with a different date and more details.

"In the year of Christ 1304 on the twenty-seventh day of the month of July, Pope Benedict died in the city of Perugia, it was said by poison. For when he was eating at his table there came to him a young man veiled and garbed as a woman, as a serving sister of the nuns of Santa Petronella, and he had in his hands a silver basin wherein were many fine ripe figs. These he presented to the pope from his devout servant, the abbess of the nunnery. The pope received them with great pleasure and, since he was fond of them, ate many of them without anyone tasting them beforehand, and then straightway he fell ill and in a few days died. He was buried in San Ercolano."

In San Ercolano, whether poisoned or the victim of a summer dysentery, he still lies.

« 13 »

It was at this time — but before the death of Benedict had forever dashed their hopes — that the Whites suddenly abandoned their policy of conciliation and once again resorted to force.

Villani, who was then in Florence, and seems even to have fought on the Black side, says that this was done at the instigation of Cardinal Niccolò.

"He cunningly plotted against the city of Florence, sending letters to Pisa, Bologna, the Romagna, Arezzo, and Pistoia, and to all the leaders of the Ghibellines and of the White party, telling them they should assemble with all their forces and with those of their friends, and that on a day named they should come to the city of Florence and drive out the Blacks."

Niccolò, Villani continues, added that he had written these letters with the knowledge and at the wish of the pope.

"The which," Villani says angrily, "was a great falsehood and lie, since the pope knew nothing thereof!"

But whether with the pope's approval and at Niccolò's urging or because they had grown desperate; whether rashly or because, with the Black chieftains in Perugia, they deemed the city leaderless and the time ripe, assemble the Whites did. Or at any rate, the White captains gave them orders to assemble. Once again at La Lastra, two miles above Florence on the Bologna road.

A goodly number almost immediately appeared.

"Twelve hundred men on horseback in white cloaks."

(Another account says sixteen hundred horsemen.)

Nine thousand foot soldiers.

A contingent — its exact size is not stated — of Bolognese, Romagnole, Aretine, and other allies.

But not the whole counted-upon tally.

Still expected was Tolosato degli Uberti with three hundred horsemen, some Pistoians and other mercenaries, with foot soldiers, and with many White refugees. They had not yet come because it was not yet the day appointed.

"Nor had the Cavalcanti, the Gherardini, the Luccardesi, and the Scolaii from the Val di Pesa" yet arrived. They too would come a day later, as agreed upon.

But unfortunately the men at La Lastra were not disposed to wait, particularly as they had friends and relatives in the city who were urging them to act swiftly.

"You are already discovered," these sent word, "and the Blacks are paralyzed with terror. Many of them now hide in this monastery or that where they are disguised as friars. But they will recover shortly. And when they get the tidings of what the Whites do, Corso and Rosso and the others will return from Perugia."

Moreover, the White leader, Baschiera della Tosa, if a patriot was a hotheaded patriot who was "swayed more by passion than by reason." Why should he delay? he cried.

"I have good troops. I should not deprive them of their victory."

On the Eve of St. Margaret's (July 20) when the heat of Tuscan summer would be the most intense, in broad daylight when their movements could be easily observed, and a day before their adherents in the city had been instructed to rise in their support, he gave the orders to advance.

This his men did, and, in the beginning, successfully.

"They came by San Gallo, and in the Cafaggio [country estate] of the bishop they drew up in formation close to San Marco." This convent, today adorned by Fra Angelico's paintings, was then without the city walls. "Their white banners were unfurled. They wore garlands of olive. And when they drew their swords, shouting 'Peace!' without doing any robbery, it was beautiful to behold. Once formed, the skirmishers on foot and on horse moved toward the city. They came to the gate of the Spadaii, since Baschiera thought that he would have friends in the city who would open it for him."

But the friends did not appear, and since, trusting these allies, Baschiera had not come "prepared with axes and other weapons to force the gates," his men were for a moment held back.

But not for long.

"The barricades of the suburbs" — made of logs and hurdles and even boards — "were contested against the Whites, but they broke them down, wounding and killing many of those who had held out against them."

Then they were in the city where their troubles began.

Many of the Blacks, shocked by their own Black outrages, had promised to join them. They did not.

"On the contrary, they made greater efforts than did the other Blacks in order to show that they were not disloyal."

The White attackers had now reached Santa Reparata — on the site of today's Duomo — and there they were assaulted by the very men they had counted on who came against them "shooting crossbows furnished with gaffles."

Next, fire broke out and threatened to cut them off from any possible escape.

At this point Baschiera lost his nerve.

"He turned his horsemen back and retreated. Their joy turned to weeping as the vanquished became vanquishers, and taking courage pursued them."

Soon they were in the country again, where many of the Whites, "overcome by the heat, flung themselves into vineyards and houses to hide themselves, and there many of them died from exhaustion."

Baschiera himself only paused long enough to abduct two wealthy nieces from the monastery of San Domenico near Fiesole. These he could use as pawns or to obtain ransom.

Then his flight continued.

"A short distance from the city, the fugitives" — sweating and streaked with sweaty dust — "encountered Messer Tolosato, who with his Pistoians was coming to meet them on the appointed day. He tried to persuade them to turn back but could not. Therefore he returned to Pistoia. With great sorrow, because he knew that Baschiera's youthful rashness had lost him the city."

« 14 »

Him and every other White and Ghibelline exile, including Dante.

For at that time — although they perhaps did not completely realize it — the gates of Florence were forever closed to them.

Or perhaps they did know it — or at least Dante did.

I am convinced of the latter, for it was at this time, and not earlier or later — I am also convinced — that Dante took the final and irrevocable step. It was at this time that he abandoned the *compagnia scempia e malvagia*, with whom he had been so ardently associated and whose cause was now in irreparable ruin.

Umberto Cosmo imagines a stormy scene.

"The separation of the poet from his friends," he says, "must have been violent. The accusations on both sides must have been vehement. Probably swords flashed."

This may or may not have been the case. Professor Cosmo understands Dante very well.

But I, for my part, cannot see the poet either shouting angrily at the pack of fools and knaves his fellow exiles always were or had become. I cannot see him confronting them with bare blade across an overturned table.

More likely, when he saw selfishness compounded by folly, and folly by cowardice, he simply came to the end of his patience.

These men who wished to risk everything while playing everything safe would not lead him back to his own city. He would only come back — and he still longed and hoped to come back, he always would — through his own efforts. But these efforts, he began to see, need not be either in the sordid realm of politics (city politics) which had once seemed to offer salvation, nor in the slaying-your-own-brothers of civil conflict.

I visualize him as facing his erstwhile colleagues with a sad and somber visage. Then, probably, he drew his cloak about him, and simply was no longer there.

XVI

Ship Without Sails and Without a Rudder

H E did not, however, disappear from the face of the earth. Instead he entered upon a new phase of his life. It was the one, incidentally, with which, next to the one in which he played the role of Beatrice's lover, we most often associate him: the *via dolorosa* of his earthly pilgrimage, when, gaunt of face and with a body that grew ever more lean, he trod mile after weary mile as he moved from one protector to another, from one lord's antechamber to the seat of honor at a second lord's table, from little town to busy city to castellated mountain fastness, often seeking only physical sanctuary — a place where he could eat and sleep and be sheltered from the weather — but just as often seeking something more.

All this Dante summarizes himself.

Convivio I, 3:

"Since that day when it pleased the citizens of the fairest daughter of Rome, namely Florence, to cast me from her bosom — that Florence wherein I was born, and where I was nourished until the very zenith of my life, and wherein, too, I long with all my heart to repose my tired soul and to end those days which have been allotted to me — I have gone as a wanderer, nay almost a beggar, through well nigh all the regions in which this tongue" — i.e., Italian — "is spoken, showing to all, against my will, the wound inflicted by fortune, a wound the blame for which is often unjustly imputed to him who has been wounded. In all truth, I have been a ship without sails and without a rudder, drifted into various ports through diverse channels by the fruitless winds which poverty breathes forth. Wherefore I have often seemed in the eyes of many whom perhaps my reputation had led to think of in another manner to be of little worth.

And not only myself did they look on with contempt, but they esteemed of very small value every work of mine, whether already written or yet to be set down."

It is a moving and a poignant cry, and it comes from the very heart of this great and tortured man at the moment when he was at last forced to recognize that the second of his two dreams had crumbled into ruins, and that from lack of experience in the ruthless world of politics — or so he thought — and because he did not understand its ways he must now pay a bitter price, even though his intentions and every innate feeling had been good.

For that reason — and because it does throw some light upon this part of his life — let us examine it in a little detail.

Since that day when it pleased the citizens of the fairest daughter of Rome, namely Florence, to cast me from her bosom.

The fairest daughter! Even when she had insulted and injured him, he still loved her!

That Florence wherein I was born, and where I was nourished until the very zenith of my life.

Here there is a slight inaccuracy. According to Holy Scripture, a man's years in this world are three score and ten, and half of three score and ten (seventy) is thirty-five. Dante, however, was thirty-seven when he was exiled in 1302. But this is close enough, and no one should quibble over two years.

And wherein, too, I long with all my heart to repose my tired soul and to end those days which have been allotted to me.

On this matter something said by Leonardo Bruni is useful.

"Here," writes this Dante biographer, speaking of one of the more important of the poet's refuges (but the words could apply to almost all of them), "he was courteously received and remained for some time, seeking by good offices" — i.e., by the support of the place's lord — "and by good demeanor" — i.e., by his own conduct — "to gain the grace of permission to return to Florence with the consent of the government of the place. And to this intent he labored much and wrote many letters, not only to those citizens who held authority, but to the people itself. And among the latter was a long epistle which began: *O popule mee, quid feci tibi?* O my people, what have I done to thee?"

Umberto Cosmo agrees with him, as do many others, including Giosuè Carducci — a scholar and a poet.

"Dante became," says the former, "all humility."

Then he adds this qualification:

"But it was a humility typical of the man. Every charge that was laid against him in respect to his conduct in his native city he scornfully refuted; his desire to return to the city he proudly affirmed; but as he stated in the proudest of his *canzoni*, the fact that he had been exiled for his work of justice he accounted an honor. To one offense alone did he confess in the envoy of the poem: that after his exile he had borne arms against his native city. But that he had been guilty of anything that merited his exile he utterly denied.

"He hoped," Professor Cosmo continues, "by such loftiness of conduct to obtain pardon, and he sought it. This was an error, because he was not understood, and the pardon was not forthcoming."

The *canzone* was the deep and carefully thought-out *Tre donne*, perhaps Dante's finest, and the three ladies it celebrates are Righteousness — "poor, as thou seest, in my repute and dress" — and her sisters Generosity and Temperance.

It ends thus:

> His sighs now held Love back. He mused apart.
> Then, by the tale beguiled,
> His eyes grew soft that just before were wild,
> And thereupon the three kinswomen did he greet.
>
> And having grasped one and the other dart,
> He cried: "Thy heads lift high.
> These arms I now do take up, these arms I.
> Rusted they are by lack of use, ye weet.
>
> "Generosity and Temperance in the street
> Go begging, and the others of our blood.
> If these be loss, then be it understood
> That they, with eyes and lips, alone should mourn
> Whom it doth most concern,
> Since on them shines the light come down from heaven.
> Not we, we fashioned of the rock eterne!
> For we who now with swords are thrust at even,
> We shall endure, and those will come again
> Who in its brightness will make it shine amain!"
>
> *Then I who in this discourse so divine*
> *Can see full well the comfort and the dole*
> *Bestowed upon these exiles worthy of soul*
> *Can glory deem the exile put on me;*
>
> *For what though chance or fortune should incline*
> *The world to transmute quite*
> *Into black flowers the white;*
> *To fall with good men greatly praised should be!*

> *And if mine eye's brave standard, fair to see,*
> *Which filled my heart with flaming and with light,*
> *By distance has been taken from my sight —*
> *I should count light that which doth weigh me down.*
> *Yet this flame has, I own,*
> *So greatly death's keys nigh to my heart came,*
> *Burned me up, flesh and bone,*
> *For which, if I'm to blame,*
> *Many a moon's gone since 't was cleansed away:*
> *That is, if repentance for a fault can pay!*

Then follows a less-than-usual double *tornata* (envoy), for — at least in many manuscripts — there is not only the customary *tornata* but a *tornata*-upon-the-*tornata*.

> *Canzone*, on thy garb let none set hand
> To look on that which a fair woman would hide.
> Enough that the bare parts be spied.
> The delicious apple to all folks deny
> Though all to take it try.
> But if by chance one day thou shouldst find one
> Who prayed thee, and a friend of virtue be,
> Then thou new colors put on
> And show to him that flower, so fair without
> That longing in loving hearts it doth bring out.

> Canzone, *birdling of the wings so white,*
> Canzone, *do thou hunt with the black hounds*
> *That did make need to me that I take flight,*
> *But who could bring a gift of peace to me,*
> *Yet do not this, not knowing what I be:*
> *Unto the wise pardon's gates ne'er closed are,*
> *For to forgive your foe is to win war.*

And what does all this mean?

Edmund G. Gardner, at least, repudiates any political implications. The *canzone* is about the three ladies who are each a moral virtue. In other words, it is a purely philosophical poem.

" 'Convert white flowers into black,' " he says in his annotations to the Temple edition of the *Canzoniere;* "i.e., blame the innocent, overturn the moral order, and invert the moral perspective of things. *There is no need to see a reference to the* bianchi *and* neri *factions which at the very most would only indirectly have suggested the imagery*."

But then he half takes back what he has said, for commenting upon the last lines of the same stanza he says this — and agrees with Cosmo.

"This half confession of offenses that penitence long ago should have obliterated recalls Leonardo Bruni's assertion that Dante had begun to assume a humble attitude toward Florence in the hope of propitiating her."

Recalls it and confirms it. For it was certainly true.

« *2* »

But perhaps even more important are the two sentences that immediately follow.

I have gone as a wanderer, nay almost a beggar, through well nigh all the regions in which this tongue is spoken.

In all truth, I have been a ship without sails and without a rudder, drifted into various ports through diverse channels by the fruitless winds which poverty breathes forth.

What were these ports — which by his definition could be anywhere from Sicily's Aegadian Isles (where even then brown-skinned fishermen pursued the tunny in their lateen-rigged vessels) in one direction, to Monaco, the Alps, and even Dalmatia in the other — which he sought in his deep spiritual or psychological turmoil?

Which were the channels his personal ship followed?

Whither did he go?

Where did he stay?

There are some students of Dante — perhaps there are many — who insist that questions like this can never be answered.

Again Edmund G. Gardner:

"There is no certain documentary evidence of Dante's movements between June 1302 and October 1306."

This is, of course, true. There is no certain evidence.

But is certain evidence necessary?

I contend not. I contend not, particularly with Dante.

For there is no one whose work is more seeded with autobiography than Dante, although he does not always label it as such, or perhaps even so recognize it. In the *Vita Nuova*, from which we have already drawn the Beatrice story. In the *Commedia*. In the *Convivio*. And also, but less frequently noted, in the *De Vulgari Eloquentia*. And by carefully examining these passages and integrating them with such documents as we have, by finding out from them and elsewhere the persons Dante knew and the places with which he was familiar, if it is not possible to reconstruct a day-by-day or even a month-by-month chronicle of Dante's *Wanderjahre*, we can at least make a shrewd guess as to its broad outlines.

And this I will attempt to do.

« 3 »

I will begin with the *De Vulgari Eloquentia.*

This book — "On writing in the Italian language," is the only really meaningful translation of its title — is an eloquent, compact, popular dissertation on the new lively tongue of marketplace and street and gutter which not only intrigued poets (as this kind of living language always will) but was beginning to creep into legal documents. It will be discussed more fully later.

But what is important now, since it was not written until Dante was well into his exile — and what must here be considered — is the light that it throws on Dante himself, for in its animadversions upon the speech spoken in Italy, all the so-called vernaculars — the local variations of such speech — of the peninsula are examined with a thoroughness of knowledge that is so detailed that, with a few exceptions which will be noted, it hardly could have been gotten from books.

All the so-called vernaculars — a large order.

I myself count thirty-six of them noted by Dante, and here set them down.

That spoken by the Romans.

"These people think that they ought to have precedence over all others, but we say that the vulgar tongue of the Romans, or rather their hideous jargon, is the ugliest in all Italy. Nor" — one more dig at his old enemy, the papal court — "is this strange, since in the depravity of their manners they seem to be more malodorous than any others."

That of the March of Ancona, and of Spoleto.

" '*Chignamente, scate sciate!*' they say." The meaning today is uncertain, but to Dante it was crude and uncouth. "Let us get rid of them, and with them the Spoletans also."

That of the people of Milan and of Bergamo.

"Let us weed them out. They say *ochiover* for *ottobre* [October]."

That of the Aquileians and the Istrians.

"They crudely belch forth, '*Ces fastu?*' [What dost thou?]"

The mountain and rural dialects of the Casentino and of Prato.

"By their exaggerated accents, they always seem discordant to city dwellers."

That of the Sardinians.

"They are not really Italians. They seem to be without a vulgar tongue of their own, imitating Latin as apes do men."

That of the Sicilians.

There were two kinds of Sicilian, Dante recognized. This he had to, for in *Sicilian* poetry written in *Sicilian*, Italian poetry knew its finest hour until he and his fellows of the *dolce stil novo* began to write.

"If we choose to take the language of the highest, it differs in nothing from that language which is worthiest of the highest praise. But if we take that spoken by the common people" — who drawl out, "*Tragemi d'este focara, se t'este a boluntate*" (Draw me from these fires, if thou please) — "no one could give it preference."

That of the Apulians.

"The speech of the Apulians is harsh, and because of their nearness to the Romans and the Anconitans they make use of shameful barbarisms."

That of the Tuscans — the Florentines, the Pisans, the Sienese, the Aretines.

"The Tuscans, infatuated by their own madness, would call theirs the illustrious language, but if we have leisure to examine their works" — i.e., the poetry of Guittone of Arezzo, Bonagiunta of Lucca, Gallo of Pisa, and Mino Mocato of Siena — "it will be found not to be curial but merely municipal."

That of the Perugians, the Orvietans, and the men from Città Castellana.

"We will not deal with them at all because of their close connection with the Spoletans."

That of the Genoese.

"If the Genoese were, through forgetfulness, to lose the use of the letter *z*, they would either have to be silent altogether or to devise some new kind of speech."

That of the Forlivese and the men of Faenza.

Dante's observations of these dialects have already been discussed — in connection with his visit to Scarpetta degli Ordelaffi.

That of the Brescians, the Veronese, the Vicentines, and the Paduans.

"The same kind of dialect" — i.e., a "harsh, bristling, and shaggy way of speaking" — "prevails among all those who say *magara* [would it were so!] with their ugly syncopations of all the participles ending in *tus* and *tas*, as in *mercò* and *bontè*."

That of Treviso.

"With these we class the Trevisans, who like the Brescians and their neighbors pronounce the consonant *v* as *f* and cut off the final syllable of the word, as in *nof* for *novem* and *vif* for *vivo*."

That of the Venetians.

"Nor do these either deem themselves worthy of the language for which we search. Do any of them doubt this? Let such a one ask himself if he has not ever said: '*Per le plage de Dio tu non veras*' [By God's wounds, thou shalt not come]."

That of Bologna — and of Imola, Ferrara, Modena, and Reggio.

"They are perhaps not far wrong who say that the people of Bologna use a more beautiful speech than the others, for they get from the Imolese the softness and smoothness of their speech and from the citizens of Ferrara and Modena a spice of sharpness characteristic of the Lombards."

However, among these people and at Reggio too the sharpness becomes a kind of roughness when they try to adopt a courtly vulgar tongue.

"That is why there has been no poet among them."

That of Parma.

"This we must consider to be even more the case with the people of Parma, who say *monto* instead of *molto*.

That of Trent and of Turin and of Alessandria.

"We say that the towns of Trent and Turin as well as Alessandria are situated so near the frontiers of Italy that they cannot produce pure Italian, so that even if their languages were as lovely as they are ear-jarring we should still say that they were not Italian. They have too many foreign ingredients."

Quite an amazing array of cities and/or regions!

Quite an amazing lot of very precise information about the languages of these cities and these regions!

But how did Dante acquire this information?

This is a question we must both pose and reply to, for it has biographical as well as literary implications.

By personal observation is the only possible answer. By listening and hearing.

But where and in what manner?

That is important too.

It is not necessary to contend that it was always in the streets and the markets — and in the palaces and homes — of those places specifically referred to. Indeed, in all probability, Dante could not have or would not have visited many of the ones named just above.

Turin is one of them. There does not seem to have been anything which would have taken Dante to Turin, and certainly not at this time of his life.

Naples is another. Apulia and Naples.

To be sure, there is a pleasant story which puts him in Naples at the court of King Robert, but political considerations alone — since Boccaccio's later patron was a strong supporter of the pope and the Black Guelphs — make this seem unlikely.

Alessandria in north Italy. Sicily. Sardinia. Milan (at this time). The March of Ancona. These also Dante probably never visited.

Nor did he need to. You have only to read Boccaccio's tales or Franco

Sacchetti's mordant anecdotes to realize that the Italian of the late Middle Ages was always on the move. In the *Decameron* — for example — you can find a Florentine in Genoa, three others in Treviso, a Perugian in Naples, a Neapolitan lady in the Lunigiana, a Pistoian in Milan, and every kind of "Lombard" in London, Paris, Algarve, or even Egypt. Sacchetti tells us (among others) of a Florentine in Ferrara, an Anconitan at Rome, a Florentine at Verona, another Florentine at Salerno and then in Apulia, a Pistoian in Carrara, and another Pistoian in the south of Italy. The list could go on and on.

Dante, then, could have heard almost any kind of Italian spoken almost anywhere he went, or he could find someone who had heard it spoken.

Let us take Sardinia as an example. Dante almost certainly never went to Sardinia.

But one of the few people of whom he spoke with a warm and almost tender regard is Nino de' Visconti of Pisa, grandson of that Count Ugolino who with two of his sons and two other grandsons was starved to death (*Inferno* XXXII) in the Tower of Hunger.

Purgatorio VIII:

> Only, I think, three steps had I descended
> To come below when I saw one who looked
> At me as if he strove to recognize me.
> It was the time now when the air darkened,
> But not so much that to his eyes and mine
> Reveal it did not what was locked up before.
> He came toward me and I came toward him.
> O noble judge Nino, how much was I pleased
> When I saw thou wert not among the damned!

But Nino was something more than a loyal Guelph — in those days Dante was a Guelph too — who had been expelled from his Arno-mouth city by the Ghibellines. He was also hereditary *giudice* — judge, but more accurately administrator — of Gallura in Sardinia's mountainous northeast. Gallura, supposedly named after the Visconti cock, was one of the four *giudicate* into which the island had been divided by its Pisan masters.

Unlike many administrators, Nino visited his province more than once, governing it with a "firm" hand and actually hanging his deputy Fra Gomita, "a vessel of every fraud" (*Inferno* XXII), for malfeasances during his absence.

He knew Sardinia well and indeed, like Fra Gomita himself (even when he was in hell), "of talking of it his tongue was never weary."

What more fitting Sardinian subject for this older man to discuss around a Caprona campfire with the young poet who was aleady so interested in the tools and the techniques of his trade than the curious and archaic language of his savage domain!

We may assume that Nino discussed it, and that Dante remembered what Nino said.

We may also assume that it was in a similar way that he learned about quite a few others of the many vernaculars which so fascinated him.

But not all of them.

Sometimes his information is too precise to be secondhand, and it seems to me that when this is the case, and *when there is other evidence (whether or not it is circumstantial) that points to his presence in this or that place,* we do not overstep our bounds to make a tentative conjecture.

Bergamo. We can say at least he *may* have been there. Forlì, Faenza, Brescia, Verona, Vicenza, and Padua. Treviso and Venice. Imola, Ferrara, Reggio, Modena, and Parma. Perhaps Trent. We can say the same.

« 4 »

It is even more probable that Dante's wanderings took him to all or to most of the places which he described vividly, and which by any stretch of the imagination can be identified with this phase of his life.

The reason for this is obvious. If you have a retentive memory and a good ear, and if the person who gives you the information has the same, you can learn much about the speech idiosyncrasies of this place or that merely by listening. (Who has not heard a Scotch accent or a Southern accent or a Western drawl or the flat and concise Down East way of speaking either seriously reported or accurately parodied?) But to describe the physical appearance — and the atmosphere — of something which you have neither seen nor heard nor touched nor tasted is something else again.

Dante, as we should know by now, had an extraordinary gift for portraying things and, in fact, nowhere is his writing finer than when he uses it in descriptions. His visual powers are unequaled. He is almost modern in his realistic accuracy.

This, largely, is because he remembers everything he looks at, and in microscopic detail.

Let us set down some of his descriptions.

Venice, for example (and we list only those places which have a possible connection with this part of his life), and the teeming anthill of its Darsena.

Inferno XXI:

As in the arsenal of the Venetians
They boil in wintertime the sticky pitch
Wherewith they do patch up their leaky vessels,
For then they cannot sail and so instead
One builds a new ship while another caulks
The hull of one which has made many voyages;
One hammers at the prow, one at the stern;
One doth make oars, another splices rope;
One doth the foresail patch, the mainsail one,
So, not by fire but by divine art,
A viscous tar did boil beneath me there.

Once — this is Wordsworth's description of Venice — did she hold the gorgeous East in fee! That *once* was in Dante's day, when from the Black Sea — and firmly based on the Galata of Constantinople, and on ports in southern Greece — to Cyprus and Alexandria, a merchant marine of thirty-three thousand *galandrie* and dromonds brought silk and spices and even cargoes of humble wheat to the Riva degli Schiavoni.

Her dockyard, whose shipbuilding and ship-repairing industries supported this fleet, employed sixteen thousand workmen. It was a sight always shown to visitors, and for obvious reasons. It would impress them with Venetian power.

Mantua and the lands above it.

Inferno XX:

Above, in fair Italia, lies a lake
Beneath those Alps that do bound Germany
In the Tirol, and it's called Benaco.
A thousand springs and more do bathe, I ween,
'Twixt Garda and the Val Camonica,
Mt. Pennine with waters that do settle there.
And its middle is an isle whereon
The bishops of Trent and Brescia and Verona
If they went there could each one give his blessing.
Peschiera, fair indeed and strong in arms
To front the Brescians and the Bergamasques,
Sits where the banks that bound it are the lowest,
And there, as it needs must, all doth pour forth
That in its bosom Benaco cannot hold,
Becoming a stream that floweth through green pastures;
And this as soon as it begins to descend
No longer Benaco but Mincio is called,
Until at Governo it meets the Po;
Nor flows it long before it finds a meadow

Where it spreads out and doth enmarsh itself,
And this malarial is in summertime.
Passing this way the cruel virgin [*Manto — the subject
        of this passage*] saw
A hummock that did rise above the fen.
Untilled it was and uninhabited.
There to avoid all human intercourse
She with her servants stopped to ply her arts,
And there she lived, there left her empty body.
Later the scattered people thereabout
On that spot gathered, knowing it to be strong
Because the bog it had on every side.
They built a city over those dead bones,
And after her who first did choose the place
Mantua called it without more augury.

Benaco is the Lago di Garda, which even to the traveler of today is somewhat breathtaking. It is almost completely surrounded by rugged, deep blue mountains (except where they are faintly scarred with the gray of bare rock or, in winter, white with snow), and at their feet, perhaps because of the lake's great depth which at one point is more than eleven hundred feet, the waters are incredibly deep blue too. Along the shore, there are (and were in Dante's time) a succession of small white villages. Sirmione, celebrated by the Roman poet Catullus. Peschiera. Desenzano. Salò (which went back to Roman times too). Toscolano. Gargnano. Riva. Torre di Benaco. Punta di San Viglio. Garda. Bardolino. Lazise. There is a castle at Sirmione, and in Dante's time there were two castles at Peschiera. The castle at Sirmione was built in 1250 by Mastino I della Scala just as the important (to us and to Dante) Scaliger family was beginning to rise to power. The castles at Peschiera — one built by the tyrant Ezzelino da Romano and the other also by the Scaligers — have since vanished, but a later one built in the sixteenth century still stands. The air is notable for its fragrance. Bergamot and laurel as well as citron, lemon, and orange grow all about, particularly on the southern-facing slopes.

From Benaco flows the Mincio, also as described by Dante. Nowhere is it a mountain stream, but soon it widens into a marsh (now three lakes) and does not flow at all.

And in the midst of this — sometimes forming a background for a stilted crane (the *gru* mentioned by Dante perhaps more than any other bird) — rises the city named after the Virgilian sorceress.

"Beyond wide stretches of pale-green water, now flat and glassy, now lightly ruffled," wrote Edwin Howland Blashfield and his wife, American artists, in 1912, "Mantua rises in a long silhouette of parapeted, tile-capped brickwork, with a silver-gray bloom born of the marsh damp. Against the sky are the towers and the curved dome of Alberti's church. In front, the town is buttressed by the bulk of the Gonzaga's castle, so vast that all the shining water seems but to be its moat, the head of the long bridge but its barbican. It is a moat, however, upon which lateen-rigged boats may sail till they reach the Mincio, then onward to the Po, and that delta which will take the traveler southward to Ravenna or northward to Chioggia, Torcello, or Venice."

Except for the church — and there were other churches and another castle — it was the same Mantua which Dante has Virgil describe in his account of "the eponymous witch-mother." It is not very different from the Mantua we can see now.

The historic landslide of the upper Adige.

Inferno XII:

> The place that we now came to for the descent
> Of the steep slope was Alpine. What you saw there
> Was such the eye turned from it. Much as was
> The avalanche which on this side of Trent
> Struck the Adige River on its flank,
> Either from earthquake or from lack of support —
> For from the mountaintop from which it started,
> Down to the plain the rocks so shattered are
> That to one coming down they give some footing —
> Such was the way down into the ravine,
> And at the far edge of this broken chasm
> Did lay outstretched . . .

Pasiphaë, as a matter of fact, the wife of King Minos, who was indecently enamored of the Minotaur!

But at the moment we are not interested in Dante's mythology but in his geography.

Benvenuto da Imola has something to tell us about the latter — at any rate about the geography of the passage in question.

"*Much as was the avalanche which on this side of Trent.* Namely, and to wit, coming from Trent to Verona.

"*On its flank.* That is, on the side of its banks.

"And note," he then added, "that the place is called Slavini by the dwellers there, and that nearby is a castle which is called Marco.

"*Either from earthquake or from lack of support.* That is, from a weakness brought about by erosion made by the swirling waters over a period of many centuries.

"And note" — a second interpolation — "that Albertus Magnus mentioned the remarkable avalanche in his books on meteors. He gave its causes. He said that mountains fell down either because their bases had been worn away, and not having bases they collapsed, or because they were torn asunder by a mighty quake, and that because of this the mighty mountain destroyed the Italian cities on the banks of the Adige River between Trent and Verona and wrought havoc upon many villas and upon many thousands of men."

The descent of the Adige, pointed out a writer of the last century, becomes more rapid between Rovereto and Ala.

"The river which glided gently through the valley of the Trent assumes the roughness of a torrent; the defiles become narrower; and the mountains break into rocks and precipices which occasionally approach the road and sometimes rise perpendicular to it. Among these wilds the traveler cannot fail to notice a vast tract called the Slavini di Marco covered with fragments of rocks torn from the sides of a mountain, or perhaps by their own weight, and hurled down into the plains below. They spread over the whole valley and in some places contract the road to a very narrow space. A few firs and cypresses scattered over the intervals or sometimes jutting out of the crevices of the rocks cast a partial and melancholy shade upon the surrounding desolation."

At thirty-nine miles (from Verona), notes a guidebook more factually, at Marco, 546 feet above sea level, the road crosses the Slavini, or Lavini, di Marco, an enormous landslip caused either by Adige ice or by an A.D. 883 earthquake.

"This enormous falling down of rocks," concluded the Reverend John Eustece, the nineteenth-century writer quoted above, "made a deep impression on the wild imagination of Dante."

The Brenta. The Piave. The Tagliamento. The Adige again. As well as Romano, the marshes near the Venetian lagoon, Vicenza, and Treviso.

Paradiso IX — Cunizza, Ezzelino da Romano's supposedly virtuous, or at any rate repentant, sister is speaking:

"In that part of the depraved, wicked land
Of Italy which lies between the Rialto
And the sources of the Brenta and the Piave
Rises a hill — it is not very lofty —
From which there came down once that flaming brand
Which wrought such great destruction on the region.
From the same root was born both he and I.
Cunizza was I called, and I shine here
Because the light of this star [*Venus, or heavenly love*]
    overcame me.

And joyously do I forgive myself
For this my lot — it does not trouble me —
Which your vulgar may find hard to understand. . . .
But see ye not that man should be excellent.
Then our first life will live again in fame.
But this thinks not the rabble that presently
The Tagliamento and the Adige do enclose.
Though it be scourged, still it does not repent.
And soon — yea, very soon — at Padua's marsh
The waters that lave Vicenza will change their color.
And where Sile and Cagnan flow side by side
One lords it now and he holds high his head
For whom the spider already weaves his web."

We may profitably leave out (at any rate, for the moment) the history which is told or implied in these lines, and need not even dwell upon the garrulous old lady who was so infatuated with her recently acquired piety.

But the places we should not leave out.

In that part of the depraved, wicked land of Italy which lies between the Rialto and the sources of the Brenta and the Piave.

By using the sources of the Brenta and the Piave as the apex of the triangle which enclosed Ezzelino's domains, Dante shows that he understood clearly that they almost came together. This implies local knowledge.

Rises a hill — it is not very lofty.

Romano, which rises gently to an eminence of not much more than six hundred feet. On it stood — and the ruins still stand — the Castello degli Ezzelini, which was built by those German robber barons of the tenth century from whom Ezzelino and Cunizza sprang.

The Tagliamento and the Adige.

This choice of rivers again implies — or seems to imply — local knowledge.

At Padua's marsh the waters that lave Vicenza will change their color.

There was a marsh to the east of Padua, and into it flowed the Bacchiglione, which rises near Vicenza.

But why did the waters of this river change their color?

Here for explanation — and further confirmation that Dante knew the bogs and quagmires of this part of Italy — turn to another vivid passage in the *Commedia.*

Purgatorio V — in which Dante addressed those in ante-purgatory who have met death violently, but who repented before dying:

I said: "Although I gaze upon your faces,
Not one I recognize, but if to please you
Anything I can do, souls born for bliss,
Speak ye and I will do it, by that peace
Which, in the footsteps of so made a guide,
Doth make me go seeking from world to world."
Then one replied: "We trust, each one of us,
In thy good offices without thine oath
If lack of power doth not thwart thy will.
I, therefore, speaking alone before the rest,
Do pray thee, if thou ever seest the land
That lies between the Romagna and that of Charles,
Thou'lt show to me the courtesy to implore
In Fano that they do make orisons
That I may purge away my grievous sins.
From that place did I come, but the deep wounds
From which poured forth the blood which was my life
Were given me amidst the Antenori,
Where I had thought I would be all secure.
This he of Este ordered, angered at me
Very much more than justice warranted.
Had I but made my flight toward La Mira
When I was overtaken at Oriaco,
I still should be up yonder where men breathe.
But I ran to the marsh, where reeds and mire
So tangled me I fell, and there I saw
Form on the ground a pool come from my veins."

This is the story. Jacopo del Cassero was a noble knight from the small town of Fano on the Adriatic coast between Ancona and Pescara. He was the son of another noble knight, Uguccione del Cassero, *podestà* of Macerata in 1268, and nephew of Martino del Cassero, who in the 1250s was said to be the most distinguished jurist in Italy.

Jacopo was also an ardent Guelph, being named by Villani as among the Guelph leaders " of a great expedition which the commonwealth made against Arezzo" in 1288, a year before Dante rode against Arezzo in the same kind of war. It was in an aftermath of this expedition that the Sienese were cut to pieces at Pieve di Toppo when they tried to ford the stagnant Chiana, in which "joust" (*Inferno* XIII), since, "naked and scarred," he did not run as nimbly as he did when pursued by black hounds in hell, Lano de Maroni, another of "the spendthrift brigade" was overtaken and slain.

As a Guelph — and because holding such an office and having the qualities needful to hold it effectively were hereditary — he was named *podestà* of Bologna in 1206, and in this capacity he waged unrelenting war against the Marquis Azzo d'Este of Ferrara, whose not altogether lovely character — he was noted "for bloodthirstiness, treachery, and avarice" — is set down by Dante more than once.

But Jacopo, who was a very rash man (*vir temerarius*, says Benvenuto da Imola), did more than use force of arms against Azzo.

"He was not," says the commentator Lana, "content with merely doing deeds. He continuously and without restraint used the most abusive language possible against Azzo. He said that he slept with his stepmother. He said that he was descended from a washerwoman. He said that he was a caitiff and a coward. His tongue never tired of repeating these villainies."

Was what happened surprising, then?

Similarly vexed, but not for the same reason, by Thomas à Becket, Henry II cried to his followers: "Will no one rid me of this turbulent priest?"

Azzo, much more violent than Henry, must have said much the same, and the same kind of action resulted.

Jacopo's term of office expired in 1297 and he declined a new appointment. He returned to Fano. But a year later, Matteo Visconti, the first of his family to become lord and tyrant of Milan, sent for him to become *podestà* there. He took ship from Fano to Venice and then started — by land and by way of Padua — for his destination.

Still among the lagoons and in fact only eight miles from Venice, at the little town of Oriaco he saw horsemen approaching. They were armed and wore the blazon of Ferrara.

What should he do? Try to ride around them to La Mira, where he might have had Paduan protection? But the Antenori (Paduans) were descended from the Trojan traitor Antenor. Might they not betray him too? Or hurriedly turn off from the road and try to hide in the morasses?

He did the latter, but soon was in mud and slime up to his waist. He could offer no resistance as Azzo's hirelings with their Ferrara swords and daggers did their work.

And where Sile and Cagnan flow side by side.

This, too, is something Dante could have seen and noted. The two rivers (the Cagnano is now called the Botteniga) meet at Vicenza, but for a while they do not mingle, the crystal-clear waters of the Sile and the soiled and turbid waters of the second stream being clearly distinguishable.

A modern writer on "the plain towns of Italy" deals with this romantically. He imagines that Dante "lingered during his wanderings at their place of junction, struck by the beauty of the swift tree-shaded streams," and further almost visualizes him as emerging from a narrow dusky medieval street "onto the broad sunny quay and the blue splashing Sile" and then on to where "the main arm of the Botteniga came roaring in under the broad stone arches of the quay, and the joined waters soon turned to the south."

Emerging to look on "in admiration."

It is not necessary to go that far. But it can and should be said that Dante at least knew about these two relatively small rivers of upper Italy and that they made a great impression on him.

Other references are more compact but often just as well visualized. Cesena.

Inferno XXVII:

> That place whose sides the Savio doth bathe
> And just as she doth lie 'twixt plain and mountain . . .

Modena — that is if we can accept the opinion of one of the more eloquent of Dante's admirers that it was in Modena that the poet was more than anywhere else stirred deeply by the church music which he described in *Purgatorio* IX:

> I turned attentively to the first note
> And then "*Te deum laudamus*" meseems
> I heard in voices mingled with sweet sound,
> And I was moved profoundly in the same way,
> By what I heard, that oftentime one is
> When people sing to organ's accompaniment
> And sometimes words you hear and sometimes not.

Pavia.

At any rate (*Paradiso* X) he described the church of San Pietro in Cieldauro (St. Peter's of the Golden Ceiling) there.

Forlì. But we already know that Dante went to Forlì.

Inferno XXVII:

> The city which withstood so long a siege
> And piled the Frenchmen into bloody heaps
> Under the Green Claws once more finds itself.

We have already noted that the Green Claws were the Ordelaffi, and that they ruled Forlì. The defeat referred to is that of a French army sent by Pope Martin IV in 1282.

Faenza and Imola.

Again *Inferno* XXVIII:

> The towns on the Lamone and the Santerno
> The young lion of the white lair doth rule —
> He who his party changes from summer to winter.

The young lion was Maghinardo da Susinana.

Verona, whose annual footrace (run, according to Boccaccio, by naked men, whose modesty made them speed the faster) for a length of green cloth is noted in *Inferno* XV; and the wickednesses of whose abbot of San Zeno is commented on in *Purgatorio* XVIII.

Padua.

In *Inferno* XV are described the embankments which protect this city from spring floods "at that time when Chiarentana feels the heat" — i.e., when the snows melt in the mountains of Carinthia.

The "white marble" of the mountains of Carrara (*Inferno* XX).

The Magra River, "which [*Paradiso* IX] parts the Genoese from Tuscany."

The much smaller Torrente Lavagna.

Purgatorio XIX — Pope Adrian V (Ottobuoni de' Fieschi, who died in 1276 after a papacy of only thirty-six days) is speaking:

> " 'Twixt Sestri and Chiaveri there pours down
> A fair and swollen streamlet. From its name
> The title of my blood doth makes its boast."

« 5 »

This much for cities, towns, rivers, lakes, and mountains. But Dante's footsteps can also — or so at least we think — be traced by noting certain of the men he seems to have known and talked to.

Certain of these have already been mentioned — in connection with the places Dante described. The Green Claws, for example. The young lion of the white lair. Giuseppe della Scala of the twisted mind and body, Alberto della Scala's depraved bastard son, into whose hands his father had unlawfully placed perhaps the noblest and certainly one of the most beautiful abbeys of all Italy.

But there were others too.

Messer Marchese of Forlì.

Purgatorio XXIV:

> I saw Messer Marchese [*in the purgatory of gluttons*],
>   who once had leisure
> To drink at Forlì with far less a thirst
> Yet even then was never satisfied.

This red-faced, pleasure-loving "gentleman of Forlì" — but he also seems to have been an excellent fighting man and may have been one of the Orgogliosi rivals of the Ordelaffi — was so notable a wine bibber that, in his city which was famous for its fiery wines, men talked of nothing else. This he found out when one day he asked his cellarer what people said of him.

"They say," said the cellarer, "that you are always drinking."

Messer Marchese smote an iron fist.

"Why do they not," he roared, "say instead that I am always thirsty?"

Asdente of Parma.

Inferno XX:

> Behold Asdente.
> That to the leather and thread he'd given his mind
> He wishes now, but he repents too late.

Master Toothless — that is what his name means, but he was given it, it was said, ironically, because his teeth were grotesquely big — "the harmless cobbler-prophet whom Dante thrust so rudely down to hell" — was probably dead by 1304, but where he lived men still either praised or denounced him.

Said Fra Salimbene:

"In those days, the Lord Obizzo, bishop of the place, invited the people's prophet, Asdente, to dinner, and diligently inquired of the future. He said that in a short while the men of Reggio and Parma would suffer many tribulations. He foretold the death of Pope Martin IV. He foretold that three supreme pontiffs should succeed, and be at discord with each other. He foretold the ruin of Modena before it came to pass. But this man is only so far a prophet that he understands the sayings of Merlin and the Sibyl and the Abbot Joachim [Joachim of Flora]. He is courteous and humble and familiar, and without pomp or vainglory."

But Benvenuto da Imola describes him as an ignorant false prophet.

Possibly Fra Dolcino, whose predecessor as leader of the Apostolic Brothers, one Gherardino Segarelli, was also of Parma.

Inferno XXVIII — in the hell of the schismatics, one of whom addresses Dante:

> "Tell thou Fra Dolcin, then, to arm himself
> (Thou who perhaps will shortly see the sun),
> If he would not soon follow me down here,
> With provender, so that when the snow holds him
> The Novarese will not gain victory
> O'er him, which otherwise were hard to win."

This was prophecy after the fact, and so of course it came true. And when Dante was close enough at hand to observe it.

Dolcino de' Tornielli, one of the many denouncers of "the wealth, arrogance, and corruption of the Holy Church" and of its divorce from Christian practices which came into being during the two and a half centuries preceding the massive reforms initiated by the Council of Trent, was said to be the illegitimate son of a parish priest. He was born north of Novara, but he and his following of "three thousand hardy young men, many noble and some rich" — and also the beautiful Margaret of Trent, who was said to be Dolcino's concubine — at first held forth and preached a sort of communism in the mountains behind Bergamo and Brescia. Then they moved into the Piemonte.

There they supported themselves by brigandry and pillage, justifying this by their belief that there was no such thing as private property. The mountain folk they battened on thought differently. Cattle thieves — even if they justified their raids with garbled verses from the Holy Scripture — were not held in high esteem by those whose wooden chalets were burned and herds were plundered. The Church supported the latter. Let there be a crusade against these heretics! An army was assembled, and it included not only men from all parts of Lombardy but even from Savoy and Provence. Dolcino and his followers withdrew into the hills between his native town and Novara, where they were trapped into submission by the heavy snowfalls of a severe winter.

This was in 1305. Thousands of them were massacred, but Dolcino and his Margaret were dragged to Vercelli, where they were paraded through the streets and then tortured, and finally — two years later, in June 1307 — were burned at the stake.

« 6 »

But if these men, and this one woman, may — but equally may not — have crossed Dante's path, there were four others in north Italy of whom he talks with such vividness and feeling that they almost certainly did. They are introduced to us in *Purgatorio* XVI. This is where Dante, having in the previous canto "taught us how to avoid the sin of anger," now shows how, on the third cornice of the place where sins are atoned, it can be expiated by passing through the intense and black, foul smoke.

Here follow his words:

> The gloom of hell and the dark night bereft
> Of every star under a desolate sky
> Overcast everywhere with heavy clouds
> N'er made unto my sight so heavy a veil

As did the heavy smoke that covered us there,
Nor one so bitter to my every sense
That it would not mine eyes let me keep open.

Hidden in the murk we hear souls singing the *Agnus Dei* — "O Lamb of God," appropriate because the Lamb of God seemed to express Christ's gentleness as well as His mercy — and one of them, as Dante gropes through the gloom, addresses the poet:

"Who art thou then who movest through the haze,
And of us speakest in the manner of one
Who still doth measure time by calendar?"

Dante tells him, and then asks for directions on how to go upward. These given him, he goes on as follows:

"With these swaddling bands
Which only death unwinds I do go up
And I have come here through anguish of hell,
And since God so hath wrapped me in His court
In manner all quite strange to modern use,
Hide not from me who thou wast before death,
But tell me, and tell if I am on the right road.
Your words shall be my escort to the passage."

The spirit does:

"I was a Lombard and my name was Marco.
I loved the world, and I did love that worth
To attain which no one longer bends the bow."

Marco Lombardo! He is the first of the four. The others will appear shortly. But only after a long and complicated discussion.

For Dante, now that he knows who the speaker is, turns to him for an explanation of something that Marco said.

"The world is thus indeed wholly bereft
Of every virtue, as thou tellest me,
And pregnant and o'erspread with wickedness,
But I do pray thee to point out the cause
That I may see it and show it unto men,
For one blames heaven, the other earth below."

"Not heaven!" cries Marco. "They are blind who ever think this! For if heaven were to be blamed, there would be no free will!"

Rather it is the man himself who, having choice, makes the wrong choice.

> "It comes forth from His hand, who dearly loved it
> Even before it was, much like a child
> That weeps and then doth laugh in baby fashion,
> The simple soul of ours which knows nothing
> Save that, having been created by its joyous maker,
> It turns eagerly to what delights it.
> At first it turns only to trifling pleasure,
> But this decieves it and it looks for more,
> Unless bridle or bit turns it aside."

Therefore, laws are needed, and indeed there are laws. But no one heeds them.

> "Laws are there, but who ever enforces them?
> No one, because the shepherd who goes before
> May chew the cud but has not hooves divided.
> Therefore the people who do see their leader
> Snatch only at those things they themselves want
> Feed on the same themselves, and naught else seek.
> Thou canst then plainly see that evil guidance
> It is that has the wicked world made bad,
> And 't is our nature that's corrupt in us."

It had not always been thus, however.

> "In the old days Rome, who the world made good,
> Two suns did have, which one and the other street
> Made plain to us, the world's and that of God.
> Now one hath destroyed the other, and the sword
> Is joined to the crook, and both together
> Must of necessity fare very ill.
> If thou believest not, consider an ear of corn,
> For every plant can be known from its seed.
> In that land which the Po and Adige water,
> Valor and courtesy were one time found
> Before the Emperor Frederick made war there.
> But now it can be confidently traveled
> By anyone who cares not — to his shame —
> To have speech with good men or to draw nigh them."

Confidently — or perhaps not quite so confidently. For Marco suddenly at least half reverses himself.

"Yet there are still three old men in whom rebukes
The ancient times the new. Slow seems the day
That God will take them to a better world.
Currado da Palazzo and good Gherardo
And Guido da Castel, who's better called,
As do the Frenchmen call him, the guileless Lombard."

Who were these three old men? That is our first question. And who was the Marco Lombardo who brought them into the story?

Fortunately we know.

Let us take Marco Lombardo first.

Marco was almost certainly a Venetian gentleman of the aristocratic Ca' Lombardi — though some say that this was not the case, and even that, because he lived much in France, Lombardo was a nickname (he was Marco Lombardo; i.e., Mark the Lombard or Italian). By profession he was a *uomo da corte* — a hard term to translate; literally it means courtier, but it really seemed to signify the kind of courtier who eats well because he speaks well and people like to have him at their table — "and he was one of the wittiest of these in the whole world."

"He was a man of noble spirit and distinguished virtue," says Benvenuto da Imola, "but quick to anger and of a proud and haughty nature."

He was also learned, says another commentator, and very skilled in matters political, adding that he was likewise noted for his generosity.

Three stories are told of him and they are all significant.

The first illustrates his pride.

He was taken prisoner in one of the frequent Lombard wars, and since he was not rich — "Thou art poor!" cries one Paolo, of the *Cento Novelle Antiche;* "Thou art poor; why dost thou not enrich thyself?" — he wrote Rizzardo da Cammino asking him to raise the money for his ransom. Rizzardo — "mourning Marco's unhappy fate" — immediately addressed every lord in Lombardy, asking them to contribute generously toward his liberation.

"But when Marco heard this he grew righteously indignant and sent a messenger to Messer Rizzardo saying that he would rather die in prison than be under so much obligation to so many.

"Then Messer Rizzardo raised the money himself."

The second tells of his openhandedness.

"Generous indeed Marco was, and whatever he gained from noble lords who had encountered misfortune he later restored to them, and he also loaned them money freely. Because of the latter, he realized, as he approached death, that much was owed to him. Therefore he made a will, and in it provided, among other things, that anyone who had property of his should retain it, and that no efforts should be made for any restitution. 'Let him who hath had from me keep it,' he said."

But the third story reveals an even more notable — and less common — quality, virtue.

At the height of his power, Count Ugolino de' Visconti — he of the Tower of Hunger story — invited Marco to a great feast at which he told him of the greatness he had won and showed him all his rich possessions.

Then he asked him: "Marco, what thinkest thou of this?"

"I think," answered Marco, "that thou art better prepared for evil fortune than any man that lives."

The count, "fearing these words of Marco's," asked him: "Why?"

"Because the wrath of God is the only thing now lacking you!" said Marco.

"And in truth," says the man who told the story, "the wrath of God soon came upon Ugolino, as it pleased God, because of his treacheries and crimes."

This much for Marco. Now the others.

Currado da Palazzo was of an old Brescian family which apparently was of French origin. Assuming that he was a mature man in 1277 when he was *podestà* in Florence and dealt with the Alighieri lawsuit, as has been earlier narrated, he was now not less than seventy. He had retired to his native town.

"There," it is related in the *Ottimo Commento*, "he lived out his days in great honor, delighting in his fine household and in matters political, for in the government of cities he had gained many rewards and won much renown."

Gherardo da Cammino deserved equally a lofty reputation, but — until Dante visited north Italy, it would appear — he was not equally well known to Dante. Or at least Dante pretends this.

"O Marco mine," he says in an omitted section of the long passage I have quoted above, "What Gherardo is this who thou sayest is left as an example of an extinct race of men and as a reproach to this our barbarous day?"

What Gherardo indeed, for who did not know this nobleman of the north?

Eventually including Dante, who has something to say of him in a book written later than the theoretical date of this encounter.

Convivio IV, 14:

"Let us say that Gherardo da Cammino had been the grandson of the basest peasant that ever drank the waters of the Sile or the Cagnano, and that this grandfather was still remembered; even then who would dare say that Gherardo was a base man?"

Who, for that matter, could help knowing him?

For as Lord of Treviso from 1283 until his death in 1306 and as head of one of the most potent families of the Trevisan March (originally they had been known as Montenara, but changed their name to da Cammino when Guecello Montenara — Wetzel of the Peaks — built Cammino Castle in 1089), they dominated and in a sense protected a whole segment of northeast Italy.

But Marco (again *Purgatorio* XVI) answered Dante as if his question were entirely reasonable:

> "Either thy speech deceives me or tries to test me,"
> He made reply, "for look, thou speakest Tuscan,
> Yet good Gherardo, it seems, thou dost not know.
> But other surname have I not for him
> Unless I take it from his daughter Gaia."

This mention of Gaia seems to cause great distress to many Dantists, for they cannot forget that one contemporary commentator said that the young lady was vain and loose-living while another stated that her devotion to amorous activities made her notorious through all of Italy. In other words, Gaia was a "gay lady" in the modern sense of the term.

But was she really?

Not so, says the Anonymous Florentine.

"Gaia was a beautiful and well-mannered young woman who resembled her father in every way. About her and her courtesy they spoke not merely in Treviso but in all the country round about."

It should be noted, however, that no such favorable judgment was ever pronounced upon Gherardo's son Rizzardo, who ruled Treviso after his father's death until his murder in 1312 by a half-witted servitor, paid, some say, by Can Grande della Scala. By all accounts, Rizzardo was a vicious tyrant.

The third of these gentlemen of the old regime and of the old-time manners, Guido da Castel, was in some ways the most courtly of all. It has been noted that he was called the guileless Lombard by Frenchmen. Some say this was because of his notable honesty. Unlike other "Lombard dogs" — the usurer with his blood-sucking rates of interest, the sharp trader with his shoddy woolens, "the scrivener [notary] who thought it a very great shame when any of his instruments proved to be other than false" — Guido never tried to take advantage of anyone. This alone deserved an adjective.

But there are others who interpret "guileless" otherwise. They say that it meant generous and hospitable.

"Messer Guido," says one of these, "devoted himself zealously to entertaining all those who passed along the French road."

I.e., the road from France over the Mount Cenis pass to the various towns of Lombardy and Emilia.

"Many armed men and many horsemen stopped with him when they came hither from France."

He fed them, says this contemporary, and gave them fresh steeds, arms, and money.

"Without any thought of repayment."

"He was," reports another, that Guido "who flourished in Reggio in the time of our poet, a prudent and a righteous man, wise in counsel, beloved and honored, for he zealously strove for his republic and was a protector of his fatherland."

In a small way, he was also a man of letters.

"This Guido was also an accomplished composer of rhymes in the vulgar tongue as can be seen in certain writings of his."

This seems to contradict the Dante statement that there was no one in Reggio who could write poetry.

But perhaps Dante meant good poetry.

Finally — and here we have one of the rare pieces of hard and specific evidence we seek so eagerly — it is stated categorically that he entertained the poet himself.

"He was a liberal man, a man noted for his liberality, and of his liberality the poet had personal experience when he was entertained by him in his own home."

« 7 »

Let us now recapitulate.

The places.

In his *De Vulgari Eloquentia*, Dante discusses the dialects and ways of speaking of at least fourteen towns in north Italy, in many cases with detailed and intimate knowledge.

At least nine of these towns he refers to again in the *Commedia*, while he shows great familiarity with at least half a dozen more, ranging from little La Mira to Mantua of the mist-enwreathed swamps. He also seems familiar with most of the rivers and many of the mountains and lakes.

The people.

He talks of a whole array of men in north Italy as if he either knew them or knew people who did.

Maghinardo da Susinana of *Faenza* and *Imola*.

The Ordelaffi of *Forlì*.
Messer Marchese of *Forlì*.
Asdente of *Parma*.
Possibly Fra Dolcino.
Marco Lombardo of *Venice*.
Currado da Palazzo of *Brescia*.
Gherardo da Cammino of *Treviso*.
Guido da Castel of *Reggio*.
And the ruling family of *Verona*.

We are now ready to put the pieces of the puzzle together. We are now ready to try to retrace Dante's footsteps.

But remember as we do so that we are at best engaged in speculation. With a few exceptions which will be duly noted, we are at best making an educated guess.

XVII

Lombardy, the Lunigiana, Lucca

H E went back to Arezzo first (this is what I deduce), following the
Arno Valley eastward, and then — after he had come to Pontassieve
— almost southeastward, perhaps passing by several castles still in friendly
hands until he came to the small, almost triangular plain over which
towered the onetime Etruscan city.

There he had paused briefly only two years before, and under its walls
he had ridden defiantly during one of the military adventures of his
youth.

It was a journey not without considerable danger. Walking, or on mule-
or horseback, he still had to elude the victorious enemy who, after La
Lastra, fanned out in every possible direction, burning and pillaging and
laying violent hands upon any of their enemy who had the misfortune to
encounter them.

"The Blacks," says Dino Compagni, "slew many of the exiles whom
they found in hiding, and they put to death many poor sick persons
whom they dragged from the hospitals. Very many Bolognese and
Aretines were taken too, and all these they hanged."

They were particularly incensed at the Bolognese and the Aretines,
since these White allies, unlike the bemused and muddled Whites themselves, boldly attacked the Porta degli Spadaii (Swordmakers' Gate) and
"carried off some of the wood of the wicket which the Blacks considered
to be a great shame done to them." They did worse than that. Says
Villani: "They removed the bolt of the said gate and, in contempt of the
Florentines, took it to Arezzo, where they set it in the church of San
Donato, their chief church."

For the record, San Donato still stands. It is now Santa Maria del Pieve, with its circular apse, three naves, and frescoes by Giotto disciples, one of the finest medieval edifices in central Italy.

But despite the risks of fleeing thither, the risks of not fleeing were even greater, for, you will remember, Dante would have been burned, not merely hanged, had he been taken. Moreover, he had friends in Arezzo, the most notable still being Ser Petracco di Parenzo, in whose house on the Vico del Orto a son, Francis Petrarch, was born on the very day that the battle of La Lastra was fought. In addition to this, Francesco Alighieri had been a recent visitor — if he was not still there — and while in the city had made certain financial arrangements for the benefit of his elder brother.

One of these had been recorded.

"May 13, 1304. It has been duly agreed in the house belonging to me, the below-named notary, with Tedescho the druggist and Baldinetto degli Scorzoni present as witnesses, that Francesco degli Alighieri, on his own statement the principle in this matter, with Capontozzo dei Lamberti of Florence at his request and urging being guarantor of the same, do each and both of them promise to pay, give back, and restore to Foglione di Giobbo, druggist, etc., twelve florins of good and pure gold upon the demand and petition of the said Foglione whenever it shall be made in the city of Arezzo, etc."

If there was a default, the amount to be paid was doubled. This was for "damages, expenses, etc." As security, certain property, not specifically defined, was pledged.

"And this I decree," wrote the notary, "shall serve in lieu of mortgage."

Twelve florins of good and pure gold!

It was not a prince's ransom, but to the harassed exile who now did not even have his erstwhile White colleagues to turn to, it must have seemed manna from heaven. Nor is it likely that this was the only provision which Francesco made for Dante. It was merely the only one of which we have positive knowledge.

It was also the only one that he would be able to make, at least for some time. For before long — actually before August of the next year, 1305 — the younger brother was in trouble too.

Again we have a document.

"In the same year and indiction and on the fourteenth day of August. Executed in the presence of Ser Giovanni, Ser Spigliato, and Tuccio Ciacchi, called as witnesses, in the *popolo* of San Piero Maggiore in the city of Florence. Lapo di Bonfigliolo and Pagno di Ristori, heralds of the commonwealth of Florence, acting on their own behalf and on behalf of the two constables of the lord *podestà*, do acknowledge and confess that they have received from Vezzo de' Vezzosi their salary and the salary of the two constables and so consider themselves well paid and content with the same."

This was for their work in attaching, as ordered, the property of "the rectors, syndics, citizens, workmen, and farmers of San Miniato di Pagnolla" to cover the amount of grain which the said Vezzo was entitled to receive from the lands of Dante degli Alighieri and his brother Francesco, *both* rebels and *both* condemned by the commonwealth, the said grain to have to be sold to raise the amount needed "to pay his salary and the salary of the men-at-arms assigned to him" for seizing the property of the said rebels.

The sum involved was thirty *soldi*. For Vezzo, for the two constables, and for an unnamed number of men-at-arms. Police service came very cheaply in those days.

But to revert to the document. In it, Francesco was clearly bracketed with his brother as a condemned rebel, nor did the fact that with his skill — not shared by Dante — in disengaging himself from political entanglements he soon extricated himself from this unhappy state of affairs change the present situation.

For the moment, his property was expropriated. For the moment — but as the records show, for the moment only — it was a big enough problem for him to take care of himself. He could do nothing for his older brother.

« 2 »

But if Dante after La Lastra came to Arezzo, he did not stay there long. There are certain possible reasons for this. It may have been because, as we have already pointed out, Uguccione della Faggiuola was no longer considered reliable by the increasingly disorganized Whites. This, however, does not seem likely, since Arezzo itself now entertained the same opinion of Uguccione and had removed him from the office of *podestà* "because of his suspicious behavior." It may have been because many of his friends, including Ser Petracco, either had left or were planning to leave the city. It may have been because Francesco could not help him anymore. It may, finally — and this seems the most likely reason — have been because, due to its geography and its political tradition, Arezzo was a natural mecca for those exiles who still pinned their hopes on military action, and Dante no longer did, and did not want to become involved.

But whatever the reason, Dante came to Arezzo, transacted a little business, saw a few friends, and went his way as he had always planned to do.

Where did he go?

The consensus is that he went to Verona — although not necessarily directly. Not necessarily without certain delays and certain stopovers which are of interest and importance.

Yet even in this matter there has been debate and argument. Not so much as to whether Dante did indeed go to *la città degna e marmorea* — the worthy and the marble city — that place which "for its glorious past leadership in warfare, literature, and art stands only below Rome and Florence and Venice," but as to exactly when he went there and who received him.

Here I must revert to a passage already cited:

> *Il tuo primo rifugio e il primo ostello*
> *Sarà la cortesia del gran Lombardo*
> *Chi in sulla scala porta il santo uccello.*

> Thy first refuge, they first hostelry
> Will be the courtesy of the great Lombard
> Who on the stairway bears the sacred bird.

But who was this *gran Lombardo?*

Alberto della Scala?

"In the first years of his flight," writes Boccaccio, "he had gone to Alberto della Scala, by whom he had been kindly received."

But Alberto della Scala died on September 10, 1301, and at that time, far from being an exile, Dante was an active political leader in Florence. He was still addressing various Florentine councils and urging them to stand firm against Pope Boniface.

Bartolommeo della Scala?

Bartolommeo was Alberto's eldest son. He had been elected *podestà* of the merchants — and hence to some extent *de facto* ruler of Verona — at the age of twenty-five. A contemporary chronicler says that he was "beloved by the people," and the *Syllabus Potestatum* "praises his wisdom, benevolence, and love of justice, and relates that all his thoughts were directed to governing his people in peace so that under his rule the Veronese prospered and grew famous."

But Bartolommeo died on March 7, 1304, and at that time Dante was almost certainly still in Tuscany.

Finally, Bartolommeo's younger brother Alboino?

Here the dates are right. Alboino reigned from 1304 to 1311. Moreover — by reason of the imperial contacts he had developed, he and Can Grande were imperial vicars — he may well have been the first of the della Scala who could lawfully use on their arms the eagle of the empire.

But — and this is much dwelt on by those who will not accept Alboino as Dante's first host — Dante said this of him in *Convivio* IV, 16:

"There are indeed certain foolish ones who think that by this word 'noble' is meant 'to be known and named by many,' and they say that it is derived from a word which means 'to know'; namely, *nosco*. This is completely untrue, for if it were true those things that were most known and most named of their kind would be the noblest of their kind, then the obelisk of St. Peter's would be the noblest stone in the world, and Asdente the cobbler of Parma would be nobler than any other of his fellow citizens, and Alboino della Scala would be nobler than Guido da Castel, whereas every one of these things is palpably false."

But how, it is argued, could Alboino della Scala be the praised and even revered "great Lombard" if Dante spoke so scornfully of him?

Umberto Cosmo gives a convincing answer.

Dante, he says, had been graciously received by Bartolommeo della Scala when he came to Forlì to Verona as ambassador from the Whites during the early days of his exile. This he remembered now, and "that memory, together with promises it is likely he received, must have induced him to seek the protection of the Scaligers."

But he had "a complex nature and, overwhelmingly conscious of his own greatness, he expected it to be recognized when it was potential rather than actual." Because it was not recognized — or not recognized to the extent he thought it should be — "there may have been some coolness between him and his hosts."

There may, too, have been — there almost certainly were — some petty slights. We will hear about them later.

These petty slights "suffice to explain how, when they were still fresh in his mind, Dante allowed himself to indulge in the sharpshooting that takes place in the *Convivio*."

But when, "perhaps as much as fifteen years later, the poet wrote his eulogy of the family in the *Paradiso*, the splendor of Can Grande had driven every spark of ill humor from his heart."

Grateful to Can Grande for his greatness and his generosity, and "with the shrewd intuition of the artist," he spoke of "the whole family rather than of an individual" — in other words, *il gran Lombardo* was neither Bartolommeo nor Alboino nor even Can Grande but the Scaligeri — and thus he "succeeded in amending without appearing to do so" his earlier harsh judgment.

I agree with Professor Cosmo.

But now back to the subject, and to his conclusion.

"No one who thinks that Dante was the author of the letter to the cardinal of Prato can think that his host was anyone but Alboino."

And who can doubt that Dante was the author of this letter?

After a brief — probably after a very brief — stay in the place to which in White defeat he had so hastily gone, it was, then, to Alboino della Scala in his city by the swiftly flowing Adige that the poet now wended his way.

3

How he got there is another matter about which we may legitimately speculate, for there was a choice of routes.

He might, for example, have found a way through the Black-held Mugello (that "pleasant, verdant" intramontane valley in the hills north of Florence) and finally, coming out on the Bologna road, have crossed into Emilia on the highway he had taken at least once before. That would have been possible, but risky.

He might have gone only as far as Pontassieve and then climbed and descended until he came to Forlì, as he had done when he was Guelph ambassador to Scarpetta Ordelaffi. That would have been risky too.

Farther to the south and east, he might (but this was the least likely of all) have gone to San Sepolcro in the fresh valley of the upper Tiber, which was only a rivulet there. Listing Dante's hosts by whom he was "suitably honored, so far as the period and their means permitted," Boccaccio names, among others, the della Faggiuola — kinsmen of that same Uguccione whose supposed unfriendliness had caused Dante and other Whites to leave Arezzo. The della Faggiuola, says Boccaccio, received him "in the mountains near Urbino." There was indeed a Faggiuola castle thereabouts — probably on the slopes of Monte Faggiuola close to the little town of Macerata Feltria.

Thence he could have descended to the Adriatic coast, passing close to San Leo, whose almost inaccessible cragtop position so impressed him. If so, he would have at least paused at Rimini, where once dwelt the Francesca of his compassionate story, and there is this much to be said for a visit to Rimini, and at this time: even as he began the *Commedia* thoroughly familiar with its politics.

Inferno XXVII:

> The mastiffs of Verrucchio old and young,
> That did such evil work upon Montagna,
> Tear with their fangs the way they always did.

The old and the young mastiffs of Verrucchio were Malatesta and Malatestino da Verrucchio, who had recently acquired control of the city by treacherously agreeing with their rival, Montagna de' Parcitati, that all mercenaries — his and theirs — should be withdrawn from the city, and then concealing theirs in various houses from which they burst forth in the middle of the night shouting: "Long live Malatesta and the Guelphs! Death to the Parcitati and the Ghibellines!"

Still it is not likely Dante traveled by this route either. It is far more likely that he took a more central route.

Up the upper Arno Valley past Subbiano and Rassina (whence through wild scenery led a difficult path to La Verna, where St. Francis received the stigmata) to Bibbiena. This part of the road passed for a short way through a narrow rocky gorge through which the river boiled tumultuously in a white foam. From Bibbiena ever higher and higher to the Passo dei Mandrioli (Shepherd's Pass). From the romantic Scotch Highlands–like Passo dei Mandrioli downward to Castrum Balnei — now Bagno di Romagna — whose healing waters were known even to the Romans. Shortly after Bagno di Romagna, Dante or any traveler would have encountered the river Savio. Here for perhaps another twenty miles the way was still rugged, but gradually the valley widened and the slopes grew gentle. Finally, he would have come to Cesena, where the road ended. Cesena was at the edge of the wide Po plain.

I believe that it was by this road that Dante made his northward journey. I believe it for the following reasons.

First, it was the shortest and most direct one Dante could have taken.

Second, it was in no way menaced by Dante's enemies. The Blacks did control many of the western Apennine slopes, but they did not threaten — nor did they seem likely to threaten — either the Casentino or any part of eastern Italy.

Third, it passed through many places where Dante would be warmly welcomed.

Bibbiena is as good an example as any.

Although Bibbiena, "stretched bowlike upon its hill, a white, graceful little town," was under the rule of a Tarlati bishop (the Tarlati were the most important Aretine family) and his fierce kinsmen, and although these Tarlati were bitter enemies of Dante's friends and protectors, the Counts Guidi of Battifolle, they also hated Florence with a deadly hate and therefore had open arms for anyone that Florence hated. Florence certainly hated Dante.

But perhaps the most conclusive argument is the great familiarity which Dante seems to have had with the country which this route traverses.

In his great passage about the death of Buonconte da Montefeltro he describes it vividly. He also refers to its most famous monument, L'Ermo — the Hermitage.

"And in regard to this," says Benvenuto da Imola, commenting upon the reference, "note that between Arezzo and Florence in the Casentino country there is a certain very holy solitude, and in it is the sanctified hermitage of Camaldoli, which was founded by the very venerable man St. Romuald of Ravenna who instituted the holy order."

A modern writer thus described it:

"After a long time the road enters the solitary forest. Presently before you, in a hollow of the hills which rise up on all sides, is a great building hanging upon the side of the narrow gorge of a torrent. Delicious green slopes scattered with oak trees rise and fall in front of it, and in the spring the slopes are strewn with rare-colored flowers."

With forget-me-nots, ragged robin, orchids, buttercups, daisies, pansies, and "the stately white asphodel"!

"Such as this must have been that lawn of Dante's poem where Leah wanders plying her fair hands to make a garland."

This may be a slightly sugared flight of fancy. It is not necessarily true that when Dante described Leah he was thinking of greensward at this particular place.

But he did know and surely visited this withdrawn sanctuary with "its stately abbot and a picturesque company of white-robed monks." Why not at this time?

« 4 »

Through Cesena ran the ancient Via Aemilia — from which Emilia gets its name — and along it, as it proceeded to the northwest, were Forlimpopoli, Forlì, Faenza, and Imola.

Near at hand was Brettinoro — now Bertinoro — on its "hill topped by a high peak crowned with cypresses." Also near at hand — and at one time or another noted by Dante — were Castrocaro (through which he passed on his earlier journey from San Godenzo to Forlì), Bagnacavallo, and Conio, the latter a castle near Forlì which has since been totally destroyed.

Brettinoro was renowned for the warm reception which it gave to strangers.

Says the author of the *Ottimo Commento:*

"Among the other laudable characteristics of the noblemen of Brettinoro were their hospitality and the fact that they would not permit anyone to make money by being an innkeeper. Instead they set up a stone column in the courtyard of the castle, and if any stranger came thither he put his hat on it and secured his horse to one of the bells there, and according to report he was then taken home by the gentleman to whom the bell belonged, and entertained as befitted his rank. In fact, this column and these bells sometimes caused strife between one nobleman and another, for everyone in those days sought the honor of entertaining those who came from afar just as now everyone seeks to avoid it."

(For the record, the "column of hospitality" still stands in Bertinoro. It is in the principal piazza. But there are now two inns and a restaurant.)

Dante, however, was less enthusiastic about this little place, and about certain of its neighbors.

Another of the enlightened and humane people to whom he introduces us in his *Commedia* is Guido del Duca of the Onesti family of Ravenna, who in the half century before Dante's birth was one of the group who ruled Brettinoro with humanity and light. So beloved was he that when he died Arrigo Mainardi, also of Brettinoro, caused the bench on which they used to sit and talk to be sawed apart, since there was no one worthy to replace him.

Dante makes him say this in *Purgatorio* XIV:

> "O Brettinoro, why dost thou not flee
> This world now that thy family [*of rulers —*
> *i.e., men like Guido*] and others
> Have left thee to escape thy evil days?"

He continues:

> "Bagnacavallo doth well to have no sons,
> And Castrocaro ill, and Conio worse,
> That take the trouble still to breed such counts."

What can we deduce from all this?

That Dante did indeed ride up to the column in Brettinoro Castle and place his cap on it? And that he was entertained there and later disillusioned? Or that this and the other references are purely literary? That he speaks merely of things that he was told about?

I think the former.

It seems to me certain that Dante at least paused at Brettinoro — where he discovered that the famed hospitality was no longer what it had been, or where perhaps he merely was (once again) not treated as he felt he should be treated — and at Cesena, Forlì, Faenza, and Imola. It is less likely that he went to Bagnacavallo. This would have taken him ten miles from his road instead of three or four as in the case of Brettinoro.

But not for long. Not even at Forlì, to which he had once come in ambassadorial estate. For he now spoke for no one but himself. To the brawling townsfolk of Cesena — having driven out its tyrant, Ciapettino degli Ubaldini, the city was now theoretically a democracy; to rough, swaggering Scarpetta degli Ordelaffi, who strutted in pillaged finery in front of San Mercuriale with its square Lombard campanile; to the temporary rulers of Faenza; and even in Imola, where Benvenuto, who would one day celebrate Dante, would be born thirty-two years later, he was now little better than the beggar which he called himself. They may well have treated him as such. But besides that, he himself knew where he was going and was impatient to get there. These were but stations on the way.

« 5 »

It is not likely that he stayed at his next halting place long either, although it must be added that about the date and the duration of this new sojourn in Bologna there is also still a certain amount of scholarly dispute.

"It is not improbable," says Edmund Gardner, for example, "that, in 1304 or 1305, he [Dante] stayed for some time in Bologna."

Others make his stay even more protracted. They say that he remained in the university city until the Guelphs were driven out of Bologna by an edict promulgated in March 1306.

In this, they have some support from certain of the earlier writers on Dante.

"He was driven out and banished from Florence with the White party, and went to the university at Bologna," says Giovanni Villani.

Presumably, add those who believe the chronicler, he supported himself by teaching there.

Boccaccio also states that Dante went to Bologna after he was exiled, and that he "stayed there a little while."

So, in effect, does Ubaldo Bastiano of Gubbio in his *Teleutelogio* (Discourse About Death), written around 1326 or 1327. In this, Death, addressing the people of Bologna, speaks of "Dante Alighieri, a poet of your times, a citizen of Florence, a teacher of your children of tender years, among human geniuses brilliant with the gifts given him by nature, and shining with the adornments of every accomplishment," but who nevertheless "lived venerously in the arms of his adulteresses."

In other words he was a good teacher there, but a lewd liver.

But all this seems to be the accretion of legend upon the basic fact that Dante did study in Bologna as a young man and may even have lived dissolutely there as other students (and not merely in Bologna) did and do.

That he went to Bologna, then, seems probable, but there is little to support either an extended stay there or a career as a teacher, and it seems more likely that he remained in the place only long enough to revisit the haunts of his youth and to talk congenially with the poets (like Quirini), the notaries, and the canon lawyers who knew him by reputation even when they did not remember him personally, and were already copying his *canzoni* and sonnets into their notebooks.

Then — possibly by way of Modena, Reggio, Mantua, and the Lago di Garda, but more probably by the shorter route which crossed the Po at Ostiglia where a half-completed castle guarded the Veronese approaches — he set out again toward the target toward which the arrow of his wanderings had always been aimed: the collection of proud castles and gleaming edifices which after Florence (and probably after Ravenna and Rome) was to be more important to him and to have a greater influence on him than any other place to which he ever would go.

« 6 »

Verona — for it is Verona about which we speak — was well fitted to fill this role, at any rate during the brief first two decades of the fourteenth century which are our present concern. For — again, after Florence, but in this case not after either Rome or Ravenna — at that time it was the most stimulating city in Italy.

(For those who like to wed fiction and fact, Dante's Verona of this early fourteenth century was also the Verona of Romeo and Juliet, if there were a Romeo and a Juliet.

Purgatorio VI — the troubadour Sordello is speaking:

> "O German Albrecht, who abandonest her [*Italy*]
> So that she has become untamed and savage . . .
> Come see *Montecchi*, come see *Cappelletti*,
> Monaldi and Filippeschi, thou that carest not!"

The Montecchi were the Montagues. The Cappelletti were the Capulets.)

But Verona and its environs had been a lively and perhaps even crowded habitation for human beings for much longer than since the time of Dante — and of Romeo. Legend says that it was founded around 100 B.C. by blond-haired Germanic Cimbri who slid down the ice-covered Alpine slopes on their shields. But even the Cimbri came late, for the S-shaped site upon the strategically important river — strategically important both in war and trade — had been dwelt in by *Homo sapiens* (probably Ligurians who, coming from the north, liked the warm protection of its gentle southward-facing hills) since the early Stone Age, and these early inhabitants were followed successively by Bronze Age Rhaetians, Gauls, and Etruscans. It was a notable city under the last.

The Romans made it great. Following the Social War, they established it — in 89 B.C. — as a Roman colony, and in consequence of, and to confirm this new importance did much building there, including, and especially, the mighty amphitheater which is smaller in size only than the Colosseum and another great amphitheater in Capua. It is said that certain descriptions in the *Inferno* are based on this amphitheater. In fact, the "whole arrangement" of Dante's lower regions with their "constantly narrowing and descending circles" may well have been inspired by this mighty Roman edifice.

The city's importance continued during the early barbarian invasions — and during some of the later ones. Theodoric the Goth made Ravenna his capital, but Verona, with its climate, was a favorite resort, particularly in summer. He built a palace there and in it spent so much time that in German legend he is known as Dietrich von Bern, Bern being Verona. Then came the Lombards, and it was at Verona that the Lombard king Alboin made the Gepid princess Rosamund drink a toast to him from a goblet made from her father's skull. Understandably, Rosamund not too long afterwards arranged to have him murdered. For some time, Verona was the Lombard capital. Under the Franks it was a capital too. Charlemagne's son Pepin frequently resided in Verona, and under his aegis it flourished. At that time it had high walls crowned with a castle, many stone bridges, and thirty churches.

But thereafter, like many another Italian city, it sank into anarchy and decay from which it was only rescued in the middle or late twelfth century by the rise of the self-governing city-state. Here its history so closely parallels that of Florence that there is no need to go into details other than to remind the reader that, as in Florence, this recovery was based on a pragmatic solution of day-by-day problems through the instruments of family and vicinity or trade self-help. But soon there was an important difference. Because of the nearness of this part of Italy to Germany with its acquisitive German emperors and its marauding and land-hungry German dukes and margraves, it was not possible to maintain a republican form of government. Self-preservation dictated a lord with *de facto* absolute powers, however these may have been kept from being *de jure* by legalistic but meaningless words.

The della Scala — the Scaligeri — succeeded the ablest but also the cruelest of these lords. Ezzelino da Romano — "Eccelin" — was an evil-looking man with black hair — *e quella fronte c'ha'l pel così nero* (*Inferno* XII) — and a swart complexion, both of which ill-consorted with his Teutonic ancestry. But he had a ruthless ability, and in short order brought Vicenza, Padua, Feltre, Belluno, Brescia, Trent, and Verona under his sway. Doing this, he restored law and order and a certain stability. But not without a savagery that shocked even his not easily shocked age. "That instrument of Satan, that Devil's executioner, that drinker of human blood" was, it is said, responsible for the execution of at least fifty thousand persons. The lucky ones were beheaded, clad in black robes as traitors to Ezzelino's theoretical overlord, the emperor. The others were burned to death, torn asunder by wild horses, or starved to death.

In those days, such cruelty may have been necessary to attain power — in fact, it almost certainly was — but it provoked a reaction. Shocked by a final outrage, the cold-blooded murder of ten thousand Paduans who fought in his army, and this because Padua, his ally, had surrendered to a common enemy, the lords of north Italy formed a league against him. They joined in "swearing a solemn oath to carry on war with fire and sword" against the tyrant "until he was either crushed or slain."

Crushed Ezzelino was. On the night of September 16, the marquis of Este surprised him at Cassano. "Turning to bay like an old boar hard pressed by the hunters," he made a fierce onslaught but shortly was seriously wounded. In the confusion that ensued he was captured. But captivity could not be endured by this fierce, hirsute man. After eleven days, he tore open his own wound, and died.

In Verona, at any rate, he was not succeeded by a return to popular government, for the Veronese had by now lost the art of governing themselves. But the new lord — or "tyrant" if you prefer the word — was as different from Ezzelino as he possibly could be.

The da Romani, if predators and robber barons of the most heinous sort, were at least a noble family of ancient lineage, its first members having come to Italy with Conrad II around 1027. But Mastino (Mastiff) I della Scala was the son of a respectable tradesman — Marzagaia says that he was a weaver, but Villani says he was a seller of ladders. *Scala* is the Italian word for ladder.

Nor did he ever hold a position which *per se* conferred upon him authority, although at one time he was captain of the people and at another *podestà* of the merchants. Nevertheless, by statesmanship based on cleverly concealed force, by tact, and by strength of character, he developed what would become a lawful *signoria* and, using but not ever claiming its powers, he ruled absolutely until he was murdered in 1277.

Mastino was succeeded by his son, and he, because Mastino had carefully seen to it that things would turn out that way, became lord of the city in fact as well as name. Almost immediately, Alberto della Scala was elected "captain and rector of all the *gastaldi* [guild officials] of the arts and of all the people of Verona." This title was for life. Shortly it was made hereditary. Thus the della Scala dynasty was founded. Counting Mastino I, it gave Verona fourteen rulers. It lasted until 1404.

Four of these Scaligeri — they have already been mentioned — have some connection with the story.

Alberto I (died in 1301), who established the dynasty. Dante saw fit to condemn him to hell (*Purgatorio* XVIII) for making his illegitimate son Giuseppe abbot of San Zeno.

Bartolommeo della Scala (died in 1304). He was lord of Verona when Dante came on an earlier mission from Forlì and from the Whites.

Alboino della Scala (died in 1311). Dante's host.

And the much younger Can Francesco, better known as Can Grande, or Big Dog, who at that time, however, was no more than a promising lad.

« 7 »

It was during the lordship of these Scaligeri — it was even during their early lordship — that there developed in the city by the Adige that lively florescence of art and letters and life that must have been one of the things that impelled Dante to seek asylum there.

This is nowhere better shown than in a sprightly doggerel poem by one Emanuele di Salamone dei Sifoni, better known as Manoello Giudeo, or Manuel the Jew, who lived in the Scaliger court and reputedly knew Dante very well.

Here are some lines from it:

> Indeed a crown
> Verona wears.
> This trumpet blown,
> This deed declares.

> Warhorse and charger,
> Fighting man, banner,
> Cuirass and sword —
> All's shine and glow.

> Hear the tramp, tramp
> Foot soldiers stamp.
> Tramp, tramp. Tramp, tramp.
> Hear how they go.

> Knights ride away.
> Flies popinjay.
> And dancers sway
> In vaulted hall.

Here lions are.
Here leopards fare.
Great rams, I swear,
Butt, one and all.

And laughter's here
That echoes far.
Ho! Ho! Ha! Ha!
Until you die!

But that is only a part of Manoello's prance and dance. "Love without wings," he tells us — I presume he means earthly as opposed to spiritual love — flourishes in chamber and hall. And to the sound of music.

Zither and tinkling lute,
Stridulent, sharp, acute,
Twangle *ting, ting*.
And here do sweet cantors,
Yea, and here troubadours
With praise of Scala's lord
Make heaven ring.

But, says the poet, there was also a serious side to life — although even as he alluded to it he was still sarcastic.

Of great Astrology
And of Theology
Here do, here doth,
Fleming and Englishman
Go *tarantara, boom, boom*,
Like loud trombone.

Here too from every land
I see them come and stand
As lord Philosophy
They argue about.

Here too from every land. Manoello elucidates this. Besides the Germans, Flemings, and Englishmen, there were "Latins" — i.e., Italians — Frenchmen, and even Saracens, and there was too the jostle and bustle of those who lived and did business there: the falconers, grooms, page boys, and other servants that were needed by a court that once entertained five thousand knights and their retainers at a single banquet. The barons, marquises, and lords, all "courteous of word," that were so dear to the Scaligeri. And, of course, the lovely ladies.

He speaks also of the entertainments — not only the music and the dancing but the tournaments, the fights between hotheaded youths armed with daggers that often ended with weasand-slitting and other bloodshed, the fights between wild beasts in the Roman arena, and the gambling that was so uninhibited that bets were even placed as to which of two trenchermen could eat the most in a given time.

It is only fair to say that Manoello's lines were written during, and almost certainly referred to, the rule of Can Grande, at which time Veronese splendor and glory reached its peak.

It was Can Grande, for example, who provided special houses for the various persons of note who were drawn to him. These houses were decorated by the best painters of the time — that assigned to soldiers with historic triumphs; that assigned to exiles with an allegory of "fair Hope"; that assigned to poets with "the school of the Muses"; that assigned to the writers of sacred themes with a painting of paradise. Which one of these sheltered Dante — who was equally an exile, a poet, and a writer upon matters sacred?

But if the lines were written about the Verona of Can Grande, at least to a degree they could apply to that of his predecessors, for that kind of Verona does not grow up in a day.

« 8 »

It was to this Verona that Dante came, riding up to its inexpugnable and nitid walls either late in 1304 or early in 1305, and it was there that he remained for an indeterminate period of time which may have been a little more than two years and hardly could have been a great deal less. In Verona, he was at once a harassed seeker for the bare means of sustaining himself, and an honored — but in his opinion, not sufficiently honored — guest.

Such an ambiguous position was not uncommon.

The great lords of the time were — as they had been since the days of the troubadours — "renowned for their generosity toward men of genius and learning" or merely "of a pleasing personality," for such liberality "served as a means of bringing honor and useful retainers to their courts, or at least of securing entertainment in their daily lives."

The Scaligeri were no exception.

Dante, therefore, was welcome in their city. But he had to share this welcome with a motley crowd which ran the whole gamut from persons of knowledge and political experience, from historians, grammarians, and astrologers, with an occasional doughty captain and more than an occasional lesser lord thrown in, down to professional jesters, buffoons, and fools.

These last, a serious historian has thought it worthwhile to point out, "were not the least honored among the guests nor the least profusely rewarded," and one is glad that he did so; for distasteful as it may have been to him, it seems highly probable that Dante was quite as often thought of as one of them as he was as a poet or a philosopher.

For that he had a sharp tongue and a ready wit is an intrinsic part of the Dante legend.

This is borne out by more than a handful of Dante anecdotes. I here give a few of them.

Anecdote one:

"While at Verona, Dante was asked how it came to pass that a shipwrecked man could escape from the sea; how a woman in labor could give birth to a child; and why the great number of the poor did not destroy the few rich.

"'For the same reason,' replied Dante, 'that the princes and sovereigns of the earth kiss the feet of a barber's son or a butcher's son when he becomes pope.'"

Anecdote two:

"Once Dante met a peasant and asked him what time it was. The countryman raised his head and looked at the sun. 'It is time to lead dumb beasts to the watering trough.'

"Said Dante: 'Who will lead you?'"

Anecdote three:

"Once upon a time there was a learned man who was stunted in his growth and as scrawny as a rat. He was in love with a lady, but she, either because of his looks or because she was chaste, would have nought to do with him. While he was in this pass, someone told him of Dante and of his renown and so he journeyed to him.

"'Messer Dante,' he said, 'I have heard of your skill and your fame. Can I have some advice from you?'

"'If I know how to give it,' replied Dante.

"Said the man: 'I have loved and do still love a lady with all that devotion which Love asks from a lover, and not only has she never granted me her favors, but she has not even contented me with a glance.'

"Dante looked at him.

"'I would gladly do anything to help you, but regarding what you ask at present, I see only one way to accomplish it. You know that women, when they are pregnant, always long for strange things. See to it that your lady becomes pregnant. Then mayhap she will long for you.'"

Anecdote four:

"Dante, that famous poet, was noted in his own days for the quickness of his impromptu replies. One day as he was returning from an excursion he met three Florentines who decided to test him. 'Good day, Messer Dante!' said the first one. 'Whence come you, Messer Dante?' asked the second. 'Was the river flooded?' queried the third one.

"Dante did not even rein in his horse.

" 'Good day,' he answered, 'and a good year. From the fair. Arse-deep.' "

But Dante, at Verona, did more than entertain his hosts and their followers — if indeed he did thus entertain them — with not exactly subtle and often crude medieval humor. As he sang for his supper in this way, he also found time for other activities which were both far more congenial to him and comported more with what we deem to have been his character.

Let us list a few of them.

It was almost certainly in Verona, and at this time, that he wrote the lost letter to the Florentines in which he asked them what wrongs he had done to them.

It is almost certain that it was here, and also at this time, that he wrote his *canzone* the *Tre donne*.

It was probably at Verona, and probably at this time, that he exchanged the poetic blows with Cecco Angiolari that led the latter to write the already-cited sarcastic sonnet in which he called Dante a Lombard lean whereas he was a stout Roman, and in which he promised to continue to cudgel him.

Beyond any reasonable doubt it was here also that he wrote his "letter to the Pistoian exile," Cino da Pistoia, which is one of the few which helps to humanize and bring down to earth the poet of the *Commedia*.

Here are some significant excerpts from this letter:

"In the warmth of your affection for me, my dearest friend, you show me signal confidence by putting this question to me: Can the soul pass from one passion to another — that is to say, from one passion to another, the nature of the passion being the same but the objects [note that the plural is used] being different, not in kind but in identity?"

This, Dante says, Cino should have answered himself, but since he has asked him to do it, he will try to do so.

"Behold there is given below a discourse in the diction of Calliope" — Calliope is the Muse of eloquence and heroic poetry — "wherein the Muse declares, in set phrase, that love for one object may die away, and then, inasmuch as the corruption of one thing is the begetting of another, love for a second one may take its place in the soul. And the truth of this, although it is proved by experience, is confirmed by reason and authority."

He then considers reason and authority.

Reason.

"Every faculty which is not destroyed after the consummation of one act is naturally reserved for another. Consequently the faculties of sense, if the organ is not destroyed, are not destroyed by one act, but are naturally reserved for another act."

Then the highly modern conclusion that the seat of love lies in a faculty of sense. Hence, it is transferable.

Authority.

The poet Ovid in the fourth book of his *Metamorphoses* tells how the sun, after he had neglected and deserted other nymphs of whom he had been previously enamored, fell in love with Leucothoe.

On love, who was a greater authority than Ovid?

"So in conclusion, dearest brother, I counsel you to arm yourself against the darts of Nemesis with such patience as in you lies. Read the *Remedies Against Fortune* which are offered to us by that most famous philosopher Seneca. And especially let not that saying pass from your memory: 'If ye were of the world, the world would love you as his own.' "

After that follows "the discourse in the diction of Calliope."

It is a sonnet.

> Companion I have been of Love since when
> The sun's swift circling made me nine years old.
> His curbs and spurs I need not then be told,
> Or how his vassals laugh or moan in pain.
> Reason or justice to put forth amain
> 'Gainst him is piping when the winds are wild
> And thinking that thereby the thunder's stilled
> And tranquil calm from tempest comes again.
> Therefore within bowshot of his arrows and slings
> In danger from them free will ever lies.
> 'T is vain that wisdom 'gainst him her shaft wings,
> For to his victim's flank new spur he plies.
> *New passion comes when the old passion dies,*
> *And 't will replace the old one's wearyings.*

For some reason a political meaning has been read into all this. Dante — or, at any rate, so say certain Dante students — is telling Cino, now himself an exile, that just as he, Dante, had to give up his love of Florence for a new love, so Cino must give up his love for Pistoia for his own new love. In both cases, the new love was Philosophy.

I find this hard to accept. It is, of course, true that Dante always interwove fact with symbolic meaning so closely that it is often hard to separate them. But in the poem actual and earthly love — the psychology of actual and earthly love — is portrayed with such knowledge that we do have to come down from the empyrean a little. It has been said that at this time Selvaggia — whom Cino celebrated in his poems — lost her husband, and that this cast on her such a pall of gloom that Cino fell into despondency too. To me, it seems more probable that it was Selvaggia herself who had either died or in some other way been lost to Cino, and that at least touched immortality, still his lot in the Adige city was not necessarily mean the end of the world.

« 9 »

But if Dante's days at Verona were not entirely wasted; if he was in better company there than that of the brawling Romagnole lords who were really *banditti* and the disgruntled and increasingly shabby White exiles who were more concerned with restoring their own fortunes than with Florence; if — in the Scaliger halls — even as he became the *uomo da corte* and sometimes the buffoon he could still write letters and poems that at least touched immortality, still his lot in the Adige city was not always a happy one.

Here again we can turn with profit to some of the traditional Dante stories.

Poggio Bracciolini tells one of them, which is repeated almost word for word in the sixteenth century by Ludovico Carbone, and again by the hack writer Antonfrancesco Doni.

"Dante was at table with the elder and the younger Can Grande" — chronology would seem to indicate he was at the table with Alboino and his later-to-be-famous younger brother — "and their servants, thinking to offend the poet, piled the leftover bones beneath his feet. As a result, when the table was cleared, all marveled at the heaped-up pile of them below where he sat. But he had a ready answer. 'Dogs [*cani* — a play on Can Grande's name] eat their bones, but I who am not a dog leave mine behind.' "

Francis Petrarch tells another. He too uses the name of Can Grande when it should more properly be Alboino.

"Dante Alighieri was a man greatly skilled in the use of the vulgar tongue, but because of his haughtiness he lived as he chose and was very outspoken in his words, something which did not greatly please the delicate ears and eyes of our princes. In consequence, when, an exile from his fatherland, he dwelt at the court of Can Grande, in those days comfort and refuge of the unfortunate, he was at first received with great honor but then gradually began to lose favor as from day to day he came to please his lord less and less. Now when this took place it happened that he went to a feast at which were present, according to the usage of the

times, mountebanks and jesters of every kind. Among these was one who
was as impudent as he could be, but who won the favor of all with his
biting and obscene words. Messer Can knew that this was very annoying
to Dante, and so he called the jester into his presence. After heaping on
him the greatest of praises, he turned to the poet. 'I am astonished,' he
said to him, 'that this man who is a fool has gained the notice and favor of
all, while you who are said to be wise cannot do the same.' 'You should
not be astonished,' replied Dante, 'for friendship comes from like manners
and like intelligence.' "

There are two points to the above two stories.

(1) That even the enlightened Scaligers often treated Dante with
aristocratic contempt.

(2) That Dante was in no way overawed by this, but paid them back
in kind.

It is a matter of record that Dante left Verona not later than sometime
in 1306. Perhaps he left earlier. It should now be easy to understand why.
But Dante was not the only one who found Dante's presence in the city
unnecessary. Princes want subservience and not sarcasm — not sarcasm
directed at themselves, at any rate; sarcasm directed at their enemies was
something different.

It is just possible that Dante left Alboino della Scala by mutual consent.

« 10 »

Where did he then go?

"After he left Verona," says Umberto Cosmo, "he continued his
peregrinations to the courts of north Italy."

To those places in north Italy, it would seem, which have already been
noted as having been mentioned in Dante's writings, and perhaps to a few
others.

Here are some possibilities.

Treviso, with its handsome Palace of the Three, and with a lord — the
good Gherardo — who with his enlightenment and his firm hand in many
ways anticipated Can Grande.

Trent, with its German people ruled by a German bishop, but geo-
graphically a part of Italy.

Brescia, which almost overlooked the Lago di Garda.

Tolomino, the castle-eyrie of Pagano della Torre, "a magnanimous lord
and a great protector of men of learning." This castle-eyrie was situated
in the mountains about thirty miles above Cividale in Friuli. It was a place
which "in summer was delightful both for its beauty and for the
incredible number of its springs and streams, for its very healthful air, for
its high mountains and its deep valleys." Looking down on the river

which flows beneath it is a high pinnacle which has long been called the seat of Dante. The peasants said that he often sat there while writing a book on — of all things! — the nature of fishes.

Finally Pola and the Quarnero, the first of which he mentions in *Inferno* XI.

With the exception of Treviso (of which more in a moment), little of this seems likely, however. If he visited Brescia and the Lago di Garda, it was probably when he was at the della Scala court, at which time he almost certainly jogged in gay company from one Scaliger castle to another — from Soave, where a famous white wine is still grown, to Sirmione and Peschiera. On one such jaunt, he could have come close enough to Trent to learn all he seemed to know about it. A visit to Cividale (and Tolomino) has all the earmarks of fantasy, as also does a visit to Istria, although in this connection Zingarelli identifies the Mount Tambernik whose massive size Dante alludes to in *Inferno* XXXII with Javornik in Slavonia (modern Yugoslavia, and the word does have a Slavic sound) and says that when this peak is mirrored in frozen Lake Zirknitz it makes one think of Dante's ice-gripped Cocytus. He implies that Dante may have seen Javornik. Certainly he heard talk of it — but of the Danube and of the far-off frigid Don, too.

But a stay in Treviso, and a happy one, is almost unchallengeable, for reasons which were stated earlier and need not be repeated.

From Treviso, Dante went to Venice.

(There, incidentally, on the Riva degloi Schiavoni, which in those days was crowded with shipping, he could have heard the Dalmatian and the Aquilian idioms which so grated on his ear, and there he could have heard about Pola.)

There is some reason to believe that, even though he may have quarreled with Alboino, he went as Alboino's ambassador.

Zingarelli, however, would have it the other way around. He says that Dante went *to* Treviso *from* Venice.

Let us hear his arguments.

"Plausible indeed," he insists, "is the conjecture of Girolamo Biscaro that Dante left to the court of Alboino for that of *Gherardo* da Cammino at the time of the war between Padua and Venice which was fought in 1304 because of a dispute about customs boundaries. To a certain extent, Verona, Mantua, and Treviso were involved in this, and because of it various treaties were drawn up between these cities by means of embassies. The position of Verona in relation to Venice was at least curious. First it made a declaration of friendship toward the latter, and even offered to mediate the dispute. Then toward the end of 1304 it abrogated this declaration and announced that it had signed a treaty with Padua. For this the Veronese were denounced in a loud voice by the doge. Now suppose that Dante had been one of those that had negotiated the treaty. He would have been as ashamed of this turnabout as if he had made it himself or as if it had been done for no other reason than to affront him. The personal characteristics" — the personal characteristics thus demonstrated — "would certainly have made it necessary for him to seek some other protector, at which point a sojourn in Treviso (where, incidentally, his son Pietro, in his rich old age, would end his days) became logical and common sense. After all, Gherardo da Cammino had been one of his fellow negotiators, and Gherardo remained faithful to his word."

The reasoning is good, but the date is a little too early.

Moreover there were other embassies — in fact, many of them.

And Dante — see San Gimignano, Rome, Forlì, and Verona itself — was already well known as a negotiator. As a skillful and successful one.

I believe that Dante went to Venice somewhat later and *from* Treviso.

But I believe that he represented Alboino and not Gherardo. Verona needed his diplomatic skill more than did Treviso.

« 11 »

Ambassador or merely visitor, however, representative of a potent lord or once again nothing more than a seeker of at least token shelter and peace of mind, Dante apparently did not stay long in the canal city either — the city built upon larch pilings with its eternal odor of backwaters and low tide.

Nor did he particularly like what he saw there.

It was not that Venice had nothing to offer him, for even then it had begun to glitter. It had for some time. Even in 1267, for example, when Dante was two years old, Martino da Canal could say that of all the cities in the world it was *"la plus belle et plus plaisant dou siècle, ploine de biouté et de tos biens"* and could add that *"les marchandises i corent par cele noble Cite com fait le eive [l'eau] des fontaines."* The pink and white marble lace of the doge's palace had at least been well begun, and, beside the wooden houses on whose rooftops even the Venetian beauties used to loll to bleach their hair, there already arose more than one of those magnificent edifices which are the glory of the city: the Ca' Quirini at the Rialto; the Ca' Zani and the Ca' Dandoli on the Riva del Carbon; the Ca' Giustiniani at San Moisé; and the Casa Falier at Santi Apostoli. The tall, graceful campanile looked down on a Piazza di San Marco which was already paved with brick, while the four bronze horses stolen from the circus at Constantinople pranced on the facade of the basilica as proudly and far more gleamingly than they do today.

But with these, the dazzle and the glitter ended. We have already spoken of the wooden houses. But even these were few. A majority of the population lived in thatch-roofed huts or hovels which were scarcely weatherproof. A majority of the streets — even then they were called *calle* or *ruge* — were not even cobbled. They were deep with mud in the not infrequent rainy weather. With mud, and with the manure left by horses, for, except on the Merceria where horses were forbidden, men rode on horseback everywhere. Even in this city of islands. Many of the larger and most of the smaller piazzas were meadows. Swine, when they were not roaming the streets, grazed on them, as did lowing cattle. The Rialto Bridge, made famous by Shakespeare and by others, was then a wooden bridge of boats.

Nor was the population in any way stimulating. In Venice at the time was, to be sure, the minor poet Ildebrandino Mezzabati of Padua, of whom Dante would say that he was the one writer in northeast Italy who at least strove "to depart from his local dialect and apply himself to a more noble language." Ildebrandino had been *podestà* in Florence, and Dante had known him there. He now could renew his acquaintance with him. He may also have seen and talked to Giovanni Quirini, although as I have already indicated it is more probable that Quirini was in Bologna. But certainly the Quirini family entertained him.

But these excepted, the Venetians he encountered, were, or so it seemed to him, a crude and self-made crew. Even to Dante, who was accustomed to the *nuova gente* Florentine merchants. They were hard-headed and horny-handed. They were seamen, either pullers at the oar or sea captains. And their language, although said to be Italian, was the crude *lingua franca* of the eastern, and for that matter of the western, Mediterranean where Spaniard, Catalan, Frenchman, Genoese, Neapolitan, Greek, Turk, and Saracen all had to find a way of doing business with each other — and the devil take language and vocabulary.

In this matter, and particularly in proof of my contention that Dante found Venice too distasteful to even think of staying there, I seek support — although at some risk — from a letter which is almost unanimously regarded as spurious. Supposedly Dante wrote it in March 1314 and addressed it to Guido da Polenta, lord of Ravenna. But it is now generally believed that it was forged by Antonfrancesco Doni, who published it in his *Zucca* in 1552.

"I had imagined to myself," it begins, "that I should here find those noble and magnanimous Catos, those severe censors of morals, in fact everything which these people in their pompous and pretentious manner would have unhappy and afflicted Italy believe that they themselves above all people represent. Do they not style themselves *rerum dominos gentemque togatam* [lords of everything and a toga-wearing people]? But what am I to say to you of the dense ignorance of these grave and reverend *signori?*"

Why, they do not even understand Latin! he went on.

"I purposed to perform my offices as your ambassador in that tongue, but no sooner had I pronounced a few words of the exordium than it was intimated to me that I must either provide an interpreter or speak to them in another language."

He tried Italian.

"Accordingly, whether from amazement or indignation I know not, I began to make a short speech in the tongue which has been known to me from the cradle, but this proved scarcely more familiar to them."

Yet why should it be?

"After all they are descendants of Greeks and Dalmatians and have brought no other contribution to this noble land than the vilest and most shameless of practices, together with the abomination of every sort of unbridled licentiousness."

Nevertheless he had tried to do his duty.

"I send you, therefore, this brief account of the mission which I have performed on your behalf."

But let there be no further missions.

"Though you may always command me, I beg you not to use me any further on such like employments. You can look for no credit from them, nor I from any pleasure."

Then the conclusion:

"I shall remain here for a few days to satisfy the natural appetite of my bodily eyes for the wonders and attractions of this place. After that I shall transport myself to the beloved haven of my rest under the gracious protection of your most kinglike courtesy."

It is argued and generally agreed that this letter cannot be authentic and for the following reasons.

(1) It is absurd to say that the Venetians could not understand Latin. Latin was the official state language in Venice as elsewhere in Italy.

(2) Guido da Polenta was not lord of Ravenna in 1314.

(3) Dante was sent to Venice to congratulate Gian Soranzo on his election as doge, but Soranzo had been elected a year and a half earlier, in 1312.

(4) The letter is in Italian rather than Latin. But all of Dante's other letters were in Latin.

(5) The style is not Dante's style but that of the cinquecento.

These arguments are hard to refute.

But that does not mean that the letter was a complete invention, for certainly parts of it are in complete accord with Dante's known views. His contempt for the Venetian language has already been recorded, and common sense tells us that there would have been more than one Venetian councillor who would have had to furrow his brows in concentration when the language of Cicero was spoken. Dante's capacity for scorn and speaking scornfully is also well known. Moreover — and especially with the passage of time — a date or the name of an addressee can be changed accidentally.

It is possible that Doni did not fabricate the letter out of whole cloth but instead garbled an actually existing letter — again either because he knew no better or to express his own dislike of Venice.

However that may have been, one thing is completely certain. Dante at no time and in no way shared the love for Venice that was felt by Petrarch, who called it "the one remaining home of liberty, peace, and justice, a city rich in gold, but richer still in reputation," or even the less precisely expressed affection felt by Boccaccio.

For one reason or another he had to go there. He did. He accomplished his business.

Then he was on his way to Padua the Learned — where he found a far more congenial atmosphere.

« *12* »

Yet even about his stay in Padua — or at any rate about certain details of his stay there — there is disagreement.

Sometime during the last century a document was made public by Giovanni Pelli. It stated that on August 22, 1306, one "Dantino, son of the late Alighiero of Florence, *who now dwells in Padua on the Via San Francesco*," appeared in the house of Signora Adelmota, widow of the late Jacopino Papafava of Carrara, as witness to the deposition by Messer Bonifazio Papafava to the effect that he had received a sum of money from Filippo, son of Messer Canto di Somaiao. The original document did not exist, but the authenticity of the copy which was made by a Paduan notary in the sixteenth century is not challenged.

From this it was deduced not only that Dante stayed in Padua, but that he lived there long enough to have his own house. Indeed, a so-called house of Dante there — it is not far from the university — is still pointed out. It is a stuccoed palace whose ogival windows seem to have been renewed with modern ironwork. In it, near the ancient muddy moat — this is the local belief — Dante lived and worked and slept while he supported himself by lecturing and reading.

Latterly, however, this has come under attack, largely because of a series of documents all dated after Dante's death and apparently referring to a man of the same name. One, dated August 31, 1339, speaks of "Dantinus, a Tuscan"; another (1345) of "Messer Dantino, son of the late Messer Alighiero"; a third (1348) of "Messer Dantino, son of the late Messer Alighiero, who was of Florence"; two others (1350) of "Ser Dantino." One of the last refers to him as a notary.

"Thus," it has been argued, "the Papafava document loses all its value, since we now have a person of the same name who outlived our subject."

But does it? Is it quite as simple as that?

The second Dantino, son of Alighiero, figures in documents which not only are found in another city (Verona) but which are from thirty-three to forty-four years later than the first document. That would give Dantino II quite a long career. Moreover, is it likely that there could be a second Dante Alighieri of Florence — for Dantino is a recognized Paduan variant of Dante — and no one know it? The Alighieri genealogy is complete and does not show one. Could it not be that another person assumed the name of Dante after Dante was both dead and famous? Stranger things have been.

In any case, it is not necessary to have this document to establish a Dante residence in Padua. We have ample other proof — proof that comes in the main from those who write about the painter Giotto.

"Dante," says Benvenuto da Imola, "praises Giotto for his artistic skill. He does this because he was a fellow citizen, because his work deserved this praise, and because he was a friend."

Because he was a friend? Benvenuto elaborates.

"It so happened that when Giotto was painting in Padua, and while he was still young" — actually he was forty years old, and Dante was forty-one — "and was painting a chapel in a place which had once been an amphitheater or a colosseum, Dante came thither. Giotto received him with great honor and took him to his house."

Other writers on Giotto tell the same story and with equal authority.

In Giotto's studio, then — or, but less probably, in a hypothetical Dante residence near the clay embankments which he describes in the *Commedia* — he and the painter at least for a while lived the gay, entertaining Bohemian life which artists and writers traditionally do.

Benvenuto and others tell a story which amusingly illustrates this.

Seated at table, no doubt, and surely with a fat *fiascone* of red wine between them, Dante and Giotto were taking their ease one day when Dante turned to the painter and asked him a question.

"Since you are the father of both," he asked, "why is it you paint such beautiful pictures and beget such ugly children?"

Giotto's sons and daughters were no better looking than Giotto and he was notably not handsome.

"Because I paint by day," he replied, "and I beget at night."

Dante wrapped himself in learning.

"That is not original," he said. "You pilfered it from Macrobius's *Saturnalia*."

But he found it worthy of a laugh.

This kind of riposte was typical of the excellent and earthy countryman whose skill and genius were to set Italian art upon its great pathway.

Here, for example, is a Boccaccio story along the same lines.

Forese da Rabatta, "though little of person and misshapen, with a flat camus face," was one of the ablest lawyers of his time. He and Giotto were great friends; they each owned country houses in the Mugello; and one day, returning from the same, they encountered each other and jogged into Florence together.

A sudden shower overtook them, and they sought refuge in a nearby farmer's house.

After a while, however, "the rain showing no sign of ceasing, they borrowed from their host two old Romagnole [coarsely woven] cloaks and two hats which were stained with age and set out again upon their way. When they had gone a little way and were all drenched, and were bemired too with the mud which their nags threw up with their feet, the weather began to clear up a little, and the two who had been silent for so long began to talk, Messer Forese, riding and listening to Giotto, who was a very fine speaker, began to look him over from one side to the other and from head to foot and, seeing him in so sorry and shabby a garb, suddenly burst out laughing without taking any thought as to his own appearance.

" 'Giotto,' he laughed, 'if a stranger encountered us who had never seen you before, do you think he would believe you to be the finest painter in the world, which you are?'

" 'Just as readily,' replied Giotto impromptu, 'as, looking at you, he would think you knew your ABC.' "

But Dante did more, while he was in that city, than spend pleasant evenings with his congenial host. It is also recorded that he watched Giotto as he worked in the so-called Arena Chapel, where, "abandoning the crude Greek [i.e., Byzantine] manner," he brought "modern painting" to life in his decorations of this handsome edifice.

Oddly enough its great good was almost the direct product of what was then regarded as a sin and an evil. We have already noted that in *Inferno* XVII Dante meets a band of usurers who are fighting off the flames and burning soil "not otherwise than dogs in summer do who ply now snout, now paw when they are bitten either by fleas or stinging flies or gadflies." One of them had as his device a sow azure on a field argent.

This was Rinaldo degli Scrovegni, who was a miser as well as a usurer, and who even as he lay on his deathbed cried for the keys to his strongbox so that no one could lay hands on his gold.

Rinaldo had a son Enrico, and this Enrico degli Scrovegni it was who determined to rebuild the ancient chapel and to commission Giotto to decorate it. He had two motives. First, it would expiate his father's offenses and keep him out of hell. (Dante, see just above, thought otherwise, but never mind that.) It would persuade the Church to allow him to inherit at least a substantial part of his father's estate, which otherwise would have been confiscated.

The world is the beneficiary. The Arena Chapel is not large, but on its side walls alone are thirty-seven of Giotto's finest frescoes. These tell the stories of Joachim and Anna (the Virgin Mary's parents), of the Virgin Mary, and of Jesus Christ. On an end wall is a circular painting of God surrounded by His angels and of Joachim being driven from the temple. Over the entrance is a *Last Judgment*. Even in their present faded state, their golds and blues and reds and greens still stir the heart. Imagine them when they were first seen — with their warm and human realism which brought God down to earth and thus into the hearts of man.

Dante saw them being painted, he saw them when they were new and gleaming, and because in one of them — the *Last Judgment* — are the devils and damned souls which he would describe in his own "Last Judgment," a question has been raised. Did he influence Giotto, or did Giotto influence him? The answer is almost certainly not either. Dante's damnation is one thing and Giotto's another. But in those days when hell and hell's fires were actually believed in, and when Giotto was painting the picture and Dante was contemplating, if he had not already begun, his poem, surely inferno and its punishment must be a subject of conversation, and an idea here, a hint there must have rubbed from one man onto the other. I am sure this happened.

« *13* »

But Padua was an interlude too. Although his days there were in congenial company — besides Giotto there were in the city a growing group of poets, historians, and scholars, of whom Albertino Mussato, chronicler and doughty captain, is merely the best known — although the university was rapidly becoming the second best in Italy, although through Enrico da Scrovegni he apparently met that Pietra da Scrovegani who some think (but I do not) was the Pietra of the Pietra poems, Dante soon was on his way again.

Wisdom dictated this, for an opportunity arose in another part of Italy which it would have been neither profitable nor prudent not to take.

Where this was, if not what it was, Dante tells us himself — implicitly in *Purgatorio* XIX, explicitly in *Purgatorio* VIII.

Let us take *Purgatorio* XIX first. In this canto is described that part of purgatory where the avaricious and the prodigal — Dante considered both vices to be the same, since they both came from an exaggerated love for worldly goods — are cleansed of their sin by being compelled to lie face downward upon the ground.

"*Ahaesit pavimento anima mea!*" the sinners cry, and Virgil encourages Dante to talk to one of them.

This he does:

> "Who thou wert, wherefore thou thy back dost have
> Turned upward, tell me, and if thou wouldst have me
> Gain aught for thee there from whence I came."

The spirit answers:

> And he to me: "The reason heaven turns
> Our backs to itself thou shalt know, but first
> *Scias quod ego fui successor Petri* [*Know thou that I was
>   a successor of Peter*].
> Between Sestri and Chiavari there rushes down
> A little river fair, and from its name
> The title of my clan doth make its boast.
> A month and little more did I prove how
> Weighs the great mantle on him who guards it from mud
> So that all other burdens seem like feathers.
> My conversion — woe is me — was late indeed,
> But when I was the Roman shepherd made
> Then I discovered what a lie is life.
> I saw that there the heart is not at peace
> And that in that life you cannot mount high.
> Then love of this life was lit up in me.
> Till that time came I was a wretched soul,
> Shut off from God and wholly avaricious.
> Now, as thou seest, I am here punished for it."

But Dante is not listening any more. Instead he has reverently fallen to his knees, for the man who is addressing him is none other than Ottobuoni de' Fieschi, nephew of the great Pope Innocent IV (who first gave the cardinals their red hats) and himself Pope Adrian V.

Adrian gently rebukes Dante, asking him why he thus abases himself, to which the poet replies thus:

> And I to him: "For your great dignity!
> My conscience stung me when I stood erect."

Then Adrian makes his great speech, and takes his farewell.

> "Straighten thy legs; yea, do thou rise up, brother!"
> He said to me. "I am a fellow servant
> With thee and all men of the great potentate.
> If ever thou that holy gospel verse
> Which *neque nubent* said didst understand,
> Thou mayst well see why I do reason thus."

Neque nubent is the opening phrase of Matthew V, 4. "They neither marry nor are given in marriage." There are no distinctions in heaven!

> "Now go thy way. I would not have thee halt,
> For thy long staying hindereth the weeping
> By which I ripen that which thou spoke of."

After that he concludes — and uses words which, if read rightly, have clear biographical importance.

> "A niece I have up there, Alagia,
> Good in herself if only that our house
> Make her not evil with its bad example,
> And she alone is left to me above."

Alagia! Remember the name!

It is not stated, to be sure, that Dante would ever come to know this lady and to tell her what her uncle thought of her. But Alagia was the wife of Moroello Malaspina, and Moroello is another matter. We have already been told of him. He was that *vapor di Marte* who crushed the Florentine Whites in a bloody battle near Pistoia. He should, therefore, have been a Dante enemy. Instead he became a protector and a friend.

This we hear about in the second of the two *Purgatorio* cantos to which reference has just been made.

Purgatorio VIII is about the good men who were late repentant. It is the canto of Dante's dear friend Nino Visconti. It is a canto in which the troubadour Sordello walks and talks with the poet and with Virgil. Appropriately, it is also the canto in which Dante meets Currado Malaspina (Moroello's cousin) of the great Malaspina family of feudal lords — they were still feudal lords in Dante's time, although feudalism was already beginning to decline — who held many a castle in the mountains between Tuscany and Genoa. These Malaspina were great fighters and generous hosts and patrons of poetry, and had been so ever since the days of Oberto Obizzo I, who died just a little after 1015.

Patrons of poetry and, in the early days, practitioners of poetry too! One of the earlier of the Malaspina, an early Marquis Albert, engaged not unsuccessfully in a poetic contest with Raimbaut de Vaquières which was not too different from the one between Dante and Forese Donati.

In *Purgatorio* VIII, Dante, after he has spoken to Nino and noted the guardian angels who hover green-clad and with drawn flaming swords, is addressed by Currado.

> "So may the lantern which leadeth thee on high
> Find in thine own free will as much of wax
> As needful is to attain the enameled summit,"
> He said to me. Then: "If thou hast true tidings
> Of the Val di Magra or of the lands nearby
> Tell them to me, for I was one time great there.
> I was called Currado Malaspina.
> I am not the old one, but descended from him.
> To mine own bear I the love here purified."

Dante answers him — and with some warmth of feeling.

> "Oh!" I replied to him. "Within your lands
> I have not ever been, but where do men dwell
> In all of Europe where they are not renowned?
> The reputation which doth honor your house
> Proclaims its lords and their dominions too,
> So that he knows them who was never there,
> And by my hope of heaven I swear to you
> Your honored race hath never put aside
> The glory of the purse and of the sword.
> Nature and custom do so privilege it
> That though its evil head lead the world astray
> It walketh straight and scorns the wicked way."

Currado is overwhelmed. Then Dante must go there, he cries; then Dante *will* go there.

> And he: "Now go. The sun will not return
> To rest times seven on the bed the Ram
> Doth cover and bestride with all four feet
> Before this will be nailed into thy head
> With stronger words than someone else's talk
> If justice doth not turn its course aside."

What does this one more "prophecy after the fact" — one more of Dante's writings about the past as if it were the future — really mean? This question is not hard to answer. Indeed, all you need is a little arithmetic. The imaginary voyage to purgatory took place on Holy Saturday in 1300. Add seven to 1300 and you get 1307. Sometime before Holy Saturday 1307, Dante left Padua and rode — or perhaps at least in part traveled by boat or barge — across Lombardy until he came to the Ligurian Apennines. These he crossed, possibly going by way of Pontremoli. Then one day he looked down on the pewter-colored ribbon of the Magra River in its small, flat, almost olive-green plain. Now he was on the borders of the Lunigiana, where he would be received in one or more of the many Malaspina castles: Sarzana, Fosdinovo, Giovagallo, Mulazzo, Villafranca, Castelnuovo.

But which ones?

Which one of the Malaspina would be his host?

For the Malaspina — already picturesquely divided into two branches, those of the *spino secco* (bare thorn) and those of the *spino fiorito* (flowering thorn), were many, and most of them would have been able — and glad — to shelter and feed our poet. Just to give an idea, living, or probably living, at the time Dante came to the Lunigiana were a Franceschino, two or perhaps three Moroellos, a Corradino, a Gherardini, a Niccolò, a Giovanni, a Lucchino, and a Manfredi. And there may have been more.

The reference to Alagia gives us a clue. Other than Currado, she was the only Malaspina specifically named in Dante's poem. But as we have noted she was Moroello's wife.

Although, then, clearly Dante did not stay — even in the Lunigiana — in any one place nor was he welcomed by only one of the Malaspina, it is obvious that Moroello was his principal host. This will become even more obvious as our story progresses. It is also attested to by Boccaccio, both in his *Life of Dante* and in his commentary on the *Commedia*.

« *14* »

But we do not have to rely upon Dante's poetry to establish the fact that at least a half year before Holy Saturday 1307, Dante (probably after visiting Modena, Reggio d'Emilia, and Parma on his way and perhaps even venturing deeply enough into the Alpe Apuana to see the lofty peak of Pietrapana which he refers to in *Inferno* XXXII) moved across the mountains into rugged northwest Italy. Nor that while he was there he was honorable and importantly employed and was not merely and still an aimless exile.

For in the notarial archives of Sarzana there are two valuable and informative documents. They are both dated October 6, 1306. They both show Dante again an ambassador.

The first one was executed at Sarzana itself, a city to which Dante must have come with mixed feelings, for it was to Sarzana that he had exiled Guido Cavalcanti and it was here that Guido was stricken with his fatal illness. Now he was an exile himself watching the damp and yellow leaves of autumn fall down and cling to the pavement. His mood must have been both mournful and nostalgic. Yet he had things to cheer him, as Guido never had. He was not waiting for fever to overtake him. He was amid friends and patrons who understood at least a part of his merit. And he was given a complicated task to accomplish, yet one he knew that he knew how to do.

This first document gave Dante plenary powers — the powers he needed as a negotiator.

Let us read it.

"In the name of the Lord, amen. We, the magnificent man and lord Franceschino Malaspina, Marquis Malaspina, do make, constitute, and ordain as our lawful procurator, agent, factor, and special ambassador Dante Alighieri of Florence for the purpose of obtaining from that reverend father in Christ my lord Antonio, by the grace of God bishop and count of Luni, and from his successors, peace, assuagement, and a perpetual end to each and every injury, war, unfriendly action, assault, burning, destruction, rebellion, wounding, homicide, and whatever crimes and enormities have been committed against the said venerable father and the church of Luni or his men and followers by the said Messer Moroello, or by Messers Moroello and Corradino, his brothers and Marquises Malaspina, or by their friends, vassals, or followers, or by the said bishop of Luni or his successors" against the Malaspina.

Franceschino guaranteed for himself — and for Moroello and Corradino — that they would ratify any action Dante took in this matter.

The second document was signed in Castelnuovo di Sarzana nearby. Castelnuovo (sometimes called Castelnuovo di Magra) is presently in ruins, but its two tall towers still look down from a steep hilltop as they did when Dante came there.

This document dealt with the treaty which Dante drew up and persuaded the bishop of Luni to sign.

It began upon a note of exultancy.

"It is a long time, it is a long time indeed, that through the overweening power of Satan, between the venerable father and lord, Lord Antonio, by the grace of God bishop and count of Luni, and those exalted noblemen Moroello, Franceschino, Corradino, and their brothers, all Marquises Malaspina, there have arisen wars, unfriendly acts, and hatreds from which have resulted slayings, woundings, blood-letting, burnings, laying waste, destruction, and many other perils, and by these the province of the Lunigiana has been greatly harmed."

But now through the intervention of Fra Guglielmo Malaspina and Fra Guglielmo of Godano, and by the negotiations of Dante Alighieri, they have followed the example of the holy pope, who said, "I give my peace unto you. My peace I leave with you."

Then followed the terms, which, although long and involved in their notarial Latin, amounted to this:

(1) On the one hand, the bishop, with Puccio and Francesco della Mosca, described as "noblemen of Fosdinovo," together with the captains and the castellans of all the towns and castles dependent on Antonio whether as bishop or as count, and, on the other hand, the followers and liegemen of the three marquises, namely the citizens of Sarzana and Sarzanella, and the towns and citizens of Carrara, Ponzano, Bibola Santo Stefano, and Bolano, did pledge themselves to "end all hostilities and strife and to bring back peace."

(2) That for the time being and without prejudice the castles of Brina and Bolano should "remain as they now are." Sometime a good deal earlier — in 1286, to be precise — these two strongholds had been seized by Antonio's fiery predecessor Enrico of Fucecchio, who had promptly beheaded the three young esquires sent by Marquis Obizzo Malaspina to protest the act. The Malaspina had swiftly seized them again, and while doing this ravaged the villages and farms and vineyards of the unhappy bishop.

(3) That "all sentences, bans, and processes made or imposed, or about to be made or imposed, in matters either temporal or spiritual by the lord bishop or by his spiritual or temporal court against the friends, subjects, or followers of the said lords marquises should be, and in fact are, lifted."

What equivalent promises were made by the Malaspina is not indicated. Perhaps a cessation of raids led by their knights with banners was enough.

This treaty was drafted in Sarzana too, and it was there attested to by the Sarzana notary Ser Giovanni di Parente in the presence of four witnesses.

Then Dante climbed to Castelnuovo, where, in the bishop's chamber and in the presence of the bishop's relatives, officials, and dependents, he affixed his own signature. As he did so he pledged that the marquises would ratify it within fifteen days, which in fact they did.

Mission accomplished, and so no wonder his cup was full! The twenty years' war was ended and on terms highly favorable to his employers!

Now he could be entertained by them in their various castles.

He was.

But particularly in Giovagallo, where Moroello held forth.

There, as the winter settled down and blizzards raged outside, he was welcomed in the great hall with its huge fire and could discuss the bards of old with the man whose forebears had been so gracious to them. And with Alagia! He always liked feminine charm.

Or he could write poetry — or exercise his pen on other matters — himself.

Write poetry himself, but not always *for* himself!

In most collections of Dante's minor poetry there is included a sonnet which the Marquis Moroello is supposed to have written to Cino da Pistoia.

It begins thus:

> Worthy indeed to find a treasure trove
> Your voice is with its sweet and Latin sound.

Nothing more appropriate could have been said of Cino

Actually it was written by Dante, who in this way repaid some of the hospitality and friendship bestowed upon him by Moroello at a time when he quite badly needed both.

« *15* »

But content as Dante was in these surroundings, and happy as his days with Moroello and with his cousins seem to have been, he did not stay indefinitely in the Lunigiana. He did not, for he could not. Tortured by various desires, not the least of which was his forever gnawing hope of being able to return to Florence, he was far too restless. Not later than the summer of 1307 and perhaps earlier, he returned — for the second or third time during his exile — to the Casentino. The Counts Guidi, who ruled there, were the same kind of heart-warming hosts as the Malaspina, and the Casentino was somewhat nearer to his longed-for city. Many of the Counts Guidi were, too, on good, if not excellent, terms with the Black government. For a while, at any rate, he would try his fortune with them.

Yet even though he left Moroello he kept on good terms with him, and it is not surprising, therefore, that when, somewhere in the Counts Guidi domains, he found himself involved once again more or less seriously with one more of those lovely ladies who never — and to the distress of some of his admirers — ceased to fascinate him, it was to this Marquis Malaspina that he addressed the one-man-of-the-world-to-another-man-of-the-world letter (with accompanying poem) that described this and explained it.

Here it is:

"So that the chains of his servant and the spontaneity of the affection by which he is governed be known to my lord, and lest false reports be spread abroad which too often prove to be the seedbed of false rumors — rumors which might prove me guilty of negligence whereas in reality I am a captive — it has seemed good to me to lay before the eyes of your magnificence the present communication.

"It befell, then, after my departure from the threshold of that court — oh, would that I were there again! — wherein I was privileged to be enrolled in the services of liberty, and very little after I had set foot near the headwaters of the Arno, carefree and happy of mind, that suddenly — woe is me! — like a bolt out of the blue, a woman appeared before me who in every respect suited my inclinations, both in her character and in her looks. Oh, how it struck me dumb to see her! But my astonishment gave place to fear when a thunderclap followed. For just as in real life its sound follows the flash, so at the sight of the flame of this beauty, Love, terrible and imperious, laid hold on me. And raging like a despot who has been expelled from his fatherland and returns to his native soil after a long exile, he slew or expelled or loaded with chains everything in me that was opposed to him.

"He slew, yea, that praiseworthy determination of mine to hold aloof from women and from songs about women, and he pitilessly banished as suspect those never-ending meditations in which I used to ponder about the secrets of heaven and earth. And finally, so that my soul might never again rebel, he fettered my free will so that it behoved me not to go where I wished but only where he wanted me to.

"Love therefore now rules me, and nought restrains him, and in what manner he doth this you may inquire from that which follows below."

"That which follows below" turned out to be a *canzone*. To those who will permit the poet to descend to earth from heaven, it is one of Dante's finest.

> Love, since I now must needs make my complaint
> For listening folk to give their ear unto
> And thus reveal myself bereft of worth,
> Give me the skill to lament as I would,
> So that the woe that I do here unloose
> Goes forth in words that do reveal my mind.
> Thou'ldst have me die, and I consent thereto,
> For who'll forgive me if I have not skill
> To say aloud that which thou makest me tell?
> Who will believe that I am so smitten?

But if thou grantest me words that match my pain,
Grant me, liege lord, before I come to die
She who's to blame will hear it not from me,
For if she knew what I do feel within
Pity would make her beauteous face less fair.

I may not flee so far she may not come
Into the place of my imagining.
I may not flee the thought that brings her there.
My foolish soul which plieth its own wit
To its own ill — evil and very fair —
Depicts her and thus forges its own torment,
Then gazes on her, and when it is filled
With the great yearning brought it by mine eyes
It falls into a rage against itself
For having fanned the flame which sorely burns it.
What word of reason and sense will ever bridle
That which has stirred so great a tempest in me?
My anguish that will not be kept within
Issues from my mouth and is articulate.

The hostile figure that still stays with me,
A conqueror, a conqueror and cruel,
And lords it o'er the power of my will,
Fallen in love with itself, doth bid me go
With heart in hand thither where she now is,
Since like to like, forever and still, doth move.
I know, though, this is snow seeking the sun,
But having no more strength I am as one
Who having fallen into another's power
Goes on his own feet to his place of death.
When I go near, methinks that I hear words
That say: "Haste! Haste! And thou shalt see him die!"
And then I turn to see if there be one
Who will protect me. Instead, I am led on
By those bright eyes which scornfully do slay me.

And I so wounded, what I do become
Thou knowest, Love, thou knowest, and not I,
Who doth remain to look on lifeless me!
And though thereafter my soul come again
Unto my heart, unconsciousness and oblivion
Have been her comrades while she was away.
When I arise once more and see the wound
Which did undo me when I was struck down,

STRAVIT QVE ANIMO CVNCTA POETA SVO ❧ DOCTVS ADEST DANTES SVA QVEM FLORE
MORS SAEVA NOCERE POETAE ❧ QVEM VIVVM VIRTVS CARMEN IMAGQ FACIT

The Michelino Dante is a tempera panel painted by Domenico di Michelino in 1465 to commemorate the two-hundredth anniversary of Dante's birth. It was hung in the Duomo of Florence, where it was used to illustrate lectures on the *Commedia*.

I may not in such wise assure myself
That I'm not all a-tremble in my fear,
And then my face from which all color is gone
Telleth what was the thunderbolt that smote me,
For although launched it was by a sweet smile,
It remained darklied o'er for a long time
Because my spirit did not trust itself.

Thus hast thou dealt with me amid the Alps,
O Love, and in the valley of that river
Upon whose banks thou didst forever rule me.
Here, whether I live or die, thou stirrest me
By virtue of that fierce, terrible light
Which, lightning-flashing, marks the path to death.
Ah woe is me, nor ladies, nor love-skilled people
Do I find here to hark to my lament.
Therefore, if she, if she do heed me not,
I may not look to succor from another.
And she who has been banished from your court,
My liege lord, doth not heed thine arrow's stroke,
For she hath forged mail of such haughtiness
That every shaft doth blunt its point thereon.
Nothing can penetrate to her armed heart.

Then the *tornata,* or envoy:

O mountain song of mine, go thou thy way.
Mayhap thou wilt see Florence, which is my land
But from her portals doth forever bar me,
Being devoid of love and stripped of pity.
And if thou goest there, go saying: "Now
My maker cannot longer war upon you,
For there whence I do come he is so bound
That if your cruelty should ever cease
He has no longer freedom to return!"

O mountain song of mine! The sincerity, the intensity, and even — at least for that day and age — the simplicity of this poem, which matched anything Dante had so far written to, for, or about Beatrice to me makes it very plain that the lines were not "allegorical" but spoke the truth, and that here amid beautiful hills so near his Florence, Dante, who was now no callow youth, had indeed been wounded by the blind bow-boy's arrows, and that this had stirred him into magnificent words.

But who was this lady on whose behalf Cupid's arrows were so unerringly winged?

Boccaccio would have her to have been a country girl, not notably beautiful, or at any rate disfigured by a goiter.

(But we have indicated earlier, the country girl referred to by Boccaccio may have been Pietra.)

Others think that she was a lady of the Counts Guidi.

In this connection, there are even a few who say that the poem was a purely literary exercise — just as Edwin Arlington Robinson is said to have composed his "Another Dark Lady" just to show how easily a love poem could be written — or, if not that, a poetic "bread and butter letter," indeed written to a Counts Guidi lady, but to thank her for hospitality received, and also to reassure her husband as to her virtue.

There are other guesses not important enough to list.

But they are all guesses, and — with one exception — any one of them could have been true.

Dante could have loved — or thought he did, and briefly — a lovely *contadina*, a shepherdess or a goatherdess or a farm girl.

He could have loved a lady of the Counts Guidi.

He could even have written a "bread and butter letter" provided there was feeling behind it.

But that the poem was a purely literary exercise — this, if not impossible, is highly improbable.

Countess or country girl, there was a real person who bewitched him with her smile and with her eyes.

« 16 »

It seems highly improbable too that the next woman with whom Dante's name is associated — namely Gentucca Morla of Lucca — did not also stir other than platonic feelings in his heart, although in this case, as perhaps in others, a caution should be added. Just because Dante's feelings were not platonic, it does not necessarily follow that a liaison resulted. For the poet in this matter was like many another man; and the fact that a man is attracted physically toward a member of the opposite sex does not mean that a physical culmination is necessary, nor that there are not other, and these even paramount, attractions. It was so, apparently, with Dante and Gentucca.

She was very much younger than he.

She was intelligent and enlightened, and she seems to have understood the things that most concerned him.

To put it mildly, he liked — he warmly liked — to be in her company. She had the same liking for him.

Dante tells us about her himself — cryptically but with very clear feeling.

Purgatorio XXIV — Dante is engaged in talk with Bonagiunta of Lucca, who, as we know, was also a poet:

> But as one looks and taketh no more note
> Of one man than another, so I to him of Lucca,
> Who most desirous seemed to be to know me.
> He murmured something. It seemed to me "Gentucca"
> I heard him whisper in that place of justice
> Where he endured the strokes that so consume them.
> "O soul," I said to him, "that seems so eager
> To speak to me, pray let me plainly hear thee
> And satisfy both thee and me with thy speech."
> "A woman is born who wears not yet the wimple,"
> Began he, "who will make to thee most pleasing
> My city, how much other men revile it.
> Now go thy way, having this prophecy,
> And if thou misinterpret that which I mutter
> The facts will some day make it clear to thee."

"The author," says Buti, who lived close to the time, "pretends that he does not understand, because, theoretically, that which Bonagiunta predicts and answers has not yet taken place — namely that during his exile he would go to Lucca, and there he would fall in love with a lady named Gentucca. This came to pass before the author wrote the passage in question. He came to Lucca and he did love a gentlewoman named Gentucca who came from Rossimpelo. He loved her because she was talented and chaste, and for no other reason."

But elsewhere she is referred to as *la bella di Dante* — Dante's mistress. Here is the story as I read it.

It became apparent to Dante after not very many months that his stay in the Casentino would not accomplish the purpose which drew him there; nor in saying this do I refer to his unsuccessful pursuit of the lady of the mountain song. The Counts Guidi either could not or did not intend to arrange for a return to Florence. So his feet became restless again and he went to Lucca, influenced no doubt by the fact that Moroello's influence was great there and in the expectation — or at least the hope — that this friend of the Florentine Blacks could and would do more for him than his Casentino lords.

In Lucca he met Gentucca, who had by then become the young bride of a moderately wealthy Lucca merchant, Cosciorino Fondora.

He met her and by mutual consent saw much of her — the young lady and the not so young poet. Because she was sympathetic and knew his poetry. Because he needed someone who was sympathetic and cared for his poetry. And that, except for certain stirrings and hopes, is all.

He had another encounter in Lucca, not as agreeable as the first one. His wife Gemma seems to have come there, even if briefly. With her were her sons Pietro and Jacopo, her daughter Antonia and possibly another daughter, and that other son Giovanni about whom nothing else is known.

Except for Gentucca, Dante liked nothing about the city, and he fleered at it as a hotbed of corruption.

Inferno XXI — one of the gargoyle-like devils is speaking:

> "Ha, Malebranche,
> Here have you one of the ancients of Santa Zita!
> Thrust him below while I go back for more
> To that place which is so well stocked with them!
> Every man there's a barrator except Bonturo.
> There no is made an aye by paying cash."

Except Bonturo!

Dante's barb was indeed poisoned. For Bonturo was not merely a barrator but, according to Benvenuto da Imola, an "archbarrator" who gave or withheld every office in the city according to what he was paid. Even Pope Boniface, on whose side he supposedly was, once was so exasperated at the extravagance of his exactions that he shook him roughly by the arm.

"Take care!" cried Bonturo. "You have shaken half of Lucca."

He was nothing if not undaunted and bold.

« *17* »

But even if Gentucca compensated for the hostility and evil ways he found, Dante did not and could not stay in Lucca long. Moroello suddenly lost his control there, his friends having been ousted in a coup, and besides this on March 31, 1309, an edict was passed which barred all Ghibellines and White Guelphs from the city and from the neighboring districts and countryside.

Once again Dante took to the road. This time he had no choice.

He went back to Moroello.

But if he went back to Moroello, it was only for a short visit. He was tired — nay, sick almost unto death — of this moving from castle to castle and from one town to another, and even among the most congenial of his hosts, even among those who loved, or protested that they loved, poetry and learning, he felt intellectually starved. How should he feed this starving? How should he begin to develop himself again? How should he at least begin to prepare to satisfy his self-chosen mission and to live up to the gnawings of his self-confidence and his ambition?

He had the answer, or, to be accurate, he knew where he could get the answer.

To do which he set out on the longest and the most adventurous of his peregrinations.

What it was you will be told shortly. But not until another matter has been dealt with — not until we have considered another aspect of Dante and his accomplishments which so far has been inadequately dealt with as we tried to piece together the story of the places he went to (and the people he encountered) and the physical and geographical aspects of this part of his life.

XVIII

Bread of the Angels and Other Matters

I REFER to Dante's activities as a man of letters, and I must refer to them. For if this son of Alighiero II had not been one of the greater — if not the greatest — writers of the Western world during the Christian era, it would hardly have been necessary for anyone to concern himself with the other things he did (and with *his* background and *their* background) during these first years of the fourteenth century. It would hardly have been worth while to pick over the sherds and fragments of remaining evidence if he had been no more than a dedicated if unsuccessful political leader in a city whose incredible future still lay ahead of it; or the inheritor, and hence manager, of a small moneylender and speculator's farm and city properties; or even if he were the foremost local intellect.

There were too many other such, and ones far easier to search out and study.

No, Dante's writing is the thing, and it is to this writing that we must now turn.

To be sure, we have not entirely neglected it. We have, for example, drawn upon the *Convivio* more than once for specific biographical information, and we have carefully examined the *De Vulgari Eloquentia* to the same end. We have adverted to four of Dante's letters — and to one supposedly apocryphal letter — to show either what he did or what he thought. For the same purpose, we have laid before the reader the *Tre donne* and the mountain song.

But nowhere have we considered these or other Dante writings done at this time as the product of Dante *vate* or Dante *poeta* (Dante the prophet or Dante the poet) — to use a stuffy word, as literature. This we will now do.

The productivity — the sum total of Dante's works during this period — was considerable.

Take the *rime* — Dante's poems — alone.

Not counting those which belong to the *Vita Nuova* cycle, the so-called *testo critico*, which was published in 1921 by the Società Dantesca Italiana in honor of the six-hundredth anniversary of Dante's death, prints fifty-six sonnets, *ballate*, and *canzoni* which are definitely listed as Dante's work. Another twenty-six are described as of doubtful attribution. (But by the law of averages some of these doubtful poems must have come from Dante's pen.) Doubtful or definitely Dante's, a substantial number of these — perhaps as many as half — were surely written between 1301 and 1308.

In addition, there are the letters.

To be sure, only the four — or, if you count the apocryphal letter, the five — letters already dealt with survive from this period. But these, clearly, are only a few from a much larger number, for Villani, Giovanni Boccaccio, and, as we have seen, Leonardo Bruni all testify that "the poet wrote many prose epistles in Latin." A number of these, since lost, were still in existence in the time of Boccaccio and even in the time of Leonardo Bruni.

Bruni looked at these letters carefully. He even reported on Dante's handwriting.

"His calligraphy was perfect," he said. "His letters were slender, long, and correctly formed."

Elsewhere — in his *Dialogue with Peter of Istria* — Bruni observes that Dante always wrote his letters with his own hand. He did not employ a scribe. And he always signed them with his own seal.

Giovanni Mario Filelfo — son of the Renaissance humanist Francesco Filelfo — went even further.

"He wrote innumerable letters."

Not *many*, but *innumerable!*

But for good reasons, this particular Filelfo is always regarded with suspicion. *Many* letters will have to do.

Finally, there are the *Convivio* and the *De Vulgari Eloquentia*.

By modern standards, they are not particularly long — the *Convivio* being seventy-five thousand words long and the *De Vulgari Eloquentia* perhaps twelve thousand — but behind every one of those words lay Dante's searchings and investigations. His "research," if you wish to call it that! And this in a time when there was none of the mechanical assistance — nor the backlog of accumulated knowledge — that we have today.

Moreover, if Dante's memory, which was good, was not phenomenal, this research would have to be renewed as he went along.

Plainly, then, we have to revise our concept of what Dante was and how he lived during these difficult days.

He was something more, we have to conclude, than merely the importunate wanderer who moved from one patron to another and was given scraps from their tables largely because that was what in those days a patron was expected to do.

He was more than a man whose abilities in one of the more difficult branches of statesmanship — diplomacy — were well established and could be useful.

He was more than someone who could write state papers, which he often did.

He was also one who, as he moved not merely from castle to city to town — traveling God knows how many hundreds of weary miles to do so, enduring God only can say what illnesses of body and spirit, putting up with rebuffs already described — but from inn to shabby inn where (ask the novelist Sacchetti or the poet Cecco Angiolari) not only was the linen soiled and foul, the food inedible, and the wine sour, but you might find that you shared your bed with a dead man, asked for more than a place where he could be seated in the huge drafty hall with its almost always smoking fireplace under a tall and handsome marble mantelpiece, or for a bench or a bed upon which to lie down.

Sometimes — indeed, more than sometimes — he was one who asked also for access to the lord's library (hoping not always successfully that it would have more than "twenty books clad in black or red" which he could consult), and for a chamber or at least a corner of a chamber, and for a chair even if it was stiff and wooden, and for a slanting wooden desk, and for parchment and for ink and for a goose quill pen.

Then, even amid the confusion and the noise which reigned elsewhere, he would be able to put down in words that which he had dredged out of his contemplation and experience: words which are still read today.

« 2 »

We have just above listed what some of these words were — or, to speak more precisely, the Dante works they went into. Poems — at least thirty or forty poems. Four or five known letters and almost certainly a great many more which have been lost. And his two treatises: the *Convivio*, which in form, but in form only, has certain resemblances to the *Vita Nuova*, and which attempted to probe deeply into every problem which concerned him; and the *De Vulgari Eloquentia*, which, among other things, is a study of the writer's available tools.

Speaking from the literary point of view, the poems are the most significant. Dante would have been a minor poet if he had not become a major one, and if the *Tre donne*, the mountain song, the *Donne che avete intelleto d'amore*, and certain of the Pietra poems (all of which have been offered to the reader) do not have the sheer lilting rosetime freshness of Folgore da San Gimignano and even on occasion Lapo Gianni — but Dante's boating sonnet addressed to Guido Cavalcanti and Lapo does — at the very least they stand side by side with the best of Cavalcanti and Cino da Pistoia.

From the point of view of history, it is to the letters we would turn. (The only exception is the letter to Cino.) Written by Dante, they show with unmistakable clarity the shiftings and uncertainties — and the mixed motives and purposes — of the Guelph leaders with whom Dante was associated. They were "official papers," if you want to call them that, but even official papers can be revealing — especially if you read between the lines.

But if you want to understand Dante himself, it is the treatises which must be read and comprehended, for in a sense they were his trial flights. They were Dante's first serious attempts to discover what he was thinking — and what Dante was thinking, when later turned into poetry, is what made him great.

« 3 »

Of the two, the *Convivio* is the more important. Even in its incomplete form — only four of a projected fifteen treatises were written — it is also the more ambitious. I believe, too, that either it was the first written or, if that cannot be accepted, that at least its writing and the writing of the *De Vulgari Eloquentia* went hand in hand.

Here, to be sure, I will run into some differences of opinion, for many Dante scholars contend vigorously that the *De Vulgari Eloquentia* was written before 1305, and hence was written first.

(At this point I should insert an aside. Writers who were either contemporary or almost contemporary believe that the *De Vulgari Eloquentia* was written much later.

Boccaccio:

"Afterwards, and when near his death, he composed a little book in Latin prose in which he attempted to give instruction in the art of writing poetry to whoever wished it and, although he seems to have had in mind to compose a book in four parts, either he did not do this before death overtook him or the others are lost, for there are only two extant."

Giovanni Villani:

"Dante composed also a little volume entitled *De Vulgari Eloquentia* of which he promised to write four books, but of these only two came into being, perhaps because of his untimely death. In it, and in strong and ornate Latin, and with many fine arguments, he reproves all the vernaculars of Italy."

But this is not likely either.)

They base this belief on internal evidence. Certain persons seem to be referred to as living in the *De Vulgari Eloquentia*, but as least one of them, John of Montferrat, was dead before January 1305. Hence the book was written before that date.

Using similar arguments, they insist that the *Convivio* must have been begun after that date. Specifically they insist that it must have been begun after March 1305 and broken off before November 1308, for it speaks of the good Gherardo — Gherardo da Cammino — as dead and he had not died until the earlier of the two dates, and it speaks of Albrecht of Austria as living and he did not die until the later one.

But this does not take into account — or at any rate brushes off — conflicting evidence, and the conflicting evidence to me is the more persuasive.

Convivio I, 5:

"This" — i.e., changes made during a thousand years in the language spoken in Italy — "I shall discuss more fully later in a book which I intend to make, God willing, on discourse in the vernacular."

I *shall* discuss more fully! The tense is future. The book on the Italian vernacular was still to be written.

Nor is it possible to reconcile this positive and unequivocal statement with another argument advanced by those who believe that the *Convivio* followed the *De Vulgari Eloquentia* — namely that the first treatise (but the first treatise only) of the *Convivio* was written and even completed and then laid aside so that Dante could turn to the *De Vulgari Eloquentia*. Not, at any rate, if you assume that such of the *De Vulgari Eloquentia* book as was completed was set down before January 1305!

For, as you have been already told, Dante, in a very early chapter of the *Convivio* (I, 3), describes himself as having been a wanderer throughout all Italy. Timewise, that would not have then been possible. Timewise, Dante had barely begun his peregrinations by the end of 1304.

« *4* »

But whenever the *Convivio* was actually begun, or whether it was set on parchment before, after, or simultaneously with the composition of the *De Vulgari Eloquentia*, its spiritual beginning dates much earlier. Its spiritual beginning took place at the same time as, and in direct consequence of, his second "new life" — the new life in which he turned away both from the lady at the window and from his gutter days with Forese Donati, and perhaps from other aberrations. At that time — that is, during the days which immediately preceded this new life — he had written at least as many as ten or a dozen of his most beautiful *canzoni* and addressed them to the lady at the window, to Pietra, and almost certainly to other ladies. They were love poems — make no mistake about it. They were as fine as any love poems ever written, although not the least intricate.

Then suddenly came the apocalypse. We have already described it. And with it new and agonizing self-appraisal.

"Such poems," in effect he told himself, "may well have been suitable to write when I was a youth, but now that I am mature they are no longer seemly."

Nor did they represent his present feelings.

What should he do about it?

The same thing that he had done before. Change the facts to make them conform to his new feelings.

This he did. Just as Beatrice — just as Bice who had been a living and a lovely Florentine — became, or would become, his beatific vision, so this other lovely and lively Florentine who had looked down on him from the balcony became my lady Philosophy.

(One wonders what her reaction was if she ever found this out.)

And just as he had put Beatrice into the *Vita Nuova*, and later would put her into the *Commedia*, so Dante put the lady at the window into a book. (Not at once, of course. Not for another ten years. He was first too deeply and disastrously involved in Florentine politics, and later in his attempts, with other White exiles, at a counterrevolution.) This was the *Convivio* — or "banquet" — we have been talking about. At this banquet, although he promised that he would take his readers away from "browsing on grass and acorns in the pasture of brute beasts," he modestly stated that he would not be able to serve them anything better than the oaten bread of his poor abilities.

But, I think you will agree, he served instead the wheaten "bread of the angels" — which bread, in his opinion, only "the blessed few" could sit at the table and enjoy.

« 5 »

It is to this wheaten bread — or oaten bread, if you still prefer it, or what have you — that we must now address ourselves. What was it like? What did it offer to the banqueter? Is it necessary to wish him — doubtfully — good appetite, or is he certain to enjoy its taste and savor?

We can best answer these questions by examining it. This — and in some detail — we now do.

To begin with, the *Convivio* consists of four treatises, and the first treatise is an introduction which really introduces.

This is a book about knowledge, Dante points out, and "all men do naturally desire knowledge." But not all men can attain it. Some are too vicious. Some have physical deficiencies — as the deaf and the dumb. Some are too preoccupied with family affairs. Some live in a place where knowledge is not available.

(This too has been said in an earlier chapter, but it should be repeated here.)

He, however, did not fall into any of those categories, for although he did not sit at the table of the blessed he at least sat at the feet of those who sat there, and so sitting gathered some of the scraps.

"Of these, I purpose to make a general banquet."

But a banquet for whom? This is the next question.

For the wretched who have seen some of the food "I have displayed to their eyes, and thereby made them the more eager."

However, let no one come to this banquet who hath neither teeth nor tongue nor palate, nor anyone addicted to vice.

"But let him come who because of family and civic cares has been kept in human hunger, and let him seat himself at the same table with all others impeded in the same way."

Thus was explained the book's title, its purpose, and its hoped-for audience.

Then some practical matters.

In this book he will have to speak of himself, and even praise himself. How justify this?

Here his reasoning is interesting.

You should never speak of yourself unless it is necessary — and here it is necessary — but if you do speak of yourself you should never speak ill.

"To dispraise oneself is directly blameworthy, because a man should tell a friend his faults in secret and there is no closer friend to a man than himself."

Self-praise, however, is equally to be avoided.

But it is "the less evil path of the two," especially when it is used "to quash infamy."

Then Dante proceeds to quash some infamy.

He tells about his exile, and in a somewhat complicated manner tells of the harm this did his reputation.

When lesser people — especially the vicious and the childish — "see a famous person, they are straightway envious, and this is why every prophet is less honored in his own country."

But his country was now all Italy, and it was therefore in all Italy that he had "perhaps cheapened" himself.

But, wheeling swiftly, he makes this a justification for writing the *Convivio*.

Because everything he had done — and himself too — was "more lightly esteemed," it "behooved him to give something of weight to the present work" by writing it "in a loftier style."

In a loftier style? Then why not in Latin? Why in Italian?

Here was a second practical matter. He discussed it practically.

Why not Latin?

First of all, Latin would not have accomplished his purpose, since it would only have expounded his ideas to the lettered who were few and not to the unlettered who were many.

(Remember, above, the banquet was for those who for one reason or another could not sit at the table of the learned. It was to be a popular book, not a recondite one.)

Second, it was not appropriate to use Latin to comment on poems written in Italian. The commentary is the servant to the writings commented on, and the servant should be familiar with, but not superior to, his master.

But why Italian?

For a brief moment he tried to use logic.

Italian was more suitable.

"The bird dog should have scent, the greyhound speed."

But then he let his heart take command.

"I was moved to using it by jealousy."

"I was moved to using it by its beauty."

"The great excellence of the vernacular of *si* lies in the fact that it is like a woman who can best be judged when she is severed from all adornment."

Finally — finally, it was *his* language.

"It was this, my vernacular, that brought my father and mother together, for it was by it that they spoke, wherefore it is manifest that it took part in my begetting and so was a certain cause of my being. This, my vernacular, led me into the way of knowledge which is our specific perfection inasmuch as it was by it that I entered into Latin, which was explained to me in it. This Latin was the path to further advances."

Furthermore, it was Italian that made possible his pursuit of poetry — a pursuit which has led him to accomplishments and renown "as is so manifest as to need no witness."

This language — and for the reasons noted — he would use in the work he had in hand.

"It shall be the new light, the new sun which shall rise when the old sun has sunk, and it shall give light unto those who are in shadows and darkness because the old sun does not shine upon them."

The Italian language, which was here for the first time glorified! And which for the first time was worthy of glory, largely because it was used by him!

« 6 »

That much for treatise I.

The next treatises continue with the book's business.

Convivio II, 1:

"Now that in my introductory discourse and under my direction the bread has been sufficiently prepared in the preceding treatise, time calls and insists that my ship depart from port. Wherefore adjusting the sail of my reason to the breeze of my longing, I enter upon the open sea with the hope of a fair journey and a secure and praiseworthy port at the end of this my feast."

The open sea — or a well-provided table?

Apparently even a great poet can mix his metaphors, which should cheer lesser writers.

But then he returned to the banquet concept. "But so that this my food may serve its purpose, before even the first viands are served I will show how it must be eaten."

But before going on any further, it must be understood very clearly what this food would be. It would be an analysis or a projected analysis of fourteen Dante *canzoni*. Just as in the *Vita Nuova* he explained the why and when of every Beatrice poem — and of certain other but related poems which were not about Folco Portinari's daughter — so in the *Convivio* he would explain the impulses which had led him to write the *Convivio* poems. Or what in 1306 or 1308 he wanted you to believe these impulses were.

He would do this under two headings, the literal and the allegorical.

"And that this may be understood, it should be understood that writing should be taken and may be understood in four ways."

The first was the literal sense, which needs no explanation.

"The second is called the allegorical. It is truth hid under a beautiful fiction."

As when Ovid says that Orpheus with his lyre made wild beasts tame.

The third was the moral sense, which does not need explanation either.

"The fourth sense is called the anagogical, and this is when a scripture is spiritually expounded which even in the literal sense, by the very things it signifies, signifies some portion of the things of eternal glory.

"The prophet says that when the people of Israel came out of Egypt, Judea was made whole and free. He meant too that when the soul goes forth from sin, it is made holy and free in its power."

Dante, however, only dealt with the first two of these.

It was enough.

For dealing with them, there was no problem faced by Dante or by any other man of his time that he did not attempt to solve. That he did so on the basis of some so-called certainties that now seem less than certain is of little moment. This will always be the case.

> Small knowledge have we that by knowledge met
> May not someday be quaint as any told
> In almagest or chronicle of old,
> Whereat we smile . . .

Thus another intellectual poet, Edwin Arlington Robinson, who wrote around the 1920s. It is obvious.

But groping is the thing, and Dante groped for some kind of answer to every subject that troubled him or puzzled him.

I will list a few of them.

Astronomy and astrology. The distinction was not crystal clear in the Middle Ages. The structure of the heavens. The significance of the heavens.

Love. The kinds and degrees of love.

The body as an instrument of the soul.

The philosopher. What he was.

Friendship and what a friend was.

The need of a supreme ruler to govern the world.

Rome and its destiny to provide this ruler.

The emperor.

Nobility and its relationship, if any, either to ancient lineage or ancient wealth.

And the four ages — adolescence, manhood, old age, and decrepitude — of man.

These in the treatises actually written.

But it is known — because he said so — that in treatise XV (the last treatise), Dante planned to discuss why beauty is made less by vanity and pride, and he also planned to tell why a favor asked for costs more than one freely given.

It is also known — and also because he said so — that in treatise XIV he would discuss justice.

In treatise VII we know that he planned to discuss loyalty (by loyalty

Dante seems to mean devotion to duty), using as an example how, "having received solace from Dido," Aeneas departed "to follow a path honorable, praiseworthy, and faithful as is written in the fourth book of the *Aeneid*."

It is thought by some that he planned to write about physical and moral courage in treatise VIII. To do this would be consistent with his character, but the supporting evidence is either nonexistent or slim.

« 7 »

It would not be possible in a book dedicated to all of Dante and not just a single one of his writings to discuss all these matters with Dante's own complexity and detail. One can only refer the reader to the *Convivio* itself. To some it may be a difficult book to read, but it is worth the effort.

But certain of its passages — though for different reasons — must be laid before the reader who would really know Dante, for they reflect both his prejudices and what he thought was true.

In Dante's day, the created universe was thought to be made of concentric heavens, but men debated on their arrangement and their numbers.

Here is Dante's dictum on the matter:

"I say, then, that in regard to the number of the heavens and their positions, various opinions have been held by many people, but the truth has at last been found!"

Only to be unfound again!

Who peopled these heavens — or rather who peopled the third heaven which was being specifically considered, since the poem under analysis was *Voi che intendendo il terzo ciel movete?*

"Substances sejunct from matter, to wit, intelligences, which are commonly called angels. And of these creatures" — once again! — "as of the heavens, divers people have held divers opinions, albeit the truth has now been found."

And the size of all this — the distance between earth and sun and planet or star?

Dante takes Venus as an example.

"This star is of so great virtue that it has extreme power upon our souls, in spite of the fact that when nearest to us it is 167 times as distant as is the center of the earth, and that is 3250 miles."

Venus then, in Dante's opinion, is 542,750 miles from the earth. There must indeed be an expanding universe, for we think it to be 25,000,000 miles distant!

And what of its, and of the other planets', significance?

"I say that by heaven I mean science, and by the heavens I mean the sciences.

"To the seven first heavens correspond the seven sciences of the trivium and the quadrivium — namely grammar, dialectic, rhetoric, arithmetic, music, geometry, and astrology. To the eighth heaven, that is the starry sphere, answers natural science, which is called physics, and first science, which is called metaphysics. To the ninth sphere answers moral science, and to the quiet heaven" — the outermost heaven — "answers divine science, which is called theology."

Going into more detail:

"I say that the heaven of the moon is like grammar." *Grammatica*, or Latin.

"The heaven of Mercury may be compared to dialectic."

"The heaven of Venus may be compared to rhetoric."

Lovers with your plausible speeches, remember this!

"The heaven of the sun may be compared to arithmetic."

"The heaven of Mars may be compared to music."

"The heaven of Jove (Jupiter) may be compared to geometry."

"The heaven of Saturn may be compared to astrology."

The other heavens have already been described.

In this part of the *Convivio*, Dante also compares the active life and the contemplative life. He had lived both. "The contemplative life is more excellent and divine." He praises reason. "The man who severs himself from reason does not live as a man, but as a beast — as says that excellent Boethius, 'He lives as an ass.' " He discusses the mechanics of vision as well as his own personal way of composing a *canzone*. He does not compose a *canzone* in "point of numbers, which is essential to music." In other words, he had begun to think of poetry as something spoken rather than sung.

« 8 »

All this is from the second treatise. He continues in treatise III.

Once again, astronomy.

Trying to explain his line "The sun sees not, who circles the whole world," he says this:

"By the world, I do not mean the whole extent of the universe, but only this region of sea and of land. In this I follow common usage, which always refers to it thus."

But what about this world?

What about its nature and its motion?

"Pythagoras and his followers declared that it [the world] was one of the stars, and that there was another [another world] made exactly like it which they called Antichthon. He said that they were both in one sphere which revolved from east to west, and that it was because of this revolution that the sun sometimes circled around and was sometimes visible and sometimes invisible."

Plato thought otherwise. The world with the seas was the center of the whole, he thought. The whole globe turned on its center, but very slowly.

"Both these opinions are refuted as false in the second book of his *On the Heavens* by that glorious philosopher [Aristotle] to whom nature revealed her secrets more than to any other. You can be assured, then" — this was Dante's considered opinion very little more than two centuries before Copernicus came to quite a different conclusion — "that this earth is fixed and revolves not, and that it, together with the ocean, is the center of the heavens."

He discusses possible meanings of the word hour.

"Be it known that hour is understood in two ways by the astronomers, one by making twenty-four hours of the day and night, using twelve for the day and twelve for the night whether the day is long or short. These are the hours the Church uses. The other is to make the day and night twenty-four hours, of which the day at one season has fifteen hours and the night nine, and at another season the night has sixteen and the day eight. These are called equal hours."

The latter are, of course, the hours we use today.

He goes into the matter of speech.

"Only man among the animals" — note that man is called an animal, the medieval becoming almost modern — "speaks and has gestures and expressions. And if anyone should say that birds talk — as is the case with the magpie and the parrot — and that certain beasts have expression and gestures — for example, the ape and certain others — I reply that it is not true that they speak nor have they gestures. They merely mimic what they see and hear."

He considers laughter — which, in a sense, is a form of speech.

"It is a sudden light which flashes from the delight of the soul."

As such, it is to be praised highly.

But laughter must be moderate.

"The book" — probably by Seneca — "*Of the Four Cardinal Virtues*" instructs us to obey this rule: Let your laughter be without loud guffaws — that is to say, without cackling like a hen."

And since the book canonized philosophy, Dante defines the philosopher.

"Pythagoras," says the poet, "when asked if he regarded himself as wise, replied that he was not wise but a lover of wisdom."

Philos, he felt it necessary to point out since the Greek language was almost entirely unknown in his Italy, meant love. *Sophia* meant wisdom. *Philosophia* — love of wisdom.

Clearly his mind roved everywhere. There was no single chamber in the house of learning that he did not seek to enter — although when he did enter he usually, if not always, found it lighted only by the wax tapers and inadequate tallow candles of his time.

« 9 »

But perhaps the most interesting and possibly the most illuminating part of the *Convivio* is its fourth and last treatise. This is the one on which he comments on the *canzone* which is usually known as *Le dolci rime d'amor ch'io solia*, but which Dante expressly insisted (*Convivio* IV, 30) be known as *Contra li erranti* — "Against the erring ones." It is the one poem among those he analyzes which in the first instance was written with a philosophical purpose. It is not a love poem later transmuted. It is not nor was it ever addressed to either a Pietra, or a woman from the Casentino, or the lady at the window, or anyone else.

So, at any rate, say most who have studied Dante.

But are they correct?

Before trying to answer, let us look at it a little — let us look, at any rate, at its opening lines.

> The dulcet lines of love which I was wont
> To seek out in my thoughts
> I must now leave, but not because I hope not
> To return unto them,
> But rather since the scornful, haughty gestures
> Which in my lady dear
> Do now appear have shut me from the way
> Of my once-wonted speech.

But what, translated into prose, does all this mean? What does it tell us about Dante's actual and intellectual biography?

Are we to take it, as Dante apparently meant us to, that his study of philosophy and all the other studies to which he applied himself had become so difficult that he must now abandon them for a while — while he prepared himself better and saw to it that he was better equipped?

Or was he actually rejected by an actual lady — the lady at the window?

If so, that story has another twist to it.

In this new version, she rejected him, not he her.

But why?

I offer this hypothesis. May she not have discovered — or had pointed out to her — that for all Dante's talk of honored ancestry, the cattleseller-moneylender's son was at best shabby genteel, and his purse shabby genteel too? In other words, that he was not good enough for her — despite his reputation and his pride?

It is, of course, a hypothesis only, but it has this to support it. In the immediately ensuing pages, Dante enters into a discussion of what true nobility really is, and this — although certain of its arguments are based on purely medieval premises — is as eloquent and persuasive as anything he ever wrote.

May he not have written this to persuade his scornful lady?

It is not impossible.

At any rate, the matter is worth pursuing a little. This I do.

Ancient lineage? Only if you have ancient lineage are you noble?

Not so, says Dante.

"If a man cannot become gentle who is low-born, or a gentle son come from a base father, then one of two absurdities must follow. The first is that there is no such thing as nobility. The other is that the human race is not descended from a single man. For if a man is always such as he was born, and if he is born such as was his father, the condition we are in must have come from the first parent. Wherefore if Adam was noble, we are all noble; and if he was base, we are all base."

Riches?

Riches do not make you noble either, for riches either come by chance — from lucky ventures — or by inheritance.

In the first instance, they are undeserved; in the second, they almost always have bad consequences.

"I affirm that inheritance by will or by succession oftener comes to the bad than to the good, and of this I will not bring any evidence, but let each man cast his eyes about in his own neighborhood."

He quotes Boethius:

"Ah me, who was he who first dug out the heavy hidden gold and the precious stones that sought to hide themselves, those precious perils?"

Again Boethius:

"Money is only good when, transferred to others by the practice of liberality, it is no longer possessed."

But if nobility does not come from either ancient lineage or long-possessed wealth, what is it?

The *canzone* tells us.

> Nobility's wherever there is virtue. . . .
> Even as heaven is where there is a star.

Virtue?

More accurately, virtues.

According to Dante — and Aristotle — there were eleven virtues. Courage. Temperance. Liberality. Munificence. Consciousness of greatness. Proper pride. Serenity. Affability. Frankness. Eutrapelia — which Dante defines as "moderation in sports," but was more probably "pleasantness in social intercourse." Finally, justice.

Have these and you were noble. You did not have to be a Uberti of Florence or a Visconti of Milan. How far, in his attempt to regain the good opinion of a lady (or for any other reason), did Dante think that he was describing himself?

« 10 »

In this fourth treatise, Dante also first ventures into waters he would explore more widely later — the problem of a world government which would (and remember that this phrase was written in the earliest years of the trecento) "abolish wars" which come from "the discords" which "arise between kingdom and kingdom."

His solution: there must be a supreme authority.

"Even as we see that aboard a ship the various tasks are directed toward a single end, to wit making the desired port after a successful voyage, and that therefore there is one who regulates all and whose voice all must obey, namely the shipmaster," so there should be one "who, considering the diverse conditions of the world, should have the universal and indisputable office of commanding the whole."

Who should this be?

The Roman emperor.

Since he will argue this matter far more exhaustively later, I will now only state his most compelling reason. God wished it — and he showed this. From the house of Jesse should come spiritual salvation and from the city on the Tiber should come temporal domination. But by Dante's chronology, which, however, was not entirely accurate, David was born and Rome was founded almost in the same year.

« 11 »

The *De Vulgari Eloquentia* — whether it was written before or after the *Convivio* — was a book of a very different kind. Indeed, it was so clearly a textbook — or its usefulness as a textbook was so apparent — that it is easy to see how by some it was assigned to a later time, a time when Dante had much more opportunity to teach, whether or not he actually did so.

But Dante, even if he were giving technical instruction of the most detailed and practical kind, was of a nature that compelled him to probe deeply into whatever he talked about, and so the book ended up by being much more than "one which gave instruction with regard to writing verses to whoever would take it," which is how, you remember, Boccaccio described it. Instead, it turned out to be what was perhaps the first serious study of what today we call comparative philology of which we have a record. As an end product, it was also a history of language and of the Italian language in particular.

Its method was pragmatic rather than analytical. His purpose, says Dante, as should be "the business of every science," was "not to prove, but to explain."

Explain language he did and very thoroughly. He began at the very beginning — at least as it is recorded in folklore and religious writing — namely, the Garden of Eden, where "we find that a woman spoke before all others. I mean the presumptuous Eve."

Eve addressed the serpent.

Or so it was set down, says Dante, forgetting Genesis II, 20, which said:

"And Adam gave names to all cattle, and to the fowls of the air, and to every beast of the field."

Which, of course, implied speech.

But even without Genesis II, 20, Dante could not accept this statement.

"We find it written that the woman spoke first, but it is reasonable for us to think that the man spoke first."

Why?

"It is unseemly to think that this so excellent act of the human race was performed by a woman before a man."

But why unseemly?

There you have the Middle Ages! Woman was an inferior being. It was through Eve that sin and wickedness came into the world.

(The Greeks had a similar theory — it was through Pandora. But one cannot help wondering what Beatrice would have thought about this? Or the lady at the window? Or Pietra? Or how it comported with Dante's sublimations, or at least idealization, of the first two?)

The first language spoken was Hebrew and the first word was El, or God.

Dante then justifies both statements.

El, or God.

"It seems absurd and repugnant to reason to argue that anything should have been named by man before God, since man had been made by Him and for Him."

The Hebrew language.

Why?

Because it was the language Christ spoke.

"The form of speech which Adam spoke was inherited by the sons of Heber whom we call the Hebrews. With them alone it remained. This was so the Redeemer could speak it — so that he could speak the language of grace, not a tongue of confusion. Therefore Hebrew was the language which the lips of the first speaker used."

Hebrew continued to be the language of all humanity for a long time — in fact, until the day when "incorrigible man, persuaded by the giant" — i.e., Satan — "presumed in his heart not only to surpass nature but the very power who works in nature, which is God. In Shinar, which was afterwards called Babel, he built a tower by which he hoped to ascend to heaven."

All men toiled at this.

"Some gave orders. Some acted as architects. Some with rules marked out the lines for masonry. Some put on mortar with trowels. Some quarried stone. Some were engaged in bringing it by sea and others by land. The rest were busied at varied occupations."

Then suddenly they were all confounded. God — as is related in Genesis II, which Dante follows closely although with some additions — angry at their overweening pride, threw them into confusion by changing their one language into many languages.

"The same language remained alone to those who were engaged in the same trade. For instance, one language remained to the architects; another to those rolling blocks of stone; another to those quarrying them. And the human race was accordingly divided into as many languages as there were different trades."

In due course, certain of these languages were carried to Europe — some of them to southern Europe (our Romance languages), some of them into northern Europe (our Germanic languages), and a last division to Greece and Asia Minor.

(Dante omits any reference to the Slavic languages, or rather he confuses them with the Germanic ones. But he has made a good and not too inaccurate beginning.)

Then he continues with the southern group.

This group itself divided, he says, "and now appears in threefold form."

What are these three forms?

The *lingua d'oc*, the *lingua d'oil*, and the *lingua di si* — "namely the Spaniards, the French, and the Italians" — all of this based on whether they *oc* or *oil* or *si* for yes.

"Those who say *oc* inhabit the western part of the south of Europe, beginning from the frontier of the Genoese. Those who say *si* inhabit the country east of the said frontier, namely that which extends as far as that promontory where the gulf of the Adriatic Sea begins, and Sicily. Those who say *oil* lie in some sort to the north of these last, for they have the Germans on their east and north, on the west they are enclosed by the English sea and are bound by the mountains of Aragon, and they are also shut off by the inhabitants of Provence and the precipices of the Apennines."

Which one was paramount among these?

All have claims, but Dante, forgetting that only a little earlier he sarcastically rebuffed the inhabitants of Pietramala, "a most populous city" — actually a country-bumpkin hamlet which even today has less than four hundred inhabitants — and all others who rate "the place of their birth the most delightful under the sun, and its vernacular above all others," awards preeminence to the *lingua di si*, "which is the language of the Italians."

He does this "on the strength of two privileges."

First, "the sweetest and most subtle poets who have written in the vernacular are its intimates and belong to its household."

Like Cino da Pistoia and his friend, he says. Cino da Pistoia's friend was Dante.

Second, "it seems to lean more on grammar." In other words, it is closer to Latin.

"And this appears a very weighty argument."

But even as what we now call the Romance group of the Indo-European family divided, according to Dante, into the *lingua d'oc*, the *lingua d'oil*, and the *lingua di si*, so the *lingua di si* itself divided.

Time did this and so did geography.

"We boldly affirm that if the ancient Pavians were to rise from the dead they would speak a language varying or different from that of the modern Pavians."

Isolation in those days of poor communications had the same effect: isolation and the tendency of groups and localities to draw in upon themselves.

Not only did those having "the same national designation as the Neapolitans and the people of Gaeta" speak differently, but what "is stranger still, the inhabitants of the same city, like the Bolognese of the Borgo San Felice and the Bolognese of the Strada Maggiore."

It is the same today. Brooklynese is different from the speech of Manhattan.

"Wherefore, if we should calculate the primary, secondary, and subordinate variations of the tongue of Italy, we would find that in this small corner of the world the varieties of speech not only come up to a thousand but even exceed that number."

Thus his analysis of the Italian language. But as he analyzed it, as — to use his own words — he "pursued the hare," there was one thing more to do.

That was to determine which of these one thousand varieties of the *lingua di si* was the best for literary purposes.

He sought the answer by carefully examining every single important Italian way of speaking, and many unimportant ones. We have already — as we traced Dante the exile's wanderings through Italy — set down many of the things he found.

But not his conclusion.

"We were hunting for an illustrious Italian language."

And after his long search he thought he found it.

But not perhaps where he expected it.

"We declare," he says, "the illustrious, cardinal, courtly, and curial vernacular language to be that which belongs to all the towns of Italy but which does not appear to belong to any one of them. It is by that that all the municipal dialects of Italy are measured, weighed, and compared."

In other words, you should take the best from every dialect in Italy and meld these into a new dialect which would be Italian.

Dante could have done this, but he did not.

"It is now recognized," says Philip Wicksteed, "that the illustrious language which Dante separates from all the local dialects of Italy is mainly based on the speech of Tuscany which he so bitterly derides."

Willy-nilly, he wrote in Tuscan because he was a Tuscan.

And his Tuscan — with only a few modifications — became Italian.

Because he wrote in it more than for any other reason — because it was the language of the *Vita Nuova* and the *Convivio* and the *Commedia* — it became the Italian which we use today.

« *12* »

That much for book I, which might well have been called "A Short History of the Origin and Development of the Italian Language." And then on to book II, in which Dante took up the main business of the *De Vulgari Eloquentia*, which was to teach writing to those who were willing enough and patient enough to learn.

This book shows Dante in a new role — Dante the pedagogue.

In this role he was as competent as he was in his other roles. He was a good teacher, careful, thoughtful, and thorough — how thorough can best be seen by examining the subject matter of the fourteen chapters which still survive.

Chapter 1. The illustrious language, declares Dante, is equally suited for use in poetry and prose, but as poetry seems to be a model for all writers he will treat of poetry. But only those who are qualified to do so should write — or, at any rate, should write poetry — in this illustrious language.

"Language is as necessary an instrument of our thoughts as a horse is to a knight, and as the best horses are suited to the best knights the best language will suit the best thoughts."

But not all have the best thoughts, consequently not all ought to use the best language.

Adornment is excellent, but "we should not describe an ox with caparisons or a swine with a belt as adorned. Rather we should laugh at them."

Chapter 2. The illustrious language should only be used in treating the worthiest subjects; namely, safety, love, and virtue. Safety Dante took to mean feats of arms.

Chapter 3. The *canzone* is the noblest form of poetry, and therefore the worthy subjects — i.e., the ones named above — should be treated in *canzoni*.

Chapter 4. The form of the *canzone*. Should classic Latin poets be imitated? (Dante's answer was yes.) The choice of a subject and its bearing on the style to be used. It could be tragedy, comedy, or elegy. Here he was groping for something that would lead him to call his great poem the *Commedia*.

"If our subject appears fit to be sung in the tragic style, we must then use the illustrious vernacular, but if it appears fit to be sung in the comic style, sometimes the middle and sometimes the lowly vernacular should be used."

He promised to treat the latter more fully later.

Chapter 5. The different kinds of line which could be used in a *canzone*. Here he is exceedingly specific. An eleven-syllable line was ideal, next came three, then five- or seven-syllable lines.

"A line of nine syllables was either never held in honor or has fallen into disuse."

Chapter 6. The construction of a *canzone* — even the arrangement of the words, which must be congruous.

Some examples which met with Dante's approval:

"Aristotle philosophized in Alexander's time."

"The praiseworthy discernment of the Marquis of Este and his munificence prepared for all make him beloved."

"Having cast the greatest part of the flowers out of thy bosom, O Florence, the second Totila went fruitlessly to Trinacria."

But it is interesting to note that Dante never wrote that way himself.

Chapter 7. Classification of the words that could be used in a *canzone.* Above all they should not be childish, feminine, shaggy, or rumpled. Best are ornamental words. These are polysyllables "which when mixed with combed-out words produce a fair harmony." *Sovramagnificentissimamente,* for example! Which itself made an eleven-syllable line.

Chapter 8. The meaning of the term *canzone.* "A *canzone* appears to be nothing else but the completed action of one writing words to be set to music."

Chapter 9. What a stanza was.

Chapter 10. The various possible structures of a stanza.

Chapter 11. The arrangement of the various parts of a stanza.

Chapter 12. How the eleven-syllable line, the three-syllable line, the five-syllable line, and the seven-syllable line should be interwoven.

Chapter 13. The use of rhyme in a stanza.

Chapter 14. The number of lines and syllables in a stanza.

But chapter 14 was never completed. It broke off in the middle of a sentence. Nor were books III and IV, in which Dante promised to treat, among other things, the sonnet and the *ballata,* even begun.

Why?

If you believe that the *De Vulgari Eloquentia* was written first, it was to turn to the far more important (to Dante) *Convivio.*

But if it was written after the *Convivio* — and if not, the *Convivio* was not finished for the same reason — its last sentence was left hanging in air because Dante no longer had time to write it.

How could he find time, since he was suddenly preoccupied with other matters?

Other matters that were of far greater moment.

It is now time to tell you what these were.

« *13* »

Once again, we will rely on Boccaccio to help us.

"I say," writes Giovanni in his *Life of Dante,* "that while the poet was most intent upon his glorious work, and had already composed seven cantos of that first part of it which he called *Inferno,* there happened the grievous accident of his exile or flight, on account of which, abandoning this and everything else, he wandered for many years with uncertain plans, with different friends and lords.

"But against what God ordains Fortune can oppose no obstacle, and therefore it transpired that someone searching for a necessary document among possessions of Dante which had been hastily rescued and put in a chest which was hidden in some church or other found the said seven cantos which had been composed by Dante, read them without knowing what they were, and then took them to a fellow citizen, Dino di Messer Lambertuccio [Dino Frescobaldi], a famous poet in Florence" — and a close personal friend of Dante even though a political enemy — "and showed them to him. At the sight of them, Dino marveled — both at the beautiful, polished, and ornate style and at the profundity of the meaning which seemed to lay hidden under the fair covering of their words. On this account and because of the place in which they were found, Dino judged them to be the work of Dante."

They must be completed, both men concluded — "if it should be feasible, so fine a beginning should have the end planned for it."

Accordingly, "they deliberated one with the other as to how they could find out where Dante was and, on investigation, they discovered that he was with the Marquis Maroello. They wrote to him, therefore, and sent him the seven cantos."

The marquis read them avidly and then, "being a man of much understanding," summoned Dante before him, showed them to him, and asked if he knew whose writing they were.

"Dante recognized them immediately and replied that they were his. Thereupon the marquis begged him that it would not please him to leave so lofty a beginning without a satisfactory end.

"Dante answered thus:

" 'In good truth, I believed that in my ruin these and many other of my writings were lost, and because of this and because of my many other troubles I had completely abandoned the high imagining which I had taken up in my work, but since Fortune has unexpectedly given it back to me, and since you think well of it, I will try to recall in my memory my first concept of it and proceed accordingly as grace is given me.'

"The magnificent work was then begun again by Dante, although he did not, as many would think, conclude it without further interruptions."

The same story is told by the same man and with the same factualness in one of his lectures on the *Commedia*.

But in this version a few details are added.

The person who instituted the search was Dante's wife Gemma; and the man who actually found the manuscript was either Dante's nephew Andrea Poggi — Tana's son — or Dino Perini, of whom we will hear more later. In conversations with Boccaccio, both claimed the honor. The cantos were found "five years or more" after Dante's banishment. That would take us at least to 1306 and probably later. Gemma was seeking deeds or other documents which would enable her to recover her dowry. She was able to do this because there was now "a more reasonable regime" in the city. The vehemence of the early persecutions was gone.

But if there were differences in small matters like this, the accounts agree in their total story. They agree that the seven cantos were found hidden in a chest or strongbox; that they were turned over to Dino Frescobaldi; that Dino sent them to Moroello Malaspina; that Moroello read them and showed them to Dante; that Dante acknowledged them to be his; and that under the marquis's persuasion he took up his long-discarded work.

These are the facts, and I do not dispute them.

But can we put flesh on them? Can we reconstruct the actual scene?

I do not think this is very difficult.

The year, to begin with, is 1308, not earlier or later, and Dante, having left Lucca, is in the Lunigiana again. Specifically, he is in a Malaspina castle, probably Giovagallo. There he works away at either the *De Vulgari Eloquentia* or the *Convivio* or possibly both.

Beatrice is not in his mind.

In the *Convivio*, he has referred to her as "that blessed Beatrice who lives in heaven with the angels and on earth in my soul" (II, 2), as "the glorious Beatrice" (also II, 2), and as "Beatrice in glory" (II, 7). But then he dismisses her almost summarily.

Convivio II, 9:

"This discourse" — upon immortality — "will be the ending of my speech about Beatrice, of whom I propose to speak no further."

In this book, he added. But he was not — at any rate, at that moment — thinking of other books.

But even as he was writing these words — or not very long afterwards — a messenger from Florence came down the road. To the castle he rode, up to its gate, across the moat, and into the courtyard. There he dismounted and asked to be presented to Moroello. He was led to the great lord and to him offered a carefully secured packet. In it was the little notebook — *quadernetto* is the Boccaccio word — which with "a number of sonnets, *canzoni*, and other such like matters" had been found by Andrea Poggi or Dino Perini.

Moroello opened it and began reading.

> Midway along the pathway of my life
> I found myself deep in a darkling wood,
> For from the right way I had surely strayed . . .

It was so grievous death was scarcely more so,
But so that I may tell the good I found there . . .

. . . the deep lake of my heart . . .

When I had rested awhile my mortal body,
Along the desert slope I once more went,
So that my surer fot was ever the lower;
When lo, and almost where began the steep,
A leopard light of foot and very swift
And with a spotted hide all covered . . .

Thus did conspire to fill my heart with hope
Of the wild beast with gaily mottled skin
The hour itself and the sweet season . . .

But not such that I was not frightened again
By sight of lion who appeared to me.
It seemed to me that he came ravening at me . . .

And a she-wolf who every appetite
Seemed to be laden with, she was so lean . . .

But this was only the beginning. It went on and on.

It told of the encounter with Virgil ("He answered me: 'Not man, but once a man!' "), of the mission of Beatrice into hell, of the gates of the infernal region ("All hope abandon, ye who enter here."), of the sad city of the virtuous heathen, of Paolo and Francesco, and then of the slimy slough in which the gluttonous like swine in the muddy streets wallowed and writhed, and finally of the fearful fourth and fifth circles in which were punished the avaricious and the wrathful.

It was, too, in an extraordinary and effectively compact meter which had never been used before. Today we call it *terza rima*. It was apparently invented by Dante.

Add likewise the fact that Moroello was probably the fourth human being — Dino Frescobaldi, Andrea Poggi, and Dante himself being the others — ever to see these lines which since have shaken the world.

They were, therefore, as astonishing as they were sublime and magnificent.

Moroello would not have been a worthy descendant of the Malaspina — the hosts of troubadours and often troubadours themselves — if he had not recognized that here behind lichened walls he had seen a vision that few had seen before.

He pressed the manuscript into Dante's hands.

"You must go on with it."

Nor is it any wonder that Dante complied with this.

For as he saw his writing — left behind, forgotten, even lost, he thought — Beatrice returned to him.

And his old words about her returned too.

"I will write that about her which has never yet been written of any other woman."

Parchment he had — for the two earth-bound books upon which he was engaged. And quill pens. And soot-black ink.

He set them before him and began using them.

"*Seguitando*," he wrote. "Continuing."

Downward he and Virgil stepped toward the bank of the foul marsh and fouler stream over which Phlegias would ferry them.

Or that is how Boccaccio tells the story.

And I am certain it is basically true. He may not actually have broken off at the end of canto VII to begin again with canto VIII. That is unimportant. But at the Moroello castle he was brought his old handiwork and a flame was relighted by it. The *Commedia* — now the *Divina Commedia* — was once again upon its way.

« *14* »

Yet even as he thus set it upon its course — and therefore had to ponder about it — it came upon him that he was not yet quite ready to do all he had to do with it. Hell perhaps, but not purgatory and certainly not paradise.

"I must make myself ready," he told himself. "I must still further temper my sword. I must fill fuller the well of my knowledge."

And since with Dante to decide was almost always to act, this he set out to do.

And in a way that fortunately we know.

In 1759, there was published in Florence a book entitled *Latinae Epistolae*, and in its proem was included a somewhat garrulous letter from one Fra Ilario, self-described as "a humble monk of the monastery of Corvo at the mouth of the Magra," and addressed to "the egregious and resplendent Uguccione della Faggiuola, among Italian lords the most illustrious."

In it, the monk tells of a strange encounter.

"I am talking," he says, "of that man whose work, with my notes upon it, I intend to dedicate to you — a man who even in very boyhood, nay, and marvelous to relate even while still an adolescent, according to what others report did try his hand at saying unheard of things, and even more marvelous did essay to make matters plain in the vulgar tongue which even the most excellent men could not set forth in Latin. In the vulgar, I say, but not that of the common herd. His words were musical."

Fra Ilario continued:

"I say then that while this man was on his way on a journey beyond the mountains and was passing through the diocese of Luni he came to our above-named monastery."

There he knocked at the portal.

"And I, seeing one whom I still did not recognize nor did the other monks — I, seeing him, questioned him and asked him what he wanted. He did not answer me but looked at me like one in a trance, and so again I asked him what he wanted. He looked long at the friars and answered: 'Peace!'

"This made me all the more curious to know who and what he was, and so I took him apart from the others. We talked a little and then I *did* know, for although before that day I had never seen him his reputation had come to me from afar."

He *did* know, and we know too. It was Dante, who had left his Malaspina castle.

They talked further.

"And when he saw that I was *all for him*" — this is a reasonably exact translation of the medieval monk's modern words — "and that I loved him for his words, he took a little book from his breast with a friendly gesture and generously put it in my hands. 'Here is part of a work of mine! I leave it as a remembrance so that you can the better remember me!' "

Fra Ilario opened it.

"And looking upon the words therein I marveled at them, whereupon he asked me the cause of this. I answered that it was because of their quality and because it seemed to me that it would have been not merely difficult but impossible to express in vulgar language a meaning so sublime."

Not only difficult or impossible but neither fitting nor seemly, the monk added.

" 'Fitting and seemly too I consider it,' replied Dante. 'In the beginning, to be sure, I first chose the legitimate language [Latin], and indeed not only chose it but commenced writing in it.

" 'Poetizing, I began thus:

> *Ultima regna canam fluvida contermina mundo*
> *Spiritibus que lata patent, que premia solvunt*
> *Pro meritis cuicumque suis . . .*

" 'But tough food you give not to lips which are still nourished by milk.'

"Thus," concluded Fra Ilario, "the tripartite offering came into my hands."

But why and where was Dante going?

Once again Boccaccio:

"He went to Paris and there he gave himself up entirely to the study both of philosophy and theology, reviewing also such of the other sciences that he had forgotten during his difficult years."

Boccaccio and others — notably Giovanni da Serravalle, who wrote in the next century — say that he also went to Oxford, but that seems considerably less likely. However, judging from his vivid description, he certainly at least saw the Flanders seacoast with its high tides which were so amazing to those who knew only the Mediterranean.

Inferno XV:

> Just as the Flemings between Wissant and Bruges,
> Fearing the flood tides that surge in on them,
> Do build their bulkheads to hold back the sea.

Villani says much the same:

"After he was driven out of Florence with the White party, he went to the university at Bologna, and afterwards at Paris and in many other parts of the world."

But in any case, he went to Paris.

And for reasons that are fairly obvious.

Just as Bologna was a rendezvous for those who studied law — both civil and canon — so the city by the Seine with its Sorbonne, its Left Bank, and its Latin Quarter already flourishing was the place to go to for theology and philosophy.

Albertus Magnus (who combined both) had taught there, and St. Thomas Aquinas had both taught and learned there.

(This we have already noted but should mention again.)

Its learning was immeasurable and even its controversies — and they were many — were wit-sharpening.

And now, as Dante took up the *Commedia* again, this was what he needed. For now even a Malaspina castle was a backwater.

He had cried: "Peace!" but that was half in desperation, for what he wanted was not peace but stimulation.

Over the mountains he would go, then, to the fountain source of learning.

But apparently he did not plan to stay there.

He would get what he wanted, then return again.

Which would be the reason for his leaving his precious manuscript in Fra Ilario's hands.

XIX

The Street of the Strawsellers

<hr>

ALMOST unquestionably he went by sea.

To be sure, there are many arguments which can and have been offered in favor of a land voyage, and some of them are not entirely unconvincing. For example, Dante plainly was familiar with the rugged terrain that lay between the Magra and southern France, and almost equally so with the goat's path which passed for a highway now that the ancient Roman coastal highway was no more and the breathtaking modern Corniche had not yet been constructed.

Purgatorio III:

> 'Twixt Lerici and Turbia, the most
> Desolate, the most landslide-shattered scree
> Compared to it a broad stairway is.

He is describing the mountain of purgatory which those who are to be cleansed of their sins must climb, and can think of no better simile.

We have already adverted to his familiarity with the little Lavagna River.

And it is clear that he knew Genoa so well that he must have visited it. Witness his concern with the stories of Michel Zanche (not very well known elsewhere in Italy), whom he placed (*Inferno* XXII) in the burning pitch of the barrators, and of Michel's son-in-law and murderer, Branca d'Oria of the famous Doria family.

The Branca d'Oria story is one of Dante's most venomous.

Inferno XXXIII — Fra Alberigo, one of the damned in the Ptolomea of murderers, is the speaker:

"He is Ser Branca d'Oria. Many years
  Have passed since he was here incarcerated."
"But I believe," said I [*Dante*], "thou dost deceive me.
  For Branca d'Oria not yet hath died.
  He eats and drinks and sleeps and puts on clothes."
"Up there," he answered, "up in Malebranche —
  There where the ooze of sticky pitch is boiling —
  Michel Zanche had not yet arrived
  When this man left a demon in his stead
  In his own body, as did a near kinsman
  Who joined with him to do the treacherous deed."

Lana, who was almost a contemporary, has this to say about the two men:

"This Michel Zanche was the intendant of the mother of King Enzo" — actually he was the intendant of Enzo's wife — "who was the bastard son of the Emperor Frederick II. And after the death of the said King Enzo, the Lord Michel took the lady for his wife. She was heiress of the judicate [district] of Logodoro in Sardinia, and there he waxed exceedingly rich through the corrupt sale of offices. Now this lady bore him a daughter, and in due course he married her to Messer Branca d'Oria of Genoa, and, as related by Dante in the next to last canto of this canticle, the said Messer Branca d'Oria, wishing to acquire the wealth of the said Lord Michel" — which he would do by inheritance if Michel were dead — "invited him to dine with him one day and for dessert had him cut to pieces."

This was in 1290, and the crime was not avenged. The living Branca still walked the streets of his city. But, said Dante in one of his most withering judgments, the living Branca was nothing more than a shell, an empty body seeming to be Branca but in reality inhabited by a friend. The true Branca had been in hell for almost two decades.

The living Branca apparently resented this.

"As is born out by ancient but most truthful writings," says Oberto Foglietta, a Genoese chronicler, "Dante, in all other respects a very worthy man, had one inborn defect which made him disliked by and distasteful to many. This was that he was so subject to partisan prejudices that often he allowed himself to be carried away by his violent feelings up to the point of madness. This quality, and his total disregard of the danger of offending powerful men with the too great freedom of speech in which he frequently indulged, led him (for reasons which I know not) to attack the name and the reputation of the Doria, and although he was often reproached for this, he continually spoke ill of them. This led the servants of Branca to conclude that they could only blunt his sharp words with deeds, and so they laid hands upon Dante in a public place and gave him a thorough drubbing.

"For which outrage," concluded Oberto, "not being able, since he was frail of strength, to meet force with force, he revenged himself with further words and with his pen."

Against Branca in the lines cited above.

But also against Genoa.

Again *Inferno* XXXIII:

> O Genoese, ye people who forsake
> All moral law, ye full of all corruption,
> Why are ye yet not hounded from out the world,
> Since with the wickedest man of the Romagna
> [*Fra Alberigo, who had murdered his brother and
> his nephew with poisoned figs*]
> I found one of ye so wicked that for his deeds
> His soul already is bathed in Cocytus
> The while his body seems to live above?

Distilling verbal poison was one of Dante's many specialties, but nowhere did he distill it with more lethal effectiveness than in the above passage — not even in his onslaught against Pisa (cited earlier in this book), not even in his many diatribes against Florence. There must have been a reason.

« 2 »

But even if there was a reason, and if the reason was an unhappy encounter with Doria bravos who humiliated him quite as much as they bruised and battered him, this could hardly have taken place at precisely this time, for *Inferno* XXXIII had not yet been written. Any traveler could have told him about the rough going between Lerici and La Tourbie (Turbia's present name). He could have learned all he knew about the Lavagna in an evening's conversation with Alagia.

But his knowledge of the sea is so precise and his familiarity with things nautical is so impressive as to make a sea voyage at some time or another almost certain. When more likely than at this time?

Most of this knowledge is made apparent by passages in the *Commedia*, some of which I here give:

Inferno V:

> I came now to a place bereft of light
> Where all did low as doth a stormy sea
> When it is lashed and beaten by cross winds.

Inferno VII:

> As sails once puffed and swollen by a gale
> Fall, all entangled, when the mast carries away.

Inferno XVI:

> Even as comes to surface he who dives
> Deep to set free an anchor that is fouled
> On reef or other deep-sea-hid obstruction,
> With arms spread outward and with feet drawn in.

Inferno XVII:

> As little skiffs lie drawn up on the shore
> Half in the water, half upon the strand.

Inferno XXII:

> Like unto dolphins when they give a warning
> To sailors with the arched curve of their backs
> So that they can make ready to save their ship.

Purgatorio II:

> We were still standing upon the sea's shore
> Like unto folk who think upon their journey
> And in their hearts go, in their bodies linger,
> When lo, as on the coming of the dawn,
> Mars doth glow ruddily through the thick mists
> Low in the west over the ocean's floor.

Purgatorio VIII:

> The hour now had come that stirs nostalgia
> In those who sail the sea, and melts their hearts
> On that day they have bidden dear friends farewell.

Purgatorio XXIV:

> Swiftly we went
> As doth a ship before a spanking breeze.

Purgatorio XXX:

> Even as the lower Wain
> Guides him who alters helm to come to port.

Paradiso II:

> O ye who are aboard some little shallop,
> And, all intent to listen, followed have
> My ship that in her singing plows the main,
> Turn back until ye see your shores once more!
> Do not sail out upon the open sea,
> For if ye lose me, ye are surely lost!
> The waters I sail were never sailed before.
> But ye, ye other few, who have reached out
> In time for food of angels by the which
> Men live here but are never satisfied,
> Ye may put forth upon the briny deep.
> Your vessel and yourselves may plow my furrow
> Before my wake becomes smooth again.

Paradiso III:

> As through translucent and transparent glass
> Or as through limpid and unruffled water
> That is not so deep the bottom cannot be seen.

Paradiso XIII:

> One time I saw a ship that swift and sound
> Had safely sailed the seas its whole long voyage
> Only to shipwreck as it entered the harbor.

Paradiso XXV:

> Just as, to rest from fatigue or to avoid danger,
> The oars which until then had lashed the water
> All stop in unison when a whistle is blown.

What does he describe in all this? Let us sum up.

The noisiness of storm waves as they are lashed into leaping fury by conflicting winds. The turquoise blue and supposedly tranquil Mediterranean is capable of such, as anyone is apt to know who has taken a small steamer from Leghorn to Bastia on Corsica and then to Marseilles. The word Dante used to describe this noisiness is *mugghia*. I have translated it "low." It would be hard to find a word more expressive.

The disordered deck scene when a ship is dismasted. Here the word Dante employs is *avvolte*, or entangled. This makes for an extraordinary visual accuracy. Sails are in a crumpled heap, and ropes a fouled-up mess. Yet only a moment earlier lines had been taut and canvas bellying.

The swimming upward of a brown-skinned diver who has released a snagged anchor. He butterflies with his arms, retracts his feet, and kicks powerfully with them. Such divers are a part of the Tyrrhenian scene. One of them, Cola or Niccola Pesce (Nick Fish), became legendary and is celebrated in the last line of one of Cecco Angiolari's sonnets. In Sicilian folklore, he is said to have dived under the island of Trinacria (Sicily), which he discovered to be supported by three marble columns, and there to have found (but he did not bring it up with him) incredible treasure.

The fishermen's boats drawn up on the sand or the shingle even as they are today.

The rainbow-hued dolphins which off every port in the Mediterranean still arch their backs as they leap and curvet around the bows of even the swiftest vessel. In Dante's time — and earlier and later — they were supposed to prognosticate foul weather.

The strange and haunting feeling that comes to all those who journey, but particularly to those who travel by sea. I must set out. It is my wish to be upon my way. This ship is ready. The hawsers are about to be cast off. And yet — and yet do I really wish to go? Do I wish to see the shores, the familiar shores, receding? Who knows if I shall ever return?

The exhilaration of a ship leaping forward like a racehorse as it is borne on its way by a fair wind.

The Wain — according to most commentators, this is the Great Dipper, but I think Dante speaks of the North Star — gleaming in the night sky, and serving almost as a beacon to mariners.

The solid sturdiness of a seagoing vessel — such as perhaps the one he sailed upon — and its contrast with shore-clinging and less seaworthy smaller craft.

A ship's wake leaping out, but astern seething and hissing until it became a flat trail that stretched into the distance.

The translucent waters — now we are near the shore — which are so clear that you can see even a small object when it is many fathoms deep.

Near the shore too, a vessel returned from a long voyage cast ashore against the mole of the very harbor from which it had once set out expectantly and which it now had almost reached on its way home.

Finally, a swift single-decked galley, its oars beating the water. But the men are weary, or a reef is seen, or known to be under the waters they are approaching. Suddenly a boatswain's whistle blows shrilly. As if paralyzed, the blades stop their motion. They hang dripping in the air.

But it is not merely in these random passages that we go to sea with Dante. We can also smell the salt with him and breathe in the air of sea venture in one of his most famous stories — that of the imaginary last voyage of Ulysses (*Inferno* XXVI) when he drives out through the Strait of Gibraltar and into unknown southern seas.

Ulysses is speaking:

When

I did depart from Circe, who detained me
For longer than a year near Gaeta,
But long before Aeneas gave it this name,
Not fondness for my son, not filial
Regard for my old father, not love's duty
Which would have brought joy to Penelope
Could tame in me the deep and burning zeal
I had to know and understand the world
And all the vices and the virtues of men.
Therefore I set forth on the boundless sea
In one ship only, and with the loyal few
Who even to the end were true to me.
Land did I always see on either hand —
Spain and Morocco and Sardinia
And all the other islands that sea laves.
I and my fellows were old — our age had slowed us —
When we at last came to that narrow strait
Beside which Hercules had set his pillars
To warn men that they should not farther go.
Seville to starboard lay, Ceuta to port
But very far astern and out of sight,
When "Comrades," cried I, "who through a hundred
        thousand
Perils and dangers have come unto the west,
In the short time of living that still remains you,
Would ye deny yourselves the experience
Of following the sun to unpeopled lands?
Consider the lofty seed from which you sprang!
You were not made to live as the beasts do
But ever to pursue valor and knowledge!"
My shipmates I so sharpened and made eager
With this short speech to venture on their voyage
That I then could have hardly held them back,
And we with one accord turned poop toward morning,
Making our oars as wings for our mad flight,
Yet ever bore we more and more to port.
Soon all the bright stars of the other pole
Shone in the night. Our own had sunk so low
They did not rise above the ocean's floor.
Five times was kindled and five times was quenched

The light upon the underside of the moon
Since we had set out upon our deep-sea passage
When there appeared a mountain, tenebrous
It was so distant. It seemed to me so lofty
That I one loftier had not ever seen.
How we rejoiced, but joy turned to lament
As there did sweep from the new land a whirlwind
Which struck and shook the forepart of our ship.
Three times around it spun us with its seas
And then the fourth time stern rose high in air
And prow plunged deep — alas so God did will it —
And then the waters closed over our heads.

Again we ask a question. Where did Dante get the specific knowledge of sea travel to a new world and another hemisphere which he used to make so convincing this description of what might almost be called a pre-Columbian voyage?

Where — to ask another question — did he get his knowledge of the Southern Cross which he hints at here and specifically refers to elsewhere?

Purgatorio I:

I turned me to the right and fixed my gaze
Upon the other pole. There I saw four stars
Which none had seen before since the first man.

Where did he get his accurate information about a storm so savage that it might almost have been a West Indian hurricane?

Paget Toynbee gives a scholar's answer to the last of these questions.

"Dante's description of the wreck of Ulysses's vessel is imitated from *Aeneid* I, 114–117," he says in his *A Dictionary of Proper Names and Notable Matters in the Works of Dante*.

Given Dante's adulation of Virgil and his saturation in his works, this is not impossible.

But there was more to the Ulysses story than the description of a violent storm. It also told of a brave venture into the unknown and what happened there, and this, even more than it reflects Virgil, reflects a waterfront yarn well known to Genoese seamen.

In 1291 — so it goes — one of their fellow townsmen and mariners, Tedisio d'Oria, together with the Venetian brothers Ugolino and Vivaldi de' Vivaldi, merchant adventurers from that city, fitted out two galleys with everything necessary for "a voyage to those parts which no one before them had made even the slightest attempt to reach." Thus equipped, and accompanied by Genoese sailors and by two Minorite friars, they "set sail for the Strait of Ceuta" — the Strait of Gibraltar — "so that by way of the Ocean Sea they might come to the lands of India carrying with them Italian merchandise."

Sail into the Ocean Sea they did, and then turned southward.

"But after they had passed the place called Gozara" — on the Atlantic coast of Africa — "no certain news was ever had of them."

Cried Jacopo d'Oria, who was a relative:

"May God, however, keep guard over them and one day bring them back safe and sound!"

But God did not bring them back — they disappeared — and there you have the Ulysses story.

Others did return, however. Two centuries before their Christopher, the Genoese were already leaving the safe and the known. They may not have rediscovered the Azores, which had been visited by the Carthaginians in antiquity — officially the Azores were not rediscovered until 1432 — and they may not even have reached Madeira, which was known to Pliny as the Purple Islands. But they had at least seen in the distance the tall snow-clad peak of Teide in the Canary Islands and they seem to have gone well past the bulge of Africa to trade for gold and ivory.

What they saw they talked about — the new stars and the old stars sunk beneath the horizon. Other things.

Dante listened.

As Shakespeare did in a London tavern and then wrote *The Tempest*, so the Florentine poet listened on a Genoese foredeck.

Listened and with attention.

Add to this the keen knowledge of ships and the sea which we have demonstrated above, and a sea voyage of more than a little length is indicated.

It does not seem to me unreasonable to feel certain that he made such a voyage, and that he made it at this time.

« 3 »

If he did, he would have gone by one of two possible routes. He might — like the seagoing vessel of his *Paradiso* II — have sailed boldly outward, guided by the stars only and not again seeing land until near Toulon. Or he might have shipped upon a craft engaged in *cabotaggio*, or coastwise trading. (John Cabot — Giovanni Caboto — and Sebastian Cabot and perhaps even the Cabots who speak only to the Lowells were, then, descendants of coastwise sailors.) In this case, he would have followed the dramatic steep seacoast of Liguria, where mountains blue-green with pines rose to a height of eighteen hundred feet within sight of the sea, and where often a sheer gray precipice fell directly into the deep water. On such a voyage, he would never be so far from land that when the right breeze blew he did not smell the perfume of the famous flowers and sometimes the more astringent aroma of the *macchia*, that thick entanglement of — among other plants — rock rose, broom, myrtle, and arbutus. Nor would he have had to have keen eyes or ears to see and hear fishermen going out to their nets or cocks crowing and other shore activities.

Whichever the route, he would have embarked at Portovenere.

(It is contended by some, to be sure, that he did go by sea but that he embarked from Genoa. This would have allowed him to travel at least part of the road whose difficulty he alluded to. It would have allowed him, after leaving the Malaspina lands, to have crossed the Slate River — Lavagna means slate and there is still a flourishing slate industry at the place — of Alagia's uncle, the Fieschi Pope Adrian. It would have given him time to incur Branca d'Oria's enmity and to earn the ill will and revenge of Branca's followers. Still, Portovenere is a more probable place of departure. For one thing it is the nearest port to Corvo. Dante could have handed his manuscript to Fra Ilario and almost straightway gotten aboard his ship.)

This Portovenere is described today as being "a picturesque little village facing a narrow arm of the sea and the island of Palmaria in the western part of the Gulf of Spezia." It has some small breakwaters or moles and a few little stony beaches and it "offers limited facilities for tourists and bathers." But from Roman days onward through the Middle Ages and at least until the time of the Emperor Charles V Hapsburg of Spain and Austria, who in the High Renaissance used it as a naval base when he moved his men against Pope Clement VII, it was something different. It was a lively and important seaport crowded with masts and shipping.

Dante, I am convinced, sailed from Portovenere, and I am convinced too that he sailed from it aboard a broad-beamed, sturdy, lateen-rigged coasting vessel, in which case he would have stopped frequently at one of the many ports upon the way. I list a few of them which were at least fishing villages in his time. Sestri Levante. Chiavari. Rapallo. Santa Margherita. Portofino. Nervi. Vareggi. Savona. San Remo. Monaco. (Of course, Genoa. He must have come ashore at Genoa. But again his encounter with Branca d'Oria's henchmen could not have taken place at this time.) And finally some of the similar places on the southern coast of France. Villefranche, for example. St. Tropez. La Ciotat.

Such stops were usual in medieval sea travel. And because — since "whenever possible the medieval merchant preferred to travel by water, restricting his overland carrying to short journeys between rivers" —

most of the anchoring vessels carried passengers who had money to spend, out would come the boatmen in their boats and the sea-weary voyagers would be rowed to the shore. There they could buy fresh food and wine that was at least potable, and find an end to the never-ending pitching and rolling. They could have — even if briefly — a minimum of comfort.

These stops were also almost necessary, for as we learn from Fra Felix Fabbri and others journeys by sea in those days were very rugged.

The traveler slept in a general cabin underneath the rowers. This cabin had no portholes and for that matter little ventilation or light. There were no berths — not, at any rate, as we today understand the word berth. There was simply a designated space in the hold on which he threw down his mattress — that is if he had been foresighted enough to provide himself with one. If he wanted to eat and to drink — other than the sorry minimum of fare which the captain by law was required to provide — he brought his own provisions, and if he wanted his food cooked he bought or bribed himself a place in the galley. That was another reason why frequent puttings into port were welcomed even if they delayed the voyage. The traveler could replenish his larder if he needed to. After all, chickens in a crate — or ducks, or geese — had as hard a life as did the passenger, and not all taken aboard when the voyage began survived more than the first stages of the trip.

Not all of the human cargo survived either. Normal to a medieval voyage were death and burial at sea. Not even the rich man who had lost his wife nor the rich wife who had lost her husband could pay the captain enough to persuade him to bring the deceased back to shore and to a church burial.

Dante did survive, however, for, as you must already know, he was for a bookman more than usually resilient and hardy. But beyond that, his *cabotaggio* was, relatively speaking, an easy business. It was the trading voyages to North Africa and Egypt and Syria — for the West traded with the paynim even as he fought him — that really took a toll.

He survived to reach his destination. Two weeks or three weeks or even longer — we do not and we cannot know — and the îles d'Hyères had been rounded. Now the vessel went northwest. To starboard lay a white and jagged coast which was leaped against by dazzlingly amethyst seas which shattered into a tangled network of foam.

All at once there was an opening.

Through it they sailed, and into a wedge-shaped harbor that was sheltered from almost every direction and that needed this shelter. It was the Phoenicians' and the Greeks' Massalia and the Romans' Massilia. It was Dante's Marsilia. It was the Vieux Port of our Marseilles.

4

It is almost certain that Dante put into this almost the world's most ancient seaport, and it is reasonable to suppose that he stayed there for more than a few days; for Marseilles is another of the places he notes and dwells upon, or at least he notes an event involving Julius Caesar — in his mind the founder of the Roman Empire — which began there, and dwells upon a man who claimed it as his home.

The event first: it was one of Caesar's most brilliant and lightning-like campaigns — but it is characteristic of a great military leader to strike as a coiled snake does — against an unprepared and astonished foe. Briefly what happened is this. In 49 B.C. civil war broke out between Pompey and his erstwhile colleague, and not only Rome but every place ruled by the Romans had to choose sides. Marseilles chose the side of Pompey. In consequence, Caesar sent his ships against it. He destroyed the Marseillais fleet, which was a large one, and began a systematic investment of the city.

But even as he did this, tidings were brought to him:

"Forces loyal to Pompey and under his legates are marshaling in northeast Spain."

"They must be destroyed before they are organized!" he cried.

Leaving a substantial part of his army with Brutus, who would one day assassinate him, he took the remainder and, in a forced march of at least one hundred fifty miles, led them to the Pyrenees.

These he crossed and, at Ilerda (now Lérida) on the Segre River, he encountered the Pompeyans. They were caught napping, for they thought him half a province away. They were utterly routed.

Dante refers to this.

Purgatorio XVIII — where those who procrastinated in the doing of good cleanse themselves by shouting examples of devoted haste:

> Mary with no delay hied to the hills,
> And Caesar so as to subdue Lerida
> Struck at Marseilles and then hastened to Spain!

The man was Fulk, a native of Marseilles, in his youth a renowned troubadour and later bishop of Toulouse, but to us notorious as one of the most ruthless of the persecutors of the Albigensians in a crusade (1208–1229) of Christians against other Christians that led to deeds more cruel than almost any that have ever been recorded.

Yet Dante saw fit to place him in the heaven of Venus.

Paradiso IX:

> "The greatest vale into which the water flows,"
> He thus began, speaking these words to me,
> "From out that sea which doth encircle the world
> Betwixt its war-torn shores 'gainst the sun's course
> Extends such distance that the zenith is
> At that place where before was the horizon.
> And in that vale I dwelt upon the shore
> 'Twixt Ebro and the Magra, whose short course
> Divides Genoa's lands from Tuscany.
> With almost the same sunset and sunrise
> Lie La Bougie and the city from which I came,
> Which warmed its own harbor with its own blood.
> Folco those people called me unto whom
> My name was known. It is this heaven
> That bears my stamp, as I the stamp of it."

Fulk is speaking, and he thus describes and identifies himself with considerable accuracy. The greatest vale is the Mediterranean, and the waters of the Atlantic do flow into it rather than the reverse. Its shores were certainly war-torn. It was not very inaccurate to say that Marseilles was halfway between the Ebro and the Magra. Actually it was nearer the Magra but not much nearer. It was almost exactly opposite North African La Bougie, from which wax candles were shipped during the Middle Ages, which is why the French word for candle even today is *bougie*.

Fulk continues:

> "For no more hotly burned the daughter of Belus
> And thus did wrong both Sychaeus and Creusa
> Than I as long as it comported with my hair;
> Nor she of Rhodope who was deceived
> By Demophoön, nor yet Alcides
> When he clasped Iole against his heart.
> Yet we repent not here, instead rejoice."

According to the mythology that we accept and that Dante accepted, the daughter of Belus is Dido, who by loving Aeneas supposedly wronged both her husband and Aeneas's wife; she of Rhodope was the Thracian princess Phyllis, who killed herself when she was abandoned by her lover; and Alcides was Hercules, who because he loved Iole was sent the fatal poisoned Nessus-shirt by his wife Deianira. But it is generally agreed that they represented Adelais, the wife of Count Barral of Marseilles; Laura, his sister; and Eudoxia, daughter of the Byzantine emperor Manuel Comnenus and wife of Count William of Montpellier.

Yet we repent not here, instead rejoice.
Why?

> "Not for the fault, which comes not back to mind,
> But for the power which ordered and foresees.
> Here gaze we on the skill which doth adorn
> So great a work, and we discern the good
> Whereby the world below turns to the one above."

This was Fulk's argument — and Dante's. By entering the Church — even though he only did it when his lady died — he had turned from earthly love to heavenly love. Hence he deserved heaven.

Dante's concept, incidentally, was the general medieval concept.

"*Folquetz de Marselha,*" says a Provençal *vida*, or brief biography, "*fo filhs d'un mercadier de Genoa que ac nom sier Amfos. E can lo paire moric sil laisset molt ric d'aver.*"

"Fulk of Marseilles was the son of a Genoese merchant whose name was Messer Amfos. And when his father died, he left him very rich in worldly goods."

He was also talented and good-looking.

"He troubadoured it very well indeed," says the same *vida*, "and was most handsome of person."

These last two qualities were all that he needed. The wealth was merely an added attraction.

Thus equipped — indeed thus overequipped — the merchant's son had no trouble whatsoever in finding patrons. Richard Coeur de Lion was one of them. As, prior to his departure for the Holy Land, Richard campaigned in Aquitaine (for he was duke of Aquitaine as well as king of England), he gathered about him in Poitiers a company of the most notable minstrels of his time. This was not inappropriate for a man whose grandfather, William of Poitiers, was a famed if somewhat bawdy poet.

Fulk was one of them.

Fulk also was received and welcomed at the courts of Alfonso VIII (of Castile) at Burgos; of Alfonso II (of Barcelona) at Barcelona; of Count Raymond V Berenger (of Toulouse) at Nîmes; of Count William VIII at Montpellier; and of Count Barral.

It was at these courts that he met the three ladies he is said to have loved, and to all of them he wrote poems. To Adelais he wrote many.

"He begged her for her love, and wrote songs about her," says the *vida*.

It adds bluntly and rather disconcertingly:

"But neither *for gold* nor for these songs nor his troubadouring did she grant him anything good in the matter of love, for which reason he always complained bitterly of love in his songs."

Dante, incidentally, found one of the songs worthy of mention.

De Vulgari Eloquentia II, 6:

"This degree of construction" — i.e., composition "which has flavor and grace and also elevation" — "we call most excellent, and this is the one we are seeking. Of this alone are illustrious *canzoni* found to consist."

Then he gives some examples.

The second one is a poem by "Folquetus de Marsilia."

> *Tan m'abellis l'amoros pensamens* . . .

> So pleasing to me is the thought of love . . .

It is written to Fulk's sweet Adelais and evidently it rang in Dante's mind, for he also paid it the complement of imitation.

Once and once only, as far as we know, did Dante attempt to write in Provençal, which in his day was still the traditional language of poetry. This is in *Purgatorio* XXVI. Arnaut Daniel is the speaker. Guido Guinicelli has just pointed him out as surpassing all others of the day whether they wrote "verses of love or prose romances."

Dante asks Arnaut who he is. Arnaut replies:

> "*Tan m'abellis vostre cortes deman,*
> *Qu'ieu no me puesc ni voill a vos cobrire:*
> *Ieu sui Arnaut, que plor e vau contan.*
> *Consiros vei la pasada folor,*
> *E vei jausen lo joi qu'esper denan.*
> *Ara vos prec, per aquella valor*
> *Que vos guida al som de l'escalina,*
> *Sovenha vos a temps de ma dolor.*"

> "So pleasing to me is your courteous question,
> I could not nor I would not conceal who I am:
> I am Arnaut, who weep as I go singing.
> With grief I see the follies of my past,
> But see with joy the hoped-for day before me.
> Therefore I pray to you, and by the goodness
> That guides you to the summit of the stairway,
> That you recall my woe when the time comes."

But it is not the tour de force and the ingenuity of writing so effectively in another language that arrests our attention at this particular moment. It is that the opening three words were taken directly from Fulk.

But why did Dante select this man to celebrate, and, we may ask equally pertinently, why did he choose the event which we alluded to and discussed just before we came to the poet?

Why of all Caesar's many victories from Gaul to Pharsalus did he pick Ilerda to honor?

Why of all the many, many poets — why, even, of all the Provençal poets — did he choose Fulk?

He was certainly not the best — or even one of the best — of the troubadours.

Jaufre Rudel, Bertran de Born, Raimbaut de Vaquières, and Peire Vidal all wrote far finer poetry, as probably did Giraut de Bornelh and even Arnaut Daniel, though modern criticism does not award him anything like the high place that Dante did.

There seems to me to be but one reason and it applies with equal force both to the lightning-like march and to the man. They were chosen because both of them Dante knew well, because both of them were old tales to him. They became old tales to him at Marseilles. Walking along the waterfront of a city that even then was an active, bustling, polyglot, and talkative haven — a city that (see just above) he had described and placed with considerable geographic accuracy — he would have heard much about the whole Mediterranean but perhaps more about things closer at hand. Ilerda — a dramatic event in local history and one which connected it (important to Dante) with the great Julius. Fulk — their son who became a great bishop, who, although born to a merchant father, had once held his own as a poet, or appeared to hold his own, with others who almost all sprang from noble and sometimes even from royal families in castles from Limoges and Perigord to Navarre.

He heard about them, and they came alive for him. When he came to write the *Commedia*, they were still in his mind.

« 5 »

We have the same kind of evidence that Dante halted at another famous city in the south of France, that he at least paused *ad Arli, ove Rodano stagna* — at Arles under the blazing Midi sun, where the swift and icy Rhone River reaches its delta to become a slow and stagnant network of bayou-like channels between flat and low islands of marshland and pasture-land, the most important of which is now known as the Camargue.

I say "the same kind of evidence," for Dante, whose cosmography sometimes seems almost like an anthology of personal experiences, de-

scribes what is still today regarded as one of the "historical sites" of Arles
with the words of one who must have looked at it.

Inferno IX:

> And as at Arles, where the Rhone grows stagnant,
> Or as at Pola near the Quarnaro,
> Which bounds Italy and washes its confines,
> The graves rise up to make the place uneven,
> So here they did and upon every side,
> Except that they were far more doleful here.
> For here between the tombs were scattered flames
> By which each one was hotter made to glow
> Than iron can be made by any skill.

"The capital of the kingdom of Burgundy, which is called the kingdom
of Arles," wrote Gervase of Tilbury, who apparently visited it a century
before Dante, "is the city of Arles, endowed with very ancient privileges.
As he was commanded to by the apostles Peter and Paul, Trophimus [St.
Trophime] converted this city to Christianity, and not long thereafter he
solemnly consecrated a cemetery in the southern part of the city in
which the bodies of the orthodox were buried."

It was soon known as the Alyscamps — it still is — from Elysii Campi,
or Elysian Fields, and legends quickly gathered about it.

"To Trophimus appeared Christ, who had again put on mortal flesh to
hallow the saint's work with His blessing, and He promised to the
cemetery and those buried there that they should never suffer from the
torments of demons even though it can be read in the gospels that demons
dwell in sepulchers."

Local tradition also insisted that "the greater part" of Charlemagne's
heroes were interred there after the twelve peers were slain at Ronces-
valles. Perhaps because it was nearer to the scene of battle than the other
of "the two especially sacred cemeteries," which was near Bordeaux,
thither they were brought — "the dead and the wounded," the former in
wagons, the latter on litters — to be put to rest in the ground made holy
by one so close to Christ. It was also said locally that those slain in the
only slightly later (796) battle when another folk hero, William of
Orange, was crushed by the Saracens were entombed there.

It can be seen today. A long double line of almost black trees stretches
away from the entrance gate and between them is row after row of
marble sarcophagi. They are still white and gleaming — except where
moss grows on them — but most of the inscriptions on them are illegible
now and probably were even in Dante's time. But what makes them
remarkable, and made them remarkable to Dante, is that — probably

because if you dug in the damp soil the grave would fill with water — they are above the ground. Thus the dead were with you and beside you and around you.

The effect is one of somber and subdued gloom, but Dante's imagination lighted it with the flaming of heaven's wrath and used these Christian sepulchers as models for the fiery open-faced tombs of his sixth infernal circle, in which heretics and Epicureans — those who said that God was not — were punished.

There were other things that Dante would have seen at Arles.

The cathedral of St. Trophime with its handsome and lacy cloister, its exquisite west porch, and its striking main portal; it is considered the most beautiful Romanesque church in Provence. A mighty amphitheater said to seat twenty-five thousand persons; this would have reminded him of the amphitheater in Verona. The ruins of Constantine's palace. A Roman theater. The obelisk. The forum. The baths. An Arab fort. And what was left of the Roman walls and Roman aqueducts.

But in the onetime Arelate of his Julius Caesar — who had twelve warships built there to use in the campaign against Marseilles which has just been noted — he describes nothing more.

It is enough. We can feel sure he went there.

It also seems likely that he went there by sea. There was a road from Marseilles to Arles, but a sea voyage would have been shorter and more logical. From Marseilles to the Rhone mouth. Up the Rhone — a very short journey — to Arles.

« 6 »

But after Arles, Dante would have had no choice. He would have had to journey by land, following the well-traveled trade route up the Rhone Valley.

In that case he would have gone through Tarascon and near Le Baux, which looks down on the twisted and contorted rocks of the Val d'Enfer, another of the places which may have provided the poet with a model for some of his infernal scenery. Le Baux, perched on a pinnacle and fully as inaccessible as his San Leo in the Romagna, was still held by some of the feudal lords whose relatives, under the name of Balzo, played such a turbulent role in Neapolitan history. The traveler — including Dante — must have eyed the heights on which stood Le Baux with understandable trepidation. The first place of importance at which he would have halted would have been Avignon.

About Dante's passing through Avignon, or even his possible staying there for a while, it is permitted — indeed, it is even desirable — to speculate.

Pope when Dante halted there, and definitely in residence, was Bertrand de Got, archbishop of Bordeaux, who had been elected at Perugia on June 5, 1305; was notified of his election and had taken the name of Clement V in southern France; and had been crowned at Lyons on November 14 of the same year.

Dante twice savagely denounces him.

Paradiso XXVII — St. Peter is speaking:

> "It was not our intent that on the right hand
> Of our successors should be seated one part
> Of Christ's people and the other part on the left;
> Nor that the keys that were committed to me
> An emblem should become upon the banner
> Of those who fight against their fellow baptized;
> Nor yet that I should be the device on the seal
> For favors that are bartered and are false,
> For which I often blush as red as fire. . . .
> O God Who doth protect us, why sleepest Thou still?
> Of our blood, Gascons, yea, and men of Cahors,
> Prepare to drink. O fair beginning,
> To what a bad end thou art destined to fall!"

Clement, it should be pointed out, was a native of Gascony.

Paradiso XXX — Beatrice is speaking; she addresses the Church:

> "The blind cupidity that bewitches you
> Hath made you like unto a little babe
> That dies of hunger yet pushes away his wet nurse
> And at that time prefect of the divine court
> Shall be a man who openly and secretly
> Shall not with him [*the Emperor Henry VII, about whom
> more in the next chapter*] march along the same road.
> But not for long then shall God suffer him
> To hold his holy office. He shall be thrust down
> To that place where Simon Magus gets his reward,
> And he of Anagni [*Boniface VIII*] goes deeper still.

That Avignon later became corrupt we have unimpeachable testimony. One of the De Sades — the family into which Petrarch's Laura married — bears witness to this with almost Petrarchan eloquence.

"It is an impious Babylon," he writes, "a living hell, a sewer of vices, the disgust of the world. One finds there neither faith, nor charity, nor fear of God, nor truth, and nothing holy, and that although the residence of the sovereign pope ought to make it a sanctuary and a fortress of religion. Of all the cities I know it is the most putrid."

But that was not in 1309.

In 1309, there really was no papal court at Avignon. The pope himself had only come there in March of that year, and then only provisionally. There was no papal palace — the enormous fortress-palace that we now see was not even begun until two papacies later. It was begun by Benedict XII sometime after 1334.

Nor did Clement, who lived modestly in a Dominican convent when he was not in one of his castles in the neighboring hills, intend to stay there permanently.

This, to be sure, is not the opinion of Ptolemy of Lucca, his confessor.

As soon as Clement was elected pope, says Ptolemy, "he determined to take up his residence in the Comtat Venaissin" and not to proceed any further.

But this is flatly contradicted by the ambassador from King Jaime II of Aragon.

"The pope has advised the cardinals that he intends to stay here [i.e., in southern France]," this man reported in 1306, "only until March of next year. Then he will dismiss his court so that they can make the journey across the mountains, while he will go to Poitiers to meet the king of France so as to persuade him to undertake a crusade and also in order to arrange a peace between him and the king of England. After that, and without stopping anywhere else, the said lord pope will go to Italy."

To me, then, it seems obvious that Dante's withering contempt for Bernard de Got developed later. At that time, and for reasons that will shortly be made apparent, Dante had high hopes of him.

Because of these high hopes, he may, to be sure, have asked to be received by Clement, but even that does not seem likely.

It is far more likely that he came to Avignon and paused there merely as a traveler; that he rode in across the Pont de St. Bénézet (*sur le pont d'Avignon*, goes the song); that he perhaps said a traveler's prayer at the twelfth-century Romanesque cathedral of Notre Dame de Doms; that if he came on the right day he looked at the market where they sold (and in neighboring towns still do) poultry, eggs, game, truffles, olives, honey, and lavender; and that he slept at some Avignon inn, where, hopefully, he was regaled with some of the Côtes du Rhine wines which had been appreciated since Roman times for their red-velvet flavor and their aroma.

Then he was on his way again.

Through Lyons — the Lugdunum of the Romans, and even in their time a flourishing commercial city — where the Saône flows into the Geneva-fed Rhone and there was an important road junction.

Almost certainly through Mâcon, near which was the famous Cluniac monastery. Very clearly Dante saw this monastery, and he remembered it and its monks.

Inferno XXIII — in which the hill of the hypocrites is described:

> Below us we did find a besmeared people
> Who walked their round with slow and painful steps,
> Weeping and seeming weary and worn-out.
> They had long robes with cowls that did fall down
> Over their eyes and were shaped in the style
> That for the monks of Cluny fashioned is.

One more sight seen in his own interminable journey!

After that Champagne.

Champagne was well known to Italians. Although bordered with forests which in those days were enormously larger than they are at present, basically it was a wide, flat, fertile chalk plain which sloped toward a network of rivers that flowed toward the English Channel. It had only recently (when Philip the Fair married its heiress) become part of the French kingdom. It was then described as "rich" — meaning agriculturally rich — but its chief claim to fame was its cycle of Champagne fairs which were held in rotation at Troyes, Provins, Bar-sur-Aube, and Lagny-sur-Seine for the wholesale distribution of goods.

To these fairs, and despite Philip's recent harsh treatment of Italians, the Lombard bankers and wool buyers resorted in great numbers — among them, incidentally, Boccaccio's father Boccaccino, who did not leave France until 1313 or 1314 — and so if Dante had chosen to pause there, he would have been among both enemies and friends.

But he did not, for he had not reached his destination.

Even at Provins, it still lay fifty miles ahead of him.

He continued to jog on.

Then all at once, beyond green fields which sloped toward the even then venerable monstery of Saint-Germain-des Prés (Saint Germain of the Meadows), he could see buildings and spires. The gray mass of the formidable fortress of the Louvre built by Philip Augustus. Notre Dame Cathedral. The city walls.

If he had chosen to, he could have crossed one of the already many bridges into a city which, if its population was probably not yet as great as the population of Florence, was still a busy, noisy, dirty place with paved streets (at least in the central section) and with a growing number of abbeys, churches, hospitals, schools, palaces, merchants' homes, and warehouses.

But his concern was not with the Parigi in which Hugh Capet, founder of the French royalty, had been — according to a legend in which Dante firmly believed — a butcher's son. His concern was with its left-bank suburb which even then was called the Latin Quarter.

There twenty thousand students lived in an almost autonomous borough which, under the king, was subject only to the university authorities. Indeed, so independent were they — except as controlled by their own masters — that once when the provost's men, trying to put down the disorders of a town and gown riot, inadvertently killed some highborn Germans, King Philip Augustus jailed the provost and then issued an order which exempted scholars and their servants from his or any lay jurisdiction.

In this Latin Quarter was a collection of narrow alleys and dark dwellings called the Vicus Straminum.

(Dante translates this Vicus Straminum as Vico de li Strami, but it was not the Rue du Fourrage, Straw Street or Street of the Strawsellers, which with the adjacent little Rue du Dante runs between the Quai de Montebello and the Boulevard Saint-Germain. It was, rather, the Straw *District*, or the *District* of the Strawsellers, called this, as Benvenuto da Imola put it, "because here were sold straw, hay, rushes, etc." to cover the damp, cold, stone floors of the unheated lecture rooms on which the students sat.)

To this Vicus Straminum Dante hied, and in it or near it he took up his residence. He was too old to be a *bejaunus* (from *bec jaune*, or yellow beak), or freshman. But even at forty-four he intended to sit, notebook in hand, at the feet of the learned and imbibe just as much knowledge as he could.

« 7 »

There is some evidence that he learned a great deal. Zingarelli, to be sure, strongly disputes the contention of many that it was as he listened and pondered on Straw Street or nearby that "he made a change of spiritual direction" — that it was in Paris that he turned from natural philosophy to the metaphysics and theology that were so intrinsic to his great poem.

This may or may not have been so, but it is at least certain that during his days on the Left Bank he did either change or modify some of his ideas in the realm of what then passed for science.

I give a few examples.

In *Convivio* II, 14, Dante explains the spots upon the surface of the moon — "*Caino e le spine*" (Cain and his bundle of thorns), he calls them elsewhere — by stating that certain parts of the satellite are less dense than others and hence let the sun's rays pass through them instead of reflecting them.

But in *Paradiso* II, certainly written after his Paris days, he specifically repudiates this theory.

Beatrice is speaking:

> And she: "Now certainly thou wilt see sunk
> In error thy belief if thou wilt listen
> Unto the argument I bring against it."

Then she launches into a long, difficult, and extremely technical explanation, which, if it seems highly strange upon the lips of the lovely Florentine, does indeed reflect the most recent opinions of the Sorbonne intellectuals.

The highly theological opinions! But, nevertheless, the highly theological opinions based on observation!

> "If rarity and virtue alone produced this,
> One single virtue would be in all things,
> This more and less distributed and so forth."

But, in God's good grace, one single virtue is not possible.

Moreover, there is another proof that the various parts of the moon cannot have different densities.

> "If this were true, it would be evident
> In eclipses of the sun, since would show through
> The light as it does through other transparent matter."

Nor can it be because the light is reflected from different distances.

> "Take thou three mirrors. Then place two of them
> Equidistant from thee. The third one more remote
> Let met thine eyes between the other two.
> Then turn toward them, and have behind thy back
> A light placed which doth strike against all three
> And to thee doth come back, reflected by all.
> Although not of the same size will seem to thee
> The light that is the farthest off, thou'lt see
> That it must shine for thee with the same brilliance,"

It is, rather, that in the divine mind "diverse virtue produces a diverse alloy."

> "From this it comes that one light from another
> Seems different, not from dense and rare.
> This is the basic principle which produces
> In accordance with its excellence the dark and the light."

Another modified opinion. In *Convivio* II, 5, Dante listed the hierarchical order of the angels as they had been set down by Brunetto Latini. You will remember that he then stated that although once there had been debate about the matter, the truth was now finally and definitely known. In *Paradiso* XXVIII, he set the order down again, but this time he follows Dionysius the Areopagite, a favorite of the schoolmen.

A favorite of the schoolmen!

Here we have another and persuasive bit of evidence in regard to the influence of Paris upon Dante.

For Paris, at least since the days of Abelard, who, as Villon put it, for the love of Héloise "*fut chastré et puis moine*," although it was a focal point for students of canon law and theology, had always had its share of those who, while they never "disputed the authority of the Church and the truths defined by it as a matter of sacred tradition," also "insisted that to supplement revelation one could rightfully employ the reason with which man had been endowed by the Creator."

This was even true of Peter Lombard — "that Peter," says Dante (*Paradiso* X), "who, as the poor widow did, offered his treasure to the Holy Church." It was true of Albertus Magnus and St. Thomas Aquinas. It was probably true of that opinionated and often bombastic Englishman Roger Bacon, who may or may not have invented gunpowder and who was so high-heartedly caricatured by the Elizabethan playwright Robert Greene in his *Friar Bacon and Friar Bungay*. It was also certainly true of Siger of Brabant.

Siger is of especial interest. A Fleming by birth, he was said to be a follower of Averroës, and in 1284 he was summoned to Orvieto by Pope Martin IV. Presumably he was to answer charges of heresy. He was murdered there by a fanatic monk. Yet Dante places him in heaven at the left hand of Thomas Aquinas.

Paradiso X:

> This one from whom they look turns back to me,
> The light is of a spirit to whose grave
> Thoughts even his sudden death seemed slow in coming.
> It the eternal light of Siger is,

> Who, as he lectured in the Street of Strawsellers,
> Did syllogize upon unpopular truths.

Dante, we may safely assume, syllogized too — and, we are certain, with the same sturdy, independent thinking that had characterized the man from Flanders.

Says Boccaccio in his biography of the poet:

"Being in Paris, and there in a *de quodlibet* discussion which was held in the schools of theology supporting fourteen different kinds of thesis brought forward by various notable men, he without even a pause collected the arguments pro and con and recited them in the same order in which they were given. Then he analyzed them and replied to the arguments which were made against them. This was deemed to be almost a miracle by the bystanders."

He made a similar statement in his *De Genealogis Deorum Gentilium:*

"This notable Florentine poet betook himself to Paris, and in that city he very often entered the lecture halls to dispute against the responses he made and the positions he took. In addition to that he was most learned in matters poetic."

But even in the *Commedia* he alludes to the academic give and take of the Seine city.

Paradiso XXIV:

> Just as the bachelor prepares yet does not speak
> Until the master puts to him the question
> To hear his reasoning, not to settle it,
> So I prepared myself.

Dante, of course, was not a bachelor. Formally or informally, he had long since climbed past that first rung on the ladder of learning. But in Paris he must have seen more than one bachelor face his ultimate ordeal — he must have heard more than one bachelor examined; he must have watched more than one bachelor as he was forced to justify to his questioner — and with the most cogent and persuasive of logic — whatever positions he had taken and set forth.

But Dante did not limit his activities in Paris to the academic world. As he had done as a young man in Florence, he walked around and observed.

Here, too, some of what he observed he would use later.

The true story of Pierre de la Brosse, for example.

Purgatorio VI:

> I saw Count Orso, and the soul separated
> From its body out of spite and out of envy,

So it is said, and not for crime committed:
Pierre de la Brosse, I mean, and let her look to it
While she for this joins not the damned flock.

Pierre de la Brosse was the physician and the chamberlain of King Philip III. When the king's son by his first marriage was poisoned, his second wife, Mary of Brabant, was accused of having had this done, and one of her accusers was Pierre. Mary's answer was — or so it was commonly believed — to accuse him of an attempt on her chastity. When certain noblemen of the queen's faction added to this a charge of treasonable correspondence with Alfonso X of Castile, he was sentenced to be hanged by the common hangman.

Now, forty years later, many still swore to his innocence, and Dante was among them.

"While he was in Paris during the days of his exile," writes Benvenuto da Imola, "he diligently examined the truth as to these crimes, and he found Pierre to have been a righteous man. Therefore, he placed him in purgatory and restored to him his good name."

In Paris — also according to Benvenuto da Imola — he learned the story of the not otherwise identified Ciampolo, or Jean Paul, the barrator-minister of King Thibaut of Navarre.

(But some say the barrator was actually Geoffroi de Beaumont, Thibaut's seneschal.)

Ciampolo, if it was Ciampolo, was the son of a father who committed suicide.

"This unhappy man was Spaniard by race and from the kingdom of Navarre. His mother was noble but his father baseborn. When by lavish spending he had squandered all his wealth, he grew despondent and hanged himself. He had a son Ciampolo."

In Paris he also learned of the Hugh Capet legend referred to above.

And in Paris he learned the Parisian way of speaking. His ears were always attuned to catch shades of local dialect.

Alluminer, they said in Paris, instead of *miniare*. We use the French word today. We speak of a manuscript as being *illuminated*. But our word for a very small portrait is *miniature*.

Dante took note of this in *Purgatorio* XI.

They said *juger* instead of *giudicare*. In *Purgatorio* XX, when he speaks of the French kings, he uses the word *giuggia*.

Clearly Paris had more than a little influence on him. Clearly he liked Paris. Even though he must have felt both angry and impotent as he watched Philip the Fair ride haughtily through the streets, clearly he felt at home in Paris. Indeed, it is more than probable that he might have stayed in Paris for a long, if not indefinite, time — and with what effect upon his writings you can make your own judgment — if events had not crystallized into a happening which made study even in this learned and congenial city seem both futile and sterile; a happening that at least briefly appeared to be Europe-shaking and that would lead him into the third of those catastrophes that in the opinion of most were what made him the man and the author whom we now revere.

XX

Alto Arrigo

To understand what this was, and why and how it came to pass, we must go back a very long time — if we believe what was accepted in Dante's day and for a long time afterward, we must go back 2061 years.

On an island in the Tiber, twelve miles from the sea and on seven of the neighboring hills, there had been established two or three centuries before a handful of palisaded villages which drew their importance from the fact that nearby was a crossing for the road, or rather track, that carried salt to the interior. They were inhabited by the Latins and the Sabines, both rude people of the Italic branch of the iron-using Indo-Europeans, who had moved into Latium about 1000 B.C., when the volcanoes in the surrounding hills were scarcely extinct.

One of these villages — it was located on the present-day Palatine hill — was called Roma, or Ruma, and its collection of thatch-roofed houses may have been in existence as far back as 1000 B.C. But it was not until 753 or 754 B.C. — traditionally under the leadership of its cattle-herder king Romulus, who had begun its walls and then slain his brother Remus for leaping over them — that it assumed hegemony over the similar villages on the others of the seven hills. Roma was not content with this. Using the "surpassing gifts for political and military organization" which its people had possessed "from the time we first hear of them," it soon conquered or merged with the kindred tribesmen who occupied much of the plain of Latium. Then it began its march.

On the road there were setbacks, to be sure. For at least two centuries, for example, Rome was ruled by the wealthy and highly civilized Etruscans of central Italy. In 397 B.C. its army was defeated by the Senones from Gaul, who then occupied the greater part of the city. Only the

Capitoline held out. It was saved, so goes the story, by the cackling of its geese — and there are always plenty of them, not all of them fowls, in capitals. In 321 B.C. another Roman army was crushed by the mountaineer Samnites, and those who survived were forced into a humiliating surrender at the Caudine Forks. And during the Second Punic War (218–201 B.C.), the whole peninsula was overrun by Hannibal, and it was only because of the skillful but unpopular tactics of Fabius Cunctator (Fabius the Delayer) that Rome itself did not disappear.

But these were only setbacks, and by 509 B.C. — the Etruscans having been driven out and a republic established — the Romans had at least pushed south to occupy a roughly quadrangular section of the lands there, a section which extended southeastward to Praeneste (Palestrina) and along the seacoast almost as far as Antium (Anzio).

Two and a half centuries later — this was in 264 B.C., when the Punic Wars began — they ruled or controlled all of Italy south of a line drawn from just north of Ariminum (Rimini) and the Gulf of Spezia, and by the time the Second Punic War ended — 201 B.C. — they ruled the whole peninsula and had reached overseas to Sicily, Sardinia, and Corsica, to the Balearic Islands, to a long but largely narrow strip in Spain that included all of its eastern, southeastern, and southern coasts, and to Dalmatia, Macedonia, Greece, and Asia Minor. When Julius Caesar, whose great-nephew Octavius would become Augustus, the first Roman emperor, died in 44 B.C., the lands ruled by the descendants of the farmers and cattle herders (and, one fears, perhaps cattle rustlers) extended from the English Channel to the Caucasus and almost completely embraced the shores of both the Mediterranean and the Black Sea. Only Britain, trans-Rhine Germany, Dacia, and Mesopotamia remained to be added.

By A.D. 130, they were. Rome now dominated the whole Western world. *Urbs et orbis*, it called itself. The city and the globe. It was indeed. No empire like it had ever been before.

« *2* »

Much has been written about this *urbs et orbis* — this empire upon which the sun did indeed set, but not for many hours. The Pax Romana (Roman Peace) is legendary. It is, of course, exaggerated. At no time was there no military action whatsoever between Eboracum (York) in Britain and Palmyra in the Syrian desert. But never have so many people in so wide an area enjoyed such relative tranquility over so long a period. Living standards were indeed low compared to today's, but at no previous time were so many people at least sure of their next meal and a roof over their heads. The rich lived magnificently. Roman writers — and the Greeks on whom they modeled themselves — were read from Londinium to Babylon. Roman architecture left its monuments from England and France to North Africa and the Middle East. Finally, there was Roman law — an amalgamation of the ancient *ius civile* (law which applied to citizens) and *ius gentium* (law which applied to the others). This Roman law has properly been described as "among those achievements of the Western world" than which "none has a greater or a better merited permanence."

But Rome's greatest contribution to those who followed her was not any one of these but their sum total. It was the name and fame of Rome which represented this sum total. Because from the Tiber village, which in the beginning was not very different from the little villages which Julius Caesar found in Gaul and Iberia and in the fog-drenched cross-channel kingdom of the Catuvellauni, the Romans had moved out slowly and methodically into every reasonably adjacent land, bringing with them their own discipline and control and with it a climate in which good and orderly things could flourish, the name Rome came to signify rule and power. Rule and power, but above all legitimate rule and power.

And because the name Rome signified rule and power, it became worth fighting for. With words, when words sufficed. When they did not, with the sword.

« 3 »

It soon was worth fighting for.

Not much more than a century after it had reached its greatest extent, the Roman Empire which carried the Roman name took the first tentative steps which would lead to its ultimate fission. Docles, the humbly born Illyrian who became the Emperor Diocletian, did two apparently contradictory things. As emperor, he made himself *dominus,* or absolute master, relegating even the famous Roman senate to the status of a board of aldermen and transferring the capital to Nicomedia in Asia Minor. Then, and apparently for administrative reasons, he divided his newly assumed power with a second Augustus and with two Caesars, one Caesar under each Augustus.

Theoretically, the second Augustus — and the two Caesars — were subordinate to the first Augustus, but after Diocletian had retired (305) to his palace in Dalmatia, things did not work out that way. From York to the borders of Persia, Augustus fought Augustus, and Caesar fought Caesar. The seeds of a divided empire were thus sown.

They came to fruit in 395, when Theodosius I in his will formally partitioned his still reasonably vast realms between his two sons, giving Arcadius the East and Honorius the West. There was now an East Roman Empire and a West Roman Empire.

Later known as the Byzantine Empire, the East Roman Empire was the more fortunate. In one form or another, it lasted almost eleven hundred years. But the West Roman Empire — in a sense, it was the true Roman Empire — endured for less than a century. During that period, there were thirteen impotent emperors or pretended emperors, only four of whom died a natural death. The last of these ironically was named Romulus Augustulus. Like most of his immediate predecessors, he had been elevated to office by a German mercenary. In 476, this particular mercenary, Odoacer, a Visigoth, decided that he wanted the name as well as the power. He deposed Romulus, sent him to a comfortable villa near Naples, and proclaimed himself King of Italy.

Italy, please note, not Rome.

Thereafter, there was no Rome — as far as the legitimate West was concerned, no Roman Empire — and except for a few and very brief interludes, very little but chaos.

The Angles and the Saxons used their flat boats to cross into England. The Franks and the Burgundians poured into France. The Visigoths invaded Spain, and then crossed the Strait of Gibraltar. The Ostrogoths, the Vandals, and the Lombards (from Langobardi, "Along the Bard River," near Denmark; not from Longi Barbi, or "Long Beards") took over most of Italy. With them they brought ruin and disorder. Rome, for instance, became a small village again, and with its aqueducts cut and the drainage system destroyed, with its once fertile *campagna* a wasteland, its inhabitants both faced starvation and were racked with malaria. This was true throughout the empire, but especially in Italy.

But the disorders were even more devastating. The Germans — and most of the invaders were Germanic — were a tribal people whose loyalty was to the clan and to the chief, and this was a natural breeder of anarchy. Anarchy was bred. Where once there had been almost monolithic rule, there were now a dozen or a score or even a hundred kingdoms (many of them petty) and dukedoms (more than a few of them powerful), to say nothing of unnumbered marquisates, grafdoms, and baronies (some of the last little more than a brigand's hideout), each one fighting to extend its generally local power.

Law had vanished — or rather the universal and logical law which had once been in effect. True, there was Germanic law — but it was tribal law, and often if not always only tribal in its application. The Four Horsemen of the Apocalypse indeed rode hard — and in this newly barbarian Europe none harder than Pestilence and Famine. There was hardly a once pleasant land or a once well-governed city or town which could now have even the necessary minimum of bare tranquility without which survival was not possible except through the protection and intervention of some strong and ruthless leader, who empirically and usually for only a short time took things into his own doughty hands — and for doing this usually exacted more than a pound of flesh.

It was this state of affairs — the state of affairs which has just been described as pertaining in the West Roman Empire — which made an attempt to resurrect and preempt the power and the prestige of Rome's name and reputation not merely inevitable but desirable, and it was a chance of history that there was available (and willing and ready, if not yet in the forefront position it would later occupy) a reasonably well-disciplined and well-organized entity which was qualified to do this.

I refer to that segment of Christianity which is now known as the Roman Catholic Church, and which operates through its chosen supreme pontiff, known today and for a long time as the pope.

This Church and the papacy which speaks for it did not come into being full-blown. In the beginning it was an underground organization — figuratively and, when you think of the Catacombs, literally — nor did its head take any more exalted title than the simple bishop of Rome. Incidentally, he is still bishop of Rome today. Nor even when he had been named patriarch was his claim to the highest place in the Christian hierarchy incontestable. There were other patriarchs — at Alexandria, Antioch, and Jerusalem, and later there would be a patriarch in Constantinople.

But when Christianity was legally and formally recognized by Constantine the Great, and when shortly thereafter it became the official state religion, the Church came out into the open, and probably because this was available and had been found to work, it organized itself along the old territorial plan of the Roman Empire. The Roman *civitas* (the city plus its dependent territory) became the episcopal see (from *sedes*, or seat), where stood the cathedral (from *cathedra*, or bishop's chair) church of the bishop, from which he governed the see. As under Rome, the sees were combined into provinces, and these were under the jurisdiction of metropolitans, who were the bishops of the principal cities in each province.

The bishop of Rome was one of these metropolitans, and with the magic reputation of the onetime empire's capital to support him it is not surprising that he soon claimed wider and then universal supremacy.

Not only was he *successor Petri* but also of the Caesars.

But it was Peter who made him this.

This was tentatively stated at least as far back as during the papacy of

Stephen I (254–257, or even before Constantine). It was unequivocally proclaimed by Damasus I, who was pope from 366 to 384.

"The Holy Roman Church," cried this Spaniard who had learned to be a Roman, "is raised above all others, not by the decrees of councils but by the words of our Lord Himself. He said to the apostle, 'Thou art Peter, and upon this rock I will build my church.' "

He made it plain that by "raised above all others" he meant both spiritually and temporally.

To be sure, and as we will see, this was later, and more than once, modified.

Nor was it always enforced with equal vigor and with complete consistency.

Nevertheless, using the Petrine doctrine as expounded by Damasus, using the forged but useful Donation of Constantine, using the authentic Donation of Pepin as a basis, pope after pope began to claim temporal lordship as well as spiritual lordship, and gradually pope after pope began to extend this claim of temporal lordship until it included every land which Rome had ever ruled, and those too which Rome had not ruled but which now were Christian. Naturally, they could not enforce this claim in the East. But in the West – in Europe, that is; in almost entirely Roman Catholic Europe – it was something few could disregard.

« 5 »

But it was not only the Roman Catholic Church, acting through the agency of its pontiffs, that laid claim to the name and fame of Rome imperial and to being its residuary legatee. The very men who had toppled the mighty edifice of the Roman Empire in due course did so too.

To be sure, their first reaction was one of wonder and of awe. To destroy Rome they had to come to Rome, and when they came their Gothic imaginations were stirred by the grandeur of its marble and its monuments; by its baths and palaces and circuses; – by its temples and its forum and its massive walls – and by the power that these represented.

This – this awe and wonder – is another of the many things observed and set down by Dante.

Paradiso XXXI:

> If the barbarians, coming from that region
> Upon which Helice [*the Great Bear*] looks down each day
> As she doth circle with the son she loves [*the Little Bear*]
> Gazing on Rome and on her mighty works

Were struck dumb when they saw the Lateran
That rose above all other mortal things,
I, who from the human to the divine
And unto the eternal from time had come,
And from Florence to a people just and sane,
With what astonishment must I have been filled!

In point of fact, it is generally thought that in this passage the poet does not refer to the original barbarian invaders — "*illi de Norvegia et Germania,*" as Benvenuto da Imola calls them — but to the hordes from all over Europe that poured into Rome in the Jubilee year of 1300. That this is probably the case is borne out by the fact that Dante makes a specific reference to the Jubilee pilgrims in the same canto:

And just as he who perhaps from Croatia
Did come to look on our Verona,
For which his hunger is not ever sated,
Doth say within himself while it is shown:
"O my lord Jesus Christ, our true God,
Was this indeed the very way you looked?"

But the barbarians of the third, fourth, and fifth centuries could hardly have been different. They too were struck dumb. They too gazed in almost mute admiration.

Then the awe vanished and they began to make claims.

In the beginning — and in most cases for a long while afterwards — these claims were modest. The earliest of the invaders from the north came peacefully and by invitation. They were content to serve the Roman Empire — and take for their reward nothing more impressive than Roman rank and Roman pay. Stilicho, for example, was a Germanic Vandal, but he accepted the command of the Roman armies, allowed himself to be named consul, and assumed the rank of *patricius,* or nobleman. Odoacer, before he overthrew Romulus Augustulus, took the same title. And even Theodoric, who set up the first truly independent Germanic kingdom of the new Italy, was willing to pay a thin sort of homage to the Byzantine emperor Zeno, and to become a consul and *patricius* too.

But even as they were thus modestly contented, even as for the most part they used the Germanic *König* (he who can) instead of the Roman *rex; Herzog* (duke) instead of *dux;* and *Graf* (count) instead of *comes,* the name and significance of Rome survived — however deeply hidden — in their barbarian consciousness. The feeling persisted — and it grew stronger and stronger as they moved further from their tribal heritage — that the word Rome meant rule.

The feeling persisted, too, that there must once again be a Roman Empire. At first, perhaps, this feeling was merely literary, and in men's minds — or possibly the Byzantine Roman Empire was still enough. But as Byzantium became isolated from the West by a massive block of still-barbarian Slavs, there became an increasing feeling that one day the West Roman Empire — again, the *true* Roman Empire — must be restored. All that was needed was a man strong enough to demand that this be done and to enforce the demand. Such a one — but after an interregnum of three centuries — did indeed appear.

His name was Karl, and although he was born in France and was the son of the French king — his father was Pepin the Short, once mayor of the palace, who had deposed the last do-nothing Merovingian monarch and put on the crown himself — he was actually a German. He was one of the Franks, or Free Men. He spoke German or a variant of German. He was Germanic in appearance — tall, yellow-haired, and with a superb physique, although Alcuin, his Englishman court-historian, notes that in his old age he inclined toward stoutness, and that he had a curiously high-pitched voice that seemed out of place in so doughty a leader. We know him as Charlemagne, or Charles the Great.

But more important than his racial heritage or his appearance was his ability. His father had been no fool, and under different circumstances he might have accomplished all his son did. As it was, Pepin firmly secured France, and then found time to conquer Lombardy and drive out King Aistulf, who had been harassing Pope Stephen II. For this Stephen made him *patricius* — the old title again — while he in turn gave the pope all of the Italian peninsula south of a line from Ravenna to the west coast, thus creating the famous Papal States, which endured until 1870.

But now circumstances were right, and Karl was ready and eager. In a reign that would last forty-three years, he had already established an empire that ran from Denmark to and into Spain and to and into Italy, and that included Frisia, Saxony, Austrasia (north central France), Brittany, Aquitaine, Gascony, the Spanish marches, Septimania (Mediterranean France west of the Rhone), Provence, Lombardy, Alemannia, Thuringia, Bavaria and Carinthia. Tributary were the Slavic lands of the Wends, the Sorbs, and the Bohemians, as well as Pannonia (in which he had defeated and destroyed the Turkic Avars, who had lived there for two centuries) and Croatia.

(His only defeat or even setback in all this came about when his rear guard, withdrawing from Moslem Spain, was annihilated by Basque mountaineers. Out of this was born the *Song of Roland*.)

He now ruled wider lands than any had ruled in the West since Valentian. It was in fact a West Roman Empire.

But he wanted the name as well as the fact, and he took steps to get it.

In 800, when he was in Lombardy where he had put on the Lombard iron crown, word came to him that Pope Leo III, whose protector he now was, had been driven from the papal city by a bloody insurrection. Charlemagne marched there, routed the rioters, and then, after examining the charges against the pope, concluded that they were false and reinstated him.

This was on December 23, 800.

Two days later he was given his reward.

"On the festival of Christmas" — Gibbon's prose surrounds it with appropriate solemnity — "the last year of the eighth century, Charlemagne appeared in the church of St. Peter; and to gratify the vanity of Rome, he had exchanged the simple dress of his country for the habit of a patrician. After the celebration of the holy mysteries, Leo suddenly placed a precious crown on his head, and the dome resounded with the acclamation of the people, 'Long life and victory to Charles, the most pious Augustus, crowned by God the great and pacific emperor of the Romans!' "

Doubtless his Frank followers clashed their approval with their weapons as they had since the time of Tacitus.

The "head and the body" of the new emperor were then "consecrated by the royal unction" and, "after the example of the Caesars, he was saluted or adored by the pontiff." He on his part paid the first fruits "in rich offerings to the shrine of the apostles."

Thus and on that day — and not without prearrangement, one feels sure — a new Roman Empire, later to be called the Holy Roman Empire, came into being. It was a Christian Roman Empire and, unlike another *Reich* which would unhappily attempt to fill its place, with only a few interruptions it was literally to last for a thousand years, passing from the Franks to the Germans and finally to the Austria of the Hapsburgs, in whose hands it would remain until it was ended by Napoleon in 1806.

One of these interruptions occurred almost immediately and should be noted. Charlemagne did not pass along his abilities to his progeny, and although a son, a grandson, a great-grandson, and the illegitimate descendant of his brother were actually crowned, for all practical purposes the empire disappeared. But in 962, Otto of Franconia, another great ruler whose territories were only slightly smaller than those of Charlemagne, brought it back to health again. He understood that to be a Roman emperor you must go to Rome. He went to Rome, where Pope John XII crowned him in St. Peter's.

From then on — and for as long as it concerns Dante and therefore us — there were two powers in Europe, each of which claimed the Roman name and the Roman authority and which were always, or almost always, in contest with each other to make this claim good.

« 6 »

It was this contest which was perhaps the most notable political feature in Europe — in the Europe of the old West Roman Empire — during the later Middle Ages. To be sure its importance can be, and often has been, exaggerated — at any rate, its importance to the ordinary man.

To the furtive-eyed peasant, for example, who lived almost like a brute beast in his straw-roofed clay-and-wattle hovel beneath the castle wall! Clad in a rough garb of homespun or leather, wearing (if he was lucky) wooden clogs for shoes, eating black bread sometimes supplemented by eggs and cheese or by such of the humbler vegetables as cabbage, turnips, or beans, trying to break up the hard earth with a crude unimproved plow, he could hardly care whether the armies with or without banners which marched by his home did so in the name of Caesar or of Christ. The starvation which resulted from burned crops and trampled fields, or from grinding taxes usually collected in services or in an ever-increasing share of his bread that he baked in his master's ovens (and he paid for the privilege of doing this), of his wine, grain, and vegetables, and even of his miserable livestock — this starvation was the same in either case.

The city artisan need care little more — although he, being more sophisticated, could at least hope that his guildsman employers would choose — and it differed from city to city, and not on ideological grounds — the side from which he could negotiate the most advantage.

But for those whose aim was power itself — for those who played the fascinating, if frustrating, game of hegemony — it was another matter. These fought for real stakes, and to the bishop who supported papal claims and the baron who supported the emperor (but sometimes it was the other way; sometimes a lord supported the pope and a great churchman the emperor) it was a life and death matter.

It was necessary to win or face disaster — and in those days, disaster could be total.

Each side, therefore, made every effort it could, and used every weapon it possessed, to secure victory.

I will name some of them.

Propaganda was used — an effort was made by both sides to influence men's minds and that in a day when psychology, let along psychological warfare, had never been heard of.

"Render therefore unto Caesar the things which are Caesar's, and unto God the things that are God's."

These words which Christ said when the Pharisee asked him whether or not he should pay taxes were quoted and requoted by the imperialists.

Then they defined them. The things which are Caesar's, they argued, were temporal and mundane rule, and this God put into the hands of Caesar — and of the Caesars — directly and without any other intervention.

"Unto God the things which are God's," responded the Church party.

But all things were God's, and the Church, speaking through its head, the pope, was God's representative on earth.

All things — including things political, since, as pointed out by St. Augustine, political institutions only existed because of Adam's sin.

They too, therefore, were under the Church's control.

Armies and arms were used. Except when Boniface marched against the Colonna, there were few, if any, Roman pontiffs before Renaissance Pope Julius II who personally put on their armor and rode at the head of their men. But many a pope organized armies against the imperialists, gave some or even much attention to their campaigns and even to the details of their campaigns, and accepted the consequences of their successes and their failures. By the very nature of their office, the emperors were military leaders.

Finally, diplomacy and even intrigue were used. When a pope was in trouble at home he sent emissaries, usually with sacks full of Italian gold, northward to stir up trouble among the dukes and margraves of Germany. Conversely, when the emperor was in trouble in Germany, he worked on the cardinals, or upon some of them, to make trouble for the pope or even to depose him. Many an antipope owed his brief glory to the bribes and the persuasiveness of an heir to the Caesars, just as many a true pope owed his office to simony. After all, bribery was cheaper than war.

This contest lasted for a very long time. At the least, it lasted from the accession of Otto to, and almost through, the life of Dante. During it, there was no decisive, or at any rate permanent, winner. Instead, the fortunes swayed back and forth.

A strong emperor, like Henry the Black (Henry III, 1017–1056), for example, could make the papacy virtually an imperial appanage. This dark-haired distant descendant of Otto was chosen emperor and spent the first years of his reign — normal and necessary — in subduing Bohemia and securing the allegiance of Burgundy and Hungary. Then he turned his attention to Italy, where a series of disreputable and dissolute popes had culminated in the election of the twenty-year-old (or perhaps twelve-year-old) Benedict IX of the infamous Conti di Tusculo family. He deposed Benedict (twice, for the Tusculans and the city mob restored him to power) and later his successors, Sylvester III and Gregory VI. Then he secured the election of his personal and German chaplain, who took the title of Clement II.

Gratefully Clement crowned him in the Vatican, and also apparently conferred the right of selecting future Roman pontiffs upon the Roman emperor, who thus ruled both Church and state.

Yet only a few pontificates and, thirty years later, Gregory VII — Gregory the Great, the second Gregory the Great — completely reversed the situation. In punishment for an ill-conceived plan to depose him, Gregory aligned the princes of Germany against Henry's successor, Henry IV, and then commanded him to appear before him at Canossa, a castle in the domains of the Countess Matilda in the Tuscan Apennines. As the snow fell on the peaks and passes, he kept him waiting for three days. Then he allowed him to appear before him as a penitent — barefooted and clad in coarse wool.

"I have done everything possible," he wrote later, "to ensure that the Holy Church, the bride of Christ, our mistress and our mother, should take her rightful place and remain free, inviolate, and Catholic."

This indeed he had. He made certain first that the Church was worthy of the position he claimed for it. He attacked abuses, the most notable of these being simony and concupiscence or even matrimony. Then — and then only — in his *Dictatus Papae*, he inflexibly reasserted papal supremacy; removed from the German emperors — and other monarchs — the right of lay investiture; and pronounced without compromise the subordination of temporal to ecclesiastical authority. And if at the end he had been obliged to flee from Rome and to die at Salerno in the realm of Robert Guiscard, his clear logic had laid a legal basis for claims to papal supremacy which often would come close to fact.

Similarly — and less than a century later — another strong emperor, Barbarossa, or Redbeard (the "good Barbarossa," according to Dante, that Frederick I of Hohenstaufen who in the legend still sleeps in his cavern, wrapped in his tawny beard and waiting to arouse Germany), again at least temporarily brought the papacy to heel.

Frederick had been elected emperor on February 15, 1152, and about two years later Nicholas Breakspear, the only Englishman ever elevated to the papal throne, was chosen pope. He became Pope Adrian IV. As was not untypical of an Englishman — particularly an Englishman in another land — this Adrian was both tactless and stubborn, and in consequence of this, he shortly became embroiled with the inhabitants of the papal city itself and Rome was placed under the pope's interdict.

Riots broke out at this. At first these were merely the horse reacting to the unexpected lash — the normal rebelliousness of a volatile and willful city — but soon they had wider implications. A revolutionist was at hand, the religious ascetic Arnold of Brescia, and he incited revolution. Restore papal decency, was his cry, by throwing out the wicked foreign pope — and presumably by then giving Rome back to the Romans. The hurled cobblestones were followed by incendiary fires. These raged in the Leonine city — papal Rome — and even at the very portico of St. Peter's.

Adrian had only one person to whom he could turn. He called on Frederick, who, jeopardizing his interests in the north, crossed the Alps and then marched to the Tiber, where he took possession of Rome, subdued it, arranged for the surrender of Arnold, whom he then had burned at the stake, and finally, as a reward, was crowned with the imperial crown by the pope's own hand.

Thereafter, temporal authority was in the saddle again. To be sure, in deference to tradition Frederick did lead the pope's white mule by its golden bridle as they proceeded through the holy city, but that was his only gesture of homage and he saw to it that there would be no more. He even created an incident to make this certain. He arranged for his chancellor deliberately to mistranslate a papal letter so that it seemed to say "bestow a fief" instead of "give a benefit." This hurt the pride of the German princes and won them to his side. Then he set four of his lawyers to studying Justinian and, as good lawyers do, they found what they were looking for: the power of the emperor is absolute.

Thus armed, he convened a diet at Roncaglia, and there even the archbishop of Milan supported him.

"*Tua voluntas ius est*" — "Thy will is law" — he told the emperor.

Indeed, if Frederick had not foolishly and needlessly involved himself in a series of disputes with the rising Lombard cities which gave the pope some extremely effective allies, he might have put temporal supremacy on a reasonably enduring basis, and perhaps — instead of being forced into a crusade and being drowned while swimming in a small river in Asia Minor — have won the struggle once and for all.

Yet, again, despite this and despite the fact that Frederick was succeeded by his forceful and able son (who, however, died at the age of thirty-two), it was only eight years after Frederick's death that the papacy fell into the hands of a man who was so determined and skillful that his twenty-three-year tenure can rightly be called the high point of the medieval papacy.

I refer to Lotario dei Conti Segni of Anagni, who assumed his office as

Innocent III. Not everything done by this unusually well-educated young Roman aristocrat (he was only thirty-seven when he was elected) today elicits unqualified approval. To give two examples, it was Innocent who inspired or at least tolerated the indefensibly savage Albigensian Crusade, and it was also during his papacy, and without more than perfunctory disapproval, that another crusade, the Fourth Crusade, set sail for the Holy Land but instead took Zara and Constantinople.

But our subject is the papacy as the heir to the power and mission of Rome and not as a forwarder of the teachings of Christ, and Innocent certainly reasserted its position in this area.

Step by step, this *"fortis, stabilis, magnanimus et astutus"* prelate (thus he is described by his first biographer) rewon authority that had been lost to Barbarossa by his predecessors. In one instance, he went even further than any other pope had gone. At the small price of condemning the Magna Carta — small because it had no effect — he not only settled the investiture problem on terms favorable to the papacy, but forced or persuaded King John to rule England and Ireland as papal fiefs.

« 7 »

But after Frederick I and Innocent III, although the papal-imperial seesaw continued to go up and down, there were, during the remainder of the Middle Ages, only one really great emperor and one really great pope. Or, to put it in another way, there was only one pope and there was only one emperor who seriously, and to a degree successfully, tried to wield the scepter of the Caesars.

The pope was Boniface VIII, about whom much — indeed enough — has been said, unless to reemphasize that his contest was with a king and not a Caesar. The emperor was Sicilian-born Frederick II, who was delivered in a silken pavilion set up in Palermo so that any who wished could see that he was his mother's son.

Frederick, a grandson of Barbarossa and on the distaff side of the Norman adventurers who had conquered Sicily, was possibly the most enlightened man to hold the imperial office in his own or any other day. He was a scientist (his book on falcons is the earliest-known ornithology book based on observation ever to be written) and a patron of science; a poet (only five of his poems survive, but they are excellent) and a patron of poetry; a thinker; a philosopher; and a lover of the good things of this world.

But most of all, he was the implacable enemy of the papacy — a papacy which, oddly enough, Ghibelline for once instead of Guelph, had elevated him to the throne to replace Otto IV Welf, who had invaded its lands.

In many ways he was the most dangerous enemy that the medieval papacy ever had, and its history during his lifetime is inextricably involved with his ambitions and his deeds.

Ambitions, incidentally, which he almost always realized!

Dante adverts to him frequently — sometimes admiringly and sometimes otherwise.

He calls him "*il secondo Federico*" in *Inferno* X, where he places him among the damned for Epicureanism side by side with Cardinal Ottaviano degli Ubaldini who, proud of his politics, said: "If there is a soul, I have lost it a thousand times for the Ghibellines!" In *Inferno* XIII, where he rebukes him for believing in trumped-up stories about treacheries on the part of Piero delle Vigne, he refers to him as Federigo and also as Cesare and as Augusto. In *Inferno* XXIII he calls him Federigo. This is where he immortalized the story — now believed to be of doubtful truth — that Frederick punished traitors by wrapping them in leaden cloaks which he then had melted. He calls him Federigo in *Purgatorio* XVI, when he alludes to some of his struggles in Lombardy.

In *Convivio* IV, 3, he refers to him as Federigo di Soave — Frederick of Swabia.

"And be it known that Frederick of Swabia, the last emperor of the Romans — I say the last up to the present time, although Rudolf and Adolf and Albrecht have been elected since his death and that of his descendants — when asked what gentlehood was, replied that it was ancient wealth and gentle manners."

He calls him Federicus Cesar in *De Vulgari Eloquentia* I, 12.

"Those illustrious heroes Frederick and his fortunately born son Manfred!" he says glowingly when he comes to his observations upon Sicilian poetry.

These are the direct references, but there are indirect references too, as when, for example, in *Convivio* IV, 2, Dante speaks of "a certain one" who "held empire," and when, in *Convivio* IV, 10, he says "the emperor" — without stating specifically who the emperor was — "not only erred in the words of his definition" — of nobility — "but also in his way of defining it."

As, also, in his famous passage about Frederick's mother.

Paradiso III — this canto deals with the heaven of nuns who have unwillingly broken their vows, and Piccarda is speaking:

> "And this the other splendor shown to thee
> On my right hand and who enkindled is
> With the illumination of our sphere

Knows all I say of me applies to her.
She was a sister and thus too was taken,
And from her brow the sweet shade of the wimple.
But even after she was returned to the world,
Against her will and against decency,
She never surrendered the veil in her heart.
This is the light and spirit of the great Constance,
Who unto the second gale from Swabia
Did bear the third and the last potentate."

Here is the story as it was widely believed at the time — among others, apparently, by Dante.

Barbarossa, hard pressed in the north was eager to extend his dominions in the south when he was made aware that the pope then regnant, Clement III, for political reasons was prepared to recognize the claims made for Constance, sister of King William, as heiress apparent to Apulia and Sicily. Here was an opportunity. Constance was a nun and more than fifty while his son Henry, recently made king of the Romans, was only twenty-eight, but what difference did that make when you considered the stakes? A nun could be absolved of her vows and Henry could put up with an old or aging wife for dynastic reasons.

She was, and he did.

"The archbishop of Palermo," says Villani, "caused her secretly to leave Sicily and come to Rome, and the Church gave her as wife to Henry, from which marriage, a little while afterwards, the Emperor Frederick II was born. And," he adds, speaking as a Florentine and a Guelph, "it was in accord with the divine will and judgment that such a wicked heir should be the result since he was born of a holy nun who was more than fifty-two years old, when it is almost impossible for a woman to bear a child — so that he was born in a contradiction to two sets of laws: the spiritual laws and the laws of nature."

But after Frederick had died — at Firenzuola in Apulia; he never went to Florence since his astrologers told him he would die there — the empire, at least in its Roman aspects, fell apart.

Indeed, for twenty-three years there was no Roman emperor at all, nor, for that matter, a king of the Romans nor even a real king of Germany, although two claimants — or pretenders, if you prefer — Alfonso the Wise (but vacillating) of Castile and Richard of Cornwall — did succeed in getting someone to elect them and were duly crowned on April 1 and April 17, 1257, respectively.

And when finally, in 1273 — and at the urging of Pope Gregory X —

an emperor was legitimately chosen, it was that Rudolf of Hapsburg whose first concern was being duke of Austria and who never even came to Italy. Nor did Adolf, who succeeded him. And when Albrecht — who with the aid of the king of England "marched against him [Adolf] and defeated him and left him on the field of battle" — came to the throne, he was indeed Alberto Tedesco — German Albrecht. He made a brave effort to take over Holland and Zeeland as imperial fiefs; sought to add Thuringia and Meissen to his domains; and, invading Bohemia, whose throne was vacant, turned "the kingdom of Prague" into such a "desert" (*Paradiso* XIX) that Dante felt it necessary to rebuke him for it. But the "garden of the empire" — Italy with Rome — never knew his footsteps nor did it feel his hand.

« *8* »

The universal papacy fared little better. Between Innocent III (died in 1216) and Boniface (elected in 1294), there were sixteen popes and few of them left any really notable mark on history. Dante only specifically mentions five of them: Honorius II for having (*Paradiso* IX) "with second crown encircled the chief shepherd of the poor brothers" — i.e., confirmed the Franciscan order; Innocent IV (*Epistola* VIII), but for his gifts as a canon lawyer not as a pope; John XXI— "Peter the Spaniard, who doth shine below in his twelve books" (*Paradiso* XII), books, incidentally, which may well have been written when he was a practicing physician and before his ordination; Nicholas III, buried head down in the hell of the simoniacs (*Inferno* XIX) and with four simoniac popes below him who are thought to have been Innocent IV, Alexander IV, Urban IV, and Clement IV; and finally (*Purgatorio* XXIV) Martin IV with his already noted propensity for eels cooked in white wine.

This does not mean that none of the sixteen had any ability. Gregory IX was a hardheaded old man whose zeal for the Church was unlimited and who used this zeal to contain even if he could not destroy Frederick II. Innocent IV was a renowned legalist and an able administrator, and he too kept the *stupor mundi* (Frederick) from complete triumph. And if Nicholas III had applied his talents to the cause of advancing the papacy with the same skill that he did toward a nepotism that was not to be equalled until the sixteenth century, he likewise would have been a great pontiff.

But not even a great pontiff was now enough, for no longer could pope contend with emperor as one of two paramount powers. He had to call on outside help, and from an entity that itself would soon own no superior. Even to fight such relatively weak antagonists as Frederick's sons Conrad and Manfred, Pope Urban IV had to call on Charles of Anjou and on France — and thus change not merely the Italian but the total picture. For although they did not know it — but we do — the universal empire after Frederick thus became an anachronism.

The words still sounded in papal bulls — like those of Boniface — or in imperial rescripts, but when you came to it, they were nothing but words. The two powers were now replaced by a multitude: England under Edward I and France under Philip the Fair were merely the most powerful. From Spain to Scandinavia, the age of nationalities could now begin. The claims of their two predecessors were reduced to theory — something for the canon lawyers and the civil lawyers to mull over, and little more.

« 9 »

Yet even a theory has a surprising vitality, especially when it is based on time-honored ideas, and it was so with the theories of papal Rome and of Rome imperial. Even as pope and emperor moved north of the Alps, the one to become captive, the other head of a German nation, the old idea of Rome as the focal point of God-decreed authority did not disappear. Like the snake, even when trampled on it would not die until sunset, and it was still afternoon. And as it seemed in its death throes an unexpected effort was made to revive it. And this time not individually but collectively. Unbelievably, a pope and an emperor who should have been antagonists at least for a brief while joined forces in a common and a sacred cause. The nations rejoiced as they hoped for the restoration of Rome to the world and the world to Rome!

This time the pope was that Bertrand de Got, onetime bishop of Bordeaux, who had taken the title of Clement V and who was living in Avignon in the modest and, in his own mind, temporary quarters we have already noted.

The emperor was the forty-year-old Henry of Luxemburg, who — according to Dante, who was of two minds about the matter — came to Italy either too late or too soon.

Purgatorio VII — Dante is speaking of Rudolf, but is looking ahead to Henry:

> "He who the highest sits and has the look
> Of having neglected what he should have done
> Is Rudolf emperor — he who might have
> Healed the wounds that Italy have slain
> *So that too late 't is for another to restore her.*"

Paradiso XXX — Beatrice is describing those in "the yellow of the sempiternal rose" in heaven:

> "And on that throne to which thine eyes are drawn
> By that crown which is placed already over it,
> Before thyself shall supper at these nuptials
> Shall rest the soul, below an emperor,
> Of high Harry [*alto Arrigo*], who to set Italy straight
> Did come there, *and before the time was ripe*."

As the saying goes, you pay your money and you get your choice. But whether Henry came late or early — and whether he could have accomplished what he sought to do at any time — come the Luxemburger did. And since this (as has already been suggested) had an incalculable effect on Dante's thinking and his writing and his doing, it is a story that must be told.

« 10 »

It began in 1304.

As we have already been told, Benedict XI, perhaps poisoned, died in Perugia on July 27 of that year; whereupon, says Villani, "there arose a schism and a great discord among the cardinals in the matter of electing a pope, and by reason of their differences they were divided into two almost equal parties."

For all practical purposes, these were the two parties which had contended with each other at the time of the election of Boniface VIII. They were now revived.

"The heads of one" — again Villani — "were Messer Matteo Rossi of the Orsini and Messer Francesco Guatani [Gaetani], who was the nephew of Pope Boniface."

In other words, committed strongly, as they must be after the outrage at Anagni, to an anti-French policy.

"The leaders of the other were Cardinal Napoleone, of the Orsini del Monte" — a branch of the Orsini who had not joined the party of Pope Boniface — "and the cardinal da Prato. These men hoped to restore their kin, the Colonna, to their former high position. Hence they were friends of the king of France, and also" — but here the connection is not apparent — "inclined toward the Ghibelline side."

Began an impasse which lasted for ten months.

The regulations originally promulgated by Gregory X but rescinded three papacies later had been renewed by Boniface and were theoretically in effect. If the conclave made no choice within three days after it had been convened, the cardinals were reduced to one dish for their midday and one for their evening meal. Eight days more and they were given only bread, wine, and water.

But despite these stringent provisions — which probably, however, were not strictly enforced — and despite the clamor of the Perugians, who, when they had nothing better to do, demonstrated noisily outside the locked palace, no candidate received the necessary votes.

Then one day the cardinal da Prato (the same Niccolò da Prato who, as would-be peacemaker between the Blacks and the Whites, had received the Dante letter we examined earlier) *happened* — or was it prearranged? — to find himself with Cardinal Gaetani in a place where they could talk privately.

"Messer Guatani," he said quietly, "we are doing the Church great harm by this matter of not choosing a pope."

"It is not of my making," said Gaetani.

"Granted," replied Cardinal Niccolò.

Then:

"But if I could find a good and honorable way to end it, would you accept it?"

"If it was good and honorable. If it did not do wrong to my friends — if it did not infringe any of our interests and rights."

"Here it is," said Cardinal Niccolò, "and you can judge it. Let each faction pick the pope — or rather both factions in a way that both have something to say in it."

"How?" Cardinal Gaetani asked.

"Let one faction, either yours or mine, choose three men from beyond the Alps" — i.e., not Italians — "suitable for the papacy. Let them choose whomsoever they please. And then, within forty days, let the other party choose any one of the three they please and make him pope."

Cardinal Gaetani was too shrewd to show his pleasure.

"I will agree if you let my party be the one to choose the three men."

For he could certainly find three men who would suit his purposes.

"I will, and I do."

"Thereupon," says Villani, "the party of Messer Francesco Guatani selected three archbishops, made and created by Pope Boniface, which were great friends of his and enemies of the king of France."

One of them was the archbishop of Bordeaux. Villani — and Dino Compagni — both call him Ramondo di Gotto. Actually, he was Bertrand de Got.

But Niccolò da Prato had to conceal a smile too, and his was the less likely of the two to be wiped off by subsequent events, for it was based on human — and Bertrand de Got's — nature.

Indeed, as he saw it, time was his only enemy. But if his only enemy, it was a dangerous one, for he had only forty days at his disposal, and his business was not right at hand.

He wasted none of them — and he wasted none of their hours or even minutes. Hastily he convened his colleagues and friends, told them what he had arranged, and persuaded them to confirm it by seal and signature.

Then couriers, provided by his friends the bankers and merchants (but provided so secretly that the Gaetani knew nothing about it), were on the road.

They reached Paris in eleven days and were ushered to King Philip's presence.

"We are from Cardinal Niccolò da Prato," they told him. "He has a candidate and can elect him pope."

"Who?" the king asked.

"Bertrand de Got. He has been your foe. That you know, and Cardinal Niccolò knows too. But this Bertrand longs for honor and for lordship, and he is a Gascon and such are by nature covetous. You can make him your friend. Cardinal Niccolò urges you to do so."

With gold and with a show of flattery.

And also, King Philip must have thought realistically, by assuming a firm and self-confident manner. After all, Bertrand de Got had not yet been irrevocably chosen.

"I rejoice greatly," he told the couriers, "and will do all I can to further and to follow Messer Niccolò's suggestions."

Then he sent his own messengers — to Bertrand.

"I urge and invite you to come and meet with me. I have urgent matters — and matters that will be to your benefit — to discuss with you."

He named a place. The monastery and fortified small town of Saint-Jean-d'Angély not far from Rochefort on the little Boutonne River and hidden by a pine forest. This would be convenient for the archbishop since it was just north of his Gironde, and it was also far enough from Paris to be safe from curious eyes and ears.

He set a time.

"Within the next six days."

The king came "with a small company" as did the archbishop, "and after they had heard Mass together and sworn mutual faith upon the altar" Philip "spoke to him good words" and told him what he had come for.

"Monsieur Archbishop," he said, "I have received messengers from

Perugia and have in my hand the power, if I will, to make you pope. If I will! It is for that reason I have come to you. For I will use those powers, I will make you pope, if you but grant six favors."

"Name them," said the archbishop.

"First, that you will reconcile me to the Church and have me pardoned for the sin I committed in the capture of Pope Boniface."

That was no problem — a pardon was but words.

"Second, that you will recommunicate me and all of my followers."

That was no problem either.

"Third, that you will grant me all the tithes of the Church for five years to pay the expenses of my wars in Flanders."

That came harder. Tithes were what the Church lived on; and on the personal side, it has already been noted, Bertrand de Got was covetous. But with the papacy in his hands, what was lost in France could be recovered elsewhere — and anyway in due course he could perhaps abrogate the agreement.

"Fourth, that you will promise to annul and destroy the memory of Pope Boniface."

Pope Boniface? Who had made him an archbishop and started him on his dizzy way up the long ladder whose summit he now neared? But he could agree to that too, and then perhaps later find a way out of it.

"Fifth, that you will restore the honors of the cardinalcy to Messers Jacopo and Piero della Colonna, and will restore them to their estate, and that when you restore them, you will make certain other of my friends cardinals too."

"And sixth?"

"The sixth favor and promise I will not tell you until both place and time are fit, for it is great and must be kept secret."

"My lord," cried Bertrand de Got, his cup full, "my lord, I now know that you love me more than any other man and that you wish to return good for evil! You have only to command and I will obey you!"

Then, says Villani, "the archbishop promised everything [that the king had asked for] on oath, and he swore to this upon the body of Christ. Besides that he gave the king his brother and two nephews as hostages. The king on his part swore to him and promised that he should be elected pope."

He was.

From Perugia to Paris to Saint-Jean-d'Angély and back to Perugia again — all this had taken only thirty-five days. There were five days of the forty still left.

They were not needed.

No sooner had word come to Cardinal Niccolò that Philip and Bertrand de Got had reached an understanding than he summoned the cardinals of the opposing faction and told them that he was ready to carry out the agreement he had made with Cardinal Gaetani.

"I will nominate one of the three men you selected, and I do nominate the Archbishop of Bordeaux."

There was not a dissenter.

"*Te deus laudamus!*" cried both the Boniface men and the Colonna faction, as back across the Alps went emissaries — this time public emissaries from the conclave — to announce to the French prelate that on June 5, 1305, he had been named high pontiff.

"I take the name of Clement V," he told them.

This might have been taken as an omen, for the last Clement — Clement IV — had been a Frenchman, Guy Foulquois of Saint-Gilles on the Rhone, and he had shown himself so assiduous a supporter of French causes that to please Charles of Anjou he caused Manfred to be disinterred and left exposed on the banks of the Verde River.

But it was not — and especially it was not by the Boniface party, who knew nothing of "the fine and subtle deceit which took place" and saw only a supposed friend in high office.

It was only when Philip bluntly ordered Clement to be crowned at Lyons rather than at Rome — and he obeyed — that they realized how badly they had been tricked.

Then their cries rang out to high heaven.

"God has punished us for our iniquities and sins."

God evidently intended to punish Clement too, for instead of a jubilee his coronation was a disaster.

As he rode through the streets of the French city — and knew that neither St. Peter's the building nor St. Peter the man was near him — a wall crowded with spectators crashed to the ground. Clement was thrown from his horse and the tiara toppled from his head. Charles of Valois — to no Florentine White's dismay — was injured by the falling rubble. Injured too — and they later died of their injuries — were the duke of Brittany; Gaillard de Got, the pope's hostage brother; and Cardinal Matteo Rossi of the outwitted Orsini, who had actually placed the crown upon the papal head. And a few days later, during some sword play following a banquet given in honor of Clement's first pontifical mass, another brother was fatally stabbed.

Small wonder that "the lawless shepherd who comes from the west" (*Inferno* XIX) often withdrew for months at a time and was accessible only to his immediate familiars. It was not merely that he was gnawed at by a painful illness which we now believe to have been cancer of the stomach. It was because he brooded, believing — and why not, since success brought only anguish and frustration? — that he lay under an evil star.

« 11 »

The second protagonist of the drama — Henry of Luxemburg — came to his office under different circumstances, but as a result of similar deviousness. This time the deviousness was on the part of Clement, who by now had learned his lesson.

It is commonly believed and frequently stated that once he was elected the Gascon pontiff did what he had agreed to do and what was expected of him, and made more than one effort to see to it that the papacy remained the tool of France. To a degree, this is true. To be sure, he did resist — and with some success — all efforts to make him condemn Pope Boniface. But that demand was unduly extreme.

But he complied with all his other agreements almost *in toto*, and he made up for his recalcitrance in the matter of Boniface by condoning if not abetting an even greater crime.

Philip had long cast hostile eyes upon the Knights Templars. Founded originally to protect pilgrims in the Holy Land and taking their name from the Temple of Solomon in Jerusalem, they had, it was alleged, become corrupt and degenerate, the principle viciousnesses charged to them being heresy in the form of black magic and devil worship, fornication, lewd living, and sodomy. But their true crime was that they were inordinately wealthy and that their wealth, which was untouchable and untaxable, was put out very successfully at usury and hence had become greater and greater.

Philip coveted this wealth, and on a witch's-brew night in 1307 he performed one of the most remarkable surprise actions ever taken. Between dawn and daylight he caused every Templar in the whole land to be seized and all their churches and mansions and possessions sequestrated. And this was a military order made up of fighting men! Torture did the rest. Although most held out even when burned slowly inch by inch, enough confessed to suit the king's purposes. He turned them over to the Church as heretics. There is no record that Clement attempted to hold him back. Indeed, he authorized the Inquisition to deal with them, and ultimately he abolished the Temple to have them executed as requested to.

But if he did this, and if he acceded to Philip's many other demands, we have good reason to believe that he did so reluctantly and only waited for a chance to free himself from royal toils.

This chance — or what he thought was this chance — soon came. Albrecht Hapsburg of Austria, that king of Germany who still techni-

cally claimed to be Roman emperor, went out a-riding on the blithe and
merry morning of May 1 in 1308. With him was his nephew John of
Austria with the faint wisp of a straw-colored moustache on his upper lip
and a rudimentary Hapsburg jaw. They were near Brugg in Switzerland,
"under the foot of the very crag from which the Hapsburg family had
sprung." Birds caroled, and the not quite Alpine meadows were multi-
colored with crocus or whitely strewn with narcissi whose coronas had a
crisped red edge. To the south, the snow-covered peaks of the Alps were
like a whitecapped sea. Hearts were high, including Albert's.

But not that of nephew John.

For some reason — possibly because his legitimacy was challenged, but
perhaps just because he expected too much — John's rights, as he saw
them, were not recognized, or so he thought.

"My uncle," he said, as the horses cantered side by side, "touching that
you acknowledge my heritage and rightful claims."

"You have no rightful claims."

"I have no claims? Am I a bastard?"

"Your words. I did not say so."

"Then have this, my legitimate uncle!"

A blade flashed and a young man galloped into the distance.

Albrecht fell to the ground, and another steed with an ornate but
empty saddle trotted homeward somewhat more slowly, and bore tidings
of what had happened to his retainers.

"The king of Germany — or, if you will, the Holy Roman emperor —
has been slain!"

There was a shocked silence, but then, and all too soon, other steeds
rode off — and were not slow — in almost every direction.

Their saddles were not empty, but carried those who were eager to
advance themselves by being the first ones to bring useful news.

"The emperor is dead. There is an imperial vacancy."

To England.

To the cities of Italy.

To the prince-electors and prince-bishops of Germany.

To Avignon.

To Paris.

Here, somewhat abridged, is Villani's account of what happened in the
last city:

"When the king of France heard of the said vacancy, he thought to
himself that by reason of the sixth promise he had exacted from the pope,
a purpose he had long had could now be carried out without difficulty,
and, with Messer Charles of Valois present, he convened his secret
council and told them what it was. It was that the Church of Rome

should elect Messer Charles king of the Romans, and that this could now come to pass since the throne was vacant. Then he revealed the secret agreement that he had made with the pope" — namely, that Clement would grant him one final wish which he would reveal later — "and asked them for their advice.

"They all encouraged him, and said that to bring this about he should use all the power of the crown and his realm. It was fitting, they said, to restore the honor and dignity of the empire to France, since in the days of old it had pertained for a long time to their forefathers, namely to Charlemagne and his successors.

"Now when the king and Messer Charles heard this, they both rejoiced greatly, and they decided that they would go to Avignon at once with a great force of barons and knights. They would pretend that they came on the matter of pressing their petition against the memory of Pope Boniface, but when they came to the court, they would demand of the pope that he now keep his sixth and last promise, and would tell him that this was the election and confirmation of Messer Charles as emperor."

It was an ingenious idea, and one very characteristic of Philip. Confronted with this show of force, neither the cardinals nor the pope himself would dare resist him, and with the empire as well as the papacy thus in his pocket — for on the basis of his Valois cousin's past career, he assumed that he would be easy to deal with and control — his France would again be the greatest power in the West.

Ingenious, but it did not come to pass.

For Bertrand de Got was now Clement V. He *had* the papacy. He did not have to bargain for it.

Nor was he unaware of Philip's designs.

"As it pleased God Who did not wish that the Church should be wholly subject to the king of France, the preparations of this king were revealed to the pope by a member of the king's own council."

The king's knights and barons, he was told, have been ordered to provide themselves with arms and horses, and in Provence alone an array of six thousand have been told to muster.

What should he do about it?

For the pope, then as now, had no divisions.

He got an answer — from an unexpected quarter.

"Holy Father," said Niccolò da Prato, "there is only one thing that you can do. Before the king comes to your presence — and with demands that you cannot refuse — you must carefully and secretly persuade the electors to proceed with their business. You must persuade them to elect an emperor forthwith. He must have been chosen before Philip has reached Avignon."

"Whom should we propose to them?" asked Clement.

"I hear," replied the cardinal, "that the count of Luxemburg is the best man in Germany, and the most loyal and bold, and the best Catholic too. I have no doubt that if with your help he comes to this dignity he will be faithful and obedient to you and to the Holy Church, and that he will do great things for both."

The count of Luxemburg? "Our dear son Henry," as he would shortly call him?

No suggestion could have been more palatable to Clement.

(It was so palatable, in fact, that he did not even pause to wonder, as we must, why Niccolò had abandoned his pro-French position.)

Henry was well known to him, as too was his brother Baldwin, whom he had recently appointed bishop-elector of Trier. They were among the few princes — other than sycophants of Philip — who had troubled to attend his coronation.

As an emperor should be, he was personable and handsome, with blond hair and a clear complexion, and his incumbent effigy by Tino di Camaino, who saw him while he lived — it is now in the cathedral of Pisa — shows him to have been a calm-faced, clean-shaven man, with high cheekbones, a broad forehead, and just a touch of sadness in his demeanor. He spoke French, but it was Luxemburg French and not the French of Paris.

"He was a wise man," wrote Dino Compagni, "just and famous, of great probity, brave in arms and of a noble race, a man of great ability and of well-tempered character. He was of middle height and well-proportioned figure, but he had a slight squint."

This was because he was nearsighted, it is said.

He did have — or perhaps this came later — the reputation of being a dreamer rather than a doer. A knight-errant rather than hard and practical. But this — in Clement's view — was no disadvantage.

Clement pondered all this.

"How can I bring such an election about?" he then asked.

How, in other words, could he communicate with the electors in such official style that they would know that the message really came from him and yet keep it secret from the cardinals, most of whom were pro-French?

Easy, said Niccolò da Prato.

"Write letters to Henry and to the electors under a small and secret seal, and at the same time I will write them and tell them in greater detail what you propose that they shall do. My letters I will send privately by my servants."

This was done.

"And as it was God's will," writes Villani, "when the messengers came to Germany and presented these letters it took only eight days for the electors to assemble at Middelburg, and there, without a dissenting vote, they elected as king of the Romans Henry, count of Luxemburg.

"This accomplished, the election was straightway made known in France and at the papal court, and the king of France, not yet knowing the manner thereof, and still making his preparations to go to Avignon, nevertheless now held himself deceived and never afterwards was the pope's friend."

« *12* »

Obviously Clement's reaction was somewhat different, nor was the exuberance of his mood other than heightened by Henry's first actions and his first pronouncements.

The imperial election took place on November 27, 1308, and before the first day of the next year he was in Aachen (Aquisgranum to the Italians; Aix-la-Chapelle). There on Epiphany — January 6, 1309 — and in the presence of the duke of Brabant, the count of Hainaut, and "all the barons and prelates of Germany," he was crowned with his first crown. The coronation took place in the ancient cathedral whose first stones had been laid by Charlemagne. This was traditional, but another bitter draught for Philip.

Then — and not too long thereafter — Henry sent a solemn embassy to Avignon, humbly to beg the pope to consecrate the new Caesar. They were to suggest a text for the sermon he would then preach. From the Book of Kings. *Dabit imperium regi suo*. He giveth rule unto His king. God, and the Church, and the pope who spoke for the Church give rule to his king — to Henry. In it would be proclaimed the superiority of papal over imperial power, and it would call for peace and the liberation of the Holy Land.

Tu dominaris potestates mari et mundi, they were to tell him. Thou shalt rule over the powers of the sea and the land.

They were to ask this question:

Quis excellentior illo, qui inter duo luminaria quae fecit Deus in firmamento coeli, maiori luminari comparatus? What is more excellent than that which, among the two lights which God put in the firmament, appears to be the greater light?

The sun (the papacy) and the moon (the empire).

Dante had already dealt with this problem and settled it. He would resettle it in favor of equal lights and then go back to his first opinion. Or appear to do so.

But the ambassadors also were to put in some good words for Henry and they did.

"Solomon," they told Clement, "was known as the peace-loving and justice-giving king. Henry is the same. He greatly esteems peace. He seeks peace and embraces it. He procures peace."

They likewise insisted to the pope that Henry's promise to take part in a crusade was not empty talk.

"Our lord, the king of the Romans, not idly nor with lip service only, but seriously intent upon the matter, promises that in his heart he places the business of the Holy Land before all other business."

Well could onetime Bernard de Got, feeling like a man escaped into the clean air, afford to respond in kind.

In his encyclical of July 26, 1309, he officially confirmed the Middelburg election.

"Him," he said, "our very dear Henry, the king-elect, we deem to be and we name, proclaim, and declare to be the king of the Romans."

To which he added, under papal seal, that he would himself crown him as Henry VII in the basilica of St. Peter's in Rome. But not for two years, counting from next Candlemas. Not until February 2, 1312.

Words, you say. But solemn papal words!

Henry was satisfied with them.

Clement was satisfied too.

For while he was outwitting Philip just as Philip had once outwitted him (he thought), he had bilked the mighty monarch who had made him, or had tried to make him, a French royal chaplain. And he had done this without raising up another rival power. How could Henry, onetime count of Luxemburg, become another Otto or a Frederick Barbarossa or a Frederick II? He would have enough trouble merely maintaining himself. And the papacy, so recently in sad estate, could return to its due eminence. Without France imposing its will on him. Without the empire either.

« *13* »

But as Clement concluded that all was now right with the world and that it would continually grow better, he had reckoned without two important matters. (We are referring to his relations with Henry of Luxemburg. His miscalculations with regard to Philip the Fair were even greater.) One was the character of Alto Arrigo (High Harry), who had now become Henricus, Divus et Augustus et Caesar. The other was the pull exerted on whoever held the imperial office by the very concept of the empire itself.

We have already called Henry a knight-errant. He was. And a knight-errant always seeks adventure or wishes to pursue a Holy Grail. But in the demands of his new office, this knight-errant had an adventure ready made for him. He had a fair lady to rescue.

The fair lady was "slave Italy," who in a strange mixture of metaphors is described by Dante (*Purgatorio* VI) as (1) "a hostelry of woe," (2) "a ship without a pilot," and (3) "the mistress not of provinces but of a house of ill repute."

What more knightly deed than to rescue her and to end her travails? What more gallant deed than to do this by leaping into the so-long-vacant saddle?

Dante (in the same canto) had put these words into Italy's mouth:

> "My Caesar, why dost thou not come to me?
> Yea, come and see how doth thy people love thee,
> And if compassion for us do not move thee,
> Then come to us for shame of thy repute."

True, it was Albrecht of Austria to whom these words were addressed. But he, Henry, would answer them.

A sign in the heavens heartened him.

"On the tenth day of May in the year 1309," writes Villani, "in the night and at the very first hour of sleep, there appeared in the heavens a very great flame. It was as large as the largest galley, and it raced from the direction of the north wind toward the south. It was seen throughout all of Italy, and was held to be a great marvel. Most men thought it meant that the emperor was coming to Italy."

Most men — including Henry.

It has already been noted that on June 2 he sent ambassadors to Clement and that one of their requests was that in due course he would be allowed to proceed to Rome, where Clement would crown him.

But although the answer, when it came, would be generally favorable, he did not wait for it.

On June 24, he tipped his hand by sending word to the Mantuans that as soon as possible he would appear in their city.

Then, with a growing retinue, he proceeded slowly to the free imperial city of Speyer on the upper Rhine, where the not disinterested flocked to him from every direction.

Most of them were Florentine exiles.

Says Albertino Mussato, himself to be an exile but a Paduan:

"Many *grandi* from Tuscany of the old Ghibelline families and of the divided Guelphs — those who through the implacability of their political foes had been forced to take the Ghibelline name — crossed the Alps to woo the king with gifts and loans."

Heartened by their numbers and their promise of help, High Harry convened an aulic council. Its members debated for a seemly length of time, and then (probably on August 21) came up with the answer he wanted.

"The emperor should go to his Italian domains as soon as he can."

There was only one in opposition. Pierre d'Aspelt, Clement's personal physician and more recently the bishop of Mainz, told Henry bluntly that it was enough for him to be king of Germany.

"You will take grave risks and run into peril if you cross the mountains," he insisted.

Some say that he was suborned by Florentine gold and it may well have been offered to him. But common sense was a more likely reason.

He was but partially successful. He did win a delay, but it was only a delay. Henry put off the expedition for a year, and he used this year profitably. He consolidated his position in the north — although later he would antagonize Germany by the heavy taxes which he would have to impose — and he protected a vulnerable flank by arranging for the marriage of his son John to Elizabeth, the heiress of Bohemia. Later John would become King of Bohemia and would be a great one, and his son Charles IV, an even greater one.

Then he turned his attention to Italy.

He was able to do this because of still-continuing papal favor.

Advised by the imperial ambassadors that the civil wars raging in Lombardy and Tuscany required prompt and firm attention, assured by Henry that he would maintain and defend every papal right and privilege, and promised that the emperor would come into Italy neither as a Guelph nor a Ghibelline but as the just and impartial sovereign of both, Clement, on September 1, 1310, issued a second encyclical which he published and sent abroad, but especially to the cities and the lords of northern and of central Italy.

"Behold the peace-loving king," he wrote, "who hath been raised above all people by the gift of grace divine. We see that he is indeed the first fruits of this grace."

Then Clement again recognized and proclaimed Henry as Caesar and repeated his promise to crown him with his own hands.

He did one thing more. He summoned a relative, Cardinal Arnaud de Faugères, and bade him meet Henry at the frontiers of Italy, where he was to receive him with every kind of honor and "ardently assist him in his noble enterprise."

That was all Henry wanted.

With all the pomp and circumstance at his disposal, with the black imperial eagle of his banner flaunting on its golden field, with lances flashing in the sunlight, and with the clash and clink of bit and bridle, he made his way to Lausanne on the north shore of Lake Geneva, arriving there on October 10.

With him were his two brothers, Valeran and Archbishop Baldwin; his wife, the lovely and devoted Margaret of Brabant; his brother-in-law, Amadeo of Savoy (descendant of the legendary Umberto Biancamano and ancestor of the kings of modern Italy); another brother-in-law, Guy of Flanders; Duke Leopold of Bavaria; and every German baron or churchman who knew which side his bread was buttered on.

With him also was an army of five thousand men, a goodly proportion of whom were plumed and belted knights. The knight-errant was followed by knights-errant.

At Lausanne he paused so that he could make ceremonial visits to both Geneva and Chambéry, and at Lausanne he also received ambassadors from virtually every Italian city except Florence.

(The Florentines had good reason for not being present. As far back as July 3, Henry had made it very plain that his goodwill did not extend to them. His own ambassadors — Louis of Savoy; Bishop Philip von Rathsamhausen; Bishop Gerhard von Wippingen of Basel; the lawyer Bassiano de' Guaschi; and Simone Filippi de' Reali, an ardent Pistoian White — had ordered them to respect imperial rights and to withdraw their troops from cities that belonged to the emperor. They had returned a rude and disrespectful answer.)

Notable among these ambassadors were the Pisans. They made lavish promises and kept them.

Then Henry was on his way again. He crossed the Alps via the Mount Cenis pass — through which, even before Hannibal, many an invader had poured into Italy — and reached Susa on the Italian side of the mountains on October 23. He had made it. The first snows, which often came early, had not yet fallen to impede him.

At Susa, he reiterated that he came in behalf of no party but on behalf of all.

Next Turin. He reached it on October 30 and remained there a week. After Turin, Chieri and then Asti.

At Asti he stayed for more than four weeks — from November 10 to December 12 — receiving impartially any Italian who came to him and in the cities that submitted to him abolishing the office of *podestà* and substituting the ancient one of vicar. Friend to all, he would nonetheless make it understood that he was the ruler.

Nevertheless, it was the Ghibellines and the Ghibelline ambassadors who were most in evidence. Among them were ambassadors from the Scaligeri of Verona offering Henry residence in that city if he needed, and ambassadors from Pisa bringing rich gifts to Margaret and the first installment of their promised subsidy to Henry. Not ambassadors but playing an ambassadorial role were many of the Uberti and other Tuscan noblemen and people of importance, including Palmieri Altoviti, who had been sentenced at the same time as Dante. Not ambassadors either but in lieu of ambassadors were the syndics of Modena and Mantua. The rulers of these cities knew that Scaliger Verona was already casting covetous eyes at them. They wanted to be sure that Henry knew that they too were his friends.

Letters came to Asti too. One of them — and friendly — was from King Robert of Naples, who would later be Henry's most implacable and effective enemy. But just now, although in June 1309 at Avignon Pope Clement had crowned him king of Sicily and Apulia, this future patron of Boccaccio and Petrarch knew that since he had an elder brother still living, his claims to the throne of Charles II were doubtful, and that he needed every friend he could find. He looked in all directions. He negotiated in Florence — with very great success, it will turn out — and at the same time wrote to Henry.

From Asti, Henry continued his triumphal progress — "as if he had been an angel of God," says Dino Compagni. He had crossed the territory of the Count of Savoy with only "a few knights" but at Asti another two thousand caught up with him, and the sight Piemontese peasants gawked at must have resembled a painting by Benozzo Gozzoli.

To and through Casale. To and through Vercelli.

At Vercelli he had another encounter which we will advert to later, for it may have a bearing on Dante. He was met there by the Marquis Moroello Malaspina, onetime Dante host. Moroello knelt before Henry and asked him to reinvest him with his lands. Henry did.

Next Novara, and then to and through Magenta, where nearly five hundred years later another Italian, Napoleone Buonaparte, would win one of his more brilliant early victories. He was now accompanied not only by Florentine and other exiles, not only by Moroello and other lords who wished to be reinvested, but by Archbishop "Maffeo" (Matteo) Visconti of Milan, who at the moment did *not* hold power in that important city and who greatly wanted to.

But, marvel of marvels, who should come out only a mile from that place to greet the emperor? Guido — Guidotto — della Torre, who *did* hold power, and who wished to continue holding it.

It is said that Guidotto intended to oppose Henry — that, in fact, "he had all his mercenaries dressed in liveries of white with a vermillion stripe" and that "he ordered many of the bridges leading to the city destroyed."

But as the emperor approached, "Messer Guidotto, seeing the great press of people going out to meet him, set out himself, and when he drew nigh he threw down his staff of office and dismounted and kissed Henry's foot."

And marvel of even greater marvels — indeed, a miracle — when the imperial party came to the Ticino, its waters were so low that they were able to wade across it without using either bridges or boats.

"This has not happened in a hundred years," said the watching peasants, who saw in it the hand of God. "It is like Moses crossing the Red Sea."

Into Milan, then, rode proudly the handsome emperor to the cheering of the populace, and to its continued cheering "he reconciled Messer Guido and Messer Maffeo and their followers."

And, says a chronicler, "he did many other noble things."

Small wonder that Cino da Pistoia hymned a paean.

"Lord, now lettest Thou Thy servant depart in peace!" he hymned.

That was in December.

A few weeks later — on another Epiphany, January 6, 1311, or exactly two years to a day after the coronation at Aachen — came the culmination. In the cathedral of Sant' Ambrogio, the archbishop of Milan crowned Henry with the iron crown of Lombardy.

(Traditionally this ceremony should have taken place in Monza. It was transferred to reward the Milanese for their loyalty.)

"This crown" — a new one, for the old iron crown of Charlemagne and others had been pawned by the delle Torre family in 1273 — "was of thin iron, in the form of laurel leaves," says Dino Compagni, "and it was burning and bright as a sword, and set with pearls and other precious stones."

Dino also says that the coronation was on December 25, 1310. The January date is Villani's and seems the more probable.

But January or December, after that the story was different. The Italians, says a historian, "had promised the mountains and the seas" to Henry. But Henry had done the same to Italy.

Now he had to begin to deliver. But if you give to one you have to take from another. And this cannot be done without stirring up a hornet's nest — even if your intentions are the best and the most honorable, even if your one aim and ultimate desire is to bring good to an unhappy land.

XXI

Porciano, Poppi, Pisa

WHILE all this — or, to be more accurate, while most of this — took place, Dante was still in Paris listening to lectures, and perhaps even giving a few, amid the rowdy students and the argumentative, but often hardly less rowdy, masters, whose unlighted (except for three or four smoking tallow candles), unheated, and crowded classrooms (if one could call them that) were conveniently located near such dispensers of interior warmth as Le Coq et Poule and La Trousse-Vache.

Said Pietro Mangiadore — Petrus Comester, Peter the Eater, but of learning not food — in an earlier century: "They hated poring over the divine writings, but they loved to see the glint of wine in their glasses."

It was still true.

In saying this, we are using a hypothetical Dante chronology more because it is plausible — and tenable — than because it is supported by any documents. Yet it does seem safe to come to the following conclusions.

(1) Because of his other activities — and particularly because of the earliest date he is likely to have left Lucca — it is as certain as certain can be that Dante had not reached the French capital, or even "the kingdom of Arles," by May 1, 1308, when Albrecht of Austria was assassinated, and it seems probable that, although he may well have reached southern France by then, he had not come to his Street of the Strawsellers by November 27, when Henry was crowned at Aachen.

(2) But it seems equally certain — all the more so since he could hardly have stayed in Paris for only a few weeks or a few months — that it was before the aulic council of July–August 1309 (at which time

The Ravenna Dante, the thoughtful effigy on Dante's tomb in Ravenna, was probably executed in 1483 by Pietro Lombardo at the orders of Bernardo Bembo, father of the humanist Pietro Bembo.

imperial councillors officially sanctioned an imperial excursion to Italy) that he had come to the Latin Quarter which was equally famous for its St. Thomas Aquinas's and St. Bonaventura's, and for its half-starved "martin's-nest dwellers" (*martinets*), the poor scholars who lodged in garrets under the eaves.

It seems safe to assume, then, that Dante was not in Paris when Philip began to assemble the plumed knights and hard-faced *routiers* with which he intended to move south to impress Pope Clement, and that he did not see the pomp and panoply and hear the heavy tramp of feet — doubtless jeered at ribaldly by the irreverent students, although the university almost always officially supported the king's position — and then the ignominious mustering out when Henry's election became known.

But he *was* on hand to hear the subsequent and noisy arguments.

Who, in theory and fact, should hold temporal power?

The pope?

Not in Dante's opinion, for since the days of Boniface Dante had equated papal power with an unprincipled attack on Florentine liberties.

The king of France?

Pierre Dubois, a lawyer at the French court, had already written that the popes had caused more wars than they prevented, that European peace could only be established by force, and that his monarch was the only one strong enough to establish it.

"He suggested," wrote G. G. Coulton picturesquely, "that the king of France should make a tame cat out of the pope and then rule righteously the whole of Europe."

But Dante's recollections of the king's interventions in his native land were not good either.

Finally, the emperor?

But this was the Ghibelline position, and by inheritance and by practice Dante was a Guelph.

Yet more and more he had found himself shifting toward a Ghibelline way of thinking.

This had begun before he came to Paris.

Convivio IV, 4:

"Wherefore" — so that the whole world may have the order and tranquility it needed for its arts and its well-being — "the whole world and everything that man is given to possess and to retain must be a monarchy — that is, it must be a single princedom ruled by a single prince. For such a one, since he possesses all things and therefore cannot desire more, can keep the kings" — the kings subservient to him — "contented in their kingdoms. Then the cities may dwell at ease, and in this ease the *vicenze* [the regions] may love one another, and in this love every household may be given its needs, and when they have been given this men may live happily. And it is to live happily that men were born."

To live happily, and not as a homeless exile.

It would be unfair to Dante to say that he was drawn to the emperor and to his cause solely because he believed that Henry would end this exile — solely because he hoped and believed that Alto Arrigo would restore to him all the things both spiritual and material of which he had been robbed. But it would be naive to assume that, even though he did not realize it, this did not greatly influence him. It did.

Henry would bring peace to slave Italy — but he would also restore Dante to the place from which he had been ousted.

And so Dante, with his pulses beating at varying speeds, listened eagerly to every rumor that was brought to Paris and to every fact reported there.

Sometimes his hopes must have soared, and sometimes days must have seemed interminable.

But then — in the summer of 1311 — came the news of a series of happenings that made Dante like an unleashed greyhound.

Henry was moving up the Rhine!

Henry was in Switzerland!

And then suddenly the tidings of all tidings that he had been waiting for.

The rider-to-be of the riderless steed had crossed the Alps. Henry was in Italy.

Word of this could hardly have reached Paris much later than the middle of October, and it may have come there sooner.

Not too long afterwards — and certainly by mid-December — Dante reacted in the only way possible.

He too crossed the Alps. He went to Italy himself.

And to the imperial presence.

This he tells us in one of his epistles.

"I, too," he writes, "who set down this letter as much for myself as for others, saw and heard in you all that imperial majesty should be, namely the utmost in loving kindness and mercy. I saw this when my hands were placed between thine, and my lips paid their debt of homage."

But where — I mean at this time, for he met him on other occasions — did he meet Henry to kneel before him and swear fealty to him?

We can only guess, of course, but a convincing case can be made for Vercelli in the western part of old Lombardy.

Dante refers to Vercelli in *Inferno* XXVIII — Pier da Medicina, condemned to hell as "a sower of discord" along with Mahomet and the

Mosca of the Buondelmonte story, is telling of the part of Italy from which he came:

> He said: "O thou whom sin does not condemn
> And whom I saw above on Latin soil
> If too great similarity doth not deceive me,
> Do thou remember Pier da Medicina
> If thou returnest ever to the sweet plain
> That from Vercelli to Marcabò slopes down."

Marcabò was a castle at the Po mouth. It, therefore, defined one end of the Po Valley, so dear to Medicina. But why Vercelli? The Po's source is many miles to the west.

A plausible explanation is that Dante knew Vercelli and saw the river there.

But an even more convincing argument that Dante came to the emperor at this city at the western limits of old Lombardy — of medieval Lombardy — is the fact that Moroello Malaspina met Henry at Vercelli.

What more likely than that Dante would have come with Moroello? He had served the Malaspina well, and when he had left Giovagallo two years or so earlier it was not as the result of some subsequent quarrel. He and Moroello had parted as friends.

What more natural that than he should ask Moroello to present him to Henry?

For he had in his baggage or in his mind — I say this because it cannot be said whether it was prepared in France or in Italy, only that it was prepared after September 1 — a sword that he had forged to use against the emperor's enemies.

This was the first of the three so-called "political" letters which he would write to advance High Harry's cause.

« 2 »

By modern standards, it is both wordy and grandiloquent, and it is hard to see it as an effective piece of political polemics. But it was not written for a modern controversy but for the early fourteenth century. There it was not only what was expected but what was demanded, and one gets the feeling that it went off very well.

"To each and every one of the Italian princes, to the senators of the sacred city, and likewise to the dukes, marquises, counts, and peoples of Italy, that humble Italian Dante Alighieri, a Florentine who has been wrongfully exiled, doth send his greetings and a prayer for peace.

" 'Behold, now is the accepted time.' Behold, now arise the signs of consolation and of peace. For a new day grows brighter, in its birth revealing the dawn that already dispels the shadows of our long-enduring tribulation. Now the breezes from the east grow fresher, the lips of the heavens turn rosy. With their sweet calm, they confirm the good things prophesied to the peoples. And we, too, who have kept a night-long vigil in the wilderness — we, too, shall see the long-awaited joy. For peace-bringing Titan" — i.e., the sun — "now climbs on high, and justice, which like the heliotrope turns dull when it is deprived of his light, will once more glitter as soon as it receives his first ray."

The strong lion of Judah, he continues, has raised up a new Moses who will lead the people of Israel back into the land of milk and honey.

"Therefore rejoice once more, O Italy, you who now deserve pity even from the Saracens! Soon you will be envied by the whole globe, since your bridegroom, the solace of the nations and the glory of thy people, Henry, the Divine, the August, and Caesar, hastens to the wedding. Dry your tears, O lady most fair, and wipe away all traces of your sorrow, for he is near who will set you free from the prison house of the ungodly, and who, smiting the evildoers with the edge of his sword, will utterly destroy them and will let out his vineyard to such other husbandmen as at harvest home will bring to him the fruits of justice."

But will he have mercy on none? Not so! Not so!

"Surely he will pardon all who sue for mercy, since he is Caesar and it is from the fountainhead of mercy" — i.e., the Church of Christ the merciful — "that all his sovereign authority flows."

But he is also Augustus, and those who do not acknowledge him he will avenge with a defeat worse than that of Pharsalia.

"Lay aside, therefore, O Lombard race, the barbarian ways you brought with you, and if there is anything of the Latin or the Trojan left among you, let this guide you lest the sublime eagle, when he swoops like a thunderbolt, may find his eaglets thrown out and the nest of his progeny usurped by raven fledglings. Up then, ye sons of Scandinavia, and show yourselves as eager as you can be for the presence of him whose coming you very rightly dread."

Do not let avarice — do not let the fear that you will have to pay tribute to him — hold you back, but come before him confessing your sins. Submit to him humbly and with a penitential psalm.

"It is not possible to kick against the pricks."

Thus much for those who had misruled Italy. And then a plea for moderation on the part of those whose wrongs would now be righted.

"But you who groan oppressed, lift up your heads now that the day of your salvation is at hand. Take up the mattock of true humility and with it break up the parched clods of your pride. With it make smooth the field of your mind."

Then the fertile valley will put forth green again — "the green, that is, that shall be fruitful of true peace."

Forgive those who had once been your enemies.

"Forbear, yea forbear from now on forward, O you who have suffered wrong with me. Then the shepherd descended from Hector" — Henry of Luxemburg — "will know you as sheep of his own fold. For although the right to punish temporally has been entrusted to him by heaven, yet he delights in correcting his children and even more in showing them mercy. That is so that he may be redolent of Him from Whom as from a single point the power of Peter and of Caesar separates and comes."

Let both parties among you realize then that peace is in store for each of them.

Rise up to meet your king, and not only rise but stand in reverent awe before his presence.

Do not say we have no lawful ruler.

"God foreordained the Roman prince, and the Church acknowledges that He later confirmed him by the word of His Word."

But God also decreed that he shared this authority with the Church.

Christ said this Himself. Born during the peace of the Pax Romana, He apportioned the world to Himself and to Caesar, and said that to each one should be rendered what was his due.

But Dante was not yet ready to carry his thinking to its later — and perhaps logical — conclusion. Christ's world, he said — and may have still thought — was the overlord of Caesar's world. This is manifested by what the Savior said to Pontius Pilate during the last meeting.

Here he refers to the "Gospel according to John XIX, 10–12":

"Then saith Pilate unto Him, 'Speakest Thou not unto me? Knowest Thou not that I have power to crucify Thee, and have power to release Thee?' Jesus answered, 'Thou couldest have no power at all against me, except it were given thee from above.' And from thenceforward Pontius Pilate sought to release Him."

But obviously Dante would not let it rest at that.

Henry had derived his power from the power that was given from above.

Clement had ratified and blessed his election.

"The Lord of heaven and earth has appointed us a king. This is he whom Peter, the vicar of God, exhorts us to honor. This is he whom Clement, the present successor of Peter, lights up with the light of his

Apostolic benediction so that where the radiance of the light spiritual is not enough the splendor of the lesser light may lend its gleam."

The lesser light? The empire?

Had Dante thus far modified the relatively modest views he held even as far back as when he wrote the *Convivio?*

Or was he trying to win friends and influence people — more specifically to keep as a friend and influence the Avignon pope — with words redolent of the old saying that you catch more flies with honey than with vinegar?

I think the latter.

Dante was trying the soft approach instead of his usual hard and forthright one. It was something he did not often do.

« 3 »

After he had written this letter, shown it to Henry, and presumably arranged for its circulation, Dante did not linger long in the north. It is possible that he accompanied Alto Arrigo to Milan. Possible, but by no means certain, and not necessarily even likely. Then he turned his footsteps south again. If, as he predicted, there was a great day coming, when it came he wanted to be near that city he both loved and vituperated — that Fiorenza which was (as he said sarcastically in *Inferno* XXVI) "so great that over sea and land thou beat'st thine wings and throughout hell thy name is spread abroad."

Umberto Cosmo says that he went to Forlì.

"The statement to this effect by Flavio Biondo," he writes, "is so precise and comes from such firsthand sources that there can be no doubt that it is true."

There in his own name, and again in the name of the other exiles, he supposedly wrote a letter to Can Grande della Scala, who had but recently joined his brother in the lordship of Verona.

Biondo's firsthand source was Pelligrino Calvi, secretary to the lord of Forlì, and according to Calvi, Dante reported to the youthful Scaliger the insolent reply given by the Florentines to the ambassadors Henry sent to them.

"They said," he told Can Grande, "that if the emperor is as wise a man as he is reported to be, he will know that the Roman princes used the Italians against the barbarians without, and not the barbarians against the Italians."

Dante continued that the Florentines told the ambassadors that they would talk about receiving the emperor at an appropriate time, and that to let the exiles return to their country actually ran counter to imperial wishes since it was the exiles who were provoking war.

Having said this, Biondo noted Calvi as reporting, Dante went on to rail so greatly against the rashness, the peevishness, and the blindness of the rulers of the city that "Benvenuto da Imola insisted that it was because of this incident that Dante hurled the epithet of blind at the Florentines," which he did in *Inferno* XV.

Zingarelli, however, takes an opposite stand. Not only is he firmly convinced that Dante wrote no such letter but he implies that he did not even come to Forlì.

"The whole account is impossible to believe," he says. "First of all, Dante had been separated from the Whites for many years, and such a letter, if it were written at all, would have been in his own name and not for the White university. His words about the barbarians have the flavor of the [later] humanists. No such thoughts were entertained in the time of Dante; at that time the emperors who called themselves Roman always had a German army. Biondo's narrative not only contradicts Villani's account of what actually happened but the procedure in other cities. Finally, nowhere in Benvenuto Rambaldi's account [Benvenuto da Imola] do you find anything about the origin of the proverbial accusation of blindness."

Despite that, there is this much to be said for the Cosmo theory.

First, even Zingarelli admits that it was not unlikely that Dante, who was "not the last to recognize" what a prodigy the twenty-year-old Can Grande was, would have taken steps to establish relations with him. Such as writing him this kind of letter, perhaps?

Second, it is true that Dante had long broken with the Whites, but despite Gustav Vinay's statement that "in Dante when he wrote the *De Monarchia*" — of which more shortly — "there was not, *nor was there ever*, any preeminent interest in politics," and his further statement that "it is very probable that in Florence Dante had neither said nor written anything that could interest his fellow citizens or us," the exact opposite was the case. Dante was a recognized political leader, and as he became an experienced one too — the hard way! — he must have learned that at least from time to time you do what is expedient. He had been disgruntled with the Whites, but now they could be useful again.

Third, Dante was well known in Forlì. He had been there before, and in a reasonably important role. And now he at least seemed close to the emperor. There is no reason that the Ordelaffi would not welcome him.

Lastly, not contradicted by anyone, Dante's ultimate destination was once again the Casentino. But given the military and political situation of 1311, not only the most expeditious but the safest way to get to the Casentino from Lombardy was by way of Forlì. Dante, therefore, certainly must have at least passed through Forlì. Whether he stayed there long enough to write a letter to Can Grande — or even whether he stayed there at all — is quite another thing.

« *4* »

Where he stayed in the Casentino — where he stayed during this particular trip to the Casentino — is another matter about which there has been debate.

In this instance, however, one cannot disagree with Zingarelli nor with his basic premise. In view of Dante's activities (both past and probable future), he says, it would not have been appropriate for him to have been the guest of a lord who was hostile to the emperor. But this leaves us with another question. Which one — or ones — of the Counts Guidi was not hostile to Henry and hence could have been this host?

Here Bishop Nicholas of Butrinto is exceedingly helpful. With a Roman notary, Pandolfo Savelli, as his colleague, and carrying credentials from both Pope Clement and Henry, he was one of the ambassadors sent by the emperor to persuade the Florentines to see the light of reason. Even at Bologna, they were received with sullen hostility, but when they reached La Lastra not only were they told plainly that they could not proceed any farther but there were clear indications that their lives and limbs were in danger.

For to La Lastra — and to the cry of "that tyrant the king of Germany is coming to destroy us" — climbed an angry and undisciplined mob with swords bared and with pikes and halberds brandished. They filled the street under the inn where the ambassadors stayed, and finally, as they shouted "Kill them! Kill them!", one of the leaders — a Megalotti and a "stout, fine figure of a man" — was thrust forward and tried to climb the stairs. Only the innkeeper, his own true blade in hand, kept him back. In the meantime, the servants of the ambassadors fled, some leaping out of the windows, others hiding under the beds.

But finally a parley was agreed upon and Nicholas was allowed to speak.

"We come only to present the embassy of the emperor."

"We will not receive it."

"We have letters from our master, Pope Clement."

"We will not read them."

"Then — and in God's name — give us only a safe conduct to leave Florence."

Through the persuasion of a onetime papal treasurer, now an important Black, and of the *podestà* and the captain, both of whom held lands in papal territory and did not wish to antagonize the pope, this was agreed to. It was agreed that the ambassadors could depart in peace and that their belongings, which the mob had already laid hands on, would be restored to them.

Not even a pretence, however, was made of keeping the second part of the agreement, and the first was only kept because a Count Guidi intervened. As Nicholas and his companion were still being hustled and bustled, Count Tegrimo rode up. With a party of his horsemen, we suppose.

"During the night, this Count Tegrimo conducted us to a castle of his called San Godenzo" — where Dante seven years before had signed an important agreement — "and there they lent us horses for our followers who now" — because of Florentine thievery — "were on foot.

"Then we were taken to another place, in which there came to us two other brothers of Count Tegrimo; that is, the Counts Tancred and Bandino. Later, we encountered another brother, Count Roger. These said they were Counts Guidi and Counts Palatine, and that of the same household were the count of Battifolle and the Count Salvatico. Likewise the Counts of Romena called themselves Counts Palatine, and they had great estates in the Romagna.

"Some of these were Guelphs and they were the richest ones. They all swore fidelity to us, and that so soon as the emperor came to Tuscany they would appear before him personally, or, if they were hindered from doing this, they would send others in their place. They swore that they would go with him to his coronation with such display as they had means for. Every one of them honored us greatly and received us with great joy, but in my estimation the Guelphs more than the Ghibellines."

Obviously the Guelphs more than the Ghibellines! The Guelphs would want to impress the emperor from whom they held their fiefs that they were his loyal vassals. The Ghibellines did not have to.

Here, then, we have a list of possible Dante hosts.

The Counts Tegrimo, Tancred, Bandino, and Roger.

Count Guido Salvatico of Dovadola.

One or another of the counts of Romena.

And Count Guido of Battifolle. This Count Guido was the nephew of the famous Guido Novello who once ruled Florence — in Manfred's name — and then left it in a panic. He lived at Poppi.

But geography — and some other considerations — eliminates some. Dovadola, for instance, is on the wrong side of the Apennines, while Romena hardly fits Dante's own description of where he was. It is not "just under the source of the Arno in the borderlands of Tuscany."

But Porciano is. It is not more than five miles — and by winding road, not as the crow flies — from where Dante's river rises on a spur of the Apennines.

Moreover, he refers to it — or seems to — in *Purgatorio* XIV when he describes the inhabitants of the upper Arno:

> Wherefore so changéd is the very nature
> Of the inhabitants of its wretched valley
> That it would seem that Circe pastured them.
> Midst filthy hogs [*tra brutti porci*] who are fitter for acorns
> Than they are for food made for human beings
> It first directs its trickle of a course.

Tra brutti porci — Porciano! The resemblance can hardly be a coincidence, and the Porciano counts — other than from the plunder of their robber-baron maraudings — derived much of their wealth from huge herds of swine which fattened on the acorns of the nearby chestnut forests.

Sometimes plundering and hog-fattening were combined. In 1289, certain of them rode into the Florentine suburbs and drove off some of the Florentine pigs. For this they were condemned and sentenced, but in 1309 — since Florence now needed friends not enemies — the sentence was revoked. This called for a celebration, and to celebrate, Count Tegrimo, with an earthy sense of humor, had the walls of his stronghold painted with a procession of porkers.

There are equally valid reasons for believing that Dante was received at Poppi too. Although their authenticity has sometimes been challenged, it is now pretty generally agreed that Dante, acting as her secretary, actually composed as well as set down on paper the three letters addressed to "the most glorious and most clement lady, the Lady Margaret, by divine providence queen of the Romans" (i.e., Henry's empress) by "G. di Battifolle, by the grace of God and of His allied magnificence Count Palatine in Tuscany" and sent them to her between the middle of April and the end of May.

G. di Battifolle was Gherardesca, daughter of Count Ugolino della Gherardesca, who with two sons and two grandsons was starved to death in the Tower of Hunger in 1288. Zingarelli says she was married to Count Guido di Battifolle; Paget Toynbee to Guido's uncle Guido Novello. She was thus either countess or dowager countess. For chronological reasons, the latter seems more likely.

These letters make interesting reading, for in their phraseology, which was subservient and yet not humble, they reveal what was expected from a noblewoman when she addressed her husband's — or her nephew's — liege lord.

The first letter expresses gratitude to Margaret for sending her news of the well-being of the emperor and of herself.

"The gracious letter of your royal benignity was seen by mine eyes joyfully, and was taken into my hands with the reverence which was its due. And when the message which it brought penetrated with its sweetness into the very depths of my mind, my heart glowed as I read it with such fervent devotion that oblivion can never blot it out, nor can I remember it without delight. For who am I that the high and potent wife of Caesar should condescend to inform me of the well-being — and may it long continue! — of herself and her husband?"

The second expresses the countess's joy at tidings received from the empress as to the emperor's triumphant progress.

"I indeed hope that the happy beginning of your reign" — which would provide, among other things, that all of "civilized mankind" should be ruled by one prince — "will always proceed from good to better."

The third letter again expresses joy that "the right hand of the Most Highest King" — God almighty — "was happily bringing about the fulfillment of the resolves of Caesar and his Augusta." It then takes up an apparent request by Margaret that Countess Gherardesca should give tangible proofs of her goodwill. Although to do this would have "a certain appearance of presumption," she will at least speak intimately — as she would not dare to if she were not sincerely devoted. Know then "by the despatch of these presents" that she and her beloved husband were "prospering and in good health" and that they rejoiced "in the welfare of their children."

The letter had this for its subscription:

"Sent from the castle of Poppi on the eighteenth day of May in the first year of the most auspicious passage into Italy of the Emperor Henry."

We thus have a "fix" that establishes both place and time.

Possibly, but improbably — and if so only for a short time — Romena; probably Porciano; certainly Poppi. These were the places which sheltered Dante and gave him a refuge. And for at least six months, but probably for longer, in the late winter, and in the spring, summer, and perhaps early autumn of this high and hopeful year of 1311.

« 5 »

What did he do while he was there? That is the next question we have to ask.

Many things is the answer — some of which we know and others we can only guess at.

We have already seen, for example, that he served as secretary to the

Countess Gherardesca, or at least as one who helped her write her letters, and we should have noted that he found in this a chance not only to further polish his style but to make cautious propaganda for the imperial cause.

It is stated that he continued with his own writing, and indeed one of his more bitter sonnets has been confidently assigned to this period.

Here it is in full:

> If Thou, Lord, see mine eyes ready to weep
> For the new anguish that lays waste my heart,
> I pray Thee, in her name who'll not depart
> From Thee, adjure them: "No such pleasures keep!"
> And then do Thou chastise with Thy right hand
> Him who doth justice stay and after flees
> To the great tyrant, there to drink the lees
> He's scattered now to destroy every land.
> This same has cast such great and icy fear
> Into Thy liege's heart that all are still.
> But Thou, fire of heaven, sky's brilliancy,
> This virtue that doth naked lie and chill,
> Lift Thou her up. With Thy veil, veil Thou her.
> Without this, peace on earth there will not be.

(It is also possible that he picked up and from time to time added to the great poem on which — Boccaccio has already told us — he did not work continuously and without interruption. But this is not the moment to talk of the *Commedia*.)

Forgetting that he was now forty-six and somewhat weary, another would have him walking, keen-eyed and alert, through the Casentino countryside as he had done when he was younger and less weather-beaten. He is described as climbing Falterona once more, and noting beneath him "a broad, deep ocean of mellow light and shade, a symphony in green and gray, with an infinite gamut of soft, delicious hues."

A final story makes him, even if briefly, a prisoner. At Porciano. Or, at any rate, it says that local legend says that he was a prisoner there, and reports that there is a tablet on a castle wall which gives an account of this.

These stories may or may not be true. It is not likely that he was a prisoner, but the walking — age forty-six or not — is not impossible, for he was restless by nature, and, as we have seen, he always liked to move from place to place.

But the most important thing he did in the Casentino was to listen.

There was plenty to listen to, for the Counts Guidi were at a kind of crossroads, and as the emperor and the Italian Guelphs moved toward an inevitable confrontation, it was clear that they would have to go one way or the other. But which?

News, therefore, was important to them — exact information about exactly what was happening — and by bribery and cajolery, they saw to it that news came to them.

News of all kinds and from all quarters.

From Florence, which was now ruthlessly and apparently securely in the hands of its Black adventurers and revolutionaries.

From Alto Arrigo in Lombardy.

From Pope Clement V, or from prelates who could and did speak for him when he did not dare to speak himself.

Even from Paris by the Seine, from France's King Philip the Fair.

The news came to the Counts Guidi, but obviously Dante heard it. Some of it in the great hall, as men wolfed down their meals and waited for orders to do something. This was rumor, not news. But surely, some of it from the Counts Guidi themselves. For if he was the Countess Gherardesca's secretary, it is quite likely that he served her nephew in a similar capacity and that he was also his adviser. His and the other Counts Guidi's.

How could it be otherwise?

He alone of those they could readily turn to had been embroiled in Florentine politics. He alone had knelt before Henry, and had written a letter which was really a manifesto for him. He alone knew Paris and Avignon and Rome. Or at least he had been to them.

So when the messages came, almost certainly Dante was permitted to look at them. And almost equally certainly, he did not like what he saw.

« 6 »

For neither in the north of Italy, nor in Florence — nor for that matter "beyond the mountains" — were things turning out as he had dreamed and planned.

Let us take Henry first. As we already know, Henry's intentions were good, and, for the day and age in which he lived, his patience and his tolerance were more than notable. Even when the Florentines rebuffed him for the first time by not sending ambassadors to Lausanne, his rebuke of them was very gentle.

"They have done ill," was all he said, "for it was our purpose and desire to have as our faithful subjects all Florentines and not merely those of one party. It was our intent to make that city our royal chamber and the finest one in our empire."

Dino Compagni confirms this attempt not to favor either side.

"The Ghibellines said: 'He will see no one but Guelphs,' " he observed. "The Guelphs said: 'He receives none but Ghibellines.' But the emperor's will was to be impartial, for each he loved as his own man and each he honored."

But events can jog the elbow, even if it is an imperial one.

In this case, it was events in Milan.

"In the said year [1311] on the eleventh day of the month of February," reports Villani, "Messer Guidotto della Torre, seeing" — or, more accurately, thinking that he saw — "himself cast out from the lordship of Milan, and Maffeo Visconti and his other enemies much in the good graces of the emperor, decided to make the city of Milan rebel."

The moment was ripe, he thought, since Henry had sent most of his knights here and there throughout Lombardy and had only a few still with him.

Guidotto's sons apparently egged their father on, for in a council convened by Henry they used such violent language against the Visconti that they were forced to flee and barricade themselves in the so-called Guasto, or Ruins, which was given this name because it stood on the site of della Torre buildings which had been destroyed in an earlier disturbance.

Maffeo Visconti and his followers attacked them there, and the resulting disorders were so serious that Henry was obliged to send his marshal to put them down. He routed the recalcitrant delle Torre. Guidotto fled to the dauphiny in France and his sons to a castle near Como.

Thereafter — although Henry still insisted that he would pardon Guidotto if he returned to his allegiance and his duty — it was difficult even to pretend to be above parties.

Says a modern historian:

"The emperor disappeared. He was replaced by the German, the barbarian, the foreigner."

In Guelph minds, that is.

In consequence, revolts flared up everywhere. In Lodi on the right bank of the Adda on the Milanese plain. In Cremona. In Brescia. In Pavia.

In part they were spontaneous, but in greater part they were fomented by Florentine gold and della Torre persuasion.

But whatever the cause, they halted the triumphal progress through his new dominions, for the emperor was obliged to deal with them.

Pavia he put off for the time being, but he sent his brother Valeran to Lodi, on whose walls as an insult the always tough-minded citizens had painted the imperial eagle upside down. Valeran took Lodi without very much difficulty; ordered half its buildings destroyed; and sentenced its leaders to death; but later for practical reasons he allowed them to buy pardon with badly needed florins.

In the meanwhile, the emperor himself rode to Cremona, but the Cremonese did not wait for his arrival. Because they had not expected this turn of events, they had not laid in provisions and were in no way prepared for a siege. Hastily, therefore, they sent ambassadors, who fell at Henry's feet and promised obedience but asked that he would rule them in his own name and not send them a vicar.

The emperor did not answer them, but after they had left his presence they were given private letters — which Henry undoubtedly had seen — and these informed the Cremonese that if they truly wanted pardon they must send citizens of good standing to beg for mercy humbly.

"They must come barefoot with nothing on their heads. They must wear only their shirts and their leather girdles must be around their necks."

This they did — the two sons of the Marquis Cavalcabò; Messer Sovramonte degli Abbati, "a very able knight"; but not the Florentine *podestà* Messer Rinieri Buondelmonti, who had fled when the first pennons of Henry's army could be seen on the horizon — and intoning what was almost a litany, they followed the still-silent emperor to the city walls.

Here his frown relaxed a little, for the gates were open in token of surrender.

He entered through one of them, and, once in the city, "he stood still, put his hand to his sword, drew it, and received them under it."

Symbolically that gave him the absolute right to punish Cremona and its citizens as he saw fit.

That was on April 20, and so far so good.

On the fourteenth of May, he was in front of Brescia and never had he been more strong or more confident.

"Henry," says Villani, "found himself with greater forces and with more numerous and with better knights that he had ever had before."

To come to specifics, six thousand of them. Of these, four thousand were Germans, Frenchmen, and Burgundians.

"They were all nobly born," an important matter in those days. By temperament and by training the nobly born — particularly those from beyond the Alps — were still Europe's best fighters.

"The rest" — two thousand, that is — "were Italians."

But these six thousand knights would not even have to fight. Their presence, led by the up-to-now invincible emperor, would accomplish his purpose. That and the fact that the Brescians were as unprovided with provisions as Cremona had been and were already "at the end of their grain."

Just appear, and it would be enough.

"When they see your camp, the Brescians will surrender at once."

And this would be an important victory.

"For if you leave Brescia alone, all Lombardy will be lost, and your opponents will make their nest there. But if you win, you will strike terror into the rest of them."

Here we have a medieval application of the modern domino theory. If you take Brescia, the anti-imperialists will understand that you mean business. But if you fail to take it, your friends will wonder if you will protect them when their own turn comes.

"Henry," says Dino Compagni, "prepared for a siege. He sent for masons and carpenters, made movable towers, dug trenches, prepared covered passageways, and gave every indication that he was ready to begin to fight."

But he failed to reckon with two things.

The first was Brescia and the Brescians.

"The city was strong and inhabited by a brave people."

The only vulnerable point was the northeastern corner, where overhanging hills came dangerously close, and here there was a fortress which the garrison of Brescia could easily — and at need — relieve.

"It was a hard city to take by storm."

The second was time, which very definitely was no longer on the emperor's side. Six months, to explain, had now elapsed since Alto Arrigo had entered Italy, and he had progressed so little that from time to time he could still see the Alps, even if only as a faint line of whitecapped surf in the distance. The Rome of his vision and Dante's was hardly a step nearer. All things considered, it may even have been farther away. And if there was a siege — and it appeared that there would be a siege — time would continue to march on.

« 7 »

Time would continue to march on, and with every hollow tick of the clocks which were beginning to appear on clock towers from Rome to London, advance — when Henry could advance again — became more difficult, for the Florentines who were the focal point of opposition had used this same time to weaken Henry's allies and organize their friends and to persuade vacillators like Clement that they must now finally and definitely choose the right (their) side.

Not that the city of the red lily did not have difficulties of its own.

"In the said year of 1311," for example, "from December to May" — in other words, at the exact time when Henry was advancing from Asti through Milan to Cremona and Brescia — "there was the greatest scarcity in Florence. A bushel of wheat cost half a florin and it was usually mixed with buckwheat."

Villani exaggerates. The price was only two thirds of that, but it was still twice the price of the year before.

"The arts and trade were never worse."

Why?

Florence was a banking city — this was the first reason — and even though the first two are White bankers, there was a serious loss of confidence when the failures of the Mozzi and the Cerchi were followed by the failure of Niccolò de' Franzi and the flight of Amerigo Frescobaldi from England. Even Black bankers like the Spini, the Pazzi, the Bardi, and the Peruzzi felt the pinch.

Merchandise — this was another reason — did not reach the marts, nor did the bales of wool and the rolls of woolen cloth that the wool processors and the wool merchants needed. The land routes had been closed or virtually closed by Henry, and now pirates from Monaco and Rapallo hovered off the mouth of the Arno and even had the temerity to land on nearby long beaches — such as those below Camaiore and at Viareggio — to seize the precious cargoes that had been put ashore there.

To be sure, Pisa was obliged by treaty to send galleys against these pirates; but would the Pisans do this?

"Let these dogs of Florentines bare their own teeth to defend their stolen bones!" they cried instead.

They had endured enough Florentine insults and injuries, and anyway they were now committed — spiritually and with their gold — to the cause of the emperor.

Finally, Florence was just emerging from the divisive consequences of the so-called "war of Corso Donati," which had led to Corso's slaying by Betto Brunelleschi's Catalan mercenaries. They had some fences to mend.

But the dogs of Florentines — and least of all those dogs of Florentines who were Blacks — were not the sort to be discouraged by matters like this. Indeed, it almost seemed as if their many difficulties stiffened their will to resist and led them to even more resolute actions, both in the military and diplomatic fields.

They strengthened the relatively new third circle of the city walls, and where it seemed necessary extended it.

"In the said year [of 1310]," writes Villani, "on St. Andrew's Day [November 30], they decided to enclose the city with moats from the Porta San Gallo to the Porta Sant' Ambrogio, and then as far as the Arno. This was because they feared the coming of the emperor. From the Porta

San Gallo to the Porta del Prato d'Ognisanti, where the walls were already built, they raised them eight cubits higher."

They welcomed King Robert of Naples as he returned from his coronation with "honors, jousts, and with presents of money," and with what amounted to *de facto* — not for a while would he become *de jure* lord too — lordship of the city.

Robert arrived in Florence on September 30 and remained there until October 24, his purpose being "to reconcile the Guelphs one with the other" — the Black Guelphs, that is — "which were divided into factions among themselves," and to discuss ways and means of opposing Alto Arrigo.

When he left — and to make sure that the Florentines neither weakened nor were compelled to weaken — he sent them his *mariscalco* (marshal, but really mercenary captain) with four hundred more Spanish-speaking ruffians. "The Tuscan League of the Bolognese, the Lucchese, the Sienese, the Volterrans, and others" — as well as Florence — would know he meant business.

The *mariscalco* was Diego de la Rat, who has been celebrated by both Cecco Angiolari and Giovanni Boccaccio.

Cecco Angiolari — in his sonnet number 135, addressed to Dante:

> I will my dear Becchina no more praise,
> Dante, but will the *mariscalco* exalt
> Who shines like a gold florin though metal base,
> Who looks like Caffa sugar, but tastes like salt,
> Who seems like wheaten bread, but is coarse rye,
> A tower seems, but is the pavement low,
> Who is a kite, but flies like falcon high,
> A hen though he cries *cock-a-doodle-doo.*

> O sonnet mine, get thee to Florence hence
> And tell the dames and damsels you find there
> Their paragon is nothing but vain show.
> Meanwhile, a hundred tales of him I'll swear
> To your good Charles, the lord count of Provence.
> I'll tan his hide for him, I'd have you know.

Boccaccio paints a somewhat more charitable picture, but he does explain both the gold florins and the invocation to the ladies.
Decameron VI, 3:

"While Messer Antonio degli Orsi was bishop of Florence" — i.e., in 1310 or later — "there came thither a worthy man named Messer Diego de la Rat who was King Robert's marshal. Now this Diego was very handsome in appearance and inordinately fond of women, and it so happened that one of the ladies of Florence who was most attracted to him was the very beautiful niece of the brother of the said bishop. And when Diego learned that, although of a good family, this lady's husband was a low fellow and very avaricious, he struck a bargain with him. He would lie with the lady one night for five hundred gold florins. Then he gilded the same number of silver *popolini*" — a coin similar in appearance to the florin but worth only one tenth as much — "and having slept with the lady, although against her will, he gave these to the husband. Which being known — "

Nothing more need be said.

The Florentines used their wealth and credit too. They also used their Florentine persuasiveness.

Florentine gold — not gilded *popolini* — aided and abetted by Florentine honeyed words, unquestionably had as much to do with the resistance of Cremona and Brescia as did the plotting of the della Torre, who tried to use revolt by these cities as a help to winning back their rule in Milan. Florentine words, aided and abetted by Florentine gold, played a principal part in reconstituting the Tuscan League and making it so formidable that even the Counts Guidi had to think twice as to the possible consequences of burning all their bridges by unreservedly committing themselves to Henry. It was Florentine determination — and probably gold and words too — that kept Lucca in line, and thus closed another gate to the south.

The Florentines also sent word — and gold with it — across the Alps. To Pope Clement in Avignon they first sent a secret agent, one Fra Bartolommeo, "the son of a money changer and a very shrewd man," and then two official ambassadors, Messer Pino de' Rossi and Messer Gherardo Bostichi, "two very able knights." To King Philip, they sent Messer Baldo Fini of Figline.

On the surface, their success was not in any way apparent.

From Messrs Pino de' Rossi and Gherardo Bostichi "much money was extracted" — by Pope Clement, who seemed to know how to "operate" himself — "and much of it was wasted, for they did not get anything they wanted."

Messer Baldo Fini made a public fool of himself.

"What colossal impudence these Florentines have!" cried the cardinal of Prato, who had changed sides once more and now was with King Philip. "What colossal impudence! With their ten louse eggs" — presumably a contemptuous reference to their florins — "they dare try anything!"

But underneath, it was otherwise.

King Philip might — at any rate for a while longer — affect a lack of concern and keep his attention fixed on internal matters, among which would soon be included the adulteries — or the alleged adulteries — of his three daughters-in-law. Pope Clement, still smiling on his protégé and possible liberator, might half agree to advance the date of Henry's coronation. But inwardly, they began to have misgivings.

Pope Clement in particular — for Pope Clement had more to fear. He wanted Henry as a foil to Philip but not as a power in his own right.

To Florence, therefore, Pope Clement sent his nephew Cardinal Pellagrù to see what he could quietly catch in the Florentine fishpond — but to be sure that no one knew that he was fishing.

The Florentines received Cardinal Pellagrù as they had received King Robert. They wanted his presence to be known even if Clement did not. The *carroccio* went out to meet him and it was escorted by a troop of lancers. Then came a procession of the Florentine clergy, and after them the Black *popolani*, some of them on horseback, others on foot.

But when the cardinal spoke, it was at a secret meeting. There the Florentine leaders told him how important it was to them — and to the pope — that Henry's coming either be prevented or delayed. For the pope's position — and for their safety — he must not be a *triumphator*.

Cardinal Pellagrù agreed.

"So, too, does Pope Clement, and when the time comes, you will have his every assistance. But not yet. And in the meantime you must not be alarmed at other actions of his."

What were the other actions they must not be alarmed at?

Here is one of them.

As Pellagrù came to Florence, other papal emissaries went to Henry.

"Clement," they reassured him, for he had heard rumors too, "will live up to his promise of crowning you with his own hands, or if not he will send duly designated legates. But before he does this you must negotiate a marriage between your daughter and King Robert's eldest son, and you must sign a treaty of friendship with Naples."

It was hardly likely that either would come to pass, Clement knew well, but it was also likely that both would be attempted, and while Henry attempted them, he hardly would move southward.

Florence, thought Clement, has offered me two weapons. I will choose what seems to be the duller one.

For he knew — and it was true — that delay would be more effective than attempted prevention. He knew that it offered far fewer risks. He knew that it had a far greater chance of success.

Dante — it must now be stated — knew it too, and it filled him with both anger and frustration. Anger at Florence for so wickedly opposing the elect of God. Frustration because the emperor did not seem to realize on what a merry dance he was being led.

He responded in the only way he could or knew how. He wrote two more letters which again were manifestos. One was to the Florentines. The other was to Henry. But like his letter to the princes, they were for all who cared to read them. They were his soldiery in his battle for the cause imperial. He wanted to deploy them where they would do the most good.

« *8* »

The letter to the Florentines first — a letter of such unbridled denunciation that it almost suggests Cicero's harangues against Cataline.

"Dante Alighieri, a Florentine in undeserved exile, to the Florentine scoundrels still there.

"The merciful providence of the eternal king who, in His goodness, rules forever in the heavens, yet does not scornfully turn aside from our affairs below — this merciful providence has entrusted to the Holy Roman Empire the direction of human affairs so that mankind may find repose under the peace of so powerful a protection and, subject always to the laws of nature, may live as the citizens of a well-ordered world."

This, he continues, is proven by the Holy Scripture. It is proven by the reason of the ancients. It is also proven by the fact that whenever "the throne of Augustus is vacant, the whole world goes astray, the helmsman and the rowers of the bark of St. Peter fall asleep, and unhappy Italy, abandoned to the whim of the mob and deprived of public guidance, is tossed about by winds and waves so baffling that no words can describe them any more than the Italians in their misery can measure them with their tears."

Beware, then, you — that is, the Florentines — "who have risen up in mad presumption against the manifest will of God." The Almighty is still a just judge.

But evidently you do not beware. Instead, "all too apt pupils in crime," you have been lured "by the gaping maw of your insatiable greed into every sin there is against the laws of God and man."

This being the case, "does not the fear of the second death make you shake and shiver — you who first and alone, dreading the yoke of liberty, have raged against the majesty of the Roman prince, he who is king of the world and God's lieutenant — and under the pretext that you are maintaining your time-honored rights, have refused to him the submission you owe, and have risen in rebellion?"

Senseless and perverse fools, do you not realize that law and order can end only when time ends? Are you not aware that, although it may be weakened, imperial rule can never be abolished? Or, like the men of a second Babel, are you trying to set up a new kind of sovereignty so that there will be one set of laws for Florence and another for Rome?

Then a suggestion which very certainly Dante hoped Clement would hear.

Would opposing and confounding Henry be enough?

If you envy the emperor, "why may it not please you to envy the apostolic monarchy in the same way? If Delia [the moon, and symbol of the empire] has a twin in heaven, why may not Delius [the sun, and symbol of the papacy] have one too?"

But then Dante turned from arguments to threats and warnings. He spoke like an Isaiah.

"If, however, you have become like the mountain of Gilboa — if your insolent arrogance has rendered you so incapable of receiving the dews of heaven that you are not afraid to oppose the eternal senate and are not even afraid of your lack of fear — will not another kind of fear shake you — the deadly and the human fear of ruin — when your inevitable shipwreck and the swift end of your outrageous robberies is seen to be at hand?"

Encircled by your ridiculous stockade, do you dare put your trust in such defenses?

If so, you are indeed blind.

"What good will it have done you to have girdled yourselves with ramparts and to have fortified yourselves with walls and towers when the eagle on his glittering golden banner swoops down?"

None at all.

Instead, the hopes that "you have vainly cherished" will in no way be advanced by your mutiny, and while you fondly dream that you are advancing your liberty you will be thrust into the prison house of slavery.

"The buildings which you have raised, not prudently to meet your needs but recklessly as palaces of pleasure — these buildings, since they are circled by no walls of a new Troy, you will see, to your grief, crumbling beneath the battering ram and then devoured by flames. Your people, which, divided against itself, now snarls, some for you, some against you, you will see united to curse you, for a starving rabble knows no fear. With remorse you will see your churches pillaged — those churches which are now thronged daily with your wives and children; the latter, puzzled and not knowing why, are doomed to suffer for the sins of their fathers. And if my soul of a prophet is not deceived, your city, worn out with its long misery, shall finally be delivered into the hands of the foreigner after the greater part of its citizens have either died the death or been made prisoners, while the few that are left to be sent into exile look on at her downfall with tears and lamentation."

In short, you will be like Saguntum (a city in Spain destroyed by Hannibal), except that it suffered while defending liberty.

Nor can Florence take any consolation from history.

The Florentines, of course, think of Parma, which won a brief victory over Frederick II.

"Instead, you should think of the thunderbolts of the first Frederick. You should think of Spoleto and Milan."

Thinking of these, the Florentines should submit to Henry and win the true freedom which is obedience to the law.

But they would not.

"O wretched offspring of Fiesole! O barbarians now to be punished for a second time! Is not knowing what will happen sufficient to strike fear in you?"

Dante thought it was.

"For to tell the truth I believe that although you wear a pretense of hope on your faces and your lying lips, you really tremble during your waking hours and start up from your dreams in alarm."

Nor would a belated repentance help the Florentines now, for "Henry, the elect of God," does not come "for his own ambitions but for the public good."

Moreover, it should not, "for a late repentance of this kind" — i.e., made in fear and not in true contrition — "will not purchase pardon but is rather the prelude to long-due punishment. 'The sinner shall be so smitten that he die.'"

« 9 »

All this was set down — or, at any rate, sent out — "on the day before the calends of April [March 31]," and it was probably set down or sent out from Porciano.

Seventeen days later — "fifteen days before the calends of May," or April 17 — and also at this Count Guidi castle, a second letter was completed and on its way.

It was addressed effulgently "to that most glorious and most fortunate conqueror, the sole lord, the Lord Henry, by divine providence king of the Romans and ever Augustus." But this time it did not come alone from Henry's "devoted servant, Dante Alighieri," but "from all Tuscans everywhere who desire peace."

This peace had been theirs, Dante began, this peace had been his and theirs "as the boundless love of God bears witness." It had been his and theirs "so that in its marvelous sweetness the hardships of war might grow less, and that in its usages we might come to enjoy the usages of His eternal kingdom."

Yea, this peace had been theirs but was now no longer.

"For the envy of the ancient and implacable Adversary who ever plots secretly against the well-being of man" — the Devil — "having dispossessed some with their own consent, has impiously despoiled the rest of us, which he could do because our champion was absent."

For that reason, continued Dante, "we have long wept by the waters of confusion, and have unceasingly prayed for the protection of our rightful king, who will destroy the minions of the cruel tyrant and set us up again under our own justice."

But now, he went on, our rightful king has appeared.

"Thou, the successor of Caesar and Augustus, have overleaped the summit of the Apennines" — he, of course, meant the Alps — "and have brought back the Tarpeian standards, so that our deep sighing has ended and the flooding of our tears has dried up. Like a long-waited sunrise, the new hope of a better age shines in Italy, and many of us, letting our longings rejoice before they have been fulfilled, sing, as Virgil did, of the reign of Saturn and the return of the Virgin."

But now doubts begin to arise as Henry lingers in the north. By some, "our sun is either believed to be pausing or suspected of retreat."

But not by Dante, says Dante. Not by Dante and his friends.

"Yet even we marvel at the sluggishness that holds thee so that, although for a long time thou hast been victor in the valley of the Po, thou dost overlook and neglect Tuscany just as if thou didst not remember — we fear that thou dost not — that the imperial rights under thy protection are not hedged in by the boundaries of Liguria, nor the Roman power cramped within the limits of Italy or even by the coastline of tricorn Europe."

Far from it! Only Amphitrite — the daughter of Oceanus, the ocean — limits them.

Said Virgil in the *Aeneid:*

> From the fair line of Troy shall one day a Caesar be born.
> The ocean shall bound his empire, his fame the stars only.

Then Dante added something he had said before, and would again.

"If the decree" — that all the world be taxed, which brought Joseph and Mary to Bethlehem — "had not gone out from the court of the most just of all governments, the only-begotten Son of God would not have chosen that moment to have been born.

"Let him, then," he continued, "for whom the whole world waits" —

let Henry, that is — "feel shame that his feet have been so long entangled in so narrow a corner of the earth. Let it not escape the attention of Augustus that Tuscan tyranny is encouraged by its conviction that he will delay, and that day by day, fomenting the insolence of the wicked, it goes from strength to strength and piles rash deed on rash deed."

He then cited the words of Curio to Caesar in Lucan's *Pharsalia.*

> While the factions waver and quake, their strength no more oaklike,
> End thou delay. Delay over the ready did harm too.
> It makes them pay the more dearly for the same task, the same toils.

This Henry owed to his own Ascanius — to his son, Prince John of Bohemia. It was, too, his duty as king consecrated — because he was holy as well as Roman and emperor.

"For thou too hast been anointed king so that they might smite Amalek and show no mercy to Agag."

But instead "throughout the winter and now through the spring" he had lingered at Milan.

What folly!

"Dost thou think to destroy the poisonous hydra by cutting off its heads?"

Alcides (Hercules) knew better. He knew that as each head was cut off, two new ones grew in its place.

"For to destroy a tree, the mere chopping off of limbs is not enough. As long as the roots are unharmed and can supply nourishment, the hateful branches will grow thicker than ever."

Then he made a point which subsequent events would justify. What would Henry accomplish by conquering Cremona? Would not Brescia then revolt — and after that Pavia, Vercelli, Bergamo, and other cities?

No, the source of troubles lay elsewhere.

"Dost thou not know, O most excellent of princes, canst thou not see from the watchtower of thine exalted highness where the stinking vixen has her lair and is safe from the hunters? Forsooth, the she-criminal does not drink from either the swift-flowing Po nor from thy Tiber. It is the headlong torrent of the Arno that her lips pollute. Florence — but thou surely knowest this — is her name."

It was Florence that was the viper that turned against the vitals of her Mother, the sick sheep that infected the flock, the incestuous Myrrha who lay with her own father.

He has more to say, but this is enough.

Then the peroration.

"Up, therefore, thou new son of Jesse! End thy procrastination! Take courage that the eyes of God look down on thee! Overthrow this Goliath with the stone of thine own strength! For when he falls, night and the shadow of its terror shall overcome the Philistines. They will flee and Israel will be delivered. Then our heritage which was taken from us and for which we have lamented without cease will be restored to us. And just as now, exiles in Babylon, we remember our holy Jerusalem, so in that day, once more citizens who live and breathe in peace, we will rejoice that we can look back on the time of our misery."

« *10* »

Thus Dante's two letters, which were eloquent if again perhaps too wordy, but it is not recorded that either of them produced any immediate effect. Immediate, however, is the important word, for in the long run they both were listened to.

Every action, it is said, produces a reaction, and in the long run both Florence and Henry reacted, although each of them reacted in a different way.

Once again, the Florentines first, for they reacted first.

To them — to "the most vainglorious of all Tuscans"; to those "eaten up by pride, envy, avarice, treachery, faithlessness, corruption, and obstinacy"; to the citizens of the city "that for shepherd had taken a wolf" (all these are additional epithets hurled by Dante) — it began, in the March days and April days of the letters, to look more and more as if 1311 would be a long hot summer.

Why not? Henry was now on the south side of the Alps, and nobody — not even Dante, despite his letter — knew what he would do next and what his capabilities were. The Florentines, on the other hand, had many promises but except for King Robert's Diego de la Rat and his Catalans they had nothing hard and firm.

Being realists, they faced this situation, and also being stubborn (or courageous and determined) and resourceful, they took steps to deal with it. They made various kinds of provisions, but all to the same end.

They continued, for example, to put more and more pressure on King Philip.

"Your Majesty has never ceased to promise us that you would come to no agreement with the emperor, and that if necessary you would move the strength of your army against him and would come in person to Rome to annihilate our common enemy."

Well, it *was* necessary, the implication was, and where was Philip?

They stepped up their appeals to the Brescians, who were holding off — and by so doing holding back — the onetime count of Luxemburg.

"Do not forget that upon your defense hangs the safety of all Italy and of the Guelphs. Do not forget, either, that the Latins should always hold those of the German race to be their enemies. They are distasteful to us in their actions, their habits, their souls, and in what they seek. It is not only impossible to be their slaves but to have any kind of dealings with them."

Men and supplies would have been more helpful, but for logistic reasons words had to suffice.

The Florentines also tried to stir up the Perugians — and others — to throw off allegiance to the emperor. They did not want imperial strongholds around and behind them.

"Shake off," they wrote, "the service in which you find yourself. Proclaim sweet liberty!"

They went further, too, when they could go farther. They could not get military assistance to Brescia, but it seemed worthwhile — since it protected an important flank — to send Diego de la Rat to Bologna. At least no imperial army would descend on them by way of the Futa Pass.

And to protect another flank they stripped their own defenses in order to reinforce the units they already had in Sarzana and Pietrasanta, and in certain of the Malaspina castles in the Lunigiana, and in other castles up and down the Arno.

They stripped their own defenses — but then did something to mimimize the dangers this might bring.

Sensibly — and with a surprising prudence in view of the emotions which had pertained for so long — they took an important new step, apparently successful, toward reducing their internal divisions.

They decided to be reasonable for a change!

A commission was set up which consisted of the six priors, the gonfalonier of justice, and twelve *savi*, two from each *sesto* of the city. It had powers to act as well as report, and, on September 2, it came up with a decree which, because of the prominent part this side-changing lawyer played in drafting it, has been known ever since as the Reform of Baldo d'Aguglione.

It provided for a limited political amnesty. Subject only to the posting of bonds to assure future good conduct, and a few other minor conditions including the payment of small fines, it permitted the return to Florence of all those who had been condemned and sentenced for political reasons provided they had been Guelphs at the time of their sentences.

Ghibellines were excluded, and — here was the catch — the Black-dominated commission could decide who were Ghibellines and who were not.

These Ghibellines were listed specifically and by name.

"It is accepted and reserved," says the last paragraph of the decree, "that each and every one of those named below shall have no benefit expressly conferred by the above provisions or by any of them, nor should they be freed, liberated, or absolved from their condemnations and banishments, but they are and remain banished and condemned in all ways as they were before the present. And the names are as follows —"

Those pardoned were about fifteen hundred in number, and the exempted from pardon perhaps less than one fourth of that.

Some of the latter are of interest.

The Uberti, who had pledged themselves to fight the Blacks in the San Godenzo agreement which Dante signed.

The Salterelli — Lapo was not as successful a side changer as Baldo.

Palmieri Altoviti.

The Scolaii; the Cerchi; Beatrice's Portinari; Dante's noble kinsmen the Elisei; the sons of Dante's turbulent cousin Cione del Bello; the sons of Ser Parenza of Incisa, among them Ser Petracco, Petrarch's father.

Giano della Bella, sponsor of the Ordinances of Justice.

(Here we have something interesting. Expelled from Florence in 1295, Giano had played no part in the events which led up to the Black revolution, yet even after sixteen years those ruling the city feared that he might still have a popular following that would bode ill to them.)

And Dante "Alleghierii," his chickens — the chickens of his two violent diatribes — having thus come to roost.

Dante lovers have forever since poured vials of their scorn upon his inclusion in this exclusion, yet to me the comment of Robert Davidsöhn seems more sensible.

"Today," he wrote in his history of Florence, "the criticism heaped upon Florence for having lost this opportunity of recalling her greatest son is violent indeed, but on looking over the facts carefully, one must agree that it is unfair. The condemnation of Dante nine years earlier was and is a disgrace to Florence. Dante was then found guilty because he defended the city against the pope, and that should have been a title of honor. But now Dante was not only an enthusiastic partisan of the German king against whom Florence was fighting not merely for her independence but for her life, but with fiery words he urged him [the emperor] to turn his arms against his [Dante's] native city. No other city, no other state, either ancient or modern, could have acted differently than Florence did when, in September 1311, it refused to annul the poet's sentence."

With this statement I find it hard not to be in accord.

« *11* »

To Alto Arrigo, 1311 brought a long hot summer too, and in his case this was literal as well as figurative. For whether the decision to besiege

Brescia was wise or unwise, once he had invested it, it would have been fatal to withdraw, and so as May ran out to become June, July, and finally August, he had no choice but to camp with his army in front of the city and hope for the best.

The best was very far from good.

Frustration — on both sides — and the unending and unbearable scorching of the Lombard sun, which at times can make even the tropics seem cool and refreshing, frayed men's nerves. The war turned savage. Even Henry turned savage.

One of the most notable of the Brescian leaders was Tibaldo Bruciati, and because this Tibaldo "had received benefit from the emperor" while he wandered in dire straits and in poverty through Lombardy with his followers Henry regarded him as a traitor.

He would treat him as a traitor, which he did.

One day Tibaldo rode out on a sortie, and "through the justice of God" (Dino Compagni) his horse stumbled and fell.

"He was seized and led to the emperor, who rejoiced greatly that he had been taken prisoner."

A court-martial was promptly arranged and the Brescian was convicted. He was "dragged around the city in an ox-hide and then beheaded."

"In like manner, those within the city behaved cruelly to those without. When they took a prisoner they placed him on the battlements so that he could be seen, and there they flayed him."

Then came plague.

(The death of the emperor's brother Valeran was no more than an episode. A "fine man and of lofty stature," he was riding around the city wearing no helmet and conspicuously clad in a bright red doublet when the quarrel from a large crossbow hit him in the neck. He lived only a few days. This may have hardened Henry, but had no other consequences.)

"The air was corrupted with the stench of the horses" — presumably slain horses — "and because the camp had so long remained there. In consequence, there arose much sickness both within and without, and a great part of those from beyond the mountains" — the Luxemburgers, the Germans, the French, and the Burgundians — "fell ill, and a great many barons died there. Others left through fear of the sickness and died on the road."

This is from Villani. He is confirmed by Dino Compagni.

"Many counts, knights, and barons, both Germans and Lombards, died there. Very many fell sick there."

One of those to die was "the valiant Monsieur Guy de Namurs, brother of the count of Flanders," and at his death demoralization set in.

Who would be safe if Monsieur Guy could die?

"The most part of the host counseled the emperor that he should depart."

But Henry did not counsel Henry this.

"Good sirs," he said instead, "it is clear that those in Brescia are in worse pass than we are. They too have sickness and death, but they have lack of victuals also. I will stay until I have taken the city."

More days passed. The grapes ripened into purple. It was September.

On September 16, Cardinal Fieschi — friendly to Henry, but in Brescia as an emissary from Pope Clement — with perhaps Cardinal Niccolò da Prato and another, came to the imperial presence with offers. The Brescians would surrender if their lives and property were spared.

They would be, answered Henry.

"The emperor" — this agreed on, and on September 18 — "entered the city, and kept the terms agreed on."

But did he?

"He caused all the walls and strongholds to be destroyed, and he exacted a fine of seventy thousand gold florins."

He also sent one hundred of the best men of the city — "both magnates and *popolani*" — from the city.

Then and then only did he think about the advice which Dante and others had given him. Four more months had elapsed and Rome was still no nearer than a mirage. He must go to Rome, striking as he did so at the only power which unequivocally barred his way.

But how?

The Apennine passes were now closed to him by the forces which Florence had assembled during his delayings, and so too were the roads along the coast or through the Lunigiana.

Then he must go by sea, and going by sea meant that he must go by way of Genoa. Disregarding, therefore — other than to pause briefly to impose his will upon Pavia — revolts and almost certain future revolts, he turned his back on Lombardy and moved as swiftly as he could toward the Ligurian Alps. These he crossed with such followers as still remained and descended the steep western slopes to Genova la Superba. Genoa was then "held by Messer Branca d'Oria" — actually it was held by Branca's son Bernardo d'Oria — "who received him honorably and swore obedience to him."

This was on October 31.

In Genoa, he would spend the next four months — four months marked by intense and sometimes successful political activity and by a second personal loss. His Empress Margaret died in Genoa, possibly herself a victim of the pestilence that walked at Brescia, since her death came less than two months after her departure. She was "a good and holy woman," "a woman virtuous even to sanctity." She was buried in the handsome, since-demolished church of San Francesco di Casteletto.

A brother and a dear wife within a few short months! Were the Fates against him?

Then "in the said year [1312], on the sixteenth day of February, he departed from Genoa with a fleet of thirty galleys."

The winds were fair and the sailors chanted as they raised the sails, but soon storms struck in.

"On account of bad weather, they were obliged to put into Portovenere and to remain there for eighteen days."

Then they continued to Porto Pisano, where Henry disembarked.

From Porto Pisano to Pisa was a scant three or four miles.

He rode these galliardly.

He entered Pisa on March 6, and was received by the Pisans as their lord.

All was festival, rejoicings, and procession.

The citizens presented him with a splendid sword and with the seventy thousand more florins they had promised they would give him when he came to Tuscany.

Now the gates were open, they cried! He would win back for them all they had lost. The winter and its snows — the thirty-year winter since Meloria — were over and gone.

« 12 »

It was at this time, apparently, that Dante rejoined the emperor — either at Genoa, as some think, or at the city near the mouth of the Arno whose white cathedral and white leaning tower he had perhaps seen in the distance across the low, flat, and sometimes marshy alluvial plain when as a youth he fought against Pisa in the Caprona campaign, but which he could now enter as a friend and not a foe.

For a Genoa encounter, we have, to be sure, only circumstantial evidence, as we have only circumstantial evidence for a trip southward on an imperial galley. Yet in each case the circumstantial evidence is reasonably convincing.

Genoa.

We know from the Branca d'Oria story — or at any rate it is a virtual certainty — that Dante did visit Genoa at some time, and it has also been pointed out that he could not have visited it in 1308, for the lines about Branca had not been written or circulated then. But on what other later occasion would he have gone there? Furthermore, Branca's son in 1312 newly ruled the place and was touchy about his father's reputation. But what better way of getting the favor of this new ruler — and the favor of a new ruler is always to be sought — than by assaulting Branca's traducer?

A trip southward on an imperial galley.

Dante had clearly seen a large naval contingent in operation on the high seas.

Purgatorio XXX:

> Just as an admiral from stern to stem
> Doth walk to see the mariners who work
> The other ships and to encourage them,
> So on the left side of the chariot . . .

But in all of Dante's life there was only one time when he could have seen an admiral commanding his fleet, and that was if he sailed with Henry on the flagship — or at any rate on one of the vessels — of the thirty-ship armada that took the emperor to Porto Pisano during that late February and early March.

But in regard to Pisa, it is another matter. We have definite and incontrovertible proof that Dante was in Pisa, and in 1312, and in that part of 1312 when Henry was there.

This is found in a letter — *Familiari* XXI, 15 — written by Petrarch to Giovanni Boccaccio in which he lamely tries to clear himself of Boccaccio's suggestion that he was jealous of his great predecessor.

"To begin with, I have no cause to hate the man. I only saw him once in my life and that was when he was shown to me in my very early boyhood. He was younger than my grandfather and older than my father. With the latter — on the same day and by the same civic tempest — he was driven forth from Florence."

In my very early boyhood. But technically, during the Middle Ages, one's boyhood was supposed to begin during one's eighth year.

But elsewhere Petrarch said explicitly that he spent this eighth year in Pisa.

"I spent my first year but not all of it in Arezzo; the next six at Incisa; and my eighth year in Pisa. Thereafter in trans-Alpine Gaul on the left bank of the Rhone River."

Petrarch's eighth year ran from July 20, 1311, to July 20, 1312.

Sometime between those two dates he was in Pisa and Dante was pointed out to him.

For Dante was in Pisa too.

13

He was there in high spirits and with exalted hopes — hopes, indeed, almost as exalted as they had been when Henry first crossed the Mt. Cenis Pass — for would not the emperor do now and at last what he had strongly urged him: crush and destroy the stinking Florentine she-fox, and let men of goodwill return to the city, and peace and evenhanded justice come back to the good Tuscan earth?

He could and would, thought Dante, and had good reasons for thinking so, for even as far back as November, while Henry was still in Genoa, he had taken some first important steps.

"At that time," writes Giovanni Villani, "he issued a proclamation against the Florentines, saying that if within forty days they did not send him twelve good men with full and plenipoteniary powers to obey him, he would condemn their property and their persons to be seized wherever they might be found."

He thought that he was playing from strength, for from the ecumenical council at Vienne, Pope Clement — who was still trying not to come out into the open — sent him word that "not being able to come in person" (to his proposed coronation) he would send Niccolò da Prato "with power to act as if he had been the pope himself."

"But the commonwealth of Florence" — by now knowing what Clement's real intentions were, and heartened by the fact that King Robert met Henry's invitation to further negotiations by sending the Florentines more troops — "did not send any emissaries at all, but instead instructed their merchants who were in Genoa to depart from the city at once."

This they did — and in the nick of time. For as soon as Henry was certain of Florentine recalcitrance, he caused all the Florentine merchandise in Genoa to be seized by his officers. If they had been there, he would have seized the merchants too.

But that was only the beginning. On December 24, a stronger move was made. Florence was placed under the ban of the empire. Her priors, the members of her councils, and all her officials were declared to be perpetual outlaws. She was declared to have forfeited her independence. The castles, towns, and cities under her jurisdiction were annexed to the empire. In addition, she was fined five thousand gold pounds.

Small wonder that the exiles — now Ghibellines by the force of circumstance — flocked to the emperor in increasing numbers, and flocked to him with high hopes.

Riccardo Ughetti with a proposal that Henry coin imperial money which alone would be valid in Italy. This would strike at the all-conquering florin.

One of the Schiatta. A Guidolotti. Palmieri Altoviti.

And Dante — renewing his pleas.

For although Leonardo Bruni makes a point of saying that Dante was not with the emperor at the time of his final confrontation with Florence — because Dante like Farinata degli Uberti did not "wish to be present at" or play a part in the destruction of his birthplace — it is not likely that he abandoned either his invectives or his call for action quite this soon.

Henry received them in the Gambacorti gardens, where he was pondering what to do about Albrecht's murderer, John the Parricide, whom he had sentenced to death at Speyer but who now walked the streets of Pisa clad as an Augustinian monk.

He listened to what they had to say.

Then he promised — and carried out his promise — strikes against Pontedera, where he captured a large train of sumpter mules, and San Miniato.

But even as his knights and men-at-arms thus probed Florentine territory, Henry was contemplating something else, and after seven weeks of not always explained delays he moved again and it was not toward Florence.

"On the twenty-third day of April," writes Villani, "*the king of Germany* left Pisa with his followers, who numbered two thousand or more mounted knights. He went by way of the Maremma, and thence without halting, through Sienese territory and that of Orvieto. After that, and without any hindrance, he came to Viterbo, which he entered peacefully since it was under the lordship of the Colonna.

"He stayed there for many days, not being able to gain admittance to Rome either by the gate of St. Peter's or by the Emilian Bridge. Both of these were held by the forces of the Orsini."

But at last he did depart and came to Montemalo.

"And afterwards with the forces that followed him without, and those of the Colonna and their party within, he assailed the fortress and strongholds at the bridge, and overcame them.

"And thus on the seventh day of May he entered Rome and came to Santa Sabina."

There he took up his residence in a hostel. But shortly — since the Orsini, despite their setback, still pressed him too hard — he crossed the city to the Lateran palace. This he made his headquarters for the ensuing struggle.

14

For there was to be an ensuing struggle and it would be a bitter one — and one in which a counted-on former ally became either an ally of or an abettor of those who opposed Henry.

I refer to Pope Clement, who now made an undisputed change of sides. "Before the Gascon had betrayed High Harry," says Dante (*Paradiso* XVII) of an earlier, happier day. Then he had perhaps counted on Clement. But now he could no longer.

Here is the somewhat cloak-and-dagger story of how the change was brought about. It comes from letters written to King Jaime of Aragon by his ambassador at the papal court. Word had come to King Philip that Clement — who alternately blew hot and cold as his fear of the French king and his hopes of being made independent by Henry were alternately in the ascendant — had just penned a letter (but not yet sent it) to Prince John of Taranto, who now occupied much of Rome at the orders of his brother King Robert and at Florentine request.

By it John was directed to surrender the Campidoglio (the strategically important Capitoline Hill) to whatever Roman senator Henry should designate. This, of course, would have meant surrendering Rome to Henry.

This must be prevented, cried Philip. And at all costs.

And so on March 28, 1312, there galloped off to Vienne, where the pope now presided over his council, the three sons of Philip — namely Louis, King of Navarre (the future Louis V of France), Philip, count of Poitiers (the future Philip V), and Charles, count of La Marche (the future Charles IV) — together with two of Philip's most effective councillors, Eguerrand de Marigny and Guillaume de Nogaret.

There to Clement they spoke plainly and persuasively.

It is against French interests to call off or to weaken John of Taranto, they said, for if Henry became master of Rome, the king of France would become a vassal of the emperor, and France would be subordinate to Germany.

It was against papal interests too. Henry now courted the papacy and Clement with lavish promises and with a show of humility, but once he had been crowned — and in St. Peter's — it would be another matter. He would then do what every other emperor had tried to do. He would try to bring the pope to heel.

Finally — and this was whispered in a tone of menace — Clement was in France (even though he was supposedly master of his own small sovereign papal state) and was surrounded by France — and by French armies.

The last argument was the most effective.

"Clement," said a Florentine only a few months later, "is a weak and indecisive man who wishes above all things to take no responsibility and to avoid all disturbances."

Obviously he could best avoid all disturbances — including, possibly, even the loss of the papacy — by acceding to Philip.

The letter was torn up in the presence of the five emissaries. Nor did the pope let things end at that. From the friend of Henry he became his implacable enemy, and joined with the French monarch in trying to bring down the man he had elevated so high.

« 15 »

With at first partial, it should be noted, and later with complete success; for the above-described action on the part of Clement — or rather his above-described decision not to act — in the long run would deal a fatal blow to Henry's cause.

In the long run! For at the moment Henry's cause still looked good. After months and even years — and many delays and uncertainties, not all of which were necessary — he was at last in the Eternal City. To be sure, he only occupied the smaller and less consequential part of it — the southern and southeastern section which ran from the Ponte Molle to the Latern (palace and church) and a little beyond. But if Prince John and the Orsini occupied the rest of the city, including the castel Sant' Angelo, his and their position was by no means secure.

Moreover, John had the usual troubles of a man who deals with allies.

The Florentines grumbled about King Berta. (King Bertha — they called Robert this because unjustly and impatiently they thought that he lacked decisiveness and was effeminate.)

The Catalan reinforcements were discontent. To make sure that Rome was defended, Florence had sent Diego de la Rat with four hundred of his knights and three hundred *almogávares* to the Eternal City. But they complained that there was no booty and that their pay was in arrears.

Nor — except at sea, where a Neapolitan fleet had attacked and dispersed a flotilla of seven galleys bringing much-needed imperial crossbowmen near the again ill-fated shoal of Meloria — were his own Neapolitans of any help. A Neapolitan army had indeed been moved to Gaetà — where it could either defend the realm or intervene — but as suddenly it was moved back to Naples, fearing either an insurrection or an invasion by Frederick of Sicily.

But then from the north came tidings of Clement's new position and John knew that he could now stand firm. He would not win a victory and then have to abandon his spoils. He could carry out his orders without misgivings.

Henry got the tidings too and promptly broke off negotiations with Robert, who was still pressing the marriage matter and who said that John had come to Rome only to attend the coronation.

"The king's offers are too late," he said, "and Messer John has come too early."

Without waiting, he then attacked the Taranto prince.

At first, he was at least modestly successful. In the white, dazzling sunshine of a Roman spring, he took the Campidoglio and the convent of the Aracoeli which stood atop it. The Orsini and one thousand Florentine militiamen retreated to the towers which the Orsini had built around the ruined theater of Pompey near the Campo di Fiore. This was on May 25. But on May 26, the emperor's fortunes changed. This day began with a second victory, for his men drove their opponents from this new refuge. But — on such small things great issues turn — they turned to strip the slain and to plunder, and when Prince John ordered a counterattack they were in disarray. In vain one of Henry's Roman allies ordered all the bells to be sounded. The citizens stayed in their houses. For six hours raged a hand-to-hand battle, and after heavy losses — among them another imperial relative, Henry's cousin Thibaut of Liége, who was murdered in cold blood after being taken prisoner — the emperor was obliged to withdraw.

He withdrew to the Lateran, where he brooded disconsolately for a little more than a month.

Then he came to a conclusion.

He could not force his way to St. Peter's, but he still held the mother church of Rome and of the world.

And half a coronation was better than no coronation at all.

On August 1, 1312, say both Villani and Dino Compagni, but actually on June 29, "Henry, count of Luxemburg, emperor and king of the Romans, was crowned at Rome in the church of St. John Lateran by Messer Niccolò, cardinal of Prato, and by Messer Luca de' Fieschi, cardinal of Genoa, and by Messer Arnaldo Pellagrù, a Gascon cardinal" — actually it was Cardinal Arnaud de Faugères — "by license of the pope and of his cardinals," who, curiously, had not withdrawn this permission.

Three weeks later — on July 21 — because his men were weary, because he feared further disorders and did not know how to cope with them, and because he did not want a Roman summer, he and his men withdrew to Tivoli, where they could look down on the elusive capital through the blurring dog-days haze.

They could look down through the haze and see the dream that had escaped them. For although they did not know it, Henry's visionary knight-errantry had reached its apogee. From now on there would be nothing but decline and fall.

I say "although they did not know it," and that they did not seems to me incontrovertible. For it was at this time — it was following his Roman disillusion and frustration — that Henry did what he should have done long before; that he struck against the head and intelligence of his enemies; that he moved against the vixen that poisoned the Arno; that he gave up his hacking at the branches to try to chop away the root of the tree.

He did this with very little delay. Sometime in August — or not more than a month after his arrival there — the emperor left Tivoli for Todi, "where he was received honorably as their lord by the inhabitants." Then he passed through the territory of the Perugians, "burning and destroying," which was easy, for the wheat fields were now the color of umber. He took Castiglione on Lake Trasimeno and then came to Cortona. Thence he moved to Arezzo, where again "he was received with great honor." At Arezzo he assembled a new army and forthwith began to move with it.

And now at last the Florentines could see hostile banners and hear the tramp of hostile feet and know that these were not men who came to make a foray but actual invaders, for on September 12 the imperial forces actually entered Florentine territory. Within days Henry took Caposevole, Montevarchi, and San Giovanni Valdarno; "came without hindrance to Figline"; and invested Incisa. On September 19, he moved even closer. On that day, Henry and his men crossed the Arno "near where the Mensola enters it" and actually penetrated the suburbs. They established their headquarters at San Salvi, where Corso Donati had been killed.

If they had done this a year earlier Henry might have taken the city, but it was now too late, for the Florentines and their leaders were now ready.

"They burned all the houses on the way," says Villani. "They called up the citizens by sounding the tocsin. The bishop of Florence armed himself" — replaced his crozier with a sword — "and hastened to defend the moats. A body of the people on foot were with him. They barred the gates and ordered the gonfalonier and his men to guard the place day and night. Within the walls on that side" — the side threatened by Henry — "they pitched a camp with pavilions, tents, and booths, and within a short time they had made palisades with portcullises out of all kinds of wood."

Nor did the other Tuscan cities fail them. Between them, Lucca, Siena, Pistoia, Prato, Volterra, Colle, San Gimignano, and San Miniato sent sixteen hundred horsemen and sixty-eight hundred foot soldiers. Bologna sent four hundred horsemen and one thousand foot soldiers; the Romagna three hundred horsemen and fifteen hundred foot soldiers; Gubbio one hundred horsemen; and Città di Castello fifty horsemen.

Against these — and the Florentine troops which must have numbered as many more — Henry, although he had "much people [possibly as many as two thousand] on foot," could oppose only eighteen hundred horsemen, of which eight hundred were "foreigners" and eager to get home. The disparity is obvious.

Nevertheless — and with the weather against him too — Henry stayed at San Salvi for nearly six weeks, making occasional raids and burning a farmhouse or two but for the most part allowing his men to enjoy the benefits of "the most fruitful and fertile harvest" that there had been for "these thirty years past." Why should he do more when he had hopes — indeed had high hopes — "of gaining the city by agreement"?

There was not even an investment or a blockade.

The gate that faced Henry was indeed locked and barred, but every other gate was left open.

"The merchandise came in and went out just as if there had been no fighting."

A "phony war," we would perhaps call it today, but more probably a war in which the emperor used force or threat of force to force negotiations. Probably face-saving negotiations. Almost certainly no more than that.

Then, almost as ineffectually as it had begun, it ended.

"On the night before All Saints' Day, and having burned his camp," Henry departed from Florence and came to the plain of the Ema, where he remained for three days. Then he removed to San Casciano, where the Pisans came to his assistance with five hundred horsemen, one hundred foot soldiers, and five hundred archers. But he hardly used them. The snows and rain had now come and there was too much "sickness among his people." Henry fell ill himself. Finally, on January 6, 1313, "he came to Poggibonizi [Poggibonsi]," which he renamed Castello Imperiale.

There he spent all that remained to him of this winter of his discontent. Spent it unhappily, for although he took a few Florentine strongholds such as Barberino and San Donato in Poggio, he and his men "suffered much want and were in great need of provisions, since the Sienese on one side and the Florentines on the other had closed the roads" by which supplies might have come.

On March 9, he could take no more, and since King Frederick of Sicily sent him twenty thousand golden doubloons with which to pay his soldiers and his debts — and promised in addition that he would soon have a Sicilian fleet there — he returned to the Pisa he had come to with plumes and panoply almost a year earlier, poor in health and shaken in his fortune, but still, with a Teutonic tenacity, refusing to give up.

XXII

De Monarchia

WHERE was Dante at this time? Where was he during the some-what more than nine months when his Alto Arrigo marched on Rome; remained there for seventy-five fruitless days; and then finally, after various halts and pauses, moved against Florence, only to end up after a grim winter in Pisa once more? Where was he during this time which was as important to him as it was to the emperor, and for similar if not the same reasons?

The truth is that we do not know — and that strictly speaking we cannot know — for except for the fact that he was in Pisa when Henry was, and for Leonardo Bruni's firm statement that he was not with Henry when Henry besieged Florence, we have only two places that make any claim upon his presence and one of these claims is pretty thin.

Yet it is permitted to hazard some guesses, and this I do, once again basing them on passages in Dante's writings — in this case, however, passages in the *Commedia*, since the *Convivio* and the *De Vulgari Eloquentia* were written long before the emperor appeared and hence could not have any bearing on the matter.

Inferno XIII:

> No green leaves, only those of somber aspect;
> No branches smooth, but gnarled and knotty ones;
> No fruits there were, but only tangled thorns.
> No brakes so rough and so entangled have
> The fierce and savage beasts that hold in scorn
> The tilled fields between Cecina and Corneto.

Inferno XXV:

> Maremma, I do think, has not as many
> Vipers as he did have upon his rump
> And up to where our human face begins.

Inferno XXIX:

> As the pain would be if from the lazar houses
> Of the Val di Chiana between July and September
> And of the Maremma and of Sardinia the sick
> Had crawled together into a single ditch,
> Such was it there, and such a stench came from them
> As doth come ever forth from pustulant limbs.

Here a geographical note should be inserted. Cecina is a small river that flows into the Tyrrhenian sea about thirty miles south of Pisa. Corneto, "a noble fortress looking down on the Tuscan sea and surrounded by a triple wall," is about the same distance north of Rome. The Maremma lies roughly between them. It was, but no longer is, a wild wasteland of contorted trees and stagnant marshlands. The wild beasts that dwelt in it were boars and bears — the Maremma boar is still famous and still hunted — with perhaps an occasional wolf or tawny-colored wildcat. It was noted for its subhuman, half-starved, fever-shaken inhabitants, the fever coming from "air and water corrupted by the south wind and the excessive heat."

Inferno XIV:

> In silence came we to where gushes forth
> From out the woods a little rivulet
> Whose redness makes me shudder even now.
> As doth from Bulicame flow a brook
> Which then is shared among the prostitutes,
> So this one took its way across the sand.

"Bulicame," says Boccaccio, "is a boiling lake near Viterbo and some say that near it are the houses of the public women. As it flows down and so that they can wash their clothes, these divert it so that a small branch comes to each room."

Benvenuto da Imola confirms its redness and a sulfurous (and hence infernal) smell, and, in his *Dittamondo*, Fazio degli Uberti says in rhyme that it seethed constantly and that if you threw a sheep into it, it would be cooked through and through in less time than a man could walk a mile.

Cooked through and through with a constant water temperature of one hundred thirty-one degrees, which is what a modern guidebook assigns to it! The guidebook also calls the water cerulean. Have they changed color?

As we have already seen, Dante also knew the Lago di Bolsena with its eels; and Montemalo; and Rome. But this knowledge could have come at another time.

But he had seen also — or we believe that he had seen — many of the other things that Henry would have come upon as he worked his way northward.

The Val di Chiana — already noted — is only one of them.

This Val di Chiana (valley of the Chiana River), says Benvenuto, was "a certain marshy, pestiferous, and fetid valley in Tuscany between Chiusi, Arezzo, and Cortona." Henry certainly passed through it as he left Perugian territory for Arezzo, and equally certainly it made an impression on Dante, for he mentions the slow flow of its waters in *Paradiso* XIII.

Far greater, however — and expressed in far more transcendent poetry, expressed in fact in some of the most transcendent poetry Dante ever wrote — was the impression made on him by Perugia and by Assisi. Here he truly soars.

Paradiso XI:

> Between Tupino and the water that leaps down
> From the hill chosen by the blessed Ubaldo
> There slants the fertile slope of the high mountain
> From which Perugia feels both heat and cold
> At her Sun Gate, and behind it weep
> Under their heavy yoke Nocera and Gualdo.
> From that slope, at the place it breaks the most
> Its steepness, on the world there rose a sun
> As our sun sometimes rises from the Ganges.
> Therefore let him who speaks words of the place
> Not say Ascesi — that would be too little —
> But Orient.

This passage serves as introduction to Dante's compact, intense seventy-five-line biography and eulogy of that "son of Pietro Bernardone" the wealthy silk merchant who "for this lady [Christian poverty] into strife with his own father ran — her for whom as for death the gates of pleasure few men do unlock," and so great was Dante's high, deep love for St. Francis, so Franciscan was he in many ways, that he need not have gone to Assisi to have written either these or any of the ensuing incandescent words.

Yet, by the same logic, it is safe to say that he would have gone there — that he must have gone there — if an opportunity presented itself, while the view from Perugia is described with such exactitude of detail, it is so much the view that we can still see from Perugia, and the feelings so much like the feelings that this view still inspires, that we must conclude that it too was something he had looked on himself. At some time or another he must have visited the city of the gryphon too.

There is one other passage which must here also be looked at as possibly pertinent to this part of Dante's life. This is the description of Fonte Avellana which Dante puts into the mouth of St. Peter Damian in *Paradiso* XXI:

> "Between Italia's two shores there rise peaks —
> They're not far distant from thy native land —
> So lofty that the thunder sounds below them.
> And there they make a mountain called Catria
> Beneath which was a hermitage consecrated
> Which one time was wholly devoted to worship."
> Thus he began his third speech unto me,
> And then continuing he went on: "Here
> Did I become so faithful to God's service
> That with no other food than olive oil
> I cheerfully endured both heat and frost,
> Content to think my contemplative thoughts.
> This cloiser one time used to yield to heaven
> Abundant harvest. Now it is so barren
> That soon this fact will be known to all.
> In that place I was Peter Damian,
> Peter the Sinner was I in the house
> Our Lady hath on the Adriatic shore.
> Little of mortal life remained to me
> When I was urged, yea dragged, to wear that hat
> Which handed is from bad man unto worse.
> Cephas [*St. Peter*] once came, came the great vessel
>   [*St. Paul*]
> Of the Holy Ghost, and they were lean and barefoot.
> They took what food they could at any inn.
> But now on each side one to prop them want
> These modern shepherds, and one to lead them —
> They have become so fat — and one to hold their train.
> They cover their palfreys with their own cloaks
> So that two beasts go under one skin.
> O patience, patience, how thou dost endure!"

"Once upon a time," says Benvenuto da Imola of this place over which presided not only St. Peter Damian but also Guido d'Arezzo, the inventor of musical notation, "it was thought by some that the author spoke of the hermitage of Camaldoli in the Casentino, which is indeed not far from the author's fatherland. But this is false, as is apparent by the name. For Catria is a tall mountain at the gateway to the March of Ancona."

"Catria," he said, and Catria it is, a 5500-foot peak in the central Apennines between Gubbio and Pergola; and there in a solitary wooded valley, itself 2100 feet above sea level, stood the monastery of Santa Croce di Avellana, founded in the tenth century and possibly even by St. Romuald, the founder of Camaldoli.

It had once enjoyed a reputation for high sanctity, says Benvenuto da Imola, its monks living like Damian on salads and vegetables dressed only with olive oil, and never touching meat. But later — by the time of Dante — it had grown wealthy and the life there was one of luxury.

There were still cells, however, and it is said that Dante lived in one of them at least briefly.

This cell was marked with a plaque.

This was first put up in 1557 by the prior Filippo Ridolfi and read as follows: "This is the cubicle which Dante is said to live in as a guest, and in it to have composed no small part of his illustrious and almost divine work." There it remained for sixty-five years. Then it was transferred to another part of the cloister. The facts now "were more truthfully known"!

Finally, Gubbio, the city of the "fierce wolf, huge and terrible," who had "appeared in the neighborhood and not only devoured beasts but men," but whom St. Francis through love — and this is one of the loveliest of the St. Francis legends — soon had trotting through the streets like a dog, having made him "gentle as a lamb"; Gubbio also claimed that Dante once resided there and probably at this time.

This evidence is offered.

A 1432 manuscript in the Laurentian Library includes a *capitolo* (*terza rima* poem) with the title: "Exposition made by Messer Bosone da Gubbio of three books of Dante, who was of his time, and whom in fact he entertained in his own home."

A manuscript of the sixteenth century has a sonnet which begins thus: "Thou who dost dwell in shadowy and cool hills." Supposedly it was written by Dante. It tells Bosone of the success Dante has had in teaching Bosone's son Greek and French.

There is a similar notice in the *Teleutelogio*.

And in the seventeenth century, a Count Falcucci bought the Raffaelli Palace in Gubbio — Bosone was of the Raffaelli family — and decorated it with an inscription which said that Dante had stayed there and filled three notebooks with his writings.

I am not convinced. Although Dante knew Bosone, who held various offices in Viterbo, Lucca, Todi, and Pisa — all of which cities Dante visited — it is unlikely that he visited him in Gubbio, and particularly at this time. At least in this matter, the *Teleutologio* is not reliable. And the sonnet is clearly the work of a local poetaster who did not know that a crow cannot sing like a skylark even if he puts on skylark feathers. How could Dante teach Bosone's son Greek? He did not know Greek. How much French he knew is problematical. Moreover, Bosone was not in Gubbio in either 1312 or 1313. He was an exile from 1301 to 1315.

But most of all, Gubbio was the last place to which Dante would have gone, for, headed by Cante Gabrielli, the worst persecutors of the Whites came from Gubbio. Go to Gabrielli's city? He was not another St. Francis who could tame the wolf.

But with the other places, it was another matter. Cecina and Corneto and the Maremma. Bulicame. Rome for the third time — Lateran Rome. The Val di Chiana. Arezzo and Cortona. Assisi and Perugia. And Fonte Avellana.

Can we not then safely conjecture the following?

That Dante, who was with Henry at Pisa, and was not with him at the San Salvi gate, *may* — but note the word is *may* — have followed his High Harry through the Maremma to Orvieto, Viterbo, and then Rome. This would have given him a close-up view of papal deviousness which at the same time permitted Henry to be crowned by authorized legates and yet prevented an effective crowning.

That he *may* have stayed with Henry the whole time that Henry was in Rome. This would have deepened the impression.

That he *may* then have followed him to Tivoli, Todi, Perugia, and possibly even to Arezzo.

But that then he left, seeking a refuge for an important purpose which will soon be apparent.

Finally this refuge *may* — I would say *may well* — have been Fonte Avellana on Catria, almost the tallest whitecapped crest in the tumultuous sea of mountains that run down the middle of Italy, and from whose summit it is reputed that on a clear day you can see the Adriatic in one direction and the shallow mirror of Lake Trasimeno in the other.

But whether at Fonte Avellana or somewhere else, he certainly did seek a refuge in the hills. A monastic refuge.

For he now needed tranquility.

He now needed tranquility and a place equipped for study, for it was at this time — although some date it as early as 1300 and others as late as 1318, I join with the consensus in assigning it to either late 1312 or early 1313 — that he left the hurly-burly of day-by-day controversy to lift his contentions into the realm of theory and philosophy by writing one of the only three books he completed, the other two being the *Vita Nuova* and the *Commedia* — and one that is equal in importance to the other two as we try to paint the portrait of the man.

« 2 »

The book is *De Monarchia* — "Concerning Monarchy." It is eighteen thousand words long and is divided into three books approximately five thousand, six thousand, and seven thousand words long respectively. Compared to the passionate and polemical letters, it was very calm indeed and always it fell back on what in those days passed for reasoned argument.

Example:

In the Middle Ages, reasoning by syllogism was deemed the proper way to reason. Throughout the book, Dante reasons by syllogism.

"This syllogism," he says on one occasion — he is talking of justice and the ruler, "is of the second figure and with intrinsic negation. All B is A. Only C is A. Therefore only C is B."

"Let A be the means by which a thing can be accomplished, and let A and B be the different means by which the same thing can be accomplished. But if A alone can do what A and B can together, then it is not necessary to call on B."

The Middle Ages also deferred to authority — mainly the authority of what had already been written or said. A quotation was more effective than an original statement.

Dante's list of quotations is impressive. I have counted two hundred seven separate ones, of which ninety-seven were from classical authors (Latin and Greek); sixty-five from the New Testament; twenty-eight from the Old Testament; nine from the Church fathers; and eight from sources which could roughly be called miscellaneous.

To divide further, Aristotle is directly quoted thirty-five times; Virgil twenty-two times; the Gospel according to St. Matthew nineteen times; the Gospel according to St. John eighteen times; the Psalms twelve times; the Gospel according to St. Luke ten times; Cicero nine times; Livy eight times; Lucan seven times; the Book of Genesis, Orosius, Ovid, and St. Thomas Aquinas (but the thinking and methods of St. Thomas pervade the book) four times each; Exodus, Leviticus, the Epistle to the Romans, and the Epistle to the Hebrews three times each; Isaiah, the Gospel according to St. Mark, St. Augustine, and the *Canticle* (an early medieval liturgy) twice each; Euclid, Homer (probably as cited by Aristotle), Ennius (probably as cited by Cicero), Vegetius, Boethius, Deuteronomy, Numbers, Daniel, the Proverbs, the Epistle to the Galatians, II Timothy,

the Epistle to the Ephesians, II Thessalonians, the Epistle to the Corin-
thians, the Epistle of James, the Epistle to the Philippians, Averroës (the
heretic, nonetheless), Peter Lombard, Gilbert de la Porrée, *De Causis*
(translated from the Arabic), Paralipomenon (Chronicles), Melissus,
Parmenides, and the *Digests* (authorized by Justinian) once each.

But despite the judicial tone and the deference to those who had lived
and written before him, Dante in reality was passionately pleading a cause
and a belief, and his calm was on the surface only.

What was this belief?

That a universal monarchy was necessary to save mankind. That it was
a provable (in Dante's opinion) fact that "a monarch or an emperor was
necessary for the well-being of the world." Further, that "when the
monarchy is under one prince, it is most like to God, and this makes it
conform to the divine intention and this is necessary for perfection."

In Dante's opinion, but not necessarily in that of others. Therefore
Dante must demonstrate it to others.

This he attempted to do.

How?

By posing and then answering three questions.

(1) *An ad bene esse mundi Monarchia necessaria sit.* Whether a
monarchy is necessary for the well-being of the world.

(2) *An Romanus populus de iure Monarche officium sibi adscivereit.*
Whether the Roman people lawfully took unto itself the office of
monarch.

(3) *An auctoritas Monarche dependeat a Dio immediate vel ab aliquo
Dei ministro seu vicario.* Whether the authority of the monarch comes
directly from God or from some minister or vicar of God.

Why?

Because it was his duty to do so.

"I hold," said Dante, "that all men on whom a Higher Being has
bestowed a love of truth should make this their first interest that just as
they were enriched by the efforts of the men of ancient times, so they too
should labor for those who come after them so that posterity will be
enriched in the same way."

He continued:

"Let there be no doubt that man is derelict indeed if he has benefited
from the common heritage and still does not make his own contribution
to the public good."

Dante included, thought Dante.

"I have often pondered on these matters," he elaborated, "and not
wishing to be accused of burying my talents, I wish not merely to
blossom but to bear fruit for the public good, and to do this by demonstrating truths which no one else has yet considered."

Which no one else has yet considered. This was a key phrase. There would be no point, for example, in explaining the nature of happiness, since Aristotle had already done this, or in writing a new treatise on old age, since this had been done by Cicero.

But there was a matter which he could still usefully treat.

"Since, therefore, among hidden and useful truths the truth about temporal monarchy is the most useful of all and the least well known — for since it leads to no immediate profit it has been neglected by all — I intend to take the kernel of this nut out of its hiding place. This I shall study for the benefit of the world, and, to my great glory, shall win the palm for being the first to do this."

To my great glory. Win the palm. Both Dantean phrases. Both phrases that made plain the motive.

I intend to. I shall.

He could, and he did.

« *3* »

Question one — but first a definition. What was the temporal monarchy?

"The temporal monarchy, commonly called the empire, is a single princedom having jurisdiction over all people living in time, or rather over these and over all their affairs which are measured by time."

Over all those peoples known to Dante. Over Trajan's Roman Empire. India and the Turks and Tatars and certainly Cathay were not included.

Well, was this kind of monarchy — was, in other words, a universal empire — necessary to the well-being of the world?

First, what was the well-being of the world?

The well-being of the world was for mankind to be able to live up to its total capacity — both in matters of the intellect and by action. To do this was to attain mortal happiness — i.e., well-being.

But man can only be able to make this total use of his total capacity — he can only become "perfect in wisdom and prudence" — if he can enjoy leisure in tranquility, so that it is only in the leisure and tranquility that comes with peace that man fulfills his proper destiny.

"Hence it is clear that universal peace is the best way of securing man's well-being."

But can universal peace best be secured under a universal emperor?

Yes, says Dante, and gives his reasons.

As Aristotle tells us — this is the first of them — when many things are directed to a single end, there must be a single director. This is true of the family — Homer says the greatest curse a father can have is: "May you have an equal in your home" — of the *borgo*, of the city, the city-state, and the kingdom.

"But if mankind as a whole" — and it does — "moves toward a preordained goal, then it needs one person to rule and govern it and that person must be called the monarch or emperor."

Mankind — to say it again — is made up of many component parts, but it is brought into harmony by a single principle.

"This harmony is achieved by one principle only, by the single prince."

Man — this is the second reason — is best when he is most like God. But God is unity.

"As a son is best when he is most like his father, so man is best when he is most like God. Therefore just as the heavens are best when they are guided by one mover which is God, so mankind is best when it is directed by one law and governed by one prince."

Whenever — this is the third reason — there is a dispute, there has to be a judge to judge it. On earth this judge must be the emperor, for if not there would be another judge who would be equal to him. Then they would have to go to a third judge and this judge would be the supreme prince.

Furthermore, the world is best when justice is most evenhanded. But where, he argues, can justice be more evenhanded than under an emperor? A supreme emperor has everything, and therefore can desire no more. He has no reason not to be impartial.

The human race — reason four — is best when it is free, but freedom cannot really exist in a democracy (Dante is thinking of Florence, which was the only democracy he knew), or an oligarchy (the rough-handed merchant-adventurer clique which ruled Venice), or a tyranny (the Lombard lords, one of whom oddly enough was Dante's so greatly admired Can Grande of Verona). No, only under a universal monarch could there be freedom.

Under such a government — and under such a government only — "the citizens do not exist for the sake of the consuls, nor the people for the sake of the king. On the contrary, the king exists for the sake of the people, and the consuls for the sake of the citizens."

Does this seem starry-eyed? Perhaps it was. Dante had lived in the world, but he was also a poet.

However, even as he argued for a single ruler, saying that things can better be performed by a single instrument than by many and that "there can only be unity if there is a single prince," he made an exception, for he was not doctrinaire.

In a sort of trecento anticipation of states' rights, he says this:

"We do not mean to say that small decisions affecting every township can proceed from the emperor, for nations, kingdoms, and cities have different characteristics which demand different laws."

He gives as an example the fur-clad Scythians of the northern steppes and the naked Garamantes who lived south of the Sahara. He perhaps thought of other, nearer ones.

Finally, he points out, his most important argument is confirmed by history.

"For if we survey the ages and conditions of man since the fall of our first parents, at no time do we see universal peace throughout the world except during the perfect monarchy of the immortal Augustus."

Q.E.D.

« 4 »

But if there was to be a single prince, why should he be the Roman prince?

On this matter, Dante uses arguments that would hardly be convincing to modern readers. Indeed, although they led to Petrarch and Cola di Rienzi — who, however, thought more of the Gracchi than of Augustus, and dreamed of restoring a Roman republic not an empire — even in Dante's time they would appeal only to the limited number of Italians who still mused on ancient glories, and to the German, or the almost German, princes in whose hands since the days of Otto the Roman power seemed to rest.

The Roman prince and the Roman people whose ruler he was had attained universal power by right, and because it was right. He and they had attained it because it was the will of God. He and they had attained it because it was the inevitable consequence of the inexorable laws of nature. He and they had attained it because they had demonstrated that he was the only person and they the only people who were capable of holding and using this power.

He and they did not have it because they had seized it. Let this be very clear.

To be sure — and here Dante used one of a debater's most disarming ploys, the acknowledgment that he had once been wrong himself — Dante had not always felt that this was the case.

"There was a time," he says, "when I too marveled that the Roman people had won dominion over the whole world, and that none withstood them, for looking at the surface only I concluded that they had not won this justly, but by force of arms alone."

But now he knew differently.

"For after my mind's eye had penetrated to the very heart of the matter, and I had seen by the most convincing signs that it was divine providence that had brought it about, my marvel ceased and gave place to a derisive scorn when I saw people meditating upon the same vain things that I once did myself" — before he became Ghibelline, at least in his thinking — "and the kings and princes agreeing on one thing only, namely resistance to their lord and their annointed one" — i.e., Henry, the Roman prince.

Divine providence! But how could he be sure that it was divine providence?

He explains.

"It was fitting" — and therefore conformed to God's purposes — "for the noblest people to be head of all the others."

But the Roman people were the noblest people.

If something is established and maintained by miracles, it is the will of God that such a thing should be. But Rome was established and maintained by miracles.

He lists a few of them.

The shield that fell from heaven while King Numa Pompilius was sacrificing. The cackling of geese that saved the capital. The hailstorm that frustrated victorious Hannibal. The young girl Cloelia's swimming across the flooded Tiber.

Whoever wills what is good for all wills what is right — and therefore, Dante implies, is God's administrator.

But the Roman people — "the holy, pious, and glorious" Roman people — "is seen to have taken no heed whatsoever for their own convenience but only to secure the well-being of the human race."

Cincinnatus, for example, who left honorable retirement at the plow to guide his nation through a time of crisis, and then returned to the plow again when the crisis was over. The elder Brutus, who sentenced his own sons to death when they conspired with the enemy. Mucius Scaevola, who burned off his own hand because he thought it had not properly defended the republic.

Here, it must be admitted, Dante strays a little. The men cited were Romans serving Rome and not the whole world.

The Roman people were fitted by nature to rule the world, and furthermore they — or their champions — demonstrated this by their frequent victories in trials-at-arms.

This clearly indicates that God was with them.

"In good truth, the judgment of God may be revealed in one of these two ways. Either by means of a direct test of strength between two contestants which is called a duel, or by several people contending one against the other as to who shall attain a goal first, like athletes when running for a prize."

He gives examples in the second category first. Throughout history there had been a contest to be the first to attain world empire. These were some of the contestants:

"Ninus, king of the Assyrians, who with his consort Semiramis sought to gain rule over the whole earth, and did indeed conquer all of Asia, but the West he never conquered.

"Vesoges, king of Egypt, who harried Asia from south to north," but was forced by the Scythians to retreat.

"Cyrus, king of the Persians," who destroyed Babylon and transferred the Babylonian Empire to Persia, "but was forced to yield his ambition and his very life to Queen Tamiris without ever having seen the West."

"Xerxes, the son of Darius," who built a bridge of boats across the Hellespont, "but was ignominiously stopped in his tracks, and failed to gain the prize."

Finally, Alexander the Macedonian.

"He came nearest of all to winning the palm of monarchy. He had already sent legates to the Romans warning them to surrender when he collapsed almost halfway on his course."

But that Rome did carry off the palm is well known, and is attested to by many.

Virgil:

> Surely one day as the years their swift way roll on
> There shall spring from the Roman line, from the blood of Teucer,
> Princes who shall extend their rule to every land, every sea.

Lucan:

> That kingdom shall be split by the sword, for the destiny
> Of the mighty people that rules land, sea, the whole globe
> Hath no place for a second.

Boethius:

> He [*the Roman prince*] doth rule with his scepter
> The people he looks on as he plunges his rays in the billows
> And those he looks on rising in the far east,
> Those whom the frigid north doth make to shiver
> And those whom the fierce south wind with its heat
> Scorches as it bakes the burning sands.

But Dante named individual contests too. Aeneas against Turnus, king of the Rutilians. The three Horatii against the three Curiatii. And with armies to support them, Fabricius against Pyrrhus, and Scipio against Hannibal.

Finally, "like testimony is offered by Christ's biographer Luke, who said that Christ chose to be born under the edict of a Roman emperor."

This was further and final evidence that Roman rule was both universal and right. For Christ, who came to redeem the sin of Adam — in other
words of all mankind — could not have been born and died under less
than universal rule. Nor could he have been born under such a rule if it
were not rightful. That would have been acceding to a wrong.

"I now think," says Dante, summing up, "that it is sufficiently proven
that Rome rightfully rules and rules rightfully the whole world."

Rome and, for Rome, the Roman prince.

The defense rests.

« 5 »

The defense rests, but only long enough for Dante to catch his breath and
to order his thinking so that he can proceed with his views on the third
problem — namely "the relations between two luminaries, the Roman
pontiff and the Roman prince," and the question of "whether the Roman
monarch, who rules the world by right, is directly dependent on God or
whether his authority comes from the successor of St. Peter, who was
entrusted with the keys of heaven."

Pragmatically this is the most important of all, for — and especially
with Clement now openly asserting that Henry was both his creature and
his vassal — if it could not be shown convincingly that the latter's
authority came from God and not the pope, Dante's dream of a universal
— and peace-seeking — world state would remain just that; it would remain
a dream.

But it must not and, if Dante could prevent it, it would not.

He sets out to do this. He first puts down and attempts to answer every
papal argument. Then he advances his own imperial arguments. In both
instances, some of them today seem curious, but they were all ingenious
and in Dante's time were found to be convincing. Following his own
order, let us examine the contentions and his refutations first. We can
then go on to his counterattack, which was equally eloquent.

Contention. There are two lights in the heaven, the sun and the moon.
The sun is the papacy and the moon the empire. But the moon shines by
the sun's reflected light. Hence the sun should rule the moon.

Refutation. This is allegory and in practical matters allegorical interpretations are dangerous. Anyway, as can be seen during eclipses, the
moon has light of its own. The sun merely makes this light brighter.

Contention. Levi the priest was the elder brother of Judah the ruler.
Therefore the Church comes before the empire in matters of authority.

Refutation. Even in the Church, seniority does not necessarily mean
authority — "as, for example, when some archdeacons are older than
their bishops."

Contention. Samuel the priest annointed Saul the king. Therefore, Saul is subject to Samuel.

Refutation. Samuel had only the specific authority conferred on him as a vicar. He could annoint Saul and nothing more.

Contention. Christ (spiritual authority) received tribute from the Magi (temporal authority).

Refutation. Christ did receive tribute from the Magi, but the vicar of Christ is not Christ and does not have the same powers.

Contention. Christ said this to Peter: "And whatsoever ye shall bind on earth shall be bound in heaven, and whatsoever ye shall loose on earth shall be loosed in heaven." This gives Peter — and his successors — power on earth and in heaven. Hence the pope is above the emperor.

Refutation. St. Peter's powers were limited to those specifically given to him. For example, he could not free a woman from marriage to one man and bind her to another while the first man still lived. He was given power in regard to heavenly matters only. The empire was a kingdom of this earth.

Contention. St. Peter told Christ that he had two swords and this meant both the temporal and the spiritual authority.

Refutation. But Christ never told St. Peter to carry two swords. Instead he told *all* his disciples to carry a sword.

Contention. When the Emperor Constantine was cured of leprosy by the prayers of Pope Sylvester, he gave Rome itself — and implicitly the powers of the Roman Empire — to the Church. On this, the Church based claims of God-willed and superior authority.

Refutation. Constantine did not have the right to give this to the Church, for it is not right for something ordained by God to destroy itself. The Church, by the same token, did not have the right to receive it.

Contention. Pope Adrian — actually it was Pope Leo IV — crowned Charlemagne. Hence the imperial powers — at any rate, those of the new Roman Empire — derive from the papacy.

Refutation. For Leo to have bestowed empire on Charlemagne was a usurpation and "a usurpation does not establish a right." Over and above that, a later emperor — Otto I — restored another Pope Leo who had been driven from office. That would seem to make the papacy dependent on the empire.

Contention. According to Aristotle, all things of the same kind are reducible to a single component. Pope and emperor are both men. Hence one must regulate the other.

Refutation. As men they are reducible to one component, but not as pope and emperor.

So much for the positive, and now the negative.

"Having set down," says Dante, "and rejected those errors on which those who assert that the authority of the Roman prince depends upon the Roman pontiff rely most strongly, it is my duty to return to and to demonstrate the true answer to the third question which in the beginning I proposed to discuss. This is that imperial authority depends directly upon the supreme source of all existence, namely God. It does not depend upon the Church."

The proofs are as follows:

(1) The imperial authority was recognized by Christians even before there was a Christian Church. Christ acknowledged that he was born and died under the authority of the emperor. Paul said that he stood at the judgment seat of Caesar where he must rightfully be judged, and later an angel told him that it was right for him to stand there. Moreover, even the donation of Constantine confirmed imperial authority. How could an emperor even wish to give away what he did not have?

(2) Nowhere in either the Old or the New Testament is temporal authority ascribed to the Church. "Every divine law is held in the bosom of the two testaments, in which bosom I cannot find anywhere that care or concern for temporal matters is bestowed upon a priest."

(3) The model of the Church is Christ, and Christ Himself said that His kingdom is not of this world.

(4) Providence, "which never errs," had set two goals for man: happiness in the world below, and blessedness in heaven. The first is the responsibility of "that protector of the world who is called the Roman prince, whose duty it is to see to it that we live in liberty and peace upon the threshing floor of this world." The duty of the pontiff is to lead us to eternal life in accordance with revelation.

This being the case — all the above being the case — it is "God, and God alone," who "elects and confirms the emperor." It is not the electors. "Their office is to proclaim what God has providentially decided." It is not the pontiff.

"It is obvious then that the temporal monarch receives his authority from the source of all authority — which source, although not divisible in the stronghold of its single being, flows out, in its superlative goodness, in many channels."

That much, and that much strongly, but then a conciliatory gesture.

"I would not, however" — this is Dante's conclusion — "wish that the truth upon this matter be so narrowly interpreted as to mean that the Roman prince is not subject to the Roman pontiff in any way whatsoever."

Far from it, since the pontiff speaks for things eternal, "and at least to a certain extent our temporal happiness is ordained by our eternal happiness."

Finally, this:

"Caesar, therefore, owes to Peter the reverence which a firstborn son owes to his father, so that enlightened by his paternal grace he himself may more brightly shine upon the world — a world at the head of which he had been placed by the One who alone is the ruler of things spiritual and temporal."

Dante thus strikes for a consensus. In his letters to the princes and peoples of Italy, to the wicked Florentines, and to Alto Arrigo, he sounded, and loudly, the trumpet for imperialist battle. But now without abandoning or even seriously modifying his partisan convictions, he at least half calls for a truce as he tries to win over those more moderate. For it has become clear to him that the imperialists without broader support could not win the battle for that single prince who would bring back order first to Italy and then to the whole world. All men of goodwill must be rallied, and some of these men of goodwill, while willing to accept his theory of imperial power, insisted — largely for reasons of theology — that even if the emperor were independent he at least must be, even if only slightly, hierarchically below the pope, who spoke for heaven, which was above the earth.

It is to these men that he addresses both his arguments and his appeal. They could be ruled by Henry without ceasing to kneel to Clement!

It was an argument and an appeal which, since it would have fatally and finally isolated the Blacks, he hoped — and I think believed — would succeed.

« 6 »

It might have if it had been made earlier, but it was now too late, for the sands of Henry's adventure had almost run out.

We have already spoken of his bleak and disconsolate winter in the valley of the Ema, at San Casciano, and finally at Poggibonsi, but even at Pisa and among friends things were only moderately better.

Yet despite an ill health that would have deterred a less resolute man, Henry's faith and his courage seem to have remained unimpaired, and he steadfastly maintained the contest.

Even while still in winter camp, he had defied Florence by imposing the same sentence he had imposed on her allies Pistoia, Volterra, Grosseto, Colle, Montepulciano, San Gimignano, and Città della Pieve. (Look at a map and you will see the Tuscan extent of the league which had been marshaled against him.) He had deprived Bishop Antonio degli Orsi (of Florence), Bishop Gherardo Malaspina (of Luni-Sarzana), and Count Salvatico and Count Guido di Battifolle (of the Counts Guidi) of their feudal rights. In addition, he had proclaimed five hundred seventeen Florentine citizens and ninety-nine prominent Black Guelphs of the Florentine countryside to be rebels and outlawed.

Now — at Pisa — he added King Robert of Naples to the list.

On April 26, his heralds read out an imperial sentence against this "son of corruption, this rebel and traitor to his imperial majesty," who had recently been made lord of Florence for a period of five years and who had forthwith sent there a French subject of his, Jacques de Cantelme, to abolish the office of captain of the people, and to act as his regent.

"Robert's realm of Apulia and the country of Provence," this said, "are hereby declared to be forfeit. He and his heir are condemned in their persons. He is a caitiff traitor."

(Robert's answer was a sarcastic manifesto "to the cities and to several rulers of the cities and castles, and to the lords of Italy." Henry of Luxemburg, this proclaimed, "is not worthy of the office of emperor. His sentence is the loquacious chatter of an old woman who grows senile.")

He persuaded Genoa to join Frederick of Sicily in promising to supply him — and their longtime enemy Pisa — with ships.

His argument:

"We have given your Opizino Spinola our imperial authority to coin florins stamped with the same image as official Florentine florins. If Florence is not brought to heel, how can you effectively circulate them?"

To replenish his army, decimated by desertion and disease, he sent "into Germany and Lombardy for fresh troops, and he made similar demands upon the Italian Ghibellines."

At the same time, he began to make thrust after thrust at strongpoints held by those who opposed him. Some of these thrusts were successful.

Pietrasanta, for example, gateway to Tuscany from Lombardy through the Lunigiana, fell to a captain of his, Henry of Flanders, and the same Henry almost took Camaiore, which controlled the Tuscan beaches.

At this last, Florence fell into a state of consternation. And of confusion. For despite the valiant conduct of the Company of the Banner — a group of their young men who truly upheld the city's honor — the *grandi* who supplied most of Florentine leadership were falling into disrepute. On the street corners it was said that they wanted power but wanted others to fight for this power. They did. Indeed, they wanted power so badly that although opposed to any emperor, they even welcomed and attempted to secure the friendship of Erhardt of Württemberg, who called himself Augustus and said he and not Henry was the rightful Caesar. Perhaps he would stir up revolts in Germany.

But these were only pinpricks and no serious attack upon Florence was made, although those historians who can always be right after the event say that this time an attack would have succeeded.

It was not made, for the Roman dream still obsessed High Harry.

"We will march south, and this time we will take St. Peter's. There will be a truly Roman crowning."

"Then you must attack Robert."

"We will attack Robert. Even if he does not defend Rome. We will attack him after we have taken Rome. We will drive him from his kingdom of Naples."

"But, sire and majesty, Pope Clement has convened the college of cardinals and has told them — without naming names, but what he means is clear — that anyone who should dare attack the kingdom of Naples will be deprived of all his rights and be excommunicated. Even if the person who did this, he said, were invested with imperial dignity."

Replied Henry:

"We do not intend to prejudice the rights of the Church, and we only oppose Robert because he has used force against us and become the tool of our enemies."

"If you do march," cried Nicholas of Butrinto, "you will suffer the fate of Frederick II."

"If God is on our side, nor pope nor Church can make us fall. And we have not offended God."

This was late in July and time was pressing, for he must act before the pope's words had their inevitable effect.

On August 8, therefore, and with banners waving, he departed from the city which had stood by him the most loyally and most joyously. By way of San Miniato he went. By way of Castelfiorentino, Castello Imperiale, and Siena. He did not stop at Siena, however, for a troop of Florentines had found shelter there and even made a sortie (it was not effective) from the Camollia Gate. Instead he camped at Pancole on the Arbia near the ancient battlefield of Montaperti.

But although hearts — Henry's heart among them — lifted at the omen, for it was here that the Guelphs of Florence had been routed and destroyed fifty-three years earlier and history might repeat itself, and although steeds caracoled and harnesses shone, underneath things were far from good.

For the scorching of another summer's sun and the fatigue caused by long days and wakeful nights as he labored in the imperial cause began to do their fatal work.

Henry's illness worsened.

What should he do?

Common sense — and some of his councillors — told him to go back; perhaps even to go back to Germany.

He did not heed it.

(How could he? He was a knight-errant.)

He did make one concession, however. To please those who served him — and loved him — he turned aside to Macereto, where there were baths.

The waters, he thought and told them, might cure him.

But they did not, and after three days he was on his way again.

He got only as far as Buonconvento — "the good convent." To that little city and its monastery he came on August 21. His condition verged upon the critical. He was too weak to stand or ride or even be carried in a litter. He was burned up with fever — the fever was even hotter than the Tuscan sun. He could not sleep.

In this condition he was laid upon a bed, where a doctor in long robes examined his urine and pronounced it to be dense and cloudy and almost red in color. Shortly afterwards a tumor appeared under his left knee. Presently his kidneys began to fail, and he was racked with pleurisy.

On August 24, the same doctor who had first examined him summoned the noblemen of his army and told them that Henry had not more than a few hours to live.

Amadeo of Savoy went to him. No one else dared.

"You must confess and must be given extreme unction."

Henry could not speak, but nodded.

Then Amadeo sent for Henry's confessor, the Dominican Fra Bernardino da Montepulciano, who administered the sacrament.

Before sundown on this eve of St. Bartholomew, Henry died.

« 7 »

As might be expected — for bad news always travels fast — the tidings spread like wildfire. It went as swiftly as courier could make horse gallop.

To Florence.

To Pisa.

To Avignon.

To Paris.

Even to Germany.

And those who heard it reacted predictably.

Said the Florentines in a letter to Lucca, and this is typical of Guelph rejoicing:

"Jesus Christ, who looketh down from the height of heaven upon us and our friends, hath prepared for us and given us a joy which could not be greater. That very cruel tyrant Henry, once count of Luxemburg, whom your and our perfidious enemies and long-time persecutors of the Church called king of the Romans and emperor of the Germans — that Henry who in the name of the empire had invaded a large part of Lombardy and Tuscany — died last Friday in the town of Buoncon-vento."

In contrast, the Ghibellines cried treachery and paid-for murder.

Fra Bernardino, on Assumption Day, they said, had poisoned both the host and the chalice he offered Henry. He had been suborned — but here the accounts differ — by Clement, by King Robert, by King Philip, or by the Florentines. This story was believed widely in such parts of Italy as were Ghibelline and also in Germany, and the belief was strengthened by the fact that Fra Bernardino was welcomed by Florence after Henry's death and that he later lived there.

It is not likely, however, that there was any truth to it.

The poets — being mainly Ghibelline — were content with hymns of praise.

Cino da Pistoia:

> Now that his mortal nature hath brought an end
> Unto the life of him in whom did dwell
> As in its home all worth and valorousness.

Then:

> Henry is emperor, and from the low
> And vicious life below God hath him called
> Unto the joyous because He deemed him worthy
> To dwell with those who inhabit His blessed kingdom.

Senuccio del Bene — Florentine and younger than either Cino or Dante:

> O weep, my life, yea weep! For now is dead
> That lord whom I did love more than myself
> And in whom lay my hopes.

But not Dante.

Unhappily — and perhaps inexplicably — we do not have any *"Per la morte de Arrigo VII"* from the pen of Dante Alighieri.

Or anything else.

So we do not have any authenticated statement as to what his immediate reactions were when that news came to him from Buonconvento which was as black as any he had ever heard.

XXIII

Can Grande's Castle and Beyond

BUT although we do not know what Dante's reaction was — what his specific and immediate reaction was — since we do not have a sonnet or a *canzone* upon the death of his hero *and written at the time*, as we have from Cino and Senuccio, it is obvious that he must have been very greatly shaken. This was the third time a dream of his had been shattered — in this case, the high dream of a world in which there could be no exiles because there would be no states but only a single and universal entity dedicated to a universal peace, the new Pax Romana of another Augustus in which all men would be united to serve the purposes of God. It is obvious that he must have been psychologically and spiritually disrupted — that he must psychologically and spiritually have been in a slough of despond.

This, too, is reflected in his writings.

Purgatorio VI:

> O slave Italy, hostelry of woe,
> Ship without helmsman in a raging storm,
> Not lady of provinces but of a brothel!

(It will be recalled that in the earlier *Convivio*, Dante referred to himself as a ship without sails and without a rudder. The phrases are strikingly similar.)

Dante goes on to see "Rome that weeps, widowed and solitary, and cries night and day." He goes on to note that "every city in Italy is filled with tyrants and each rustic clown that joins a party becomes another Marcellus." He goes on to describe Florence with some of his most icy sarcasm.

My Florence thou needst have no argument
With this digression. It does not concern thee —
Thanks to thy people, who so very shrewd are.
Many [*many elsewhere is implied*] have justice at heart
   yet loose the arrow slowly,
Since without thought it comes not to the bow.
Thy people have justice at the tip of the tongue.
Many refuse to take the common burden.
Thy people are so ready with an answer
They say "I'll do it!" even before they're asked.
Then be thou happy. Thou hast good reason to,
Being rich and being at peace and being wise,
And that I speak the truth the facts make plain.
Athens and Lacedaemon, who made
The ancient laws and were so civilized,
Give little hint of right and virtuous living
Compared to you who make so carefully combed-out
Provisions that until the middle of November
Lasts not that thread which in October you spun.
How many times within thy memory
Laws, yea, and coinage, and officials and customs
Thou hast changed, and called one back, exiled another.
If thou rememberest thyself and seest the light,
Thou'lt see thyself like unto a sick woman
Who finds no rest upon her featherbed
And ever turning seeks to ease her pain.

Historically, of course, the above lines — all of the above lines — refer to an earlier time. They refer to the earlier imperial vacancy which preceded Henry's election and not the present one. They refer to the revolutions which drove Dante from his city. But they were not written at that time, and they equally reflect the mood of a time much closer to that when they were written. They equally reflect the mood of 1313.

« 2 »

Yet it must not be concluded from this that Dante immediately and irrevocably withdrew from all concern with the affairs of Italy and of the world to devote himself singlemindedly to the soul-stirring project with which he is forever (and, in the minds of some, solely) identified. It must not be concluded that he now plucked this flower safety (his crowning achievement) from this nettle danger (all that he had endured). It must not be concluded that he now and finally tempered the sword, that he now and finally sublimated his agonies into an ecstasy that would take him to and beyond the stars.

Far from it! Much too resilient was he by nature and, even as he reached for the empyrean, too great were his ties with the earth.

Nor was the time yet ripe for such a withdrawal, for the battle still continued, and Dante was never one to desert the banner of the things he stood for as long as it waved bravely, no matter how it seemed to be hopelessly ringed by foes.

The battle still continued? To be more specific, Florence on the one hand (with King Robert of Naples as her captain and ally, and also master), and the imperialists and the Ghibellines, urged on by Pisa and later by other cities, on the other, still carried on their contest for the control of Italy.

Bands of horsemen still galloped through many a village and pillaged many a farmer, and there was maneuver and countermaneuver in the Valdelsa (where a warrior archpriest almost delivered Colle to the Ghibellines) and before Arezzo and near Pistoia and San Miniato. There were raids — by Volterran Guelphs and Pisan Ghibellines — in the territory of San Gimignano too, but the San Gimignanese ended them by signing, and not at any great cost, a five-year neutrality pact with Volterra. Their vineyards were now safe.

To be sure — on the whole and despite setbacks, for some of the above-noted raids were in Florentine territory — the advantage seemed to lie with the city of shopkeepers. How could it be otherwise? The Ghibellines now lacked a leader, since Alto Arrigo was not only dead, but buried.

After Henry had closed his eyes, the German and the other foreign knights, the knights of Lombardy and the Pisans — they alone had remained faithful to his cause, the men of Todi and Spoleto and the Ghibelline noblemen of the Casentino, the Marches, the Romagna, and the Maremma having trickled off homeward — slowly brought his body back to the place from which he had set out, and there (in Pisa), at the city gates, the dead monarch was met by three thousand men and women all in garb of mourning. The next day solemn obsequies were celebrated in the white-marble Duomo where only a few weeks earlier Masses had been held to pray for Henry's success. Then "with great sorrow and also with many honors" he was interred.

"This," said Giovanni Villani, "was the end of the Emperor Henry, and let no reader marvel that his story has been told to the end by us and that we have not [at the same time] recounted the other happenings and occurrences in Italy and in other provinces and lands. There are two reasons for this. First, all Christians, and even the Greeks and Saracens" — note that Greeks and Saracens are linked together, both being considered schismatics — "were so concerned with his doings and his accomplishments that no other events which took place elsewhere seemed noteworthy. And second, because of the multifold and diverse successes which came to him during the short span of his life, it was firmly believed by intelligent men that he would certainly have conquered the kingdom [of Naples] and taken it from King Robert" if he had lived.

For Robert, Villani explained, "made but little preparations for its defense."

But Henry did not live, and now Robert was safe and so was Florence. Or were they?

Certain of the Pisan Ghibellines thought not.

All that was needed, they thought, was a new Ghibelline leader, and they were sure they had one. Fadrique of Trinacria. Frederick of Sicily.

Frederick had already showed his Ghibelline hand. It was he, it will be remembered, who sent sacks filled with gold coin to Henry in the latter's winter of desperation at Poggibonsi.

And now he came himself. Thinking we do not know what thoughts but certainly they were concerned with what would most advantage him, he sailed from Palermo with a fleet of fifty galleys and an impressive number of Spanish and Sicilian foot soldiers and knights.

The port backed by yellowish mountains sank out of sight. The wind was light. The blue sea sparkled.

Did he plan to join forces with Henry, and then march south to Rome and the kingdom? Or would he give only naval support? Would he sail between blue Ischia and even bluer Capri into the Bay of Naples, drawing Robert back to defend his harbor and his castles?

If he asked himself these questions, he did not have to answer them, but instead had a different decision to make. For even before he stepped ashore at Piombino — which he did on September 5 — he was met at sea by Henry of Flanders, who told him that the Emperor Henry had departed from this world. Then a fishing vessel brought him other tidings. Later they turned out to be false but at the moment he believed them.

"John of Bohemia" — Alto Arrigo's son — "has crossed the Alps and with an army."

Now there was a new set of problems. How should he handle them?

Should he join John, becoming his ally as he might have been his father's?

Should he patch up peace with Florence and the Florentines? They might then make Robert abandon any designs he had on Sicily.

Or should he return to Palermo and there devote his own energies to defending his own island? Should he forget foreign help and helping foreigners?

These questions he weighed carefully as his ships continued north, and he still weighed them as he disembarked at Piombino.

There he was met by Pisan emissaries.

"I have come only," he told them, noting how they looked avidly at his military and naval might, "I have come only to pay homage to the man upon whose side I would have fought, but whom I never saw in life."

"Do so, sire," they said.

But when he had ridden the fifty or sixty miles along the Tuscan coast; when he had crossed the Cecina, gone through the then-little fishing village of Livorno into Pisa and then to the Camposanto; when he had knelt there at the tomb of Alto Arrigo, they addressed him otherwise.

"We invite you to appear before our council."

This he did, and there they made him an offer.

"Take up, sire, the command laid down by Henry, and if you do this we will make you lord of Pisa and thus *de facto* lord of the Ghibellines. March your armies toward the south, and sail with the combined fleets of Pisa, Genoa, and Sicily against our common enemy."

Against King Robert, that is. The Pisans would be able to deal with Florence themselves.

Frederick hesitated. There were dangers, he indicated, but — but he would risk those dangers.

If — for there was a condition.

"Renounce your sovereignty of Sardinia and give it to me. I will confer it on my brother. Then I will risk doing what you want me to."

Give up Sardinia?

But from Sardinia came an important part of Pisan revenues, and from Sardinia, strategically placed, whatever hope Pisa had of once again becoming a great sea power.

"This we cannot do," they told Frederick.

"What you ask, I will not do," he answered.

Nor did he, but returned to Piombino as fast as steeds could take him and set sail for Palermo whence he had come.

It is thought by some — notably Philalethes, but even Paget Toynbee says that "it was doubtless this want of sympathy with the fate of Italy that aroused Dante's wrath" — that it was this has made Dante so hostile to King Frederick. For hostile he certainly was.

Convivio IV, 6:

"Pay attention to who sits at your side, ye enemies of God who have grasped the scepters of the rule of Italy. It is to you I speak, Charles [Charles II of Naples] and Frederick [our Frederick of Sicily], and to you others who are lords and tyrants. Ye would do better to fly low like the swallow than to wheel loftily over vile things like a kite!"

De Vulgari Eloquentia I, 12:

"*Tarantara!* What sound is now uttered by the trumpet of the new Frederick? What is that now made by the tocsin of the second Charles? What but 'Come, ye butchers! Come, ye false dealers! Come, ye henchmen of avarice!' "

Purgatorio VII:

> Jaime and Frederick have their father's realms.
> They do not have his heritage of virtue.

Paradiso XIX:

> The avarice and the cowardice shall be seen
> Of him who doth the isle of fire guard,
> There where Anchises died in his old age.

Paradiso XX:

> And him thou seest in the down-bent arc
> Is William, whom that very land doth mourn
> Which weeps that Charles and Frederick are still living.

It should be noted, however, that both the *Convivio* and the *De Vulgari Eloquentia* were written long before Frederick declined — unless greatly bribed — to pick up Alto Arrigo's sword. His refusal to become lord of Pisa could not, therefore, have been what first made Dante look on him with scorn and contempt. But it may have heightened and intensified feelings he already had.

« 3 »

But if "the honor of Sicily" — this was another of Dante's contemptuously sarcastic phrases for Fadrique — was somewhat less than honorable in that he went off sulking because the Pisans would not pay a price that he would not have even dreamed of taking if Henry were still emperor, this did not cause the Ghibellines — again the Pisan Ghibellines — to give up their cause as lost. The scent of victory had been too recently and too pleasantly in their nostrils, for they had shared without reservation Villani's opinion as to what would have been the probable outcome of Henry's expedition; they also felt certain that with Robert tamed, they could bring Florence to heel and see it sue for peace — that Florence, whose money-changer machinations (but not military skill, for in the field they had won as often as the Florentines) had reduced their once-proud city to the status of a second-class power.

They refused — they refused resolutely — to see this scent dissipated. Nor needed they to.

Not if they did the right things. Not, in particular, if they chose the right leader now that Henry was dead and Frederick had failed them.

And we have already met him.

He was that Uguccione della Faggiuola whom we saw holding the office of *podestà* in Arezzo during Dante's early days of exile, but who gave it up because of intrigues with Pope Boniface and Corso Donati, and since then had been a sword for sale and a stirrer up of (to him) useful discord, though after that one deviation always on the Ghibelline side.

A man who always looked out for himself? Possibly. But also one of the age's ablest soldiers.

And one of its most handsome.

A surviving portrait — it is not contemporary, but surely was based on a contemporary picture — shows a fine-looking man with dark hair, an aquiline nose, and dark, intent, intelligent but selfish eyes. That would have been Uguccione in the 1290s. But now in 1313, the sixty-three-year-old warrior had snow-white hair and his face was lined by rugged living and by his cares. Nevertheless, says one who surely knew him, neither his energy nor his zeal nor his physical resilience had in any way been impaired. In armor and in the saddle, he was still a young man.

Other things that have been noted about him. He spoke softly — this may have been to conceal the fact that he weighed things carefully — but he acted decisively. When he made a decision, he abided by it. He was strong and well built — strong and well built even after all these years of strenuous living. Indeed, only one fault has been charged to him — other than his restless ambition. He was as dedicated a trencherman as Messer Marchese was a dedicated wine bibber. This is recorded by Petrarch. He was nine years old when he saw Uguccione, and he was so impressed with his prowess at the table that he averted to it in his *De Viris Illustribus*, written some sixty years later.

Uguccione was now in Genoa, where he was serving as Henry's imperial vicar. But with Henry dead — and with no assurance that the office would be renewed by Henry's successor — perhaps he would like new employment.

The Pisans hoped so. They would try to find out.

Pisan emissaries, therefore, sailed north and confronted Uguccione.

"We have been authorized to ask you to become leader of the Ghibelline forces."

"With what powers and holding what offices?"

"Pisa will make you her war captain (commander in chief), *podestà*, and captain of the people."

They defined the authority of these posts.

"I accept," said Uguccione.

He must have said so immediately, for the time involved was very short.

You will recall that Frederick of Sicily did not step ashore until September 5, and then needed some time to ride to Pisa and for negotiations. Yet on September 30, Uguccione assumed the powers which had been offered to him.

It was a new day after a dark night — even if a short dark night — for the city at the Arno mouth.

"Once again," writes Robert Davidsöhn, "and in a manner far more splendid than it did twenty-five years ago when Guido da Montefeltro commanded, the glory of victory lighted up the banner of the Pisan Ghibellines."

Maybe "hopes of victory" would be a better phrase, for although the crowds cheered as the grizzled old warrior from the Massa Trabaria stepped from his barge onto one of the already-paved *lungarno*'s for a triumphal march through the city, there were only hopes but not yet either glory or achievement.

Soon, however, glory — and achievement — seemed nearer.

Uguccione was a soldier's soldier, and the soldiers he could count on reacted accordingly. It has already been noted that after the death of Henry there was widespread abandonment of the imperial cause. Most of the *scarsafedi* were Italians who feared neighboring Florence, but there were a few from the north, and among these was a company of German and Luxemburger knights led by Baldwin of Montcornet and Thomas of Siebenforn, the latter Henry's chamberlain. They had come with high hopes. On their banners was depicted the head of Conradin of Swabia, the grandson of Frederick II, who had been beheaded in the marketplace of Naples. They would avenge Conradin and this blot on German honor. Henry's death had made this impossible and they had turned north. But now they were intercepted by hard-riding messengers.

"The Ghibellines have a new leader. They can use your services again."

"Who is he?"

"The lord of Faggiuola."

Uguccione della Faggiuola! Under Uguccione, doughty and resolute, and like most Ghibelline barons of the Apennine crests probably of German descent, they could and would fight, and perhaps, even, they would accomplish their mission.

They wheeled in a half circle and turned south again. (The dust stirred up by the maneuver must surely have been seen by disconcerted Florentine outposts.) Soon German gutturals and Luxemburg German-French could be heard in Pisan streets as the taverns were filled with this returned soldiery, all of them thirstily drinking Italian wine.

They set an example to others too.

Many a Pisan knight had put down his arms and gone home when the others did, but now they took them up again. Perhaps a thousand did.

With these added to the Germans and the Luxemburgers, Uguccione now had the nucleus of a respectable army. In horsemen alone, he had eighteen hundred men at his disposal. And the number grew daily.

He now had power as well as powers.

« 4 »

This power he used wisely and well. Trained by long years of difficult and bitter partisan struggle, Uguccione did not have to be told that Pisa alone would not give him an adequate base from which to carry out the purpose for which he had been appointed — namely to topple the Florentines and the Guelph Tuscan League which Florence had organized. He did not have to be told that he must broaden this base — that he must construct a Pisan Ghibelline League to counterbalance it, or at least that he must find reliable allies, allies that were close at hand and not in distant Germany or even among the cities of Lombardy, such as Verona or Milan.

This he set out to do as promptly as possible. But first he had a nearer task. He must make Pisa itself understand who was its master. For it would not do to enter upon foreign adventures — or even foreign negotiations — if everything were not in order at home.

He did this in a single swift, dramatic act. Hardly had he assumed power when the Pisan government — possibly if not probably with his knowledge — sent emissaries to King Robert at Naples with instructions to negotiate either a peace treaty or an armistice. They returned with a peace treaty. Between Robert and Pisa on the one hand; and between Pisa and Florence, Lucca, Siena, and Massa Marittima on the other.

But a peace treaty was the last thing Uguccione really wanted, and when (1) King Robert failed to live up to its terms, and (2) the *anziani*, Pisa's governing body, called on him to dismiss his German and his Luxemburger troops, this gave him the opportunity he sought.

Without ceremony, he ordered the arrest of Pietro Bonconti (who had come to him with the order to dismiss the troops), his father Banduccio Bonconti (who was one of the *anziani* at the time peace negotiations were authorized), and the city chamberlain Vanni de' Verdi, the last apparently on the theory that he was inclined toward the Guelphs. Under the pain of torture, he made them confess to capital crimes. The most heinous of them: they had accepted Florentine money to arrange a peace that Florence would like.

But not a peace that would be in the interests of Pisa. They had betrayed their city.

"Spread this abroad," said Uguccione. His agents did.

In particular they went among the laboring people who were easily aroused, and soon the streets and alleys were filled with shouting artisans.

"Death to the ambassadors!" they cried. (The ambassadors who had negotiated the peace treaty.) "Death to the Guelphs! Death to Banduccio, the traitor peacemonger!"

In the meantime, the Germans and the Luxemburgers rode through the city. With their standard, a live tame eagle, flying above them, they pried into any corner from which opposition might come. They made certain that no one — but no one — would threaten their pay.

In this atmosphere, it was not difficult for the judges to sentence the two Bonconti and their colleague to death for treason. They did and the three were forthwith beheaded.

Then — on the next day — Uguccione summoned all citizens to the cathedral to exercise their *balìa* and confer power on him. They did this *viva voce*, giving him supreme command in war and peace for a period of ten years.

"Many grumbled," says a historian, "both at the executions and at the seizure of power, but fear kept them from speaking."

Among other things, fear of the Germans and the Luxemburgers, who now understood very well that if it had not been for his intervention they would now be upon the road again and with their hire unpaid.

With this popular approval — arranged, perhaps, but clearly and loudly spoken — he had accomplished what he needed to accomplish. He had made his position in Pisa impregnable and secure.

It was then, and then only, that he took the next logical step — extension of his power to another city. In this case to Lucca, some forty-eight miles west of Florence upon the right bank of the Serchio River and up to now one of her more reliable allies, a town of well-built walls and a strong fortress, about which we have heard something already and will shortly hear more.

Yet even in his dealings with Lucca, the old warrior began by hiding his mailed fist in a velvet glove. He tried negotiations first. Apparently, too, he tried them successfully, for somehow he persuaded the Lucchese to cede to him Cerretello — once Pisan, this castle had been taken by Florence in 1312 and then given to Lucca — as well as Asciano and Viareggio, and to promise him Bietina and Buti. More important, he also persuaded Lucca to recall her Ghibelline exiles — including nineteen of the Interminelli family, one of whom, Castruccio Castracani, Machiavelli would idealize almost as he idealized Caesar Borgia — in return for Pisa's recall of the Guelphs.

Not until this was accomplished did he show his hand. But then he did.

"In the said year of 1314," reports Villani, "the Ghibellines having been restored to the city, and Uguccione pressing the Lucchese hard to give back their property to them, which the Guelphs who had appropriated it were reluctant to do" — and also to turn over Bietina and Buti, which they had not yet done — "Uguccione plotted an act of treachery with Interminelli, who had been recalled, and with the Quartigiani and the Pogginghi and the Onesti. In consequence, on June 14 disturbances suddenly broke out with hand-to-hand fighting, and when Uguccione came to the gates with the Pisans and their army, the Prato postern was yielded to him by these people, and he and his men entered the city."

King Robert's vicar Messer Gherardo da San Lupidio could have stopped this, says Villani — he and the Lucchesi Guelphs. But they were quarreling among themselves and had few horsemen and even fewer foot soldiers. The Florentines dallied at Fucecchio, fearing to come nearer lest Uguccione change his plans and invade their territory instead.

"For which reason the vicar and the Guelphs, not being able to defend themselves, rode out of Lucca and came to Fucecchio and to Santa Maria a Monte and to other castles in the valley of the Arno, and the city was sacked and pillaged by the Pisans and the Germans, who carried off all its wealth. This sack lasted eight days, and friend and foe alike were robbed. The strongest prevailed, and there were many slayings and many fires. Among other things, the papal treasure, which Cardinal Montefiore had brought from Rome and from the Campagna and from the Patrimony (of St. Peter) and had left in San Frediano at Lucca, was seized by Uguccione and his German ruffians and by the Pisans and was carried away to Pisa."

One must go back a long time, cries Villani, to find a day when a city suffered such misfortune and loss and such destruction of person and property through party warfare as on this occasion did Lucca.

A measure of this loss!

The renowned silkworkers of the city, who "were famed throughout the West" for the Byzantine splendor of their brocades, not merely were robbed of the costly stuffs in their warehouses, but their looms were either broken to pieces by the looters or burned. They left the city and were welcomed by Florence and also by Venice and Bologna. Some of them returned but not all, and those who did not return carried their skills elsewhere. Lucca's silk monopoly was gone forever.

But not its strategic position, which was now in Uguccione's hands.

This hold, incidentally, he proceeded to consolidate as rapidly as possible. With the assent of Castruccio — who after all could afford to wait, since Lucca was his own city and he was loved there — he set up his son Francesco as captain and *podestà*.

But that was only a beginning.

A month later — on July 13, 1314 — saying that he did this in the name of the Holy Roman Empire and of the Ghibelline party in Italy, he decreed a perpetual alliance between Lucca and Pisa and proclaimed himself captain-general of their joint forces as well as of the forces of every city or stronghold under their or imperial control. Among the latter were at least twenty-seven Lucchese towns and castles, most of which he could hardly have taken by storm but which now promptly if not cheerfully accepted his overlordship.

For the moment no one gainsaid him, and so there was a new balance of power in northern Tuscany. Florence — Black Florence — which hitherto had been master here, now (except at a few castles such as Montecatini which were held by the Lucchese Guelphs) had withdrawn behind her walls, where she was threatened by a newly organized state which had become at least her equal.

« 5 »

As far as I know, it has nowhere and by nobody been suggested that Dante was with or near Uguccione during any part of this time, and specifically it has not been suggested that he returned to Pisa after the death of Henry or that he either accompanied the Ghibelline warrior to Lucca or followed shortly after him. Yet in my judgment at least the last of these possibilities must be given serious thought.

Boccaccio, to be sure, says this explicitly of Dante and what he did at this time: "Without making any further efforts in regard to his return [to Florence], he passed over the Apennines and went to the Romagna." But Boccaccio was in error, for we know as positively as we can know anything that the poet was in Lucca in 1315 and it seems to me that arguments for his having come there in 1314 are very convincing, for not later than July 1314 he took a new very strong political stand and one that he would hardly have dared to take except under the protection of a powerful and friendly lord.

This stand was taken in the realm of papal rather than imperial politics and came about because of a sudden but not unexpected happening. Il Guasco — Dante's despised Pope Clement — was no more, and another one of the poet's post-dated prophesies had thus come true.

Paradiso XXX:

"The prefect of the heavenly forum [*Clement V*] will be
In that time one who openly or secretly
Will not with him [*Henry VII*] proceed down the same road.
But short will be the time God suffers him
To hold the holy office. He will be thrust down
Where Simon Magus deservedly is
And will push him of Anagni lower still."

Simon Magus — Simon the Sorcerer — was a man from Samaria who had been converted by St. Philip and who later offered money to St. Peter to bestow on him the gift of the Holy Ghost. Thereafter all traffic in spiritual offices was known as simony. Beatrice is speaking and she tells Dante that in due course Clement will be sent to the hell of the simoniacs, thrusting Boniface (him of Anagni) even deeper into its flames.

And so it came to pass. Exhausted by his devious struggles in which he was first for Henry and then against him; tormented by his involvement in the destruction of the Templars — not because there was either justice or pity in his heart but because he feared the consequences to his and the Church's reputation and hence influence; wracked by his agonizing disease, less than a year after the death of the emperor Bernard de Got departed from this world too.

Says Villani:

"In the year 1314, on the twentieth day of April, Pope Clement died. He was on the way to Bordeaux in Gascony" — his native and beloved Bordeaux with its smell of ships and wine kegs — "and when he crossed the Rhone at Roquemaure, he fell ill and died."

Then he added his own and sulfurous hellfire.

"It is related that while the said pope still lived a favorite nephew of his died, and he commanded a great master of necromancy to reveal what had befallen this nephew's soul. When the said master had finished his spells, he caused one of the pope's chaplains, a very courageous man, to be transported by demons who set before his eyes and showed him a palace in which was a bed of burning fire on which was the body of the said dead nephew, and they told him that he was sentenced thus for simony. Then in his vision he saw another palace opposite the first one, and they said it was being prepared for Pope Clement. Now the said chaplain reported this to the said pope and after that he never was glad."

Continues Villani:

"After Clement was dead and his body had been left all night in a church and with many lighted candles around it, his coffin caught fire and was burned as was his body from the waist downward."

« 6 »

But whatever the agency, dead the pope was and once again alive came
Dante's hopes. His Roman hopes. For there would now be a new pope
and might he not be made a Roman one? Two lights had once lighted the
world. Might not one of them be lighted again?

Dante thought so.

And the promoter of a Roman empire half reversed himself to become
the promoter of a Roman papacy.

He sought a goose quill and found parchment.

"To the Italian cardinals, Dante of Florence," he began.

(This is not the original heading, but the letter must have began something like this.)

To Cardinal Niccolò de Prato, Cardinal Napoleone Orsini, Cardinal
Guglielmo de' Longhi, Cardinal Francesco Gaetani, Cardinal Jacopo
Colonna, and Cardinal Pietro Colonna. Only six in number out of a
college of twenty-four, but if they held together they might accomplish
what he wanted them to.

Then he plunged into the matter under consideration, which was the
choosing of a new pope.

"How doth the city sit solitary" — how doth Rome sit solitary — "that
was full of people! How is she become as a widow! She that was great
among the nations, and princess among the provinces."

Here we have something a little curious — or it seems so. You will
perhaps remember the above words, for you have seen them before.
They were the words with which Dante began his never-published Latin
letter on the death of Beatrice. At that time, he used them about Florence
deprived of this lady. Now he used them about Rome deprived of her
pope. Yet it is not curious that they were taken from the prophet Jeremiah's Lamentations. For Dante was trying to be a prophet too.

He continued with a biblical prophet's somber warnings.

"The greed in days of old of the chiefest among the Pharisees which
made the ancient priesthood an abomination not only brought to an end
the ministry of the sons of Levi, but brought siege and ruin on the chosen
city of David. So it was, therefore, that the prophet too often lamented
the holy Jerusalem as undone."

He would have lamented Rome too. For Rome was "the sacred
sheepfold" that Christ meant "when he said: 'Peter, feed my sheep!' " and
it was Rome that "the same Peter, and likewise Paul who preached to the
Gentiles, consecrated with the shedding of their own blood."

But now Rome was abandoned and sorrowing, and not of necessity or because it was ordained by the stars, "but because you, making sorry use of the freedom of will, have made this your choice."

You! Dante lashed out the word. But who is meant by you?

The cardinals! The princes of the Church who are responsible for ruling the Church, ruling it and guiding it!

"You are, as it were, the centurions of the front rank of the Church militant."

And what had they done with their centurionship?

"Neglecting to guide the chariot of the Bride of the Crucified along the road that lies before you, you have gone from your path in the same way as did the false charioteer Phaeton. You whose duty it was to enlighten the flock that follows you through the wild crags of our pilgrimage here below have led them and yourselves to the edge of the precipice."

What else?

"You have scorned the fire that fell down upon your altars. You have sold doves in the temple. But give heed to the scourge! Give heed to the thunderbolt! And do not make light of the patience of Him who awaits your repentance."

Now who am I to say all this? This was Dante's next question.

"Yea, may you not well ask: 'Who is this man who, not fearing the swift punishment of Uzzah, sets himself up to protect the ark?' "

They may well ask this, for "truly I am one of the least of the sheep in the pasture of Jesus. I have no pastoral authority because I have no wealth."

But I do have the grace of God which made me what I am, and I am burned up with zeal for His house.

"Moreover, even from the mouths of babes and sucklings have been heard verities which are pleasing to God. This is the justification for my boldness. And besides this I have the authority of the Philosopher who in his system of morals taught that truth is to be preferred to friendship."

The Philosopher — that is, Aristotle.

And what are some of these truths — which he told them not in order to provoke them to railing but to make them blush?

"Each one of you has taken greed for his wife — greed which is the mother not of piety and righteousness but of sacrilege and wrong. Indeed, not charity but the daughters of the horseleech have become your daughters-in-law."

In other words, it is the lust for worldly wealth and worldly power that has misled them.

"All except the bishop of Luni."

Another one of Dante's sarcastic thrusts, for Gherardino da Filattiera of the Malaspina family, bishop of Luni from 1313 to 1321, was notable for his greed.

Nor did they hold true to the religion of the Church fathers.

"Your Gregory [Gregory the Great] now gathers cobwebs. Your Ambrose [bishop of Milan and converter of St. Augustine] lies forgotten on a bookshelf, as does your St. Augustine. So too do Dionysius [Dionysius the Areopagite], your St. John of Damascus, and your Bede. Instead you cry up the *Speculum* [a medieval lawbook much used by those who sought wealth], Innocent [the legalist Innocent IV], and him of Ostia [another canon lawyer]. The former sought God as their end and highest good. The latter tell you how to get riches and benefices."

One thing more:

"But, Fathers, suppose not that I am the phoenix of the wide world." According to Bruno Latini, there was only one phoenix. "Everyone is mumbling or muttering or thinking or imagining what I say aloud."

Even Balaam's ass spoke the Lord's words. So did he.

"Be you ashamed therefore."

But remember that heaven could pardon them.

Under what conditions?

"If you show repentance which in turn will bring amendment."

If they made amendment.

But what amendment?

And now Dante came to the point of the letter.

For the letter did have a point.

"It behooves you to keep in your mind's eye, and in such measure as your power of seeing permits you, the present condition of the city of Rome, something that would arouse the pity of Hannibal himself, not to say others. She is now bereft of both the one and the other of her luminaries." In other words, she had neither pope nor emperor. "Hence she sits solitary and widowed as has been said above."

This, of course, should be the concern of all the cardinals.

"But most of all it should be the concern of those of you who knew the Tiber when you were little children."

The *Roman* cardinals!

"For although it is the duty of all Italians to love the capital of Italy as the common source of their civilization, it is rightly held to be even more your part to reverence it, since in your case it is also the source of your very being."

The Roman cardinals — but two of them in particular.

"Thou above all, Orsini, that thy colleagues who were removed from office may not forever remain stripped of their glory and that by the authority of the Apostolic lord they may resume the time-honored insignia which they undeservedly were compelled to lay down! Thou also, thou adherent of the other Trasteverine faction, that the anger of the deceased pontiff may grow green [presumably, may cool down] in thee."

Orsini — Ursa, or Bear, in the Latin text — was Napoleone Orsini del Monte, and in spite of his name he belonged to the Colonna (anti-pope) rather than to his own kinsmen's pro-Boniface faction. The "adherent of the other Trasteverine faction" was Francesco Gaetani. He was Pope Boniface's nephew, and an enemy to the Colonna and to Cardinal Napoleone.

But let them forget such old enmities and join hands — with each other and with the two other Roman and the two other Italian cardinals.

And let them then right the wrong that was done when Clement V was elected.

For they could right it if they wished to and would. They could right it "if you" — that is, the Italian cardinals — "who were responsible for this wandering afield shall with one accord fight valiantly for the Bride of Christ, and for the see of the Bride which is Rome, and for our Italy, and to speak more broadly for the whole body politic of mankind which is now on pilgrimage on this earth."

In other words, if they returned the papacy to Rome.

"If you, fighting gloriously in the arena of a contest already begun, accomplish this, you will surely hear '*Gloria in excelsis*' as the disgraced Gascons, who are burning with avarice and striving to usurp the glory of Italy, become an example to posterity through all the coming years."

« 7 »

But the "*Gloria in excelsis*" was not heard — not in Dante's lifetime!

To be sure, the Italian cardinals did give some indication that they had heard what Dante said and they at least tried to effect a compromise. Knowing that they were hopelessly in the minority, they realized that they could not elect an Italian, but it occurred to them that they might elect a non-Italian who would be friendly to their ideas. Their choice was Guillaume de Mandegot, who was cardinal-bishop of Palestrina. Because he was a Frenchman, they hoped that he would be acceptable to the Gascons and to King Philip, who controlled the conclave. Because his see and source of revenue was in Italy — and because he himself now had his residence there — they felt that he would bring the papacy back to the Tiber.

The French party evidently thought or feared the same thing, for they took action of the very strongest sort to make sure it did not come to pass. What this was is reported in an encyclical letter sent by the six Italian cardinals to their "brothers and very dear friends" of the Cistercian monasteries of Cîteaux, La Ferté, Pontigny, Clairvaux, and Mormond.

"While we and the other cardinals were in the bishop's palace at Carpentras after the death of Pope Clement for the purpose of choosing in conclave the future pope, and while we, the Italian cardinals, not seeking our own advantage but that of God, looked for a man who would hold up the pillars of the Church, guiding the same Church while reforming it, suddenly the Gascons assembled a great multitude of foot soldiers and armed knights and, led by Bertrand de Got and Raymond Guilhem, nephews of the [late] lord pope, who either feared justice under his successor or thought that with violence they could take possession of the house of God by hereditary right, forced their way into the city and cruelly slew many Italian retainers.

"They also set fires in various parts of the city and, not content with this, they invaded the very hostelries in which we lived and to the blare of trumpets threatened the most savage war against us.

"After that they surrounded the conclave itself, shouting: 'Death to the Italians! We want a pope! We want a pope!' "

At this point discretion seemed quite clearly the better part of valor and, in no way prevented by the French cardinals, who were glad to have them go, Cardinal Napoleone, Cardinal Niccolò da Prato, and the other four arranged to have a small opening broken through a rear wall through which they slipped into the night.

They were not detected — or perhaps it was thought wiser not to detect them, since they were leaving. Soon they were on the road. Through Orange to the Rhone they went, and then up the Rhone to Valence.

This was on July 24. They wrote the letter on September 8.

September 8, *1314*.

But it was not until nearly two years later — it was not until August 7, *1316* — that almost the longest interregnum in all papal history ended, and then only after certain of the Italian cardinals — they had now returned to the conclave — defected and the new king of France, Louis X, known as Louis the Obstinate, had intervened.

The man chosen was Jacques d'Euse, archbishop of Avignon and cardinal-bishop of Oporto.

He took the name of John XXII.

"He was," says Villani, "a poor clerk and his father was a shoemaker."

Villani either spoke spitefully or was badly informed. Cardinal d'Euse was not of noble birth, but his father — at least by the standards of Cahors, which was a rich and money-minded city — was a wealthy and successful tradesman, and as during his boyhood and youth Jacques moved from university to university (although it is said by some that he did not begin serious studies until he was forty-four, actually as a young man he studied both in southern France and in Naples), he was accustomed to having money in his purse and to the shrewd practices of a merchant.

This Pope John XXII was the last pope named during Dante's lifetime, and just as he had denounced earlier popes who served or served themselves, so Dante denounced John too. One of these denunciations has already been cited, for d'Euse was one of the Caorsini at whom he hurled his imprecations (*Paradiso* XXVII) in the same passage in which he denounced Pope Clement.

But in another passage he had words for John alone.
Paradiso XVII:

> But thou who writest only to unwrite,
> Know thou that Peter and that Paul who died
> To save the vineyards that thou wastest still live.
> But thou canst say: "So strong is my desire
> For him whose wish it was to live alone
> And who because of a dance won martyrdom
> That I know neither Paul nor the Fisherman."

Here is an explanation of the above and somewhat cryptic words. On the Florentine florin was the image of John the Baptist — "him whose wish it was to live alone" — and it was said Pope John was so devoted to this florin that he had forgotten his duties as successor to St. Peter and preacher of the words of St. Paul.

That he was devoted to the golden coin is clearly demonstrated by an action he took later. This, although it came after the death of Dante, should be set down, for it clearly reflects earlier actions which could have led Dante to his strictures.

"In 1322," writes Villani, "Pope John caused to be minted in Avignon a new piece of gold money of the same weight and gold content and appearance as the gold florin of Florence, and it had nothing to distinguish it from the florin except that beside the lily was the name of Pope John. He was much blamed for this because it was clear he wanted it to resemble the florin of Florence."

But anything that was minted and could be spent or hoarded was coveted by this acquisitive old man — he was nearly eighty when he was elected pope and lived to be ninety, at least according to Paget Toynbee, although some say he was five years younger — and he knew how to get what he so loved.

"No one," says Robert Davidsöhn, "understood better how to benefit financially from ecclesiastical promotions and vacancies, and woe to the promoted prelate who declared himself bankrupt or unwilling to pay."

He was like a spider who lived in a spiderweb, but his flies were the coin of the realm — the coin of any realm. It is variously estimated that this successor to the humble fisherman left a fortune of from seven hundred fifty thousand to eighteen million gold florins when he died!

« *8* »

Dante's letter to the Italian cardinals — Dante's unsuccessful letter to the Italian cardinals, for Jacques d'Euse, become Pope John XXII, made no move whatsoever to take the papacy from Avignon — was not the only epistle which he wrote at approximately this time. A second of the not more than thirteen surviving letters which can be ascribed to Dante with any confidence was also written during the two years that followed Henry's death. It was personal in its nature, yet it too had political implications or at least a political background, and these must be understood to really understand the letter.

It was written in 1315, and we will begin by saying that the situation in Florence was very different in that year from what it had been in 1313 when a messenger had come riding in to bring them the tidings from Buonconvento. Theoretically, to be sure, the war was over, since the gallant and persistent emperor no longer threatened. But the consequences of trying for a good six years to save Italy singlehandedly — or at least of trying to organize the defense of Italy — were again felt everywhere.

The cupboard was again bare — this was to be expected, since for two years most of the surrounding fields had been ravaged and grain shipments from abroad were blocked by Pisa — and a drought so severe that there was no water to turn the Arno mills made it unlikely that it would soon be filled again. The treasury was empty too, and new taxes had to be levied. Among them that relative innovation, an income tax. Even the clergy had to pay it! And business was in such disarray that a moratorium had to be declared on private debts.

To add to all this, the enemies of Florence, instead of disappearing, now encircled the city. This was largely Uguccione's doing. Secure in his rule of Pisa and Lucca, he had used this security and the strength it gave him to negotiate alliances with Can Grande della Scala of Verona, with the Bonacolsi of Mantua, and with the Pazzi and the Ubaldini of the upper Valdarno. While he raided Florentine territory near Empoli and in the Valdelsa, carrying off men and cattle, and while the others did the same near and above Pontassieve, he began preparing for thrusts on a large scale. He would move three thousand knights and twenty thousand foot soldiers into the Val di Nievole. If he succeeded there — and we now know that he did — Florence would be in serious trouble.

Small wonder, then, that the city seethed. The plain people, who did not care whether Blacks or Whites ruled them as long as they were fed, began to move into the streets. It was necessary to call upon Count Carlo di Battifolle — a relative of Dante's Count Guido — to ride in with two hundred Sienese horsemen to put them down. The merchant (who paid two pennies tax on the *libbra*), the money changer, the judge, the doctor, and the tailor (who paid two and a half percent), the dyer and the tanner (who paid one and two thirds percent), and the butcher, the school-teacher, the owner of a bath, the cook, the worker in the stone quarries, the shop employee, the porter, and even the cleaner of latrines, all of whom paid various decreed amounts, began to wonder if the Black government was all it had promised to be. Even the bankers modified their support. Why lend money if you couldn't force repayment? Many governments would have fallen.

But the Black government was not the kind that would give up easily, nor did it. If its old friends had weakened — and they had only weakened, they had not become enemies — it would strengthen its position by getting new friends.

How?

By doing what it had done four years before!

By recalling a substantial number of the exiles, who thus recalled would stand gratefully at the side of those who had recalled them.

On May 15, 1315, on June 2, on September 3, and on December 11, 1316, therefore, it published a series of amnesties. Only the first of them is of interest to us, but it is of paramount interest, for on it was the name of Florence's forever most famous exile.

Dante Alighieri could return to his native city.

Word of this was hurried to him at Lucca, and as he received it, his heart leapt; but then it sank again, for there were conditions. Could he accept them?

His friends urged him to, but could he? Could he honorably? Could he and be true to Dante?

Here is his decision. It is contained in a letter apparently written to Teruccio di Manetto Donati, Gemma's brother and therefore Dante's brother-in-law.

"From your epistle, which I received with the respect it deserves and read with every care, I learn that my return to Florence has occupied your mind and heart. I am very grateful to you, all the more so since it is a rare thing indeed for an exile to find friends. And since my reply to what you have written may not be of the sort that certain of the fainthearted would approve, I earnestly beg you that it may be carefully examined and considered by you before judgment be passed upon it.

"I gather, then, from a letter from your nephew and mine, as well as from those of various friends, that under the terms of a decree lately proclaimed in Florence dealing with the return of exiles, I may be given pardon and return at once provided I pay a certain fine and submit to the shame of an oblation. These two conditions are truly as ridiculous as they are ill advised. I mean that those were ill advised who conveyed them to me. Not you! For in your more discreet and thoughtful letter no hint of such conditions was made."

Such conditions! Such shameful and insulting conditions, for the oblation meant that to win pardon the supposed malefactor had to enter a Florentine prison — if he were not a prisoner already — and from thence, clad in sackcloth and with a fool's cap on his head and a lighted candle in his hand, walk through the streets of Florence to the baptistery of San Giovanni, where a sponsor offered him to God and the Baptist!

In other words, he had publicly and humiliatingly to acknowledge guilt.

But he, Dante, would admit no guilt and so his pen dug parchment.

"Is this then the gracious way in which I am to be recalled to my native city after the anguishes of almost fifteen years of exile? Is this the reward of an innocence which is manifest to the whole world? Of the sweat and the unending toil of study? Far be it from the friend and companion of philosophy to commit such a rash act of humility as to submit himself almost like a felon in chains as Ciolo degli Abbati and other criminals have done! Far be it from a preacher of justice who has endured wrong to pay a compensation to those who have injured him just as if they were his benefactors!"

Then the conclusion.

"No, Father" — Teruccio was a priest — "it is not by such a road that I will return to mine own land, but if you first, and then others, find another way that does not sully the good name and the honor of Dante, I will tread it with no laggard's steps. But if by no such road may Florence be entered, then I will never enter Florence. For look you, can I not gaze upon the face of the sun and of the stars wherever I may be? Can I not under any sky contemplate sweet truth unless I first disgrace and dishonor myself in the eyes of the people and the state of Florence? And I will not lack bread!"

I will not lack bread!

His hackles were indeed ruffled. This phrase showed it.

So did another phrase.

And I will not grovel in the dust like Ciolo degli Abbati!

Ciolo, whose misdeeds were proverbial, like Dante had been excluded by name from the 1311 Reform of Baldo d'Aguglione. He was a noted sponger whose apology for appearing at a banquet to which he had not been invited was: "I am not to blame. You are to blame for not sending me an invitation."

I will only return if I can come with head high and proudly!

This was in late May, and it was not until October and November that Florence answered him.

With two new sentences!

October 15, 1315.

"In the name of God, amen. Below written are the condemnations and sentences of condemnation given, published, and proclaimed by that noble and puissant knight Messer Raniero del fu Messer Zaccaria of Orvieto, royal vicar in Florence, and consented to by his judges, against each and every Ghibelline and rebel against the city of Florence . . .

"Inasmuch as we have cited and summoned each and all of the above" — the Ghibellines and rebels and even suspected Ghibellines — "to appear before us and our court within a certain time and there give assurance that they will observe their bounds" — stay in the places of confinement assigned to them — "and inasmuch as they have taken no care to appear, we pronounce them contumacious and in contempt. And we again cite them to appear before us within a certain time to make their excuses if they can, and if they do not appear within that time and thereafter fall into Florentine hands, they will be led to a place of justice and there the head of each and every one of them will be cut from his shoulders until he does utterly die."

Dante, to be sure, is not specifically mentioned, but we know that he must have been among those sentenced, for on January 9, 1343, Jacopo Alighieri, his son, agreed to pay the Florentine treasury eight gold florins so as to be permitted, as his mother's heir, to recover half interest in a farm at Pagnolle which had been confiscated from his father "Durante, called Dante, son of Alighieri of Florence," who had been condemned by Cante Gabrielli in 1302 and by Raniero of Orvieto in 1315.

November 6, 1315.

"In the name of God, amen. Here are the banishments and outlawries published and proclaimed by the noble knight Messer Raniero di Zaccaria of Orvieto, royal vicar for the city and state of Florence, against the below-written Ghibellines and rebels for the below-written disobediences and contumacies in respect to the punishments and banishments set down hereafter and pronounced in the council of his judges."

The sentence of decapitation was repeated and to it was added another sanction. The "below-written Ghibellines and rebels" were declared outlaws as provided under the laws of Florence, and each and every citizen of Florence was authorized "to offend them in their possessions and their persons freely and with impunity."

In other words, to murder them if they encountered them and to appropriate any property they might still have. In Florence, under Florentine law. Anywhere else with Florence protection.

In this decree, Dante *was* listed, for here are those named in his *sesto* of the Porta San Piero:

"All of the house of Portinari" — Beatrice's kin — "except Manetto, Folchetto, Serragallo, Torrigiano, Puccio, Segno, Andrea, Portinari, and Franchetto, brothers; and Accerito di Manetto, Andrea del fu Renzo, Benozzo, Giovanni di Manetti, Gherardo Falchi, and Andrea di Renzo, all of these Portinari too. They have paid their fines.

"All of the house of Giuochi except Lamberto Lapi and Filippo di Gherardi, who have paid their fines.

"Dante Alhegherii and his sons!"

This, in my opinion, was his absolute spiritual nadir. This, I submit, rather even than the death of Beatrice, or his expulsion from Florence, or the death of Alto Arrigo, and certainly rather than when he realized that he could not bring the pope back to Rome, was when he reached the bottom of his own personal bottomless pit. It was at this time that he came to the end of the psychological road.

Yet — happily — the end was a beginning and his nadir led the way to his zenith. For just as in his great poem he went from hell to heaven, so now from his own hell he turned toward paradise. The paradise of doing what he was destined to do, and what he had promised to do. And now he was ready. Stripped of his *impedimenta* — the word means baggage, but in this instance, at least, its Latin form is more expressive — reconciled to his loss of the world, he was now prepared to resume his immortal journey.

He would begin to do so very soon.

« 9 »

But not at Lucca. Except for Gentucca, who had provided him with the pleasant interlude of 1308 but was probably now more concerned with her aging and ill husband (Cosciorino wrote his will on December 15, 1317, and there is no reason to believe he lived much longer), and except for the protection provided by Uguccione, Lucca had too little to offer him. It was, to be sure, near Florence, but after the decrees of October 15 and November 6, that no longer mattered. In all other respects, now that its silkworkers had gone, it was a turbulent small town which was largely noted for the bloody violence of its feuds and perhaps as the birthplace of

Bonagiunta Orbicani, the minor poet who so greatly admired Dante but had been dead these fifteen or more years.

And now even his protector was no longer available. Castruccio Castracani had seen to that.

On August 29, 1315, Uguccione and his allies had smashingly defeated the Florentines at Montecatini — the Florentine loss, ten thousand slain and seven thousand taken prisoner — but after that he had fallen into a lethargy which was the natural consequence of a good fifty years of hard campaigning, and the young Lucchese nobleman, with his shock of red-gold hair which he never covered in rain or shine or even in battle, took advantage of this to set up a power base of his own. Putting aside for the moment the genial manners and the gift for witty retorts which had won him many friends, he wrote a letter to Frederick (Hapsburg) of Austria, one of the two pretenders to the imperial throne, and urged him to make him imperial vicar. Frederick did, and in this capacity Castruccio suddenly seized Massa di Carrara of the marble quarries and executed thirty of its leading citizens for treason.

Since the treason consisted of agreeing to hand over Massa to Uguccione — to whom as lord of Lucca it rightfully belonged — Uguccione struck back.

On April 10, Neri della Faggiuola, Uguccione's son and *podestà* of the city ever since his brother Francesco had been killed at Montecatini, received orders from his father to arrest Castruccio and confront him with the choice of either surrendering Massa and "all other castles and lands" which he had illegally seized or being executed by the public hangman.

But Neri lost his nerve.

"Convinced by the strong arguments of his advisers and his followers, he neither dared nor wished to do what his father ordered, but instead sent for Uguccione" — who was in Pisa — "and urged him to set out for Lucca with some of his knights and carry out the execution himself."

Uguccione did — but only got as far as Monte San Giuliano (now Monte Pisano) halfway between the two cities. Then tidings came to him that Pisa was in revolt. Through the streets had surged the populace, led by one Coscetto da Colle, and to the palace in which Ugucionne and his household dwelt.

"Liberty! Long live the people! Death to tyranny!"

Thereafter they had looted the palace and killed all of Uguccione's servants, and had proclaimed a new lord, Count Gaddo de' Gherardeschi, unquestionably a descendant of Count Ugolino of the Tower of Hunger story.

Uguccione hesitated. Should he return to Pisa or go on to Lucca to his son?

He returned to Pisa, only to find that the walls were manned and the gates shut in his face. He could only take the city by force and he did not have the force.

So he departed a second time for the city of Lucca.

But he was now descredited, and found this city ready to break from his hands too.

"Castruccio! Long live Castruccio!" rang through the streets.

Then:

"Kill Uguccione! Slay Uguccione! Death to the tyrant!"

The same cry in two cities! The lion, the grizzled but heroic lion, was a hunted fox.

There was only one thing to do. Uguccione did it. He released Castruccio, who forthwith leaped upon a horse and galloped through the streets of Lucca, cheered by the citizens. Then he surrendered to him and asked for his protection.

Then and there, the young Lucchese demonstrated that he was in no way the typical Renaissance lord and tyrant. He refused to take revenge on Uguccione and Neri but instead had them conducted to the gates of the city and bade them to begone.

They obeyed him. Taking no chances, father and son galloped up the Serchio Valley to the "noble castle of Verrucola," which looked down from a lofty peak in the Garfagnana (high mountain valley northwest of Lucca). There they were received by Spinetta Malaspina, some kind of cousin of Dante's host Moroello. But they did not stay with him for long. Instead they crossed the mountains to Modena and then Mantua. Finally — but not long afterwards — they came to Verona, where they were received warmly by Can Grande, who made Uguccione commander in chief of his cavalry and later *podestà* of Vicenza.

« *10* »

It is my firm conviction that Dante also came to Verona at approximately this time. It is my opinion, in other words, that Dante either preceded Uguccione to Can Grande's castle — perhaps leaving Lucca after his scornful rejection of Florence's offer of amnesty — or, more probably, followed him there and after not very great an interval.

To be sure, there is no hard evidence for such a conclusion. There is no piece of paper or parchment, for example, that says that the poet was in Verona at such and such a time.

But the circumstantial evidence is very appealing. I give some of it. Dante's glowing words about Can Grande in *Inferno* XVII; these have

already been set down. Their possible echo in his description of the greyhound in *Inferno* I. The strong likelihood that the Veronese nobleman
was the D.V.X. (*dux*, or leader) of *Purgatorio* XXXIII. All these make it
almost certain that Dante had personal contacts with Can Grande when
the latter was a mature great captain and not a promising youth of fourteen.

This, incidentally, is the D.V.X. passage:

> But not at all times without heir shall be
> The eagle which left his feathers on the chariot
> Whereby it became a monster and then prey.
> For I see certainly, and therefore tell it,
> That near are those stars now, and are secure
> From any stop or stay, that bring a time
> In which a five hundred [*D*] and a ten [*X*] and a five [*V*]
> Sent unto us by God shall slay the harlot
> Together with the giant that runs with her.

But who was meant? Who would destroy the oppressors of Italy?

Henry VII? But Henry was dead and his mission had failed before
these lines were written.

Uguccione? The same, for Uguccione died in 1319. But besides that,
Uguccione, who changed sides more than once, hardly met Dante's
specifications.

A purely idealized leader and no specific person, or if any person was
meant, the Savior Christ?

This was Benvenuto da Imola's thought about the greyhound and it
could be applied to D.V.X. too.

Others reached the same conclusion. D.X.V. — for in the *Commedia*
the words were written in that order — stood for *Dominus Xtus Victor*
(the Lord Christ Victor).

Or, finally, Can Francesco, known as Can Grande, della Scala?

This is the majority opinion and, speaking for the majority, W. W.
Vernon, one of the last century's great Dante scholars, writes as follows:

"All things, therefore, concur in making it intellegible and probable
that D.V.X. is Can Grande della Scala — an opinion adopted by some of
the ancient commentators."

To be sure, some of the "all things" which he offers in evidence are at
least curious.

"If we write down the name and qualification of Can Grande as 'Kan
Grande de Scala Signore de Verona,'" he reports Giuseppe Picci as
saying, "and compute numerically the initials and prepositions, we have

the following result: K = 10; G = 7; d = 4; e = 5; S = 90; S = 90; d = 4; e = 5; V = 300."

Total, 515.

I, however, prefer less esoteric mathematics.

(1) Charlemagne was crowned Holy Roman emperor in 800.

(2) If you add D.V.X .(515) to 800, you have 1315.

(3) In 1315, Can Grande, twenty-five years old, and master of Verona since 1311, began to demonstrate that he was the outstanding Ghibelline captain in Italy. Twenty-five too, as has been noted before, was the age at which during the Middle Ages you entered manhood. In 1315, Can Grande became a man officially. In 1315, he could become D.V.X.

« 11 »

But it is not necessary to rely on *Inferno* I or *Inferno* XVII or *Purgatorio* XXXIII to come to the conclusion that Dante visited Verona — his third but not his last visit to the city — precisely during this period of his life.

Effectively, he says so himself. Probably in 1319 — but certainly no later than August 25, 1320 — he wrote a long letter to Can Grande dealing with his *Commedia*. It will be discussed fully in a later chapter, but its opening paragraph should be adverted to here and now.

"The praise of your renowned magnificence which wakeful fame spreads abroad as she flies so variously affects various people that it lifts up some into the hope of good fortune and casts others down into the fear of being destroyed. Indeed I once concluded that the report she brought must be extravagant and beyond the realm of truth, since the deeds she narrated went far beyond any other deeds of modern time. Where-fore — and so that doubt might not keep me too long in great suspense, just as the queen of the South [the queen of Sheba] sought Jerusalem, and as Pallas sought Helicon, so did I hie me to Verona so that I could examine with my own trustworthy eyes the things about which I had heard. There I did indeed see your splendor. There I was the witness of, and the partaker in, your generosity. And there just as formerly I was convinced that the tales told about you were more than a little fulsome so now I realized that it was the facts themselves that were beyond measure. And so it came to pass that whereas earlier, and from hearsay alone, I had been — although with certain reservations — your well-wisher, now that actually I saw you I became your servant and friend."

But when could Dante have witnessed this Can Grande splendor? When could he have participated in Can Grande's generosity?

Certainly not in 1302 or even in 1305–1306, the probable dates of Dante's two earlier visits to Verona, for at that time the greatest of the

Scaligers was still a younger brother who did not even share the lordship with his older brother Alboino.

It must have been later — at least after 1308, when at the age of eighteen Can Grande became joint lord of the city, but more probably after 1311, when on Alboino's death he became sole ruler. Not until then could Can Grande have glittered as he walked in golden panoply. Not until then could he have been so generous that it was dazzling to Dante or to anyone.

But there is no time after 1308 or 1311 when there seems to be any likelihood that Dante could have come to the new white knight of Ghibelline aspiration — the white knight who still rides in marble with his cloak blowing in the wind over his tomb near Santa Maria Antica — before that time in 1315 when he rebuffed Florence's offer of conciliation and was chastised by her anew in turn.

It must, then, have been either late in 1315 or early in 1316 when he came to the city on the Adige — with high hopes in his soul, and perhaps even with a sonnet by Can Grande, who, it seems, was a poet as well as a warrior, on his lips or in his heart.

This sonnet celebrated the young lord's alliance with a new Caesar — or more accurately one of the new Caesars — Frederick of Hapsburg.

> O Guelphs, now that the prince of Austria
> Hath taken great Can Grande in his embrace
> Ye had best flee, and that at a swift pace,
> Lest this Theodoric pursue ye fast and far.

It went on to warn them of spirit-crushing defeat, to say that they would be entangled in their bad fortune as swine are herded one against the other, and to declare that the rich would not be saved by their wealth, that this was the judgment of God, that it would not avail them to call on "their" King Robert, and finally that the "holy empire" would bring joy to its faithful by reason of a great disaster in the Orient — which, however, is now taken to refer not to a Byzantine defeat in Armenia but to the promised destruction of King Robert's fleet off the *eastern* part of the Ligurian Riviera.

With high hopes and in a mood of exultation.

But for reasons that we do not know — but we know that he had not quarreled with his benefactor — he did not stay there long.

« 12 »

Boccaccio tells us in some detail where he went next.

"In those days" — in the days after the death of Henry — "the Lord of

Ravenna, a renowned and ancient city in the Romagna, was a noble knight whose name was Guido Novello da Polenta. Trained in liberal studies, he bestowed high honors on men of ability, and especially on those who surpassed their fellows in learning. Now it came to his ears — and this was more than he dared hope for, although he had long heard reports of his genius — that Dante was in the Romagna and in dire straits, and he decided to welcome him and honor him. Nor did he wait for this to be asked of him, but reflecting in his generous mind how men of his talent must feel shame at begging favors, he approached him with offers of his own and requested him as a special favor the very thing that he knew Dante must ask of him — namely that he would graciously consent to live with him. Since the two desires — that of the inviter and that of the man invited — were the same, and since Dante was extremely pleased with the liberality of the noble knight, and, finally, since necessity compelled him, he went to Ravenna without waiting for another invitation. There he was honorably received by the knight who revived his failing hopes with sympathetic encouragement, gave him in abundance all that was appropriate, and kept him there for many years — indeed until the end of his life."

There are, to be sure, minor inaccuracies in this account, but they are not more than minor.

It is at least an exaggeration to say that Dante was "in dire straits." Can Grande would have been surprised to hear this. Moreover his name and fame were now such that there was hardly a lord in Italy — or out of it — who would not gladly have fed him and clothed him just to have him in attendance. By the same token, it is not true that he accepted Guido Novello's invitation because "necessity compelled him." He accepted it because he wanted to accept it — because it seemed wise to do so. It is also not correct to say that he came to Ravenna from an unspecified place in the Romagna. We know that he was in Lucca and are confident that he was in Verona. His visit, or visits, to the Romagna were at an earlier time.

But the main facts still stand.

Dante *was* enthusiastically urged to come by a noble lord who sincerely liked to "bestow high honors on men of ability."

He *did* go to the city near the Adriatic shore which once (in Umbrian pre-Roman days) had been a collection of hovels on the little islands of the Po delta and then became successively a principal Roman naval base (under Augustus), the chief city of the Byzantine exarchate (under Justinian and his predecessors and successors), and the capital and final resting place of Theodoric the Goth.

He *did* stay there for the rest of his life.

« *13* »

But when did this take place? When did he leave Verona for this *ultimo* (last) — as opposed to *primo — rifugio?*

Experts differ. Indeed, Corrado Ricci, who has devoted an enlightening volume to the study of Dante's last years, lists substantially more than a dozen Dante scholars who between them — some for one date, some for another — argue for every single year between 1313 and 1320. He himself argues that the poet could not have gone to Ravenna before October 1316 nor much later than that, and that he probably went there in 1317.

This, briefly, is his reasoning.

(1) Guido da Polenta's immediate predecessors were his uncle Bernardino and his other brother Lamberto. Both of these were rabid Guelphs. Bernardino, among other things, had been named *podestà* by the Florentine Blacks — he died while he was holding this office — and the two had been among those who fought most strenuously against the Emperor Henry. Dante, now Ghibelline, could hardly have come to Ravenna while they lived. But Guido Novello had remained aloof, seemingly — despite a successful or partially successful war against the Venetians near Commacchio — more interested in the arts and enlightenment than in war. When, therefore, he became lord of Ravenna, it was something different. But Lamberto — the last of the two — did not die until June 22, 1316, and Guido did not succeed him until the following October.

(2) Pietro Alighieri and a number of others were excommunicated on January 4, 1321, for not having among them paid the sum of 575 florins plus 55 florins costs for various benefices which had been bestowed upon them. Pietro's benefice was the Church of Santa Maria Zenzanigola, which has since been destroyed, and there is considerable evidence that Pietro had held it for "a long time." This could not have been less than since 1317.

(3) In Dante's exchange of Latin poems with Giovanni del Virgilio, there is also evidence that the poet had been in Ravenna for a long time. We will take this up later.

(4) In 1318, and extending into 1319, an epidemic raged in the Romagna. Even the dead could not always be buried. It seems unlikely that Dante would have come to Ravenna while this raged, but if he came later he would not have stayed in the city for a long while. He must have come before it began.

I agree with Signor Ricci. I am satisfied that it was in 1317 that Dante left Can Grande and journeyed toward the Adriatic shore.

Was it in winter?

Then, at least from time to time, there would have been gray skies and either drizzling rain or raw damp snow as he made his way to Ferrara — in which city he is placed by a scatological story in which he outwits the jester Gonella and causes him to be smeared in his own filth — and then around or across the Valli di Comacchio, where he might have seen the stilted birds he loved to describe.

But if it was spring — and if he came before the epidemic began it must have been — the journey would have been pleasanter.

Outside, and particularly to the north of Ravenna, there was mile after mile of brown and reedy marsh, where, as a modern writer puts it, "descendants of Sidonius's frogs croak in Aristophonic chorus."

But in spring the brown turned green and was strewn with lilies, orchids, and iris — suggesting, as the same writer puts it, "the color scheme of the Byzantines [and] the more vivid hues of the mosaics."

On higher ground — and to the left — was the *pineta* (pine forest) known to Boccaccio and Byron, and described by Dante.

Purgatorio XXVIII:

> Eager to search now both within and without
> The divine forest, deep and verdant green,
> Which to mine eyes made shadowy the new day,
> I did not longer wait but left the slope
> To walk slowly, slowly over the ground
> Which everywhere around was filled with fragrance.
> A dulcet air that scarcely seemed to stir
> Or move then lightly touched my brow
> With no more force than has a gentle breeze
> By which the trembling leaves without delay —
> Each one of them are moved toward the part
> Where throws the sacred mountain its first shadow,
> Yet were not so much bent from standing straight
> That little birds poised on the highest treetops
> Did not still practice their enchanting arts
> But filled with joy they greeted the morning hours
> As singing still they fluttered among the verdure,
> Which echoed the same burden to their rhymes
> As doth reverberate from branch to branch
> In the pine woods by the Chiassi shore
> When Aeolus unlooses the Scirocco.

Last of all, the city itself, with its moody, nostalgic, sometimes sad splendor; the city of the great lawgiver whose portrait in mosaic is in San Vitale ("Caesar I was and am Justinian" — *Paradiso* VI); of Julius Caesar, who sent the eagle southward when he marched from it to cross the Rubicon (also *Paradiso* VI); of such exquisite churches (San Vito, Sant'

Apollinare Nuovo, Sant' Apollinare in Classe, and others) that he could derive from one of their altarpieces one of his more magnificent similes ("fire through alabaster" — *Paradiso* XV); the city of the tombs of Galla Placidia and Theodoric; the city described by another poet, Fazio degli Uberti, who lived less than a generation later, as "so old its walls seemed to be made of glass."

And finally, the city of a young lord who asked nothing while he gave much.

It must have been with much the same feelings — the feelings of intense relief — as a medieval captain had when his ship sailed behind the protecting moles of a secure seaport after a long and dangerous voyage that Dante rode in through the northern gate of the city and then to the palace of the eagle of Polenta — Guido's arms were an eagle half argent, half gules, on a field or — who bade him be as welcome as he was eagerly awaited.

XXIV

To the Eternal from the Temporal: An Account of the Commedia

IT was in this city by the shallow Adriatic Sea with its many lagoons and its many salt marshes — it was in this city in which, if he had not found "a people just and sane" (*Paradiso* XXI), for these are not found this side of heaven, he had at least found a just and sane ruler — it was in this city of Byzantine memories and a bird-filled pine forest that Dante brought to a conclusion that great masterwork which he called *Commedia* (by him pronounced *Com-ay-*DEE-*ah*), but which even as early as Boccaccio (see his *Trattatelo in Laude di Dante*) was referred to as *la divina Commedia*, or the *Divine Comedy*. And because this *Divine Comedy* was here concluded, and because it is as the author of this *Divine Comedy* that Dante is almost always and very rightfully remembered, it is fitting and necessary that we consider it now.

This does not mean that this poem was his only achievement. Surely this is apparent to everyone who has followed his career thus far.

There were his other writings, and all of them were good and some were excellent.

To sum up — and review — there was the *Vita Nuova*, which he wrote when he was less than thirty.

There were his lyrics of the *dolce stil nuovo*. At least half a dozen of them are among the brightest jewels in the tiara of Italian poetry.

On the lighter and more high-hearted side, there were the hunting sonnet and the boating sonnet and the entertaining rough-and-tumble *tenzone* with Forese Donati.

There was the *Convivio*, which attempted to do for philosophy what

The Yale Dante, attributed to the school of Angelo Bronzino *c.* 1575 but possibly of earlier date, is the finest Dante portrait in the United States. It can be seen at the Yale University Art Gallery in New Haven, Connecticut.

the *Vita Nuova* did for love. There were the *De Vulgari Eloquentia* and the *De Monarchia*.

Then too there were his activities in the world of diplomacy and politics. These we have reviewed in detail.

But things like this were done by other Florentines, for if there was no other *Vita Nuova*, many another Florentine wrote acceptable poetry, possibly not as great as even Dante's minor poetry, but still distinguished. Other Florentines wrote treatises — if not on language and the empire, then on the law and medicine. There were other gay young Florentine blades who later became serious citizens; other and more successful managers of inherited property; other students of philosophy; others who served as prior or on a Florentine council; and there were many other ambassadors.

But there was no other author of the *Commedia*.

There could not be, for there was no other *Commedia*. It was not only outstanding. It was, and still is, unique.

Professor Thomas G. Bergin says this of it in his recent book *Dante:*

"The *Commedia* may fairly claim to be the greatest poem in our tradition. T. S. Eliot says that after Shakespeare and Dante 'there is no third,' but no single work of Shakespeare can be compared with the *Commedia* in its scope."

There is a third, of course. Homer. But with this one exception, the statement can stand.

Dr. Bergin gives a reason for assigning this first place to the *Commedia*. It combines spontaneity with erudition.

Here he turns to Giovanni Battista Vico, whom he describes as the first discoverer of the true Homer. Vico, he says, applied the adjective "sublime" to the *Commedia*, but says that Dante would have been more sublime if he had known nothing of scholastic philosophy or of Latin.

"But," says Dr. Bergin, "it is precisely the combination of these erudite elements with the 'barbarous' purity of Dante's inspiration that gives the *Commedia* more depth than the Homeric poems."

I agree.

I, however, have another way of comparing and evaluating the three poets.

In a sense — although perhaps this is oversimplifying — Homer and Shakespeare turned outward: Homer to write in the *Iliad* — although of course this tale of Troy is much more than that—the most stirring and magnificent *chanson de geste* ever penned, and in the *Odyssey* the most glorious seaman's yarn ever set down, a seaman's yarn that had the good fortune to have been written by a great poet; Shakespeare to create and lovingly people a world of his own, a world which extended from

Cleopatra's Egypt to Macbeth's Scotland and Hamlet's Denmark, and included both Bottom's rustic fairyland and Prospero's Bermudian island, but which was still, in his own words, "a stage."

Dante, instead, turned inward, and there, because he is not merely "a kind of Everyman" but Everyman himself, we find ourselves. His world —I speak specifically of his world in the *Commedia*—is a pilgrimage— an interior pilgrimage, to be sure, a pilgrimage of the spirit—and on it we are all fellow pilgrims. It is a religious pilgrimage. But that is fitting, for man — atheists and agnostics included — is a religious animal quite as much as he is a political animal, and even those of us who cannot literally believe in its terms, can deeply and personally share Dante's progress from hell through purgatory to heaven.

We can, and have, and still do.

Earlier in this book, I set down the story told by Sacchetti (who was born when men who had known Dante still lived) about the poet's angry reaction to a donkey driver who was reading — but garbling — Dante's poetry as he hurried his overladen little animal through the city streets. But I have heard a gondolier in Venice, a cab driver in Florence, a waiter in Rome, and a bartender in Connecticut do the same — but with feeling and accurately.

Likewise a hotelkeeper in Naples. And a businessman in Milan. And (less surprisingly) an artist in Siena.

Nor were these the only ones. On my first trip to Italy, I landed in Trieste and came by train to Venice. In my carriage, I sat next to a distinguished-looking gentleman who, after helping me with my baggage and telling me what to tip the porter and then showing me a gold medal which he had been given for a lecture on Shelley, in perfect English delivered to me such a learned talk on Dante that I thought he must be the most distinguished Dante scholar in the land.

Later, as we walked toward our respective gondolas, he handed me his card. After his name were the words Senatore del Regno.

But he was not a scholar who had won political preferment. He was a man of state affairs and politics who loved — and wished to share this love — the greatest poet of his land.

« 2 »

Now what is this piece of writing which has so fascinated so many people and for so long? What is this greatest poem of our tradition? What is the matter and the meaning of this *Commedia* which later, and for the very best of reasons, came to be called divine?

At the risk of restating what has been a thousand times stated, and proclaiming the familiar as a novelty, I will try to tell you.

(1) It is the story, in something just a little more than fourteen thousand almost always terse and meaty lines, of the literal, if imaginary, journey of one Dante Alighieri degli Alighieri from the *selva selvaggia* which lay just outside of hell's gate through hell and purgatory and paradise, and then into the very presence of God eternal, guided at first and principally by Virgil (the actual and Roman poet Virgil); and then, but more briefly, by Cato; and finally by Beatrice, who had once been Bice Portinari. This journey takes place in actual space and time. It begins, for example, just before dusk on the eve of Good Friday 1300. I say "just before dusk," for Dante commences *Inferno* II by saying: "The day departed and the darkening air released all earthly creatures from their toil." In 1300, this Good Friday fell on April 8, but for Dante's purposes it was March 25, for March 25 was believed by most in the Middle Ages to be (a) the true date of the Crucifixion, and (b) the date of the Creation, which, they said, took place in 5232 B.C. He reached purgatory on Easter Sunday. In paradise he was beyond and outside of time.

(2) It is a moral and didactic fable with allegorical and anagogical meanings.

In other words, the reader must always have a divided attention. He must always be conscious of what the poem actually says, but behind this he must be aware of what it means symbolically.

For making the above statements we have, incidentally, the best of all possible authorities, namely Dante himself. In the letter to Can Grande whose introductory paragraph we already quoted, he first justifies the existence of bonds of friendship between persons of superior station (Can Grande) and their inferiors (himself) and then goes on to proclaim himself the former's "most devoted servant and friend" and to declare that he values this friendship as "a most precious treasure."

He continues thus:

"Therefore since it is taught as one of the dogmas of moral philosophy that friendship is both made equal and preserved by acting as equals, it is my sacred duty to preserve this equality by making some return for the benefits you have conferred on me. For this reason, I have often and at length examined such insignificant gifts as I can offer, and I have found nothing more suitable for your outstanding worth than the sublime cantica of the *Commedia* which is graced with the title of *Paradiso*. This then, with the present letter to serve as a superscription, I inscribe, offer, and, in a word, commend to you."

But before he inscribed, offered, and commended, he would explain.

"I will become a commentator and write down a few words of introduction."

This he did.

"There are six points of which examination must be made before one begins any didactic work. The subject. The author. The form. The purpose. The title of the book. The branch of philosophy to which it belongs."

Three of these — the subject, the form, and the title — Dante would deal with now, for they applied to the whole work. The others he would deal with later.

The subject first.

"For the elucidation of what is to be said, it must be known that the meaning of this work is not simple but rather what can be called polysemous, or having many meanings, for the first meaning is that which is conveyed by the letter and the next meaning is that which we hold to be signified by the meaning. The first meaning may be called literal and the second allegorical or mystical."

He turned back to an example he had used in the *Convivio* — the psalm "When Israel went out of Egypt" — and repeated the two meanings, literal and allegorical, he had given it there.

(Dante more than once used the same argument twice.)

Then he added two other meanings:

"If we look at it in the moral sense, the conversion of the soul from the pain and grief of sin into a state of grace is intended, and if we look at it anagogically, the passing of the sanctified soul from the bondage of this world into the freedom of eternal glory."

Then his conclusion.

"The form is twofold as well: the form of the treatise and the form of the treatment. The form of the treatise is threefold because it is divided in three ways. The first division is when the work is divided into three canticas. The second is when each cantica is divided into cantos. The third division is when each canto is divided into rhymed lines. The form of the treatment is poetic, fictional, descriptive, digressive, and figurative. In addition to this, it is explanatory, analytical, probative, putative, and explicit in examples."

Finally, the title.

"The title of the book is: *Here begins the Comedy of Dante Alighieri, a Florentine by name but not by nature,* and to understand this it is necessary to know that comedy gets this name from *comos,* meaning village, and *oda,* meaning song. Hence comedy is, as it were, a village song. Now comedy is a certain kind of poetical narrative that differs from all others. It differs from tragedy in that tragedy is admirable and peaceful in the beginning but in the end it is fetid and horrible. It is said that tragedy is so called from *tragos,* a goat, and *oda.* It is, as it were, a goat song — that is to say, foul as a goat."

And how did this apply to Dante's *Commedia?*

"From all this it is clear that the present work should be called a comedy, for if we look at the matter it deals with, in the beginning it is horrible and fetid, for this is hell, but in the end it is fortunate, to be longed for, and pleasing, for it is heaven. Moreover its manner of speaking is uninstructed and modest, for it uses the vulgar in which even women in the marketplace do their gossiping."

But what was this material? What was the *Commedia*'s subject?

To sum up, "The subject of the whole work in its literal sense is the state of souls after death. It is this, pure and simple, and without limitation. And from the allegorical point of view, the subject of the whole work is mankind itself, who will receive reward or punishment from divine justice in accordance with its deserts, according to whether — having free will — man is worthy or unworthy."

In other words, the literal pilgrimage, described literally, of Dante of Florence.

And an allegorical pilgrimage of — the word cannot be repeated too often — Everyman.

To understand the *Commedia* then — and Dante, whom the *Commedia* "crowned and mitred" — we must examine it in both categories. This we will do.

« 3 »

The literal meaning must be dealt with first, for it is the literal meaning that first confronts the reader. It is the literal meaning that we must read, mark, and inwardly digest if we are to pass on to any other meaning. It was the literal meaning too that early won the *Commedia* its wide readership, or perhaps listenership would be more accurate, for it was heard on the piazza or the street corner quite as often as it was perused in the study or the law office: a listenership that included the old woman of Verona whom Dante heard muttering about his scorched beard, and our famous donkey driver, and the notaries of Bologna, and noble princes and lords from the Casentino to Lombardy to the Adige.

It is the literal meaning that first wins it readers today. The scholars and those who explain the book come in later.

Says Dorothy Sayers, the writer of popular and successful detective fiction who became one of the more enlightened Dante scholars, on this matter — and she ought to know, for she knew how to win a wide audience for herself:

"The ideal way of reading the *Divine Comedy* would be to start at the first line and go straight to the end, surrendering to the vigor of the storytelling and to the movement of the verse, and not bothering with any historical allusions or theological explanations which do not occur in the text."

It is the *ideal* way — and for anyone on his first encounter with Dante the *only* way, although a modern reader may be a little handicapped by not knowing about persons and events which in Dante's time were as familiar as yesterday's headlines. For Dante — this also is Miss Sayer's opinion, and one must agree with it — was "simply the most incomparable storyteller who ever set pen to paper," and you cannot truly enjoy a good story if you clutter up your mind with too many footnotes.

The most incomparable storyteller, who in this case regales us with an incomparable travel story.

For just as much as *The Travels of Marco Polo*, which was finished (1298) only two years before Dante's pilgrimage began, the *Commedia* is a story of the things which were seen and done and heard in a journey to strange and distant lands. In Marco Polo's case, Cathay and the Indies. In the case of Dante, the lands beyond the grave.

« *4* »

Like Marco Polo's book, which begins with the simple statement, "In the time when Baldwin II was Emperor of Constantinople, and in the year of our Lord 1260, Niccolò, the father of the said Marco, and Maffeo, the brother of the said Niccolò, embarked in their own vessel," the *Commedia* begins without circumlocution.

Midway upon the pathway of his life, says Dante, he finds himself lost in a wild woodland, his way toward the delectable mountain blocked by three fierce and ravening beasts: a leopard "light and very swift and covered with a spotted hide," a proud-maned lion "slavering with hunger," and finally a lean she-wolf.

From these, he tells us, he flies in terror and indeed might have gone back whence he came had his way not been barred by someone "who from long silence was most weak of voice."

Dante turns to him.

> "Have pity on me," I did cry to him,
> "Whoever thou mayst be, shade or real man!"

The shade looks up.

> He said to me: "Not man. Man I once was,
> And those who did beget me Lombards were,
> And both of them indeed were Mantuans.
> *Sub Julio* was I born, though late in his life,
> And lived at Rome under the good Augustus

> In the days of the false and lying gods.
> I was a poet, and sang of the just
> Anchises who did come from Troy
> After the proud towers of Ilium were burned."

Virgil! It must be Virgil! It was Virgil! Dante cries out in joy.
"Thou art my master and thou art my author!" he cries.
Then:

> "Thou art alone the one from whom I took
> The fair style which has won me so much glory."

After that, he begs Virgil to help him.

Virgil replies that although the wolf will indeed be driven off by the greyhound — whom we have already identified with Can Grande — and although this greyhound will restore the Italy for whom the ancient Roman heroes died, Dante himself can only make the longed-for ascent if he goes by another road. He can only make it if he first goes through "an eternal place" where he would hear "the cries of the despairing creatures racked with pain who do bewail their coming second death." Thereafter he would come to those "who are contented in their flames because they hope they'll come when 't is allowed unto their blessed ones." Then — and then only, and guided by "a fitter one than I" — would he reach heaven and see God.

> I answered him: "Poet, I do entreat thee
> And by that God who was not known to thee,
> So that I may escape this evil and worse,
> That thou do lead me on the road thou toldst me
> Until I come unto St. Peter's gate . . ."
> Then he went on, and I did follow him.

Did follow him — but not without one further effort to turn back.
For Dante still doubted.

"Am I qualified" — this paraphrases a long passage in *Inferno* II — "and is my strength sufficient? True, others have descended into hell. The father of Silvius [Aeneas], as was told in Virgil's poem, and the chosen vessel [St. Paul]."

> "But I, why should I go there? Who permits it?
> I am not Aeneas, and I am not Paul.
> For this nor I nor other thinks me fit.
> Therefore if I commit myself to go
> I greatly fear my going may prove folly."

Virgil looks at him sternly.

"If I understand you rightly, you are smitten with vile cowardice. Put it away from your heart. I will tell you why I came to you and pity you."

He does — and not briefly:

> "I was among those who suspended are
> When did a lady summon me so fair
> That I did beg her that she should command me.
> Her eyes shone even brighter than the stars,
> And she began to speak with soft low tones
> And with an angel's voice. These were her words:
> 'O thou most courteous, courteous Mantuan soul
> Whose flame is still renownéd in the world
> And shall be long as shall the earth endure,
> A friend of mine, but not a friend of fortune,
> Has been so set upon the desert
> That he would turn his feet back on his way.
> Yea, I do fear he's gone so far astray
> I may have come too late to succor him
> If I believe what I have heard in heaven.
> Then haste thee. With the beauty of thy speech
> And with aught else thou needst for his deliverance
> So aid him that I may be comforted.
> And I am Beatrice who bid thee go.' "

Beatrice!

Yes, and she was sent by her who is "so moved by pity that she reverses stern judgment." This is the Virgin Mary, who saw Dante in his dire straits and to the lady he once had loved sent St. Lucy, the patron saint of clear seeing.

> " 'Beatrice,' she said, 'true praise of God,
> Why rescuest thou not him who so loved thee
> That he for thee did leave the vulgar crowd?' "

"Never on earth," Beatrice said to Virgil "were men so swift to seek their good or flee their hurt as I was after these words were spoken. I came to you trusting in your noble speech."

And when he saw the tears in her shining eyes, Virgil goes on, he did as she bade him and rescued Dante from the beast that barred his way.

The poem continues — but now Dante is speaking:

> Then did such goodly courage fill my heart
> That I began to speak as one set free:
> "O she, compassionate soul that succored me,
> And courteous thou who did obey so swiftly
> The true, true words that she did speak to me!
> Thou hast so filled my heart up with a longing
> To make this journey with those words of thine
> That I do come back to my first intention.
> Now go. There's but one will among us two.
> You leader, you my lord, and you my master." . . .
> I entered on the deep and savage way.

« 5 »

It is a way which we cannot describe in detail without making a long book out of a chapter, yet it is a way whose broad outlines must be set down.

First (*Inferno* III), the gate of hell and its inscription:

> "Through me one goes into the sorrowing city.
> Through me one goes into eternal pain.
> Through me one goes unto the lost people.
> Justice did move my high creator;
> I was made by the divine power
> And by supreme wisdom and primal love.
> Before me nothing there is was created
> Except eternal things, and I will last eternally.
> All hope abandon, ye who enter here."

Next, the limbo of the "uncommitted" — in modern parlance, the fence sitters and the ones who played it safe. These were the ones who were neither for the right nor for the wrong, the ones who were "hateful both to God and to his enemies."

They are many in number. Behind a whirling banner, Dante saw "so long a train of people that I could not have believed death had undone so many.

"These wretches who were never yet alive" are stung by hornets and wasps until their faces stream with blood which mingles with their tears and as it falls is devoured by noisome worms. Dante recognizes some but only gives us the basis for recognizing one — the unhappy Pope Celestine V, whom we have already met. In modern times, Rudyard Kipling, in his poem "Tomlinson," reintroduces us to one of those who might have found a home there. Tomlinson has "read," has "felt," has "guessed" — but he has never done a spontaneous good deed, nor committed a hot-blooded sin, and St. Peter will not let him in and the Devil will not waste his coals on him.

All this takes place in *Inferno* III, where ante-hell is described. In *Inferno* IV, Dante comes to the first circle of true hell, that limbo where dwell the illustrious pagans whose only sin, says Virgil who was one of them, was that they had lived before Christ or without serving Him, and whose only punishment is that they must live in longing without hope.

The list of those encountered there is a catalogue of the ancient great. They have been named in an earlier chapter.

These dwell in "a noble castle" surrounded by sevenfold walls, which some take to be the three intellectual and the four moral virtues and others as the three studies of the trivium and the four of the quadrivium. It is protected on all sides by a stream, and within is a meadow green as emerald.

It is in this canto that Dante sets on himself so high a value that it might disturb us if time had not proved it to be correct.

Homer, Horace, Ovid, Lucan, and, for the moment, Virgil stand together and engage in conversation.

Then:

> After together they had talked awhile,
> They turned to me and gave a sign of greeting,
> And at this my good master smiled a little.
> Then on me they bestowed even higher honor.
> For they so welcomed me into their company
> That I was sixth of these great intellects.

Limbo is hell, but it is still not quite hell, and Dante leaves it to come (*Inferno* V) to circle two, which is the circle of the lustful. Here, to be sure, the punishments are still light, for lust — as Dante knew well — was at worst no more than an aberration of love, and he of all people could not be too hard on it. Still, there are punishments. The light has gone, and there is weeping and wailing. It is in this circle that he encounters Paolo and Francesco and here too he meets the oldtime legendary lovers.

Thereafter, however, Dante moves into truly infernal regions where "new torments, yea, and new tormented ones did I about me see where'er I moved, wherever I did turn and fix my gaze."

We have a beginning in *Inferno* VI, where the circle of the gluttonous is described:

> I am in the third circle, that of rain,
> Eternal and accursed, icy and drenching,

That never changes in amount or kind.
Enormous hailstones, muddied water, snow
Furiously descend through the dark air.
The ground that they fall down upon doth stink.
Cerberus, a beast savage and hideous,
With his three heads in doglike fashion barks
Over the people who are here engulfed.
Red eyes, he has, and a beard greasy and black,
A swollen belly and sharp claws for hands.
The rain makes them howl as hounds do,
And they make one flank shelter for the other.
The unholy wretches turn from side to side.

This is where he meets Ciacco — Master Hogfat.

But even gluttony is not the worst of sins, and the horrors grow even more shaking as he descends lower.

Circle four (*Inferno* VII), guarded by Pluto, "the great enemy," with his strident "*Pape Satan, pape Satan aleppe!*" — chilling gibberish which Benvenuto Cellini says was derived from the "*Paix! Paix! Satan! Paix! Paix! Allez! Paix!*" which was grimly intoned in French courts of law. This is the circle of the avaricious and the prodigal. Here groaning spirits roll enormous weights. One clashes with another and it must all be done over again. No individual is named, but Virgil tells Dante that among them are popes and cardinals.

Circle five (*Inferno* VIII). This is reached only by crossing the "marsh which is called Styx," and beneath this marsh, making its surface bubble as from some foul methane gas, are "the souls of those whom anger overcame." It was here that Dante sees Filippo Argenti.

Circle six. The circle of the heretics. Here (*Inferno* IX and X) in their blazing tombs are those who hold that "the soul dies with the body." Epicurus "with all his followers." Frederick II. Il Cardinale — Cardinal Ottaviano degli Ubaldini, uncle of the Archbishop Ruggieri who brought about the death of Count Ugolino. According to Fra Salimbene, he was "a handsome and a noble man," at whose table he found "abundant wine and every kind of delicacy." And, of course, Farinata degli Uberti and Cavalcante degli Cavalcanti.

Circle seven. This is the last circle of what might be called upper — as opposed to middle and to lower — hell, and here Virgil and Dante stumble down a slope described as alpine which is guarded by "the infamy of Crete . . . that was conceived in the pretended cow" — i.e., the Minotaur. This is the circle where the violent are punished, and it is divided into three lesser circles for reasons which Virgil explains in *Inferno* XI.

"From every wickedness which earns heaven's hate
Injustice doth result, and this result
Doth harm to someone either by force or fraud.
But because fraud is peculiar to man alone
It more displeases God, wherefore more deep in hell
The fraudulent are sent, more pain assails them."

This explains middle and lower hell, but now he explains the part of hell he and Dante are entering:

"The next circle belongs to the violent,
But since violence is done to three persons
It has been formed into three separate rounds.
Against God, against oneself, against a neighbor
Force may be used — against these or their possessions —
As you shall hear, and you shall hear the reasons.
Violent death or wounds that painful are
May be inflicted on a neighbor; on his property
Pillage and arson and unlawful seizing.
Therefore manslayers and those who assault,
Pillagers and plunderers, these doth torment
The first round, and torments them in diverse bands.
A man on himself may lay violent hands
Or on his own goods. Therefore in the second
Round must needs repent — must needs repent in vain —
Whoever doth himself rob of your world [*commits suicide*]
Or gambles or squanders away his wealth
And so must weep where he should joyful be.
Violence may be done to Deity
By Him denying and blaspheming Him,
And therefore doth the smallest round impress,
And with its seal, both Sodom and Cahors,
And him whose heart speaks scornfully of God."

« 6 »

Virgil and Dante now enter these rounds. They see and sometimes talk to more of the sinners.

The violent against their neighbors. Their round is guarded by the centaurs, described (*Inferno* XII) as "swift-running beasts," who are led by Chiron. He, as the two poets approach, "did take a dart and with its notch did his beard then push back against his jaws." The sinners here are punished by being "sunk unto the eyebrows" in the red and boiling stream of Phlegethon. Among them are Alexander the Great, Dionysius of Sicily, Ezzelino da Romano, Obizzo d'Este, Guy de Montfort of

England, Attila "who was a scourge on earth," Pyrrhus, Sextus Pompey, and the two Riniers, Rinier of Corneto and Rinier Pazzo, contemporary brigands.

In Dante's mind, the centaurs may have had another role besides guarding Phlegethon.

These mythical creatures, half horse and half man, are said by some to represent the armed horsemen of the *condottieri* (mercenary captains) whose blood and smoke already hung heavy over Italy.

The violent against themselves. Here (*Inferno* XIII) are the suicides, who are punished by being turned into living trees which are torn at by harpies until their branches drip blood. Dante only names one of these — Pier delle Vigne, Frederick II's chancellor and also a very fine poet. Dante tells his story — it is one of his finest. He breaks a branch and the trunk cries out to him: "Why manglest thou me?" Then, at Virgil's urging, he tells his tale.

"I held the key to Frederick's heart," he begins. In other words, he was Frederick's closest and most trusted adviser.

Dante has him say this:

> "I brought such faith unto that glorious office
> That doing this I lost both sleep and strength.
> But then that harlot [*envy*] that never from the household
> Of Caesar did her whore's eyes turn away . . .
> Inflamed — and against me — the minds of all,
> And these inflamed did so inflame Augustus
> That all my joyful honors became woes."

They did indeed. In 1249, Pier, then at the height of his power, was falsely accused of treason by those jealous of his influence, and Frederick impulsively had him imprisoned and blinded. He killed himself — either at Pisa or San Miniato — by dashing his head against the prison wall.

Pier puts it thus:

> "My mind, now tortured by this disdainful scorn,
> Thinking by dying to escape from this,
> Made me, who just was, unjust to myself."

In this canto, Dante also discusses the spendthrifts, and it is interesting to note that he places them in the same *cerchietta* as the suicides, that of those who do violence to themselves.

Finally (*Inferno* XIV through XVII), the violent against God, nature, and art — the blasphemers, the sodomites, and the usurers.

Of the blasphemers, of whom (*Inferno* XIV) he sees "many herds"

who either walk about or lie sprawling on an expanse of sand on which
fall burning flakes of fire, he names only one — Capaneus of Thebes, and
Capaneus is a pagan. Of the usurers, poised at the edge of the abyss and
bitten at by the same falling flames, he says (*Inferno* XVII) a little more,
but this has been already related when Dante's visit to Padua was discussed.

Certain parts of his account of the *cerchietta* of those who did violence
to nature have also been discussed earlier, but they must be spoken of
again now, for it is in this *cerchietta* (*Inferno* XV) that Dante meets
Brunetto Latini and shows by his treatment of this almost father to him
that it is a libel on his integrity to say that he wrote a poem about the
lower regions so that he could put his enemies in hell.

He puts his friends there too — when they have done wrong — and
among these there was none nobler nor more dear to Dante than Ser
Brunetto. Of him and the other sodomists, Dante says this:

> Not contempt but grief
> Does your sad state within me set so deep
> That long it will be ere it wholly leaves me.

It is an almost modern attitude.

« 7 »

But that is the end of hell's upper reaches, and now Dante and Virgil
come to the deep gulf which separates them from middle and lower hell,
and to Geryon, "the beast with the pointed tail" who crouches there and
who is the symbol of fraud — the sin which in its various aspects is
punished below.

Dante (*Inferno* XVII) describes Geryon thus:

> His face the face was of an honest man,
> So gracious was it in its outward aspect,
> But all his trunk like to a serpent was.
> He had two claws, all hairy to the armpits;
> His back and chest and each one of his sides
> All painted were with many knots and circles. . . .
> And as up there among the German guzzlers
> The beaver settles down to take its prey,
> So did the beast so fierce and wicked lie
> Upon the rim that bounds the sand with stone.

And now, Virgil tells Dante, you must descend into the pit on the back
of this monster. Dante shakes as one does with a quartan fever. But then

he sees Virgil mounted on the beast and "like a servant who dutifully follows a good master" he climbs onto Geryon too. Geryon wheels and descends, and Dante, still as frightened "as Icarus was when he felt the wax melting in his wings," clings to him. But at last, like a hawk stooping, he lands gently, and Dante is at the foot of the jagged cliff. He is in circle eight — sometimes known as Malebolge, or Evil Pouches. This is the circle of the fraudulent, those — for Dante had a comprehensive but, it seems to me, accurate concept of fraud — of every kind.

This Malebolge, according to Dante (*Inferno* XVII) "all stone of iron color, and a wall goes round it," is divided at its bottom into ten valleys.

These are the *bolge* — purses, pockets, holes in the ground — which gave its name to it. As he descends (*Inferno* XVII–XXX) ever deeper and deeper, Dante examines them one by one.

Bolgia one — that of the seducers and panders, who are scourged by horned serpents. It is here that he meets Caccianemico. And Jason, who oddly enough is thought of as having seduced Medea.

Bolgia two — that of the flatterers. These go about puffing with their snouts and smiting themselves with their palms. Among them are Alessio Interminei of Lucca and the whore Thais from a play by Terence whose exaggerated speech to her lover was thought to be comedy.

Bolgia three — that of the simonists. In this *bolgia* Dante sharply denounces Constantine for having giving temporal power to the pope. Nicholas III and Boniface VIII are here. It is almost a *bolgia* of popes.

Bolgia four — that of the diviners. Here, in appropriate punishments, the heads of the sinners are turned backwards upon their shoulders. Who are some of them? Manto, the founder of Virgil's Mantua. (Incidentally, the Greek word for diviner is *mantis*.) Tiresias. Aruns the Etruscan. Of Dante's time, Guido Bonatti of Forlì, a tiler by trade, whose prophecies greatly influenced Guido da Montefeltro; and Asdente the cobbler.

Bolgia five — that of the barrators. We have already discussed this *bolgia* and the Hallowe'en-like, almost trick-or-treat antics of its devils in connection with the accusation of barratry lodged against Dante. It can be only added that this is the only place in the *Commedia* where there is comedy not in the Dantean sense but as the slapstick horseplay that appealed so greatly in the Middle Ages and still does.

Bolgia six — that of the hypocrites, who are punished by being made to walk slowly and forever weighted down with leaden cloaks and cowls. Here we find the Fra Catalano and the Fra Loderingo who ruled in Florence when Dante was a boy.

Bolgia seven — that of the thieves. Dante comes to this *bolgia* after some feats of climbing which are so accurately described that it is one of the passages that makes many insist that he was an accomplished alpinist.

Here he meets the crude and vulgar Vanni Fucci and the five Florentines Agnèl Brunelleschi, Buoso Donati, Puccio Sciancato, Cianfa Donati, and Francesco Cavalcanti. Here too we have at least one scene so grotesque that it can hardly be equaled by a gargoyle on a Gothic cathedral. Agnèl and Buoso are changed into serpents and then into one serpent before his horrified eyes.

Bolgia eight — that of the false councillors. There are so many that they are like fireflies on a summer hill. Among them, turned into flames, are Ulysses and Guido da Montefeltro, whose stories have already been told.

Bolgia nine — the sowers of discord, whose bodies are cleft and mangled as in those days was a traitor's when he was hanged, drawn, and quartered. Foremost among them is Mohammed, whom Dante regarded as the divider of the Christian religion rather than the founder of a new one. Mohammed is horribly described. He is ripped from chin to the part that breaks wind. His entrails hang between his legs. His vitals appear "with that foul sack which excrement makes of that which swallowed is." I go into this in gruesome detail to show that as Dante went deeper and deeper toward the infernal center of the earth, his writing — and the punishments he described with it — became more and more cruel and savage. No longer are the damned souls merely blown aimlessly by the wind, like those of Paolo and Francesca.

Bolgia ten — that of the impersonators, the alchemists, and the false coiners. Here the damned are afflicted with a loathsome and eternal scurvy, and here we find Griffolino of Arezzo, the alchemist Capocchio, Gianni Schicchi, and Master Adamo. Yet, understanding that Dante was logical as well as implacable, we cannot help wondering at finding them there. Were their sins greater than the sins of some in the *bolge* above them?

« 8 »

But even below circle eight — even below Malebolge, in which he lingered for so many cantos and lines — is circle nine, where traitors to God and man are punished, and Dante, with Virgil leading him, goes to this circle too. It is the farthest he can go. It is at the bottom of a dark well — literally "a dark well," for the words in Italian are *puzzo scuro* — and to it he is gently lowered by Antaeus, one of the giants (the others are Ephialtes, Nimrod, and Briareus), who reminds Dante of Monteriggione and whom he variously describes as "tall as three Frieslanders" (say almost twenty feet), "full five ells without the head" (about the same), and "thirty great spans" (a few inches more) "down from the place where a man buckles his cloak." The head is said by him to be as large "as is the pinecone at St. Peter's in Rome."

Here — for treachery is cold — he finds himself in a place as frigid as the upper reaches of hell had been blazing hot, and here, in a lake that is frozen into ice so thick that one of the Apennines or of the Dolomites could have fallen on it without breaking it, are the traitors to their kindred or their country.

He lists four-and-twenty of them, and could have listed as many more. Alessandro and Napoleone degli Alberti, who slew each other after a dispute over their deceased father's land in the Val di Sieve. King Arthur's Modred. Focaccia of the Cancellieri of Pistoia, from whose murder of a youthful kinsman came the fatal division of the Guelph party into Blacks and Whites. Sassol Mascheroni. Bocca degli Abbati. Buoso da Duera, who gave free passage to the French invading Italy in 1265. Tesauro de' Beccheria, beheaded (1258) by the Florentines for conspiring with the Ghibellines. Ganelon. Tribaldello of Faenza, who betrayed the Ghibellines just as Tesauro had betrayed the Guelphs.

Below these, and frozen into a single hole, were Ugolino and his enemy the Archbishop Ruggieri, while in Ptolomea, even below these, were Branca d'Oria and Fra Alberigo of Faenza.

But not even Ptolomea was the nethermost place in hell. Below Ptolomea was the Giudecca, where Satan himself was, the once-bright fallen angel, and where were punished the three archtraitors of all: Judas Iscariot, who betrayed Jesus Christ — and through him the Christian Church — and Cassius and Brutus, who betrayed Julius Caesar — and through him the Roman Empire.

They and their plight are thus described by Dante in *Inferno* XXXIV:

> Oh how it seemed to me a mighty marvel
> When I did see three faces in his [*Satan's*] head.
> One was in front, and that vermilion was.
> The other two were joined unto this one
> Exactly over the middle of each shoulder,
> And all of them were joinéd at the crown.
> The right one seemed to be between white and yellow;
> The left the color seemed to be of those
> Who dwell in that place where the Nile descends.
> Under each one there came forth two great wings
> Of the size fitting for so huge a fowl:
> Sails on the sea I never saw like these.
> They had no feathers, but like to those of a bat
> Was their appearance. He kept beating them
> So that three winds did issue forth from him,

And this it was that kept Cocytus frozen.
With his six eyes he wept, and over three chins
Tears did come dripping down, and bloody foam,
And in each mouth he tore with his teeth,
And as a hackle does, one of the sinners.

But imagination could go no farther. Nor can Dante, for the first stage of his journey is completed.

Virgil tells him this:

"A new night rises. It is now the time
For us to take our leave. We have seen all."

They do. With Dante clasping him around the neck, the Roman poet descends "from tuft to tuft between the tangled hair and frozen crusts."

Then suddenly Dante becomes aware that although they have not changed their direction, they are no longer descending but mounting.

Why?

He is on "the other side of the center." He is climbing toward the southern hemisphere.

And he could reach it.

Down there — and from Beelzebub as far
As is his tomb in length — there is a place
Which is not known by sight, but by the sound
Of a small rivulet that splashes down
Through a cleft in the rock which it has worn
As it winds downward, and at gentle speed.
The leader and I upon that hidden road
Did enter to return to the bright world,
And without pausing for any rest
We clambered up, he first and I the second,
Until I saw some of the beautiful things
That heaven wears, through a round opening.
Thence we came out to see again the stars.

« 9 »

Thence we came out to see again the stars!

But only for a short while. For "the sweet color of oriental sapphire" which is frosted with these trembling diamonds — including the four stars of the Southern Cross, which had never been "seen before but by the first people" (Adam and Eve) — is rapidly being succeeded by one of the most exquisitely described dawns in all literature. "The fair planet which comforts those in love" — Venus, the day star — begins to make the Fishes, with which it is in conjuction in April, grow paler. A dawn breeze traces crepelike crinkles on the distant sea. The sky turns white and rosy. Then it turns orange. Last, the sun arises, "arrowing the day and with his keen missiles shooting Capricorn from midheaven" and flooding everything with intense light.

It is at this time that a vessel swift and light — for Dante stands upon a seashore — comes speeding across the water toward where he stands. It is steered by a heavenly helmsman and on it are a thousand spirits. They are all singing "*In exitu Israel de Aegypto*," now cited by the poet for the third time.

They fling themselves on the beach and then turn to Dante and his two companions, for he has now been joined by a white-bearded old man who is Cato of Utica, Dante's noblest and most austere of pagans.

"If you know, show us the way to the mountain!" they cry.

The mountain! But what mountain? The mountain of purgatory, the second of the three regions where dwell those who had lived on earth and had then died — the place where sins are not punished but atoned for because the sinners repented before their death.

And the spirits who thus cry to him? Who are they?

They are pilgrims to this mountain on which, one by one, their sins will be removed from them. They are travelers to the light of heaven.

Dante looks at them, but Virgil speaks for him.

"We do not know the way any more than you do. We are strangers like yourselves. And we came here by a road harder than any road that you trod."

They are pilgrims and travelers.

Dante thinks about this.

If he does not know the way he can find it, he thinks.

He will be a traveler and a pilgrim too.

« *10* »

He will be a traveler and a pilgrim too, in a region which was his own invention. Dante's hell was the hell that was believed in by almost everyone in the Middle Ages, a grotesque elaboration of concepts supplied by Greek mythology, the Gehanna or Topheth of the Hebrews, and certain words of Jesus Christ himself. It was the hell officially accepted by the Church. The same can be said of his paradise. Here and there — notably when he comes to the heavenly hierarchy and the exact order of precedence among the angels and archangels, the powers and dominions, the seraphim, the cherubim, and the thrones — he seems to have his own opinion. But his main concept is the official one.

His purgatory, however, he devised himself. The official Church view was that purgatory was a sort of temporary hell, and it was placed underground. To some extent, moreover, its punishments were those of hell, except that they did not last forever. But Dante's purgatory was a place where you aspired upward. Its punishments were not chastisements but cancellations. Indeed, purgatory was a place where you literally cleansed yourself, and if sometimes — if indeed almost always — the purgations seemed like punishments, this was appropriate and accepted. There is a homeopathic medicine for the soul too.

Obviously it was not underground. It could not be — and be consistent — for purgation — as we know and Dante knew — needs flooding daylight, and — as we know and Dante knew — evil things prosper in dank cellars, and in the dark. By the same token, it must also be in another hemisphere, for in his concept of it, a geographical and spiritual juxtaposition to the world which Dante thought was the only world was essential. In the terms of his philosophy, it must be the exact opposite and yet a copy of this world — a sort of photographic positive from its photographic negative. This being the case, it seems to me logical that he should have chosen to place it on what I hope is neither facetious nor inaccurate to call a South Sea island, an island illuminated by the sun by day and the stars by night and wrapped always by a translucent atmosphere and laved by a bland sea.

On this island, a truncated cone rose from a relatively gentle shore, and on its lower slopes is ante-purgatory. It was here that those who had delayed in repenting — who repented only in their dying moments — underwent their first purgation by having to endure still more delay. Above this was a valley, in which (*Purgatorio* VII) "gold and fine silver, cochineal and white lead, the dye of indigo lucid and clear, emerald when it has just been newly cut, all these by the color of the grass and the flowers that grew in that small vale would have been surpassed," and above the valley a precipice so sheer that you must be carried over it by an angel.

Atop the precipice was the gate to purgatory — contrast this with hell's gate — which creaked and was rusty so little was it used, and within the gate was purgatory itself, divided into seven terraces, one for each of the seven deadly sins. The terraces were themselves arranged into three groups. Group one dealt with love misdirected — and note that every pardonable sin comes from love misused — and here we find the proud, the envious, and the wrathful. Group two was for love defective, and here we have the slothful. Group three was for love excessive — the avaricious, the gluttonous, and the lascivious.

Above all was the earthly paradise, where grass — again, as green as emerald — was strewn with "red and yellow flowerets" and waters which were so pure that no one on earth could even imagine them flowed in two rivers — Lethe and Eunoe — which Dante compares to the Tigris and the Euphrates, possibly because in the old legend the Tigris and Euphrates flowed through the Garden of Eden.

It was in this earthly paradise that in a sense the *Commedia* came to its climax. But that will be related in due course.

« *11* »

But now Dante climbs just as he had descended when he was in hell, for he is on his way to God and God is above us. And here should be noted also certain other differences. When Dante was in hell, his journey was continuous. He paused neither for rest nor for refreshment. In purgatory, however, he mounts upward only when it is day. The reasons for this have already been suggested. For another thing, Virgil is no longer his only guide. On the terrace of the avaricious — and prodigal — he encounters Statius. Dante describes him as a native of Toulouse, but actually he was born in Naples *circa* A.D. 61, and according to medieval legend (which was believed by Dante but was definitely not true) he became a Christian when he read Virgil's fourth *Eclogue*, which (also in the medieval belief) prophesies the coming of Christ. Hereafter Dante has two guides, and in this connection it should be noted that Virgil from this point on seems less and less sure in his answers. More and more frequently he turns to Statius — the Christian poet as opposed to the pagan poet — for assistance. Statius can help him out with matters beyond his ken.

For a third and final point of difference, the *Purgatorio* is a cantica of increasing explanations and expositions. The accurate if often acidly pithy observations of the *Inferno* are replaced with increasing frequency by dissertations. This is the cantica which contains the lengthy essay on the sad and fallen state of the Romagna. It is the cantica of Sordello's lament for Italy. It is the cantica of art criticism and literary criticism — the cantica in which he meets Oderisi of Gubbio and Bonagiunta and Arnaut Daniel, and in which he talks about Cimabue and Giotto as well as Il Notaro and Guittone and Guido Guinicelli.

Yet for all that it is still a logical extension of the *Inferno*, for it deals with a realm which is still part of the physical world, and through it — except in the one instance when in a dream St. Lucy lifts him through the air to the rusty gate — Dante moves by physical means and with mortal reactions. He is, for example, out of breath after a steep climb, and as he moves along a narrow ledge which tops a lofty cliff he understandably demonstrates both fear and caution.

Also — but he will do this in the *Paradiso* too — he explains the general with the specific. Lust is not an abstract figure like a monster in a miracle play but an actual man or woman who was lustful. It is, of course, so with all the other sins. Consequently the *Purgatorio*, like the *Inferno*, contains a series of always interesting and sometimes dramatic encounters.

Here are some of those he meets.

Purgatorio II. Casella, who not only enraptures Dante with his singing but — more important — all the other souls who wait for entrance.

Purgatorio III. Manfred, the gallant son of Frederick II, who was condemned by the Church, which literally caused his remains to be buried in an unknown grave, but who was forgiven by God because he repented.

Purgatorio IV. The lazy Belacqua.

Purgatorio V. Buonconte Montefeltro. La Pia.

Purgatorio VI. Sordello.

Purgatorio VII. The *fainéant* kings. "Rudolf the emperor." Ottokar of Bohemia. Philip III of France, whose fleet was destroyed in 1295 and who thereafter returned to Perpignon, where "he fell gravely ill of a fever and the flux" and died. He was the father of Philip the Fair. Peter of Aragon. Henry III of England.

Purgatorio VIII. Nino Visconti and Currado Malaspina.

It should be noted that all of this occurs in ante-purgatory, the description of which takes up eight cantos and 1115 lines, some of them as beautiful and as moving as any Dante wrote. It should be noted, too, that none of the purgations have yet begun and that, except as they are hurried along by Cato, who, bidding them to make haste, scatters them like doves feeding in a wheat field, most of them continue in their old ways.

Casella still twangles his lute. Manfred is still the proud imperial prince. He wants his daughter to be told that he is destined for heaven. Belacqua, "who shows himself more indolent than if laziness had been his sister," sits clasping his knees as he rests against a stone. Buonconte and La Pia march in a long procession chanting *"Miserere"* but are otherwise unpunished. Sordello, the nobleman poet, sits like a crouching lion. The kings, although one of them beats his breast and another lays his hand upon his cheek and sighs, mainly lie thinking green thoughts in a green shade. Nino is still the good Nino who wonders about his wife and daughter, and Corrado Malaspina is still the worthy descendant of mountain aristocrats who also patronized the bards.

But in true purgatory the atonements begin. Even Dante's atonements, for at its entrance, after he has mounted three steps of white marble, perse stone, and porphyry, an angel of God traces seven P's (P for *peccato*, or sin) upon his brow.

Then he comes to the terraces, seven in all, and thereafter he mounts from one to another. As he leaves each terrace, one of the P's is expunged.

Let us look at these terraces.

Terrace one is where pride is punished. It is described in cantos X through XII. Here — and I name only those who have already appeared in this book — Dante finds Oderisi and Provenzan Salvani. On the sculptured walls of this terrace are depicted examples of humility — the Virgin Mary saying "*Ave*" to the angel; King David dancing before the ark of the covenant; Trajan comforting the poor widow who had lost her son. On the pavement are mosaics of the proud brought low. Here those being chastised move with figures bent "like to a corbel that supports ceiling or roof" and these figures humbly intone the Lord's Prayer. Dante shows some agitation in this terrace, for as we have noted, pride is one of his especial failings.

Terrace two (cantos XII through XIV) is where envy is punished. The envious are clad in coarse haircloth, and their eyelids are sewn shut "as those of untrained sparrow hawk one sews when it will not keep still." Here Sapia is, and here is Guido del Duca. Here too are some magnificently nostalgic lines (spoken by Guido) which must have suggested to Ariosto in the sixteenth century the words with which he began *Orlando Furioso*:

> *Le donne e i cavalier, li affani e li agi*
> *Che ne invogliava amore e cortesia.*

> The ladies and the knights, the toils and diversions
> To which we were moved by love and courtesy.

Terrace three (cantos XV through XVII) is where anger is punished. Among the angry is Marco Lombardo, and some of his anger — against the Church and against the degeneracy of the age — Dante must surely have found well directed. It is on this terrace that Virgil (in *Purgatorio* XV) magnificently explains that all sin is love disordered. Let us apply this to anger. Anger comes because what you love fails in what you expected of it.

Terrace four (canto XVIII) is where sloth is atoned for. Here the slothful keep running and running, and as they run they shout examples of olden-time zeal.

"Make haste, make haste," they cry, "lest time be lost for loving too little and that the zeal for good make grace turn green again."

Terrace five is that of the avaricious and the prodigal. It is described in cantos XIX, XX, and XXI, and on it we find Pope Adrian V and Hugh Capet.

It is upon this terrace of the avaricious that Dante and Virgil encounter Statius, and about this meeting a little more should be said. Not long after they have parted from Hugh Capet, Dante feels the mountain shake as though it were falling, and thereafter comes the cry of *"Gloria in excelsis"* from all who stand about. A chill seizes him "such as seizes one who faces death," and for a while he — and Virgil too — "stood motion-less and in suspense." But shortly — and as he is still struck with wonder — a shade appears and, following some direct and pointed questioning, explains.

This is a place which is free from change, he explains. It knows neither rain nor hail nor dew nor snow nor hoarfrost. There are no rainbows here. There is not even the dry vapor which, according to Aristotle, hidden in the earth, escapes to cause earthquakes.

There are no earthquakes — with one exception.

> "Lower down perhaps it trembles a little or a lot,
> But caused by the wind hidden in the earth —
> I know not why — up here it has never trembled.
> Up here it doth tremble only when some soul
> Feels itself pure and so may rise or set out
> On its ascent, and then a loud shout follows."

The earth's trembling was for him, the spirit continues. The shout was for him. For he has lain here five hundred years and now his purgation is complete.

Then he identifies himself:

> "Men in the world still speak my name. 'T is Statius.
> I sang of Thebes and then of great Achilles,
> But fell beside the way under the second burden.
> The ardor in me was lit by the spark —
> And how indeed it warmed — from the divine flame
> From which more than a thousand have been kindled.
> I mean the *Aeneid* — for this a mother was,
> And was a nurse unto my poetizing.
> Without it not a dram would I have weighed,
> And to have lived up there during the time
> When Virgil lived, I to one sun more would have con-
>   sented
> Than I did owe in this my banishment."

And now follows one of Dante's most charming scenes:

Virgil turns to him with a look that bids him to be silent and the poet obeys, but Statius notes a smile on Dante's face which the poet cannot conceal. He asks the reason.

Dante hesitates.
"Do not fear to speak!" says Virgil.

> I therefore: "Thou dost wonder now perhaps,
> O ancient spirit, at my smiling thus,
> But I would wish a greater wonder to seize thee.
> He who doth guide mine eyes to look on high,
> That Virgil is from whom thou didst derive
> The power so to sing of gods and men.
> If thou didst think I had another reason,
> Put it aside as false and credit only
> The words that I have spoken unto thee."

Instantly Statius falls to his knees as he seeks to kiss Virgil's feet, but Virgil restrains him.

"Thou art a shade. It is a shade thou seest," he says.

"Let that prove," cries Statius, "how deep is my love for you since it made me take a shade for a solid substance."

Thereafter there are three poets instead of two, and as three poets they proceed upward.

« 12 »

They proceed upward to the two terraces that still remain to Dante — to the terrace of the gluttonous, where he meets Forese Donati, starved and emaciated, and Bonagiunta of Lucca; and to the terrace of the lustful, where he meets Guido Guinicelli and Arnaut Daniel.

Finally (*Purgatorio* XXVII) they come to a wall of fire beyond which, an angel of God tells them, they cannot go unless they pass through it. But do not fear, the angel says. Enter into it, and do not be unmindful of the singing beyond.

Now follows a tense and dramatic moment. Dante is shaken with fear. He becomes, to use his own words, like one who is laid in the grave. He remembers burnings he has witnessed and is ready to turn back.

But Virgil — with Statius at his side — urges him on. "Here, indeed," he says, "there may be torment, but not death. Even on Geryon's back I brought you to safety. Will I not do so here, which is nearer to God? If you stay in the flame a thousand years it will not harm you. Try it with the edge of your garment and see."

Dante still hesitates, and then Virgil makes his final argument.

"This wall is all that lies between thee and Beatrice!"

Says Dante:

> As, at the name of Thisbe, Pyramus
> Dying did lift his eyes to gaze on her
> On that day when the mulberry turned red,
> So did my stubbornness soften.

He turns to Virgil, and, "as if he were tempting a child with an apple," the latter says to him: "What! Are we going to stay on this side?"

Then Virgil himself plunges in, bidding Dante to follow him, and Statius to follow Dante.

> As soon I was in it, into boiling glass
> I could have cast myself to cool myself
> So past all measure was the burning there.
> But my sweet father — and to comfort me —
> Did talk of Beatrice as he went.
> He said: "I seem to see her eyes already."
> Guiding us was a voice that canticled
> Beyond it. Giving all our heed to this,
> We came out to the place where one ascends.

They come out, and find that the sun is now setting. But still they climb until suddenly it is dark and, "ruminating and gazing at the stars," Dante falls asleep. He dreams of Leah (the active life), who picks flowers and who tells him who she is, but goes on to speak of Rachel (the contemplative life), who sits at her mirror all day. We are both satisfied, says Leah.

With that it is dawn, and Dante wakes to find the great masters already risen. With them he mounts a few steps farther, his eagerness giving him feathers to fly with.

And then suddenly he is at the place he has been climbing to for so long.

Here (*Purgatorio* XXVII) is how he describes this moment:

> When all of the long stair had under us
> Been set and we were on the top of it,
> Upon me Virgil did affix his eyes
> And said: "The temporal and the eternal fire
> Thou'st seen, my son, and art come to a point
> Where of myself I can discern no farther.
> I've brought thee here with understanding and skill.
> Take henceforth what thou willst for thy guide.
> Thou'st forth come from the steep ways, from the narrow.
> Look on the sun that shines now on thy brow.
> See thou the grass. See thou the flowers and trees

Which of itself the earth doth bring forth here.
Until to thee come the fair eyes rejoicing
Which weeping bade me go to rescue thee
Thou mayest sit, thou mayest walk among them.
Expect no longer word nor sign from me.
Free, upright, healthy now thy judgment is.
It would be wrong now not to do its bidding.
Over thyself I crown and mitre thee."

Over thyself I crown and mitre thee!

Over Dante the man mortal, and Dante the man spiritual. For he was now truly the captain of his soul and the master of his fate. True, he had one more atonement to make, but in this he did not need the help of Virgil or of anyone else. He was now tempered to make it himself.

« *13* »

It is at this point that the *Commedia* moves rapidly toward one of its climaxes.

Dante now stands on the threshold of paradise lost — the Garden of Eden, the earthly paradise — but he is prevented from entering by "a stream which to the left did with its little waves incline the grass which grew upon its bank." On the far bank is a lovely lady. Later we will hear her called Matelda, and she has been variously identified with the great Countess Matilda who gave her vast Tuscan lands to the Church — this is improbable — and with a German nun, Mechteld von Hackeborn, who died in 1298 and whose descriptions of the earthly paradise may have influenced Dante — this is at least possible — and with an otherwise-unknown friend of Beatrice.

This Matelda walks opposite him — on the other side of the stream — along the waters, and it is she who cries out suddenly: "My brother, look and listen!" as she points out a triumphant procession that is approaching with a chariot drawn by a gryphon which, Dante says, is more splendid than any ancient Rome had used "to gladden Africanus or Augustus."

But it is not the splendor of this procession — and it is the most splendid that any mortal eyes have seen — that brings Dante's heart into his throat.

It is this.

As voices sing "Come with me, my spouse, to Lebanon" and "Blessed art thou who comest," and as the new day makes the "eastern parts of the sky all rosy, the rest serene and fair," a lady appears. She is "girdled with olive over a white veil, and under a green mantle she wears a flame-colored garment."

Dante does not have to be told who she is, for as he sees her he feels "old love's great power." It is she whose "virtue had already purified him before he was out of his boyhood."

Nevertheless, he still turns to Virgil, "like," he says, "a child that runs to his mother." But Virgil has vanished.

The lady speaks:

> "Dante, because Virgil hath gone away,
> Weep thou not, do thou not yet weep,
> For thou must still weep for another sword."

She continues:

> "Look on me well. I, I am Beatrice.
> But how dost thou dare draw nigh to the mountain?
> Dost thou not know that here man is made happy?"

Beatrice! It is indeed Beatrice! Then "the ten years' thirst" had at last been quenched and he had fulfilled the almost impossible promise which he made as he finished the *Vita Nuova*.

In his exultation, he can hear the angels singing: "Our hope is in Thee, O Lord." But then he remembers her stern words and his spirits sink "as a candle melts in fire," for he realizes that there is one thing more that he must do before he can move upward.

Beatrice — although the angels now seemed to chant: "Lady, why dost thou so shame him?" — tells him what this is:

"God's lofty decrees would be broken if Lethe were crossed and its life-giving waters tasted without some scot of repentance which makes you shed tears."

She then asks him if he will confess, and Dante describes what ensues:

> Confusion, yea, and fear, together mixed,
> Did snatch from out my mouth so loud a yea
> That even to hear it you must see it too.
> Then as a crossbow breaks when it is drawn
> With far too great a strain, both cord and bow,
> And the bolt hits the mark with far less force,
> So I broke down under the heavy charge,
> Pouring forth tears and breathing heavy sighs . . .
> I then said weeping: "The things of the world
> With their false pleasure turned aside my steps
> As soon as your fair face from me was hidden."

This is a beginning but it is not enough, as Beatrice makes more than clear to him:

> And she: "Hadst thou kept silent or denied
> What thou confessed hast, not less known would be
> Thy fault: by such a high judge is it known!
> But when doth come forth from a man's own cheeks
> Indictment of his own sin, then in our court
> The grindstone doth indeed blunt the sword's edge.
> Nevertheless, so that thou bearest the shame
> Of thine own straying and thus another time
> When Sirens tempt thee thou may stronger be,
> Cease from thy sowing of tears and hearken to me.
> Then thou wilt hear how in another direction
> My buried flesh should have caused thee to go.
> Never did nature or art present to thee
> Such marvel as those fair limbs in which I
> Enclosed was, and they now crumbled to dust,
> And if this highest wonder failed thee
> Because I died, what other mortal thing
> Should have inveigled thee to long for it?
> Truly thou shouldst have, when the first shafts sped
> Of things deceptive, shouldst have risen up
> To follow me who was no longer mortal.
> Nor oughtest thou to have bent thy pinions downward
> To look for other blows — whether young girl
> Or other vanity that lasts not long.
> A nestling doth indeed wait two or three,
> But in the sight of a full-feathered bird
> In vain is net spread or is arrow shot."

But with this lecture — and with a sharp summons "to lift up his beard," which is taken to mean that Beatrice wants him to realize that his sins were committed as a mature man — the lady of his long waiting seems to have felt that he had been punished enough.

"The nettle of remorse" would do the rest, and when it has, he is plunged into Lethe and is in the earthly paradise where Beatrice told him he could for a little while be "a forester" but after which he would be with her "a citizen of that Rome in which Christ is a Roman."

A little while — but long enough for a detailed description of the Corpus Christi-like procession which he had seen in broader outline from across the river. And the enthronement of Beatrice in this procession.

Then he ends the cantica — and with a strange abruptness.

Purgatorio XXXII:

> If I had, reader, larger space in which
> To write, I would at least sing in part
> Of the sweet draught that never would sate.

This was the Eunoe, which had the same power of making him remember his good actions that Lethe had of making him forget his bad ones.
One must be immersed in it before one could come to heaven.

> But since now all the sheets have been used up
> That were prepared for this, the second cantica,
> The curb of art will not let me go further.
> I came forth from the holiest of waves
> Reanimated as new plants are
> When they have been renewed with new foliage,
> And I was pure and ready to mount to the stars.

« 14 »

It can and has been argued that this is the poem's true apogee — that when he enters the earthly paradise, Dante has gone as far as he or any other man can go. There is some merit to this argument, for this is certainly the end of Dante's mortal pilgrimage — the end of his human comedy, if you want to call it that.

But we are dealing with a *divine* comedy — those who renamed it this were correct in doing so — and in a divine comedy there was a further realm to visit. Dante had descended into hell and then climbed the mountain of purgatory. He must now soar to the empyrean. Otherwise the book would not be complete.

Dante tells of this final soaring in the *Commedia*'s third cantica, the *Paradiso,* and in his telling of it we find some of his most transcendent and luminous writing. But how could it be otherwise? For in this cantica — and he more than once said so — he was describing the indescribable, and in so doing he had to make the reader believe that it had been described to him and that he, like Dante, had seen things immortal but with mortal eyes.

Yet for all this — for all the mysticism which in its glow and fervor can only be compared to that of Joachim of Floris and certain of the seventeenth-century English metaphysical poets — it contains some of the most human and most vividly understandable passages in the whole *Commedia*. And some of the most readable.

Many of these have already been set down, but they should at least be mentioned again so the picture of the *Paradiso* may be complete.

The lines about Corso Donati's sister Piccarda in *Paradiso* III. The story of her abduction has already been told, but not her reaction to the fact that, although it was through no fault of hers that she did not keep her vows, God will not admit her to a higher heaven than the heaven of the moon.

Here it is in her own words:

> "Brother, this will of ours is quieted
> By virtue of charity. This makes us wish
> Only for what we have, nor thirst for more.
> If we did wish to be more on high,
> Then our desires would discordant be
> With His desire who doth here assign us . . .
> For it is in *His* will we find our peace."

The story of the Roman Empire as related by Justinian in *Paradiso* VI. Here in 111 ringing lines which march as did the ancient legions to the sound of blaring trumpets is the history of the second chosen people from the days when the eagle "made its abode in Alba for three hundred years" until the time when it was menaced by the "new Charles," Charles of Anjou's son Charles II, during the youth of Dante. It is compact but complete. "The wrong done of the Sabine women"; "the woe of Lucretia"; the wars against Brennus and Pyrrhus; the defeat of Hannibal; its spreading out "even to the Rhine" and then to the East, because of which "the woeful Cleopatra still weeps"; the crossing of the Rubicon; and the vengeance of Titus against the Jews — all these are mentioned and many things more. And at the conclusion Justinian, as a lawgiver should, denounces both the Guelphs and the Ghibellines — the first for opposing Rome's standard with "the yellow lilies" — i.e., France — and the second for appropriating to a party the emblem which should belong to all.

The story of man's redemption — why an all-powerful God permitted man to fall and why he will be redeemed again. This is narrated by Beatrice, who speaks like a theologian, in *Paradiso* VII.

The already-told stories of Charles Martel, Cunizza, and Fulk of Marseilles. They are found in *Paradiso* VIII and IX, which deal with the heaven of Venus. It was a heaven in which Dante felt much at home.

The biographies of St. Francis and St. Dominic. These are told in *Purgatorio* XI and *Purgatorio* XII — that of St. Francis by St. Thomas Aquinas, who was a Dominican, and that of St. Dominic by St. Bonaventura, who was a Franciscan. It would be hard to imagine more effective brief accounts of "the little poor man" and of "God's athlete" — of the two men and of their impact on the age. Characteristically, each ends with a denunciation of the order to which the narrator belongs. The Dominicans now seek strange food, the food of riches and ecclesiastical office, says St. Thomas. There is mold in the Franciscan wine cask, says St. Bonaventura.

The lines dealing with Cacciaguida in *Paradiso* XV, XVI, and XVII.

Finally, the stories of St. Peter Damian (*Paradiso* XXI — the heaven of Saturn) and of St. Benedict and the founding of his order in *Paradiso* XXII.

All these are set down in a poetry that grows ever more stately and yet somehow still preserves a lucid simplicity that makes it — at least to the educated, and to the educated of Dante's day as well as ours — as easily digestible as the poetry in the two earlier canticas.

Yet there are some passages in this cantica of which this cannot be said. There are some passages which are hard and difficult even to the most penetrating mind. There are some passages which require much more than ordinary mental faculties, much more than ordinary powers of concentration.

Some of these have already been set down.

Beatrice's explanation of why the moon has spots (*Paradiso* II).

Beatrice's explanation of man's redemption (*Paradiso* VII).

And very much earlier in this book (chapter III), Dante's understandable inability to comprehend why a man born on the Indus who did not worship Christ because he had never heard of Christ should be eternally damned.

Here (*Paradiso* XIX) is the ringing answer given by the heavenly eagle — in this case representing divine justice:

> "Now who art thou to sit in judgment's seat
> To judge a thing a thousand miles away
> With the short vision of a single span.
> Certes, for him who subtilizes with me,
> If Holy Scripture did not stand above him,
> There would be wondrous opportunity for doubting.
> Oh earth-bound animals! Oh ye gross minds!
> The primal will, which of itself is good,
> From itself, which is supreme good, has never moved,
> And all is just that is consonant with it.
> No good created draws it to itself,
> But it, raying forth, is cause of that good."

To explain, the Scripture teaches you that the judgments of God cannot always be found out. But they are just, because they are His judgments. That should be enough.

But there are at least two other passages which have not been mentioned yet and should be.

Paradiso VIII. Here Charles Martel — Dante's only virtuous French prince — tells Dante why there is diversity of character. He tells why one man is born a Solon, another a Xerxes, another a Melchizedek.

> "That nature which revolves and is the seal
> Of mortal wax doth do its duty well
> But does not discriminate between one man and the other.
> Hence it does come to pass that Esau differs
> From the seed of Jacob, and Quirinus comes
> From so mean a father that we say his ancestor was Mars."

In other words, God in His wisdom permits the influences that rain down on man from the various heavens to hit as chance directs. Otherwise all men, having a common first father, would be exactly alike.

Paradiso XIII. St. Thomas Aquinas explains how it can be that Solomon, although "in wisdom he was without a peer," is not equal in wisdom to Adam or Christ.

> "Know thou he was a king and sought such wisdom
> Only as he needed to be a worthy king
> And not to know what the number was
> Of the movers here on high or if *necesse*
> When 't was contingent a *necesse* made . . .
> Or if in a half circle could be made
> A triangle which no right angle had."

God — to reduce this to terms which are more easy to comprehend — gives only such wisdom as is needed. Solomon needed only a king's wisdom. Adam and Christ needed more.

All these encounters and words take place in the heaven of Jupiter or lower, and after listening to the last of them — this is the one about the Hindu — and perhaps understanding it, Dante, with Beatrice still beside him, continues his ascent.

It is now that he talks to St. Benedict and St. Damian. It is now too (*Paradiso* XXII) that he "looks down on the little threshing floor" — the earth — "which makes us all so fierce" and sees it all "from its hills to its river mouths." This was an extraordinary descriptive tour de force on the part of Dante, writing almost six and a half centuries ago, but we who have seen photographs taken by the astronauts do not have to extend even slightly our imaginations to visualize what he said.

After that, the triumph of Christ.

"Behold it!" Beatrice cries.
Says Dante (*Paradiso* XXIII):

> Just as — and in her clear, clear plenilune —
> Trivia smiles amid the eternal nymphs
> Who point the heavens to their last confine,
> So saw I far above a thousand lanterns
> A sun that did enkindle everyone
> As ours enkindles the supernal shows,
> And through its living light did more than shine
> A lucent substance, and it gleamed so brightly
> Upon my visage that I could not bear it.

It is the Son of God, with the Virgin Mary, and surrounded by a "circling melody" of the souls of the blessed.

And then out of a wheeling of glad souls issues a fire. It is St. Peter, "to whom our Lord left the keys"; St. Peter, "that baron" of the celestial hierarchy, who in Galilee "did walk on the sea."

St. Peter questions Dante on faith.

Dante (*Paradiso* XXIV) replies thus:

> "As the truth-telling pen
> Did write it, Father, of thy beloved brother,
> Who with thee did set Rome on the good path,
> It is the evidence of things unseen."

Shortly thereafter — and after more questioning and elaboration of answers, and after St. Peter, by blessing him and again wheeling, assures him that he has "pleased" him with his speech — a second light moves toward him.

Beatrice (*Purgatorio* XXV):

> "Look! Look! There is the baron
> For whose sake pilgrims to Galicia go."

It is St. James, and St. James catechizes him on hope.
Dante answers this question too:

> "Hope," said I, "is the certain expectation
> Of future glory, the which doth produce
> The grace divine and merit which goeth before."

These words are almost a direct quotation from Peter Lombard. Fortunately they come to Dante's mind.

Finally (*Paradiso* XXVI), St. John questions him about love, or, as is more commonly said, charity.

Here Dante gives no precise answer, but says that good is the Alpha and Omega of everything, and that everything that is good comes from love.

This seems, however, to satisfy St. John, and at this point — for his vision had been taken from Dante — "from mine eyes every mote did put to flight Beatrice with the bright radiance of her own." His sight has been restored, and he can now look upon heaven again.

He does, and with an ever-increasing awe and wonder. He talks with Adam. He listens to St. Peter denounce the Church he had founded. He sees the heavenly hierarchy and hears Beatrice describe the creation of the angels. Beyond a river of light he sees the celestial rose, and St. Bernard explains its order to him in detail.

Then suddenly the beatific vision. He looks upon God Himself in the form of an inordinately intense bright point of light.

And looking upon God, he cries out both at his joy and at the impossibility of describing this.

Paradiso XXXIII:

> Oh how inadequate my speech is! How it fails
> My high conception!

He continues:

> As the geometer who doth all he can
> To square the circle but he cannot do so,
> Hard though he think about the principle,
> Such — such indeed — was I at the new sight.
> I wished to see how did the image conform
> To the heavenly circle and how it was placed there.
> But this too much was for my feeble wings,
> Or would have been had not my mind been smitten
> By a flash of lightning which made all things clear.

What was it that was thus made clear? Dante cannot answer, for it was beyond anything mortal eyes had ever seen except, perhaps, for St. John of the Apocalypse.

He acknowledges this and then ends the poem:

> For this high fantasy I lacked the power,
> But now my desire and my will revolved
> Like to a wheel that is moved evenly,
> By the love that moves the sun and the other stars.

« 15 »

Thus the literal story ends but, as we and almost everybody else knows, the *Commedia* is something more than a literal account of Dante's journey through hell and purgatory and heaven to Beatrice and then to God. Dante was a preacher as well as a poet and, as he almost but does not quite say in his letter to Can Grande, it is his hope that, progressing in his great poem, he will be able to point a moral even as he adorns a tale and that the moral will be listened to and absorbed even while the tale is being enjoyed.

This he will do by means of allegory, which, according to the dictionary, is "the veiled presentation, especially in a figurative story, of a meaning metaphorically implied but not expressly stated," but which elsewhere has been called "dramatized metaphor."

Dante's book, then, as Dante himself has already told us, must be read allegorically as well as literally if it is to be completely understood; and so, although it would be neither practical nor useful to go in detail into a subject upon which a whole library of volumes and papers — many of them at odds with each other in their conclusions — has been written, it is useful and in fact necessary at least to go into the broad outlines of Dante's approach and to examine some of the more significant points.

Here they are:

(1) The *Commedia* in its very deepest meaning symbolizes a grail search — a search for the grail of salvation.

(2) In this search Dante is not merely Dante the Florentine — Dante the son of Alighiero degli Alighieri — but mankind.

(3) Virgil is not merely the revered greatest of the Latin poets and Dante's literary idol (as well as his guide and master) but reason or philosophy or classical (i.e., pagan) learning.

(4) Beatrice is not merely Bice Portinari but revelation.

(Some say that Beatrice is theology or the Church, and Professor Charles S. Singleton in an eloquent and extremely well-reasoned book identifies her with Christ. I find the first two too cold, and I cannot quite go along with the third one. It seems to me to go too far.)

(5) Finally, mankind — or Everyman — as it seeks for salvation can be guided only up to a certain point by the powers of the intellect — reason, philosophy, learning — and after that the guide must be revelation. It can reach God only by revelation through the means of faith, hope, and charity, which descend on it through the Holy Ghost.

This outlines the principal allegorical scheme, but below it there is a myriad of lesser allegories and of lesser allegorical and symbolical meanings. Some of these should be given — if only so that the reader can look for and understand the rest.

In *Inferno* I, for example, the three beasts are not merely literal savage and ravening wild animals but lust (the leopard), pride (the lion), and covetousness (the she-wolf), and the greyhound is not only a specific though never-named future leader but civic righteousness.

In *Inferno* III, Charon is not merely the infernal ferryman who carries the damned souls into hell but the horror felt by the unrepentant who realize too late that death has come.

In *Inferno* VI, three-headed Cerberus is not merely the three-headed dog who guards his particular circle but the slavering bestiality which is the natural punishment and the natural consequence of gluttony and self-indulgence.

But perhaps the most complex as well as the most discussed and argued about of his meanings within the meaning is the allegory hidden in the pageant which Dante is permitted to see in the later cantos of the *Purgatorio*. Much of this has been discussed earlier in this chapter, but not the climax.

In this (*Purgatorio* XXXII), Dante sees in order the following things:

(1) "The bird of Jove" which sweeps down from the sky, tearing out not merely flowers and leaves but the very bark of a tree.

This has been taken to mean the persecution of the Church under Nero and Domitian.

(2) "A fox that did of all good nourishment seem starved." This fox flings itself upon the body of the chariot but is driven off by Beatrice.

It is said to represent Arianism and other early heresies.

(3) An eagle that leaves the chariot feathered with its own feathers.

This is said to be the so-called Donation of Constantine, which supposedly made the papacy a temporal power.

(4) A dragon that thrusts its tail into the wagon and, withdrawing it "as a wasp withdraws its sting," drags out the bottom of the cart and carries it away.

This is Mohammedanism.

(5) The chariot covered once again with plumage. This is "offered perhaps with good intention," but it is like "dog grass in a fertile soil."

This is the Church's new enrichment by Pepin and Charlemagne.

(6) The "holy structure" putting horns on all its parts — three on the shaft and one at each corner.

This is the resultant corruption of the Church.

Seventh, and finally, there appears to Dante a harlot sitting on the chariot and beside her is a giant who kisses her over and over again. "But because she turned her lewd and wandering eyes on me, her savage paramour beats her from head to foot. Then he looses "the monster" and drags it through the wood "so far that he made the wood a screen between me and the harlot and the strange brute."

The harlot, we are supposed to understand, is the Roman curia and the giant the royal house of France. The forest is Avignon, to which the papacy had been dragged.

But what about Dante's own role in this, for he puts himself right into the middle of the allegory.

"Because she turned her lewd and wandering eyes on me."

What does this mean?

Does it mean that when Dante was ambassador to Pope Boniface the Church tried to win him to her services?

Or — and this seems more probable — that Clement really and seriously listened to the arguments Dante presented in the *Convivio* and in the first of his political letters? That he really and seriously meant to break with Philip the Fair and permanently take the side of Alto Arrigo? Or what?

There are other allegories too, and the Dante reader must be prepared to look for all of them. He must try to understand them. To do this, he must ask questions.

Is, for example, the Old Man of Crete (*Inferno* XIV) the Old Man of Ovid's poem or does he symbolize divided loyalty?

Why is Cato, a suicide, admitted to purgatory (*Purgatorio* I) while Pier delle Vigne, also a suicide, is sentenced (*Inferno* XIII) to hell? Is this merely Dante's estimate of the two men, or is there a hidden meaning?

Is three-faced Satan of *Inferno* XXXIV accidentally three-faced, or is this because he is a trinity as God is, but a trinity of evil?

What is the significance (*Purgatorio* VIII) of the serpent which is driven off by the flaming swords of two guardian angels just after Dante meets Nino Visconti and before he meets Currado Malaspina?

Why (*Purgatorio* XXI) does Dante confess to Beatrice? Why *must* he confess to her? Is it a purely human catharsis? Does he pour out his heart because he must pour it out to feel at peace again, and to whom can he better pour it out than to the woman whom he loves? Or does this symbolize the confession itself? That — and the Church believed this — one must not merely repent but must confess before one is forgiven?

I could continue indefinitely.

The reader could continue indefinitely too. He could and should and, if Dante has won him, he will.

« *16* »

And that Dante has won him — or at least that Dante has won many of him, has won many readers, is not debatable. It is common knowledge and proven fact.

But how? That is the first question. What were his means and his tools?

Why was he beginning to be read in his own trecento? Why is he still read and loved by many today?

The first reason I have already suggested. It is because he is Everyman, and because we who read him have in us something of Everyman too.

The second reason was more important in his time than it is today. It is that he dealt with things that were believed in and were of vital moment. Take hell as a beginning. To most of us today, hell — and I mean a literal hell with licking flames and demons and not just a psychological concept — is a purely literary idea. But in Dante's day it was as real as the streets and squares of Florence or the canals of Venice.

In this connection, a story in Villani's chronicle is illuminating:

"On the first of May 1304, just as it had been the custom in the good old days for companies and bands of merrymakers to go through the city in joyous festival, so now they assembled in various parts of Florence, and one district vied with another in seeing who could put on the best show. They of the Borgo San Frediano customarily were the most skillful in devising novel and diverting pastimes, and they now published it abroad that all who wanted to have news of the other world should hie them to the Carraia Bridge, and near it on the Arno they constructed a floating stage on which they made representation of hell. They had flames and other torments, and on it were men disguised as demons, while others had the appearance of naked souls who had once been people. These they put to one kind of torment or another, and there were cries and shrieks and tumult which were fearful and horrible to hear, and because of this many people came to the bridge to look on. It was wooden from pile to pile and was so overladen that without warning it gave way in many places and fell, carrying the people with it. As a result many were either crushed or drowned and many were badly injured. What had started as a pastime became the real thing, and many indeed went by death to get tidings of the other world, with lamentation and sorrow to the whole city."

But Dante gave them news of the other world too. He gave it to them in the *Commedia* — and in a language they could understand and against a background that no one had any trouble whatsoever in relating to his own experience.

This is something that can hardly be stressed too much. Dante, as we have seen, was many things, but he was also Dante the realist; Dante who listened accurately and saw accurately, and who set down accurately what he heard and saw. In this respect, he is like no one else in the Middle Ages as perhaps can best be seen by comparing his forthright simplicity with the ornate prose of Boccaccio, a prose which remains ornate even in the raciest tales of the *Decameron*. In many ways, we do not find a comparable accuracy until almost modern times.

Let us illustrate by looking at his dialogue.

Whether in heaven or in purgatory or in hell, whenever Dante meets a Florentine he or she talks (and thinks) like a Florentine, and by this I do not mean that he or she speaks the vernacular as opposed to Latin. I mean that the local idiom is used — the special highly localized way of speaking that was used only on the streets or in the marketplaces of Florence, and not even in Prato or Signa or Fiesole or Pontassieve. This is equally true of any Bolognese, Romagnole, or Lombard who happened to cross his path.

But Dante's differentiations — the differentiations which he used to convey reality go even further than that.

His noblemen speak like noblemen (Guido del Duca — *Purgatorio* XIV); his gentlemen of the old school like gentlemen of the old school (Marco Lombardo — *Purgatorio* XVI); his crude plainspoken citizens like plainspoken citizens (Ciacco — *Inferno* VI); his well-bred scholars like gentlemen and scholars (Brunetto Latini — *Inferno* XV); and his lewd rogues like lewd and filthy rogues (the incredibly foul Vanni Fucci — *Inferno* XXIV).

His gift for conveying a sense of reality also extended to his portrayal of setting or scene. According to Wordsworth, "Heaven lies about us in our infancy," and so did Dante's heaven — and his hell and his purgatory too — for in great part it was built out of images which had lain about him and his contemporaries for as long as he and they could see and observe.

That this is so should have long since become apparent to the reader, for this book is strewn with Dante similes — and it should be noted that Dante was perhaps the greatest user of similes in the history of writing — by which he conveyed the look and feeling of life eternal in terms of this temporal world.

It is not necessary to repeat them here or to set down any more, although the temptation is strong.

Except one.

Purgatorio X:

> O ye vainglorious Christians, wretched, weary,
> Who in the ailing vision of your mind
> Still put your trust in your backsliding steps.
> Do you not understand that we are worms
> Born to become the angelic butterfly
> That flies to justice without any defense?

Why does your mind then soar so loftily
Since, as it were, ye are defective insects,
Even as a worm that has not yet developed?

We are worms born to become the angelic butterfly!
Even as he reaches toward heaven — and this case reaches toward it magnificently — he does so in terms of our earth.

But it is not enough for a great narrative to convey reality.

It must always hold the reader's attention, and it has been correctly said that this can only be done when the narrator constantly forces the reader to ask eagerly: "What happened next?"

This Dante clearly does. The *Commedia* is at once a story and a collection of stories. But whether our Florentine is telling of Paolo and Francesca, or of the last voyage of Ulysses, or of Count Ugolino in the Tower of Hunger, or any other of the dozen or so stories which are scattered through it; or whether instead our concern is with the total story which was the most unequaled love story of all time — the story of the transformation of Bice Portinari, that slip of a Florentine girl whom Dante loved and lost and was unfaithful to and then loved again, into Beatrice, who was in God's presence with the blest — the answer is the same. He tells it splendidly, and with every legitimate narrative device.

With humor, for example, which was sometimes playful, as in various of his exchanges with Virgil and in his account of Virgil's meeting with Statius, and sometimes robustious and even scatalogical, as in the Malacoda episode in *Inferno* XXI. With pity and compassion. With pathos. And with stern judgment when neither friendship nor enmity made the scales other than even in his hands.

He makes use too of the irrelevancies and asides by which an author can keep attention from flagging. One of these is his reference to the story of the inventor of chess (*Paradiso* XXVIII). This man asks the king of Persia to reward him with one grain of wheat on the first square, two on the second, four on the third, and so on. The final total runs to twenty figures, or beyond the tens of quintillions.

But most of all he wins his audience because he tells them the most daring fable ever invented. "To the eternal from the temporal" is his description of it. And he has now become one who can take us there. This he does.

« *17* »

How did this come about? How did Dante become one who could do this? This has a place in our account of the poem.

When did Dante write the *Commedia?*

Where?

The first question is of a kind that — given our fragmentary knowledge of man's pertinent interior psychological chemistry — is difficult or impossible to answer, not merely in the case of Dante but with anyone else.

Let us take Shakespeare as an example. William Shakespeare was the son of a Stratford citizen who was a glover by trade and who also held certain minor municiple offices. At the age of eighteen he married a woman nine years older than himself — possibly because he had to — and, living somewhat wildly, got into difficulty with the law because of alleged poaching activities. Thereupon he left home. He went to London and was drawn to the theater, where at first he supported himself by holding the horses of the patrons and later in a better way as an actor. Then he became what is today known as a playdoctor, rewriting — possibly for his own company — bad plays so as to make them suitable for production.

All he added, it has been said, was genius. But it was quite an *all*, as anyone knows who has ever seen these plays on any stage, even a bad one.

Now how did this glover's son, brought up in a provincial and narrow small town, find the qualities which enabled him to construct his many works, most of which were more profound and more beautiful, had more wit and feeling, and showed more sense of the wonder and tragedy of the world than those of any other English writer who has ever lived —perhaps any other man who wrote drama anywhere and in all time? Other glovers' sons have come from country towns of London.

Or take Homer. According to tradition, Homer — born in either Smyrna, Colphon, Salamis, Rhodes, Argos, or Athens, or in Kyme, Ithaca, Chios, Pylos, Sparta, or even Egypt or Babylon — was a professional bard who, as he became old and poor and blind, wandered from city to city in Greek Asia Minor telling his stories. But there have been other blind bards who were also old and poor. And none of them wrote the *Iliad* or the *Odyssey*.

It is so with Dante Alighieri. Let us repeat what has been said before. He was the son of a father and the nephew of uncles whose paramount interest was in making money, and that not always by entirely respectable means. In those days, anyone who loaned money or speculated in lands was suspect. He had no education — or little education — that many other Florentines did not have. He acquired a certain amount of experience — and *kudos* — in Florentine politics, but so did Dino Pecora, a butcher, and Dino Compagni, the silk merchant. And if he wrote poetry, he was not the only young Florentine to do this — many whose poems still survive in anthologies ending up as bankers and businessmen and notaries.

And then the *Commedia*, which is as unparagoned in its realm as the plays of Shakespeare and the two epics of Homer are in theirs. Perhaps more so.

Now what metamorphosed Dante into a man able to write the *Commedia?* How did the worm become this butterfly?

The usual answer has already been more than once hinted at if not specifically given. Dante was hammered into shape by the triple blows of his three catastrophes.

First, when he was a boy and then a young man, he loved a young woman as any young man might do, except that — because he was a poet and because being a poet he wrote down this love and then, also because he was a poet, he believed his own words — he loved her a little more deeply and a little more profoundly than did other young men. And then this young woman died.

Second, he substituted love for his city for love for the young lady, and as he had served the young lady, he served Florence. He served her with all the ability he had, with all his heart and his soul. And because he had served his city — or had tried to serve it — and did not clearly understand the savage ruthlessness and lack of principle of politics (then as now), he was exiled. He who had done right, who *knew* he had done right, who had done right for no ulterior purpose was exiled; was told that he must pick up his scrip and go; was told that he must never again see the city in which he — and his parents and his parents' parents before them — had been born and in which he hoped to die.

Third, his dreams growing, he substituted love for a universal empire for his love for his city, and he devoted every skill he had to bringing about this empire. But the cause failed, Henry died at Buonconvento — and there were no heirs to Henry.

Man would now not be joined together under a single God-chosen ruler to fulfill the purposes of God even though God had seemed to will it.

This answer cannot be dismissed entirely. Victorian as it may be, we cannot entirely put aside the thought that God must indeed char the wood ere he can limn with it; for if Beatrice had not died, he would not have had the vision that made his poem possible, and if — Carlyle is right — Dante had not been driven from Florence, the ordinary preoccupations of family and civic life would have left him little time to put pen to paper. As we have noted, he said in the *Convivio* that this could happen. Finally, if Henry had become both a crowned and effective emperor, he might well have missed some of the more important experiences that took him to the *primum mobile* and beyond.

And yet — and yet this only partly tells the story. For surely there were others who have loved and lost, others who have met personal and political disaster, and others who have seen their dreams shattered. But there is only one *Commedia*.

So we turn full circle and our beginning is our end. With Dante, as with every other genius — and not merely in the realm of letters — the answer is that we do not know.

« 18 »

Question two: when was the *Commedia* written?

Here we do not so much have no answer as a choice of answers, for there are various valid-seeming theories, and for each of them there are well-presented supporting arguments.

In this matter, Boccaccio sets the outside possible limits.

We have already set down his account of how sometime after Dante's exile the first seven cantos of the *Commedia* were accidentally found and shown to Dino Lambertucci, who in turn forwarded them to Moroello Malaspina. If this can be believed, not only was the poem begun but some 942 of its lines had been written before he departed from Florence forever in the autumn of 1301.

Boccaccio tells a very similar story about the last thirteen cantos. It was Dante's custom, he says, whenever he had finished six or seven cantos to send them to Can Grande, and only after the latter had seen them could anyone who wished to do this make a copy. This he continued to do until he came to the cantos above mentioned. These he had completed but he had not yet sent them when he died.

He had not only not sent them but they could not be found, and indeed after some time had elapsed hope of finding them had been so far abandoned that Dante's sons Piero and Jacopo "had almost decided to finish their father's work."

But at this point, a miracle intervened. "To Jacopo," says Boccaccio, "who was much more zealous in this matter than his brother, there appeared a marvelous vision which not only took away from him his folly and presumption, but which told him where the thirteen missing cantos were."

Here is what happened, the source being Pietro Giardino, "a worthy citizen of Ravenna and a long-time disciple of Dante's," who told it to Boccaccio.

"Eight months after the death of Dante, Jacopo came to my house just before daybreak and told me that that night as he slept his father had appeared to him clad in shining raiment and with a strange light shining in his eyes."

" 'Are you alive?' Jacopo said he asked him.

" 'Yes, but in the true life, not ours.'

" 'And before passing to this true life did you complete your work? And if so where are the missing parts? We could never find them.'

" 'Yes, I completed it.'

" 'Then he took me by the hand,' said Jacopo, "and led me to the room in which it was his custom to sleep when he still lived the life of the living. He pointed out a certain place in this room and told me that there I would find what I had been seeking for so long a time. I then awoke, and I could not forebear coming to you to tell you this. I have marked the place very well in my memory. Will you come with me so that we may find it together?' " Giardino could and did.

Although it was still a long time until dawn, he accompanied Jacopo to Dante's old home and to his bedchamber. Against the wall there they saw a piece of matting.

"Lifting this gently," continues Boccaccio, "they found a little niche which neither of them had ever seen before, nor had they known that it was there, and in it they found some writings all mildewed by the dampness of the wall and so near to rotting that they would have crumbled into pieces if they had stayed there any longer. These they carefully cleaned and read, and saw that they contained the thirteen missing cantos. Thus was the work which had been so many years a-completing completed."

So many years! In the Boccaccio version, the *Commedia* was begun before 1301 and finished not less than twenty years later.

Others insist, however, that the *Commedia* was composed during a much shorter period of time, but as to what this shorter period of time was there is by no means agreement. One theory — and many accept it — holds that the *Inferno* was composed before Henry came to Italy (i.e., before 1310), the *Purgatorio* during his campaigns, and the *Paradiso* after Henry's death. Another theory contends that the *Inferno* was begun in 1313 and the first cantos of the *Purgatorio* by May 1315. Barbi suggests that the work was commenced in 1307 or thereabouts; Edmund Gardner that "it may have been begun between 1306 and 1308" and that "portions of the *Inferno* and the *Purgatorio*" were "composed before the catastrophe of 1313."

To help us resolve these conflicting opinions we have — other than Boccaccio's perhaps not altogether unromanticized story — only a few hard or reasonably hard facts.

(1) Francesco da Barberino, discussing Virgil in his *Documenti d'Amore*, makes this statement: "This man Dante Alighieri in one of his works, which is called the *Commedia*, and which deals among other things with infernal matters, constantly commends Virgil as his master." It is contended that Barberino was in Provence from 1309 to 1313 but that he then returned to Italy in time to know and to be able to quote from the *Inferno*. If this is so, at least the *Inferno* was circulated by 1313.

(2) Passages from the *Inferno* — "Charon, the demon with eyes like red-hot coal" (*Inferno* III) and "O thou who comest to the house of pain" (*Inferno* V) — are copied on the front and back covers respectively of a parchment register of criminal sentences belonging to Tieri di Gano di Useppi of San Gimignano, notary of the Bolognese *podestà* Niccolò Bandini. This register covers the first semester of 1317.

(3) Dante's epistle to Can Grande refers to the *Paradiso* in terms that make it certain that it either had been commenced or was about to be. (but not as something already completed). This letter was probably written in 1319.

(4) In one of his *Eclogues* — we will deal with these shortly — Dante seems to say that ten cantos of the *Paradiso* had now been written. This eclogue is also ascribed to the same year.

To sum up, the *Inferno*, or parts of it, may have been written — and published — by 1313 and must have been by 1317. At least parts of the *Paradiso* must have been written by 1319.

But there is one other matter that has some bearing on attempts to date the *Commedia*.

How was it written?

Did Dante begin with the first line and continue to the end without changing a word and without ever looking back to alter or interpolate?

Or did he revise the poem from time to time, and from time to time make later insertions?

Two statements by two early commentators seem to support strongly the first possibility.

The *Ottimo Commento*:

"I heard Dante say that never did a rhyme make him say anything other than what he wished to say, but that many a time he had made his rhymes say things that they would not for other poets."

Benvenuto da Imola:

"When Dante first set about the composition of his poem, all the rhymes in the Italian language presented themselves to him in the guise of so many lovely maidens, and each in turn humbly petitioned him to give him a place in his poem. In answer to their prayers, Dante first summoned one and then the other, and assigned to each an appropriate place in his composition, and when it was completed it was seen that no one of them was left out."

Others, however, take the opposite point of view.

Says Edmund Gardner:

"After the death of Henry, Dante may well have revised and completed these two canticles."

That is, the *Inferno* and the *Purgatorio*.

He cites an allusion to the death of Clement V in *Inferno* XIX as an example of such a revision.

Here is why this matter is of moment.

If the poem was written without ever turning back, then at the very earliest no canto could have been written before an event referred to in it had taken place, for Dante was no Manto and no Aruns. Thus an "earlier than this it could not have been written" could be set down for many parts of the poem.

But if Dante did turn back, if he did alter and amend, then this method of dating is no longer valid.

I myself incline to this latter point of view.

Dante's objective — whether he knew it or not — was to put down all he thought and felt about everything, and it seems hard to believe (a) that given the circumstances of his life, he could have written a poem which accomplished this — and the *Commedia* did — in a short time (even the short time of six to eight years which some chronologies would have it) and (b) that he would leave out anything that added to its white-hot fire simply because that meant going back to find the appropriate place for it.

It seems to me, rather, that composing the poem took up a very substantial part of Dante's life — that he may well have scratched out certain tentative beginnings not very long after the *Vita Nuova* (even though he was then in no way ready to complete it) — and that, as Boccaccio tries to tell us, he continued at the writing of it almost until the end of his life.

« *19* »

Where was the *Commedia* written? That is the third and final question. In what place, or more probably in what places, did Dante turn its concept into words.

In Florence?

If Boccaccio can be believed, yes. But only the first seven cantos.

Yet even in this matter we have two difficulties.

(1) In Florence — and at that time — Dante was so deeply involved (after he gave up his dissolute days and then his days of study) in the affairs of the city that it is difficult to see when he could have found the time and the tranquility to work on such a poem as the *Commedia*.

(2) Ciacco's famous prophecy of White overthrow and Black triumph was made in *Inferno* VI. But — and here the theory of interpolations is all that saves us — those lines could not have been written until later.

Nevertheless, we cannot dismiss the possibility that some of the poem was written, or at least roughed in, in Florence.

And after Florence, where?

The answer is everywhere.

In the Casentino. With Moroello Malaspina. In Paris. At Fonte Avellana. In Verona.

And in many other places.

Written and then put down and then taken up again. For he was pursued by a hound of heaven, and he always had the *Commedia* with him. Here he added a *terzina* and there a canto, and always he was tormented by it as by a demon. It was this that — in his own description — made and kept him haggard and gaunt.

Indeed there is only one thing we can say about the when and where of the poem with reasonable certainty. He completed it at Ravenna. Yet even here there are some details to argue about. Some of those who have studied Dante feel that when he came to the Adriatic city he had already finished both the *Inferno* and the *Purgatorio* and that he had only the *Paradiso* left to do. Others feel that he had only come as far as the end of *Purgatorio* XXVII and that not only the *Paradiso* but those cantos of the *Purgatorio* which deal with the earthly paradise were written in Guido da Polenta's city.

The better case can be made for the second conclusion, for not only does the magic portraying of the *pineta* occur in *Purgatorio* XXVIII but the mood of the last six *Purgatorio* cantos begins to be the mood of the *Paradiso* and basically that was a mood of exaltation and calm.

It was a Ravenna mood — it was a mood induced by this new home and final refuge. For now at last he had found the kind of patron he needed. We have already seen enough of Francesca's nephew to know that though able and enlightened, he was not a Count Guidi or a Moroello Malaspina, and he was clearly not a Can Grande della Scala. But he knew what Dante needed and he gave it to him. A house of his own within and somewhere near the city walls. Not a room in the lord's palace. A garden. A study. And, part of this and more important, peace and tranquility.

These things he used well. Calmly and deliberately — as a man who weighs each step carefully before he takes it and yet goes forward — he continued toward his goal.

There are 14,333 lines in the *Commedia*. Of these either 4758 or 5655 — according to whether the last thirty-three or the last thirty-six cantos — were written in Ravenna. If they did not have the street-corner and marketplace popular appeal of certain parts of the *Inferno*, they were the most golden that he or any other poet had ever penned.

XXV

Tityrus in Ravenna

IT is pleasant to record that as he did this, as he wrote these lines whatever their number, as he moved toward the attainment of the almost unattainable, he was able — and for the first time since he had ridden to Rome upon the already lost cause of trying to work out some sort of accommodation between the Florentine Whites and Pope Boniface — to lead an untormented and idyllic life not only in the ideal surroundings just outlined but in the company of those who admired him and whom he loved. It may seem odd to speak of Dante's "old age" since he was only fifty-two when he came to Ravenna, but we must do so, for time did its work faster in those days than it does now and Dante was, and knew he was, old. It is pleasant to record that, as far as he was able, he had a happy old age.

This does not mean, of course, that every anguish had departed from his heart. Most notably, he was still haunted by his dream of the city of his boyhood and by his hope that somehow and in some way he would be allowed to return there.

The proof of this: *Paradiso* XXV was definitely written in Ravenna, and in *Paradiso* XXV — although it was an aside which had no real relation with the progress of the poem — he said this:

> *Se mai contingua che il poema sacro —*
> *Al quale ha posto mano e cielo e terra*
> *Sì che m'ha fatto per più anni macro —*
> *Vinca la crudeltà che fuor mi serra*
> *Dal bell' ovile ov'io dormii agnello,*
> *Nimico ai lupi che li danno guerra,*

Con altra voce omai, con altro vello,
Ritornerò poeta, ed in sul fonte
Del mio battesmo prenderò il cappello;
Però che ne la Fede che fa conte
L'anime a Dio quivi entra' io, e poi
Pietro per lei si mi giro la fronte.

If ever it should happen that the sacred poem —
To which both heaven and earth have set their hand
So that it's kept me lean these many years —
Shall conquer the cruelty which doth bar me
From the fair sheepfold where I slept as lamb,
Enemy to the wolves that ravaged it,
With other voice than then, with other fleece,
I will return as poet, and at the font
Of my baptism will put on the crown,
Because into the faith that makes account
Of souls to God there I did enter, and afterwards
Because of this St. Peter encircled my brow.

Biographically speaking, the important phrase in this moving flood of words is "with other voice than then, with other fleece," and the meaning could hardly be more clear. If Florence, if my Florence which I love with all my heart and soul even though I have so often and so bitterly assailed her — and as a matter of fact he could not lightly break with old habits, and in this passage ("enemy to the wolves that ravaged it") he still did — if this Florence will only let me come back to her again, I will not come as the mouthpiece of a political faction. I will come only as a poet — as a Florentine poet — and ask only to be crowned as a poet on the steps of my Bel San Giovanni and thereafter to be allowed to live in peace.

But even as he made this plea, Dante knew full well that his wish would not be granted and that he must accept his fate and the duties that doing this imposed on him and the consequences of discharging these duties.

He must continue with his *Commedia,* undeterred by anything or anybody, and there would be plenty of things and persons that would try to deter him. For, as he himself noted (*Paradiso* XVII), in his journey "down through the world that is forever bitter and up the mountain from whose lofty summit I was uplifted by my lady's eyes and through heaven from light unto light, I have learned that which if I do retell it will have for many a bitter savor."

Should he be silent then? Should he who had already made so many enemies "be a timid friend to truth" for fear of making more?

His answer — it is put into the mouth of Cacciaguida in the same
canto — is a resounding no:

> "A conscience darkened
> Either with its own or with another's shame
> Will find thy speaking to be very harsh.
> Nevertheless, all falsehood put aside
> And make thy vision wholly manifest,
> And let them scratch indeed then where they itch.
> For if the words thou sayest shall be unpleasant
> At the first taste, life-giving nourishment
> They shall become when they have been digested."

He must go on with his immortal poem. Doing it, he must tell the un-
varnished truth.

« 2 »

But, as we will now see, he did so under ameliorated circumstances. The
ship which had so long drifted aimlessly without sails and without a
rudder had at last found a safe and sheltered port.

Moreover there were those there to welcome him and to make his days
good ones.

Who were some of them?

His son Pietro heads the list. Pietro was already beginning to be a
person of substance and stature, the benefices we have already discussed
providing him with enough revenue not only to support himself but
perhaps to help his father.

(Later Pietro Alighieri would become distinguished and wealthy both
in Verona and Vicenza, in proof of which Renato Piattoli has recorded
twenty-eight documents dating from May 19, 1332, to July 19, 1358. In
these Pietro is described variously as "judge and general delegate of the
podestà"; "delegate of the *podestà*"; "general delegate of Guido da
Correggio, *podestà*"; "judge and general vicar of Guido da Corregio,
podestà"; "judge of the commune"; "vicar of the *podestà* of Vicenza";
judge and vicar of the *podestà* of Vicenza"; and judge and councillor of
that magnificent lord, the Lord Can Grande della Scala." But now he was
still content to live in his father's house, listen to his father's words, and
absorb enough of his father's thinking to write a commentary on his
father's book which, if not as detailed as other commentaries, at least has
the virtue of being authoritative.)

Dante's second son — originally Dante's third son, but Giovanni was
now dead — was in Ravenna too. Jacopo was less able — in a worldly

sense — than Pietro, and less successful too. He never had any great position or great wealth. But as a writer — for both sons wrote — he had slightly more ability and, if that be possible, he was the more loyal to his father and later to his father's memory.

His possible role in finding the last cantos of the *Commedia* we already know, but it was also Jacopo who put together the first complete manuscript of the poem and sent it (on April 2, 1322) to Guido da Polenta, who had by then been driven from Ravenna and was captain of the people in Bologna. He accompanied it with a sonnet which in part went thus:

> So that indeed the beauties, O my lord,
> That this my sister beareth as a light
> May have, and of thy courtesy, escort,
> This present part of it I send to you . . .
> I send it to you first. Correct it please,
> And if you find it worthy, praise it too.

Dante would have liked the first lines and the last one. But the request in the next to last line would hardly have pleased him, for he had written the poem as he wished it to be written. But there were certain conventions in medieval good manners. A clerk must write so — and so only — if he wrote to a lord. And Jacopo was a clerk.

Also to her father came Dante's daughter, who, after his death, entered the nunnery of Santo Stephano all' Ulivo, where she took the name of Sister Beatrice. In my opinion this was Antonia. In 1350 — when she was close to, if not more than, fifty years old — Boccaccio brought her a gift of ten golden florins from the republic of Florence, which had now forgiven Dante and tried to honor him posthumously in this way. In the Dante house she perhaps served as housekeeper, for Gemma, although she could have rejoined her husband, remained in Florence shrewdly taking care of her property and with, some say, another daughter, about whom, however, except for this bare statement, nothing is known.

« 3 »

But besides two sons and a daughter, Dante had friends in Ravenna.

Had them or more probably *found* them, for with one possible exception there is no evidence that he knew any of them before he came to the relatively small Adriatic city in which — although it had only seven thousand inhabitants as compared to thirty-two thousand in Bologna and more than fifty thousand in Florence — Guido da Polenta had somehow or other managed to assemble a small group of stimulating and accomplished people.

Among them the most notable – but perhaps because of his strong pro–Pope Boniface and anti–White Guelph past the least closely associated with Dante – was Raimondo Concoreggio, archbishop of Ravenna. Raimondo was a native of Milan and the scion of a noble family there. In 1285 and 1286 he studied at Bologna, and it is suggested that Dante may have known him then. In the latter year, although he had not yet obtained his law degree, he was invited to practice law in Sodi at the not small salary of forty imperial *libbre* a year, which same would be increased to fifty *libbre* if and when he got his degree. At this time he put on holy orders, and thereafter his rise was steady. He became Bishop of Vicenza and next papal envoy to Philip the Fair. He returned to Italy in 1300 and was forthwith made papal vicar in the Romagna and, in 1302, rector of the Flaminian Way.

In the latter capacity he set up his residence at Forlì, where he soon so antagonized the Ordelaffi that they arranged to have him set upon by their bravos, who almost murdered him. Indeed his recovery was regarded as a miracle, but recover he did and thereupon returned to his duty, in doing which he so tamed the unruly Romagnoli that at least for a while there was law and order in this lawless province.

It was at this time that the earlier Polenta lords – Guido's father Ostasio and his uncle and his brothers – learned of his abilities and after a bitterly contested election succeeded in having him named archbishop. The surprising thing is that he accepted.

Accept he did, however, and thereafter administered the archbishopric in his usual ruthless, able way. But even as he did this – and as he did it continued to intervene in European and Italian politics, trying to prevent some of the more flagrant injustices in the proceedings of the Templars, helping the monks of St. Francis's La Verna restore the monastery, negotiating between Henry VII and the Lombard cities, and offering his assistance to the Black Guelphs of Florence and king Robert of Naples – he did not forget either culture or matters of the mind. Here, like so many in the trecento, he anticipated the coming Renaissance.

Among other things – and in Ravenna – he founded a library or libraries.

Of these the most renowned – and the best – was the Cartilegio near the Duomo. It had as large a collection of historical and theological writings as any library in eastern Italy.

Historical and theological writings! These surely were consulted by Dante, for there is both history and theology in that part of the *Commedia* which was written in Ravenna.

He must surely have come to know the archbishop at the same time.

Another close to him at Ravenna was Pietro Giardino, who has already been mentioned more than once. Pietro was a notary.

A third was Menghino Mezzani. Menghino was a notary — and a poet too.

Besides these were Bernardo Cannacci, who composed the Latin lines to Dante which begin "To these evils I yield not." These can still be seen near the tomb of Dante; Niccolò Carnevali and Achille Matarelli, both lawyers; and possible the chronicler Geremia Gotto, who wrote a history of the Romagna which has since disappeared of which the source, Geremia said, was that Guido Bonatti whom Dante put in hell as an astrologer.

But perhaps the two nearest to him — except for his sons and daughter — came from his own Tuscany. They were Dino Perini of Florence and Francesco da Milotti of Certaldo. Dino was the grandson of another Dino Perini who had been a Florentine merchant, and he was possibly the *"Dinus Forentinae aetatis nostra gratissime dicacitatis adolescens"* — "Dino of Florence, the same age as we are, and a youth whose conversation was witty and pleasing" — of whom Petrarch talked many years later. Possibly but not certainly, for there were many Florentine Dinos. Francesco da Milotti was a distinguished physician — distinguished and apparently successful. He had patients in Forlì, Bologna, and Imola as well as Ravenna. Showing that there were no unshatterable class distinctions, his only daughter Caterina was married to Giovanni da Polenta, Guido da Polenta's brother.

It is also possible that Giotto came at least briefly to Ravenna during Dante's stay there. If so, Dante would surely have entertained him. He would have entertained him and also watched him at his painting as he had done a dozen or so years earlier in Padua.

"At that time," says Vasari — and although he is cloudy as to the exact date he seems to be talking of a year between 1316 and 1322 — "Giotto was in Ferrara, and when it came to the attention of Dante the Florentine poet that he was there, he arranged things so that he would be brought to Ravenna, where he was now living in exile, and there he had him paint for the Polenta lords some fresco stories on the walls of the church of San Francesco. They were reasonably good."

Because Vasari is not always notable for his accuracy — he was never reluctant to accept legend as fact, especially when it made for a good story — this statement has been received by many with some skepticism, all the more since there are no supporting documents. But it was definitely established by Crowe and Cavalcaselle, the nineteenty-century historians of Italian art and artists, that Giotto was away from Florence in

1318, and in 1920 a group of paintings was discovered in another Polenta-endowed church, San Giovanni Evangelista, which are pretty generally accepted as Giotto's work. Perhaps Vasari merely got his churches wrong.

Finally, we have the generous and tactful Guido da Polenta himself. For although Guido may not have been a member of the Dante coterie in the strictest sense of the word, it is unthinkable that he was not a frequent visitor at the Casa Alighieri. After all, who had brought Dante to Ravenna and why?

He had much to learn and something to contribute. In necessary measure, he did both.

« 4 »

How did Dante occupy himself here? How did he occupy himself in this city which had received him with such open arms and where he now was in such congenial company? How, that is, besides working steadily away at the completion of the *Commedia?*

For there are those who say, nor is their contention unreasonable, that despite the fact that at least one third of the poem seems either to have been written or put into final shape at Ravenna, this would not have been enough to absorb all his energies — energies, incidentally, which had shown no signs whatsoever of burning out with the years. It is also suggested that if indeed he did not have an official post at the Polenta court, he might well — in spite of Guido's many favors — have wished a source of personal income. An independent source, for he was still, as he had always been, independent and proud.

In this connection, Boccaccio offers a theory which has convinced many:

"Dante, then, lived in Ravenna for many years under this noble lord, and here by his teachings he trained many scholars in poetry, and especially poetry in the vulgar tongue. In my judgment, he was the first one to glorify this tongue and to make it esteemed among those of us who are Italians, just as Homer made his language esteemed among the Greeks and Virgil his among the Latins. Before him there was no one who had the feeling for it and the resolution to make this poetry with its numbered syllables and its end-line consonance [rhyme] an instrument for serious artistic endeavor. Hitherto it had only been used for the lightest sort of love trifles."

His textbook, Boccaccio implies, was the *De Vulgari Eloquentia*, which, as you will remember (chapter XVIII), the author of the *Decameron* contends was written at this time and for this purpose. It was not — except possibly but not probably the unfinished book II. But it still could have been used.

Because of this Boccaccio statement and for other reasons, it is thought by many — and by some firmly believed — that Dante held some kind of chair in a supposed University of Ravenna. That he became a teacher with a fixed stipend and with regular classes.

Edmund Gardner is among the former. He at least tentatively accepts the Boccaccio thesis.

"It is possible," he writes in his *Dante*, "that Dante held some kind of a professorship in the local university. Scholars and disciples came to be instructed in the poetic arts, among them, it would seem, Guido da Polenta himself."

But with Corrado Ricci there are neither ifs nor buts.

"Alighieri," he says, "did not go to Ravenna as an exile supported by Guido da Polenta. Many notices compel us to believe that he came there as a reader in vulgar rhetoric at the *studio*."

He supports this contention by citing the opinion of many other Dante scholars. Scheffer-Boichert, he says, considers it to be almost certainly historical truth. Scartazzini after "repeated examinations" is forced "to admit that in truth Dante was in Ravenna in the capacity of a reader or instructor." Macri-Leone, Pasquale Papa, and Edward Rod find the idea ingenious.

So does Michele Barbi.

"It is a hypothesis," Signor Ricci quotes him as saying, "which to us seems happy enough, even if in substance it is based only on the words of Boccaccio and those who copied him."

One of those who copied Boccaccio was Saviozzo da Siena. In his *terza rima* commentary on Dante, he says this:

> Here for the first time Dante began to read
> In vulgar rhetoric, and thus made plain
> To many his poetic harmony.

But there were other relatively early writers who said the same.

Grannozzo Manetti is one of them.

"At Ravenna, therefore, where he dwelt for many years and indeed for the remainder of his life," he writes, "Dante indeed taught poetry to not a few distinguished men. Not a few distinguished men of more than average intelligence he so instructed in their maternal tongue that there were not many of them that could not be called poets in the vulgar."

Signor Ricci also cites the opening words of one more of the many anecdotes about Dante which in those days went their round.

"It so happened that Dante because of the divisions of those parties which were called the Blacks and the Whites was banished from Florence and forbidden to come nearer to it than one hundred miles. Wherefore he wandered about the world and particularly to those places in which he knew there were famous schools, and then after much time had gone by he established himself at Ravenna with Guido da Polenta, who was its lord."

But Ravenna, he says firmly, was one of the said places. It had been at least since the sixth century, when Procopius in his description of Byzantine Italy had noted schools of *grammatica* and eloquence there.

We are therefore asked by these men to imagine Dante in a cap and gown and facing a roomful of students to whom he taught the important art of speaking well and writing well as applied to poetry in Italian. Day by day and every day and for an arranged salary. In this picture he is not, of course, another Magister Romanus like the Magister Romanus who taught him and other Florentines in his own youth. Those who listened to him were not schoolboys but men. But nevertheless he is a paid lecturer and a paid teacher and trammeled by the task's routine.

« 5 »

But Dante pedagogue — even Dante this king of pedagogue — is a concept that others find completely untenable. Among these is Francesco Novati. His arguments — and those of most who take the same position — are roughly as follows:

(1) Although there is evidence that there was teaching at Ravenna, there is no evidence that there was a *studio* or a university there. Nor is it reasonable to suppose there was one.

To be sure — this is Novati's contention — it is reasonably certain that from the sixth century to the tenth there were schools in the city which taught some of the more advanced subjects, but thereafter three centuries lapse in which the place seems to have been in a scholastic doldrums — at any rate above the elementary level — nor does the appointment in 1304 of one Leone of Verona to teach grammar and logic to the young people of the city contradict this. His salary was to be twenty-five *libbre*, less almost by half, if you remember, than beginner lawyer Concoreggio was to get in Lodi. This does not indicate an important position. But there was no reason for there to have been a university in Ravenna. Little more than fifty miles away — and almost forty of these along the Via Emilia — was Bologna with its truly famous university. The Ravennati could go there.

(2) It is stated that Dante taught rhetoric in the vulgar. But in the Middle Ages all teaching was in Latin.

Then Novati sums up positively, if somewhat scornfully, in these words:

"We can say this without hesitation. No Italian university before the sun of the Renaissance shone high above the horizon would have received among its band of instructors a master who, following in the footsteps of Cicero, imparted the principles of vulgar eloquence and taught his disciples to compose sonnets or *canzoni,* or who commented on and spoke about the sonnets and the *canzoni* of others just as he would have explained the poems of Virgil or Horace. Can it be imagined then that this could have taken place in Ravenna during the first twenty-five years of the trecento and when the *Divine Comedy* had hardly begun to be circulated, being largely only recited in bits and pieces by the *canta-storie*" — along with tales about King Arthur and his Round Table and poems about Charlemagne and his twelve peers?

But no sooner has he made this pronouncement than he half contradicts himself.

"As I say this, I do not want to deny in any way that in Ravenna at the court of the courteous lord of Polenta the 'divine old man' was surrounded by an elect and numerous crowd of students and admirers of his genius and his learning who were eager to draw on the treasure house of his instructings."

Over and above this, certain of Novati's statements are demonstrably inaccurate, notably the one about the *Commedia,* for at least the whole of the *Inferno* and much of the *Purgatorio* were known to a great many others than those who listened to them recited at street corners. Nevertheless, common sense and a reasonable examination of what is probable support Novati's conclusion rather than that of Boccaccio, Ricci, and Gardner.

Even as recently as the early part of this century, there was a local legend of a small country lane not very far from Ravenna and on the banks of a half-stream, half-drainage canal called the Scolo Lana. It was known as Poet Lane or Street of the Poets because Dante and his companions supposedly liked to stroll there.

Not in the classroom, then, but on this Vietta degli Poeti, or in the *pineta* with its bird song and its breezes, or under an arbor in his own garden, Dante used to walk and talk. Following him and ever ready to gather up the gold of wisdom which he must have scattered so lavishly were the persons we have enumerated above. His two sons, revering their father and already preparing to preserve his memory. The notary and the notary who wrote poetry. The composer of inscriptions in Latin. The two lawyers. The writer of a Ravenna chronicle. The young Florentine student and the physician from Certaldo. Sometimes — but only on the occasion of a visit to Ravenna, which may have been brief — Giotto. And sometimes Guido Novello himself.

And if you wish to use your imagination, perhaps Antonia too. Antonia bearing a plate or a wicker tray laden with pears and plums and peaches and figs and swelling grapes. Or on occasion a brimming *fiasco* of foaming Romagna wine. For conversation — especially learned conversation — is thirst begetting, and even the Gospel tells us to take sometimes a little wine for the stomach's sake — and for the spirit's sake too.

But imagination is not necessary. It is enough to know that Dante, who had always gladly learned, now gladly taught — but only his followers and his friends.

This I believe to be the true story of Dante instructor, and that it is the true one seems to me to be substantiated by a very charming episode — or really series of episodes — which took place at almost exactly this time.

There was in Bologna a talented young professor, Giovanni del fu Messer Antonio, who taught *grammatica* at the university there from 1319 to 1323 — some say from 1318 to 1325 — and in particular expounded the poetry of Virgil, Statius, Lucan, and Ovid. His was the only chair of poetry in an institution which specialized in law, and because as he taught this poetry it became apparent to all and sundry that he loved Virgil above all poets — that he loved him just a little this side of idolatry — his students and soon everybody knew him as Giovanni del Virgilio.

But if he idolized Virgil and loved the other classic poets, he was not too narrow in his views to read poetry in the vernacular, and even, within limitations, to admire such poetry, provided it at least approached conforming to his high standards.

Some poetry of this kind now came into his hands. He was given a copy of that part of the *Commedia* which had by then reached Bologna. He read it, and then read it avidly, at first only noting that its author was as devoted to Virgil as he was and then suddenly and almost reluctantly that it was by a great poet.

But it was by a great poet, he realized in dismay, who did not write in Latin but instead in the language — in the *ephemeral* language, for it changed from year to year if not from day to day — of the base mechanics and the sordid businessmen of his money-minded city. How could he so squander his genius? Only the language of Cicero and Caesar — and of Virgil — could guarantee immortality.

(This was an idea that would not be thought unusual until almost modern times. Even as late as the seventeeth century, John Milton seriously considered writing his *Paradise Lost* in Latin.)

But the writer of this poem deserved immortality and must be made to seek it. He must be compelled or cajoled into abandoning a course which was so wasteful of his talents. He must be compelled or cajoled into writing a new poem, but in the ancient language. This del Virgilio undertook to do.

And with a poet's weapons. Retiring to his study, he wrote in Virgilian hexameters a piece of poetry which he called a *carmen*, or song. This he sent to Dante.

It began thus:

> Auspicious mouthpiece of the Pierides [*Muses*], who with new songs
> To the world dost bring delight while the tree of life
> Thou dost make flourish as thou settest the threefold limits
> That souls may win by their worth; the wicked falling to Orcus;
> Those seeking the stars winning Lethe; the blessed, lands beyond the sun,
> Why — why alas — to the crowd only dost give things of such import,
> While we, grown pale with longing, have naught of your prophet's fare?

Why? Why indeed? For to do so, del Virgilio continues, is a misuse of time. A common man could as well draw dolphins to the sound of his lyre, the village fool solve the riddle of the Sphinx, as you could teach the mob to understand your hell and heaven. Come! Come! How can you be "sixth of that great company," how can you be worthy of him who led you to heaven if you use vulgar speech? Virgil whom you so admire did not sing in the language of the marketplace. Nor did he choose a subject fit only for harlequins at a country fair.

Nor need Dante.

For just as there was a language available so were there nobler subjects right at hand.

> Tell how Jove's armor-bearer in winged flight sought the stars!
> Tell how a plowman trampled the flowers and the lilies!
> Tell of the Phrygian stags torn by the hound of Molossis!
> Tell of the Ligurian mountains and the ship of Parthenope!

To explain, give up your poem about heaven and hell and instead celebrate in Latin the exploits of your beloved Henry VII. Write an epic about Uguccione della Faggiuola's victory at Montecatini. Take for your subject the defeat of the Paduans by Can Grande della Scala. Relate how King Robert and his Neapolitan fleet carried their war to the very threshold of the republic of Genoa.

If you do this, your fame may reach Herculean Gades — Cadiz, which was beyond the Strait of Gibraltar — in one direction and the flooding

Danube and the famous island of Pharos in the other and thence to the lands where Dido ruled of old.

And if you do this, one thing more. I myself — I, Giovanni del Virgilio — with my own hands will place a crown of laurel on your brow in front of my applauding students!

I myself — if you deem me worthy!

To use a modern equivalent, Giovanni would see to it that Dante was made in effect "an honorary doctor" by one of the two most distinguished universities in the world.

« 6 »

Obviously, Dante could hardly have been other than flattered, for here was praise from a man — and by implication from a place — whose praise counted and was never lightly given.

His response showed that he appreciated this fact. For although he would not accept del Virgilio's invitation, and for reasons he would shortly give, he replied to the poet-professor in a manner which the latter would surely appreciate and which, since he wrote himself, he would recognize had taken thought and time. He answered Giovanni del Virgilio with a Virgilian eclogue — a very winning Latin poem which both imitates and parodies the Roman poet he and Giovanni both so revered. In it he casts himself as Tityrus, an aging shepherd. With him is Meliboeus, a young shepherd. Meliboeus is Dino Perini. Reclining under an oak tree, they tend their flocks together.

Meliboeus speaks first:

"Tityrus, what does Mopsus want? What wants he? Tell me," he said.

Mopsus, the third person in the eclogue, is Giovanni del Virgilio.

Tityrus smiles and at first does not answer, but as Meliboeus continues to importune him finally he does.

But with a lecture:

"You fool! You stupid fool!" I said. "Your goats your care
Should be when of your meager fare you do not complain,
And those pastures should be unknown where lofty Menalus
With his peak even when the sun's at noon doth keep in shadow
And where many colored flowers do inlay the grass."

Those lofty pastures are Bologna, where, even Tityrus admits, Mopsus plays his reed so wondrously beside silver willows and splashing streams that even the lions come down from the mountains, forgetting their rage.

Obviously — all the more after this glowing description — Meliboeus persists. The young shepherd wants to go thither — with Tityrus. Then he could learn the songs Mopsus was singing and teach them to his goats — to his students.

And Tityrus could take him.

But Tityrus could not and would not. He is better off where he is, he says. True, in that city where others wrangled in the courts of law Mopsus has dedicated himself to the Muses. But he grows pale and wan doing this. He does not prosper.

In explanation, it should be noted that Giovanni del Virgilio is reputed to have had considerable difficulty in collecting even his inadequate salary.

Besides — and it is thus he answers Meliboeus's anguished plea for him not to rusticate in Ravenna forever — it is now too late, at any rate as far as Bologna is concerned.

> "O Meliboeus, vanished, yea blown away by the wind,
>   And all the poets and their glory and their renown.
>   The Muses have but scantily maintained the studious Mopsus."

But besides that, there was another place — and here he echoes *Paradiso* XXV, which must have been written at approximately the same time — to which he wished to go if he ever left Ravenna and where, rather than in Bologna, he hoped to be given the poetic crown.

> "Were it not rather better my triumphant locks
>   Once auburn should hide beneath the laurel their silver
>   Beside my native Arno if I should ever come there."

"If you should ever come there!" cries Meliboeus. "But don't you know that time is fleeting? The very goats we first bred are growing old. When will this happen?"

When, replies Tityrus, "all the heavens about the earth and all my star-born souls" are as well known as hell is. Cannot Mopsus give him even that time?

"Mopsus!" cries Meliboeus. "Why Mopsus?"

Tityrus explains thus:

> "Have you not noted the scorn with which he greets
>   My *Comedy?* He calls it idle women's chatter which stales upon their lips.
>   He says the Castalian sisters [*Muses*] would shame to acknowledge it."

"Then how will you win him over?" asks Meliboeus.

"It will be easy," replies Tityrus.

He tells how:

> "I have a ewe well known to you and by far the choicest
> Of the whole herd, and her milk so abundant is
> That she can scarcely support her udder's weight.
> Under yon rock she feeds upon the lush grass.
> Not jostling the herd, she pastures alone,
> Yet, although she is never driven, comes in willingly
> At milking time. From her I will milk, then,
> With skillful hands ten measures and send them to Mopsus.
> Meanwhile take thou charge of the butting herds
> And crunch with your teeth the hard crusts we get for food."

"I will send him," Dante is saying, "ten cantos of my *Paradiso*."

That should be enough.

« 7 »

It is pleasant but not surprising to be able to record that his young admirer responded in kind — with a so-called responsive eclogue which showed that even if he still insisted that Latin and not Italian was the only truly immortal language, he was a great deal more than a crusty if still youthful pedant. The idyll is allowed to continue, for clearly Giovanni is delighted both by Dante's light and playful good humor and by the fact that it was now very clear to Giovanni that he could write Latin almost as skillfully as he wrote his native tongue.

"Divine old man!" he begins, and dealing with his eclogue I will for the most part summarize. "You shall be Maro's heir" — Virgil's heir, for Virgil's name was Publius Virgilius Maro — "or indeed you shall be Maro's self. And I hope — although I cannot wish for you to return to the ungrateful city — that your silver hairs will there indeed be crowned by Phyllis. But in the meantime come here. Come here where marjoram and other herbs are fragrant and where poppies bring reposeful sleep. Alexis [not identified] will strew your couch with thyme. Nisa [a lady, but also not identified] will bathe your feet. The young and old will come to see you."

Then he added a final tempting morsel:

"Muso will be here."

Muso was Albertino Mussato, the poet-historian whom Dante had surely known either in Verona or Padua. Like Dante, Mussato was now an exile. He had been driven from his native Padua.

"But I dream in vain," he concludes, "for even if I should persuade you, Iolas [Guido da Polenta] would not permit you to leave the cave which he has given you."

Yet he still refused to give up hope.

"What do I hear?" he says. "Why does yonder heifer low? It is because her udders are heavy too. Then I will rise and run to milk her, and with the milk fill ample bowls in which to soften the crusts which I will give Tityrus if he comes here."

Obviously this milk was a poem written by Del Virgilio.

If he comes here — and if he wishes his Bolognese admirer's offering!

For to send milk to a shepherd is presumptious.

"So spoke I," is the eclogue's conclusion. "I and my comrades. Then the sun rose upon the mount."

« *8* »

Iolas never did, or perhaps Dante never asked him to, for his cave — his cottage — suited him well. But he did reply to Del Virgilio with a second eclogue, which, however, it is thought generally, did not reach the latter during Dante's life. Indeed, because of this, and because it is written in the third person, there are some who do not think it was the work of Dante. They suggest that it was written after his death by one of his disciples. This to me does not seem likely, however. Its style and its thinking are too much like that of the first eclogue. If he wrote one, he wrote both.

Technically as well as in substance, it completes the cycle. It brought the eclogue to where and what an eclogue classically should be. For not only does it report a conversation between shepherds — this had been done in the first eclogue and was a *sine qua non* of pastoral and bucolic poetry — but it transfers the scene to Sicily, the home of Theocritus, the first writer of this kind of poetry, and that is where a true eclogue should take place.

It begins with a lovely, if purposefully artificial, description of midday. Wing-footed Eous and "the other steeds" the other three steeds which with Eous drew the chariot of the sun — have reached the zenith. The sunlit trees and rocks which at other times "would spread a longer shadow on the grass" stand out sharply above a countryside that seems to blaze. It is intensely hot, and therefore Tityrus and Alphesiboeus (Francesco da Milotti), who is with him, betake themselves to a refreshing woodland of linden and plane trees. There Tityrus, "freighted with his years" and content to breathe in the fragrance, dozes beneath a maple tree.

Alphesiboeus speaks to him.

All things should be where they belong, he says. The souls of men are borne upward toward the stars. Swans swim whitely on the Cayster River. Fishes swim in the sea, and they forgather there. Hyrcanian tigers maraud in the Caucasus Mountains. Serpents swarm in Lydia.

He continues:

> "Then I should wonder, my fellow shepherds should wonder too,
> Why those caves fit for the Cyclops, those arid rocks
> Beneath Mount Etna, should be pleasing unto Mopsus."

Tityrus is about to answer when Meliboeus comes up. So hard has he run that he is gasping for breath, and so "the older shepherd," having "lifted up his hoary locks," asks the panting youth what the important tidings are that have caused him so to strain his lungs.

Meliboeus tries to compose himself for a reply, but before he can utter a word his pipe itself begins to play a tune. "It happened on the lush well-watered banks where Reno and Savena." It is the renewed invitation — the invitation renewed in the responsive eclogue — to visit Bologna.

This time Tityrus seems on the point of accepting, but Alphesiboeus interrupts.

> "O venerated old man, the sweet dew-spent fields of Pelorus
> Would you thus leave to hie you to the cave of the Cyclops?"

"Why not?" cries Tityrus, doubtless to the delight of Meliboeus. "And why do you thus plague me?"

"Why?" asks Alphesiboeus. "Why?"

Then he answers:

"Don't you realize that the singing pipe conveys to you the same kind of message that the reeds did to Midas when, counseled by the god of wine, he turned the moist Pactolian sand to gold? Fortunate sage, do not trust the flattering bait which would draw you to a seaside realm that is strewn only with volcanic pumice. And besides — do not do such a wrong to the dryads of our grove" — presumably the women of Ravenna who were drawn to Dante as women were everywhere — "do not do such a wrong to your flocks."

"This you must know, O more than half of my heart," says Tityrus. "Mopsus offered his love to me because he believes that having fled affrighted from Pyraneus's evil heart" — i.e., having been driven from Florence as an exile — "I must perforce live between the Po mouth and the Rubicon. He commends the Aetnean seacoast as better. He does not know that we live upon the tender grass of a mountain in Sicily."

He pauses.

"Yet even at that," he continues, "Mopsus could persuade me to leave this place and go to his cave if I did not fear Polyphemus."

Who is Polyphemus?

As usual, there have been many guesses and many opinions. To those who like symbolical interpretations, Polyphemus is no specific person. Instead he represents the general depravity and corruption of Italy. Others suggest he is the city of Bologna, once friendly to Dante's Whites, now a Black ally. Those who believe he was a single individual offer the following possibilities: Romeo Pepoli of the renowned Pepoli family, leader of the Bolognese Black Guelphs until he was driven from the city in 1321; King Robert; Diego de la Rat; and two Florentine *podestà*'s (this presumes that the hand of Florence reached out that far), namely Ranieri di Zaccaria and Fulcieri da Calboli.

Corrado Ricci suggests still another person. He ingeniously convinces himself that Polyphemus was a man who bore the not entirely glorious name of Venetico Caccianemico. This, of course, was not the Venetico Caccianimico whom Dante had put into hell for shamelessly selling his sister to Azzo (or Obbizzo) d'Este. This Venetico had died before 1300. It was rather his grand-nephew of the same name, who was also known as Zenga. Dante feared, argues Ricci, that he might try to avenge the harsh strictures he had made against the first Venetico, just as bravos hired by Branca d'Oria's son had avenged his strictures against Branca.

King Robert, however, is the most likely of these. Polyphemus was not merely a Cyclops but the chief of the Cyclops. He could hardly have stood for anyone less.

But whether he was King Robert or someone else, or no one but instead a symbol, he gives Alphesiboeus the argument he needed.

"Who does not fear Polyphemus?" he cries. "Polyphemus whose jaws forever drip with human blood?"

He lists certain of his victims. Acis, loved by Galatea. The followers of Achaemenides, who, trapped in the cave after they had been left behind on Sicily by Ulysses, were devoured one by one.

Then he perorates:

"Dear as my life, I pray that never a dreadful longing
May urge thee to let Reno and her naiad [*Savena*] lure thither
The illustrious head which the Pruner speeds to crown
With leaves undying which the heavenly Virgin hath plucked for him."

Tityrus must remain where he is. Honors are coming. Honors — and here there is the sad note that he himself knew that his sands were running out — even if only in heaven.

The older shepherd makes no reply, but his smile indicates that he has listened and been convinced. The shadows lengthen. The air grows chilly. The shaggy goats wend their way homeward.

The poem ends thus:

> Meanwhile Iolas the prudent, hid near at hand,
> Had heard all that was said and told it to us.
> He told it to us and we, Mopsus, tell it to thee.

« 9 »

What is all this about?

What is the significance and meaning of this little group of poems?

Why are they important?

Is it because, as Wilmon Brewer suggests, they mark the first competent attempt — after an interval of one thousand years — to restore the ancient pastoral poetry in its classic loveliness and beauty?

This certainly they do, for, as Brewer also points out, they not only show Dante at his most mature but they also combine keen observation of nature with "the harmonious blending of diverse materials," and to this "they add a genial humor very rare in the pastoral, and at times an unusual solemnity" because of the great issues they discuss. They led too to a reestablishment of Arcadia in the geography of the imagination and to a kind of writing that is reflected in the works of such diverse authors as Sannazaro, Tasso, Guarini, Spenser, Shakespeare, Cervantes, Lope de Vega, and even Milton.

Or is it because they contain hidden — and often not hidden — biography?

This they do too.

They definitely establish for the first time, or confirm it if we believe our other sources, not only the pattern but many of the details of his life in Ravenna. They enable us to set down with some confidence this the penultimate chapter of his life.

What do they establish or confirm?

(1) That he was content with the way his days went. That his goats — his students or disciples — were well fed, and that if at times he thought it necessary to make the conventional complaints of a poet about the meager fare and crusts of bread on which he had to live he was, generally speaking, satisfied with his cave — his little house — and with his condition.

(2) That he lived in Ravenna for at least a reasonable length of time. Not less than four years, for it would take that long for his newly weaned kids to become fully mature goats.

(3) That the writing of the *Commedia* went well. The ewe, you will remember, from whose udders Tityrus sent ten brimming pails of milk to Mopsus came in willingly at milking time.

(4) That he had the friends already noted and that of them the two most important and dear to him were Dino Perini and Francesco da Milotti. A careful reading of the eclogues would seem to indicate that Dino was the paid and formal teacher which Dante was not. It is also interesting to note that the hint that Dante was not very far from his last days comes from Francesco da Milotti, who was a physician.

(5) There were at least some in intellectual Bologna who deplored two things. First, that Dante insisted on writing in Italian. And second, that he had withdrawn to what seemed to them a cultural backwater.

Giovanni del Virgilio was the spokesman for this group, and the eclogues show, as we have already seen, that he extended to Dante two invitations to come to Bologna and that he twice refused them.

The eclogues give some of the reasons. But the basic reason was that Ravenna provided him with all that he needed. The backwaters of Giovanni del Virgilio were to him a sheltered and deep pond.

This does not mean that its surface was not ever ruffled. Quite the contrary, as will be indicated by three more of the many anecdotes which were circulated about him and which were widely believed.

Dante, says the first of them, was very speculative and contemplative — we would say absentminded — and one day as Mass was being celebrated he was so preoccupied with other matters that he neither knelt when the host was lifted nor removed his hat. Some of his enemies saw this and hastened to the archbishop — to Archbishop Concoreggio — and charged Dante with being a heretic.

The archbishop summoned him into his presence and asked him if the charges were true — if he had neither knelt nor removed his hat.

"It is," replied Dante, "but here is the reason. My mind was so intent upon God that I did not remember what my body was supposed to do. But these men of ways so evil had their eyes more on me than on God. If their eyes had been on God, they would not have seen what I did."

Another story tells of a jealous scholar.

He listened as a group of other scholars were discussing — and with great reverence — Dante's enormous store of knowledge. Finally he could contain himself no longer.

"You are discussing the knowledge of a rogue!" he cried angrily.

"Why a rogue?" he was asked.

"Because," he blurted, "because —" Then he caught himself. "Because Dante in his poetry has said everything that is worthy of memory and renown and has left nothing for the rest of us."

A third story tells of another charge of heresy.

A learned Franciscan friar, who held the office of inquisitor, once confronted Dante in a Ravenna church.

"Are you that Dante who says that he went to hell and purgatory and heaven?" he asked him.

"I am Dante Alighieri of Florence."

"Oh," said the inquisitor, "then you are the one who goes about writing *canzoni* and sonnets and other such trash."

Dante nodded.

"You would do better to write a book in Latin and to have it based on the Church of God, for the trifles you have written will bring you to the bad end you deserve."

Dante made as if to answer that he would be glad to, but the inquisitor interrupted him.

"I have no time now, but we will meet on such and such a day" — and he named one — "and I will then see what you know about these matters."

Dante went off to his room and there "he wrote that *capitolo* which is called the 'little creed,' and in it he set down the whole Christian faith." On the appointed day, he showed it to the inquisitor, who marveled at it. And thereafter he and Dante became good friends.

This "little creed" — it is only twelve lines long, and begins "I believe in God and hope for life eternal" — is generally regarded as apocryphal, but its story and the other two stories show some of Dante's harassments and annoyances.

They were only harassments, however, and as the eclogues show he still found the vales and woodlands of Trinacria (Sicily — but here Ravenna) cool and refreshing. So when Francesco da Milotti (Alphesiboeus), plainly sent to him by Guido da Polenta (Iolas), came to him with his arguments against leaving, he was in a frame of mind to listen to them.

It was tempting to think of himself in Bologna, an oracle for worshiping students and surrounded by the adulators — but undoubtedly the intelligent adulators — whom Giovanni del Virgilio would have provided.

But it was more sensible to remain in Ravenna.

He decided to be sensible. He decided to stay.

« *10* »

Stay he did. With two exceptions — one of which came to no good end — he never departed from the Polenta city which he had thoughtfully chosen, living there the life which has been described and with a spiritual self-possession which was appropriate — and perhaps necessary — but somewhat new.

His first absence took place either late in 1319 or very early in 1320 and involved him in the fringes of an extremely curious episode. This was the grotesque effort made by Galeazzo Visconti, the lord of Milan, to persuade one Bartolommeo Cagnolati to kill Pope John XXII by means of incantations and spells. The whole story is too complicated to set down in full detail, but its essence is this. Cagnolati, a Milanese clerk, pretended to be a sorcerer, and Galeazzo sent for him and had a servant put into his hands a silver statuette of a naked man. It was about a palm in height, and had "*Jacobus papa Iohannes*" written on its forehead. On its breast was the symbol of Saturn and the word Amaymon. Amaymon was the name of a devil.

"I wish you to use this to slay the pope," he said, and then outlined a witch's brew of strange ingredients he should also use, among which was the sap of aconite which Cagnolati was said to possess.

"Burn these and chant certain spells and you will accomplish my purpose."

Cagnolati refused.

"I have no aconite. At the urging of a holy friar, I threw it away."

He was dismissed, having first been made to swear that he would say nothing of what he had been asked to do.

But instead of keeping his oath, the fellow hastened to Avignon, where he formally accused Galeazzo of the crime and for this was rewarded with one hundred florins.

Then, foolishly, he returned to the Visconti, who threw him into prison and kept him there for forty-two days, after which they fined him and released him but kept him under surveillance by their spies.

It was well they did, for they soon needed him again. Galeazzo Visconti had given the statuette to one Pietro Nani, a dependent of both Can Grande and Uguccione della Faggiuola. Nani claimed knowledge of magic arts and said that he could use them to destroy Pope John. But when he failed, and for the failure blamed the fact that the pope was protected by "a serpent's horn given him by Countess Marguerite de Foix," Galeazzo again summoned Cagnolati.

He showered him with favors and then took him to Piacenza, where he led him into a secret chamber.

"Know you," he whispered to him there, "that the pope is enemy not only to us but to the whole Ghibelline cause, and that it is necessary that he be removed from this world!"

Cagnolati nodded but made no sign that he was prepared to help in doing this.

"Know you further that I have summoned Messer Dante Alighieri of Florence to come to me on this business but that I still want to put it in your hands."

"I would be content to have Dante undertake it."

"But know you," said Visconti finally, "that under no circumstances whatsoever would I permit Dante to come into this matter, and that under no circumstances whatsoever would I have told him about it, and that I want you to undertake it because I have confidence in you."

Obviously he would not have told Dante under any circumstances, for there were at least two circles in Dante's hell in which Dante could and probably would have placed him.

Cagnolati now changed his tune. He pretended to accept and was given the statuette. Then for the second time he fled to Avignon, reaching it on September 11. He made a second deposition and was rewarded with a fat pension on which he lived very prosperously for nine years.

Now what can we make of all this?

Is it gibberish? Or did Galeazzo really send for Dante, whom he really believed to be a sorcerer and an enchanter?

Although improbable, this is by no means impossible. Throughout the Middle Ages, Virgil was thought of as a magician quite as much as a poet. He was said to have possessed a horse of bronze which prevented all the horses of Naples from becoming swaybacked; a bronze fly which as long as it stood on his doorsill kept the whole city free from flies; and a magic storeroom in which meat could be kept for six weeks without spoiling. It was told of him that he had made a statue of a bowman with drawn bow and arrow ready to fly, and that as long as this arrow was kept pointed at Vesuvius it would not erupt. It was related that he built the Castel dell' Ovo upon an egg. It would stand as long as the egg remained unbroken.

And Dante was a disciple of Virgil. He was a disciple in poetry. Why not in magic too?

The answer is we do not know. We do not know, that is, whether Galeazzo summoned him, or, if he did, whether Dante answered those summons and then departed scornfully when he discovered what was wanted of him.

But we do know that he was in Mantua — and at the time. Mantua is very near Piacenza.

We know because he himself tells us so. He tells us that he was in Mantua and that while he was there "a certain question fell into dispute"; it was debated by many, he says, but, "because in arguing they looked only at the surface but did not penetrate to the truth," it was never resolved.

The question: "the location and the shape or form of two elements, namely water and earth," and specifically "whether water in its own sphere — that is, within its own natural boundaries — was in any place higher than the earth which rises from the water and which we call the inhabited world."

To have something unresolved went against the grain with Dante, especially when it was unresolved because of superficial arguments.

"Wherefore," he said, "since I was brought up from my boyhood to love truth, I could not dissuade myself from further discussing the matter, but instead determined to tell the truth about it and to refute the arguments of those on the other side. This I did equally from love of truth and hatred of falsehood."

Further discuss it he did, but not in Mantua, where minds clearly — at any rate, as Dante saw it — were far too muddled to make this worth his effort. He discussed and he did not — also in his own opinion — leave it unresolved.

"This philosophic matter" — here is his own opinion of his own accomplishment — "was settled *once and for all* under the rule of that unconquered lord, the Lord Can Grande della Scala, representing the Holy Roman Empire."

Settled once and for all, "except for," as he felt compelled to inter-polate bitingly, "a few who, burning with excessive charity, will not accept the invitations of others and who, parading their humility, poor pensioners of the Holy Spirit, refused to be present at the talk lest they should seem to endorse the excellences of someone else."

"It was settled" in the sanctuary of the blessed Helena — the little chapel of Sant' Elena under the very shadow of the Duomo — "and before the assembled clergy of Verona."

Except, of course, the few noted just above.

"This was done one thousand three hundred and twenty years from the Nativity of our Lord Jesus Christ. The day was the seventh from the ides of January and the fourteenth before the calends of February."

January 20, 1320. His sojourn in Mantua could not have been much before that.

The talk itself — the 4500-word *Quaestio de Aqua et Terra,* a very odd and pedantic lecture which perhaps took an hour to deliver — would hardly be worth even mentioning if it were not that Dante delivered it and that, next to the very last cantos of the *Commedia,* it was the final thing to come from his pen.

It is entirely medieval in its presentation, and yet it seems hard to believe that even in those days anyone took seriously the arguments which Dante uses. One of them: the noblest element must be higher than a less noble one. Earth was the noblest element.

But even as we say this — and even in this curious opus — we see Dante groping toward something closer to what we would now call a scientific approach.

We must rely upon our senses and our reason, he says.

"For by our senses we perceive that throughout the wide world water flows downward to the sea, whether northern or southern, eastern or western."

And our reason tells us that this would not happen unless the sources of these rivers and the courses of their channels were not higher than the sea.

But then he reverts to the medieval.

Why were they higher, and furthermore why was the northern hemisphere lifted up and higher than the southern hemisphere?

The answer: it is God's will.

"Let men desist, therefore; let them desist from searching out things which are beyond our understanding, and let them search only to such point as they may. Then they may draw themselves to immortal and divine things to their utmost power and may give over things which are too great for their power."

Let them desist from searching out things which are beyond our understanding. The recognition that there are things beyond our understanding is part of what makes Dante — even medieval Dante — somebody we still listen to. For beyond each door there is another door, and as we penetrate through the atom to what makes the atom and then to what makes those things that make the atom we will find that beyond each answer there is another question, and that there is no end in sight. Dante knew this seven hundred years ago, even though he expressed it in terms which we might not use today.

« 11 »

There is no reason to believe that Dante remained in Verona any longer than was needed for him to set people right upon this matter of the land and the sea, and, of course, to call on and to pay his respects to Can Grande.

Then he returned to Ravenna — and gladly.

This time he meant to stay there.

"I now return to Ravenna," he told Cecco d'Ascoli, the strange, often vindictive, always eloquent poet who after Dante's death met the death

Dante always feared; namely, he was burned at the stake. "And I will never leave any more."

He had no reason to, he thought.

But within a few months, or at any rate within a year, something beyond his control — and probably even beyond the control of Guido da Polenta — intervened and forced him to change his plans.

XXVI

The Last Mission. The End

IT took place in an area in which Dante had several times demonstrated more than the average competence — that of diplomacy and the negotiations between lord and lord or state and state. For geography — geography and the inevitable clash of interests which, given the character and ambitions of the two protagonists, resulted from this geography — had brought a direct confrontation between Ravenna and her most powerful neighbor, and in this the poet was called on to intervene.

Here a careful examination of the right kind of map of northeastern Italy will help a good deal. Beginning at Cattolica, just north of Focara — named for its watch fires which warned seamen of the adverse, stormy winds which are so often found there and where in 1312 Guido del Cassero and Angiolello da Carignano (*Inferno* XXVIII) were drowned at the orders of Malatestino-of-the-One-Eye da Rimini — was a seventy-mile stretch of sandy beaches which extended at least to the mouth of the Po. Behind it — at least in the northern part — was the *pineta*, much larger then than it is today. And behind the *pineta* — although technically the seacoast was part of it too — was the Romagna itself, mainly forested mountains — but some of them were steep and bare — and fertile plains.

In this small province lived some of the most backward and ignorant peasants in all Europe and some of the most turbulent lords. Benvenuto da Imola tells a story about one of the former.

One day as Guido da Montefeltro held court in Forlì a rustic from the hills (*rusticus montanus*) came to him to deliver a cartload of pears and Guido very graciously asked him to stay to dine.

"I cannot," he said, "for it is going to rain."

"But my astrologer" — this was Dante's Guido Bonatti of *Inferno* XX — "has examined the heavens and he says it will not."

"My donkey," replied the peasant, "knows more than your astrologer. When he came out of his stall his ears stood up and he twitched them."

"Will it be a heavy rain?"

"Yes, my lord, for he twitched them out of the ordinary."

The sun shone, and he rode off to the laughter of the bystanders.

"But within an hour," reports Benvenuto dutifully, "it began to thunder, and there was such a downfall it could be called a deluge."

But despite the ignorant peasants — and sometimes their ignorance was of a less comic nature; despite the ruinous floods which often submerged whole villages, the devastating earthquakes, and the plagues of locusts; despite the fact that large parts of it were *montagna* where bears and wolves marauded and where only sheep- or goat-grazing and charcoal-burning could be carried on; and, finally, despite the depredations of the above-named turbulent lords — the land was so infested with these brigands that farms were fortified and the inhabitants of Spoleto were astonished when Giraldus Cambrensis from distant Britain crossed the Apennines to them without being robbed — despite all this, it was still — relatively speaking — not poor.

It produced, so it was said, grain, wine, oil, fish, meat, salt, eggs, and cheese. Faenza was celebrated for its *fava* beans, Cesena for its figs, and Forlì for its aromatic herbs. I leave out its manufactures, although the pottery of Faenza would later become famous throughout the world as *faïence*, while Faenza linen, using Romagnole flax, had been made and was known since Roman days. "Romandiola," said Benvenuto da Imola, "among all the Italian provinces is the most pleasant, and it is the most productive of all good things." This was only partly local pride.

« 2 »

Obviously, Ravenna — and its Polenta lords — did not dominate the whole province. This was indeed a place where every villager tried to be a Marcellus, tried to make himself a tyrant. It would be so until the days when Romagnole Sforza Attendolo (1369–1424) dropped his plow to become a *condottiere* and subsequently to found the dynasty that supplanted the Visconti in Milan. To name a few, Guido da Montefeltro and then the Ordelaffi ruled in Forlì; Maghinardo da Susinana and then the Manfredi in Faenza; the Alidosi and others in Imola.

In point of fact, Ravenna did not even dominate the whole seacoast. In the southern part — after you had crossed the Rubicon — were Rimini with its own powerful lords and — before you came to this small, famous river — Cesenatico, which has been variously described as the little fishing village it still is and as a small town built as recently as 1302 as a military seaport for Cesena, a dozen or so miles inland. The latter is probably true.

But in the northern part of the Romagna coast, from Comacchio southward — or *sometimes* from Comacchio southward, for Comacchio more than once changed hands — to Cervia with its salt pans, in whose piazza a traveler could see "a hill of white sand, gleaming like marble," described as only one of the "many mountains" of the same, Ravenna ruled supreme.

It controlled thirty miles of coast, and because of their location these thirty miles were, speaking strategically, the most important miles.

(Rimini to the south had some overseas shipping and served as an *entrepôt* for Ragusa — Dubrovnik — and for such commerce — it was not much — as there was with Dalmatia. But it did little business with the hinterland and could not dominate it.)

It had, too, a seaport of a sort, for Ravenna was only three miles inland during the fourteenth century instead of the seven that it is now, and Chiassi, the Roman Classis, if it was silting rapidly and so could only handle "little small ships," as the Venetians contemptuously called them, could handle a fair number of them.

To protect these and the modest foreign trade they carried, to safeguard them and this expanse of shore from Slavic pirates who would be as eager to raid the Ravennati as they were to trade with Rimini, to protect its salt trade — almost their monopoly — and possibly to extend its influence, it is not surprising that Ravenna turned its thoughts toward the sea. Guido da Polenta was less swashbuckling than his father or his uncles and his cousins, but he was still a Romagnole lord who believed in taking and keeping. It is not surprising that he might have tried to establish his city as at least a minor maritime power.

« 3 »

Unfortunately, however, north of him was a major maritime power. Beyond the reticulated mouths of the Po, beyond its marshy delta, were more sandy beaches and then twenty-five miles of narrow *lidi* (barrier bars which rose high enough above the water to be habitable) backed by a shallow lagoon.

In the midst of this lagoon — like a seagull nesting on the water or like sapphires and rubies in the sunlight, and near at hand were those other nesting seagulls, Murano, Burano, Mazzorbo, and Torcello — stood Venice. With its outposts established wherever ships could sail or men traded, we have already suggested that it was one of the world's most resplendent cities.

It was also one of the world's most successful ones. Not only did it, as Wordsworth put it, "hold the gorgeous East in fee," but it sought to make the West pay tribute too.

"The Venetians are greedy men," says Fra Salimbene. "They are stubborn men and outrageous men, and they would gladly make the whole world submit to them if they but could. They treat the merchants who come to them very badly. They sell to them at high prices, and they lay many tolls upon the same man in the same voyage. If any merchant brings any goods to Venice, he cannot take them back with him. He must sell them whether he wishes to or not. And if a ship is driven into their harbor by any misfortune, it may not leave until its captain has sold them all its cargo."

Presumably at any price they chose to offer.

They justified this by pleading motives of piety.

"It was God's will that drove the ship to us," Fra Salimbene reports them as saying. "We cannot go against God's will."

And they would brook no rival. Whether it was bickering among the quarreling Frankish knights of the Morea (this was the Peloponnesus, and the bickering hurt Venetian trade); or what they — the Venetians of all people! — were pleased to call Byzantine treachery and deviousness; or merely what they deemed to be a threat to their access to the Terra Firma (their name for the mainland of Italy), they met anything that infringed on, or even seemed to infringe on, their interest with immediate action. This usually got results.

Fra Salimbene — again Fra Salimbene — tells us of one of these occasions:

"The Venetians," he says, "had taken a fifty years' lease" of a castle which commanded the mouth of the "Ravenna canal." This castle — although Benvenuto da Imola says that the Venetians built Marcabò rather than leased it — was almost certainly the Marcabò of Pier da Medicina (*Inferno* XXVIII), and the Venetians had acquired it — or built it — so that they "could control the navigation of the river and compel all inbound traffic to submit to their control." The "Ravenna canal" was probably the Po di Primaro, which in those days — for the course of the Po has radically changed more than once — was the principal mouth of the river and not very far north of Ravenna.

But now the lease had expired, and instead of pulling out the Venetians moved in a greater force than ever and tore down the castle's wooden walls to replace them with ones of stone.

Then and then only did they take off the mask.

"They utterly closed the canal to the Lombards so that they could draw no supplies from either the Romagna or the March of Ancona. Yet if it had not been for this hindrance they might have drawn from these places corn and wine and oil, fish and flesh and salt and pigs and all the other good things necessary for man's life."

Competition thus removed, the Venetians, laden with goods that could not be gotten anywhere else, moved in bag and baggage, and "their trade methods were so astute and their *visdomini* [consuls] were such active political agents that the Bolognese found themselves outbought and outsold even in their own districts."

In self-defense the latter were compelled to build their own fortress also at the mouth of the Po di Primaro, and for a while the two fortresses glared at each other.

"Then the Venetians came up with a great fleet and with engines for siege, and they battered the castle with mangonels and catapults. But the men of Bologna defended it valiantly, and the Venetians retired."

But not permanently, for the men of Venice, when they had set their minds on anything, never gave up. They waited for two or three years, by which time some three to five hundred of the Bolognese "had died by reason of the unwholesomeness of the sea air" — swamp air is what he should have said — "and the multitudes of fleas and gnats and flies and gadflies."

Then they indicated that they would receive a Bolognese ambassador. This man, Fra Peregrino di Polesino, a Franciscan, came to them, and with him the Venetians consented to make what they called a generous peace. The Bolognese need not destroy the castle. They could dismantle it. They did and gave the wood to the Franciscans of Ravenna!

« *4* »

This was in 1269, but the Venetians were no less greedy fifty-two years later. In 1321, they were no less stubborn and outrageous and, if they would not necessarily "gladly make the whole world submit to them," they certainly were no more willing to share Po navigation — or control of Adriatic coastal waters — with anyone else than they had been when Bologna threatened to make them do this in the years of the Po di Primaro war.

Nor would they.

But this time it was not Bologna who threatened or seemed to. It was Ravenna. At last under able lordship — it had been since the Polentas seized power in 1270, and now this power was consolidated — the city down whose streets emperors and then exarchs had walked when Venice was little more than a collection of shacks built on larch pilings like the lake dwellings of their Bronze Age *terramare* ancestors, this city dared to lift up its head. Its salt, the salt that came from its Cervia — and because of poor refrigeration, salt was like gold in the Middle Ages; cities rioted when it was not delivered — it dared to sell on its own terms. It engaged in coastal trade without always troubling to comply with Venetian regulations. Its ships may have even entered the great river, for Marcabò had been destroyed in 1312.

This could not be tolerated, nor would Venice tolerate it. But first a justification must be found — or invented — for even in those days a state did not like to appear to be the aggressor. This Venice did.

"The Ravennati," cried her doge Giovanni Soranzo, "have seized our ships and killed one of the captains and his crew, and they have wounded others without any provocation whatsoever and while our two cities were at peace."

It is entirely possible that this was true. The distinction between piracy and legitimate warfare was not clearly drawn in those days and, as a Sacchetti story makes plain, the seadogs of the *lito Adriatico* were rough fellows who were quite ready, after a shore evening of drinking, to move in upon an inn *cum fustibus et cum lanternis* (with cudgels and with lanterns) and with an intent to murder and rob all within. They would not have been less ruffianly on the high seas, and certainly a ship of Venice would have seemed a fair prize to them, particularly since the Venetians were hated for their arrogance by all seamen.

But, equally, the story of this *zuffa* (scuffle), as it came to be called, may have been a total fabrication. It is immaterial. For Venice wanted a pretext and now she had one, and of it she would avail herself to the utmost.

But first she must prepare her citizens. They must know that war was imminent.

On August 11, 1321, therefore, the doge convened the great council.

"Relations," he told it solemnly, "between us and Ravenna grow worse from day to day."

This was an understatement. Almost certainly relations with Ravenna had already been broken.

Then and then only did he proceed toward action.

On August 17, he summoned to his presence Niccolò di Marsilio and directed him to proceed to Forlì. There he must present himself to Cecco Ordelaffi, its lord. He must tell Cecco that the doge had listened carefully to the proposals made by Cecco's own emissary, Giacomo de' Bianchi, on the matter of a joint war against Ravenna, that he agreed with them, and that he urged Cecco to begin hostilities as soon as possible.

"Inform him that I have made arrangements to have three thousand gold florins sent to him as soon as this can be done. This is in part payment for the three hundred knights he is supplying."

He would pay the rest as soon as Cecco reopened the campaign "against the damned and evil city that is the enemy of both of us."

The doge also directed Niccolò to promise and pledge Cecco in the name of Venice that no peace would be made with Ravenna without first advising Cecco and the Forlivese and including them in its terms. He was also to promise that for the duration of the war Venice would provide Forlì with salt and grain. This would be made part of a formal agreement provided that the city of Forlì on its part swore orally, and incorporated this in a written agreement, that it would make war and continue to supply the agreed-upon horsemen.

An ambassador charged with a like mission was sent to Rimini too. But evidently without much hope. For in a letter which he carried to Pandolfo Malatesta, its *podestà* and brother of Francesca's Paolo, in which the doge set down the injuries "done to us by Guido da Polenta and the city of Ravenna" — including the attack upon Venetian ships — and in which he promised vengeance for these "crimes," he merely cautioned Rimini against any breach of neutrality.

"Under no circumstances," he warned, "are you to permit troops coming to the assistance of Ravenna to pass through your territory. This would be considered an unfriendly act and one that showed that you are an enemy of the Venetian signory and wish to do it harm."

Messages of similar import were delivered by an ambassador to independent-minded Cesena and by accredited emissaries to Imola and Faenza. Neither on the right nor on the left was Ravenna to receive any help.

But Venice was, it appeared, and from the place which could deliver such help most effectively. On August 22, couriers from Niccolò di Marsilio disembarked on the Riva degli Schiavoni and strode urgently to the doge's palace. They bore the Ordelaffi answer.

"Cecco," he had instructed them to report, "has formally promised the doge and the council that he will declare himself the enemy of Ravenna and will forthwith move against it with every foot soldier he has and with two hundred horsemen. In a month he will increase this number to three hundred. He swears that he will be an enemy to this city which is so hostile to Venice and that he will attack it with courage and with all his strength, and that he will inflict on it every kind of damage, desolation, destruction, and ruin that he can, and that he will continue to do this until it either sues for peace or for a truce."

Even as he said this, the Ordelaffi fighting men began to move, and this made any question of who was right and who was wrong — who lied and who was telling the truth — purely academic.

Guido da Polenta was no coward but he was not a fool and, as word came to him of lances flashing in the sun as the Forlivese, led by Cecco, who like his brother Scarpetta was one of the best fighting men in north Italy, moved toward Ravenna not even twenty miles away, he could not but conclude that he was caught between the two prongs of a pincers. Forlì by land, and Venice by sea and land. He had no choice. He must seek to end hostilities.

« 5 »

But how? That was now the question.

There was only one way, he realized. By bowing to the inevitable. By sending to Venice an ambassador of his own with full powers and with instructions to use these powers in any way he could to bring about an agreement which would call off the dogs of war.

Moreover, an ambassador was available.

Who?

Who but the one man at his court — besides Archbishop Concoreggio — who had ambassadorial experience; who had served as Florence's emissary to San Gimignano and then to Pope Boniface; who had probably served as ambassador from the White party to Scarpetta Ordelaffi (this incidentally, and the fact that he had done some services to Scarpetta, would be an added advantage, since Forlì would be involved in any negotiation); and who, finally, had successfully settled a long-standing dispute between the Malaspina lords and the bishop of Luni?

Who but Dante Alighieri degli Alighieri?

He was the one and obvious choice.

It should not be thought, however, that he was eager to go. Almost certainly Dante was not. Hardly more than a year before, he had returned from his almost pointless journey to Mantua, Verona, and perhaps Piacenza, and this voyage he had then sworn would be his last.

Besides that, there is some evidence that his health had begun to fail, and even for a well man August by the canals is something less than alluring. It was less so then than now.

But Dante had — among his many other qualities — a stern and rigid sense of duty. He also liked to fulfill his obligations.

And surely he was under obligation to Guido da Polenta.

Late in August, Guido da Polenta sent for him.

"I would like you to go to Venice and negotiate."

To Venice! Of all places, to Venice! We have seen long since how distasteful he found it.

But Guido had asked him and this left him no alternative. He accepted and was on his way.

Or so we think, for we have only one account of this which would prove to be Dante's last mission — in fact, his last act in this world — and it is not by a contemporary. But Filippo Villani was the nephew of Giovanni Villani — who, incidentally, is one of the few others who state specifically that Dante was sent to Venice — and the son of Matteo Villani. Both of these were contemporary and may have given their nephew and son his information.

"Guido da Polenta," he writes, "had little confidence in his own strength, but he imagined that the eloquence and reputation of Dante might turn away from him his impending ruin. So he imposed on him the task of obtaining peace by means of fair words. Dante freely undertook this mission and, after a difficult journey, anxiously approached Venice. But the Venetians had little knowledge of eloquence, and moreover were so apprehensive of the marvelous powers of persuasion which were reported to be possessed by the poet that, for fear of being turned from their high-handed purpose, they refused his repeated requests to lay his case before them. And not only that. When the poet, who had not obtained an audience and was now stricken with fever, asked to be given an escort and also to be allowed to return by sea aboard a coasting vessel, they refused him. This was the insane thought that struck them. They had put the whole power of war and peace into the hands of their admiral, and they feared that if they allowed Dante a safe conduct by sea he would be able to make this admiral turn any way he wanted to by threatening to expose him to contumely. The poet, therefore, had to endure the hardships of a voyage by land and, when he reached Ravenna, he died within a few days."

It should be stated at the outset that there are certain details in this story that cannot, and should not, be believed.

For example, it is not likely that the doge and his council refused to listen to Dante. Almost certainly they did listen to him, for it was only six weeks later that they told a second and more official delegation from Ravenna that Guido must surely know that it was the wish of Venice "to live in peace" with his "city and people." It was simply that they wanted more specific terms, including a promise that he would return booty that the Ravennati were alleged to have seized and assurance that the Ordelaffi would be included in any treaty.

Nor is it likely that the Venetians refused Dante permission to return by sea because they feared that he would subvert their admiral. Venetian admirals are not so easy to persuade. And anyway there was a better and more compelling reason for a return to Venice by land, for, if short, the sea voyage was apt to be stormy and even dangerous, particularly at this time of the year. Moreover, in view of the fact that Ravenna and Venice were at the point of war, it is not likely that any ships plied between the two cities.

But we can and must believe the basic facts. That Guido da Polenta did fear that he did not have the military — and certainly not the naval — force to resist the two cities which moved against him. That he had confidence in Dante's eloquence. And that therefore he sent Dante to Venice to plead his case for him.

Dante did this but was not successful in his plea, although apparently he laid the ground for a future success. This being the case, and probably also because he had Venetian proposals to report and because he was now ill — by now very ill — there seemed no reason to linger. He would return to Ravenna. This he did wearily and by land.

The probable way is well known, for it was the one taken by almost all. First by boat — or perhaps even by gondola — down the long lagoon past what we now call the Lido, past Malamacco, past Palestrina, and to Chioggia. From there — and now on dry land — to Loreo between the Po and the Adige. Next to the Po itself.

(Here, it should be noted, and at the Adige, there was an intricate network of the river and canals. There must have been a half dozen crossings on the long flat rafts that served as ferries.)

Then, rising from green fields, an exquisite golden brown tower some nine stories in height and crowned by a conic top which had almost the shape of the cap worn by a magician and, facing it, extraordinarily beautiful cloisters and magnificent gardens.

It was the Benedictine monastery of Pomposa, founded by Archbishop Aurelian of Ravenna in 523. Little of it was newer than the eleventh century.

Here Dante rested for a while — just as Henry VII had rested at Macereto before he came to Buonconvento — and for the same reason.

Then he was on his way again. He went near but around the Valli di Comacchio — home of the *Anopheles* mosquito, which — with the malaria it carried — was fatal to Dante now and five centuries later would bring about the death of Anita Garibaldi.

After that he was on high ground and, weak though he must by now have been, he could smell again the fragrance of his pine trees. But that was all. For now, as Filippo Villani indicates, he was near the end.

« 7 »

He came to it on the night of September 13 to September 14.

"But since the ordained hour comes to all," writes Boccaccio, "Dante, who had fallen sick in the middle of his fifty-sixth year" — actually it was in the middle of his fifty-seventh year — "and who had received the sacraments humbly and with devotion, and who had reconciled himself to God by his contrition for all that he had done against His will, rendered up to his creator his wearied spirit. This was in the month of September in the year of Christ 1321 on the day of the Holy Cross. I do not doubt that it was received into the arms of his most noble Beatrice, with whom — and in the sight of Him who is the highest good — he now lives most joyfully in that life whose happiness never shall have an end."

Some of the romantic have tried to reconstruct the scene. They portray — and one painting does this very vividly — a gaunt-faced and laurel-crowned poet, embraced by his sons and daughters and surrounded by kneeling priests, with friends and a grave-faced Guido da Polenta standing in the background.

But doubtless anyone who had been there would have witnessed something less dramatic. He would have seen an emaciated man tossing upon his pallet as he had once described Florence tossing. Perhaps Antonia cooled his brow with her dutiful hand or Pietro and Jacopo performed some necessary errand. Without question, Francesco da Milotti was there to do what medicine could for his friend and his patient.

And then suddenly — and around the sickbed only, for the swallows still piped around the eaves and the street noises continued — there was only the silence that comes when the sick man breathes no longer. There was only the sudden unbelief.

« 8 »

The next day — or very shortly thereafter — came public obsequies. These were arranged for by Guido da Polenta.

"This magnificent knight" — once more Giovanni Boccaccio — "had the mortal remains of Dante placed upon a funeral bier. This had been adorned with the symbols of poetry" — the laurel leaves which Dante in his last eclogue had indicated were already being picked for him — "and he had it carried upon the shoulders of his most distinguished citizens to the church of the Minorite Friars."

This was Fra Salimbene's austere and simple basilica of San Francesco, built in the middle of the fifth century, but since, and even before Dante's time, remodeled more than once. It stood, and still stands, near the center of the medieval and modern city, and got its name — originally it had been St. Peter and St. Paul's — because since 1210 it had been the property of the Conventual Franciscans.

"They bore it thither with all the honors which he deemed to be due such a distinguished person, and when it had been followed there with almost official lamentations he had it placed in the stone coffin in which it still lies. After that, as is the custom in Ravenna, he returned to the house in which Dante had lived, and there he himself made a long and eloquent address in which he both praised the learning and merit of the deceased man and tried to console those whom he had left behind him in this life of woe."

Giovanni Villani seems to confirm this.

"In Ravenna," he says, "before the door of the principal church" — San Francesco was not the principal church, but never mind, it was, given Dante's Franciscan feelings, the most appropriate one, and it was not very far from the Duomo, which was — "he was buried with much honor and in the garb of a poet and a philosopher."

In his robes of a teacher, and with a crown of laurel on his brow.

The author of the *Ottimo Commento* does the same, but more ecstatically.

"At his burial," he writes, "he had greater honors than has been paid anyone since Octavius Caesar. This was because he was honored both in the writings and by the presence of a multitude of doctors of learning."

Apparently, too, there was a memorial service in Florence. Azzo II, abbot of the Badia whose tierces and nones rang bells of memory in Dante's ears as he wandered through Italy and perhaps even as far as the English Channel — Abbot Azzo who had ruled the abbey since 1297 and is said to have been a very close friend of Dante's — "mindful of this friendship," says a historian of the Badia, "and of the worth of the man, with the highest ceremony and as a sign of gratitude celebrated solemn offices and sacrifices for him in this our church."

It is suggested that Dante's brother Francesco and his wife Gemma played a part in arranging this.

But that was all, for it is not recorded that the earth shook at his passing as the mountain of purgatory did when Statius was admitted to heaven; nor did ambassadors ride out to the four corners of the world as they did when pope or emperor departed from this life, even though he would one day rule over a realm vaster than any ruled by any pope or emperor. His death was not announced in the marketplaces, and if it was whispered there, as it probably was, prices did not rise or fall. Heralds did not proclaim it on the street corners as a matter of public concern.

« 9 »

Only one thing more.

As he concluded his funeral oration, Guido da Polenta announced that if he lived and prospered he would build for Dante "such a distinguished tomb that if nothing else Dante had done had made him memorable to posterity, this tomb would." Then he called on the poets of the land to write poems in his memory. One of them, he said, would be used as Dante's epitaph.

The poets responded in great numbers.

Pieraccio Tedaldi, a Florentine poet living in the Romagna who, although he loved a Romagna lady, celebrated in poetry his weariness at staying there.

He wrote a sonnet to "our sweet dear master" whom "the ultimate enemy now unbridled" had taken away from them.

"I mean that high author, Dante Alighieri," he said.

An anonymous — but not *the* Anonymous — Florentine.

Bosone da Gubbio, who addressed his poem to Emanuele Giudeo, the useful poetaster of Verona whom we already know, and whom he incongruously condoled for two losses: that of his mistress and that of Dante.

Cino da Pistoia.

And in Latin — and the Latin poems were more pertinent since the epitaph would be in Latin — Menghino Mezzani, Giovanni del Virgilo, and others.

Boccaccio saw these Latin poems, and after noting that they were many in number and that they were not used because Guido "by great misfortune lost his estate" — less than a year after Dante's death, he was driven from Ravenna and forced to take refuge in Bologna — he says this of them:

"They were shown to me long afterwards, and seeing that they had never been put on the tomb because of the accident just mentioned, and also deeming that what I am now writing, although not a material tomb, still may serve as that would have served to preserve Dante's memory, I judged that it would not be inappropriate to add them here. But it is only necessary to insert one of them. And having examined them all, I consider the most worthy in form and in meaning to be fourteen verses by Messer Giovanni del Virgilio of Bologna. Here they are:

Theologus Dantes, nullius dogmatis expers,
Quod foveat claro philosphia sinu:
Gloria musarum, vulgo gratissimus auctor,
Hic iacet, et fama pulsat utrumque polum:
Qui loca defunctis gladiis regnumque gemellis
Distribuit, laicis rhetoriciscque modis.
Pascua Pieriis demum resonabat avenis:
Atropos heu letum livida rupit opus.
Huic ingrata tulit tristem Florentia fructum,

Exilium, vati patria cruda suo.
Quem pia Guidonis gremio Ravenna Novelli
Gaudet honorati continuisse ducis,
Mille trecentis ter septem Numinis annis,
Ad sua septembris idibus astra redit.

Theologian Dante, to whom not unknown were
All things nurtured in philosophy's famed bosom,
Glory of the Muses, yet author pleasing to the crowd,
Lies here but his fame goes out to either pole.
He to the dead, brandishing his twin swords,
Their places assigned, speaking both plainly and rhetorically.
Lastly he made pastoral poetry with his Pierian reeds,
Until dark Atropos — alas — put an end to his joyous task.
On him ungrateful Florence bestowed the sad fruit
Of exile. His fatherland was indeed cruel to its bard.
But Ravenna can rejoice thereat, for she held him
In the bosom of her honored lord Guido Novello.
There in the year of our Lord one thousand three hundred
    and thrice seven
On the ides of September did he return to the stars.

Let us examine these carefully, for they sum up how he seemed to one of his more enlightened contemporaries and how he now seems to many even today.

Theologian Dante.

Stiff as that sounds, was he not a theologian, for was not his great masterwork based on theology?

To whom not unknown were all things nurtured in philosophy's famed bosom.

That describes him too, for according to the lights of his day, he was a philosopher.

Glory of the Muses, yet author pleasing to the crowd.

The *Commedia* was as great a poem as has ever been written, but it was reduced to a language that almost anyone could understand.

He to the dead, brandishing his twin swords — of justice and of mercy — *their places assigned.*

This is obvious.

Lastly he made pastoral poetry.

Well, here del Virgilio does indulge himself, yet who can blame him? Dante did write pastoral poetry, and this pastoral poetry would win the Bolognese professor-poet immortality. Giovanni del Virgilio would be remembered because of it.

And did not Florence exile him and Guido Novello welcome him?
And finally did not he return to the stars?

« *10* »

I think so, and I think that among them he shines today more brightly than
ever, for no longer does he belong only to the notaries of Bologna, or to
the street-corner crowds who craned to hear his verses, or to the few
noble lords who patronized him. Now he belongs to the whole world.

Boccaccio — in the book from which we have just cited the story of
Dante's funeral; in the lectures he gave in front of the church of Santo
Stefano (Dante's church of Santo Stefano, the one attached to the Badia,
not the one near the Ponte Vecchio); in his letters to Petrarch; and in
determined pleas to the Florentine government — was the first to bring
into being what might be called Danteolatry if it were not that Dante
deserved this worship.

It has ever since continued to grow. To give a few examples, the city
which had once rejected him in the late fifteenth century officially
invited the poet's four-times great-grandson to transfer himself from
Verona to Florence. But this great-great-great-great-grandson was content in Verona where he and his forebears had prospered, and he
declined. In 1529, Pope Leo X commissioned Michelangelo to design a
tomb for Dante — it would be in Santa Croce — and thereafter, using all
his papal authority, made such a determined effort to have his bones
brought back to his native city that the monks of San Francesco had to
hide them. They did this so successfully that they were not found until
1865.

Nor — except during the seventeenth century — did this reputation
show any signs of abating, and in the nineteenth century it grew even
greater, for during the Risorgimento, Dante became the national — and
the nationalistic — poet of Italy. His attacks on Hapsburg emperors like
Rudolf and Albrecht were used to arouse feelings against the hated
Austriaci. Indeed, so great was his hold on the Italian imagination that during Fascist days admirers of the late and not lamented Mussolini insisted
that the *veltro* who would save Italy was Il Duce. Mussolini was, it so happens, born "between Feltro and Feltro," thus conforming to the Dantean
prophecy.

But now even the seas do not bound and limit him, nor his own land.
Much has been made — by those who forget that Dante never attacked
the Catholic faith but also by some of those who say he spoke for it — of
the fact that in 1965, the year of Dante's seven-hundredth anniversary, a
pope called on all who listened to do honor to his memory. But more
could be made of another fact; namely, that not only in the Germany and

France and England and Scandinavia that he knew but also in a Japan which he had never heard of — or, if he had heard of it, it was only as Marco Polo's mysterious Cipango — and in the Americas which would not be discovered for nearly two centuries, and even in the Antipodes where, in his imagination, rose the mountain of purgatory, men read him and love him and then study him and try to understand him.

And who can say that this is not as it should be?

Candeli, Italy, 1924 — Greenwich, Connecticut, 1966

Bibliography

ALIGHIERI, DANTE. *The Convivio*. Translated by Philip H. Wicksteed. Temple Classics. London, n.d.
——. *The Divine Comedy*. Translated and with comments by John D. Sinclair. New York, 1959.
——. *The Latin Works*. Temple Classics. London, n.d.
——. *Le Opere di Dante. Testo critico della Societa dantesca fiorentina*. Florence, 1960.
——. *The Portable Dante*. New York, 1947.
——. *The Vita Nuova and the Canzoniere*. Translated by Thomas Okey and Philip H. Wicksteed. Temple Classics. London, 1948.
ALIGHIERI, JACOPO. *Chiose alla critica dell' Inferno*. Florence, 1915.
ALIGHIERI, PIERO. *Petri Allegherii super Dantis ipsius genitoris comoediam commentarium*. Florence, 1845.
ALLEN, A. M. *A History of Verona*. London, 1918.
ANCONA, ALESSANDRO D'. *I Precursori di Dante*. Florence, n.d.
AQUINAS, ST. THOMAS. *On the Truth of the Catholic Faith* (*Summa contra gentiles*). New York, 1964. See also other writngs by Aquinas.
BARBADORO, BERNARDINO. "La condenna di Dante." *Studi danteschi* II, 1920.
BARBI, MICHELE. "Un altro figlio di Dante?" *Studi danteschi* V, 1922.
——. "Brunetto Alighieri alla battaglia di Montaperti." *Studi danteschi* IV, 1921.
——. "Contributi alla biografia di Dante." *Bullettino della Società dantesca italiana* NS VIII, 1892.
——. "Dante a San Gimignano." *Bullettino della Società dantesca italiana* NS VI, 1889.
——. "Dante e l'arte di medici e speziali." *Studi danteschi* I, 1920.
——. "Fra gli antenati Dante." *Studi danteschi* II, 1920.
——. "Giovanni di Dante Alighieri e la dimora del poeta in Lucca." *Studi danteschi* VI, 1923.
——. "Guido Cavalcanti e Dante di fronte al governo popolare." *Studi danteschi* I, 1920.
——. "L'iscrizione di Dante nell' arte di medici e speziali." *Studi danteschi* XVII, 1933.
——. *The Life of Dante*. Berkeley and Los Angeles, 1954.
——. "La tenzone di Dante con Forese." *Studi danteschi* IX, 1924.
——. "L'ufficio di Dante per i lavori di San Procolo." *Studi danteschi* III, 1921.
——, and PIATTOLI, RENATO. "La Casa di Dante." *Studi danteschi* XXII, 1938.
BELLONI, ANTONIO. "L'usuriere Vitaliano." *Giornale storico della letteratura italiana* XLIV, 1904.
BERGIN, THOMAS G. *Dante*. New York, 1965.
BLASHFIELD, E. H., and BLASHFIELD, E. W. *Italian Cities*. New York, 1912.

BOCCACCIO, GIOVANNI. *Il Commento alla Divina Commedia e gli altri scritti intorno a Dante.* Bari, 1918.

———. *Life of Dante.* Translated and with an Introduction and a Note on the Portraits of Dante by G. R. Carpenter. New York, 1900.

BOETHIUS. *The Theological Tractates and the Consolation of Philosophy.* Cambridge, Mass., 1953.

BRANCA, VITTORIO. *Rimatori del dolce stil novo.* Genoa, Rome, Naples, and Città di Castello, 1941.

CAGGESE, ROMOLO. *Firenze dalla decadenza di Roma al Risorgimento d'Italia.* Florence, 1912.

CARLYLE, THOMAS. *On Heroes, Hero-Worship, and the Heroic in History.* London, n.d.

Casa di Dante Alighieri in Firenze, La. Relazione della commissione instituta della giunta municipale de' 17 marzo 1866. Florence, 1869.

CAVALCANTI, GUIDO. *Le Rime.* Florence, 1881.

CHUBB, THOMAS CALDECOT. *The Life of Giovanni Boccaccio.* New York, 1930.

———. *The Months of the Year: Twelve Sonnets by Folgore di San Gimignano.* Sanbornville, N.H., 1960.

CICERO. *Essays on Old Age and Friendship.* New York, 1926. (Another translation is available in the Loeb Classical Library.)

COMPAGNI, DINO. *The Chronicle of* ———. Translated by Else C. M. Benecke and A. G. Ferrers Howell. London, 1906.

COMPARETTI, DOMENICO. *Virgilio nel medio evo.* Florence, 1896.

COSMO, UMBERTO. *A Handbook to Dante Studies.* Oxford, 1950.

———. *Vita di Dante.* Bari, 1930.

CRESCINI, VINCENZO. *Del Discordo trilinguo attribuito a Dante.*

DAVIDSÖHN, ROBERT. *Firenze ai tempi di Dante.* Florence, 1929.

———. *Storia di Firenze.* Florence, 1956-1965.

DAVIS, CHARLES T. *Dante and the Idea of Rome.* Oxford, 1957.

DEBENEDETTI, S. "Un nuovo documento di Dante e di Francesco Alighieri." *Bullettino della Società dantesca italiana* NS XIV, 1907.

DEL LUNGO, ISODORO. *Beatrice nella vita e nella poesia del secolo XIII.* Milan, 1891.

———. "Dante in Lunigiana." (In *Dante e la Lunigiana.*) Milan, 1909.

———. *Dante ne' tempi di Dante.* Bologna, 1888.

———. *Dell' esilio di Dante.* Florence, 1881.

———. *Dino Compagni e la sua cronica.* Florence, 1880.

———. "Un documento inedito del priorato di Dante." *Bullettino della Società dantesca italiana* IV, 1890.

———. *La donna fiorentina del buon tempo antico.* Florence, 1900.

———. *Firenze e Italia nella vita e nella poema di Dante.* Florence, 1925.

DELLA TORRE, ARNALDO. "Scritti danteschi pubblicati in occasione del VI centenaio della nascita di F. Petrarca." *Bullettino della Società dantesca italiana* NS XIII, 1905.

D'ENTRÈVES, A. P. *Dante as a Political Thinker.* London, 1952.

DIEHL, CHARLES. *Venise.* Paris, 1931.

Documents Concerning Dante's Debts. Tenth Annual Report of the Dante Society. Cambridge, Mass., 1891.

ELIOT, T. S. *Dante.* London, n.d.

FINZI, MARCELLO. *I falsarj nell' Inferno dantesco.* Florence, 1925.

FRULLANI, EMILIO, and GARGANI, GARGANO. *Della casa di Dante. Relazione con documenti al consiglio generale del commune di Firenze.* Florence, 1965.

GARDNER, EDMUND G. *Dante.* London, 1923.

———. *Dante's Ten Heavens.* London, 1904.

GENTILE, LUIGI. "Di un documento per l'anno di nascimento di Dante." *Bullettino della Società dantesca italiana* V-VI, 1891.

GILSON, ÉTIENNE. *Dante the Philosopher.* New York, 1929.

GRANDGENT, CHARLES H. *Discourses on Dante*. Cambridge, Mass., 1924.
HARE, CHRISTOPHER. *Dante the Wayfarer*. New York, 1905.
HASKINS, CHARLES H. *The Rise of the Universities*. Ithaca, 1957.
HOLLIS, CHRISTOPHER (editor). *The Papacy*. New York, 1964.
LARNER, JOHN. *The Lords of the Romagna*. New York, 1965.
Le Cento Novelle Antiche. Milan, 1825.
LIVI, GIOVANNI. *Dante, suoi primi cultori, sua gente in Bologna*. Bologna, 1918.
LODGE, ELEANOR C. *The End of the Middle Ages*. London, 1928.
LUCAN. *Pharsalia*. Translated by Robert Graves. Baltimore, 1935.
MASSERA, ALDO FRANCESCO (Ed.). *Sonetti burleschi e realistici dei primi due secoli*. Bari, 1940.
MOLLAT, GUILLAUME. *Les Papes d'Avignon*. Paris, 1949.
MOLMENTI, P. G. *La Storia di Venezia nella vita privata*. Torino, 1885.
MOORE, EDWARD. *Studies in Dante*. Oxford, 1917.
NARDI, BRUNO. "La Tragedia d'Ulisse." *Studi danteschi* XX, 1937.
NICASTRO, S. "L'avo di Dante in Prato." *Archivio storico pratese* IV, 1921.
NOYES, ELLA. *The Casentino and Its Story*. New York, 1915.
Ottimo Commento della Divina Commedia di Dante. Pisa, 1827.
PALMEROCCHI, ROBERTO. *Cronisti del trecento*. Milan and Rome, 1935.
PAPANTI, GIOVANNI. *Dante secondo la tradizione e i novellatori*. Livorno, 1873.
PIATTOLI, RENATO. "Gli Alighieri a Prato nel secolo XIII." *Studi danteschi* XVII, 1933.
———. *Codice diplomatico dantesco*. Florence, 1950.
———. "Geri del Bello e Bellino di Lapo suo nipote." *Studi danteschi* XVIII, 1934.
———. "Geri e Cione del Bello a Prato nel 1280." *Studi danteschi* XVI, 1932.
PREVITÉ-ORTON, C. W. *The Shorter Cambridge Mediaeval History*. Cambridge, 1953.
RAGG, LONSDALE. *Dante and His Italy*. New York, 1907.
RAJNA, PIO. "Il Casato di Dante." *Studi danteschi* III, 1921.
———. "Per la questione dell' andata di Dante a Parigi." *Studi danteschi* II, 1920.
RAMBALDI, BENEVENUTI, DA IMOLA. *Comentum super Dantis Aldigherij Comoediam*. Florence, 1887.
RICCI, CORRADO. *L'ultimo rifugio di Dante*. Milan, 1921, and Ravenna, 1965.
ROSSETTI, DANTE GABRIEL. *Dante and His Circle*. London, 1892.
SACCHETTI, FRANCO. *Le Novelle*. Florence, n.d.
———. *Tales from Sacchetti*. Translated from the Italian by Mary G. Steegman with an Introduction by Guido Briazi. London, 1908.
SAYERS, DOROTHY L. *Further Papers on Dante*. London, 1957.
SCHACHTER, NATHAN. *The Mediaeval Universities*. New York, 1962.
SCHEVILL, FERDINAND. *The History of Florence*. New York, 1936.
SINGLETON, CHARLES S. *Dante Studies*. Cambridge, 1965.
SISMONDI, J. C. L. *A History of the Italian Republics*. London, 1917.
STALEY, EDGECUMBE. *The Guilds of Florence*. Chicago, 1906.
STEPHENSON, CARL, and LYON, BRYCE. *Mediaeval History*. New York, 1962.
SYMONDS, JOHN ADDINGTON. *An Introduction to the Study of Dante*. London, 1899.
TANNER, J. R., PREVITÉ-ORTON, C. W., and BROOKE, Z. N. *The Cambridge Mediaeval History*, Volume VI. Cambridge, 1957.
TOLDO, P. "La frode di Gianni Schichi." *Giornale storico della letteratura italiana* XLVIII, 1906.
TORRACA, FRANCESCO. *Nuova studi danteschi*. Naples, 1912.
TOURING CLUB ITALIANO. *Guida d'Italia*. Milan, 1935–1963.
TOYNBEE, PAGET. *Concise Dictionary of Proper Names and Notable Matters in the Works of Dante*. Oxford, 1914.
———. *Dante Studies and Researches*. New York, 1902.
———. *A Dictionary of Proper Names and Notable Matters in the Works of Dante*. Oxford, 1898.
VANDELLI, G. "I 'Fori' del 'Bel San Giovanni.'" *Studi danteschi* XV, 1931.
VERNON, WILLIAM WARREN. *Readings on the Inferno of Dante*. London, 1884.

———. *Readings on the Paradiso of Dante.* London, 1900.

———. *Readings on the Purgatorio of Dante.* London, 1889.

VILLANI, GIOVANNI. *Chronicle.* Translated by Rose E. Selfe and edited by Philip H. Wicksteed. London, 1906.

———. *Le Vite d'uomini illustri fiorentini.* Venice, 1748.

VIRGIL. *The Aeneid.* Translated by C. Day Lewis. Garden City, 1953.

VITTORINI, DOMENICO. *The Age of Dante.* Garden City, 1953.

VOSSLER, KARL. *Mediaeval Culture.* New York, 1929.

WICKSTEED, PHILIP H. *Dante and Aquinas.* London, Toronto, and New York, 1959.

——— (translator). *The Early Lives of Dante.* London, 1904.

———. *From Vita Nuova to Paradiso.* Manchester, London, and New York, 1922.

WILKINS, E. H. *The Life of Petrarch.* Chicago, 1961.

———. *Petrarch's Later Years.* Cambridge, Mass., 1959.

———, and BERGIN, THOMAS G. *A Concordance to the Divine Comedy.* Cambridge, Mass., 1965.

WILLIAMS, EGERTON R., JR. *Plain Towns of Italy.* Boston and New York, 1913.

ZENATTI, ODDONE. *Dante e Firenze.* Florence, n.d.

ZINGARELLI, NICOLA. *La Vita, i tempi e le opere di Dante.* Milan, 1948.

It should be noted that the above-named books and studies form only a small part of the voluminous accumulation of writings about Dante. A complete list would make a small volume in itself. Nor does it include every book or study which I myself have turned to. I have set down only such examinations of Dante as seem to have influenced me as I wrote his biography.

Those who wish to pursue the matter have ample realms in which to travel, and as guides to them — not only the best, but the most available — I suggest that they consult the "Biographical Note" at the end of Michele Barbi's *The Life of Dante;* the footnotes and references in Thomas G. Bergin's indispensable *Dante;* the bibliographical suggestions in Umberto Cosmo's *A Handbook to Dante Studies;* the outdated but still useful "Bibliographical Appendix" in Edmund G. Gardner's *Dante;* and the notes at the end of each chapter of Zingarelli's *La Vita di Dante,* together with Aldo Vallone's "*Supplemento biografico* (1921–1948)" at the end of volume II.

Dante's own works should be read too, and for those who unhappily cannot read him in Italian and — where necessary — in Latin, there is a plethora of translations. Above — except for those in *The Portable Dante,* which include Laurence Binyon's *Divine Comedy* and D. G. Rossetti's *Vita Nuova* — I have included only one for each book, but there are many more. In the card index of the Yale University Library alone I found listed at least seventy persons who have translated or paraphrased or retold either the whole of the *Commedia* or parts of it. It is not necessary to list them all, but no one should overlook Charles Eliot Norton's prose translation, or the verse translations of Melville Anderson Best, Geoffrey L. Bickersteth, H. F. Cary (the old standby), Jefferson

Butler Fletcher, Henry Wadsworth Longfellow, and Lawrence Grant White, to say nothing of the modern (in their approach) translations of John Ciardi and Dorothy L. Sayers. Very useful also are the late Miss Sayers's introductions to *Hell* and *Purgatory*, particularly the former.

Other translations of other books which should not be overlooked are William Anderson's translation of the *Convivio*, Wilton Brewer's translation of the *Eclogues*, Charles H. Latham's and Paget Toynbee's translations of the *Epistolae*, and Donald Nicholl's translation of *De Monarchia*. Most of these have useful notes too. And, if only for its introduction, Gustav Vinay's translation of *De Monarchia* should also be examined, although it translates Dante's study of universal empire into Italian rather than English.

Yet despite this *embarras de richesse*, I have throughout this book used my own renderings into English for all of the poetry and much of the prose. This is not because of any over-selfconfident belief that I could surpass or even equal the better of my predecessors. It is simply because I have found it necessary to consider everything that Dante wrote in two lights: (1) as magnificent poetry and eloquent, if not magnificent, prose; (2) as a source of both exterior and interior biography. The latter in particular made it important to make sure that the English version conveyed to the last detail the precise meaning which I was convinced that the poet had meant to convey. For that reason I had to use my own translations.

But the reader could not ever be allowed to forget that he was not reading a diary, however self-revealing Dante often was. For that reason it was necessary to translate the poetry into poetry (I have mainly used blank verse, since *terza rima* would have forced me to take too many liberties), and the prose into a not too modernized facsimile of Dante's splendid words.

A Note on the Illustrations

I F Dante had lived three, or even two, centuries later than he did — or if he had lived in ancient Rome — the problem of an authentic Dante portrait would not exist. Everyone is familiar with the realistic statue-portraits of eminent Romans, and in later Italy, beginning at least with Filippino Lippi, Botticelli, Ghirlandaio, and Piero della Francesca and reaching an apogee with Raphael, Andrea del Castagno, Bronzino, and above all Titian, there was a mort of accurate portraiture which set down the faces of the day.

Dante came into the world too soon for this, however, and there is only one portrait of which it can be stated incontrovertibly that it was painted by an artist who had seen the living poet. This is the Giotto portrait in the Bargello in Florence which was discovered behind a layer of whitewash on July 21, 1840. The late R. T. Holbrook and others insist that it was ruined by an incompetent restorer, who, among other things, changed the green of Dante's gown into dull brown so as not to offend the reactionary sensibilities of the grand duke of Tuscany, who saw in the red, white, and green which Dante wore in honor of Beatrice the colors of Risorgimento Italy. Ruined or not, it is an excellent and revealing picture and is used as the frontispiece of this book.

The only other Dante portrait which could have been contemporaneously executed is the so-called Torrigiani death mask, but most students feel that this was done much later. They assert, in one reason which they give for believing this, that the art of making death masks, practiced by the ancients and then lost, had not yet been rediscovered. Holbrook feels this very strongly, and gives the following as the probable pedigree and sequence of Dante portraits: (1) the Giotto portrait; (2) the miniature in Codex Palatinus 320; (3) the Naples bust; (4) the Torrigiani death mask and the portrait in Codex Riccardianus 1040; (5) all modern portraits.

For obvious reasons, then, I have included the Palatine miniature, the

Naples bust, the death mask, and the Riccardiana portrait, and to them I have added these three others:

The effigy on Dante's tomb in Ravenna, which may have been done in 1483 by Pietro Lombardi in the pay of Bernardo Bembo, father of the great humanist Pietro Bembo. I include it because it shows a grave and thoughtful Dante we would like to believe in.

The Michelino Dante in the Duomo at Florence. This is perhaps the original Dante portrait which is the most often looked at; although, because of its numerous reproductions, more people know the Naples bust.

The so-called Yale Dante in the Jarves collection of the Yale University Art Gallery in New Haven, Connecticut. This is by a long shot the best Dante portrait in the United States, and it is a fine piece of work in its own right. It shows a more than slightly acidulous Dante.

One final word on Dante portraits. In the *Commedia*, Dante refers to his beard, and Boccaccio speaks of him as bearded in his *Vita di Dante*. But every authenticated portrait shows him as clean-shaven.

Index